PRAISE FOR ISRAEL AND THE NATIONS

"This fine collection of essays, the second to emerge from an international collaboration of scholars that took place in Bratislava, both broadens the geographical scope of the discussion concerning Paul 'within Judaism' and serves to move it forward in significant ways. This volume will be particularly significant for the ongoing discussion of the relationship between Paul's conception of a mission to the gentiles and Jewish expectations about the place of the nations in the end-time redemption of Israel." —**Terence L. Donaldson**, Lord and Lady Coggan Professor Emeritus of New Testament Studies, Wycliffe College, Toronto

"This extraordinary rich collection of essays deals with an issue that is at the heart of Paul's theological thinking. It gathers an international group of scholars who are well renowned for their historical and exegetical expertise. The variety of the contributions demonstrates convincingly that it is only a multi-perspective approach like this one that can be regarded as a suitable way to properly treat the issue that is in the focus of this volume. No one who wants to deal with this book's subject can do without this book."—**Michael Wolter**, University of Bonn

Israel and the Nations

Paul's Gospel in the Context
of Jewish Expectation

Edited by František Ábel

LEXINGTON BOOKS/FORTRESS ACADEMIC
Lanham • Boulder • New York • London

Published by Lexington Books/Fortress Academic
Lexington Books is an imprint of The Rowman & Littlefield Publishing Group, Inc.
4501 Forbes Boulevard, Suite 200, Lanham, Maryland 20706
www.rowman.com

6 Tinworth Street, London SE11 5AL, United Kingdom

Copyright © 2021 by The Rowman & Littlefield Publishing Group, Inc.

All rights reserved. No part of this book may be reproduced in any form or by any electronic or mechanical means, including information storage and retrieval systems, without written permission from the publisher, except by a reviewer who may quote passages in a review.

British Library Cataloguing in Publication Information Available

Library of Congress Cataloging-in-Publication Data

Library of Congress Control Number: 2021931035

ISBN: 9781978710801 (cloth)

ISBN: 9781978710818 (electronic)

∞™ The paper used in this publication meets the minimum requirements of American National Standard for Information Sciences—Permanence of Paper for Printed Library Materials, ANSI/NISO Z39.48-1992.

Contents

Acknowledgments   vii

Preface   ix

PART I: PAUL THE APOSTLE IN THE CONTEXT OF JEWISH ESCHATOLOGICAL APOCALYPTICAL NOTIONS

1   The Making and Unmaking of Jews in Second Century BCE Narratives and the Implication for Interpreting Paul   3
Genevive Dibley

2   Paul and the Joining of the Ways: Ordering the Eschaton, Preparing for Judgment   25
Anders Runesson

3   From Aristeas to the Apocalypse of Abraham: A Survey of Some Hellenistic Jewish Texts Relating to the Issue of Israel and Its Relationship to the Other Nations   49
Eric Noffke

4   What Eschatological Pilgrimage of the Gentiles?   61
Matthew V. Novenson

5   Eschatological Universalism, the Nations, and the Jewish Apocalyptic Paul   75
Loren T. Stuckenbruck

6   Did the LXX of the Twelve Prophets Contribute to the Eschatological Opening to the Nations?   87
Patrick Pouchelle

| 7 | Paul between Judaism and Hellenism
Imre Peres | 103 |

PART II: THE SPECIFICS OF PAUL'S MESSAGE CONCERNING END-TIME REDEMPTION OF ISRAEL AND ITS ROLE TOWARDS THE NATIONS (*ETHNĒ*)

8	*Israēl* (and *Israēlitēs*) in Paul, Particularly in Galatians *Michael Bachmann*	121
9	Bending Knees and Acknowledging Tongues (Phil 2:9–11): The Nations' Loyalty to the God of Israel in the Shadow of the Empire *Kathy Ehrensperger*	149
10	'But It Is Not As Though the Word of God Had Failed': Israel as a Sub-Text in Romans? *William S. Campbell*	165
11	The Ins and Outs of Paul's Israelite Remnant *Joshua Garroway*	187
12	The Gentile as Insider and Outsider in Paul's Letter to the Romans *Kenneth Atkinson*	199
13	"If you are called a Judean . . ." (Rom 2:17): Paul and his Interlocutor *Markus Öhler*	219
14	"All Israel Will Be *Saved*" or "*Kept Safe*"? (Rom 11:26): Israel's *Conversion* or *Irrevocable Calling to Gospel the Nations*? *Mark D. Nanos*	243
15	Paul, the Israelite, on Israel and the Gentiles at the End of Time: Reflections on Rom 9–11 *Karl-Wilhelm Niebuhr*	271
16	*Pesher* Concerning Righteousness (Romans 10:5–13) in Relation to the Response of Jews and Gentiles to the Gospel *František Ábel*	289

Index of Authors	317
Index of Subjects	325
Index of Scripture References and Ancient Sources	339
About the Contributors	351

Acknowledgments

Just as in the first volume, I would like to thank Professor Neil Elliott for his strong encouragement and valuable advice during the preparation and achievement of this project, including in editing both its volumes as such. I express my gratitude to the publisher, Lexington Books/Fortress Academic, for accepting also the second volume of the project for publication.

Special thanks also go to all those who pulled their weight and offered help during the preparation as well as the holding of the conference, especially to my colleague Adriana Belanji Biela, and the whole conference staff as well, postgraduates Ivan Belanji, Eva Guldanová, Simona Kapitáňová, Michaela Prihracki, Valéria Terézia Dančiaková, and students who together helped us with material and organizational provision. I express my gratitude also to Pavol Bargár, Rabbi Mikhailo Kapustin, Miroslav Kocúr, Martin Kováč, and Ondrej Prostredník, who were instrumental in hosting individual sessions, and whose contributions to the discussions enhanced the value of the conference. Without the help and work of all these colleagues, students, and friends, the conference could not have be achieved and run successfully.

František Ábel
Editor

Preface

The contents of this book present the findings of the conference *Paul's Message and Jewish Eschatological Notions Concerning Israel's Role Towards the Nations*, which took place on 10–13 September 2019 in Bratislava. It is the second volume of the research project entitled "Paul within Judaism—New Perspectives" (VEGA 1/0103/18), supported by the Scientific Grant Agency of the Ministry of Education, Science, Research and Sport of the Slovak Republic and the Slovak Academy of Sciences (VEGA), for the years 2018–2020, with its home base at the Evangelical Lutheran Theological Faculty of Comenius University in Bratislava.

While the first volume, *The Message of Paul the Apostle within Second Temple Judaism* (Lanham: Lexington Books/Fortress Academic, 2020)—presenting the findings of the first conference taking place in October 2018—contains the responses of a wider range of scholars to the dynamics of various approaches to Paul's message, from the traditional as well as the new perspectives on Paul, this volume presents the findings of continuation of discussions concerning Paul's message in its historical context, particularly focusing on one of the most important topics among the later Second Temple eschatological conceptions of Judaism: particularly the notions of the end-time redemption of Israel and its relation to the Gentiles, the non-Jewish nations (*ethnē*).

Despite the complexity of these notions and their interpretations, an important query about the status of non-Jews is coming to the fore in research. Since the Jewish scriptures contain a variety of approaches to the non-Jewish nations, the answer is not unambiguous. This query becomes all the more pressing when these notions are related to messianic ideas. In that context, this wide range of Jewish descriptions of the non-Jewish nations and their fate is joined by the questions of what God's purpose for Israel and the Gentile nations (*ethnē*) is and how God communicates with the nations through Israel. These questions were just as important for the Jewish majority population in Judea and Galilee, as they were for the Jewish communities in the Diaspora, where Jews inevitably interacted daily with the non-Jewish majority. Moreover, the urgency of these questions was strongly intensified by messianic expectations, especially in the Judea and Galilee of the first century CE. The rationale in each case was primarily Jewish monotheism: the conviction of God as the sole, universal deity, the Creator of the universe, a God who continues to exercise sovereignty over the created order of the world, including all the nations within it. Naturally, notions of the eschatological redemption of Israel had to embrace its relation to non-Jewish nations, making for varied concepts of how to view the issue.

Therefore, it is no surprise that this concept, emphasized by its connection to contemporary Jewish messianic expectations, holds a key role in Paul's theologizing. Paul, the Jew and Pharisee, was also trying to comprehend and resolve all these questions, and thus to grasp the point of God's purpose for Israel and the Gentile nations. The question of how God's vocation of Israel, relating to the messianic expectation, impacts upon non-Jewish nations was for him a crucial one and the most urgent.

In this regard, we must be aware that Paul, as well as his Jewish contemporaries after they became the followers of the Jesus Christ movement, did not break new ground in the comprehension of the Jewish scriptures and notions of them, as if they had found out a completely different mode of their interpretation. Quite the contrary: all that related to this new messianic movement still had to situate itself within the Israel narratives, traditions, and notions as they were conveyed in the scriptures of Israel. In other words, Paul's message was part and parcel of intra-Jewish dialogue. However, that intra-Jewish dialogue was being progressively disrupted, primarily on account of the tragic events occasioned by the Jewish revolts against the Romans in Judea and Galilee in the latter half of the first and the first half of the second centuries CE, and was suspended for a long time, due to the developing prominence of rabbinic Judaism on one hand and patristic Christianity on the other hand. The negative impact of this "parting" manifests itself, among other ways and perhaps primarily, in the approach to and interpretation of Paul's message. As time progressed, Paul, the Jew and Pharisee, the apostle of the Gentiles, came to serve as a unique example of religious conversion, from "particularistic and legalistic" Judaism to "universalistic" Christianity. The outcomes of this are the diverse forms of Christian interaction with Jews and Judaism, continuing to echo down the centuries and having a predominantly negative character.

Therefore, a paradigm shift, especially in the field of Pauline research, is something which should be reckoned as both significant and necessary, and at the same time considered to be a common ground of current New Testament research. All the aforementioned key facts and aspects have to be taken into consideration when discussing Paul's message. We have to approach and grasp Paul's message, as well as the message of the whole first generation of Christ-followers, primarily in its historical context, particularly in the context of the Graeco-Roman Hellenistic world of the first century CE, an inseparable part of which was also the Jewish phenomenon in all its variedness and complexities.

This approach was also applied in practice at the conference and in its findings. Working on the historical context, the participants were focusing on the specifics of contemporary Israel's eschatological expectation towards the Gentile nations and Paul's manner of dealing with it, from various angles and approaches. The contents of this volume attest to the inherent importance and significance of the topic. First come the contributions that concentrate on Jewish eschatological expectations in a more general sense. Here, the authors, in researching available contemporary literary sources, focus on specific aspects of Second Temple Judaism and consider the connections between textual reflections and social reality. In this way, they aim better to understand Paul's own theologizing concerning this topic. The authors of the ensuing contributions focus directly on selected parts of Paul's message in passages from Philippians, Galatians, and especially Romans, aiming to grasp the point and better to explain and formulate Paul's own expectation concerning the end-time redemption of Israel and the participation of the nations (*ethnē*) in that event. Irrespective of the differences between the authors in their particular approaches to the topic as well as the distinctions between their findings, what is significant is the common agreement that Paul's message has to be considered and interpreted in its historical context, meaning within Second Temple Judaism, and that scholars should avail themselves of the relevant methods of historical-critical exegesis and hermeneutics.

For the organizers and the faculty, as well as Comenius University in Bratislava as an institution, this conference proved to be a second excellent event arising from this research project. Moreover, it was a second very special opportunity to host a group of world-respected scholars engaging in Pauline research, particularly Kenneth Atkinson, Michael Bachmann, Daniel Boyarin, William S. Campbell, Genevive Dibley, Kathy Ehrensperger, Paula Fredriksen, Joshua D. Garroway, Mark D. Nanos, Karl-Wilhelm Niebuhr, Eric Noffke, Matthew V. Novenson, Markus Öhler, Patrick Pouchelle, Anders Runesson, Loren T. Stuckenbruck, and Mikael Winninge. The organizers appreciated the fact that several of them attended both conferences, thereby showing their interest in the continuation of these discussions, and were also glad that the second meeting made space for other participants besides, which enriched the program and also the scale of particular approaches to the topic. The ample participation in this conference is of significance to the research project, and it also confirms its importance and value. Moreover, the extended representation of the home faculty at the second conference, as shown by the list of participants, is proof of the fulfillment of one of the main goals of the project, namely, to introduce and implement the *Paul within Judaism* perspective into the Slovak academic environment.

This volume is the outcome of all those discussions and represents sixteen contributions offering a varied scale of opinions and stances concerning Paul's message in the context of Jewish eschatological expectation. In this regard, the content structure of the volume is divided into two parts, the first of which contains the contributions focusing on the topic in its broader context of various aspects of Jewish eschatological apocalyptical notions in order better to understand Paul and his own message, and the second of which is devoted to particular points of Paul's message in that context. Overall, we hope that this second volume of the research project will reveal its potential just as the first one did, and that it will likewise confirm the necessity of continuing in discussion about Paul's message and its theology in its historical framework and context, in the effort to solve the ever-present enigmas relating to Paul's Jewishness, and thus to better understand what it meant to be a Jew while remaining with a perception of the new era in Jesus Christ and its final consummation. Finally, we hope that it will motivate further research of the topic, including in Slovakia and other Central European countries, such as the Czech Republic, Hungary, and Poland as well. As such, it is an ever-present invitation and motivation to further research of Paul's message in its historical Jewish context, changing the hermeneutic paradigms and seeking to ascertain the next relevant outcomes so that we are better able to understand what Christian identity means, or should mean.

Participants in the conference, *Paul's Message and Jewish Eschatological Notions Concerning Israel's Role Towards the Nations*; Bratislava, Slovakia, September 10–13, 2019 (the names of contributors to this volume are marked with an asterisk):

Atkinson, Kenneth	University of Northern Iowa in Cedar Falls, USA*
Ábel, František	Comenius University in Bratislava, Slovakia*
Bachmann, Michael	University of Siegen, Germany*
Boyarin, Daniel	University of California, Berkeley, USA
Campbell, William S.	University of Wales, Trinity Saint David, UK*
Dibley, Genevive	Rockford University, USA*
Ehrensperger, Kathy	University of Potsdam, Germany*

Fredriksen, Paula	Hebrew University, Jerusalem, Israel
Garroway, Joshua D.	Hebrew Union College—Jewish Institute of Religion, Los Angeles, USA*
Nanos, Mark D.	University of Kansas, USA*
Niebuhr, Karl-Wilhelm	Friedrich-Schiller-Universität, Jena, Germany*
Noffke, Eric	Waldensian Theological Faculty in Rome, Italy*
Novenson, Matthew V.	University of Edinburgh, UK*
Öhler, Markus	University of Vienna, Austria*
Peres, Imre	Comenius University in Bratislava, Slovakia*
Pouchelle, Patrick	Centre Sèvres, Paris, France*
Runesson, Anders	University of Oslo, Norway*
Stuckenbruck, Loren T.	Ludwig Maximilian University of Munich, Germany*
Winninge, Mikael	Umeå University, Sweden

Part I

PAUL THE APOSTLE IN THE CONTEXT OF JEWISH ESCHATOLOGICAL APOCALYPTICAL NOTIONS

Chapter One

The Making and Unmaking of Jews in Second Century BCE Narratives and the Implication for Interpreting Paul

Genevive Dibley

It is clear from their desire to become circumcised that the gentile-Jesus-followers of Galatia understood their faith in Jesus as the Christ to have effectively constituted their conversion to Judaism. They had, after all, accepted the Jewish God, a Jewish messiah, Jewish scriptures, Jewish ethics—one could forgive all parties concerned for thinking these Jewish-acting ex-pagans were in some fashion becoming *actual* Jews. Though Paul squarely blames the Galatians' desire to be circumcised on the work of outside influencers, visitors who had come to Galatia sometime after he had left the province, it would have been an entirely natural assumption on the part of the Galatians that they would need to be circumcised in order to complete their transformation into Jews.[1] Even without the influence of the visitors, the Galatians would have likely arrived at the conclusion that they needed to be circumcised on their own. Circumcision was a central, covenantal component in the Abraham narrative, a mandate which carried with it a dramatic ultimatum—in essence, *cut yourself or be cut off* (Gen 17:14). It is hard to imagine how the Galatians, desiring as they did to be claimed by Abraham's God, could have reasoned to any other conclusion.

How exactly Paul came to hear of the Galatians' intention to complete their conversion is not clear from his letter. Whatever his source, he seems to have deemed the intel reliable – the Galatians intended to submit to circumcision in keeping with the Jewish law. There is no hint in the letter that the Galatians were debating the merits of convert circumcision or that they were seeking Paul's counsel on the matter. Paul, for his part, did not prevaricate—under no circumstances, he wrote, should the converts allow themselves to be circumcised. The intensely singular focus in Galatians on circumcision, the vitriol, the length of the sustained argument over six chapters, leaves an impression of impassioned urgency on Paul's part—that he imagined the knife to be poised and the Galatians prone as he anxiously penned his letter.

THE PROBLEM

Paul is seemingly nowhere more un-Jewish than in his insistence that the gentile converts in Galatia remain uncircumcised. Having encouraged the gentile-Jesus-followers in every other aspect of their lives to act ever more Jewishly, appealing repeatedly to Torah in support of his propositions,[2] Paul's response to the Galatians' intention to be circumcised likely was at the time, as it is now, perplexing. Had he followed his prohibition with a simple declarative statement along the lines of "and now for something new . . . the righteous need no longer be Jews" or something to that effect, matters would have been greatly clarified. The problem arises in Paul's protracted, some might argue tortured, attempt to tie the movement to Abraham (here one must read: *Judaism*) while maintaining that the Christ-confessing-Jewish-acting-ex-pagans should not be circumcised.

A SOLUTION

In the vein of the *Paul within Judaism* perspective,[3] Matthew Thiessen has proposed a most interesting reading of Paul's stance forbidding convert circumcision. Borrowing from modern ethnographic theory, Thiessen sifts the evidence of the letters through the sociological matrix of *primordial–constructivist* ethnicity construction.[4] Primordialism posits ethnicity as a phenomenon inherent to the structure of human society and thus essential, stable, and irreducible. The constructivist understanding, by contrast, holds that ethnicity is a construct, a convention of society and thus transient and malleable. "Some Pauline scholars have attempted to bring such ethnographic theory to bear on Paul's thinking. Implying that Paul is self-consciously a constructivist—Paul redefines Jewishness in order to include gentiles in the people of God."[5] Thiessen counters that scholars have it the wrong way round. Paul, he claims, was an ethnic primordialist. Accordingly, Thiessen asserts, Paul would have understood *Jewishness* and *gentileness* to be "divinely instituted identities,"[6] holy and profane, cast and fixed from birth, immutable and therefore non-transferable.

Paul's primordialism, Thiessen reasons, would have in turn dictated an essentialist understanding of the rite of circumcision. The Abrahamic covenant mandated eighth-day circumcision (Gen 17:12, 21:4; Lev 12:3). The author of Genesis further stipulates: *Any uncircumcised male who is not circumcised in the flesh of his foreskin shall be cut off from his people; he has broken my covenant* (Gen 17:14).[7] The author of the book of Jubilees (2nd cent. BCE) demonstrated a deep concern for the timing of the ritual and the consequences for getting it wrong:[8] *This law is (valid) for all history forever. There is no circumcising of days, nor omitting any day of the eight days because it is an eternal ordinance ordained and written on the heavenly tablets. Anyone who is born, the flesh of whose private parts has not been circumcised by the eighth day does not belong to the people of the pact which the Lord made with Abraham* (Jub. 15:26a [trans. VanderKam, 91–92]). Because adult gentile circumcision could not be performed on the eighth day of life according to the prescription of the Law, gentiles by default could not preform the circumcision *of the Abrahamic* covenant. In the primordialist Jewish ritual world, anything other than eighth-day circumcision was futile.

According to Thiessen then, it was not that Paul thought gentile Christ followers *need not* convert to Judaism but that they quite literary *could not* convert to Judaism. It was not that Paul found fault with the Law or fault with Jewish ethnocentrism but rather that Paul, like the author of Jubilees, read the Law literally. There simply was no path to conversion.

By inverting the poles of orientation, Thiessen cleanly acquits Paul of the anti-Judaism smear that has dogged readings of the epistles for centuries. Paul emerges a hero advocating gentile inclusion via baptism into Christ all while upholding the Law. It is an elegant solution. The problem is, however, at least in Galatians, Paul seems *mighty* worked up over the prospect of the Galatians's circumcision if it was the case that gentile adult circumcision was merely ineffectual.

ESTABLISHING A LINE OF INQUIRY

Thiessen's reading of Paul as a primordialist as a means of explaining his stance on circumcision is certainly plausible. His book, *Paul and the Gentile Problem*, is thick with well-researched arguments—one is spoiled for choice as to where to begin a line of inquiry. Yet as I weigh his argument, stepping back from the nuance of his reasoning, the piece of the puzzle that most nags me about this theory is Paul's desperation in Galatians that the converts not circumcise themselves. Paul seems to perceive a level of threat in the proposition of the converts' circumcision that is not fully satisfied by an appeal to the eschatological expectation that gentiles had to remain gentiles in order to justify God's claim to be *Lord of all*.[9] If, as Thiessen contends, gentile circumcision doesn't work to make gentiles Jews, then it would be the case that even if the Galatians had circumcised themselves, they would still *be* gentiles, just mangled ones.

What follows is a narrative tour of four, second century BCE texts, 1 Maccabees (1 Macc), Judith (Jdt), and Greek Esther (Add Esth), that include gentile circumcision as a story element, and Jubilees (Jub.) that interpolates the origin narrative of the covenant of circumcision in its rewriting of Genesis. It is a collection of texts that had been circulating in the culture for two centuries by the time Paul and his compatriots engaged the idea of gentile conversion and whether such converts should be circumcised.

CONVERTS BY COMPULSION: 1 MACCABEES

1 Maccabees recounts the story of the Jewish revolt against the Seleucid Empire. The plot of the narrative is driven by issues of national-religious identity. The movement of individuals between identities—Jew and Greek—with their associated loyalties signified by circumcision, was the warrant for war on both sides of the conflict in this retelling.

As the author of 1 Maccabees presents the conflict, the war was precipitated on the Jewish side by the desire of a contingent in Jerusalem to adopt Greek civic customs, namely by the building of a gymnasium in Jerusalem (1 Macc 1:14). The original audience of 1 Maccabees was left to intuit the attendant social pressures the establishment of such an institution would have placed on a circumcised man in the Greco-Roman culture which promoted nudity but which abhorred the public display of the glans.[10] The author then tells the reader that Jews *made themselves uncircumcised*, ἐποίησαν ἑαυτοῖς ἀκροβυστίας (1 Macc 1:15a), in order to participate in the gymnasium according to Greek custom.

While there were various methods by which a man could disguise a congenitally inadequate foreskin, camouflaging a circumcision was a more difficult proposition. The creative use of a *kynodesme* or a carefully positioned gourd with a well told story could conceal a circumcision in situations where male nudity was the *de rigueur*. However, the use of such aids ran the risk of failure and quite literal exposure.[11] The "Cadillac of correctives,"[12] as Robert Hall puts it, for the ritually inflicted defect[13] of circumcision in the Greco-Roman world was *epispasm*. Aulus Celsus (c.25 CE) describes the surgery: *the surgeon would cut around the glans freeing the sheath of skin surrounding the shaft of the penis, pull the skin forward and dress the wound carefully so that the skin would reattach to the glans leaving a foreskin*, a procedure he assures his reader was *not so very painful* (Celsus, Med. 7.25.1 [Spencer]).[14]

The term the author of 1 Maccabees used in describing the body modification of the Hellenophiles of Jerusalem was ἀκροβυστίας, uncircumcision. What did the author intend his reader to think the Hellenophiles were doing? The author of 1 Maccabees indicts the Hellenophiles of Jerusalem not for *concealing* their circumcision but for *undoing* their circumcision, for making it as though they had not been claimed at birth by their parents and community for YHWH. Ἀκροβυστίας was the opposite of περιτομή, circumcision. As the state of περιτομή for a Jewish male was achieved by surgical removal of the foreskin, so achieving its opposite, the state of ἀκροβυστίας, of becoming uncircumcised for a circumcised Jewish male, would seem to logically imply the surgical reversal of that circumcision. The author of 1 Maccabees appears to have charged the Jewish Hellenophiles of undergoing *epispasm*.

Assuming this to be the case, the question then is: did *epispasm* make a circumcised man born to a Jewish family a gentile? For the author of 1 Maccabees the answer seems to have been *yes*: Καὶ ἀπέστησαν ἀπὸ διαθήκης ἁγίας καὶ ἐζευγίσθησαν τοῖς ἔθνεσιν καὶ ἐπράθησαν τοῦ ποιῆσαι τὸ πονηρόν, *and [they] removed the marks of circumcision, and abandoned the holy covenant. They joined with the Gentiles and sold themselves to do evil* (1 Macc 1:15b). Men doing such a thing had willfully abandoned Israel's covenant with God, the very essence of what created and defined Israel according to sacred tradition. Having thrown off the covenant, their birthright, they had instead covenanted themselves to the Greeks, *yoking* themselves to the gentiles, *selling* themselves to do evil. This language of "yoking" and "selling" conjures images of slavery, evoking passages like Leviticus 26:13 *I am the LORD your God who brought you out of the land of Egypt, to be their slaves no more; I have broken the bars of your yoke and made you walk erect* (also Ezek 34:27). The value judgment is explicit—rejection of circumcision was a rejection of the covenant it represented and the identity derived from it.[15] It was tantamount to a willful resubmission to slavery under the gentiles. To the mind of the author of 1 Maccabees, those who availed themselves of *epispasm* were apostates, disloyal traitors.[16]

From the desire of the Jerusalem Hellenophiles to make Jerusalem a Greek polis and become Hellene themselves, the author of 1 Maccabees turns to Antiochus IV's desire to *likewise* make Jerusalem a Greek polis and the Jews Hellene. The emperor's support of the pro-Helene reformers in Jerusalem turned into a calculated and vicious campaign of forced Hellenization in Judea after Jason's 169 BCE attempt to regain the high priesthood from Menelaus while Antiochus was in Egypt. Interpreting events in Jerusalem as a coup, Antiochus issued the *gezerot* outlawing the practice of all particular Jewish cultural customs on pain of death (1 Macc 1:42, 50), his express goal, according to 1 Maccabees, was the erasure of Jewish difference that *all should be one people* (1 Macc 1:41). The particular Jewish cultural customs targeted were the *chukim,* the ordinances of kashrut, sabbath, circumcision, and possession of a copy of the Torah.

The king's project, ill-advised and poorly executed as it was in Judea, nonetheless revealed the emperor's constructivist conception of identity—a belief that identity was malleable and transient by nature, a thing capable of being shaped and forged in the crucible of empire. Antiochus came by this view honestly, no less than Alexander the Great had tried a similar social/cultural experiment to bind his far-flung empire together. Not only was Antiochus a constructivist, believing that identities could be shed and alternatively adopted, but all the gentiles of his kingdom and a good number of Jews, according to the author of 1 Maccabees, also believed the practice of the Seleucid religion and observation of Seleucid customs capable of converting non-Hellenes into Hellenes: *All the Gentiles accepted the command of the king. Many even from Israel gladly adopted his religion; they sacrificed to idols and profaned the sabbath* (1 Macc 1:43). Antiochus's attack on the religious rituals and sacred spaces of the YHWH cult, the incitement of the people to despise the religion of their ancestors, was designed to that end—to separate the people from their god in an effort to realign the people's orientation, fidelity, and sense of kinship to the empire. The effort and expenditure the Seleucids exhausted on this project, sending inspectors and soldiers to every town in Judea to enforce the edict, testify to the fact they believed not only that such mass conversion was possible, but that it would work to their advantage.

It was not only the Jerusalem Hellenophiles or the Seleucids or "all the gentiles" of the kingdom who believed it possible to abandon the religion-culture of one's birth and adopt another, the Jewish resistance fighters clearly thought it as well. All sides in the conflict as represented in 1 Maccabees perceived ethnic/cultural identity as contingent. When the Maccabean rebels succeed in pushing the Seleucid army out of the territory of Israel, the insurgents' first order of business was to tear down the pagan altars and then forcibly circumcise all the uncircumcised boys found within the borders of Israel (1 Macc 2:44–46). Executed within the sphere of Maccabean influence, compulsory circumcision served to score the reestablished border in the flesh of the *am ha'aretz*. In the inversion of this *gezerah*, Mattathias reached for the same political solution sought by his nemesis Antiochus: unity in conformity. As the Jewish rebels reclaimed the land physically, so they reclaimed the bodies of those on the land. In the neat narrative world of 1 Maccabees, circumcision accomplished this homogeneity in a single knife stroke.

Under the flag of zeal for the Law (1 Macc 2:27), the appropriateness of compulsory circumcision as a response to a Jewish military victory is simply assumed in 1 Maccabees. Circumcision, however, was only one of several practices particular to Jews outlawed by Antiochus. One might imagine Mattathias could have equally forced the observance of the Sabbath or ordered the slaughter of all pigs in Judea in redress of the other injustices suffered by the faithful. Circumcision was surely the more dramatic choice as it involved blood, pain, fear, disfigurement (of a type), if not also a bit of levity when one imagines the hunt for the miscreants. Yet in his reclamation, the Mattathias of 1 Maccabees selected a single signpost to mark his victory: circumcision. This in turn advanced an extremely literal, provincial, embodied view of Jewish identity. To be *in* Israel, you must *be* Israel.[17] To *be* a Jew, you must *look* like a Jew. To *look* like a Jew was to *be* a Jew. Certainly, the presentation in 1 Maccabees vastly oversimplified the varied and complex nature of Jewish religious identity.[18] Yet simplify the author did and in doing so established circumcision as the supreme metonymy for Jews and Judaism. It does not necessarily follow from this that the author of 1 Maccabees was the originator of this figure. What is at issue is the fact that when circumcision does surface in its metonymic capacity as an identity marker for Israel in the second century BCE, it does so without rival in the climactic moment of reversal in a pivotally significant national legend. 1 Maccabees was, of course, a piece of political propaganda. Such campaigns, if they are waged successfully, reduce the message to the most salient, emotionally compelling signposts. 1 Maccabees presented circumcision as the standard defining Jewish national-religious identity and a mark capable of resignifying a gentile body within the territory of Israel as a Jewish body.[19] While historians rightly question the historicity of the author's portrayal of the conflict,[20] what remained long after the historical Mattathias and his sons first rallied the resistance against their Seleucid suzerains was the author of 1 Maccabees' interpretation of Jewish resistance and the ritual symbol representing their righteous struggle – an interpretation disseminated to a wide audience over successive generations. As Salman Rushdie notes in *Midnight's Children,* "Sometimes legends make reality, and become more useful than the facts."[21]

CONVERTS OUT OF SELF-PRESERVATION: ESTHER

The book of Esther (4th century BCE) makes an intriguing claim that the Persian proletariat, in a bid to avoid being slaughtered by the Jews following the edict of Ahasuerus in 8:10–12, either *became Jews* or *professed/pretended to be Jews* (מתיהדים) *because the fear of the Jews had fallen upon them* (Esth 8:17b). What the author imagined these gentiles to be doing in this brief reference is debated by scholars. Were the Persians of Esther attempting to pass as Jews only in the moment of threat or was the author asserting that they actually became and remained Jews?²² Here, however, we are up against the limits of the narrative presented. Esther is a novella, not a historical recounting. The gentiles' conversion/pretense to be Jews in 8:17 was a detail in service of illustrating the complete and total reversal of the fortunes of the Jews themselves satisfying a conscribed narrative arc. As Hadassah was concealed among the king's haram under a Persian name,²³ her family of origin unknown ostensibly to aid her survival, so the Persians must then conceal their origins or in fact become Jews in order to survive. ²⁴ Esther was a story about Jews for Jews. Having served their narrative purpose, the author felt no compulsion to sketch out a long-term socio-religious identity of the fictive Persians in question.²⁵ Acknowledging the operating constraints on the narrative, the lack of detail on this point does not necessitate the conclusion that the author and his intended audience did not have a precise idea of what מתיהדים would have involved for the Persians.²⁶

As one imagines the scene in the moment of Jewish ascendancy, the fearful Persians would have had to credibly present themselves as Jews *to Jews*, offering some significant evidence of their loyalties. The inherent ambiguity in Esther 8:17 as to what the Persians were doing to present themselves as less of a target to their would-be Jewish attackers was clarified for later readers the following century in the translation and expansion of the Esther tradition in the Septuagint.²⁷ Esther 8:17 received an explanatory gloss adding the detail that *many of the gentiles were circumcised and lived according to Jewish custom/became Jews out of fear of the Jews* (Add Esth 8:17b). The redactor of Greek Esther thus makes clear—the Persians circumcised themselves in order to escape certain death.²⁸

While the redactor of Greek Esther make explicit that the Persians circumcised themselves, it is likely the intended readership of the MT Esther tradition assumed as much. Circumcision, however, was a sacred rite in Judaism. Clarifying this assumption, the redactor of Greek Esther was compelled then to make clear what that action *meant*. He added that the Persians *lived according to Jewish custom* post circumcision and so became Jews. In the gloss, any ambiguity concerning the Persians in Esther 8:17 is eliminated. Their circumcision marked their conversion, a transfiguration born out in their living.

While psychological studies of conversion tend to focus on the convert as an individual, the act of conversion equally involves the *community* with which the proselyte desires to be identified. To be a *convert* as opposed to an imitator, or a voyeur, or even a stalker, requires the acceptance of the convert by the desired group, a recognition and validation of the convert's claimed identity.²⁹ Even in the fictive world of Greek Esther, one would imagine that the Persians suddenly acting Jewishly would have been noticed by the Jews themselves—Jews who would then have been in a position to identify Persian pretenders on the day of reckoning. Even if the Persian-pretenders had been able to infiltrate the Jewish community unnoticed, the newness of their circumcision would have presented an issue, if their aim was to merely pass as a Jew in the moment of danger.

The book of Esther is unusually attentive to the months and days on which events occur. Supposing the *fear of the Jews* fell on the Persians immediately upon learning of Mordecai's edict and that, afraid for their lives, they circumcised themselves that very same day, only nine months in Hebrew Esther and eleven months in Greek Esther would have elapsed between the earliest possible date for the Persian's circumcision and the Persian massacre on the 13th of Adar. While the wound would have taken on average three weeks to heal,[30] the scar would have taken one to two, even three years to mature and fade.[31] If the scenario the reader is intended to imagine was that, to escape death, the Persians were required to prove their claim to Judaism by demonstrating their circumcision, the fresh purple scar would have given them away as only recently having undergone the operation. In Greek Esther 9:1–2 addition D, the Persians learn of the edict sanctioning their destruction on the same day as the planned massacre. In this addition it would not have been a scar the Persians presented to the Jews to spare their lives but an open wound. Either way, it would have been evident to the Jews on the 13th and 14th of Adar who was a Jew-from-birth and who was a pretender on inspection. As neither the author of MT Esther or LXX Esther demonstrate the least reticence about killing thousands of fictive Persians it is worthy of note that the newly-circumcised-Jewishly-acting-Persians were not said to be murdered alongside the Jews' sworn Persian enemies (Est 9:5–16, Add Est 9:5–16). This would suggest not that the Persians got away with their subterfuge,[32] but rather, that on the basis of their demonstratively fresh circumcision alone, the Persians were accepted by the Jews of the Esther tradition *as Jews*.

CONVERTS BY CONVICTION: JUDITH

The character of Achior in the book of Judith (2nd century BCE) is the case of a willing, eager convert to Judaism.[33] The narrative introduces him as part of the Assyrian general Holofernes' war council. As the leader of the Ammonites, a vassal of the Assyrian Empire, and Israel's near neighbor to the west across the Jordan River, Achior was in the position to offer intelligence to Holofernes in his campaign against the Northern Kingdom of Israel. His report to the council detailed a succinct, suspiciously deuteronomic understanding of the theory of Israel's military power (Jdt 5:16–21). Achior advised the general that Assyria's only chance against Israel lay not with the great man's prowess or his vast army, but rather with whether Israel was in good standing with her patron deity. If Israel went to war with the help and protection of YHWH, the Assyrians, Achior warned, would surely be defeated.

Whether Achior was a God-fearer the text does not say. His speech is suggestively conformist to the late Second Temple period Jewish theological worldview. Within the narrative, those of the council and Holofernes himself certainly take Achior's report as evidence that his loyalties and allegiance lay with Israel. The general accuses Achior and the Ammonites of being *mercenaries of Ephraim,* seizes Achior and hands him over to the Israelites at Bethulia for him to die with Israel in the upcoming battle (Jdt 6:1–13). The narrative unfolds, and upon witnessing the dramatic deliverance of the Jews from the Assyrians, Achior decides to fully switch alliances and become an actual Jew: *Achior, having seen all the God of Israel had done, believed in God exceedingly. He circumcised his uncircumcised flesh and was added to the house of Israel and remains so to this day,* ἰδὼν δὲ Αχιωρ πάντα, ὅσα ἐποίησεν ὁ θεὸς τοῦ Ισραηλ, ἐπίστευσεν τῷ θεῷ σφόδρα καὶ περιετέμετο τὴν σάρκα τῆς ἀκροβυστίας αὐτοῦ καὶ προσετέθη εἰς τὸν οἶκον Ισραηλ ἕως τῆς ἡμέρας ταύτης (Jdt 14:10). Achior's conversion and incorporation into Israel was accomplished by circumcision *solus.* Circumcision made him a Jew and a Jew he remained.

Like the story of Esther, the tale of Judith was a Jewish story about the Jewish heroine, Judith, and the miraculous deliverance of Israel brought about by her cunning. The gentle-turned-Jew, Achior, was only a supporting character. Given a single line, his conversion was an ancillary detail. So why include it at all? After all, Achior had already found refuge among the Jews, he already knew where the axis of power lay, why then in this tale did the author additionally turn him into a Jew? The answer may lie with the Hebrew prophets' expectations regarding the fate of the gentiles, namely, that the enemies of Israel would be destroyed and that the remaining nations would turn to God and respect Israel (e.g., Isa 66:14–21). Within the narrative world of Judith, the conversion of Achior was the accompaniment to the humiliation of Holofernes illustrating the dual prophetic expectation: Holofernes the annihilation, Achior the turning. Their respective nationalities, Assyrian and Ammonite, represented the worst of Israel's enemies near and far.[34]

Two of the more famous prophetic passages envisioning the eschatological turning of the gentiles are found in Isaiah and Micah: *"[M]any nations shall come and say: 'Come, let us go up to the mountain of the LORD, to the house of the God of Jacob; that he may teach us his ways and that we may walk in his paths'"*(Isa 2:3) and *"For out of Zion shall go forth instruction, and the word of the LORD from Jerusalem"* (Mic 4:2c). These passages and others like them, however, leave the details aside of what *exactly* it might look like for gentiles to walk in the path of the Lord. Ostensibly it would seem to mean that gentiles, convicted of the truth of the Jewish *Weltanschauung,* would follow the Law and therefore observe the ethical commandments, the Sabbath, the festivals, and—in the absence of a prohibition against it—the rite of circumcision. Achior is presented in Judith as a gentile, deuteronomically-oriented, convicted of the theological propositions of Judaism, and submitting to *circumcision*—the first command any Jewish male observes (albeit done on his behalf as an infant). By this act, the circumcised male lays claim to the community as a Jew and is in turn claimed by the community as a Jew. It is a natural implication of the prophetic vision that in desiring to become a Jew Achior would submit to circumcision. It is an assumption that notably gave the author of Judith no pause. Achior's conversion by circumcision was stated simply, and in brief, requiring no supplement justification or explanation, the logic of such an action clearly apparent to both author and audience.

EIGHTH-DAY CIRCUMCISION AND THE QUESTION OF CONVERTS: JUBILEES

Seemingly on the opposite end of the spectrum regarding circumcision is the book of Jubilees. In rewriting his source material in response to the evolved convictions of his own community and his rhetorical agenda, the author of Jubilees offered a second century BCE interpolation of the command given to Abraham to circumcise all of his house in Genesis 17:12–14.

> This law is (valid) for all history forever. There is no circumcising of days, nor omitting any day of the eight days because it is an eternal ordinance ordained and written on the heavenly tablets. Anyone who is born, the flesh of whose private parts has not been circumcised by the eighth day does not belong to the people of the pact which the Lord made with Abraham but to the people (meant for) destruction. Moreover, there is no sign on him that he belongs to the Lord, but (he is meant) for destruction, for being destroyed from the earth, and for being uprooted from the earth because he has violated the covenant of the Lord our God. (Jubilees 15:25–26 [trans. VanderKam])[35]

The ordinance in Jubilees is harsh, a child suffering an extreme penalty for the non-compliance of his parents.[36] While the author of Jubilees does put some spin on the ball, in actuality he has only underscored the threat present already in Genesis 17: *Throughout your generations every male among you shall be circumcised when he is eight days old. . . . Any uncircumcised male who is not circumcised in the flesh of his foreskin shall be cut off from his people; he has broken my covenant* (Gen 17:12a,14).

In thinking about Paul and his gentile problem, the question has been focused on whether circumcision could turn a gentile into a Jew. Jubilees 15, however, demonstrates the reverse. A violation of the covenant of circumcision—a circumcision left undone or done at the wrong time—turns a born Jew effectively into a gentile.[37] The sons of procrastinators or the non-observant were "considered uncircumcised from the viewpoint of the halakhah"[38] and so condemned as *people (meant for) destruction.*

It has been widely assumed by commentators that such a strict interpretation of the ordinance of circumcision eliminating lax Jews from consideration as *sons of the covenant*, particularly when read with the exclusivist tradition of Ezra-Nehemiah, wholly disregarded any possibility of gentile conversion to Judaism—full stop.[39] But did the author of Jubilees have in view prohibiting gentile conversion by his instance for the absolute timing—*eight days or nothing*—for the observation of circumcision?

To be capable of violating the covenant, one first had to be *under* the covenant. On the subject of circumcision, Jubilees served to warn Jews, not to inform gentiles. However, the question remains, does the absolute timing—*eight days or nothing*—for the correct observation of circumcision exclude gentile conversion by default? Gaming the scenario out, let us suppose a gentile man became enamored of Judaism. He desires to convert fully to Judaism via circumcision and live as a Jew but becomes convinced that he cannot because the ritual of circumcision cannot be performed on the eighth day of *his* life as prescribed. He accepts his fate and lives as a God-fearer. But what if, damned by his own disadvantageous birth, the God-fearing gentile sought to correct this timing deficit in the next generation and he has his congenitally gentile son circumcised on the eighth day—would that child then be a Jew? If so, eighth-day circumcision would pose only a generational barrier to gentile conversion. In the form of his son, a significantly motivated gentile father could theoretically convert his family even if he himself never makes it to the Promised Land.

Further complicating the idea that the strict eighth-day circumcision imposed on Jews in *Jubilees* would have been read as a barrier to gentile conversion is the author's unqualified transposition of Genesis 17:23–27 in *Jubilees* 15:23–24. In both texts, neither Abraham, nor Ishmael, nor the men of his house, nor the foreigners with him were eight days old when they were circumcised. There is no indication in either text there was even an eight-day old baby boy in the camp. The failure of the author of Jubilees to offer a parenthetical limiting the midrashic potential of the late timing of Abraham and his household's circumcision leaves a conspicuous literary gap if the exclusion of gentile conversion was anywhere in the author of Jubilees' mind. The handholds for scaling the obstacle of the eighth-day mandate binding on those already within the covenant is in plain sight in both Genesis and Jubilees for who would make the case for gentile conversion. The fact of the matter is that the visitors to Galatia, about whom Paul was so exercised, could have argued their same case for gentile convert circumcision from Jubilees 15 as much as from Genesis 17. That the author of Jubilees did not sew up these rather obvious literary gaps indicates that he did not have gentiles in view in Jubilees 15 one way or another.

An interesting control passage for understanding how the author of Jubilees understood the eighth-day circumcision obligation would have been the story of Zipporah's circumcising of Gershom in Exodus 4:24–26. Though Moses failed to circumcise his son as stipulated in the covenant of Abraham, the tradition holds that Gershom was not cut off from the people (Judg 18:30). The author of Jubilees, however, omitted the tale in his rewriting and we are none the wiser as to how he would have reconciled this story with his strict eighth-day mandate. Perhaps the most that can be said is that there is not enough information to be able to persuasively argue how the author of Jubilees's understanding of the covenant of circumcision as it related to Jews would have informed his opinion as to whether a gentile might convert to Judaism through circumcision.

THE RHETORICAL PITCH OF PAUL'S LETTER TO THE GALATIANS

To say that Paul 'opposed' the position advocated by the visitors to Galatia is an understatement. *I am astonished,* he writes the newly minted converts, *that you so quickly have been turned from the one who called you by the grace of Christ to a different gospel* (Gal 1:6). He emphatically, pedantically reiterates portions of his argument as though his readers were particularly dull: *Even if we or an angel from heaven should preach a gospel other than the one we preached to you, let him be eternally condemned! As we have already said, so now I say again—if anyone is preaching to you a gospel other than what you accepted, let him be eternally condemned!* (Gal 1:8–9; other examples 1:10–12; 4:20). He belittles his audience: *You foolish Galatians! Who has bewitched you?... Are you so foolish?* (Gal 3:1–3). He savages his opponents: *I wish those who disturbed you would mutilate themselves* (Gal 5:12). He all but throws up his hands in frustration at the end of the letter, *let no one make trouble for me; for I carry the marks of Jesus branded on my body* (Gal 6:17). No other subject, not even the Corinthians' denial of the bodily resurrection, provoked a rebuttal in the tenor or on the scale of Paul's letter to the Galatians.

Adjectives one might assign Paul at the moment he penned this letter are frustration, exasperation, confusion, hurt, indignation, anger, worry, or desperation. If the problem with the Galatians' impending circumcision was that it would simply not work, according to Thiessen, Paul's shrill rhetorical pitch seems hardly warranted. In fact, Paul argued something far more extreme than that there was simply *no need* to observe circumcision in the messianic age or that circumcision would *not work* to make the Galatians Jews—Paul insisted that the circumcision of the converts posed a *first-order threat* to the realization of the messianic age itself. His warning could not have been more dire—should the Galatians submit to being circumcised, the work of Christ would be negated (Gal 1:4; 2:18–21; 4:11; 5:1–10).

Clearly Paul wanted to preserve the otherness of the Galatians—to keep their bodies gentile even as he counseled them to act ever more Jewishly. This was in keeping with the Jewish eschatological expectations of the period which had evolved an expectation of a coming reclamation of the gentiles as gentiles in the divine final righting of the world.[40] However, if the rhetorical pitch of Galatians is understood to be one of anxiety provoked by the perception of a threat, and we understand that component to be interpretively significant, then again it is hard to imagine the Galatians' desire to follow the Law in all its aspects would have provoked such a drastic response from Paul. Paul's reaction is simply not commensurate with the offence.

One could equally imagine Paul receiving word of the converts' intention to circumcise and seeing it as a teaching opportunity, a chance to come again alongside this congregation he had some hand in forming to expand their understanding, even delighting in their commitment, misguided as it may have been. Paul was likely an excellent rhetor, or he would not have met such missional success. There were so many ways to approach this problem of the Galatians' desire to be circumcised, Paul's biting frustration and thick midrashic prose seem aimed directly at neutralizing the threat, less at bringing the Galatians to enlightenment.

Surely the practice of circumcision was a matter of debate, tradition, rejection, reverence and alternatively indifference among the lay Jews of the late Second Temple period. In the surviving literature of the culture in which circumcision is mentioned or otherwise discussed, the value and obligation of the practice of the rite are assumed, a central component of orthopraxy for Jews. Even Philo who allegorized the meaning of circumcision was nonetheless harshly critical of Jews who failed to perform the physical ritual (Philo, *Migr.* 89–93). For Jews, circumcision was both an obligation and a privilege.

The late Second Temple witnesses testify: the categories of *Jew* and *gentile* were fixed, an immutable binary of being signified by circumcision. While the categories were fixed, the people who embodied them, however, were not. Circumcision—its presence, absence, or performance—made and unmade Jews.[41]

Thinking rhetorically through Galatians, attuned structurally to the presence and absence of arguments, not just what Paul did say, but what he could have said and didn't—I find myself ultimately unpersuaded that the ineffectual nature of adult gentile circumcision could have been a sufficient motivation for Paul's distress in Galatians. The perceived level of peril would suggest Paul rather believed the opposite to be true—that adult gentile circumcision worked all too well in making gentiles Jews. Paul did not want the Galatians to circumcise themselves because he believed they would, by that single act, become Jews. Paul *needed* the Galatians to remain gentiles in accordance with his eschatological vision of the divine righting of the world.⁴² The threat was that the Galatians, who had accepted the Jewish God, a Jewish messiah, Jewish scriptures, and Jewish ethics, with a minor surgery could slip entirely into Israel, becoming cultically indistinguishable. This appears to me to be the trajectory Paul is desperate to arrest because it was, to his mind, entirely possible for the Galatians to become Jews.

NOTES

1. "From a Jewish perspective, without social conversion—that is, without the integration of a gentile into a Jewish society—there is no conversion at all; the gentile remains a gentile. . . .What must a gentile do in order to achieve social integration into the Jewish community? The only empirical or 'objective' requirement that our sources reveal is circumcision for men." Shaye J. D. Cohen, *The Beginnings of Jewishness: Boundaries, Varieties, Uncertainties* (Berkeley, CA: University of California, 1999), 168–69. Only "[a]fter the time of Justin and his promulgation of *Verus Israel* [2nd century C.E.], becoming a Christian (or follower of Christ) meant something different—it no longer entailed becoming a Jew. . . ." Daniel Boyarin, *Border Lines, the Partition of Judeo-Christianity* (Philadelphia, PA: University of Pennsylvania, 2004), 73.

2. Usually introduced with the formula καθὼς γέγραπται. For extensive discussion see Stanley E. Porter and Christopher D. Stanley, *As It Is Written: Studying Paul's Use of Scripture* (Leiden: Brill, 2008).

3. The goal of the *Paul within Judaism Perspective* is to read Paul as an authentic, coherent Jewish thinker in continuity with his tradition not in opposition to it. For discussion see Mark D. Nanos, "Introduction," in *Paul within Judaism: Restoring First-Century Context to the Apostle*, ed. Mark D. Nanos and Magnus Zetterholm (Minneapolis, MN: Fortress Press, 2015), 1–30.

4. Matthew Thiessen, *Paul and the Gentile Problem* (New York, NY: Oxford University Press, 2016), 7.

5. Ibid.

6. Ibid.

7. All biblical quotations are taken from the NRSV unless otherwise indicated.

8. Thiessen, *Paul,* 77–82.

9. Mark D. Nanos, *The Mystery of Romans: The Jewish Context of Paul's Letters* (Minneapolis, MN: Fortress Press, 1996), 179–201.

10. Robert G. Hall, "Epispasm: Circumcision in Reverse," *BR* 8 (1992): 52–57. At issue was propriety—it was a social *faux pas* in the context of a Greek gymnasium to have the glans of a man's penis exposed. "The Greek standard of modesty held that the foreskin should cover the glans. Visible glans in an uncircumcised man was taken as a sign of arousal and was thus considered indecent within the arena. To prevent mishaps, many athletes wore the *kynodesme,* a strand of colored string that looped around the foreskin, closing it tightly over the glans" (David L. Gollaher, *Circumci-*

sion: A History of the World's Most Controversial Surgery [(New York, NY: Basic Books, 2000)], 13–14).

11. See Martial, *Epigrams*, 7.82.

12. Robert G. Hall, "Epispasm and the Dating of Ancient Jewish Writings," *JSP* 2 (1988): 71–86.

13. Louis H. Feldman, *Jew and Gentile in the Ancient World: Attitudes and Interactions from Alexander to Justinian* (Princeton, NJ: Princeton University Press, 1996), 155.

14. Reference is made to this procedure in the *Testament of Moses*, 8:3.

15. Josephus defined a convert from their Jewish heritage as one who hates Jewish customs: *As for Antiochus he . . . thought to give* [the pagans] *a demonstration of his own conversion* (μεταβολή), *and his hatred of the Jewish customs*" (Josephus, *J.W.* 7.3.3 [Whiston]; also, Josephus *Ant.* 12.5.1). Conversely, he defined a convert *to* Judaism as one who embraces Jewish customs (*Ant.* 13.9.1).

16. Josephus, *Ant.* 12.241. See Erich S. Gruen, *Heritage and Hellenism* (Berkeley, CA: University of California Press, 2002), 29–31; and Lester L. Grabbe, *Judaism from Cyrus to Hadrian* (2 vols., Minneapolis, MN: Fortress Press, 1992), 278–79.

17. In the consolidation of Hasmonean power, Jannaeus destroyed three cities "because [the] inhabitants would not bear to change their religious rites for those peculiar to the Jews" (Josephus, *Ant.* 13.395 [Whiston]).

18. As Cohen observes, "[f]or both Jews and gentiles the boundary line between Judaism and paganism was determined more by Jewish observance than by Jewish theology" (*From the Maccabees to the Mishnah* [(Philadelphia, PA: Westminster, 1989)], 61).

19. Of the forced conversion of the Idumeans, Josephus wrote: *Hyrcanus . . . permitted* [the Idumeans] *to stay in that country, if they would circumcise their genitals, and make use of the laws of the Jews; and they were so desirous of living in the country of their forefathers that they submitted to circumcision, and the rest of the Jewish ways of living; at which time therefore this befell them, that they were hereafter no other than Jews* (Josephus, *Ant.* 13.9.1 [Whiston]). That the conversion of the Idumeans was compulsory gave Josephus seemingly no pause as to their legitimacy. Herod the exception that proves the rule, see Benedikt Eckhardt, "'An Idumean, That Is a Half Jew. Hasmoneans and Herodians between Ancestry and Merit," in *Jewish Identity and Politics between the Macabees and Bar Kokhba: Groups, Normativity and Rituals*, ed. Benedikt Eckhardt (Leiden: Brill, 2013).

20. Erich Gruen suspects with good reason the historicity of the 1 Maccabees account that significant numbers of Jews were availing themselves of epispasm (*Heritage and Hellenism*, 29–30). However, the historicity of the events in Jerusalem are less at issue in this line of inquiry. The author of 1 Maccabees presented this act of becoming ἀκροβυστία as treason against God and the nation, the clear going over to and aligning with the oppressing foreign power. Whether or not this actually happened or is a stylized accounting by an author in support of his rhetorical purposes is beside the point. It was how it was memorialized for posterity.

21. Salman Rushdie, *Midnight's Children* (New York: Penguin Random House, 1991), 47.

22. Amidst this dearth of narrative clues, commentators looking to dismiss the idea of gentile conversion in Esther have cited the expressed motivations of the Persians —namely, that they are motivated out of naked self-interest not wanting to be murdered—as evidence in favor of the Persians pretending to be Jews in Esth 8:17. There is perhaps a tantalizing though tenuous precedent, however, for the envelopment of a mass of gentiles into the assembly of Israel in Exodus 12:38. A great mixed company comes out of Egypt with the Hebrews. The motivations for the multitude's departure are not given in the text. Their leaving *with* Hebrews following the tenth and final plague of the death of the first born is at least suggestive of the idea that they too are fleeing for their lives—that, having taken stock of the situation, thought their chances of survival better with the Hebrews and God. The text leaves the reader to believe that the multitude was simply folded into Israel, absorbed, and so saved. Holding open the possibility of such a reading, the mixed company might be compared in motivation to the Persians who feared the Jews and so attempted to become in some manner Jewish to survive. For discussion on the motivation of the Persians, see Cohen, *Beginnings* 175–97; John Dunne, *Esther and Her Elusive God: How a Secular Story Functions as Scripture* (Eugene, OR: Wipf & Stock, 2014), 61. For discussion on the motivation of the mixed multitude, see Shaul Magid, "The Politics of (Un)Conversion: The 'Mixed Multitude' ('Erev Rav) as Conversos in Rabbi Hayyim Vital's 'Ets Ha-Da'at Tov' JQR 95, 4 (2005), 625–66; David Tuesday Adamo, "A Mixed Multitude: An African Reading of Exodus 12:38," in *Exodus and Deuteronomy*, ed. Athalya Brenner and Gale A. Yee (Minneapolis, MN: Fortress Press, 2012), 67–78.

23. Hadassah/Esther's identity as a concubine of Ahasuerus, part of his house and holdings, calls into question the ease with which modern commentators assume for her the ability to retain her identity as a Jew. This might obscure a radical feminist moment of a woman's identification over and against that of her husband.

24. Jon D. Levenson, *Esther: A Commentary* (Louisville, KY: Westminster, 1997), 117.

25. Had the author extended the story, it would be interesting to learn if he imagined the Persians of Esther continuing with the ruse beyond the 13th of Adar—the new Jewish hegemony compelling them to raise their children as Jews resulting in their assimilation. Though a fiction, the reality and the threat of assimilation over successive generations would not have been an abstraction to readers. The curtain on the tale of MT Esther, however, falls with Mordecai and the Jews at the apex of their political fortunes with no indication as to whether the ascendency of the Jews extended past his lifetime.

26. For discussion, see Adele Berlin, *Esther* (Philadelphia, PA: Jewish Publication Society, 2001), 80; Levenson, *Esther,* 115–17.

27. On the relation of the tradition see, Michael V. Fox, *The Redaction of the Books of Esther: On Reading Composite Texts* (Atlanta, GA: Scholars Press, 1991), also Francisco-Javier Ruiz-Ortiz, *The Dynamics of Violence and Revenge in the Hebrew Book of Esther* (Leiden: Brill, 2017), 16–20.

28. It is a presumption that the Persians preformed self-circumcisions. As written, the text does not preclude a reading that has the Persians presenting themselves to a mohel to be circumcised.

29. Joshua Iyaduria, "Religious Conversion and Social Transformation," in *The Encyclopedia of Psychology and Religion*, ed. David A. Leeming (Boston, MA: Springer, 2014).

30. J. H. Rogers, E. Odoyo-June, W. Jaoko, and R. C. Bailey, "Time to Complete Wound Healing in HIV-Positive and HIV-Negative Men Following Medical Male Circumcision in Kisumu, Kenya: A Prospective Cohort Study" *Public Library of Science ONE* 8: 4: e61725 (2013).

31. Ardeshir Bayat, Duncan McGrouther, and Mark Ferguson, "Skin Scarring," *BMJ* 326 (2003): 88–92.

32. The reading of the Persians' circumcision as a trick the Persians played and got away with cuts strongly against the developed arc of the narrative. The Jews are the ones who discover hidden plots and lay traps in Esther. It is a carnivalesque narrative of complete and total reversals. A reading in which the Persians somehow fool the Jews makes the Jews dupes and the reversal of their fortunes incomplete.

33. The story of the conversion of King Izates is also relevant here, but as Paul would not have had access to Josephus's text, it is omitted. For discussion, see Mark D. Nanos, "The Question of Conceptualization: Qualifying Paul's Position on Circumcision in Dialogue with Josephus's Advisors to King Izates," in *Paul within Judaism*, 105–52; Lawrence H. Schiffman, "The Conversion of the Royal House of Adiabene in Josephus and Rabbinic Sources," in *Josephus, Judaism, and Christianity*, ed. Louis H. Feldman and Gohei Hata (Detroit: Wayne State, 1987), 293–312; Gary Gilbert, "The Making of a Jew: 'God-Fearer' or Convert in the Story of Izates," *USQR* 44 (1991): 299–313.

34. While much is made of the detail that Achior was an Ammonite and Ammonites along with Moabites were forbidden in Deuteronomy 23, it is difficult to read Judith as an argument actively advocating for Ammonite/gentile inclusion along the lines of Ruth.

35. James VanderKam, *The Book of Jubilees. A Translation*. Corpus Scriptorum Christianorum Orientalium 511. Scriptores Aethiopici 88 (Louvain: Peeters), 1989.

36. The Mishnah, by contrast, allows for a delay in cases of illness or for the Sabbath (*m. Šabb.* 19:5).

37. Todd R. Hanneken, *The Subversion of the Apocalypses in the Book of Jubilees* (Atlanta, GA: SBL Press, 2012), 100.

38. Michael Segal, *The Book of Jubilees: Rewritten Bible, Redaction, Ideology and Theology* (Leiden: Brill, 2007), 236.

39. Example, Hanneken, *Subversion*, 222.

40. Paula Fredriksen, "Judaism, the Circumcision of Gentiles, and Apocalyptic Hope," *Journal of Theological Studies* 42 (1991), 558–64; Paula Eisenbaum, *Paul Was Not a Christian: The Original Message of a Misunderstood Apostle* (New York, NY: HarperOne, 2009), 96–98.

41. Though relevant, space prohibits discussion of the conversion of gentile women to Judaism.

42. For detailed discussion, see Genevive Dibley, *Abraham's Uncircumcised Children: The Enochic Precedent for Paul's Paradoxical Claim in Galatians 3:29* (Berkeley, CA: UC Berkeley ETD, 2013).

BIBLIOGRAPHY

Adamo, David Tuesday. "A Mixed Multitude: An African Reading of Exodus 12:38." In *Exodus and Deuteronomy: Texts and Context*, edited by Athalya Brenner and Gale A. Yee, 67–78. Minneapolis, MN: Fortress Press, 2012.

Bayat, Ardeshir, Duncan McGrouther, and Mark Ferguson. "Skin Scarring." *British Medical Journal* 326 (2003): 88–92.

Berlin, Adele. *The JPS Bible Commentary: Esther.* Philadelphia, PA: Jewish Publication Society, 2001.

Boyarin, Daniel. *Border Lines: The Partition of Judeo-Christianity.* Philadelphia, PA: University of Pennsylvania, 2004.

Bringmann, Klaus. *Hellenistische Reform und Religionsverfolgung in Judäa. Eine Untersuchung zur jüdisch-hellenistischen Geschichte (175–163 v. Chr.).* In *Abhandlungen der Akademie der Wissenschaften in Göttingen. Philologisch-Historische Klasse 3. Folge, Nr. 132*, 149–52. Göttingen: Vandenhoeck & Ruprecht, 1983.

Celsus. *De Medicina.* Translated by W. G. Spencer et al. 3 vols. Loeb Classical Library. Cambridge: Harvard University Press, 1938.

Cohen, Shaye J. D. *From the Maccabees to the Mishnah.* Philadelphia, PA: Westminster, 1989.

———. "Respect for Judaism by Gentiles according to Josephus." *Harvard Theological Review* 80, no. 4 (1987): 409–30.

———. *The Beginnings of Jewishness: Boundaries, Varieties, Uncertainties.* Berkeley, CA: University of California, 1999.

Dunne, John Anthony. *Esther and Her Elusive God: How a Secular Story Functions as Scripture.* Eugene, OR: Wipf & Stock, 2014.

Dibley, Genevive. *Abraham's Uncircumcised Children: The Enochic Precedent for Paul's Paradoxical Claim in Galatians 3:29.* Berkeley, CA: UC Berkeley Electronic Thesis and Dissertation, 2013.

Eckhardt, Benedikt. "'An Idumean, That Is a Half Jew.' Hasmoneans and Herodians between Ancestry and Merit." In *Jewish Identity and Politics between the Maccabees and Bar Kokhba: Groups, Normativity and Rituals*, edited by Benedikt Eckhardt, 91–115. Leiden: Brill, 2013.

Eisenbaum, Paula. *Paul Was Not a Christian: The Original Message of a Misunderstood Apostle.* New York, NY: HarperOne, 2009.

Feldman, Louis H. *Jew and Gentile in the Ancient World: Attitudes and Interactions from Alexander to Justinian.* Princeton, NJ: Princeton University Press, 1993.

Fox, Michael V. *The Redaction of the Books of Esther: On Reading Composite Texts.* Atlanta, GA: Scholars Press, 1991.

Fredriksen, Paula. "Judaism, the Circumcision of Gentiles, and Apocalyptic Hope." *Journal of Theological Studies* 42 (1991): 558–64.

Gilbert, Gary. "The Making of a Jew: 'God-Fearer' or Convert in the Story of Izates." *Union Seminary Quarterly Review* 44 (1991): 299–313.

Gollaher, David L. *Circumcision: A History of the World's Most Controversial Surgery.* New York, NY: Basic Books, 2000.

Grabbe, Lester L. *Judaism from Cyrus to Hadrian*. 2 vols. Minneapolis, MN: Fortress Press, 1992.

Gruen, Erich S. *Diaspora: Jews amidst Greeks and Romans*. Cambridge: Harvard, 2002.

———. "Hellenism and Persecution: Antiochus IV and the Jews." In *Hellenistic History and Culture*, edited by Peter Green, 238–64. Berkeley, CA: University of California, 1993.

Hall, Robert G. "Epispasm and the Dating of Ancient Jewish Writings." *Journal for the Study of Pseudepigrapha* 2 (1988): 71–86.

———. "Epispasm: Circumcision in Reverse." *Bible Review* 8 (1992): 52–57.

Hanneken, Todd R. *The Subversion of the Apocalypses in the Book of Jubilees*. Atlanta, GA: Society of Biblical Literature Press, 2012.

Iyaduria, Joshua. "Religious Conversion and Social Transformation." In *The Encyclopedia of Psychology and Religion*, edited by David A. Leeming, 1513–514. Boston, MA: Springer US, 2014.

Jewett, Robert. "The Agitators and the Galatian Congregation." In *The Galatians Debate*, edited by Mark D. Nanos, 334–47. Peabody, MA: Hendrickson, 2002.

Josephus, Flavius. *The Antiquities of the Jews. The Works of Josephus*. Translated by William Whiston. Peabody, MA: Hendrickson, 1987.

———. *The Wars of the Jews. The Works of Josephus*. Translated by William Whiston. Peabody, MA: Hendrickson, 1987.

Levenson, Jon D. *Esther: A Commentary*. Louisville, KY: Westminster, 1997.

Livesey, Nina E. *Circumcision as a Malleable Symbol*. WUNT 2.295. Tübingen: Mohr Siebeck, 2010.

Longenecker, Richard N. *Galatians*. Word Biblical Commentary 41. Dallas: Word, 1990.

Magid, Shaul. "The Politics of (Un)Conversion: The 'Mixed Multitude. ('Erev Rav) as Conversos in Rabbi Hayyim Vital's 'Ets Ha-Da'at Tov." *The Jewish Quarterly Review* 95, no. 4 (2005): 625–66.

Mørkholm, Otto. *Antiochus of Syria*. Copenhagen: Gyldendal, 1966.

Nanos, Mark D. *Reading Paul Within Judaism: Collected Essays of Mark D. Nanos, Vol. 1*. Eugene, OR: Wipf and Stock Publishers, 2017.

———. "The Inter- and Intra-Jewish Political Context of Paul's Letter to the Galatians." In *The Galatians Debate*, edited by Mark D. Nanos, 396–407. Peabody, MA: Hendrickson, 2002.

———. *The Mystery of Romans: The Jewish Context of Paul's Letters*. Minneapolis, MN: Fortress Press, 1996.

———. "The Question of Conceptualization: Qualifying Paul's Position on Circumcision in Dialogue with Josephus's Advisors to King Izates." In *Paul within Judaism: Restoring the First-Century Context to the Apostle*, edited by Mark D. Nanos and Magnus Zetterholm, 105–52. Minneapolis, MN: Fortress Press, 2015.

Neusner, Jacob. "The Conversion of Adiabene to Judaism: A New Perspective" *Journal of Biblical Literature* 83 (1964): 60–66.

Nolland, John. "Uncircumcised Proselytes?" *Journal for Study of Judaism* 12 (1981): 173–94.

Park, Eung Chun. *Either Jew or Gentile*. Louisville: Westminster, 2003.
Philo. *Questions and Answers on Genesis*. Translated by Ralph Marcus. Philo: Supplement 1. Loeb Classical Library. Cambridge: Harvard University Press, 1953.
Porter, Stanley E., and Christopher D. Stanley, eds. *As It Is Written: Studying Paul's Use of Scripture*. Leiden: Brill, 2008.
Priest, John. *The Old Testament Pseudepigrapha, Vol. 1*. Edited by James H. Charlesworth. New York, NY: Doubleday, 1985.
Räisänen, Heikki. *Paul and the Law*. Philadelphia, PA: Fortress Press. 1986.
Rogers, John H., Elijah Odoyo-June, Walter Jaoko, and Robert C. Bailey. "Time to Complete Wound Healing in HIV-Positive and HIV-Negative Men Following Medical Male Circumcision in Kisumu, Kenya: A Prospective Cohort Study." *Public Library of Science ONE* 8: 4 (2013): e61725. Cited April 20, 2020. https://doi.org/10.1371/journal.pone.0061725.
Ruiz-Ortiz, Francisco-Javier. *The Dynamics of Violence and Revenge in the Hebrew Book of Esther*. Leiden: Brill, 2017.
Rushdie, Salman. *Midnight's Children*. New York, NY: Penguin Random House, 1991.
Schiffman, Lawrence H. "The Conversion of the Royal House of Adiabene in Josephus and Rabbinic Sources." In *Josephus, Judaism, and Christianity*, edited by Louis H. Feldman and Gohei Hata, 293–312. Detroit: Wayne State, 1987.
———. *Who Was a Jew? Rabbinic and Halakhic Perspectives on the Jewish-Christian Schism*. Hoboken: Ktav, 1982.
Schürer, Emil. *The History of the Jewish People in the Age of Jesus Christ (175 BC–AD 135)*. 5 vols. Peabody, MA: Hendrickson, 1994.
Segal, Michael. *The Book of Jubilees: Rewritten Bible, Redaction, Ideology and Theology*. Leiden: Brill, 2007.
Suetonius. Translated by John C. Rolfe. 2 vols. Loeb Classical Library. Cambridge: Harvard University Press, 1915.
Thiessen, Matthew. *Paul and the Gentile Problem*. New York, NY: Oxford University Press, 2016.
VanderKam, James. *The Book of Jubilees. A Translation*. Corpus Scriptorum Christianorum Orientalium 511. Scriptores Aethiopici 88. Louvain: Peeters, 1989.

Chapter Two

Paul and the Joining of the Ways
Ordering the Eschaton, Preparing for Judgment

Anders Runesson

INTRODUCTION: FROM PARTING TO JOINING

"Paul and the Parting of the Ways" has a nice ring to it, the beauty of alliteration merging with layers of historical claims and so, rhetorically, reinforcing the legitimacy, as it were, of the quest itself. But at the core of the metaphor, deep inside that very quest which it ostensibly describes but in truth controls, lies hidden assumptions undermining the project as such, leaving us trapped in the contemporary rather than illuminated by the historical. For he, the historical Paul, knew not the word "Christian," and of "Christianity" he had never heard. Whatever happened in that Damascene moment was embedded in and interpreted by the mind of a self-proclaimed Israelite; indeed, a Hebrew and a son of Abraham (Rom 11:1; 2 Cor 11:22; cf. Gal 2:15; Phil 3:4–5).[1]

Woe to us, then, if we ask for a parting between a known and a void projecting back at us our own mirror image; between an ancient way of being and our neighborhood church down the street. Paul was, indeed, not a "Christian," and for some "Christianity" he could not have left Judaism. This has been shown in study after study, from angles in ample number, forming a foundation from which we may now proceed to deepen our understanding of the apostle to the gentiles.[2] For the quest for the historical Paul, as the quest for the historical Jesus, does not end, but begins with the insight that he was a Jew, practicing Judaism, indeed proclaiming Judaism.[3] The task still pending is thus not *if*, but *what kind*, *how*, and *why*? This chapter is mostly concerned with the *how*, as it relates to the gentile Other, touching also on the *why*. Some preliminaries will, in the following, set the scene. I will then present a threefold entry point for understanding Pauline difference, before adding, at the very end, a word on how Paul tends to be approached today by most churches, and how this differs from the Paul of history.

If we accept that the Pharisees, like the rabbis after them, believed that there would be a resurrection from the dead,[4] preceding the divine act of judgment necessary to set things straight as Heaven was about to interfere with human governance decisively and for good, then Paul's Pharisaic identity was not challenged but, in many ways, confirmed on the road to Damascus. It was a moment of blinding insight—rather than a calling—that time was much further ahead than he had previously assumed. Something was actually happening, and he, Paul, was drawn into a sequence of decisive events leading up to and preparing for the End. Critical for what subsequently developed into his calling were the small face-to-face groups, or associations, whose patron deity was the God of Israel, worshipped by some through a Messianic lens.[5] In terms of the latter, such groups were already spreading slowly but surely in the eastern Mediterranean, North Africa, and all the way to Rome. Catering, as did all associations, to diverse networks associated with neighborhoods, households, occupations, ethnic-geographical or immigrant connections, or cultic preferences,[6] group membership in these institutions was often—but not always—mixed between Jews and non-Jews, slaves and free, men and women.[7] It was within these types of institutional settings, habitually called "synagogues" or "congregations" by modern scholars, that the post-Damascene Paul's sense of purpose was formed. It is not sociologically unreasonable to hypothesize, then, that the institutional structures within which Paul's conceptual world was adjusted influenced the way in which his sense of time was modified, as well as his understanding of what now needed to be done in order to prepare for the inevitable.[8]

Among the numerous possible analytical entry points emerging from a basic description of the Pauline context such as this, what interests us here more specifically is the ethnic diversity in membership that was common in these types of small groups, both Jewish and Graeco-Roman.[9] In such a setting, the acute insight that the God of this specific ethnic group, the Jews, had initiated a cosmic and historical-political process leading to a final judgment and renewal of the entire world (cf. 1 Thess 4:13–5:11; Rom 3:25–31; 1 Cor 3:13–17; 4:5; 11:29–32; 15:49–56; 2 Cor 5:10) would very likely and instantly have led to questions about how this would affect those in one's immediate context, those who in various ways constituted the plausibility structure that maintained the meaning system within which everyone operated on a daily basis (cf. Rom 1:16–2:13).[10] In other words, these diverse small face-to-face groups, whose patron deity was the God of Israel, set the agenda for what issues were going to be the most pressing ones as people involved began preparing for the End. Theology, defined as the attempt to map and therefore also merge worldview and reality, thus inescapably had to place at the top of the agenda the fate of the non-Jews.[11]

The "why" of the urgency of the location of non-Jews in the present eschatological moment is, then, best or at least first, answered sociologically. In most groups, based on their membership, the approach simply had to be "universal" in some sense of that word. But how, more precisely, this was theologized would differ depending on a number of factors, too numerous to list here. For Paul, it seems quite clear that, far from a parting of the ways in which entities split, or are urged to split, from one another, his vision was a *joining of the ways*; a process in which a "wild olive shoot" is grafted in "to share the rich root of the olive tree" together with the "natural branches" (Rom 11:17–18). But this metaphor, indeed the vision as such, is still so general that even Matthew's Gospel could have included it, despite the fact that Matthew arguably, in terms of the non-Jewish other, entertained an end-time scenario quite opposite to that of Paul.[12]

The real issue in the early Jesus movement, after Jesus's death,[13] is not the "if," or even the "why," of gentile inclusion. We have no evidence that any followers of Jesus rejected the idea that non-Jews should be made aware of the coming end of the world and offered a way to survive this turbulent transformation of creation.[14] Rather, the issue was *how* exactly this should be done. It is around this "how?" that boundaries were drawn and conflicts arose; indeed, this is what constituted the core of the gentile problem, as any solution to it would have major implications for Israelite, or Jewish, self-understanding. Shedding further light on what is often referred to as Paul's "universalism," and how he got there—what changed when he joined the Jesus movement—will help us understand better what was at stake as this messianic movement spread from the land of Israel to take root in the Diaspora. Indeed, it may assist us in nuancing our perception of the distinctiveness of Christ-Centred Judaism in relation to other forms of Judaism.

UNIVERSALISM THROUGH PARTICULARISM?

It is quite common to approach the study of the place of the gentile "Other" in ancient Judaism, including in the Jesus movement, through the prism provided by the terms "universalism" and "particularism." These words, however, are so general and malleable that they can be, and have been, used by scholars to mean very different things, resulting in confusion when conclusions are drawn and compared.[15] For example, should one understand mission, or recruitment, by a group directed to people beyond that group as a sign of universalism, based on the global nature of such outreach and the openness of the group to accept converts? Or should such activities, and the self-understanding and group identity implied by them, be seen rather as a sign of a particularistic view of salvation, as such an endeavor would likely be motivated by beliefs aligning with Cyprian's dictum *extra ecclesiam nulla salus*? Or, again, would it be an expression of particularism or universalism to understand one's own way of life as intertwined with the ethnicity of the group to which one belongs, but not considering salvation to be dependent on either group membership or ethnicity and, as a consequence, be uninterested in a proselytizing mission?

In a previous study,[16] I have suggested that due to the susceptibility of these terms to confusion and misunderstanding, they should be avoided altogether in scholarly discourses in favor of alternative ways of defining the location of the "Other" on the conceptual maps of insiders.[17] To my mind, there are three basic aspects to our question, each opening up for a limited number of reactive possibilities, here listed under the respective aspect with some non-exhaustive examples in footnotes serving a heuristic purpose:

1. Ethnic status
    a. Closed-Ethnic religion (no converts accepted into an ethnoreligious group).[18]
    b. Open-Ethnic religion (converts accepted into an ethno-religious group).[19]
    c. Non-Ethnic religion (rejection of ethnicity as a meaningful category in relation to group membership).[20]
2. Salvation
    a. Salvation-inclusive religion (People outside the group may be considered for salvation under certain circumstances, without conversion).[21]
    b. Salvation-exclusive religion (The boundaries of the group mark the limits of salvation).[22]
3. Mission[23]
    a. Proselytizing Mission (Aim: incorporation of the missionized into the missionary's group).[24]
    b. Ethno-Ethic Mission (Aim: modification of the behavioral patterns of people outside the missionary's group, but not through incorporation).[25]
    c. Inward Mission (Aim: modification of the beliefs and practices of the missionary's own group).[26]

As for mission, each of the three types may be subdivided into active and passive practices and postures. That is, mission in any of these categories can be understood as an effect not only of an active address to the person(s) missionized, but also an expected change of behavior of the outsider in light of their perception of the behavior of the ingroup itself; the former describing a centrifugal movement and the latter expecting a centripetal effect.[27] Since both active and passive versions of all types of mission existed in ancient Judaism, including the Jesus movement, this distinction adds further nuance as we read in context, aligning certain texts with others in ways otherwise invisible.

As we seek to understand better Paul's position on how to order the eschaton while preparing the nations for the coming judgment, organizing the complexities of the issues that arise according to this type of analytical framework reveals some interesting patterns of thought and how they developed as Paul joined the messianic movement. We shall discuss each of these aspects in turn.

Gentile Inclusion: Ethnicity

The issue of the relationship between the ethnic status of the worshipper and the nature of the deity worshipped lies, as we have noted, at the center of the complex problems facing the Jesus movement as it expanded in the Diaspora. This was not unique to the Jesus movement, though, as Judaism was at home in the Diaspora well before the arrival of the Christ-followers, and other Graeco-Roman cults connected with a specific people, like the Egyptian cult of Isis, also had long experienced an increasing interest among non-native worshippers.[28] The meshing together of traditions that had previously been ethnically specific can also be seen in the Greek Magical Papyri, where aspects of Jewish traditions and worship can appear in spells dedicated to Egyptian and Greek deities, and vice versa. Indeed, even in the archaeological record, as Leonard Rutgers pointed out almost thirty years ago and as has been confirmed by many since then, Jewish and non-Jewish individuals and groups intermingled in most areas of society, such that it is often "extremely difficult, if not impossible, for modern scholars to decide with which religion users of charms and amulets identified themselves."[29]

De-ethnosizing processes such as these, as related to membership profiles in group settings where ethnic deities were worshipped, were thus in the air when Paul began to develop an understanding of what his destabilising Damascene experience might entail. His—as well as other messianics—solutions to the gentile problem should thus be understood as variations on a common socioreligious theme, rather than construed as an idiosyncratic reaction embedded in a unique and socially isolated process.

Paul's original position on the ethnic aspect of our problem, at least if we are to believe Gal 5:11, was that of an open-ethnic perspective, which allowed for, perhaps even encouraged, non-Jews to join the Jewish ethnos as they opted to seek the favor of the God of the Jews: "Why am I still (*eti*) being persecuted, if I am still (*eti*) preaching circumcision? In that case, the offense of the cross has been neutralized[30] (*katargeō*)."[31] The Paul we know from the letters, however, turned violently against those who declined to undergo the same change of mind he himself did, asking them to "cut it all off" rather than unsettle those whom he counted among his (gentile) friends (Gal 5:12). As Paul prepares the nations for the final divine reckoning, the order in which he is now convinced God wants to find the *ekklēsia* at the eschaton reflects the world as he knows it, i.e., divided up in two parts, representing the totality of humankind: Israel and the nations (1 Cor 7:17–18; Rom 3:29). Those who were called as Jews must thus remain Jews,[32] and the same rule applies to the gentiles.

Why? A reasonable explanation for this pattern of thinking—in addition to the fact that this way of dividing the world was part of the Jewish worldview more generally, and also, for that matter, part of the way all ethnic groups understood their world[33]—would be that, for the Paul we know from his letters, if people began changing their status as a consequence of their newly found cultic loyalties, it would imply that God had overdone it when the Spirit had been eschatologically poured over them all *regardless* of their ethnic (or other) status. Indeed, a self-imposed obligation to make changes in one's status, post-Spirit reception, presumably in order to better fit into what one perceived to be God's plan, would be tantamount to a rejection of the Christ-event itself, which had inaugurated the final sequence of history before the eschaton, including the universal releasing of the Spirit. For an individual "in-Christ" to take such a step would indicate a fundamental lack of trust in the fact that the God of Israel was also the God of the nations (again, cf. Rom 3:29). It would place the believer outside Christ (cf. Gal 5:4), jeopardizing salvation itself, as all lack of *pistis* would.[34]

Paul's change of mind, having interpreted as divine Spirit possession what he encountered among ex-Pagan gentiles, as Paula Fredriksen has called the non-Jews heeding Paul's call,[35] is thus best described as a move from an open-ethnic approach allowing individuals from other ethnic groups to join the Jewish *ethnos*, to a closed-ethnic position, refusing, on theological grounds, non-Jews entry into the Jewish *ethnos*. To keep everything together, saving both Jews and non-Jews, Paul has to, and does, create an overarching category, a globalized Christ[36]—an emperor of sorts, ruling the nations—in which a salvific "unity in diversity" may be found.[37] It is critical to note here that Paul argues that his change of mind is vital for the deliverance of the nations; within the *ekklēsia* nothing less, nothing more than diversity will do. In other words, since salvation is found within the *ekklēsia*, ethnic diversity becomes a salvific category intertwined with and dependent on an institutional reality, which is, in its structures, theologized.³⁸ This leads us to the aspect of salvation and the question of whether Paul's letters display a coherent view on this matter, which may be categorized as either inclusive or exclusive.

Gentile Inclusion: Salvation

As noted above, our source material presents us with two basic attitudes: a salvation-inclusive and a salvation-exclusive position. To repeat, the former refers to the notion that individuals outside one's own group may attain salvation without joining the in-group (i.e., without conversion), and the latter suggests the opposite: outside the group, there is no salvation. Where between these two poles on the spectrum should we place the apostle to the nations?

We need to note, first of all, that Paul, as a Christ-follower, adopted a certain kind of salvation-inclusive position with regard to those among his own people who decline the offer of joining the "in-Christ" group (Rom 11:26, 28–29). Seen in first-century context, this is quite a remarkable stance, considering what Paul, as so many others of his contemporaries, had invested in making the claim for Christ as savior of all. There appear to be at least two key matters of conviction that explain this theological inclusiveness: (a) For Paul, God cannot abandon his promises (Rom 9:6, 14; 11:28–29). This foundational belief, surfacing most clearly in Romans,³⁹ seems to function as a hermeneutical hub from which other theological assertions extend like spokes on a conceptual wheel, moving the Pauline rhetoric in certain directions. (b) The Jewish people is and will always remain a people, and to this ethnic group Paul himself belongs (e.g., Rom 9:3–5; Phil 3:5).

Seen in light of (a) above, it appears as if Paul's sense of a shared ethnic identity leads him to seeing peoplehood as a salvific criterion, indeed a sine qua non for inclusion in the coming kingdom. He is thus able to claim not only that, regardless of the current situation, in the end all Israel will be saved (Rom 11:26), but also that Israel—as an ethnic category, beyond those united "in-Christ"—is playing, and will continue to play a decisive role as the world inches closer to the end; indeed, the part of Israel that has declined the "in-Christ" offer in fact makes possible reconciliation between God and the nations, and, when that time comes, they will be instrumental to the process in which the dead will be resurrected (Rom 11:15).⁴⁰

This emphasis on ethnicity as a primary salvific category may explain why, when Paul theologizes the position of the nations, Abraham, together with the Spirit, become so important (cf. Rom 4, esp. vv.11–12, 16–17; 8:14; Gal 3:6–9). Indeed, Christ in and of himself seems not to be enough to save the nations, as Paul in his theological argument also needs to make siblings of Jews and gentiles by referring both to Israel's foundation, through Abraham, and the Spirit: "For all who are led by the Spirit of God are children of God [. . .] and if children, then heirs" (Rom 8:14, 17). Christ's achievement, in the context of gentile inclusion, is to activate this eschatological process, unleashing the Spirit. It is not that gentiles now become Jews, of course (cf. Gal 5:2–6), or that ethnic identity, including Jewish ethnic identity, is made null and void. If that would have been the case, the discursive function of Abraham would have been difficult to explain, as it requires the notion of distinct categories being unified, not nullified.[41] Rather, it is the promise to Abraham, that he become the father of many people-groups, not only of Israel, which is now fulfilled.

For non-Jews, this type of theo-ethnic reasoning points to a salvation-exclusive stance,[42] in which a redemption coordinated by the God of Israel is salvifically dependent on the people of Israel, both those who had joined the Christ, and those who had declined this offer. Thus, as a consequence, as the eschaton approaches, those from among the nations who are not joined to Abraham, alongside Jacob, are doomed. This is, as far as I can see, the inevitable implication of the inheritance-approach Paul adopts as he aims to explain the basics of salvation; if not children, then not heirs (cf. Rom 8:17, and also 4:11, 16). Contrary to the position of Jews who have declined the in-Christ offer, but who are still understood as children and, ultimately, therefore also heirs based on God honoring his ancient promises (Rom 11:28–29), there is in Paul's theology no plan B for the gentiles. Paul's pattern of salvation seems to be, thus, asymmetric. This emerges as an inescapable conclusion when his approach to redemption is studied through the prism of his theo-ethnic convictions, which lie at the very foundation of his theology of salvation and splits the salvific light of the Christ into a spectrum of colors. It is true that Paul mentions on one occasion that an unbelieving husband is made holy through his believing wife, and vice versa, and that their children therefore are holy (1 Cor 7:14). But apart from such specific cases—in which genealogical discourse still plays a decisive role[43]—Paul does not have much positive to say about gentiles outside Christ.[44] In sum, Paul thus combines a closed-ethnic outlook with a salvation-exclusive stance as far as non-Jews are concerned, indeed an intriguing position to take, one which can only be explained by his globalized 'in-Christ' theology combined with his theo-ethnic convictions.

Before we move on to the final aspect of Paul's approach to gentile inclusion as part of his plan to join the distinct ways of Jews and non-Jews—i.e., the issue of mission—just a word on the much debated and often misunderstood issue of dual covenants, or Sonderweg, in Paul's writings. In brief, the notion of a Sonderweg refers in this context to the idea that there would be—and Paul would be a witness to this pattern of thought—two paths to salvation: one for Jews, without Christ but with Moses, and one for gentiles, with Christ. While some New Testament exegetes, perhaps most famously Lloyd Gaston,[45] have indeed argued such a notion to align well with Paul's writings, this is not the position taken by most scholars, myself included, identifying with the so-called Paul-within-Judaism perspective. To be sure, even in antiquity some (Jewish) believers in Jesus argued precisely that Moses was for Jews and Jesus for gentiles—and that those Jews who followed both Moses and Jesus lived in the best of worlds.[46] But this is not, in my view, what we see in Paul. The apostle to the gentiles does claim that, in the end, all Israel, meaning all Jews, will be saved, as a people, including those who during their lives declined the "in-Christ" offer. God's covenant with them stands (Rom 11:26–29). When bringing up the reluctance of many Jews to accept the Jesus-offer, Paul refers this to the will of God—not to these individuals themselves, as if their sin, but rather as them being part of God's plan for the world, a precondition for the process of the joining of the ways between Jews and non-Jews. Paul simply states that this is all part of the divine mystery; it is God's secret (Rom 11:25, 33–36). In other words, while in reality, in the historical and socioreligious lives of the men and women involved, this means a Pauline acceptance of these two alternative ways of being as paths ultimately leading toward salvation, in terms of the eschatological realization of that salvation and the mechanisms behind it, Paul prefers to remain silent and refer to God's mysteries. And, as Krister Stendahl once said in a public talk at Lund University in the 1990s, rejecting the idea that he himself would identify with the two-paths solution, this silence on Paul's part is hermeneutically significant.

Gentile Inclusion: Mission

Paul's theology (and practice) of mission follows closely from his position on the ethnic issue, and therefore presents us with a complicated "in-between" scenario. As we noted above, proselytizing mission is based on the conviction that in order to be salvifically effective, the effort must result in the inclusion of the other—in this case the gentile other—into the group to which the missionary him or herself belongs. But since Paul has an ethnically based two-tier system, with two subgroups (Jews and non-Jews) within his overarching group identity marker ("in-Christ"), this terminology needs to be somewhat modified. Paul does not—emphatically not, as we have seen—want non-Jews to attain his own status as a Jewish member of the *ekklēsia*.[47] But he does want to include them precisely as non-Jews "in Christ," and he does require them to leave behind their old cultic habits, not only their lamentable ethical behavior, since for Paul cult and ethics are intertwined (cf. Gal 2:15; 4:8–10; 5:16–21, 24; cf. Rom 1:23–24, 28–32).

In other words, Paul's position cannot be described as proselytising mission, since its purpose is not to fully include those missionized in the group to which he himself belongs—i.e., the Jewish-messianic core of the Jesus movement. Neither can it be described as ethno-ethic mission, as Paul very much requires his non-Jewish converts to stop worshipping their old gods and join, exclusively, the cult of the God of Israel, i.e., the God of his own people; to become ex-pagan gentiles. His approach to mission, as reconstructed from his letters, falls just in-between these two variants. If we bring the above conclusion to bear on this situation, namely that Paul at one point embraced an open-ethnic stance towards gentiles, but that he had a radical change of mind and moved towards a closed-ethnic position (Gal 5:11), we find that his approach to mission aligns well with the ethnic aspect of his theology. Paul's practices related to gentile inclusion thus changed from proselytizing mission, which for him led to no persecution, to what we may call an inclusive ethno-ethic missionary strategy, which did cause him suffering, indicating that his was a minority position.

What brought about this change of mind is difficult to say. If one assumes that the shift in Paul's theology and practice of mission followed after his Damascene moment, then one would have to add further factors explaining why he, specifically, came to this conclusion, since some members of the Jesus movement maintained that non-Jews joining the Jesus movement had to be circumcised in the process to become full members.[48] There was no consensus on missionary practices in the first century; becoming a follower of Jesus did not automatically lead to a position on the matter. Likewise, if the change is understood as having taken place sometime after Paul became a Christ-follower, we would need more evidence in order to fully comprehend why he changed his mind. Was there a change of socioreligious setting? Was he convinced through certain people's arguments? Other people's authority seems not to have been enough for Paul to modify either his beliefs or his practices.[49] Be that as it may. In the end, all we can say is that the Jew Paul engaged in a mission to save the non-Jewish world, and that the type of mission he applied as a tool grew from his convictions about the salvifically significant role of ethnicity as the world was coming to an end.

A final point before we conclude. As is clear from Gal 2:9, the Paul of the letters had a distinct appreciation for differences in missionary strategies as they applied to Jews and non-Jews respectively, declaring that Peter was assigned the task of the inward mission to their fellow Jews, while Paul himself was to take on the outside world, the nations. One may, of course, wonder why such a division would be necessary in the first place, if it would not have been for the fact that these missions were perceived of as different in nature, involving distinct practices and messages addressed to the respective audiences based precisely on their ethnic identity.[50] Paul's acceptance of such different missions based on the missionized individuals' ethnicity speaks in favor of us understanding Paul's own view of the Christ-event to mean different things to Jews and gentiles respectively, as we have also argued above.[51] The implication of this is, of course, that Paul would have understood himself not to have lived like a gentile, but like a Jew, thus confirming what so many scholars who in one way or another identify with the Paul-within-Judaism perspective have argued for many years: Paul was a Jew, bringing a Jewish message of salvation to a non-Jewish world—a Judaism for gentiles—so that the ethnic other, too, may survive the eschaton; indeed, so that the nations become a sacrifice that Paul, as if a temple priest, could bring forth to the God of Israel (Rom 15:16; cf. 12:1).

In the end, Paul's understanding of the state of the world and the role of Israel and the gentiles in the current moment and in the soon-to-come eschaton, as this is described in Romans 11, even suggests that he, the apostle to the nations, would no longer embrace a mission to the Jews. Not because he had given up on their salvation, or that he simply avoided the topic since it was not his task, but precisely because Paul was convinced that the status of Israel as he found it in his own days, with most Jews not joining the Jesus movement, was the work of God; that it was part of God's plan to bring both them *and* the nations to ultimate salvation. A mission to Jews, then, would seem to contradict God's plan for the present, and, indeed, undermine Paul's own work bringing the number of the gentiles destined for salvation to its full (Rom 11:25). In the meantime, awaiting the eschaton, Paul says, God's love for the entirety of Israel is firmly anchored all the way back to Abraham, Isaac, and Jakob, and can never be undone (Rom 11:28–29).[52] This, and not any human missionary activity, is the basis of Israel's salvation.

CONCLUSION: FROM JOINING TO PARTING

Having become convinced that Jesus had been resurrected from the dead—as noted, a confirmation of his Pharisaic belief in the resurrection of the dead[53]—and that this resurrection inaugurated the final sequence of history before Israel's God's decisive intervention in human governance and politics, Paul developed an understanding of his call to be the salvation of the nations, in their "full number" (Rom 11:25). Preparing the nations for the ultimate divine judgment act, after God had moved on from the long period of time when he had left sins unpunished (Rom 3:25–26), Paul sought to order the world so that it matched what he understood to be the state in which God wanted to find it. This meant, as Richard Last has argued,[54] primarily to organize institutions—associations—which reflected the diversity that he deemed salvifically appropriate.[55] Not surprisingly, the basic form of diversity that took up most of the time and effort of the apostle to the nations was ethnic in nature, since salvation was, for him, an ethnic category. A joining of the ways between Jews and gentiles was for Paul thus not just a general wish to convince the world that the Christ had significance outside the Jewish people. The joining of the ways of the nations with those of the Jewish people lay at the very core of both his theological convictions and his socio-institutional program.[56]

If we put aside the general and, in my view, analytically inappropriate terms "universalism" and "particularism," and direct the spotlight to the details of how Paul perceived that things needed to change for his ideal vision of the eschatological order to materialize as he prepared the nations for divine judgment, the following tripartite pattern emerges: (a) With regard to Ethnic Status, Paul moved from an open-ethnic stance to a closed-ethnic position, insisting on ethnic diversity within the people of God in order to make visible his theological conviction that "God shows no partiality" (Rom 2:11): (b) Shifting to the Aspect of Salvation, Paul adopted a salvation-exclusive position in his approach to the nations, keeping for Israel a salvation-inclusive vision, based on their location on his conceptual map as being instrumental for the salvation of the world as a whole: (c) Finally, building on the other two aspects, Paul left behind his previous approach to mission as proselytising and embraced instead an inclusive ethno-ethic mission, aiming to position the gentiles alongside, but distinguished from, Jews like himself "in-Christ."

In sum, then, for Paul the salvation of the world depended on a joining of Jews *as* Jews and gentiles *as* gentiles under the umbrella of the overarching "in-Christ" identity. This salvifically efficient arrangement makes institutionally tangible the core conviction that the God of Israel is the God of the whole world (Rom 3:29–31); an organizational proclamation through membership profiles that God will not be partial as he brings history as we know it to an end through a decisive judgment act (Rom 2:4–11; 10:12–13; 1 Cor 12:13; Gal 3:28). This intense Pauline commitment to maintaining diversity within the *ekklēsia*—indeed, ultimately his particular theo-ethnic notion of divine mercy and justice—was, however, soon to be forgotten in the emerging mainstream (non-Jewish) churches. To put things in perspective, perhaps a brief and broad brush-stroke comparison may be useful, based on the three aspects we have explored above.

In terms of ethnic status, while Paul came to embrace a closed-ethnic position, the later mainstream churches rejected ethnicity as a salvifically significant parameter altogether and developed a non-ethnic stance.[57] As for Paul's composite approach to salvation, maintaining Israel as a necessary category even outside the Christ alongside his salvation-exclusive approach to the non-Jewish world, the churches to come abandoned complexity and nurtured primarily salvation exclusivism.[58] Finally, as much as Paul's mission strategy, his inclusive ethno-ethic stance, was dependent on his position on ethnicity and salvation, the changing hermeneutics in the non-Jewish churches led to an adoption of a proselytizing mission.

It was especially the move to a non-ethnic position in the emerging mainstream churches that turned on its head the very point of departure not only for Paul's strategizing on gentile inclusion, but also the theological foundation behind it. What was for Paul an ethno-religious matter of course—that Judaism (in its Christ-oriented form) was the gift that would save even the non-Jews—morphed, in the hands of the Church Fathers, into an archetypal heresy. What began as a variant of Jewish teaching for gentiles was thus transformed into gentile teaching for Jews. Or, if a metaphor be allowed, those who opened their home to receive and save the Other as the divine reckoning was approaching were themselves thrown out and declared unfit for the kingdom by those whom they had tried to rescue.

Remarkably, all of this could be and was done claiming support from Paul. Of course, the path eventually chosen by the majority was controlled by political, cultural, and socio-institutional forces unknown to Paul, but which became crucial as Christian theology mapped—and merged with—new religio-political realities. These forces, rather than Paul,[59] explain how and why Christianity reorganized the eschaton and created the salvific otherness between Jews and non-Jews that Paul sought to overcome. Analyses of the hermeneutical aerobics involved in this process, and their disastrous outcomes over centuries for the Jewish people in particular, may help us not only to understand better the Paul of history, but also the history of Paul, from Late Antiquity until today. Such understanding is bound to highlight also our own choices as interpreters as well as the nature and discursive role of historical analysis itself for how we perceive of and shape the world. A self-reflective scrutinizing of our methods and motives—an academic response of sorts to the Delphic *gnōthi seauton*[60]—is, after all, an integral part of the scholarly pursuit. Indeed, in this regard Abelard's approach, echoing Aristotle, still provides guidance, insisting that questioning "is the first key to wisdom. . . . For by doubting we come to enquiry, and by enquiry we perceive the truth."[61]

NOTES

1. On Paul's understanding of the meaning of "Israelite," a group to which he says he himself belongs (Rom 9:3), see Rom 9:4–5: "They [i.e., Jews, also those who had declined the 'in-Christ' offer] are Israelites, and to them belong the adoption, the

glory, the covenants, the giving of the law, the worship, and the promises; to them belong the patriarchs, and from them, according to the flesh, comes the Messiah, who is over all, God blessed forever. Amen."

2. Pamela Eisenbaum, *Paul Was Not a Christian: The Original Message of a Misunderstood Apostle* (New York, NY: HarperCollins, 2009). See also Matthew Thiessen, *Paul and the Gentile Problem* (Oxford: Oxford University Press, 2016); Paula Fredriksen, *Paul: The Pagans' Apostle* (New Haven, CT: Yale University Press, 2018). The foundation for such historical readings of Paul was laid by several scholars, beginning decades ago, including Krister Stendahl (for a summarizing account of his thinking, see his *Final Account: Paul's Letter to the Romans* [Minneapolis, MN: Fortress Press, 1995]). See also the work of Mark D. Nanos, *The Mystery of Romans: The Jewish Context of Paul's Letter* (Minneapolis, MN: Fortress Press, 1996) and more recently Kathy Ehrensperger, *Paul at the Crossroads of Cultures: Theologizing in the Space Between* (London: Bloomsbury, 2013,) and William S. Campbell, *The Nations in the Divine Economy: Paul's Covenantal Hermeneutics and Participation in Christ* (Lanham, MD: Lexington Books/Fortress Academic, 2018). The history of research on Paul in this regard is helpfully discussed by Magnus Zetterholm, *Approaches to Paul: A Student's Guide to Recent Scholarship* (Minneapolis, MN: Fortress Press, 2009). See also now Jacob P. B. Mortensen, *Paul among the Gentiles: A Radical Reading of Romans*, NET 28 (Tübingen: Narr Francke Attempto, 2018). The special issue on Paul, *JJMJS* 5 (2018), evaluates the contribution by E. P. Sanders forty years on and discusses the very latest advances in Pauline scholarship. See also the condensed but illuminating overview of scholarship on Romans by Laura Salah Nasrallah, *Archaeology and the Letters of Paul* (Oxford: Oxford University Press, 2019), 181–87, noting especially Stendahl's contribution, along with Stowers, as reconstructing a Paul "speaking within Judaism" (187).

3. See especially Paula Fredriksen, "Judaizing the Nations: The Ritual Demands of Paul's Gospel," *NTS* 56 (2010): 232–52.

4. On diverse expressions of such convictions in ancient Judaism, seen within its wider North African and Near Eastern context, see Alan F. Segal's magisterial work *Life after Death: A History of the Afterlife in Western Religion* (New York, NY: Doubleday, 2004); on the period around the turn of the era, see 351–96 (the Pharisees discussed on pages 379–82); on the rabbis, see 596–638. See also Claudia Setzer, *Resurrection of the Body in Early Judaism and Early Christianity: Doctrine, Community, and Self-Definition* (Leiden: Brill, 2004). As Setzer notes, while there existed a great diversity of understandings of afterlife in Jewish texts from the second century BCE to the first century CE, "[t]he first time resurrection occurs as a doctrine by which others identify a certain group is the case of the Pharisees, reported by three sets of sources as a group that upholds resurrection" (18). For Josephus's description of Pharisaic beliefs as compared to Paul, note *BJ* 2.163 and 1 Cor 15 (Segal, ibid., 381). In Acts 23:6–9 Paul is portrayed as establishing a bridge between himself as a Pharisaic Christ-follower and other Pharisees precisely through a reference to the resurrection of the dead as a shared conviction. Quoting Setzer again,*Life After Death*, 30: "Oddly, it sounds as if preaching resurrection is the offence and Jesus is incidental."

5. On Christ-groups and other groups honoring the God of Israel as their patron deity understood within the overall institutional framework provided by ancient associations, see most recently the important work of John S. Kloppenborg, *Christ's Associations: Connecting and Belonging in the Ancient City* (New Haven, CT: Yale University Press, 2019), and Richard Last and Philip Harland, *Group Survival in the Ancient Mediterranean: Rethinking Material Conditions in the Landscape of Jews and Christians* (London: T&T Clark, 2020).

6. For in-depth discussion of these five categories of associations, between which there were some overlap, see Philip A. Harland, *Associations, Synagogues, and Congregations: Claiming a Place in Ancient Mediterranean Society* (Minneapolis, MN: Fortress Press, 2003) 28–53.

7. Source material related to these types of groups are conveniently collected and analyzed in John S. Kloppenborg and Richard S. Ascough, *Greco-Roman Associations: Texts, Translations, and Commentary. I: Attica, Central Greece, Macedonia, Thrace* (BZNW 181; Berlin: De Gruyter, 2011); Philip A. Harland, *Greco-Roman Associations: Texts, Translations, and Commentary. II: North Coast of Black Sea, Asia Minor* (BZNW 204; Berlin: De Gruyter, 2014).

8. On the connection between Pauline theology and the nature of the (pre-Pauline) institutional structures of Graeco-Roman and Jewish associations (or synagogues) within which and into which he spoke, see Anders Runesson, "Placing Paul: Institutional Structures and Theological Strategy in the World of the Early Christ-believers," *SEÅ* 80 (2015): 43–67.

9. Cf. the de-ethnosizing processes taking place in the membership of other contemporary ethnic cults, such as the cult of Isis, which opened up ethnic deities for worship by people of various ethnic and geographical backgrounds, extending the reach of the deity beyond the people-group from within which the cult originated. There are many examples of such expansion of the membership base of worshippers. Note also the diversity in terms of gender and social status common is associations; cf., e.g., SEG 46:800=GRA I.72, which lists the names of members of a Zeus Hypsistos group in Pydna, Macedonia (inscription dated to 250 CE). The names include 31 men, three women; slaves, freed people, citizens, and non-citizens. For an example of a predominantly, or exclusively, female group, members having enough wealth to make their own offerings to their gods, see, e.g., Philippi II 340/L589=GRA I.71 (dated to first or second century CE [?]).

10. "Plausibility structure" is sometimes defined in slightly different ways. For the purpose of this chapter, I follow Bruce Karlenzig, "Plausibility," in *Encyclopedia of Religion*, ed. William H. Swatos Jr. (Walnut Creek, CA: AltaMira Press, 1998), 364, who refers to "the sociocultural context or 'base' for meaning systems." Cf. Peter L. Berger, *The Sacred Canopy* (Garden City, NY: Doubleday, 1967).

11. In addition, based on the mixed membership of many associations, definitions would have been key from the very beginning of the movement of the position and status of slaves in relation to the free, as well as of women in relation to men.

12. For a detailed discussion of the status of non-Jews in Matthew's Gospel, see Anders Runesson, *Divine Wrath and Salvation in Matthew: The Narrative World of the First Gospel* (Minneapolis, MN: Fortress Press, 2016), 343–433. Matthew's vi-

sion seems to be closest to that of Paul's worst opponents, those he wished would "cut it all off" (Gal 5:12; cf. Acts 15:5). For a comparison between Paul and Matthew in this regard, see Anders Runesson, "Beyond Universalism and Particularism: Re-thinking Paul and Matthew on Gentile Inclusion," in *Paul and Matthew among Jews and Gentiles. Essays in Honour of Terence L. Donaldson*, ed. Ronald Charles (London: Bloomsbury, 2021), 99–111. It is of importance, though, to note that in the end Paul and Matthew had the same aim, namely, to save the non-Jewish Other; they differed only regarding the methods to be used to achieve this goal.

13. The historical Jesus had not addressed this issue in any detail as far as the sources can tell us (on the contrary according to Matt 10:5–6), which also explains the fact that those who came after him seems to have been at a loss as to how to approach the problem when the movement began to spread beyond the Jewish people. This fact, again, speaks in favor of historical reconstructions of the spread of the movement primarily within settings already displaying mixed (ethnic) membership, whereas Jesus himself focused his operations on non-mixed Jewish civic institutions ("synagogues") in the land.

14. On the transformation of creation as a whole, cf. Rom 8:19–22. Such openness towards gentile inclusion in salvation—not necessarily in Israel—was quite common, though not universal, in other forms of Judaism, earlier than, contemporary with, and later than Paul. Some texts, however, quite obviously authored in a context of oppression by gentiles, envision the annihilation or enslavement of non-Jews in an eschatological future, and some trajectories, while allowing for the salvation of the non-Jews did not allow for their incorporation into Israel as proselytes. It is on a map of such diversity of Jewish approaches to the religio-ethnic other that we need to locate the Pauline solution, which was only one of several within the Jewish Jesus movement. Key publications discussing these issues are Terence L. Donaldson's, *Judaism and the Gentiles: Jewish Patterns of Universalism (to 135 CE)* (Waco, TX: Baylor University Press, 2007); David C. Sim and James S. McLaren, eds., *Attitudes to Gentiles in Ancient Judaism and Early Christianity* (London: Bloomsbury, 2013).

15. See discussion in Anders Runesson, "Particularistic Judaism and Universalistic Christianity? Some Critical Remarks on Terminology and Theology," *Journal of Greco-Roman Christianity and Judaism* 1 (2000): 120–44. Also published in: *Studia Theologica*, 54:1 (2000): 55–75. Cf. Peder Borgen, "Proselytes, Conquest, and Mission," in *Recruitment, Conquest, and Conflict: Strategies in Judaism, Christianity, and the Greco-Roman World*, ed. Peder Borgen, Vernon K. Robbins, and David B. Gowler (Atlanta, GA: Scholars Press, 1998), 57–77, where he argues that the "sharp distinction between particularism and universalism does not do justice to the historical data [. . .] Particularism and Universalism are not mutually exclusive concepts when applied to Jewish and Christian history and self-understanding" (57).

16. See n. 15.

17. For example, what is often called theology of religions; the way the insider understands and locates other religious traditions on his or her larger conceptual-theological map, assisting them in making sense of their own place in a reality in which non-corroborating truth claims about the nature and role of human existence in the universe compete.

18. For example, the Book of Ezra; various strands of rabbinic tradition; traditional forms of Samaritanism.

19. For example various other and more dominant strands of rabbinic tradition; most modern forms of Judaism.

20. Most modern forms of mainstream Christianity. Ancient cults such as, e.g., the widespread cults of Isis, Jupiter Dolichenos, and Mithras, which were originally connected to an ethnic-geographic area, also developed to be unbound by ethnic requirements in terms of general membership. Even in such cases, though, it should be noted that ethnicity could still play a role within groups in terms of status and access to certain offices. For example, priests of the cult of Jupiter Dolichenos continued to be exported from Syria, although it seems these priests could, in turn, also train non-Syrians to become priests; see Anna Collar, *Religious Networks in the Roman Empire: The Spread of New Ideas* (Cambridge: Cambridge University Press, 2013), 139.

21. Book of Jonah; Rabbinic tradition and most mainstream forms of Judaism today.

22. Cyprian's *extra ecclesiam nulla salus*. Such perspectives, in various forms, have often been foregrounded in mainstream Christianity, even though other more inclusive trajectories have existed throughout Christian history and today.

23. I have revised the terminology somewhat here since my first publication of this approach in 2000, and discussed at some length the idea of "mission" in Graeco-Roman society, Judaism, and among Christ-followers, whether Jews or gentiles, in: Anders Runesson, "Was There a Christian Mission before the Fourth Century? Problematizing Common Ideas about Early Christianity and the Beginnings of Modern Mission," in *The Making of Christianity: Conflicts, Contacts, and Constructions*, ed. Magnus Zetterholm and Samuel Byrskog (Winona Lake, IN: Eisenbrauns, 2012), 205–47. On mission, and how mission may be defined, see also the important study by Martin Goodman, *Mission and Conversion: Proselytizing in the Religious History of the Roman Empire* (Oxford: Clarendon, 1995).

24. Eleazer's position in Josephus's story of the royal house of Adiabene (*A.J.* 20.34–48). The traditional Christian form of mission is today questioned in some Christian denominations understanding mission primarily as providing aid and relief during and after natural and political catastrophes, assisting others in need, and sharing knowledge and resources with nations in need of improving their infrastructure, etc. (Mt 25:31–46 is often referred to in such contexts, suggesting that Mt 28:18–20 should be understood as referring back to, and enjoining, the embodied practices outlined there).

25. For example, the Book of Jonah; Ananias's position in Josephus's story of the royal house of Adiabene (*A.J.* 20.34–48). For discussion of this Josephan text in relation to Paul, see Mark D. Nanos, "Paul's Non-Jews Do Not Become 'Jews,' but Do They Become 'Jewish'? Reading Romans 2:25–29 within Judaism, alongside Josephus," *JJMJS* 1 (2014): 26–53 (http://www.jjmjs.org/).

26. The historical Jesus, but also the most common form of mission in Judaism, Christianity, and many other traditions.

27. For example, the idea of gentiles being attracted to Zion when the time was right, without active Jewish missionary activity. Note also the different approaches

within the Jesus movement, even sometimes in the same text (Mt 2:1–2; 8:5–13; 10:5–6; 15:21–28; 28:18–20). John's Gospel declares that love among insiders is a sine qua non for outsiders' recognition of their identity as followers of Jesus, implying that no missionary efforts will succeed without this criterion having been fulfilled first, presenting, thus, an understanding of mission as at its core centripetal and passive (John 13:35; cf. Isa 61:9).

28. On this, see Runesson, "Was There a Christian Mission?" Physical evidence for this popularity can be seen in the Isis statues and temples erected in several port towns in Asia Minor (she became a patron deity of sailors and merchants among many other things), the establishment of two Sarapis cults on Delos. But the spread of these cults spanned the entire Mediterranean world; see discussion in R. E. Witt's classic work, *Isis in the Graeco-Roman World* (London: Thames and Hudson, 1971), 46–58, 256–59; map on pages 56–57. Lucien's *Metamorphosis* is of key interest here, as it describes in some detail rituals involved.

29. Leonard V. Rutgers, "Archaeological Evidence for the Interaction of Jews and Non-Jews in Late Antiquity," *AJA* 96 (1992): 101–18, here 108. Although also mostly dealing with the Late-Antique period, there are many insights to be gained by reading Eric C. Smith, *Jewish Glass and Christian Stone: A Materialist Mapping of the "Parting of the Ways"* (London: Routledge, 2017).

30. NRSV has "removed."

31. For the purpose of this chapter, I will leave open the question of whether this approach belongs to Paul's previous or current life in Judaism, respectively. The point here is the (major) shift from one position to another, a shift which the historical Paul beyond doubt went through and which was interpreted by him as of crucial importance for the order in which the God of Israel wanted to find the world before the arrival of the son of God and the final judgment. For the view that Gal 5:11 refers to Paul's pre-Damascus approach to non-Jews, see Terence L. Donaldson, "Paul within Judaism: A Critical Evaluation from a 'New Perspective' Perspective," in *Paul within Judaism: Restoring the First-Century Context to the Apostle*, ed. Mark D. Nanos and Magnus Zetterholm (Minneapolis, MN: Fortress Press, 2015), 277–301, here 299, n. 39; so also Thiessen, *Gentile Problem*, 37–41. For a position that understands the passage to speak of both of Paul's positions, and, consequently his change of mind, as belonging to the period after he joined the Jesus movement, see Douglas A. Campbell, "Galatians 5:11: Evidence of an Early Law-Observant Mission by Paul?" *NTS* 57 (2011): 325–47. See also the discussion by Karl-Olav Sandnes, *Paul Perceived: An Interactionist Perspective on Paul and the Law*, WUNT 412 (Tübingen: Mohr Siebeck, 2018), 83–89, which moves in a different direction altogether, understanding the passage as countering an (incorrect) understanding and representation of Paul by his Galatian opponents, and thus not referring to a change of mind at all.

32. Circumcision implying full Torah observance; cf. Gal 5:3.

33. Such a worldview would not in and of itself prohibit an openness for individuals to cross ethnic boundaries and become proselytes, although some Jewish writings would reject this possibility. See Matthew Thiessen, *Contesting Conversion: Genealogy, Circumcision, and Identity in Ancient Judaism and Christianity* (Oxford: Oxford University Press, 2011).

34. More detailed discussion of this argument is found in Anders Runesson, "Paul's Rule in All the *Ekklēsiai* (1 Cor 7:17–24)," in *Introduction to Messianic Judaism: Its Ecclesial Context and Biblical Foundations*, ed. David Rudolph and Joel Willits (Grand Rapids, MI: Zondervan, 2013), 214–23. For the connection between *ekklēsia*/association membership and salvation, see also Richard Last, "What Purpose Did Paul Understand His Mission to Serve"? *HTR* 104:3 (2011): 299–324, here 324: "For Paul, salvation comes to those 'in Christ,' and those 'in Christ' should identify themselves as different from others by virtue of their membership in a congregation of Christ-believers." See further below.

35. Fredriksen, *Paul*, 74.

36. Cf. William S. Campbell, *Paul and the Creation of Christian Identity* (New York, NY: T&T Clark, 2008), 157, on Paul as constructing several sub-identities as a nested hierarchy of identity, "of which being in Christ is the primary."

37. Interesting here is a comparison with Josephus's story about the events in Adiabene (*A.J.* 20.38–48), Ananias arguing (but not theologizing) that it is quite possible to "worship God without being circumcised, even though he [the king] did resolve to follow the Jewish law [τὰ πάτρια τῶν Ἰουδαίων] entirely" (20.41). One may add that even with Ananias's solution to a difficult political situation, following the law in this way without circumcision would require God's forgiveness; it is thus not presented by Josephus as an ideal or divinely ordained solution ("He added, that God would forgive him, though he did not perform the operation, while it was omitted out of necessity, and for fear of his subjects"; 20.42). For Paul, of course, the opposite is true. On the other hand, Ananias's opponent, Eleazer the Galilean, would not be willing to count on such divine lenience, urging the king to undergo the operation, which he also did. For Eleazer, it is not enough to read the law, one must also practice it in all its parts (20.43–48; cf. Matt 7:21–23). On the Adiabene story, see Donaldson, *Judaism and the Gentiles,* and Nanos, "Do They Become 'Jewish'?"

38. On Paul's theology as intertwined with and making use of institutional structures, see Runesson, "Placing Paul."

39. But cf. also the covenantal hermeneutics behind Gal 3:17.

40. On the meaning of reconciliation (*katallagē*), cf. Paul's use in Rom 5:11, where Christ is the subject.

41. That is, applying a different set of metaphors, Paul is not advocating a melting-pot scenario in which differences are mixed into a new, third entity, but rather a mosaic-style solution, in which the different colors of the tesserae are maintained but brought into a new pattern, contributing to an overall image in which such tesseral distinctiveness is a sine qua non for the art to make sense.

42. Cf. however, Charles H. Dodd, *The Epistle of Paul to the Romans* (London: Hodder and Stoughton, 1932), 184–87, who argues that Romans 11 implies a full universal salvation for humanity, not only for Israel (note esp. the chart on page 187).

43. The unbelieving spouse seems to relate to the believing partner as that partner relates to Israel through Abraham, but apart from the criterion of *pistis*. A theology of salvation by association, as it were.

44. Contrary to Matthew's Gospel, which in 25:31–46 outlines a theology of salvation aligning quite closely to the rabbinic concept of righteous gentiles. For discussion of this Matthean passage, see Runesson, *Divine Wrath*, 414–28.

45. Lloyd Gaston, *Paul and the Torah* (Vancouver: University of British Columbia, 1987).

46. Such claims are found in the Pseudo-Clementine *Homilies* 8.5–7. For discussion, see Karin Hedner Zetterholm, "Jewish Teaching for Gentiles in the Pseudo-Clementine Homilies: A Reception of Ideas in Paul and Acts Shaped by a Jewish Milieu?" *JJMJS* 6 (2019): 79–82; cf. Annette Yoshiko Reed, "'Jewish Christianity' after the 'Parting of the Ways': Approaches to Historiography and Self-Definition in the Pseudo-Clementines," in *The Ways That Never Parted: Jews and Christians in Late Antiquity and the Early Middle Ages*, ed. Adam H. Becker and Annette Yoshiko Reed (Tübingen: Mohr Siebeck, 2003), 189–231, here 213–17. On Jewish followers of Jesus, Reed writes: "Both H[omilies] 8 and R[ecognitions] 4 exalt those whom some scholars might call 'Jewish Christians' (or even 'Christian Jews') in the sense of people who view the Torah and the Gospels as equal in soteriological value" (217).

47. As noted above, for Paul there is a very real and, in terms of his theological worldview, functionally defined difference between Jews and non-Jews in the *ekklēsia*, so that any eradication of the ethnic boundary is understood as a contradiction of God's will, a sign of a lack of *pistis*, and, ultimately, a disqualifier as far as the kingdom is concerned (cf. Rom 3:1–4, 29–31; 1 Cor 7:17–24; Gal 5:3–4).

48. For example, Acts 15:5, noting here that these people, like Paul, are identified as Pharisees.

49. Critical changes of behavior of people within the movement, especially regarding the issue of ethnicity and different forms of belonging, are, of course, attested in the Pauline correspondence itself. When Cephas is accused of making changes to his behavior and missionary strategies in relation to gentiles in Gal 2:11–14, switching to a stance aimed at making gentiles live like Jews (*iuodaizein*; Gal 2:14), Paul mentions social pressure from authorities, ultimately having their orders from James in Jerusalem, as the cause for his change of mind. On different views on the timing of Paul's own change of mind, see n. 31 above.

50. It can hardly be a matter of sheer convenience, since if the message would have been the same for all those missionized, a geographic division between the various Jewish missionaries would surely have been preferred.

51. That Paul's rhetoric was not always easy to decipher even among his early readers is well known, as is also explicitly stated in 2 Pet 3:15–16, where the topic is the timing of the return of the Christ. More interesting for our purposes here is the evidence that some people also claimed that Paul was misunderstood precisely with regard to the issue of ethnic distinction as key to the adopted missionary strategies and their results. The rumours reported in Acts 21:20–22 rest on the assumption that Paul would not have made such a distinction, and taught not only non-Jews but also Jews not to circumcise—i.e., the very opposite of the practice of the Pharisaic Christ-followers of Acts 15:5, who also rejected ethnic-based distinctions within the Jesus movement, but from a different angle. This view is, however, rejected by both the highest authority in Jerusalem, James, and Paul himself, as these figures are portrayed

in Acts, and thus clearly also by the author of Acts, as this author, as also the Paul of the letters does, argues for a unity in diversity within the people of God, a joining of the ways between Jews and gentiles.

52. Cf. Num 23:19.

53. The phenomenon of resurrection in itself was likely not the problem for Paul before joining the movement, but rather the 'now' and the 'who,' the latter aspect also affecting and modifying various ideas about the messianic figure and this figure's role in Israel and the world.

54. Last, "Purpose."

55. Cf. Gal 3:28.

56. These two—theology and institution—were, for Paul, simply two sides of the same coin, the latter a manifestation of the former, and, consequently, serving as an embodied and constant reminder of the message he proclaimed.

57. To be sure, such a position does not exclude application of ethnic discourse, understanding Christians as a "third-race." On this, see Denise Kimber Buell, *Why This New Race: Ethnic Reasoning in Early Christianity* (New York, NY: Columbia University Press, 2005). The terminology applied here rather foregrounds the step away from a theo-ethnic focus on the people of Israel as sine qua non for the salvation of the nations, a focus essential to the earliest Jesus movement, including Paul, as it began expanding outside the Jewish people.

58. It should be noted, though, that Cyprian (cf. above, n. 22) was never fully accepted, as some theologies have been more open than others. It was not until the Second Vatican Council, however, that such more open trajectories, also in relationship to the Jewish people specifically, were developed more fully in depth and reach.

59. Sandnes, *Paul Perceived*, 51, alludes to a similar hermeneutical dynamic, which removes Paul from direct continuity with the later theological choices of the churches: "It seems Paul's Damascus experience and his Gentile mission brought into being a theology that contributed to a process gradually moving toward a parting of the ways, although that was not at all his intention."

60. Perhaps, among the multifarious expressions of the reception of this dictum, the initial lines of Alexander Pope's poem *Know then Thyself* from *An Essay on Man, Epistle II*, catches best the sense fitting the context here: "Know then thyself, presume not God to scan//The proper study of mankind is Man."

61. Peter Abelard, prologue to *Sic et Non*, in *Medieval Literary Theory and Criticism c. 1100–1375: The Commentary Tradition*, ed. A. J. Minnis and A. B. Scott (rev. ed.; Oxford: Clarendon, 1988), 99–100. Quoted from: *The Bible in Medieval Tradition: The Letter to the Romans*, trans. and ed. Ian Christopher Levy, Philip D. W. Krey, and Thomas Ryan (Grand Rapids, MI: Eerdmans, 2013), 31.

BIBLIOGRAPHY

Abelard, Peter. Prologue to *Sic et Non*, in *Medieval Literary Theory and Criticism c. 1100–1375: The Commentary Tradition*. Revised Edition. Edited by A. J. Minnis and A. B. Scott. Oxford: Clarendon, 1988.

Berger, Peter L. *The Sacred Canopy*. Garden City, NY: Doubleday, 1967.
Borgen, Peder. "Proselytes, Conquest, and Mission." In *Recruitment, Conquest, and Conflict: Strategies in Judaism, Christianity, and the Greco-Roman World*, edited by Peder Borgen, Vernon K. Robbins, and David B. Gowler, 57–77. Atlanta, GA: Scholars Press, 1998.
Campbell, Douglas A. "Galatians 5:11: Evidence of an Early Law-Observant Mission by Paul?" *NTS* 57 (2011): 325–47.
Campbell, William S. *The Nations in the Divine Economy: Paul's Covenantal Hermeneutics and Participation in Christ*. Lanham, MD: Lexington Books/Fortress Academic, 2018.
———. *Paul and the Creation of Christian Identity*. New York, NY: T&T Clark, 2008.
Collar, Anna. *Religious Networks in the Roman Empire: The Spread of New Ideas*. Cambridge: Cambridge University Press, 2013.
Dodd, Charles H. *The Epistle of Paul to the Romans*. London: Hodder and Stoughton, 1932.
Donaldson, Terence L. *Judaism and the Gentiles: Jewish Patterns of Universalism (to 135 CE)*. Waco, TX: Baylor University Press, 2007.
———. "Paul within Judaism: A Critical Evaluation from a 'New Perspective' Perspective." In *Paul within Judaism: Restoring the First-Century Context to the Apostle*, edited by Mark D. Nanos and Magnus Zetterholm, 277–301. Minneapolis, MN: Fortress Press, 2015.
Eisenbaum, Pamela. *Paul Was Not a Christian: The Original Message of a Misunderstood Apostle*. New York, NY: HarperCollins, 2009.
Ehrensperger, Kathy. *Paul at the Crossroads of Cultures: Theologizing in the Space Between*. London: Bloomsbury, 2013.
Fredriksen, Paula. "Judaizing the Nations: The Ritual Demands of Paul's Gospel." *NTS* 56 (2010): 232–52.
———. *Paul: The Pagans' Apostle*. New Haven, CT: Yale University Press, 2018.
Gaston, Lloyd. *Paul and the Torah*. Vancouver: University of British Columbia, 1987.
Goodman, Martin. *Mission and Conversion: Proselytizing in the Religious History of the Roman Empire*. Oxford: Clarendon, 1995.
Harland, Philip A. *Associations, Synagogues, and Congregations: Claiming a Place in Ancient Mediterranean Society*. Minneapolis, MN: Fortress Press, 2003.
———. *Greco-Roman Associations: Texts, Translations, and Commentary. II: North Coast of Black Sea, Asia Minor*. BZNW 204. Berlin: De Gruyter, 2014.
Karlenzig, Bruce. "Plausibility." In *Encyclopedia of Religion*, edited by William H. Swatos, Jr., 364. Walnut Creek, CA: AltaMira Press, 1998.
Kimber Buell, Denise. *Why This New Race: Ethnic Reasoning in Early Christianity*. New York, NY: Columbia University Press, 2005.
Kloppenborg, John S. *Christ's Associations: Connecting and Belonging in the Ancient City*. New Haven, CT: Yale University Press, 2019.
Kloppenborg, John S., and Richard S. Ascough. *Greco-Roman Associations: Texts, Translations, and Commentary. I: Attica, Central Greece, Macedonia, Thrace*. BZNW 181. Berlin: De Gruyter, 2011.

Last, Richard. "What Purpose Did Paul Understand His Mission to Serve"? *HTR* 104:3 (2011): 299–324.

Last, Richard, and Philip Harland. *Group Survival in the Ancient Mediterranean: Rethinking Material Conditions in the Landscape of Jews and Christians.* London: T&T Clark, 2020.

Levy, Ian Christopher, Philip D. W. Krey, and Thomas Ryan, eds. and trans. *The Bible in Medieval Tradition: The Letter to the Romans.* Grand Rapids, MI: Eerdmans, 2013.

Mortensen, Jacob P. B. *Paul among the Gentiles: A Radical Reading of Romans.* NET 28. Tübingen: Narr Francke Attempto, 2018.

Nanos, Mark D. *The Mystery of Romans: The Jewish Context of Paul's Letter.* Minneapolis, MN: Fortress Press, 1996.

———. "Paul's Non-Jews Do Not Become 'Jews,' but Do They Become 'Jewish'? Reading Romans 2:25–29 within Judaism, alongside Josephus." *JJMJS* 1 (2014): 26–53.

Nasrallah, Laura Salah. *Archaeology and the Letters of Paul.* Oxford: Oxford University Press, 2019.

Reed, Annette Yoshiko. "'Jewish Christianity' after the 'Parting of the Ways': Approaches to Historiography and Self-Definition in the Pseudo-Clementines." In *The Ways That Never Parted: Jews and Christians in Late Antiquity and the Early Middle Ages*, edited by Adam H. Becker and Annette Yoshiko Reed, 189–231. Tübingen: Mohr Siebeck, 2003.

Runesson, Anders. "Beyond Universalism and Particularism: Re-thinking Paul and Matthew on Gentile Inclusion." In *Paul and Matthew among Jews and Gentiles. Essays in Honour of Terence L. Donaldson*, edited by Ronald Charles. London: Bloomsbury, 2021, 99–111.

———. *Divine Wrath and Salvation in Matthew: The Narrative World of the First Gospel.* Minneapolis, MN: Fortress Press, 2016.

———. "Particularistic Judaism and Universalistic Christianity? Some Critical Remarks on Terminology and Theology." *Journal of Greco-Roman Christianity and Judaism* 1 (2000): 120–44.

———. "Paul's Rule in All the *Ekklēsiai* (1 Cor 7:17–24)." In *Introduction to Messianic Judaism: Its Ecclesial Context and Biblical Foundations*, edited by David Rudolph and Joel Willits, 214–23. Grand Rapids, MI: Zondervan, 2013.

———. "Placing Paul: Institutional Structures and Theological Strategy in the World of the Early Christ-believers." *SEÅ* 80 (2015): 43–67.

———. "Was There a Christian Mission before the Fourth Century? Problematizing Common Ideas about Early Christianity and the Beginnings of Modern Mission." In *The Making of Christianity: Conflicts, Contacts, and Constructions*, edited by Magnus Zetterholm and Samuel Byrskog, 205–47. Winona Lake, IN: Eisenbrauns, 2012.

Rutgers, Leonard V. "Archaeological Evidence for the Interaction of Jews and Non-Jews in Late Antiquity." *AJA* 96 (1992): 101–18.

Sandnes, Karl-Olav. *Paul Perceived: An Interactionist Perspective on Paul and the Law.* WUNT 412. Tübingen: Mohr Siebeck, 2018.

Segal, Alan F. *Life after Death: A History of the Afterlife in Western Religion*. New York, NY: Doubleday, 2004.

Setzer, Claudia. *Resurrection of the Body in Early Judaism and Early Christianity: Doctrine, Community, and Self-Definition*. Leiden: Brill, 2004.

Sim, David C., and James S. McLaren, eds. *Attitudes to Gentiles in Ancient Judaism and Early Christianity*. London: Bloomsbury, 2013.

Smith, Eric C. *Jewish Glass and Christian Stone: A Materialist Mapping of the "Parting of the Ways."* London: Routledge, 2017.

Special Issue on Paul. *JJMJS* 5 (2018).

Stendahl, Krister. *Final Account: Paul's Letter to the Romans*. Minneapolis, MN: Fortress Press, 1995.

Thiessen, Matthew. *Contesting Conversion: Genealogy, Circumcision, and Identity in Ancient Judaism and Christianity*. Oxford: Oxford University Press, 2011.

———. *Paul and the Gentile Problem*. Oxford: Oxford University Press, 2016.

Witt, R. E., *Isis in the Graeco-Roman World*. London: Thames and Hudson, 1971.

Zetterholm, Karin Hedner. "Jewish Teaching for Gentiles in the Pseudo-Clementine Homilies: A Reception of Ideas in Paul and Acts Shaped by a Jewish Milieu?" *JJMJS* 6 (2019): 79–82.

Zetterholm, Magnus. *Approaches to Paul: A Student's Guide to Recent Scholarship*. Minneapolis, MN: Fortress Press, 2009.

Chapter Three

From Aristeas to the Apocalypse of Abraham

A Survey of Some Hellenistic Jewish Texts Relating to the Issue of Israel and Its Relationship to the Other Nations

Eric Noffke

Paul of Tarsus is universally known as "the apostle to the nations."[1] Since the time of his calling on his way to Damascus, he has always considered himself as sent to preach the Gospel among the nations, and this is what he did for the rest of his life. In this way he had placed himself at the center of the most important change that occurred in the mission of the Jesus movement, that at the beginning was addressed to Israel and its lost sheep.[2]

If we want to understand how and why the early Christians (or at least part of them) decided to open their mission to the pagan nations, we have to consider that at least since the days in which Nebuchadnezzar destroyed Jerusalem, there had been Jews living among the foreign nations. The diaspora had a growing influence on Jerusalem and Judaea. Just to give an example, Ezra and Nehemiah, who reformed Judaism during the Persian empire, were coming from the Babylonian diaspora, which had been capable of developing some connection with the Persian court. It was especially during the Hellenistic time, though, that the Jewish diaspora grew exponentially and elaborated various ways to interact with the pagans, with their religion, and especially with their highly refined Hellenic culture. When the Christians opened their *ekklēsiai* to the pagans, then, they inherited at least three centuries of Jewish-Pagan interaction. But what kind of interaction did they actually have? It can be helpful to review some of the attitudes that the Hellenistic Jews adopted on the issue, in order to understand what (if any) influence they had on Paul and his comprehension of Israel's role towards the Nations (leaving aside the very common polemic against the pagans). The aim of this chapter is to provide some data on the diaspora context of Paul's mission to the pagans (the topic of this conference).

THE *LETTER OF ARISTEAS*

The *Letter of Aristeas*, a Jewish text usually located in Alexandria and dated to the second half of the second century BC, witnesses to a very sophisticated form of Judaism, and defends a model of possible coexistence with the Nations: God's election of Israel doesn't exclude pagans from the possibility of recognizing the unique God.

The document is well known because it tells the legend of the translation of the Septuagint, but actually this is only the occasion to develop a much longer narrative focused on the meeting between well-educated Jews and Gentiles. The story, in the form of a letter from Aristeas to Filocrates, tells how the decision to translate the Law of the Jews for the famous Alexandrian library was taken by the king Tolomaeus, who sent an embassy to the high priest Eleazarus in Jerusalem, asking for translators. Before sending the delegation, the king orders to free all the Jews who had been deported and enslaved by his father, paying himself the necessary amount of money for their ransom. The texts of the edict and of the letter to Eleazarus are given (as well as the high priest's answer). Much space is then dedicated to the description of the generous gifts sent to Jerusalem, which gives to the author an opportunity to describe the temple and its life as well as the city of Jerusalem and the surrounding countryside. After these descriptions, there follows a report of the dialogue between some ambassadors and the high priest, about some purity rules, which are interpreted allegorically: far from being a form of superstition, Judaism is presented as a rational and reasonable religion. When the delegation returns to Alexandria with the seventy-two translators (six for each of Israel's tribes), they are immediately introduced to the king as special guests in the course of seven banquets in their honor (prepared according the Jewish dietary rules), a good chance for the king to pose individual questions to all his guests concerning the art of good government. It is only after this long description that we are briefly told about the translation and its astonishing accomplishment. Having done their job, the translators can return to Jerusalem.

What is striking in the *Letter of Aristeas* is the atmosphere of full mutual understanding among Jews and Gentiles at the king's court. They are all highly educated people, trained in the Greek *paideia*, which allows the Greeks to have a full understanding of the one God and recognize His power over the whole world. In the words that follow, it is clearly stated that He's the same God for everyone, even if they call Him with different names:

> These people worship God the overseer and creator of all, whom all men worship including ourselves, O King, except that we have a different name. Their name for him is Zeus and Jove. The primitive men, consistently with this, dem-

onstrated that the one by whom all live and are created is the master and Lord of all. (*Let. Aris.* 16)³

Of course, Israel's unique status is clearly in the mind of the author of this Letter, but we are referred to it only once in a short invective against idolatry:

> In his wisdom the legislator, in a comprehensive survey of each particular part, and being endowed by God for the knowledge of universal truths, surrounded us with unbroken palisades and iron walls to prevent our mixing with any of the other peoples in any matter, thus kept pure in body and soul, preserved from false beliefs, and worshiping the only God omnipotent over all creation. [. . .] So, to prevent our being perverted by contact with others or by mixing with bad influences, he hedged us in on all sides with strict observances connected with meat and drink and touch and hearing and sight, after the manner of the Law. In general everything is similarly constituted in regard to natural reasoning, being governed by one supreme power, and in each particular everything has a profound reason for it, both the things from which we abstain in use and those of which we partake. (*Let. Aris.* 139–140, 142–143)

Even if the Greek paideia can lead to the only God, according to Aristeas the Jews have one advantage with respect to the pagans, namely, the Law that was revealed to Moses instructs them about God through a specific way of life. It's an elitist point of view, of course, because implicitly it excludes the average persons, who were excluded from a higher education and, consequently, could not get rid of idolatry. But, in principle, there is one humankind that has the means to recognize the only true God and to live according to wisdom. In other words, according to Aristeas, the educated Greek doesn't need to convert to Judaism in order to be saved. On this issue, we need to remember that in this writing salvation is related only to this earthly existence: there is no hint that allows us to think that there was an openness to eternal life; it's the same perspective that we find in the Old Testament.

The whole Letter, then, is designed to defend the principle that Jews and Greeks can know the same God, expressing in this way the highest level of inclusiveness reached by Hellenistic Judaism. It's also interesting to note one more comment made by Aristeas about the Jewish translators:

> I admired these men tremendously, the way in which they gave immediate answers which needed a long time (to ponder), and while the questioner had thought out details in each case, those answering gave their replies immediately one after another—they were manifestly deserving of admiration to me and to the audience, but especially to the philosophers. All who will inherit this narrative will, I think, find it incredible. (*Let. Aris.* 295–297)

The *Letter* is most probably addressed to the other Jews, but its fictive frame is aimed at saying that the pagans can be fascinated and positively struck by Israel's wisdom. Was that a real situation at a certain point for Alexandrian Judaism, or was that just a dream or an illusion? It could have been so in the second century BC, when the Jewish community reached the highest level of integration in Ptolemaic society.

One doubt remains: what about the pagan rites the king was obliged to perform? Aristeas never talks about the pagan cult, which would have been the limit that no Jew could trespass without losing his/her own identity. This problem remains hidden under the surface of such an optimistic writing.

Even if such an openness to Hellenistic culture is peculiar to the *Letter of Aristeas*, the idea that a pagan who abandons idolatry can find the real God without being obliged to convert to Judaism can be found in other highly Hellenized authors such as Philo from Alexandria. Even if he's actually mainly interested in reading the Bible using the tools provided by Greek philosophy, it's quite noteworthy to see both his openness to the pagan world (he doesn't try to convert the pagans, but proselytes are nevertheless welcomed) and his strong consciousness of Israel's superiority among the nation (due to God's Law, of course). In *Mos.* 2.43–44, for instance, we find a description of the yearly celebrations for the translation in Greek of the Torah that ends with an important comment:

> Therefore, even to the present day, there is held every year a feast and general assembly in the island of Pharos, whither not only Jews but multitudes of others cross the water, both to do honor to the place in which the light of that version first shone out, and also to thank God for the good gift so old yet ever young. But, after the prayers and thanksgivings, some fixing tents on the seaside and others reclining on the sandy beach in the open air feast with their relations and friends, counting that shore for the time a more magnificent lodging than the fine mansions in the royal precincts. Thus the laws are shewn to be desirable and precious in the eyes of all, ordinary citizens and rulers alike, and that too though our nation has not prospered for many a year. It is but natural that when people are not flourishing their belongings to some degree are under a cloud. But, if a fresh start should be made to brighter prospects, how great a change for the better might we expect to see! I believe that each nation would abandon its peculiar ways, and, throwing overboard their ancestral customs, turn to honoring our laws alone. For, when the brightness of their shining is accompanied by national prosperity, it will darken the light of the others as the risen sun darkens the stars. (*Mos.* 2.43–44)

We get here the impression on one side of a wide group of people with a pagan background sympathizing with the Jews at least on occasion of a Holiday like this and on the other side of a Jewish community open to such a sympathy and company. Should we infer from this openness that the Jews considered those Gentiles to be clean from idolatry? It looks like that, on a more popular level, there was some kind of acceptancy of gentile sympathizers, at such a level that they felt like eating and partying together.

JOSEPH AND ASENETH

We meet a whole different perspective in the novel *Joseph and Aseneth*, which was most probably composed in Alexandria in the course of the first century BC, before Augustus conquered Egypt in the year 30 BC. It tells a new version of the Biblical story (see Genesis 41): Joseph is visiting the house of Aseneth during his trip across Egypt while preparing the country to face the seven years of famine that are expected. Here he meets Aseneth, who falls in love with him. But, being a pagan, she is rejected with contempt by Joseph, and this brings her to a radical rejection of her former life in idolatry: she humbles herself and goes through a deep conflict with her family when she literally throws her idols out of the window. After a week of mourning and fasting she is finally welcomed by an angel in God's people, and her name is written in the book of life.

> And the man said to her, "Remove the veil from your head, and for what purpose did you do this?" For you are a chaste virgin today, and your head is like that of a young man. And Aseneth removed the veil from her head. And the man said to her, "Courage, Aseneth, chaste virgin. Behold, I have heard all the words of your confession and your prayer. Behold, I have also seen the humiliation and the affliction of the seven days of your want (of food). Behold, from your tears and these ashes, plenty of mud has formed before your face. Courage, Aseneth, chaste virgin. For behold, your name was written in the book of the living in heaven; in the beginning of the book, as the very first of all, your name was written by my finger, and it will not be erased forever. Behold, from today, you will be renewed and formed anew and made alive again, and you will eat blessed bread of life, and drink a blessed cup of immortality, and anoint yourself with blessed ointment of incorruptibility. Courage, Aseneth, chaste virgin. Behold, I have given you today to Joseph for a bride, and he himself will be your bridegroom forever (and) ever." [. . .] "And behold, I am going away to Joseph and will tell him about you everything I have to say. And Joseph will come to you today, and see you, and rejoice over you, and love you, and he will be your bridegroom, and you will be a bride for him forever (and) ever." (*Jos. Asen.* 15)[4]

We see here a quite different perspective from the *Letter of Aristeas*, in many respects. First, all contacts between Pagans and Jews that could cause a form of pollution are avoided (e.g., Joseph eats at a different table than that of

Aseneth and her family). Second, here we find the story of a pagan rejecting all her former life as garbage (to use Paul's words in Philippians 3:8): before Joseph prayed for her, she was blind and had no clue of the true God. Third, the real life is the eternal one in God; but more than with an apocalyptic perspective, here we have to deal with a very interesting form of mysticism. With these premises, it's clear that a pagan can be saved only through a full conversion to the God of Israel. Abandoning idolatry is not enough: it's necessary to fully become part of Israel and to have the name written in the book of life. Interestingly enough, though, we have here the conversion of a woman, not of a man: of course this was inevitable with the story of Aseneth, but it's not by chance that this specific story was used to talk about conversion to Judaism and also that this is one of the very few explicit descriptions of a conversion. This probably means that this more radical understanding of conversion was restricted to a minority among the Jews.

APOCALYPSE OF ABRAHAM

This curious apocalypse, usually dated at the end of the first or early second century AD, and related to writings like *2 Baruch*, *4 Ezra* (all texts that reacted to the destruction of Jerusalem in 70 AD),[5] survives only in Old Slavonic and tells us the story about Abraham abandoning idolatry and being welcomed by God through His angel. After being blessed with the promise of a people and having stipulated a pact with God, he is given a vision of the destiny of his people. In this book's perspective, humankind is divided in two groups: Israel and the other nations. Here election is clearly not enough, because observance of the Law is indispensable to overcome Azazel's deception and to gain eternal life, but the first striking fact is that Abraham the converted is never told to undergo circumcision. Does it say something about the idea of conversion of the author of this apocalypse?

The second interesting element is that in most of the book, idolaters seem to have no hope, and in the whole book the only conversion story that is told is that of Abraham. But, while in the vision of chapters 15–29 the destiny of the other nations seems to be doomed because of idolatry, suddenly a surprising fact occurs when it comes to the end times:

> And I looked and saw a man going out from the left, the heathen side. From the side of the heathen went out men and women and children, a great crowd, and they worshipped him. And while I was still looking, those on the right side came out, and some insulted this man, and some struck him and others worshipped him. And I saw that as they worshipped him Azazel ran and worshipped and, kissing his face, he turned and stood behind him. And I said, "Eternal, Mighty

One! Who is this man insulted and beaten by the heathen,⁶ with Azazel worshipped?" And he answered and said, "Hear, Abraham, the man whom you saw insulted and beaten and again worshipped is the liberation from the heathen for the people who will be (born) from you. In the last days, in this twelfth hour of impiety, in the twelfth period of the age of my fulfillment I will set up this man from your tribe, the one whom you have seen from my people. All will imitate him, . . . (you) consider him as one called by me [. . .] It is he who will test those of your seed who have worshipped him in the fulfillment of the twelfth hour, in the curtailing of the age of impiety. (*Apoc. Ab.* 29.4–14)⁷

The interpretation of this passage of the vision is quite controversial, especially because some scholars suspect a number of Christian or Bogomil interpolations. Most of the scholars identify this unnamed person with Jesus, and what makes this text interesting for our research is that it looks like that the author of this apocalypse gives him a positive role (he is sent by God to be *the liberation from the heathen for the people who will be [born] from you*). This interpretation is possible only at the light of verse 29.9b, where it is rather stated that this man comes from Israel.⁸ But this is probably a Christian interpolation aimed at correcting the Jewish text in order to identify this man with Jesus. If this is correct, and whoever this person is (a *Nero redivivus*?), here we have a reference to some kind of mingling between Jews and Gentiles in the times preceding the End.

The *Apocalypse of Abraham* can be considered, then, an example of a possible and original development of the two attitudes towards the pagans we have met so far: even if (following the well-attested apocalyptic negative attitude towards the pagans) the main interest remains on Israel's eschatological destiny, God has chosen to save some pagans, as we also see in a passage that occurs at the end of that vision (*Apoc. Ab.* 29.19–20). According to Rubinkiewicz,⁹ verse 20 is corrupted and translates consequently. Enrietti doesn't consider the verse corrupted and translates: "They will be humbled by me, when they will see that I rejoice of those who rejoice with my people and of those who welcome anyone who converts to me."¹⁰ If this translation is correct, according to the *Apocalypse of Abraham* at the End of Times those pagans who sympathize with Israel will find salvation. Again, we see a case in which recognition of the true God and benevolence towards Israel are enough for a Gentile to be saved and, like Abraham in this story, doesn't have to circumcise.

IZATES FROM ADIABENE

I would like to sum up this brief survey with one intriguing story told by Josephus in his *Antiquities*. It's the story of some illustrious converts from the middle of the first century AD, queen Helena from Adiabene and her son, king Izates. When they were residing at Charax Spasini, *a certain Jewish merchant named Ananias visited the king's wives and taught them to worship God after the manner of the Jewish tradition.* Also Izates converts and would like to be circumcised, but he's restrained by his mother and Ananias himself: they are worried that the people of Adiabene would refuse a Jewish king. He (Ananias) *told him, furthermore, that God Himself would pardon him if, constrained thus by necessity and by fear of his subjects, he failed to perform this rite.* Izates is convinced by these words, as long as Eleazar, another Jew from Galilee, arrives at court and sees him reading the Torah. He *had a reputation for being extremely strict when it came to the ancestral laws, urged him to carry out the rite. For when he came instead of carne to him to pay him his respects and found him reading the law of Moses, he said: "In your ignorance, O king, you are guilty of the greatest offence against the law and thereby against God. For you ought not merely to read the law but also, and even more, to do what is commanded in it. How long will you continue to be uncircumcised"?* The king decides to be immediately circumcised. It's possible to understand Josephus's approval of Eleazar's words in his final comment. Contrary to Elena's and Ananias's concerns, God preserved Izates and his children from all threats: *God thus demonstrated that those who fix their eyes on Him and trust in Him alone do not lose the reward of their piety* (quotations from *Ant.* 20.34–48).[11]

In this story we find an example of two different points of view on conversion to Judaism. On one side, we have Ananias, who didn't consider it necessary for a pagan to circumcise, especially when it could have been politically dangerous, as long as the idols were abandoned. On the other side was Eleazar who, showing a more radical interpretation of the Law, wanted the king to fully convert and undergo circumcision. Interestingly enough, the first option is represented by a merchant, not a person with religious purposes in his life, while the second is depicted as a very strict religious person.

This story reveals how the debate was still open on the matter in that time, but we don't get the impression of a missionary religion. On the contrary: there were some Jews that proselytized, but most of the times, like in Joseph and Aseneth's story, it was probably a matter of mixed couples or single individuals fascinated by such a different religion. In other words, of course for the Hellenistic Jews Israel was a light for the nations, but for most of them the pagans were supposed to look for the light themselves and come to Israel, if they wanted; only a few Israelites actually tried to bring the light to the pagans as missionaries.[12]

The issue of proselytism must have been debated at that time, leaving to those pagans who were fascinated by Judaism several possibilities open: being just a sympathizer or a God fearer or accepting to become a proselyte and being welcomed as a full member of the Jewish people (at least by some Jews). We don't know, though, what kind of contact with pagans was allowed according to the different groups: would a Jew share a meal at the same table with a God fearer or a sympathizer? The same dynamics were reproduced in the first Christian congregations, at least until Paul came to change everything.

ANY HELP IN UNDERSTANDING PAUL'S THEOLOGY?

As we get to the early Christianity, it can be stressed that—unlike mainstream Judaism—we are now dealing with a missionary movement, and a very committed one. The turn of the ages, the fulfillment of God's promises has arrived with Jesus's resurrection: now it's necessary to spread the news to all the world. But a problem arose as soon as some pagans started to be interested in the Gospel and were joining the *ekklēsiai*. In that moment the new movement found itself dealing with the same dynamics that characterized the life of a synagogue and its relationship with the pagans. But there was something new, that asked for a quick and different solution. Judaism was the religion of some million people, with synagogues everywhere: there was enough room for every kind of expression and understanding of this ancient religion and no group was capable (or wanted) to impose a general rule in dealing with sympathizers and proselytes. The net was so wide, uniting different forms of Judaism and competing interpretations of the Law, that today we have quite a hard time in defining the borders among the groups within Middle Judaism.

Jesus's followers, on the contrary, constituted a prophetic movement involving a rather small number of people, but moved by a strong missionary impulse, convinced of being, through God's Spirit, the renewed people of God. There wasn't much room for different comprehensions of this new mission without creating violent conflicts. And this is what happened, especially over the issue of the pagans' conversion: eating together or at separate tables could become a "life or death" issue (Galatians 1 and 2; Acts 15).

Paul the Pharisee was most probably in the line of Eleazar in pursuing the need for the Gentiles to be circumcised, if they wanted to be saved on the Last Day. But Paul the follower of Jesus, the apostle to the Nations had rejected the Mosaic Law as a means of salvation: circumcision was not only unnecessary, but as he contest in the letter to the Galatians, it could become a way to reject the salvation offered to every person by God in Jesus. His faith in God's grace through Jesus the Christ fully explains his rejection of circumcising the Gentiles who had come to faith. But we should also remember that as a Hellenistic Jew, he probably had also the experience of those who, like in the

Letter of Aristeas, just didn't see the need to have the pagans who rejected the idols to also fully become part of Israel: once the idols are abandoned (for whatever reason), the Gentiles can stand in front of God with a serene heart and be blessed by Him even if they didn't circumcise . . . And sit at the same table with the Christians with a Jewish background.

Quite different was the point of view of the missionaries sent by the Pharisaic oriented congregation in Jerusalem, who were strict in asking the pagans to circumcise and obey the main Jewish laws. Even if the first-century Jerusalem was a Hellenized city, also among its elite we don't see as many signs of the everyday interaction with the pagans as we see in the diaspora. It is quite probable that the general feeling towards the pagans (if they were the object of any interest at all) was that they needed full conversion in order to be saved at the final judgment. Note that Josephus's Eleazar came from Galilee, another region with a large majority of Jews and limited contacts with the pagans, especially in the countryside, the homeland of Jesus and of his brother Jacob.

Once challenged in Antioch by Jacob's emissaries on the issue of Gentile's conversion to Judaism in order to be saved in Christ, Paul had one more good reason to theologically explain why he didn't agree at all on the issue of the Gentiles' circumcision, lest Jesus's death and resurrection became useless.

NOTES

1. See for example Rom 1:5; 11:13–14; Gal 1:16.
2. See Mat 10:5–6; 15:24. We are probably dealing with original words of Jesus, at least on the basis of the criterion of embarrassment. What is striking is that this teaching seems to be in line with that of James the brother of Jesus as we see, e.g., in the fact that his emissaries in Antioch refused table communion with the former Gentiles (Acts 15; Gal 1–2)—namely, accepted full communion only with other Jews. Are we to suppose, then, that James was in continuity with Jesus when he expected the pagans to convert to Judaism in order to become part of the Jesus movement, or is Matthew here influenced by the later teaching of James and put it on Jesus's lips?
3. All quotations from the *Letter of Aristeas* are from the translation of Shutt, in *The Old Testament Pseudepigrapha*, vol. 2, ed. James H. Charlesworth (New York/Auckland: Doubleday, 1985).
4. Translation by F. H. Colson, *Philo, vol. 6*, Loeb Classical Library 289 (Cambridge, MA/London, U.K.: Harvard University Press, 1994).
5. The possible place of composition of this work is still debated, either the diaspora or Judaea.

6. Mario Enrietti (in Paolo Sacchi, ed. *Apocrifi dell'Antico Testamento* [Brescia: Paideia, 1999]) refers the complement "by the heathen" to the verb worshipped, and not to "insulted and beaten," probably in coherence with what is said in 29.5.

7. Translation by Rubinkiewicz, in *The Old Testament Pseudepigrapha, vol. 1*, ed. James H. Charlesworth (New York/Auckland: Doubleday, 1983).

8. In this way, for example, John J. Collins, *The Apocalyptic Imagination* (Grand Rapids, MI: Eerdmans, 1998), 229–30. According to Nickelsburg "The vision (vv 3–6) is better read as a description of the anti-God figure who attracts Gentiles to him and leads some Jews astray," playing in some way a role similar to that which Azazel has for the Jews (George W. E. Nickelsburg, *Jewish Literature between the Bible and the Mishnah*, 2nd ed. [Minneapolis, MN: Fortress Press, 2002, 287]; see also Sacchi, ed. *Apocrifi dell'Antico Testamento*, 104). According to Nickelsburg, there is only a small Christian interpolation in 9b (the reference that this person comes from the Jewish side and not, as in v. 4, from the pagan side of the picture).

9. Translation by Rubinkiewicz, in *The Old Testament Pseudepigrapha, vol. 1*, ed. James H. Charlesworth, 1983.

10. "Saranno da me umiliati quando vedranno che gioisco di chi gioisce col mio popolo e di chi accoglie coloro che si convertono a me."

11. Translated by Louis H. Feldman, *Josephus. Jewish Antiquities, vol. 9, book 20*, Loeb Classical Library 456 (Cambridge, MA/London, U.K.: Harvard University Press, 1996).

12. The issue whether Judaism was a missionary religion during the second temple period is the object of a very intense scholarly debate. Until the middle of the twentieth century, there was a certain degree of agreement that there was a mission to convert the Gentiles. The Greek translation of the Old Testament and the use of typically pagan literary genres were seen as targeted to the conversion of the pagans, in the spirit of Mat 23:15, that seems to refer to a mission of the Pharisees all over the world. It has been mainly Victor Tcherikover (*Hellenistic Civilization and the Jews* [Philadelphia, PA: Jewish Publication Society of America, 1959, reprint ed. Peabody, MA: Hendrickson, 1999]) who convincingly stated that all this literature was addressed to Hellenized Jews and not much to the Hellenistic world, stressing the fact that we almost lack any witnesses of actual conversions. The strong effort of Louis H. Feldman (*Jew and Gentile in the Ancient World* [Princeton, NJ: Princeton University Press], 1993) to convince the scholarship that Judaism was totally committed to proselytism among the pagans didn't fully succeed, and other contemporary scholars, like John M. G. Barclay (*Jews in the Mediterranean Diaspora* [Edinburgh: T&T Clark, 1998]) or Lester L. Grabbe (*A History of the Jews and Judaism in the Second Temple Period, vol. 2: The Coming of the Greeks: The Early Hellenistic Period [335–175 B.C.E.]* [Edinburgh: T&T Clark, 2011]), prefer to picture a more multifaceted Judaism open to converts, but with more than one idea on the matter and almost no proof of organized missionary programs.

BIBLIOGRAPHY

Barclay, John M. G. *Jews in the Mediterranean Diaspora*. Edinburgh: T&T Clark, 1998.

Charlesworth, James H., ed. *The Old Testament Pseudepigrapha*. Vol. 1. New York, NY and Auckland: Doubleday, 1983.

———. *The Old Testament Pseudepigrapha*. Vol. 2. New York, NY, and Auckland: Doubleday, 1985.

Collins, John J. *The Apocalyptic Imagination*. Grand Rapids, MI: Eerdmans, 1998.

Colson, F. H., trans. and ed. *Philo*. Vol. 6. Loeb Classical Library 289. Cambridge, MA/London, U.K.: Harvard University Press, 1994.

Feldman, Louis H. *Jew and Gentile in the Ancient World*. Princeton, NJ: Princeton University Press, 1993.

———, trans. *Josephus. Jewish Antiquities*. Vol. 9. Book 20. Loeb Classical Library 456. Cambridge, MA/London, U.K.: Harvard University Press, 1996.

Grabbe, Lester L. *A History of the Jews and Judaism in the Second Temple Period. Vol. 2: The Coming of the Greeks: The Early Hellenistic Period (335–175 B.C.E.)*. Edinburgh: T&T Clark, 2011.

Nickelsburg, George W. E. *Jewish Literature between the Bible and the Mishnah*, 2nd ed. Minneapolis, MN: Fortress Press, 2005 [2002].

Sacchi, Paolo, ed. *Apocrifi dell'Antico Testamento*. Brescia: Paideia, 1999.

Tcherikover, Victor. *Hellenistic Civilization and the Jews*. Philadelphia, PA: Jewish Publication Society of America, 1959. Reprint ed. Peabody, MA: Hendrickson, 1999.

Chapter Four

What Eschatological Pilgrimage of the Gentiles?

Matthew V. Novenson

It shall come to pass in the latter days that the mountain of the house of the LORD shall be established as the highest of the mountains, and shall be raised above the hills; and all the nations shall flow to it, and many peoples shall come, and say: 'Come, let us go up to the mountain of the LORD, to the house of the God of Jacob; that he may teach us his ways and that we may walk in his paths.' (Isa 2:2–4 = Mic 4:1–2 RSV)

On this mountain, the LORD of hosts will make for all peoples a feast of fat things, a feast of wine on the lees, of fat things full of marrow, of wine on the lees well refined. And he will destroy on this mountain the covering that is cast over all peoples, the veil that is spread over all nations. (Isa 25:6–7 RSV)

And the foreigners who join themselves to the LORD, to minister to him, to love the name of the LORD, and to be his servants, everyone who keeps the sabbath, and does not profane it, and holds fast my covenant—these I will bring to my holy mountain, and make them joyful in my house of prayer; their burnt offerings and their sacrifices will be accepted on my altar; for my house shall be called a house of prayer for all peoples. (Isa 56:6–7 RSV)

I am coming to gather all nations and tongues; and they shall come and shall see my glory, and I will set a sign among them. And from them I will send survivors to the nations, to Tarshish, Put, and Lud, who draw the bow, to Tubal and Javan, to the coastlands afar off, that have not heard my fame or seen my glory; and they shall declare my glory among the nations. And they shall bring all your brethren from all the nations as an offering to the LORD, upon horses, and in chariots, and in litters, and upon mules, and upon dromedaries, to my holy mountain Jerusalem, says the LORD, just as the Israelites bring their cereal offering in a clean vessel to the house of the LORD. (Isa 66:18–20 RSV)

> Many peoples and strong nations shall come to seek the LORD of hosts in Jerusalem, and to entreat the favor of the LORD. Thus says the LORD of hosts: In those days ten men from the nations of every tongue shall take hold of the robe of a Jew, saying, 'Let us go with you, for we have heard that God is with you.' (Zech 8:22–23 RSV)

> Then everyone that survives of all the nations that have come against Jerusalem shall go up year after year to worship the King, the LORD of hosts, and to keep the feast of Sukkot. (Zech 14:16 RSV mod.)

These are all justly famous, rhetorically powerful oracles from the classical Hebrew prophets envisioning an eschatological future when gentiles will forsake their idols and their weapons of war and make pilgrimage to Jerusalem to worship the living God and learn his ways.[1] But Paul, apostle to the gentiles and a virtuosic interpreter of the prophets, cites precisely none of these texts. None at all. Not so much as an allusion or an echo.[2]

What are we to make of this fact? It would seem that the apostle has missed a trick. Given Paul's urgent need to justify his gentile mission,[3] these classic eschatological pilgrimage texts are low-hanging fruit, surely. And yet, Paul never avails himself of any of them. That is to say, Paul never actually makes the interpretive move that many modern critics have thought must have lay at the back of his mind. As E. P. Sanders—to cite one pre-eminent example—has written, "Paul's entire work, both evangelizing and collecting money, had its setting in the expected pilgrimage of the Gentiles to Mount Zion in the last days."[4]

Others before me have pointed out this curious feature of Pauline intertextuality, most importantly Terence Donaldson in his excellent 1997 book *Paul and the Gentiles*.[5] Donaldson goes on to conclude that, because Paul does not cite these texts or invoke this tradition, he must have thought of his gentile mission not as a performance of an eschatological script at all but rather as a form of Jewish proselytizing, only proselytizing for *Christ*-adherents rather than *Torah*-adherents.[6] I disagree with Donaldson's conclusion (because I think there are other eschatological scripts Paul might have been performing; more on this below), but we have Donaldson to thank for troubling the eschatological-pilgrimage-of-the-gentiles hypothesis, which was in need of troubling. The solution, I argue in this chapter, is not to take the eschatological pilgrimage tradition as a given and to reject it (as Donaldson does), but rather to refuse to take it as a given, to interrogate and deconstruct it, and then to see what options lie open to us.

Hence the title of this chapter: "*What* eschatological pilgrimage of the gentiles?" This is one of those secondary-literature stock phrases that we use thinking we know what we mean by it, but I want to suggest that in fact we do not. The phrase papers over a great deal of actual diversity in the relevant texts from the classical prophets, few or none of which (depending how we count them) Paul himself actually cites anyway. What we have here is a conspicuous mismatch between *explanans* and *explanandum*, between the putative tradition on the one hand and the relevant Pauline texts on the other. It is this mismatch that I want to explore and, hopefully, to resolve.

To be sure, there is such a thing as an eschatological pilgrimage-of-the-gentiles tradition attested in a number of texts from the Second Temple period.[7] But—I would want to insist—to be deserving of the name, a text should clearly attest all three aspects: eschatology, pilgrimage, and gentiles (as the marquee oracles from Isaiah, Micah, and Zechariah cited above all do). And we find all three aspects, for instance, in Tobit's address to the city of Jerusalem in the prayer of Tobit 13:

> O Jerusalem, the holy city, he will afflict you for the deeds of your sons, but again he will show mercy to the sons of the righteous. Give thanks worthily to the Lord, and praise the King of the ages, that his tent may be raised for you again with joy. May he cheer those within you who are captives, and love those within you who are distressed, to all generations forever. Many nations will come from afar to the name of the Lord God, bearing gifts in their hands, gifts for the King of heaven. (Tob 13:9–11 RSV)

And in the Hellenistic Jewish prophecy of *Sibylline Oracles* 3:

> And then all the islands and cities will say . . . 'Come, let us fall on the ground and entreat the immortal king, the great eternal God. Let us send to the temple, since he alone is sovereign, and let us all ponder the law of the Most High God' . . . From every land they will bring incense and gifts to the house of the great God. There will be no other house among men, even for future generations to know, except the one which God gave to faithful men to honour. (*Sib. Or.* 3.715–719, 772–775; trans. Collins)

And probably also in a climactic scene near the end of the Animal Apocalypse:

> The Lord of the sheep brought a new house, larger and higher than the first one, and he erected it on the site of the first one . . . And all the sheep were within it. And I saw all the sheep that remained. And all the animals on the earth and all the birds of heaven were falling down and worshiping those sheep and making petition to them and obeying them in everything. (*1 Enoch* 90:29–31; trans. Nickelsburg and VanderKam)

These and other related texts have all been much discussed.[8] I take what I think is an uncontroversial majority view that these texts carry the baton, so to speak, of the eschatological pilgrimage-of-the-gentiles ideal from Isaiah, Micah, and Zechariah before them. So far, so good.

The problems arise when we come to Paul. As I have said, although he cites the prophets (especially Isaiah) copiously,[9] Paul never cites any of classic eschatological pilgrimage texts noted above. Nor does he bring all three of our key elements—eschatology, pilgrimage, and gentiles—together anywhere in his own prose. Paul's letters are full of eschatology, and of gentiles, but none of those gentiles ever takes hold of the hem of the robe of a Jew for directions, none of them ever makes *aliyah* to Mount Zion. (Admittedly, there is the case of Titus in Gal 2:1–3: "I went up to Jerusalem with Barnabas, bringing Titus along." But Titus does not go up. Paul goes up, and brings Titus along with him. And he goes up not to worship at the temple but, apparently, to show Titus off to the chief apostles.)

One might possibly see—and quite a few interpreters have seen—a hint of the eschatological gentile pilgrimage motif in Paul's collection of money from the gentile Christ-assemblies abroad to give aid to the poor among the saints in Jerusalem (mentioned in 1 Cor 16:1–4; 2 Cor 8:1–9:15; Rom 15:25–31). Indeed, ever since the mid-twentieth-century work of Johannes Munck and Dieter Georgi, this account of Paul's collection has become quite influential, even standard.[10] As David Downs has argued, however, Paul nowhere portrays the gathering or the delivery of the collection as a pilgrimage of the gentiles.[11] Most importantly, it is Paul himself, not the gentile donors, who will bring the offering to Jerusalem.[12] And he will deliver it not to the temple on Mount Zion but to the Jerusalem Christ-assembly, for distribution to its poorest members.[13]

Some recent interpreters—even ones who are otherwise deeply skeptical of Luke-Acts as a historical source—have thought that the rumor in Acts 21:28–29 that Paul sneaked his gentile companion Trophimus past the court of gentiles into the inner courts of the temple[14] is a smoking gun: Paul actually tried to trigger the eschaton by dragging a newly holy-in-Christ gentile across the sacred boundary.[15] But one lone Ephesian does not a pilgrimage make. And anyway, this is Luke's story, not Paul's. (And even Luke says it was a rumor, that Paul did not actually do it.) And nothing Paul himself says hints at such a scheme. According to his travel itinerary in Romans 15, Paul will go up to see the brothers-in-Christ in Jerusalem, as he has done several times before (Galatians 1–2). Only this time, he will come bearing gentile money.

But if the collection for the poverty-stricken saints in Jerusalem is not an eschatological pilgrimage of gentiles, what then? Well, there is one other key text that we have yet to consider. I have claimed that Paul never cites any of the eschatological pilgrimage texts from scripture, but some of my colleagues would say that this claim of mine is an error of fact. I have missed out, they would say, Paul's crucial citation of Isa 11:10 at Rom 15:12:[16] "And again Isaiah says: *There shall be the root of Jesse, even he who rises to rule over the gentiles, in him the gentiles will hope.*" This is a crucial citation, indeed, but it is not an exception to the rule that Paul never cites any of the eschatological pilgrimage texts from scripture. Here is one of those instances where, I think, we do not really know what we mean by the phrase "eschatological pilgrimage of the gentiles." Or, if we do know what we mean, then we are using it sloppily. We are either confused or willfully imprecise. Let us consider this imprecision.

One of my muses for the argument of this chapter is the Hebrew Bible scholar J. J. M. Roberts, in particular his excellent 2004 article "The End of War in the Zion Tradition."[17] Roberts argues that even the *bona fide* eschatological pilgrimage oracles noted at the beginning of this chapter presuppose a starkly imperialistic vision of divine governance. About Isaiah 2 (=Micah 4)—"Many peoples shall come and say, 'Come, let us go up to the mountain of the LORD' . . . He shall judge between the nations, and shall decide for many peoples; and they shall beat their swords into plowshares, and their spears into pruning hooks" (Isa 2:3–4)—Roberts writes: "The reason the nations can discard their weapons of war is that they are all vassals of Yahweh, and as his vassals, they are not permitted to go to war against one another to settle their disputes; instead their disputes will be settled by Yahweh's binding arbitration issued from the imperial capital in Jerusalem."[18] For his part, Roberts is particularly concerned to argue against those interpreters who see the "swords into plowshares" image as a straightforwardly pacifist ideal.[19]

What is more, Roberts also differentiates between this ideal *politeia* in Isaiah 2 and the related but different one in Isaiah 11. About Isaiah 11:10—"In that day, the root of Jesse shall stand as a sign to the peoples; him shall the nations seek, and his dwellings shall be glorious"—Roberts writes: "Rather than the divine mountain being exalted to catch the attention of the nations, it is the king from the root of Jesse who stands out like a flag, and it is to him that the nations go to inquire."[20] Isaiah 2 (and 25 and 56 and 66, and Micah 4, and Zechariah 8 and 14, all cited at the beginning of the present chapter) have a gentile pilgrimage to Zion but no messiah. Isaiah 11 has a messiah but no gentile pilgrimage. It is surely no accident that Paul cites the one oracle and not the others.

And in fact, Paul cites not the proto-MT Hebrew (as represented, e.g., in 1QIsaiah^a) but the Old Greek version of Isa 11:10, which has even more messiah and even less gentile pilgrimage than its Hebrew *Vorlage*. Whereas in the Hebrew the Davidic king rises *la-nes amim*, "as a sign to the peoples," in the Greek he rises ἄρχειν ἐθνῶν, "to rule over the gentiles" (perhaps mistaking *nes*, "sign, flag," for *nasi*, "prince, ruler"). And whereas in the Hebrew the nations "enquire after him" (*yidroshu*), in the Greek they "hope in him" (ἐλπιοῦσιν). It is this Greek version that Paul cites in Rom 15:12, painting a picture not of the eschatological pilgrimage of the gentiles to Zion but rather of the eschatological subjection of the gentiles to the messiah.[21] The full passage, in context, reads as follows:[22]

> Christ became a servant of circumcision for the sake of the truthfulness of God, so as to confirm the promises to the patriarchs, and [a servant] with respect to the gentiles for the sake of his mercy, so as to glorify God, as it is written:
>
> *For this reason I will confess you among the gentiles,*
> *and I will sing to your name.* [OG Ps 17:50 = 2 Kgdms 22:50]
> And again it says:
> *Rejoice, O gentiles, with his people.* [LXX Deut 32:43]
> And again:
> *Praise the lord, all you gentiles,*
> *and let all the peoples praise him.* [OG Ps 116:1]
> And again Isaiah says:
> *There shall be the root of Jesse,*
> *even he who rises to rule over the gentiles,*
> *in him the gentiles will hope.* [OG Isa 11:10]
> (Rom 15:8–12)

This catena of four scripture citations is meant to bear out Paul's claim in v. 9 that Christ became a servant of the *gentiles* for the sake of God's mercy: The one thing that all four scriptural excerpts have in common is the keyword ἔθνη, "gentiles." In addition, the first and the last excerpts have in common the theme of the Davidic messiah in his role vis-à-vis the gentiles: the latter excerpt obviously ("the root of Jesse rises to rule"), the former excerpt in its immediate context. "For this reason I will confess you among the gentiles, and I will sing to your name, O Lord, who magnifies deliverances for his king, and does mercy for his christ [i.e., messiah, anointed], for David and his seed forever" (OG Ps 17:50–51 = 2 Kgdms 22:50–51).[23]

My point here is that it is inaccurate to call the citation of Isa 11:10 in Rom 15:12 an eschatological pilgrimage reference. And because this is the only citation of Paul's that is even in the vicinity of the eschatological pilgrimage motif, I think we are better off not appealing to that motif at all for the purposes of interpreting Paul's gentile mission. There is, however, an eschatological script here,[24] just not the particular script that we usually hear mentioned in this connection. There is nothing here about the gentiles making pilgrimage to Zion, but everything about their being subjected to the messiah. The messiah rises to rule the gentiles, and the gentiles obey him. As Paul himself puts it later in the same chapter, "Christ works in me to bring about the obedience of the gentiles [ὑπακοὴν ἐθνῶν]" (Rom 15:18).[25] Paul mentions "Zion" only twice, both times in Isaiah quotations (Isa 28:16 in Rom 9:33; Isa 59:20 in Rom 11:26),[26] both expressly with reference to Israel, *not* the gentiles.[27] Gentiles-in-Christ (like Jews-in-Christ, presumably) have the Jerusalem *above* as their metropolis (Gal 4:26), not the present Jerusalem (Gal 4:25), which perhaps is why Paul does not exhort them to make pilgrimage to the latter.[28]

I do not know why the eschatological pilgrimage-of-the-gentiles hypothesis has come to command such wide assent in the field. I would speculate, though, that is has to do with a popular and intuitively sensible—but, I think, finally mistaken—threefold rubric of ancient Jewish views of the fate of gentiles. This rubric goes roughly as follows: Some ancient Jews thought that gentiles would be destroyed in the final judgment (e.g., *Jubilees*; *4 Ezra*); others that gentiles would, or could, become proselytes and thus be saved (e.g., Judith; *Joseph and Aseneth*); still others that gentiles would remain gentiles but renounce idolatry and make pilgrimage to Zion (Isaiah 2; Zechariah 8; etc.). Given those three options, many of us have, of course, opted for the lattermost as the closest fit with Paul: He clearly does not believe that all gentiles will be destroyed; but he equally clearly opposes gentiles becoming proselytes via circumcision; hence he must hold to the eschatological pilgrimage paradigm.

The mistake is thinking that there are only three options. In fact, there are more, even *many* more, depending how finely one wants to parse it. Some "gentile destruction" texts imagine the gentiles being dispatched judicially (in a last judgment), others extra judicially (in a last battle). Some "gentile conversion" texts reason that gentiles must convert in the quotidian present, others that they will have an eschatological opportunity to do so. Some "gentiles remain gentiles" texts imagine that individual gentiles *who keep the Noachide laws* will be spared, others that individual gentiles *who have Christ-faith* will be spared, still others that gentiles *from nations that did not oppress Israel* will be spared. And however they are spared, some of our texts imagine them being subdued by the messiah, others imagine them licking the dust of the feet of the Jews (with no messiah to be seen), still others imagine them making pious pilgrimage to Mount Zion. And so on. My point is that our texts make a very wide range of creative moves,[29] and we only hamstring ourselves as interpreters if we reduce them all to just a few simple templates.

In Paul's discourse, we find eschatology and gentiles, to be sure, but not pilgrimage. And this is a problem for the eponymous hypothesis, because it is pilgrimage in particular that is the hallmark of this putative tradition. Paul's gentile mission, I think, aimed to bring about not the eschatological *pilgrimage* of the gentiles but the eschatological *obedience* of the gentiles.[30]

Of course, a combination of these two ideas is easily conceivable, and was in fact conceived of by, for instance, Psalms of Solomon and the Animal Apocalypse. In those texts—arguably, but one has to argue the case—the gentiles *both* make pilgrimage to Mount Zion *and* obey the messiah.[31] I would say, however, that the Psalms of Solomon and the Animal Apocalypse are simply more creative than Paul is in this respect. Although Paul surely knew Isaiah 2 every bit as well as he knew Isaiah 11, he only chose to appeal to the latter in interpreting his gentile mission. I strongly suspect, though I cannot prove, that the reason for this choice was that only the latter text has the root of Jesse, the messiah from the seed of David, which is the one thing Paul's gospel cannot do without.[32]

NOTES

1. This chapter benefited a great deal from critical discussion at our conference in Bratislava. I am especially grateful to Kathy Ehrensperger, Paula Fredriksen, Joshua Garroway, and Anders Runesson for their incisive questions and suggestions. Any remaining faults in the chapter are mine alone.

Inasmuch as no other classical prophetic texts clearly attest all of these features, this list can be said to be comprehensive. (But on the afterlives of these oracles, see further below). A very fine discussion of this whole tradition is given by Heikki Räisänen, "Zion Torah and Biblical Theology: Thoughts on a Tübingen Theory," in Räisänen, *Jesus, Paul, and Torah: Collected Essays*, trans. David E. Orton, JSNTSup 43 (Sheffield: Sheffield Academic, 1992), 225–51.

2. By my count. The nonoccurrence of citations is demonstrable. The one near-miss is 1 Cor 15:54, where Paul quotes (what we recognize as) the Theodotian text of Isa 25:8: "Death is swallowed up in victory," but nothing from the preceding verses that mention gentile pilgrimage (Isa 25:6–7). The nonoccurrence of allusions is harder to establish, but I think it quite clear. The editors of NA28, more generous than I in this respect, identify three in their "Loci Citati vel Allegati": Isa 56:7 in Phil 4:18 ("their burnt offerings and their sacrifices will be accepted on my altar"//"I received from Epaphroditus the gifts you sent, a fragrant offering, a sacrifice acceptable and pleasing to God"); Isa 66:20 in Rom 15:16 ("they shall bring all your brethren from all the nations as an offering to the LORD"//"[Paul's] priestly service of the gospel of God, so that the offering of the gentiles may be acceptable"); and Zech 8:23 in 1 Cor 14:25 ("ten men from the nations of every tongue shall take hold of the robe of a Jew, saying, 'Let us go with you, for we have heard that God is with you'"//"falling on his face, [the unbeliever] will worship God and declare that God is really among you"). But in none of these cases would Paul have needed the supposed prophetic source text in order to say what he says. They only look like allusions if one presupposes that Paul has an eschatological gentile pilgrimage motif in mind, which is precisely the question before us.

3. On which see J. Ross Wagner, *Heralds of the Good News: Isaiah and Paul in Concert in the Letter to the Romans* (Leiden: Brill, 2002); and John M. G. Barclay, *Paul and the Gift* (Grand Rapids, MI: Eerdmans, 2015), 449–561.

4. E. P. Sanders, *Paul, the Law, and the Jewish People* (Philadelphia: Fortress, 1983), 171. This view is very widespread in the secondary literature, including—to cite just a few leading lights—Hans-Joachim Schoeps, *Paul*, trans. H. Knight (Philadelphia, PA: Westminster, 1961); Ferdinand Hahn, *Mission in the New Testament*, SBT 47 (London: SCM, 1965); Halvor Moxnes, *Theology in Conflict* (Leiden: Brill, 1980); Markus Barth, *The People of God*, JSNTSup 5 (Sheffield: Sheffield Academic,1983); Peter Stuhlmacher, *Paul's Letter to the Romans*, trans. Scott J. Hafemann (Louisville, KY: WJK, 1994 [German original 1989]); Karl-Wilhelm Niebuhr, *Heidenapostel aus Israel*, WUNT 62 (Tübingen: Mohr Siebeck, 1992); Paula Fredriksen, *Paul: The Pagans' Apostle* (New Haven, CT: Yale University Press, 2017).

5. Terence L. Donaldson, *Paul and the Gentiles: Remapping the Apostle's Convictional World* (Minneapolis, MN: Fortress Press, 1997), here 194: "Paul's statements about the Gentile mission stubbornly resist any attempt to force them into the Procrustean bed of eschatological pilgrimage patterns of thought . . . [Note] the virtual absence of eschatological pilgrimage texts. Such texts were plenteous and close at hand. Given Paul's desire to ground the Gentile mission in scripture, there would have been plenty of opportunity to cite such texts if he had so desired."

6. Donaldson, *Paul and the Gentiles*, 304: "Both before and after his conversion, he was convinced that [gentiles'] one hope of salvation was to become part of the people of Israel. His conversion can be understood as a shift from a paradigm in which membership in Israel was determined by Torah, to one in which it was determined by Christ."

7. On which see Terence L. Donaldson, *Judaism and the Gentiles: Jewish Patterns of Universalism (to 135 CE)* (Waco, TX: Baylor University Press, 2007), 670–78.

8. See Jill Hicks-Keeton, "Already/Not Yet: Eschatological Tension in the Book of Tobit," *JBL* 132 (2013): 97–117; Andrew Chester, "The Sibyl and the Temple," in *Templum Amicitiae: Essays on the Second Temple Presented to Ernst Bammel*, ed. William Horbury, JSNTSup 48 (Sheffield: Sheffield Academic, 1991), 37–69; Devorah Dimant, "Jerusalem and the Temple in the *Animal Apocalypse* (1 Enoch 85-90) in Light of the Qumran Community Worldview," in Dimant, *From Enoch to Tobit*, FAT 114 (Tübingen: Mohr Siebeck, 2017 [Hebrew original 1983]), 119–37.

9. See Dietrich-Alex Koch, *Die Schrift als Zeuge des Evangeliums* (Tübingen: Mohr Siebeck, 1986); Richard B. Hays, *Echoes of Scripture in the Letters of Paul* (New Haven, CT: Yale University Press, 1989); Christopher D. Stanley, *Paul and the Language of Scripture*, SNTSMS 74 (Cambridge: Cambridge University Press, 1992); Timothy H. Lim, *Holy Scripture in the Qumran Commentaries and Pauline Letters* (Oxford: Clarendon, 1997); Florian Wilk, *Die Bedeutung des Jesajabuches für Paulus* (Göttingen: Vandenhoeck & Ruprecht, 1998); Wagner, *Heralds of the Good News*.

10. See Johannes Munck, *Paul and the Salvation of Mankind*, trans. Frank Clarke (Atlanta, GA: John Knox, 1959 [German original 1954]); Dieter Georgi, *Remembering the Poor: The History of Paul's Collection for Jerusalem* (Nashville, TN: Abing-

don, 1992 [German original 1965]); Keith F. Nickle, *The Collection: A Study in Paul's Strategy*, SBT 48 (Naperville, IL: Allenson, 1966); Burkhard Beckheuer, *Paulus und Jerusalem* (Frankfurt: Peter Lang, 1997).

11. David J. Downs, *The Offering of the Gentiles: Paul's Collection for Jerusalem in Its Chronological, Cultural, and Cultic Contexts* (Grand Rapids, MI: Eerdmans, 2016), 3–9. See also the earlier criticism leveled by Leander Keck, "The Poor among the Saints in the New Testament," *ZNW* 56 (1965): 100–29.

12. One might invoke as counterevidence 1 Cor 16:3: "When I [Paul] arrive, I will send those whom you [Corinthians] accredit by letter to carry your gift to Jerusalem." But the stated purposes of these Achaean couriers is safekeeping, not symbolic pilgrimage. And in any case, by the time he writes Romans 15, Paul has apparently resolved to deliver the collection himself.

13. Rom 15:25–28: "At present, I am going to Jerusalem with aid for the saints. For Macedonia and Achaia have been pleased to make some contribution for the poor among the saints at Jerusalem; they were pleased to do it, and indeed they are in debt to them, for if the gentiles have come to share in their spiritual blessings, they ought also to be of service to them in material blessings. When therefore I have completed this, and have delivered to them what has been raised, I shall go on by way of you [in Rome] to Spain."

14. Acts 21:28-29: "[Jews from Asia] cried out, "Men of Israel, help! This is the man who is teaching men everywhere against the people and the law and this place; moreover he also brought Greeks into the temple, and he has defiled this holy place." For they had previously seen Trophimus the Ephesian with him in the city, and they supposed that Paul had brought him into the temple."

15. For example, J. Albert Harrill, *Paul the Apostle: His Life and Legacy in Their Roman Context* (New York, NY: Cambridge University Press, 2012), 72–74; Fredriksen, *Pagans' Apostle*, 244.

16. Indeed, this very point was made to me by Christopher Zoccali at an SBL session on the topic. Zoccali has argued that Rom 15:12/Isa 11:10 is indeed evidence of an eschatological gentile pilgrimage motif in Paul (Christopher Zoccali, *Reading Philippians after Supersessionism* [Eugene, OR: Cascade, 2017], 35–44). He is quite right about the importance of the citation, but not about its connection to a pilgrimage motif, for the reasons I adduce here.

17. J. J. M. Roberts, "The End of War in the Zion Tradition," *HBT* 26 (2004): 2–22. And see Roberts's other essays on related themes in his *The Bible and the Ancient Near East: Collected Essays* (Winona Lake, IN: Eisenbrauns, 2002).

18. Roberts, "End of War," 6.

19. See in particular H. W. Wolff, "Swords into Plowshares: Misuse of a Word of Prophecy?" *Currents in Theology and Mission* 12 (1985): 133–47.

20. Roberts, "End of War," 11.

21. On these aspects of Old Greek Isaiah 11, see further Wagner, *Heralds of the Good News*, 317–27; Matthew V. Novenson, "The Jewish Messiahs, the Pauline Christ, and the Gentile Question," *JBL* 128 (2009): 357–73. And on the theology of Old Greek Isaiah more generally, see J. Ross Wagner, *Opening the Sealed Book: Old*

Greek Isaiah and the Problem of Septuagint Hermeneutics, FAT 88 (Tübingen: Mohr Siebeck, 2013).

22. My translation. On the difficult syntax of the opening sentence, I follow J. Ross Wagner, "The Christ, Servant of Jew and Gentile: A Fresh Approach to Rom 15:8–9," *JBL* 116 (1997): 473–85. With Wagner, and *pace* Joshua Garroway ("The Circumcision of Christ: Romans 15:7–13," *JSNT* 34 [2012]: 303–22), I think it most likely that διάκονον περιτομῆς, "servant of circumcision," here means *not* "agent of circumcision," i.e., "circumciser," but rather "servant of the people Israel." But see Garroway's ingenious argument to the contrary as developed in *Paul's Gentile-Jews: Neither Jew nor Gentile, but Both* (New York, NY: Palgrave Macmillan, 2012).

23. On this latter reference, see Novenson, "Jewish Messiahs."

24. *pace* Donaldson, *Paul and the Gentiles*.

25. On this underappreciated theme, see the classic discussion by Paul S. Minear, *The Obedience of Faith* (London: SCM, 1971).

26. "[Israel] stumbled over the stumbling stone, as it is written, *Behold, I am laying in Zion a stone that will make men stumble, a rock that will make them fall; and he who believes in him will not be put to shame* [Isa 28:16]" (Rom 9:33); "In this way all Israel will be saved, as it is written, *The deliverer will come from Zion, he will banish impiety from Jacob* [Isa 59:20]" (Rom 11:26).

27. On Zion in Romans 9–11, see further Wagner, *Heralds of the Good News*.

28. On the Jerusalem above in Galatians 4, see Michael B. Cover, "Now and Above, Then and Now (Gal 4:21–31): Platonizing and Apocalyptic Polarities in Paul's Eschatology," in *Galatians and Christian Theology*, ed. Mark Elliott et al. (Grand Rapids, MI: Baker, 2014), 220–29. As Paula Fredriksen helped me to clarify in our discussion in Bratislava, I understand Paul to expect that, at the imminent parousia of Jesus and resurrection of the righteous dead, all people-in-Christ will be translated directly to the Jerusalem above. The cosmology and anthropology underlying such a scenario are brilliantly explained by Matthew Thiessen, *Paul and the Gentile Problem* (New York: Oxford University Press, 2016), 129–60.

29. Many of which are detailed in the other chapters in the present volume.

30. See further Novenson, "Jewish Messiahs."

31. On these texts, see further Patrick Pouchelle's and Genevive Dibley's chapters in the present volume.

32. I have made this case in full in my *Christ among the Messiahs: Christ Language in Paul and Messiah Language in Ancient Judaism* (New York, NY: Oxford University Press, 2012). Other important interpretations of the messiah motif in Paul include Stanley K. Stowers, *A Rereading of Romans: Justice, Jews, and Gentiles* (New Haven, CT: Yale University Press, 1994); Joshua W. Jipp, *Christ Is King: Paul's Royal Ideology* (Minneapolis, MN: Fortress Press, 2015); Fredriksen, *Pagans' Apostle*.

BIBLIOGRAPHY

Barclay, John M. G. *Paul and the Gift*. Grand Rapids, MI: Eerdmans, 2015.
Barth, Markus. *The People of God*. JSNTSup 5. Sheffield: Sheffield Academic, 1983.

Beckheuer, Burkhard. *Paulus und Jerusalem*. Frankfurt: Peter Lang, 1997.
Chester, Andrew. "The Sibyl and the Temple." In *Templum Amicitiae: Essays on the Second Temple Presented to Ernst Bammel*, edited by William Horbury, 37–69. JSNTSup 48. Sheffield: Sheffield Academic, 1991.
Cover, Michael B. "Now and Above, Then and Now (Gal 4:21–31): Platonizing and Apocalyptic Polarities in Paul's Eschatology." In *Galatians and Christian Theology*, edited by Mark Elliott et al., 220–29. Grand Rapids, MI: Baker, 2014.
Dimant, Devorah. "Jerusalem and the Temple in the *Animal Apocalypse* (1 Enoch 85–90) in Light of the Qumran Community Worldview." In Dimant, *From Enoch to Tobit*, 119–37. FAT 114. Tübingen: Mohr Siebeck, 2017. Hebrew original 1983.
Donaldson, Terence L. *Judaism and the Gentiles: Jewish Patterns of Universalism (to 135 CE)*. Waco, TX: Baylor University Press, 2007.
———. *Paul and the Gentiles: Remapping the Apostle's Convictional World*. Minneapolis, MN: Fortress Press, 1997.
Downs, David J. *The Offering of the Gentiles: Paul's Collection for Jerusalem in Its Chronological, Cultural, and Cultic Contexts*. Grand Rapids, MI: Eerdmans, 2016.
Fredriksen, Paula. *Paul: The Pagans' Apostle*. New Haven, CT: Yale University Press, 2017.
Garroway, Joshua. "The Circumcision of Christ: Romans 15:7–13." *Journal for the Study of the New Testament* 34 (2012): 303–22.
———. *Paul's Gentile-Jews: Neither Jew nor Gentile, but Both*. New York, NY: Palgrave Macmillan, 2012.
Georgi, Dieter. *Remembering the Poor: The History of Paul's Collection for Jerusalem*. Nashville, TN: Abingdon, 1992. German original 1965.
Hahn, Ferdinand. *Mission in the New Testament*. SBT 47. London: SCM, 1965.
Harrill, J. Albert. *Paul the Apostle: His Life and Legacy in Their Roman Context*. New York, NY: Cambridge University Press, 2012.
Hays, Richard B. *Echoes of Scripture in the Letters of Paul*. New Haven, CT: Yale University Press, 1989.
Hicks-Keeton, Jill. "Already/Not Yet: Eschatological Tension in the Book of Tobit." *Journal of Biblical Literature* 132 (2013): 97–117.
Jipp, Joshua W. *Christ Is King: Paul's Royal Ideology*. Minneapolis, MN: Fortress Press, 2015.
Keck, Leander. "The Poor among the Saints in the New Testament." *Zeitschrift für die neutestamentliche Wissenschaft* 56 (1965): 100–29.
Koch, Dietrich-Alex. *Die Schrift als Zeuge des Evangeliums*. Tübingen: Mohr Siebeck, 1986.
Lim, Timothy H. *Holy Scripture in the Qumran Commentaries and Pauline Letters*. Oxford: Clarendon, 1997.
Minear, Paul S. *The Obedience of Faith*. London: SCM, 1971.
Moxnes, Halvor. *Theology in Conflict*. Leiden: Brill, 1980.
Munck, Johannes. *Paul and the Salvation of Mankind*. Translated by Frank Clarke. Atlanta, GA: John Knox, 1959. German original 1954.
Nickle, Keith F. *The Collection: A Study in Paul's Strategy*. SBT 48. Naperville, IL: Allenson, 1966.

Niebuhr, Karl-Wilhelm. *Heidenapostel aus Israel*. WUNT 62. Tübingen: Mohr Siebeck, 1992.

Novenson, Matthew V. *Christ among the Messiahs: Christ Language in Paul and Messiah Language in Ancient Judaism*. New York, NY: Oxford University Press, 2012.

———. "The Jewish Messiahs, the Pauline Christ, and the Gentile Question." *Journal of Biblical Literature* 128 (2009): 357–73.

Räisänen, Heikki. "Zion Torah and Biblical Theology: Thoughts on a Tübingen Theory." In Räisänen, *Jesus, Paul, and Torah: Collected Essays*, 225–51. Translated by David E. Orton. JSNTSup 43. Sheffield: Sheffield Academic, 1992.

Roberts, J. J. M. *The Bible and the Ancient Near East: Collected Essays*. Winona Lake, IN: Eisenbrauns, 2002.

———. "The End of War in the Zion Tradition." *Horizons in Biblical Theology* 26 (2004): 2–22.

Sanders, E. P. *Paul, the Law, and the Jewish People*. Philadelphia, PA: Fortress Press, 1983.

Schoeps, Hans-Joachim. *Paul*. Translated by H. Knight. Philadelphia, PA: Westminster, 1961.

Stanley, Christopher D. *Paul and the Language of Scripture*. SNTSMS 74. Cambridge: Cambridge University Press, 1992.

Stowers, Stanley K. *A Rereading of Romans: Justice, Jews, and Gentiles*. New Haven, CT: Yale University Press, 1994.

Stuhlmacher, Peter. *Paul's Letter to the Romans*. Translated by Scott J. Hafemann. Louisville, KY: WJK, 1994. German original 1989.

Thiessen, Matthew. *Paul and the Gentile Problem*. New York, NY: Oxford University Press, 2016.

Wagner, J. Ross. "The Christ, Servant of Jew and Gentile: A Fresh Approach to Rom 15:8–9." *Journal of Biblical Literature* 116 (1997): 473–85.

———. *Heralds of the Good News: Isaiah and Paul in Concert in the Letter to the Romans*. Leiden: Brill, 2002.

———. *Opening the Sealed Book: Old Greek Isaiah and the Problem of Septuagint Hermeneutics*. FAT 88. Tübingen: Mohr Siebeck, 2013.

Wilk, Florian. *Die Bedeutung des Jesajabuches für Paulus*. Göttingen: Vandenhoeck & Ruprecht, 1998.

Wolff, H. W. "Swords into Plowshares: Misuse of a Word of Prophecy?" *Currents in Theology and Mission* 12 (1985): 133–47.

Zoccali, Christopher. *Reading Philippians after Supersessionism*. Eugene, OR: Cascade, 2017.

Chapter Five

Eschatological Universalism, the Nations, and the Jewish Apocalyptic Paul

Loren T. Stuckenbruck

INTRODUCTION

It is routinely regarded as self-evident that Paul's gospel was universal, with its emphasis on forming a community of faith among non-Jews who are put on equal footing alongside Jews before God. As far as the early Christ-movement is concerned, Paul was not alone in anticipating an eschaton that, in some sense,[1] embraces or reaches humanity as a whole. Among writings that would become part of "the New Testament," the Lukan double-volume takes on momentum in this respect, with the risen Jesus referring to "repentance and forgiveness of sins" to be proclaimed "to all nations" (Luke 24:47) and then declaring to the disciples that they "will be my witnesses in Jerusalem, in Judea and in Samaria, and to the ends of the earth" (Acts 1:8). Similarly, Matthew's gospel famously concludes with Jesus's directive to his closest followers that they should "make disciples of all nations" (Matt 28:19). Finally, in the Book of Revelation, the visionary John is given to see a new Jerusalem where "the nations will walk by its light, and the kings of the earth will bring their glory into it" (Rev 21:24). However, it is Paul's correspondence with faith communities, composed between 49/50 and 56 CE, that offer earliest written evidence within the early Christ movement for a spread of faith that is "universal" in scope.[2] Though Galatians can be given attention in this respect (see Gal 3:26–29; 6:11–16), Paul's universalizing "all" language is most explicit in his letter to the Romans.

In Romans, several texts can be cited in this connection. The letter presents the focus of Paul's mission to non-Jews as predicated on a twofold conviction: he lays claim to a human condition of sin and death for which there is no exception, and he expresses hope that God's purpose for the cosmos as a whole will have its way (see below). With regard to humanity's propensity to wrongdoing, one could refer further to Romans 3:9 ("for both Jews and Greek, *all* are under sin"), 3:23 ("*all* have sinned and fall short of the glory of God"), and 5:12 ("death came to *all* humans . . . *all* have sinned"). By contrast, on the positive side, one may think of Paul's programmatic statement in Romans 1:16 that his "gospel" is "for *all* who have faith, for the Jew first and also to the Greek" or, even more so, in 11:32, where he declares that "God has imprisoned *all* in disobedience that he may be merciful upon *all*."[3] With the latter text in mind and under the assumption of theological coherence in the letter as a whole, we may ask what events Paul thought would lead to such an all-embracing conclusion. For this, the argument in Romans 11 itself would seem to provide an answer in several stages, namely, that, following (1) a rejection of Jesus as Messiah by most Jews, (2) a "fullness" (πλήρωμα) of non-Jews will be taken up into the people of God (v. 25b), so that, then, (3) "all Israel will be saved" (v. 26b). Thus, Paul presents his mission to non-Jews as sandwiched between God's activity on behalf of Israel, with largely negative and positive results. The resonance of Paul's gospel among non-Jews participates in setting the stage for a universalizing soteriology in the eschaton. Thus, the precondition of maximum inclusion of non-Jews (their "fullness") becomes a key link in the chain of events leading to a globalizing end.

THE NATIONS IN ROMANS 15:7–13

While envisioning unity between both Jewish and non-Jewish believers, Paul returns to envisioning an *oikoumene* for which he directs his hope near the end of the letter (15:7–13). Here, prior to outlining his past itinerary and concerns relating to upcoming travel to Jerusalem (15:14–21 and 22–32, respectively), he projects onto an ideal future the kind of unity he has just commended to the "strong" and "weak" non-Jewish and Jewish believers in Rome (14:1–15:6). In this part of chapter 15, Paul states less about Jewish unbelief (cf. 11:20) and emphasizes, again with Jewish salvation-historical privilege in mind, that Christ became "a servant of the circumcision . . . in order to confirm the promises of the patriarchs" (15:8; cf. 9:4; 11:28). This matrix, anchored in "promises," is lightly contrasted with "mercy," which is now being shown as a new state of things among non-Jews ("the nations"; 15:9; cf. also 9:22), who are now in a position to worship God (15:9). While Paul is clear about Israel as the chronological and exemplary foundation for his gospel, *how* it is that the gospel has come to non-Jews in his own mission remained something for him to explain. His attempt to do so rests largely on the disappointing response to the Christ-event among Jews, a response that he attempts to reconcile with divine will, which he maintains underlies a certain "hardening" (cf. 9:18; 11:7, 25) or "blindness" (11:8–10) on their part.

Significantly, without explaining how it is that the nations will come to glorify God, Paul cites several traditions in rapid succession: these are Psalm 18:50 (Rom 15:9; par. 2 Sam 22:50), Deuteronomy 32:43 (15:10), Psalm 117:1 (15:11), and Isaiah 11:10 (15:12). Although these passages play an explicit role in Paul's argument, their function is declarative, so the worship of God among the nations affirmed in 15:9 is an outcome that is already anticipated in the sacred tradition. The quotation from Psalm 18:50, introduced by the phrase "it is written," consists of words spoken in the first person: "I will confess you among the nations and sing praise to your name." The speaker in both Psalm 18 and 2 Samuel 22 is David, and if the Davidic voice is retained by Paul, the subject is the one who worships (as one thanking God for victory in battle over his enemies), not the nations themselves. The nations, however, are not simply the enemy over whom the Davidic voice has been given to triumph; they are also those *among whom* God's power is declared. The relation between the "I" of the text and the non-Jews' worship of God is at this point unclear. The citation from the Song of Moses in Deuteronomy 32:43 in 15:10, introduced by the impersonal "it (the sacred tradition) says," takes the argument a step further: "Rejoice, O nations, with his people." Here, the jubilation (perhaps worship is implied) enjoyed by God's people Israel is enjoined upon non-Jews. In Paul's argument, the worship of Israel's God among non-Jews is expressed as a matter of imperative. This call to worship is restated, introduced simply by "and again," in the quotation from Psalm 117:1 in 15:11: "Praise the Lord, all you nations, and may all the peoples praise him." Here the imperative is combined with the third-person exhortative that, again, makes the worship of non-Jews a matter of divine injunction. Although God is the object of the worship, the call to engage in this activity is being understood as driven by divine will. Finally, Paul explicitly quotes the prophet Isaiah ("and again, Isaiah says"): "There shall be a shoot of Jesse; and the one who rises up to rule over nations, in him nations shall place their hope." The focus of this quotation is implicitly and plausibly christological, that is, the "shoot of Jesse" is deemed to be Christ, the Messiah, whose advent fulfills what the prophet anticipated. Unlike the context of Psalm 18 cited in verse 9, "nations" here are not presented as inimical (i.e., to one ruling over them), but rather as those who have hope. The messianic promise, though essentially one that relates to Jewish hope, is here made to address the hope of non-Jews, who are now included.

How is this "hope" for non-Jews to be understood in light of the scripture citations in Romans 15:9–12? The declaration of God's victory by the Davidic voice over oppressive rule "among the nations" distinguishes between non-Jewish overlords, on the one hand, and those non-Jews who suffer under their oppressive rule. The Christ figure, discerned in the root of Jesse in Isaiah 11, represents a form of just rule and, therefore, hope that they can be delivered.[4] The praise of God in Psalm 18 is transformed into the worship of God among non-Jews who are also given reason to hope. In this way Paul can be said to inscribe non-Jews into Jewish tradition.

Thus far, I have focused briefly on teasing out an inner logic to the catena of texts being interpreted by Paul in Romans 15:9–12. It remains to be asked, however, what premise allows Paul to adopt such reasoning. Was Paul engaging in "scripture" interpretation of a sheer intertextual nature, or does his appeal to the sacred texts in Romans 15 assume a thought structure that can be ascertained if we consider additional Jewish sources? While considerable attention has been given to a number of varied "universalizing" traditions both inside and outside the Hebrew Bible, it is my contention that more can be said by drawing the early Enochic tradition into the conversation. Here, I am not thinking so much about the Animal Vision (1 En. 85–90), to which some attention has been given,[5] but rather the earlier tradition found in the Book of Watchers at *1 Enoch* 6–11.[6] Before doing so, it is helpful to provide a brief reminder of traditions preserved in the Hebrew Bible so that the "Enochic" contribution can be more clearly discerned.

THE NATIONS IN THE HEBREW BIBLE AND THE ENOCHIC BOOK OF THE WATCHERS (1 EN. 6–11)

When envisioning the future relationship between Israel and the nations, many texts in the Hebrew Bible think of the latter's ultimate subservience to Israel as they come to recognize the God of Israel (so, e.g., in Isa 18:7; 45:14; 60:3–12; 66:23; Zech 8:23; 14:16–19; Ps 22:27 and 86:9). Though several of these passages anticipate that the nations will worship God (Isa 66:23; Zech 14:16–19; Ps 22:27 and 86:9), there is little expectation that they will convert *per se*. Beyond this, texts such as Isaiah 2:3 and Micah 4:2 anticipate that nations will respond to instruction emanating from Israel by walking "in his [God's] paths." The main framework within which such texts operate is one that centers on Jerusalem, especially the Temple, which after all is held to be the center of the divine presence. Thus, Israel has been singled out as "a kingdom of priests and a holy nation" (Exod 19:5–6) to be representatives of God's activity on earth. The predominating vision of the future is one that involves the nations' pilgrimage to Jerusalem as they recognize the futility of their gods (cf. Jer 16:19).

When turning to 1 Enoch 6–11, one likewise encounters the expectations that the nations will worship God. The author(s) of 1 Enoch 10:20–22 anticipate that God will instruct Michael, one of the primary angels, to prepare for an ideal time of eschatological bliss. The text reads:

> (20) But as for you, cleanse the earth from all uncleanness, and from all injustice, and from all sin and godlessness. And eliminate all the unclean things that have been done on the earth. (21) And *all* the children of humanity will become righteous, and *all* the peoples will serve and bless me, and they will all worship me.[7] (22) And the entire earth will be cleansed from all defilement and all uncleanness. And no wrath or torment will I ever again send upon them, for all the generations of eternity. (translation my own)

The narrative context leading up to this conclusion of redemption history does not feature the story of Israel (unlike the Apocalypse of Weeks in 1 En. 93:1–10 or the Animal Vision), but is rooted in events prior to and after the Flood. The conclusion, as given here, loops back to the opening of 1 Enoch 6, with which the section begins, namely, a storyline that closely adheres to Genesis 6:1–2. The Ge'ez version to 1 Enoch 6:1–2, largely in agreement with the Greek Codex Panopolitanus, reads: "When the children of humanity had increased in those days, beautiful and comely daughters were born to them. And the watchers, the sons of heaven, saw them and desired them. And they said to one another, 'Come, let us choose for ourselves women from the daughters of humanity, and let us sire children for ourselves.'"

What follows is, of course, a narrative that departs substantially from Genesis 6: the angelic beings carry out their expressed intent and sire giant offspring. While the rebellious angels teach humans practices associated with instruments of violence, "magical" and divinatory knowledge, and beautification techniques (1 En. 8:1–3), their offspring, the giants, engage in a series of violent acts that threaten the existence of the environment, including birds, reptiles, fish, and humans whose enslavement to farm the earth is unable to satisfy their appetites (7:3–6).

When the souls of those murdered by the giants raise a complaint mediated by four prominent angels (8:4–9:11), the divine response is multidimensional. First, as in Genesis 6–8, there is to be a destruction of the earth from which Noah, "a plant," is to be saved to ensure the survival of humanity (10:1–3; cf. also vv. 6–7). Second, God instructs Raphael and Michael, respectively, to bind and consign the wayward angels Asa'el (10:4) and Shemihazah and his companions (10:11–14) to a prison-like existence until the time of a final judgment. Third, the angel Gabriel is sent against the giants (called "bastards" and "hybrids"), who will war against and destroy one another (10:8–10; cf. also v. 15). What emerges after these punishments is the destruction of "evil deeds," on the one hand, and the appearance of "the plant of righteousness and truth" (10:16), on the other, for which the Noahic figure in 10:1–3 serves as a prototype. Those associated with the plant of righteousness, who will "escape" (v. 17a—either the destruction by the Flood or the destruction of evil deeds), are described as "the righteous ones" who can enjoy long and reproductive lives (10:17). This plant, in turn, functions as a predecessor—or better, as a bridge—in the narrative to the children of humanity who will become righteous in 10:21 and worship God. While no genetic relation connects the plant of righteousness and truth in 10:17 with the children of humanity in 10:21, the tradition is modeling eschatological expectation (an *Endzeit*) on a saving event of the past (an *Urzeit*, given in 10:1–3 and 16–17).

This narrative, despite its vagueness, is distinct in a number of ways from texts in the Hebrew Bible mentioned above. Unlike the latter, the future worship of God by all humanity will be preceded by a comprehensive purification carried out by the archangel Michael. This "holy" state is a precondition for their worship.[8] Furthermore, the Enochic tradition makes no explicit mention of several features one might expect from a pious Jewish tradition. There is no explicit mention of covenant or covenant faithfulness, there is no reference to either Abraham or Moses, nothing is said—as elsewhere in the early Enoch tradition (except, perhaps, for the Apocalypse of Weeks at 1 En. 93:6)—about the Torah, nor is anything stated about sabbath observance of circumcision. Moreover, the text states nothing about humanity and the peoples of the earth coming to Jerusalem, though the language of worship (see n. 8) may imply participation in a cult. The text opens up the possibility that "cult" can be understood in a virtual sense, and that the cleansing of the earth mentioned in 10:20 and 22 envisions ritual purity beyond Jerusalem, whether in "the land" in a narrower sense or in "the earth" more broadly. The text, in any case, anticipates an eschatological outcome on such a grand scale that it does not remain with "the plant of righteousness and truth" in 10:16, but comes into play regardless of location.

The correlation between *Endzeit* and *Urzeit* is fundamental to the Enoch text's eschatology. Since the foundation for the eschaton reaches back to beginnings, it is less important that there be an unbroken chain between the plant of truth and righteousness and all humanity in *1 Enoch* 10:16–22. So, the universal worship of God stands within the framework of beginnings of two kinds: Noah, on the one hand, and increase of humanity, on the other.

First, there is Noah. A significant feature in the text where Noah, who remains nameless, is introduced is the naming of his father as Lamech; he is the "son of Lamech." By naming his father, the text expresses the legitimacy of his parenthood, something that stands in direct contrast to the illegitimacy of the giants; as "bastards" and "hybrids," they represent an illegitimate form of existence because they were sired by angels who have acted out of rebellion (1 En. 6), and they embody an unsanctioned mixture between what is heavenly and what is earthly (cf. 15:3–8). That a contrast between Noah and the giants is a deliberate motif underlying the text is made clear, given the stories circulating about the nature of his birth. In both the *Genesis Apocryphon* (1Q20 ii 1–v 26) and 1 Enoch chapters 106–107, parallel versions about his birth emphasize, despite some differences, that Noah is *not* a giant. Lamech his father, suspecting that the unusual appearance of the newborn child is actually the product of a rebellious angels who has impregnated his wife, has to consult Enoch in order to find out what has happened. In doing so, through his father Methuselah, Lamech learns that Noah is his child after all and, if we follow the less fragmented storyline in 1 Enoch 106, is the one through whom God will preserve the human race from the coming destruction.[9] The Noahic figure functions, then, as the quintessential human being whose existence reflects that with which humanity was endowed at creation. The righteous and all those who will worship God stand in continuity with him and can be understood to be his heirs. Noah, not Abraham,[10] is the progenitor of the righteous; he represents a new start that, beginning with a faithful base in Israel (10:16), will absorb and embrace humanity as a whole, wherever they happen to be.

The other correlation between *Ur-* and *Endzeit* reflects the correspondence between all humanity in 1 Enoch 10:21 and the humanity who increase on the earth in 6:1–2. Before the wayward angelic beings arrive on the scene, the text innocuously states that humanity was on the increase and that to them beautiful daughters had been born. What the lusting angels do, by binding each other with the oath and by taking the human women to sire offspring, is turn the created order on its head. Human integrity is violated, first as women are taken to produce illegitimate offspring (7:1–2) and, second, as women and men are given instructions to fashion products and engage in activities that are to be regarded as contemptible and oppressive. As the giants destroy different categories of creation (wildlife, agriculture, and humans), the created order as described in Genesis 1 (days three, five, and six) is threatened with extinction. The trouble-free beginning, followed by such a drastic downturn, is outshone by the worship of God by all humanity in the eschaton. The environment, previously threatened with complete destruction, will flourish with reproductivity as never before: the earth "will be tilled in righteousness" (10:18), and vines and seeds will each multiply by the thousand (10:19). And, even during the events marked by violence and punishment (in 7:3–8:3 and 10:1–15), the essential integrity of humanity is left intact.

Why does the time of Noah and the Flood acquire such importance for the Enoch tradition in chapters, where the Enoch figure himself is not even mentioned? It is because the period, as no other, illustrates the divine defeat of evil in a sacred past on such a global scale. This principled, proleptic yet definitive overcoming of evil drives the vision of eschatological bliss and worship. Without God's intervention through angelic and human agency, a new beginning for all humanity is unimaginable. Though the time during which the text was produced is one in which evil is seen as a force that continues to pose very real danger (cf. 1 En. 15:11–12), evil itself has become a power that, within the storyline, has already been defeated and is biding its time until the destruction for which it is destined (10:6, 14; cf. 16:1). As such, the tradition evinces a certain confidence that a salvific outcome for humanity has been set in motion that will reach its zenith when God shall be worshipped by all.

A RAPPROCHEMENT OF *DENKSTRUKTUR* BETWEEN THE BOOK OF WATCHERS AND PAUL

If we return to Romans and to the Pauline correspondence more generally, the Noahic storyline does not serve as a point of departure. Paul's terms of reference, probably based on his Jewish and Jewish-Christian interlocutors, were different and based on Torah. He remains concerned with covenant, and agitates over dietary restrictions, sabbath observances, and circumcision that get in the way of his plea that all, whether or not they adhere to these facets of Jewish practice, can lay equal claim to belonging to the people of God. That Paul's appeal to Abrahamic faith as prior to the giving of the Torah on Mt. Sinai would have been convincing to those who were debating him is doubtful, as for them Torah observance could even have been attributed to Abraham himself (so, e.g., in the *Book of Jubilees*) and can be said, with or without being identified with wisdom, to have been operative in creation itself. Nevertheless, his attempt to drive a wedge between humanity at the beginning (Adam; Rom 5:12) and Abraham (Rom 4; Gal 3), through whose faith the cosmos falls heir (Rom 4:13, 17), and a later advent of the Torah (Rom 5:20; Gal 3:19) shows a similar concern as the Book of Watchers to ground his advocacy for "faith" in a beginning that is foundational for a salvific state of things in the eschaton. For Paul this eschaton, manifested through the coming to faith among non-Jews, was already under way. Their worship of God, anticipated in Deuteronomy 32:43 and Psalm 117:1, had for him already become an emerging reality that has yet to reach its peak when a "fullness" comes in (Rom 11:25). In addition, for him the essential defeat had taken place in a recent time, interwoven with Jesus's death and resurrection, a "Christ event" that he attributes to the faithful activity of God.

For all the differences between the early Enoch tradition in the *Book of Watchers* and Paul, it is possible to consider a certain rapprochement in thought structure between them. The Book of Watchers does not, as Paul, derive the nations' worship of God from a definitive event in the very recent past. However, the firm conviction in 1 Enoch 6–11 that in the past God has intervened to seal the ultimate fate of forces that threaten to destroy and lead humanity astray reflects a perception of the world in which this defeat of evil could already become manifest.[11] The tradition remains vague about whether non-Jews can already participate in this state of affairs. However, they too are the beneficiaries of sociopolitical and cultural forces that oppressed humanity (symbolized in the activities attributed to the rebellious angels in 1 En. 8:1–3). Although there is nothing in the text that expressly maintains such participation among non-Jews (indeed, this is assumed by the later Enochic texts in 1 En. 90:38–39; 91:14; and 105:1–2), the theological foundation for this has already been laid, and, in principle at least, the door is held open to this possibility. Deliverance from the forces of evil and oppression shall include, if not already, the nations and peoples of the earth. Thus, Paul's appeals to scripture in Romans 15:9–12 sit comfortably with a Jewish tradition in which Jerusalem-centered worship and observance of Torah are not held up as definitive criteria for belonging to God's people, who whether they are Jew or non-Jew, are the beneficiaries of a hope based on divine activity to defeat evil in the past. In this sense, Paul's "universalistic" discourse, in both the setting of the problem and the solution, is not too remote from Jewish tradition. Indeed, it may be thought to have been resourced by one Jewish thought structure in order to address a Jewish complex of tradition whose discourse revolved around different terms. The hope of "the nations" so advocated by Paul (cf. Rom 15:12), recalibrated along the lines of Christology, remains firm in the conviction that the global and eschatological worship of God is guaranteed.

NOTES

1. For an orientation to the notion of "universalism" in both Paul's thought and Second Temple Jewish tradition, see Gudrun Holtz, "Universalism," in *Encyclopedia of Second Temple Judaism*, ed. Daniel M. Gurtner and Loren T. Stuckenbruck (2 vols.; London: T&T Clark, 2019), 2:809–12. For more thorough studies, though with varying emphases, see Daniel Boyarin, *A Radical Jew: Paul and the Politics of Identity* (Berkeley, CA: University of California Press, 1994); Terence L. Donaldson, *Judaism and the Gentiles: Jewish Patterns of Universalism (to 135 CE)* (Waco, TX: Baylor University Press, 2007); Gudrun Holtz, *Damit Gott sei alles in allem. Studien zum paulinischen und frühjüdischen Universalismus*. BZNW 149 (Berlin: De Gruyter, 2007); and Aaron Sherwood, *Paul and the Restoration of Humanity in Light of Ancient Jewish Tradition*. EJEC 82 (Leiden: Brill, 2013). While Boyarin and Donaldson focus on the Diaspora as a context in which Jewish tradition could mitigate Jewish

"particularism" and Holtz struggles, while including more discussion of Qumranic sources, to explain how the nations' eschatological redemption as part of God's eschatological reign should have functioned as part of Paul's Jewish heritage—in this regard, it is interesting to note how little attention she gives to the Enoch tradition. Alongside the more often cited *Sibylline Oracles* 3:772–795 and Josephus's *Antiquities* 8.116–117, Sherwood gives more weight to Enochic tradition and the *Book of Tobit* (*Paul and the Restoration of Humanity*, 151–75, 189–201), as does Ronald Herms's study of the theme in relation to the Johannine Apocalypse, in *An Apocalypse for the Church and for the World: The Narrative Function of Universal Language in the Book of Revelation*, BZNW 143 (Berlin: De Gruyter, 2006), 61–77 and 120–37.

2. How much this remains within or departs from what can be found in Second Temple Jewish tradition has and remains a major question in Western scholarship since Ferdinand Christian Baur, driven by a supersessionist ideology, drew a clear line between Paul's universalism, on the one hand, and Jewish ethnic-national particularism, on the other; see Ferdinand Christian Baur, *Paul, der Apostel Jesu Christi. Sein Leben und Wirken, seine Briefe und seine Lehre* (Stuttgart: Becher & Müller, 1845), 535–612.

3. Whereas Rom 1:16 puts the gospel on offer to all who have faith and therefore does not project what the ultimate outcome will be, in 11:32 Paul goes a step further: just as he insists that God's faithfulness in redemption history will lead to "all Israel" being saved in 11:26a, so also God's purposes will attain a *telos* that embraces "all" that includes humanity as a whole.

4. Cf. David I. Starling, *Not My People: Gentiles as Exiles in Pauline Hermeneutics*, BZNW 184 (Berlin: De Gruyter, 2011), 160 and n. 204: the "response to the victory of God over the Gentiles rulers opposed to God's people and his messiah" in Ps 18 "does not rule out a reading in which Gentiles are pictured as rejoicing in the defeat of their overlords by the messiah, coming under his saving lordship as conquered enemies and joining with him in the praise of God" (as in Deut 32:43).

5. On the Animal Vision and the motif of eschatological conversation or transformation of Gentiles (1 En. 90:27–38), see esp. Patrick A. Tiller, *A Commentary on the Animal Apocalypse of 1 Enoch*. EJIL 4 (Atlanta, GA: Scholars Press, 1993), 19, 385–88; George W. E. Nickelsburg, *1 Enoch 1: A Commentary on the Book of 1 Enoch, Chapters 1–36; 81–108*, Hermeneia (Minneapolis, MN: Fortress Press, 2001), 406–07; Herms, *An Apocalypse for the Church and for the World*, 120–36; Sherwood, *Paul and the Restoration of Humanity*, 189–201; and Genevive Dibley, "Abraham's Uncircumcised Children: The Enochic Precedent for Paul's Paradoxical Claim in Galatians 3:29" (PhD Diss., University of California at Berkeley and Graduate Theological Union, 2013). For a reading that de-emphasizes an absorption of Gentile into the house of Israel, see Donaldson, *Judaism and the Gentiles*, 110–17. Although it is tempting to find an important precedent for a Pauline view of the nations in the Animal Apocalypse, there is more to say about the foundational tradition in the Book of Watchers, as will be attempted here.

6. The discussions of this passage by Donaldson (*Judaism and the Gentiles*, 100–03) and Sherwood (*Paul and the Restoration of Humanity*, 152–64), though of-

fering some important observations, do not in my opinion explore its value for Rom 15 far enough.

7. For v. 21 the Grk. Codex Panopolitanus omits "and all the children of humanity will become righteous" through homoioarcton, so that the Geʻez tradition preserves the more complete and textually reliable reading.

8. The Grk. Codes Panopolitanus refers to this worship with the verb λατρεύοντες, which on that level of tradition may even imply priestly activity in a cultic setting.

9. For a much fuller account, see Stuckenbruck, *1 Enoch 91–108*, CEJL (Berlin: DeGruyter, 2007), 606–89 (esp. 676–77).

10. As emphasized in the Apocalypse of Weeks at 1 En. 93:5; on Abraham as the essential progenitor for "faith," see also Matt 1:12; 3:9 (par Luke 3:9); 8:11 (par. Luke 13:28); John 8:31–59; Rom 4:9–13; and Gal 3:6–9; 3:29.

11. For further discussion of this aspect of Enochic theology and its impact on early Christian notions of time (Synoptic tradition, Fourth Gospel, Acts, and Paul), see Loren T. Stuckenbruck, "The Myth of Rebellious Angels: Ethics and Theological Anthropology," in *Anthropologie und Ethik im Frühjudentum und im Neuen Testament*, ed. Matthias Konradt and Esther Schläpfer. WUNT 322 (Tübingen: Mohr Siebeck, 2014), 163–76; and *The Myth of Rebellious Angels*, WUNT 335 (Tübingen: Mohr Siebeck, 2014), 161–256.

BIBLIOGRAPHY

Baur, Ferdinand Christian. *Paul, der Apostel Jesu Christi. Sein Leben und Wirken, seine Briefe und seine Lehre*. Stuttgart: Becher & Müller, 1845.

Boyarin, Daniel. *A Radical Jew: Paul and the Politics of Identity*. Berkeley, CA: University of California Press, 1994.

Dibley, Genevive. "Abraham's Uncircumcised Children: The Enochic Precedent for Paul's Paradoxical Claim in Galatians 3:29." PhD Dissertation. University of California at Berkeley and Graduate Theological Union, 2013.

Donaldson, Terence L. *Judaism and the Gentiles: Jewish Patterns of Universalism (to 135 CE)*. Waco, TX: Baylor University Press, 2007.

Herms, Ronald. *An Apocalypse for the Church and for the World: The Narrative Function of Universal Language in the Book of Revelation*. BZNW 143. Berlin: De Gruyter, 2006.

Holtz, Gudrun. *Damit Gott sei alles in allem. Studien zum paulinischen und frühjüdischen Universalismus*. BZNW 149. Berlin: De Gruyter, 2007.

———. "Universalism." In *Encyclopedia of Second Temple Judaism, Vol. 2*, edited by Daniel M. Gurtner and Loren T. Stuckenbruck, 809–12. London: T&T Clark International, 2019.

Nickelsburg, George W. E. *1 Enoch 1: A Commentary on the Book of 1 Enoch, Chapters 1–36; 81–108*. Hermeneia. Minneapolis, MN: Fortress Press, 2001.

Sherwood, Aaron. *Paul and the Restoration of Humanity in Light of Ancient Jewish Tradition*. EJEC 82. Leiden: Brill, 2013.

Starling, David L. *Not My People: Gentiles as Exiles in Pauline Hermeneutics*. BZNW 184. Berlin: De Gruyter, 2011.

Stuckenbruck, Loren T. "The Myth of Rebellious Angels: Ethics and Theological Anthropology." In *Anthropologie und Ethik im Frühjudentum und im Neuen Testament*, edited by Matthias Konradt and Esther Schläpfer, 163–76. WUNT 322. Tübingen: Mohr Siebeck, 2014.

———. *The Myth of Rebellious Angels*. WUNT 335. Tübingen: Mohr Siebeck, 2014.

———. *1 Enoch 91–108*. CEJL. Berlin: De Gruyter, 2007.

Tiller, Patrick A. *A Commentary on the Animal Apocalypse of 1 Enoch*. EJIL 4. Atlanta, GA: Scholars Press, 1993.

Chapter Six

Did the LXX of the Twelve Prophets Contribute to the Eschatological Opening to the Nations?

Patrick Pouchelle

INTRODUCTION

Scholars are now more aware of the diversity of Ancient Judaism. It is therefore a recent trend in the research on universalism to define several patterns concerning this notion. After assessing whether Judaism is universalist or particularistic,[1] scholars are more inclined to pay attention to the diverse forms of dealing with nations in the biblical literature and in the Jewish traditions. To my knowledge, the first explicit attempt is from Donaldson.[2] He presents four patterns of inclusion of gentiles in the covenant with the God of Israel: (1) the God-fearer, in which non-Jews worship the God of Israel and participate in some Jewish regulations; (2) the conversion model, in which non-Jews are assimilated in the Israel community through conversion;(3) the Ethical monotheism model, in which Jews and non-Jews share the same system of value; and (4) the eschatological expectation, in which non-Jews will enter the covenant in the last days only. Another assessment is given by Simkovich.[3] She focuses on the concept of eschatological universalism only, suggesting that Donaldson was not sufficiently precise in this matter. She offers five models: (1) Israel as subjugators of the nations;(2) nations recognizing Israel as standard-bearer, acknowledging the Israelite God, but without being part of the covenant; (3) the assimilation of nations to Israel; (4) the universalized worship model, in which the nations will worship the Israelite God without becoming part of Israel; and (5) the ethical universalism model, in which the boundary between Israel and the nations fade away because Israel and the nations are conceived to share common ethical value. The main thesis of Simkovich is that only the fourth and fifth models are really universalism. The fourth model is hardly to be found in the Hebrew Bible, and the fifth one appears only in the Hellenistic Jewish literature. Probably the patterns were more diverse than described by Donaldson and Simkovich.[4] For this reason, Simkovich's work has been criticized.[5] Nevertheless, I would like to focus on one simple fact—both Donaldson and Simkovich neglect the Septuagint (LXX). This is especially a surprise as Simkovich, for instance, asserts that it is precisely in Alexandria that the Jewish thought might have explored more widely the question of universalism.

The legend of the old Greek translation of the Hebrew Bible is that it has its origins in a request made by king Ptolemy to show the highest achievement of Jewish thought. This production, which was a translation of the Hebrew Scriptures, was recorded in the Letter of Aristeas. In it, the Letter suggests that the result of this endeavor showed the ascendency of Jewish culture and thought over that of the Hellenistic philosophy of the day. Given its Hellenistic backdrop, it is therefore a common view to see in the LXX signs of greater universalism. Hence, for Bertram, the specialist of the LXX in the *TDNT*, this is taken for granted.[6] However, one should never forget that his views were biased as he conceived the LXX as a unified corpus, which it is not. He also sees the LXX as the preparation for the NT and implicitly opposed the presumed universalism of the Christians to the particularism of the Jewish people.[7] These views proved to be false: the LXX is not the necessary step to Christianity, and the Hebrew Bible shows that the Judaism is also universalist.

For these reasons, recent research on the LXX is rightly more prudent on determining theological insight in the LXX.[8] In fact, the translators usually did their best to translate the text they had. In my opinion, the notion of patterns, as defined by Donaldson or Simkovich, could help us to delve deeper into the question of the "universalism" of the LXX. I do not want to emphasize these patterns, the way they are defined, and if they really represent what texts have to offer. What is more important is that this notion of patterns leads us to go over the question of whether the LXX is more or less universalistic than the Masoretic Text (MT). LXX may rather exhibit a tendency toward some specific patterns of universalism against those witnessed in the MT.

The frame of this chapter does not offer the place to produce an exhaustive study. I will focus on the twelve minor prophets. It is presumably translated by one translator. Modern LXX scholarship is more aware of the specificity of each translator of the LXX. So, what will be said about universalism in the LXX of the Twelve prophets will obviously not be accurate for other translations. Five key examples (Amos 9:12; Obad 21; Mic 4:2; Zeph 3:9–10; Zech 2:15) of eschatological expectations in the MT will be compared to their version in the LXX, paying attention to whether or not the differences could be attributed to the translator or to the original text available to the translator (also called the *Vorlage*).

AN EXAMPLE OF SEPTUAGINT UNIVERSALISM? AMOS 9:11–12

Owing to its use in Acts 15:17, Amos 9:12 is the most important argument to prove that "LXX openly emphasizes God's universalism."[9] In the MT, God is affording his people consolation by promising it that it will be victorious over Edom, probably understood as a symbolic name of "All the nations" which oppressed it:

בַּיּוֹם הַהוּא אָקִים אֶת־סֻכַּת דָּוִיד הַנֹּפֶלֶת וְגָדַרְתִּי אֶת־פִּרְצֵיהֶן וַהֲרִסֹתָיו אָקִים וּבְנִיתִיהָ כִּימֵי עוֹלָם:
לְמַעַן יִירְשׁוּ אֶת־שְׁאֵרִית אֱדוֹם וְכָל־הַגּוֹיִם אֲשֶׁר־נִקְרָא שְׁמִי עֲלֵיהֶם נְאֻם־יְהוָה עֹשֶׂה זֹּאת:

> On that day I will raise up the booth of David that is fallen, and repair its breaches, and raise up its ruins, and rebuild it as in the days of old; in order that they may possess (יִירְשׁוּ) the remnant of Edom (אֱדוֹם) and all the nations who are called by my name, says the LORD who does this. [NRSV]

The syntagma "to be called by one's name" most probably means here "to possess" (see 2 Sam 12:28). The Hebrew vision is clearly that of revenge. The LXX, on the contrary, offers something radically different:

> ἐν τῇ ἡμέρᾳ ἐκείνῃ ἀναστήσω τὴν σκηνὴν Δαυιδ τὴν πεπτωκυῖαν καὶ ἀνοικοδομήσω τὰ πεπτωκότα αὐτῆς καὶ τὰ κατεσκαμμένα αὐτῆς ἀναστήσω καὶ ἀνοικοδομήσω αὐτὴν καθὼς αἱ ἡμέραι τοῦ αἰῶνος, ὅπως ἐκζητήσωσιν οἱ κατάλοιποι τῶν ἀνθρώπων καὶ πάντα τὰ ἔθνη, ἐφ' οὓς ἐπικέκληται τὸ ὄνομά μου ἐπ' αὐτούς, λέγει κύριος ὁ θεὸς ὁ ποιῶν ταῦτα.

> On that day I will raise up the tent of David that is fallen and rebuild its ruins and raise up its destruction, and rebuild it as the days of old; in order that they may seek, those remaining of humans and all the nations upon whom my name has been called, says the Lord God who does these things. [NETS]

The tone seems here clearly universalistic, particularly if we, like most of the modern translations, accept the Lucianic recension "in order that they may seek me" or if, together with some manuscripts, we follow the quotation made by Acts 15:17 "in order that they may seek the Lord." However, what seems to be the oldest state of the Greek text does not offer any accusative to the verb "to seek." In fact, one could suggest that the differences between the Greek text and the Hebrew originate from the translated Hebrew text. Indeed "humans" may well be a translation of "Adam" (אדם), read instead of Edom (אדום), a simple difference of vocalization allied with a defective writing.

Moreover, in the LXX, ἐκζητέω "to seek" frequently corresponds to the Hebrew דרשׁ "to seek" which is graphically and phonetically close to ירשׁ, "to possess." In Hebrew, the verb דרשׁ could be used intransitively to mean "to investigate." For instance, in Judges 6:29, some people investigate in order to know who has profaned an altar. Should this meaning be correct, the LXX version would be less "universalistic" than expected: The nations will investigate to know who restored the tent of David. We could understand that the nations, seeing the miraculous restoration of Israel, will acknowledge that the Israelite God is mighty.

In my opinion, the Lucianic recension offers a later stage. Grammatically, the intransitive construction of ἐκζητέω is odd, or at least infrequent. This could be an impetus for scribes to add "me" so as to correct what sounds odd to their ears. This version could have been adapted to "the Lord" by the author of Acts 15:17 to fit the context.

The Lucianic recension was more in line with eschatological expectations where nations could search God. This kind of expectation is not unattested in the Hebrew Bible. See, for instance, Isaiah 65:1, a text resonating with the Lucianic version of Amos 9:12 regarding the notion of the call of the divine name:

> I became evident to those who did not consult me; I was found by those who did not seek me. I said, "Look! Here I am," to a people who have not called upon my name.

Hence, the Lucianic version could have been coined as a reminiscence of such expectations. A more definitive conclusion about the history of transmission of Amos 9:12 could not be reached, but this verse could not be used to prove a greater emphasis on universalism in the LXX as, on one hand, the difference originated from the Hebrew text[10] and not from the translator and, on the other hand, the sentence is not so universalist, even in Greek. Even its most universalistic version, the Lucianic one, could be compared to other Hebrew text, like those in the third Isaiah. More precisely said, the history of transmission of Amos 9:12 shows at least three different patterns of expectations concerning nations: 1) In the MT, Israel will subjugate the nations. 2) In the Old Greek, where ἐκζητέω is intransitive, the nations will acknowledge the true God; nothing is said about a potential conversion. 3) In the Lucianic version and in Acts 15:17, where ἐκζητέω is transitive, the nations will seek God and probably worship God.

These patterns could be adapted to the decision of the Council of Jerusalem where Amos 9:12 is quoted. The apostles didn't arbitrate between universalism and particularism; they arbitrated between different views of universalism. In fact, they translated an eschatological expectation, which is getting realized to a specific Halakha: which regulations could be expected from the arriving nations to follow? Some were ready to accept the nations as part of the Jewish people (model of assimilation), whereas Paul did not accept this model. The decision of the council was to ask the Gentile to follow the Noahic Torah (a model of universalized worship according to Simkovich, i.e. nations were not part of the specific covenant with Israel but worship the God of Israel). The choice of the apostles to quote Amos 9:12 in a version close to the Lucianic one confirms their view: nations will seek the God of Israel, but nothing is said about their assimilation to the people of Israel.

AN EXAMPLE OF NON-UNIVERSALISTIC TONE IN THE LXX, OBADIAH 21

The Prophet Obadiah, one of the shorter texts of the OT, is an oracle against Edom. Its ending has been used by Simkovich as an example for the first model—Israel as subjugator of the nations—especially the last sentence:[11]

וְעָלוּ מוֹשִׁעִים בְּהַר צִיּוֹן לִשְׁפֹּט אֶת־הַר עֵשָׂו וְהָיְתָה לַיהוָה הַמְּלוּכָה׃

The saviors (מוֹשִׁעִים) shall go up to Mount Zion to rule (שפט) Mount Esau; and the kingdom shall be the LORD's.

In the LXX the tone is different:

καὶ ἀναβήσονται ἄνδρες σεσῳσμένοι ἐξ ὄρους Σιων τοῦ ἐκδικῆσαι τὸ ὄρος Ησαυ, καὶ ἔσται τῷ κυρίῳ ἡ βασιλεία.

The men who are rescued shall go up from Mount Sion to punish (ἐκδικέω) Mount Esau and the kingdom shall be the Lord's (NETS slightly altered).

In fact, the Hebrew *Vorlage* of the LXX is here close to the MT. The Hebrew form מושעים has been understood as a *hophal* rather than a *hiphil* (like many modern translations of the Hebrew Bible) and the verb שפט has been understood not as ruling but as taking revenge, a meaning belonging to the semantic field of punishment. This is attested in MT,[12] and we could discuss with Simkovich here if שפט really meant "to rule" here, but not simply "to judge" or "to condemn." In the LXX, the Greek verb ἐκδικέω correspond, another time to שפט in 1 Sam 3:13 where God judged the house of Eli owing to the sins of his sons and in 2 Chronicle 22:8 where Jehu judged the house of Ahab.

Finally, and this is precisely the most dramatic shift, a preposition מִן may well have been put before the "mountain of Zion" transforming the verb "to go up" from a probable liturgical or juridical meaning to a military one explaining why the translators understood שׁפט as "to take revenge."[13] In the LXX, Israel will attack Edom and will execute judgment on it, and not rule over it.

As in Amos, the difference between the MT text and the LXX is more probably due to a different *Vorlage* (the addition of מִן) than to a bias of the translator. In this textual tradition, Israel is not even the subjugator of Edom but will simply punish it or exact the retribution it deserves. At the extreme, there is no concept of universalism witnessed by the LXX, only the hope for a future victory of Israel over the oppressing nations.

AN EXAMPLE OF A LESS OPEN STANCE TOWARDS THE NATIONS IN THE LXX: MICAH 4:2

In an eschatological passage, Micah 4:2 (a passage almost identical to Isaiah 2:3) expresses the hope that nations will go up to Jerusalem to be taught by God himself. The texts are very similar so that one has probably been borrowed by the other.[14] In this verse the difference between the two prophets is minimal, only עם "people" in Isaiah instead of גוי "nation" in Micah:

וְהָלְכוּ גּוֹיִם רַבִּים וְאָמְרוּ לְכוּ וְנַעֲלֶה אֶל־הַר־יְהוָה וְאֶל־בֵּית אֱלֹהֵי יַעֲקֹב וְיוֹרֵנוּ מִדְּרָכָיו וְנֵלְכָה בְּאֹרְחֹתָיו כִּי מִצִּיּוֹן תֵּצֵא תוֹרָה וּדְבַר־יְהוָה מִירוּשָׁלָ͏ִם׃

And many nations (Isaiah: peoples) shall come and say: "Come, let us go up to the mountain of the Lord, to the house of the God of Jacob; that he may teach us his ways and that we may walk in his paths." (Mic 4:2)

The translation of Isaiah is relatively closed to the Hebrew text apart from the end where the translator seems to avoid a semantic repetition of "in his paths" after "in his ways":

καὶ πορεύσονται ἔθνη πολλὰ καὶ ἐροῦσιν Δεῦτε καὶ ἀναβῶμεν εἰς τὸ ὄρος κυρίου καὶ εἰς τὸν οἶκον τοῦ θεοῦ Ιακωβ, καὶ ἀναγγελεῖ ἡμῖν τὴν ὁδὸν αὐτοῦ, καὶ πορευσόμεθα ἐν αὐτῇ· ἐκ γὰρ Σιων ἐξελεύσεται νόμος καὶ λόγος κυρίου ἐξ Ιερουσαλημ.

And many nations shall go and say: "Come, let us go up to the mountain of the Lord and to the house of Jacob, and he will declare to us his way, and we will walk in it." (Isa 2:3)

In the translation of the prophet Micah, on the contrary, there is one big difference. In Hebrew God himself will teach the nations; in the LXX, this is the house of the God of Jacob, that is to say Israel:

καὶ πορεύσονται ἔθνη πολλὰ καὶ ἐροῦσιν Δεῦτε ἀναβῶμεν εἰς τὸ ὄρος κυρίου καὶ εἰς τὸν οἶκον τοῦ θεοῦ Ιακωβ, καὶ δείξουσιν ἡμῖν τὴν ὁδὸν αὐτοῦ, καὶ πορευσόμεθα ἐν ταῖς τρίβοις αὐτοῦ· ὅτι ἐκ Σιων ἐξελεύσεται νόμος καὶ λόγος κυρίου ἐξ Ιερουσαλημ.

and many nations shall come and say: "Come, let us go up to the mountain of the Lord, and to the house of the God of Jacob; and they will show us his ways and we will walk in his paths." (Mic 4:2)

The difference could originate from the Hebrew *Vorlage* which may have contained what would have been vocalized by the Masoretes as וְיוֹרֻנּוּ instead of וְיֹרֵנוּ. As for Amos 9:12, this is a difference in vocalization along with a defective writing. If the MT is older here, we could be tempted to see in the textual tradition witnessed by the LXX an avoidance to see God himself speaking to the Nations. Again, whatever the reason why the LXX is different, one could observe that the LXX is not less or more "universalist" than the MT; it only conveys another model. In the MT, God himself taught the nations, as if they were his own people. In the LXX this role is attributed to Israel who is becoming the educator of the nations. Moreover, most probably, the difference originated from the *Vorlage*.

A HESITATION BETWEEN SEVERAL MODELS: ZEPHANIAH 3:9–10

In the MT, these two verses are at the beginning of the second part of the book, dealing with the conversion of the Nations:

כִּי־אָז אֶהְפֹּךְ אֶל־עַמִּים שָׂפָה בְרוּרָה לִקְרֹא כֻלָּם בְּשֵׁם יְהוָה לְעָבְדוֹ שְׁכֶם אֶחָד׃
מֵעֵבֶר לְנַהֲרֵי־כוּשׁ עֲתָרַי בַּת־פּוּצַי יוֹבִלוּן מִנְחָתִי׃

At that time, I will change the speech of the peoples to a pure speech, that all of them may call on the name of the Lord and serve him with one accord. From beyond the rivers of Ethiopia my suppliants, my scattered ones (עֲתָרַי בַּת־פּוּצַי), shall bring my offering (Zeph 3:9–10).

The Hebrew text contains a very difficult Hebrew syntagma עֲתָרַי בַּת־פּוּצַי (linked together by the accentuation in the MT). This part has sometime been interpreted as secondary because some reliable manuscripts of the LXX does not have anything corresponding to that. Barthélemy correctly observed that this absence does not mean that the Hebrew parts were absent, as the translator may well have had the same issue as us and simply decided to skip this difficult passage. Barthélemy therefore thinks (with some doubt however) that the Hebrew syntagma is original. He suggests "those who worship me, my community of scattered one" will bring offerings to God.[15] In the LXX, the absence of correspondence gives to the passage a universalistic tone without any reference to the diaspora:

ὅτι τότε μεταστρέψω ἐπὶ λαοὺς γλῶσσαν εἰς γενεὰν αὐτῆς τοῦ ἐπικαλεῖσθαι πάντας τὸ ὄνομα κυρίου τοῦ δουλεύειν αὐτῷ ὑπὸ ζυγὸν ἕνα. ἐκ περάτων ποταμῶν Αἰθιοπίας οἴσουσιν θυσίας μοι.

Because at that time I will change the language upon peoples for her generation, so that they all might call upon the name of the Lord, so that they might serve him under one yoke. From the ends of the rivers of Ethiopia, they shall carry my sacrifices. (Zeph 3:9–10)

This is all the nations whose language has been changed by God[16] that will bring offerings. Moreover, they will be gathered under one yoke. Here, the Greek ζυγός "yoke" surprisingly correspond to שְׁכֶם "shoulder." The MT could be compared to Num 7:9 where the Kohathites have the charge to carry all under one shoulder (i.e,. all together) the holy things for the cult. The Talmud (*Avodah Zarah* 24a) uses this verse to explain that gentiles will accept all the divine commandments. The LXX may witness such belief if we accept ζυγός as a metaphor for the law.[17] In this case, the model is here the one of assimilation.[18]

However, the textual history of the Greek version is very complicated. Some strong manuscripts offer προσδέξομαι ἐν διεσπαρμένοις μου "I will take in my scattered ones" corresponding to עֲתָרַי בַּת־פּוּצַי. The verb προσδέχομαι, whose presence is unexpected, has two meanings, "to await, to endure" or "to take in favor, to agree, to welcome." The second meaning seems better here. Nonetheless, this verb is normally used transitively, which is not the case here. Two different interpretations could be given. First, either the object is implicit and God will welcome *them*, that is to say the nations, and place them in the Jewish diaspora.[19] That would be a kind of assimilation model. Or, a second interpretation, which supposes an implicit conjunction, is that God will take some people from those who are scattered, for giving offerings. According to this second interpretation, nations remain separated from the scattered Jews.[20]

The Lucianic recension offers here something that looks like a double translation: προσδέξομαι ἱκετεύοντας με τῶν διεσπαρμένων οἴσουσιν θυσίας μοι "I will take those of the scattered one who beg me, they shall carry my sacrifice." Here, it seems that only the righteous people in the diaspora are dealt with. However, the sentence is grammatically odd, as οἴσουσιν has no clear subject. That is probably why some witnesses, like Theodoret of Cyrus, offer προσδέξομαι ἱκετεύοντας με υἱοί τῶν διεσπαρμένων οἴσουσιν θυσίας μοι "I will take those who beg me, the sons of the scattered shall carry sacrifice to me." Whereas the nations could be denoted by ἱκετεύοντας με, only Jews from the diaspora will offer the offering to God.

This is a nice example where it seems that the translators, scribes, and revisors read a difficult Hebrew text and gave birth to several versions in which each tradition offers different models of universalism.

For MT, only the diaspora is concerned by the sacrifice, whereas in the Old Greek, all the nations could offer the sacrifice. For the other Greek versions, the interpretation is more ambiguous: either the nations will be included in the diaspora, or the nations will be welcomed by God, but only the diaspora could offer the sacrifice, or only the diaspora is welcome by God, in an interpretation close to that of MT.

A REAL SYSTEMATIC TREND IN LXX? ZECHARIAH 2:15

This passage was used by Simkovich to illustrate the model of assimilated nations.[21] For her, when the prophet said, "I will dwell in your midst," he was declaring that God was speaking to his united people: Israel and the nations.

וְנִלְווּ גוֹיִם רַבִּים אֶל־יְהוָה בַּיּוֹם הַהוּא וְהָיוּ לִי לְעָם וְשָׁכַנְתִּי בְתוֹכֵךְ

> Many nations shall join themselves to the Lord on that day, and shall be my people; and I will dwell in your midst. (Zech 2:15)

However, we could also understand this another way: "Nations shall be my people *but* I will dwell in your midst." Hence, all the nations belong to God, but God only dwells in Israel and this is why Israel could acknowledge the saying of the prophet. This is in line with what follows: "The LORD will inherit Judah as his portion in the holy land, and will again choose Jerusalem." This text is, nevertheless, unclear. In a sense, the LXX clarifies it:

> καὶ καταφεύξονται ἔθνη πολλὰ ἐπὶ τὸν κύριον ἐν τῇ ἡμέρᾳ ἐκείνῃ καὶ ἔσονται αὐτῷ εἰς λαὸν καὶ κατασκηνώσουσιν ἐν μέσῳ σου

> And many nations *shall flee* to the Lord on that day and shall become a people *to him* and *they will tent* in your midst. (Zech 2:15)

We could see three main differences. Let's begin by the simplest: "to him" instead of "to me." This appears to me as rather insignificant. Probably "to him" was caused by the absence of God as subject of the following verb.

Indeed, and this is the second difference, this is no more "I" (that is to say God) that will dwell in your midst but "they" (the nations). These two differences could originate to the *Vorlage* (לו instead of לי for the first difference and ושכנו instead of ושכנתי for the second one).

In the textual tradition witnessed by the LXX, it looks like that all the nations will be like *gerim* among Israel. Nothing is said about the statute of the strangers here, but a study on the third difference with the MT will help to delve deeper in that topic. Indeed, at the beginning of the verse, the nations are said to flee to the Lord rather than to join to him. This difference could not be easily explained by the Hebrew text. It is due either to a different verb in Hebrew or to the translator. At a first sight, such difference contributes to soften the belonging of the nations to the people of God. They will only be refugees, not citizens! They will flee to the Lord; they will not be attached to him (unlike in Isaiah 56:3, for instance).

In Isaiah and Jeremiah, we find other sentences where the LXX has the verb "to flee" where Hebrew has something different in a similar context. In Jeremiah 27[50]:4–5, this is Israel and Judah who will come back to the Lord. In Hebrew, they will join together to the Lord. In the LXX, the same verb as in Zech 2:15 has been rendered by "to flee":

ἕως Σιων ἐρωτήσουσιν τὴν ὁδόν, ὧδε γὰρ τὸ πρόσωπον αὐτῶν δώσουσιν· καὶ ἥξουσιν καὶ καταφεύξονται (MT וְנִלְווּ) πρὸς κύριον τὸν θεόν

Until Sion, they will ask the way, for here they will put their face, and they will come and *flee* to Lord, the God.

Lev 26:25, where Israel is cursed, might be of some help. When God will bring the sword against his people, they will withdraw in their cities (Hebrew אסף). The translators of the LXX have interpret the verb correctly (which is better known for denoting "to gather") by translating it with καταφεύγω. The withdraw has been understood as a gathering for refuge for Israel and Judah. Perhaps the translator of Jeremiah had such a text in mind.

Twice in Isaiah, καταφεύγω appears in a context of opening to the nations, with no clear explanation from the MT. Isaiah 54:15 is a difficult Hebrew text. This verse repeats thrice the root גור with the infrequent meaning of "to attack" "to be hostile":

הֵן גּוֹר יָגוּר אֶפֶס מֵאוֹתִי מִי־גָר אִתָּךְ עָלַיִךְ יִפּוֹל׃

If anyone stirs up strife, it is not from me; whoever stirs up strife with you shall fall because of you. (Isa 54:15)

The translator of Isaiah, or a different Hebrew tradition, understood גור according to its main meaning, "to dwell somewhere as alien and dependent":

ἰδοὺ προσήλυτοι προσελεύσονταί σοι δι' ἐμοῦ καὶ ἐπὶ σὲ καταφεύξονται

Look! Strangers [converted people?][22] will come to you through me and flee to you.

The end of the verse in Greek is quite different from the MT. The translators of Isaiah are famous for easily adapting their Hebrew *Vorlage*, so that it is possible that they interpret contextually. The link with Zech 2:15 is made even a little bit stronger in some manuscripts (notably the Vaticanus) where is found after ἐμοῦ the following sentence: παροικήσουσι(ν) σοι "they will dwell beside you" (the verb παροικέω could correspond to שכן "to dwell" attested in Zech 2:15, but only twice in Ps 93[94]:17; 119[120]:6).

The second text is Isaiah 55:5. This is another eschatological text:

הֵן גּוֹי לֹא־תֵדַע תִּקְרָא וְגוֹי לֹא־יְדָעוּךָ אֵלֶיךָ יָרוּצוּ לְמַעַן יְהוָה אֱלֹהֶיךָ וְלִקְדוֹשׁ יִשְׂרָאֵל כִּי פֵאֲרָךְ׃

See, you shall call a nation that you do not know, and a nation that do not know you shall run to you, because of the LORD your God, the Holy One of Israel, for he has glorified you. (Isa 55:5)

Here, "you" is requested to call an unknown nation. The identity of "you" and "nations" is not so clear. Whatever the Hebrew interpretation, the Greek version, by using the plural (interpreting גוי as singular collective) denotes the eschatological coming to Jerusalem as a flight:

ἔθνη, ἃ οὐκ ᾔδεισάν σε, ἐπικαλέσονταί σε, καὶ λαοί, οἳ οὐκ ἐπίστανταί σε, ἐπὶ σὲ καταφεύξονται ἕνεκεν τοῦ θεοῦ σου τοῦ ἁγίου Ισραηλ, ὅτι ἐδόξασέν σε.

The nations, that do not know you, will call upon you, and the peoples who do not know you, will flee to you because of the Lord your God, the holy one of Israel, for he has glorified you.

The reason why the translators of Isaiah used καταφεύγω is uncertain. In Isaiah 54:15, the description of Jerusalem as a mighty city a few verses above could lead to see in her a city who could offer asylum to the defeated nations. The remaining parts of the nations are punished by God. Isaiah 55 belongs to the same line of argumentation. The verb καταφεύγω may well have been used to develop the meaning of רוץ "to run" or to harmonize with Isaiah 54:15. Indeed, in these two verses of Isaiah, the context is similar.

Jeremiah 27[50]:5 shows that the return of Judah and Israel has been conceived as a refuge to God. The example of Isaiah 54 and 55 manifests that this notion has been also attributed to the foreigners, either as real proselytes or as simple foreigner. The eschatological status of these foreigners is not explicit. It remains unclear if they completely belong to Israel or not. However, their relationship with God is nevertheless explained as a military disaster. As Judah and Israel were punished, scattered, and came back, so the nations will be punished and will go to God seeking refuge in Israel conceived as a secure place.

Simkovich has rightly noticed that the notion of refuge is of huge importance in the text called *Joseph and Aseneth*.[23] This is a love story written in Greek,[24] originating from Alexandria. Joseph meets Aseneth who fell immediately in love. But Aseneth is a polytheist, daughter of a pagan priest. She felt a deep sorrow and converted herself to the God of Joseph, rejecting her idols. Then an angel came down and declared:

Καὶ οὐκέτι κληθήσει Ἀσενέθ, ἀλλ' ἔσται τὸ ὄνομά σου πόλις καταφυγῆς, διότι ἐν σοὶ καταφεύξονται ἔθνη πολλὰ καὶ ὑπὸ τὰς πτέρυγάς σου σκεπασθήσονται λαοὶ πολλοί, καὶ ἐν τῷ τείχει σου φυλαχθήσονται οἱ προσκείμενοι τῷ θεῷ διὰ μετανοίας.

"And your name shall no longer be called Aseneth, but your name shall be City of Refuge, because in you many nations will take refuge with the Lord God, the Most High, and under your wings many peoples trusting in the Lord God will be sheltered, and behind your walls will be guarded those who attach themselves to the Most High God in the name of Repentance. [OTP]

Many biblical notions merge in this simple sentence. At least, note the emphasis on the fact that the Nations are many, as in Zech 2:15. One should also note the verb πρόσκειμαι which corresponds precisely to לוה in Isa 56:3. What is interesting is the merging of the flight of the nations with that of the city of refuge, where the inadvertent murders could take refuge so as to avoid the avenger of the blood of the victim. Concerning the nations, this could mean that the nations are in a state of being sinners, as they have oppressed Israel. Yet, in fact, they did not know what they did. Therefore, like an inadvertent murderer, they could take refuge in Aseneth, an example of "conversion embodied," so as to avoid the judgment of God. In my opinion, this is a later stage of thinking. The several occurrences studied in the LXX rather show the asylum as occurring after the divine judgment and after the nations have acknowledged who is God. The text *Joseph and Aseneth* shows that this tradition has been received and expanded.

CONCLUSION: WHAT ABOUT PAUL?

After having made a short survey of five key examples of openings to the nation in the twelve prophets, we could draw some conclusions. Amos 9:12 has been frequently used to show the universalist nature of the LXX. In fact, this question of characterizing the LXX as a whole as more or less universalist than the MT is not really pertinent. Like the notion of messianism,[25] that of universalism was not so big an issue for the translators. Limiting ourselves to the translators of the twelve prophets, we have observed that the differences between the MT and the LXX are frequently due to a different Hebrew *Vorlage*, or even a difference in vocalization of the same Hebrew text. It is therefore unwise to attribute this potential shift to the translators. Second, this potential universalistic "shift" is far from being systematic in the twelve prophets. We could even observe some sentences where the Greek text seems to offer less possibility to the nations to join the Israelite God (Obad 21, Mic 4:2). In fact, they are not less or more "universalistic"; they just offer other patterns of universalism. Few of them are unattested in the MT.

Yet, Zechariah 2:15 reveals what may be a unique trend in the LXX, shared by Jeremiah and Isaiah and received until a later text like *Joseph and Aseneth*. Nations will take refuge in Jerusalem and will become refugees. The fact that this idea is shared by many translators and that the verb "to flee" may correspond to a different Hebrew word are arguments for attributing this shift to the translators. Yet, their motivation remains obscure. They may have wanted to express the idea that nations will be oppressed by God and will flee as a mark of their condemnation. In a way similar to the Jewish people, nations are offered the ability to acknowledge the God of Israel and be welcomed by him, as witnessed by Jeremiah. However, their status as "converted" is not clearly defined in these verses.

This short survey should be completed in many ways, including studying other pieces of translations, like Isaiah, Job, Proverbs, or even the Pentateuch. Owing to the lack of time, I do not want to go deeper into the interpretation of the LXX as a whole, but I would like to make this discussion clear: Although the simple fact that the LXX was in Greek, the most important language of its time and obviously a condition for delving deeper into the notion of universalism, one should avoid without qualification to present the LXX as a universalistic text. Put another way, if, as McKnight has observed, the LXX could be understood as "the first step of toward a missionary religion" and perhaps Simkovich would add "toward a more Ethical universalism," this is only because it finally gives access to the Bible to a broader audience. As McKnight still accurately observes, that means neither of the other steps were "taken shortly after" nor that they originated in the LXX only.[26]

Let us finish with an open question. If the notion of asylum for nations is important for the LXX, why do the NT in general and the Pauline corpus in particular neither use it nor quote Zech 2:15? It seems that such a text would have been an argument for the welcoming of the gentiles into the Christian communities. Yet, καταφεύγω is used only twice in the NT: once in Acts 14:6 in a context where the verb does not convey any theological nuance (except if we see in the flee of Paul and Barnabas an indirect allusion) and once in Heb 6:18 where the author of the letter includes the reader in an "us" who have taken refuge. Again, this could be an indirect allusion to Zech 2:15, but the link seems to me rather weak. Paul neither uses this verb nor alludes to these prophetic verses.[27] That does not mean that the LXX should be neglected in the research on Paul. Rather, it should be dealt with as a witness among others, obviously not more but also not less.

NOTES

1. I think the last time this question was raised is in 1999: James D. G. Dunn, "Was Judaism Particularistic or Universalist?" in *Judaism in Late Antiquity*, part 3, vol. 2: *Where We Stand: Issues and Debates in Early Judaism*, ed. J. Neusner and A. J. Avery-Peck (Leiden: Brill, 1999), 57–73.

2. Terence L. Donaldson, *Judaism and the Gentiles: Jewish Patterns of Universalism (to 135 CE)* (Waco, TX: Baylor University Press, 2008).

3. Malka Z. Simkovich, *The Making of Jewish Universalism: From Exile to Alexandria* (Lanham, MD: Lexington Books/Fortress Academic, 2017).

4. See notably the contribution of Matthew Novenson in this volume.

5. For instance, Lester R. Grabbe, review of Simkovich, Malka Z. *The Making of Jewish Universalism: From Exile to Alexandria*. Lanham, MD: Lexington Books/Fortress Academic, 2017, in http://enochseminar.org/pdfs/RES-2019.01.03-Lester-Grabbe-on-The-Making-of-Jewish-Universalism.pdf [consulted on January 16, 2020].

6. For example, "The universalism of LXX piety finds characteristic expression in Da. 9:6" (*TDNT* 2:364)

7. Georg Bertram, "Praeparatio Evangelica in der Septuaginta," *VT* 7 (1957): 225–49; "Septuaginta-Frömmigkeit," *RGG* 3 (1961): 1707–9.

8. See, for instance, Scot McKnight, *A Light among the Gentiles* (Minneapolis: Fortress Press, 1991), 60, for universalism; and more generally, see Karen H. Jobes and Moisés Silva, *Invitation to the Septuagint* (Grand Rapids, MI: Baker Academic, 2000), 288–96.

9. Claude Tassin, "Universalisme," *Dictionnaire critique de théologie*, ed. Jean-Yves Lacoste. Quadrige (Paris: Presses Universitaires de France, 2002), 1210.

10. Jan Joosten, "Une théologie de la Septante?" *RTP* 132 (2000): 35–37.

11. Simkovich, *The Making of Jewish Universalism,* 13.

12. See, e.g., 1 Sam 3:13, see also *HAL* or *DCH*.

13. Marguerite Harl, *Les douze Prophètes. Joël, Abdiou, Jonas, Naoum, Ambakoum, Sophonie*. La Bible d'Alexandrie 23.4–9 (Paris: Cerf, 1999), 112–13.
14. See, for instance, Ralph L. Smith, *Micah-Malachi*. Word Biblical Commentary 32 (Dallas, TX: Word Books, 1984), 36–37.
15. Dominique Barthélemy, *Ézéchiel, Daniel et les 12 Prophètes*, Volume 3 of *Critique textuelle de l'Ancien Testament*. OBO 50/3 (Göttingen: Vandenhoeck & Ruprecht, 1992), 911.
16. Here the Greek supposes the Vorlage בדורה. The resulting meaning is not clear. See Harl, *Les douze Prophètes*, 366.
17. See Harl, *Les douze Prophètes*, 366.
18. For other insight in the so called "universalism" of the LXX of Zephaniah, see M. Harl, *Les douze Prophètes*, 326–28.
19. Perhaps a similar perspective in the codex Washington followed by some Coptic versions: δεόμενοι μου εν τοῖς διεσκορπισμένοις οἴσουσιν θυσίας μοι "those who pray me in those who are scattered shall carry sacrifice to me," with the same ambiguity: did the one who prays belong to the diaspora or is he included to it?
20. See Harl, *Les douze Prophètes*, 367.
21. Simkovich, *The Making of Jewish Universalism*, 16–17.
22. For a discussion of this meaning, see, for instance, Matthew Thiessen, "Revisiting the προσήλυτος in 'the LXX,'" *JBL* 132 (2013): 333–50.
23. Simkovich, *The Making of Jewish Universalism*, 74.
24. See the contribution of Eric Noffke in this volume.
25. See Jobes and Silva, *Invitation to the Septuagint*, 297–300.
26. McKnight, *A Light among the Gentiles*, 60.
27. See the contribution of Matthew Novenson in this volume.

BIBLIOGRAPHY

Barthélemy, Dominique. *Ézéchiel, Daniel et les 12 Prophètes*. Volume 3 of *Critique textuelle de l'Ancien Testament*. Orbis Biblicus et Orientalis 50/3. Göttingen: Vandenhoeck & Ruprecht, 1992.

Bertram, Georg. "Praeparatio Evangelica in der Septuaginta." *Vetus Testamentum* 7 (1957): 225–49.

———. "Septuaginta-Frömmigkeit." *Religion in Geschichte und Gegenwart* 3 (1961): 1707–9.

Donaldson, Terence L. *Judaism and the Gentiles: Jewish Patterns of Universalism (to 135 CE)*. Waco, TX: Baylor University Press, 2007.

Dunn, James D. G. "Was Judaism Particularistic or Universalist?" In *Judaism in Late Antiquity*. Part 3, vol. 2: *Where We Stand: Issues and Debates in Early Judaism*, edited by J. Neusner and A. J. Avery-Peck, 57–73. Leiden: Brill, 1999.

Grabbe, Lester L. Review of Simkovich, Malka Z. *The Making of Jewish Universalism: From Exile to Alexandria*. Lanham, MD: Lexington Books/Academic Fortress, 2017. http://enochseminar.org/pdfs/RES-2019.01.03-Lester-Grabbe-on-The-Making-of-Jewish-Universalism.pdf [consulted on January 16, 2020])

Harl, Marguerite. *Les douze Prophètes. Joël, Abdiou, Jonas, Naoum, Ambakoum, Sophonie*. La Bible d'Alexandrie 23.4–9. Paris: Cerf, 1999.

Jobes, Karen H., and Moisés Silva. *Invitation to the Septuagint*. Grand Rapids, MI: Baker Academic, 2000.

Joosten, Jan. "Une Théologie de la Septante?: Réflexions méthodologiques sur l'interprétation de la Version grecque." *Revue de Théologie et de philosophie* 132 (2000): 31–46.

McKnight, Scot. *Light among the Gentiles: Jewish Missionary Activity in the Second Temple Period*. Minneapolis, MN: Fortress Press, 1991.

Simkovich, Malka Z. *The Making of Jewish Universalism: From Exile to Alexandria*. Lanham, MD: Lexington Books/Fortress Academic, 2017.

Smith, Ralph L. *Micah-Malachi*. Word Biblical Commentary 32. Dallas, TX: Word Books, 1984.

Tassin, Claude. "Universalisme." In *Dictionnaire critique de théologie*, edited by Jean-Yves Lacoste, 1209–211. Quadrige. Paris: Presses Universitaires de France, 2002.

Thiessen, Matthew. "Revisiting the προσήλυτος in 'the LXX,'" *Journal of Biblical Literature* 132 (2013): 333–50.

Chapter Seven

Paul between Judaism and Hellenism

Imre Peres

SOME REMARKS ON TODAY'S RESEARCH ON PAUL

At the beginning I would like to state that Paul was a rather complicated person as a human, as a Jew, as a missionary, and as a Jewish and then as a Christian theologian.[1] Since the time of Albert Schweitzer (1875–1965)[2] research of him has shown that it is not easy to exactly define his personality, his theology, and his thinking. I see Paul's research to date marked by his own theological issues, his responses to the impulses from state or local government, from the churches, from the Jewish persecutors, or from the false teachers. The picture created from this mosaic is therefore still quite varying to this day. The tendencies to portray Paul as a purely Jewish theologian in the research of the "New Perspective on Paul" also do not show a firm unity, and this effort has several directions and also new/newer perspectives of the New Perspective.[3] Research shows how complicated it is to paint a reliable compact picture of Paul. What we should assume in it is: (1) On one hand the reality that the apostle Paul, in his personal depth as a theologian, is certainly much more Jewish than we previously thought. (2) On the other hand, with hindsight the question stands out whether he really is only a Jew, or also a Hellenist, or even better: whether he was a Hellenistic Jew, possibly even a Jewish Hellenist.[4]

These questions have been dealt with several times in research on Paul. And yet, they occur again and again, and they drive us to deeper and more complex observations. Certainly, it is important to partially research Paul. The results of this make sense for research on Paul and are certainly useful for the picture of Paul. However, it can be easy for us to make mistakes in this, and with it if we research Paul only partially (and tend to do so with biased preunderstanding) without a firm, clear, thorough, complex concept. How would it be possible? In this moment it is difficult to say it briefly.

In my contribution, I would like to open a little the narrow wall around Paul—until now also from us—or at least find a few windows where Paul thinks, speaks and acts not only as a Jew but also as a Hellenist. Or even better: how Paul is presented and works as a person shaped by Judaism and also by Hellenism—in spite of his diversity in theology still as a unified person with a unified faith. It is this "Hellenistic side" of his personality that I will try to uncover now a bit as I see it. And in this I would like to have a small belief that by looking at Paul one can also shed a little more light on "Pauline Judaism."⁵

WHAT SHOULD "PAULINE HELLENISM" MEAN, HOW I UNDERSTAND IT?

When Paul expresses himself as a "Hellenist" as I define him, it means several things to me. It is necessary to make several things clear in advance.

- It is about his—probably—direct quotations from the works of the Greek authors.
- It can also be allusions to the works of the Greek authors.
- It can also refer to schemes that come as Paul's literary product.
- It can concern his reflections in the Greek way which he uses to react to the impulses from his environment.
- This also includes his knowledge of Greek/Roman sport, life of soldiers, cult and religion, philosophy, ancient customs and rites (rituals), cemeteries and afterlife beliefs, etc.
- His positive attitude towards society and state authorities, his Roman citizenship, which he also uses for his defense.
- The defense of the Hellenistic communities for whom he wanted to be a shining example as their missionary.

I take these motifs and elements into account when Paul speaks from the position of Hellenism or the ancient religion, culture, literature, and Greek-Roman education.

CONCRETE REFERENCES TO PAULINE HELLENISM, VERY BRIEFLY

In this chapter, I would like to briefly point out the concrete examples of where, in my opinion, Paul speaks or reacts as a Hellenistic theologian. In his speeches and letters, Paul quotes several ancient authors—for example,

Aratus (Acts 17:28), Euripides (Acts 26:14), Menander (15:33), and others, which is not so easy to precisely identify.[6] Paul should have had knowledge of the works of these authors.

Paul positions himself to protect the Hellenistic communities from the Jews who persecute him so often,[7] or from the Synod in Jerusalem (Acts 15), or from the false teachers. This position (or self-reflection) can also grow from the fact that he saw himself as the light for the Gentiles in the mission of his life (Acts 13:47).

The letters of the apostle also show a Hellenistic picture. In these he brings his proclamation to the congregations in the form that was common in Hellenistic letters. In his article *"The Hellenistic Letter-Formula and the Pauline Letter-Scheme,"*[8] Detlev Dormeyer points out that when he considers, e.g., a letter from Pliny the Sabinianus, that it shows a rich resemblance to Paul's epistle to Philemon.[9]

Paul's attitude, e.g., to the meat for the gods was quite tolerant, which a proper Jew could never accept. He saw no theological risk in this. Paul is massively Hellenistic here. He is equally "tolerant" in the question of gods, whose existence he can allow. He has two methods here: In the mission to the Greeks he can imagine the existence of any gods in the universe (1 Cor 8:5–6),[10] but of course in submission to Jesus Christ, who is the absolute Lord over them. Of course, he is then consistent in the churches and says that there are no other gods. Paul is Hellenistic-free here.

A special sphere of discovery of Pauline thought is his memories of the past persecution of Christians. There are repeated instructions for this in his letters.[11] The nature of these instructions is fairly simple and has several facets: He publicly acknowledges that he used to persecute Christians.[12] He never denied this fact. Generally, he talks about it in the context where he characterizes his life. He recognizes that he did this persecution as the theologian of Judaism. But the persecution did not lead as a dispute against the pagans, but against the Jews (i.e., the potential Christians), who—in his opinion at the time—went astray from the correct Torah and temple religion (i.e., to the Christ-Messiah faith).

Paul could not have any right to chase the Greeks or Romans (Pagans) and transport them to Jerusalem. Especially not the Romans, who were really born Romans and who were under the protection of the emperor. It is very interesting that Paul never apologized for his past persecution. There is a feeling of sadness in his memories, but it does not provide any compensation or does not ask for forgiveness. Why not? Probably because he did not understand his deeds as a human failure or godless mistakes, but simply as a wrong orientation in life due to Jewish theology, and as a poorly understood (nationalistic) tradition. He replies theologically to this problem only where he wants to emphasize his conversion: before he was against Christ and Christians, today he is a new person in Christ. This argument does not actually speak about Christians but about himself.

To give an example of a good description of the persecution of the apostle Paul, read what Andreas Lindemann wrote:

> "With regard to the statement that Paul had acted as a persecutor as a ἀγνοῶν, the tendency observed in Paul is clearly shifted; and there is also a clearly different perspective with regard to the image of Paul in the book of Acts: the pursuit activity which the Pharisee Paul was very conscious of, now becomes something like an oversight, it was an error for which the persecutor was basically not responsible. Paul himself never writes in the preserved letters that the persecution of believers in Jesus was an act of unbelief, the ἀπιστία, on the contrary, he had been convinced that in faithfulness to the 'fatherly traditions' he did God's will. Accordingly, Paul does not write that he was a sinner as a persecutor or had acted under the power of sin; the revelation of Christ that was given to him is therefore not interpreted by him as salvation from sin or as forgiveness of sins."[13]

This example already shows well where and how the apostle Paul appears from the Hellenistic pastoral ground. That should be enough for our arguments.

I will analyze in more detail and fairly extensively a special topic for Paul, namely the Pauline doctrine of reconciliation. This topic is typical for research on Paul because it shows well where and how Paul argues as Jewish and contra-Jewish, Hellenistic and yet contra-Hellenistic.

PAULINE RECONCILIATION: THE ESCHATOLOGICAL HOPE OF GOD'S JUDGEMENT SEAT

In Apostle Paul's theological concepts, the doctrine of reconciliation, along with those of justice and personal hope for eternity, play a very important role. In research we ask about the roots of this teaching. Which sources were decisive for the Pauline views? Has he been inspired[14] only by the knowledge of what he considers to be an insufficient theology and practice of Judaism, according to which reconciliation, justice before God and the hope for eternal life from the works and due to the preservation of the Mosaic laws, is impossible? Or did he also know other sources?

In the following I will show that Paul was inspired for these ideas among others also by the Hellenistic environment, more precisely by everyday life, the cultic folk practice, and the afterlife ideas that had prevailed in popular belief. When analyzing ancient Greek tomb texts, it can be seen that in these the deceased are often described as people without mistakes and sin, who were good in word and deed, just, clever, and too beautiful in appearance or too young in age; in addition, people who had lived for their homeland or others, achieved important prizes or successes in life, etc. All these give them the personal prerequisites for a maximum positive afterlife hope. Their reconciliation is actually some kind of "self-reconciliation" or "self-justification." Nevertheless, or precisely because of this, based on his Jewish Torah knowledge, Paul could also be inspired on the pagan background to create a deep doctrine of reconciliation.

In the Pauline writings, the reconciliation statements are concentrated in two groups: *Directly by Paul* in theology for the Corinthian church (2 Cor 5:18–20), and in Romans (Rom 5:10–11; 11:15). In the *Deuteropauline literature*, the idea of reconciliation is taken up in the Letter to the Colossians (Col 1:20–22) and in the Letter to the Ephesians (Eph 2:16). We can say with Christian Wolff that "surely this statistical finding suggests that there is an original Pauline interpretation of the work of salvation."[15]

There is currently a discrepancy in the question of the emergence of the idea of reconciliation in Paul, which is based on two lines that Helmut Merkel defines as follows:[16] There are exegetes who link the New Testament reconciliation statements especially to the Hellenistic environment. Martin Hengel, Ferdinand Hahn, Cilliers Breytenbach, and others emphasize this thesis. Another direction in this question is represented by New Testament scholars, such as Otfried Hofius,[17] who seek the origin of the Pauline idea of reconciliation in ancient Judaism. In their experiment, they go to Deutero-Isaiah's theological statements (Isa 53). According to Helmut Merkel, this path only leads to the destination through many detours, so the result is not entirely convincing.[18]

In today's discussion, the argumentation is also directed at the question of whether the theory of reconciliation was a central topic in Paul's theological system. This is mainly denied by the Catholic theologian Joachim Gnilka,[19] who believes that reconciliation is an important word for Paul, but—because it is rare in his letters—it should not be placed at the center of the apostle's theology. Of course, the New Testament scholars of the reformation theological heritage see it differently.

TWO REMARKS ON THE "GREEK-STYLE" RECONCILIATION

I suppose—and that is why I insert this here—that Paul's reconciliation statements do not only lead to Eschaton in history as a logical conclusion and consequence of God's concrete act of salvation in Jesus's death on the cross. Of course, it is very important, and also necessary in terms of salvation history. But the idea of reconciliation as a theological statement on the problem of guilt and sin can in principle be eschatologically motivated for Paul. In my opinion, it comes from two sides:

Generally, on the part of humankind there is a will or a tendency to live well, better, and even better, which applies not only to life on this side but also to life after death. This longing is common for the Gentiles, Jews, and also Christians. Those who had or have an anticipation of life in the other world want to have the hope that they will enjoy happiness after death. That is why the pagans—as we shall see—wanted to convince themselves and mainly the gods that they are not guilty of any offense or wrongdoing, that they did not live badly, that they were good people in principle, and that they have the prerequisites that should ensure them a good place in the afterlife. The pagans are afraid of the wrath of the gods or of the revenge of the gods.[20] That is why they trivialized guilt and sin: Thus, they built a kind of self-righteousness or self-reconciliation for themselves with regard to the afterlife. However, such eschatological hope is dangerous according to Paul. So, Paul could also—I emphasize the *also*—come to the problem of hope for the afterlife and reconciliation from the pagan eschatology.

On the other hand, the Greeks faced daily confrontation with death,[21] that the gods—mainly the underground ones—are evil, terrible, relentless, without mercy and understanding. Nevertheless, the Greeks hoped that in the hour of death or in the underground court, the gods would not be so severe, that they would take pity on the poor soul that they would not send them to the Hades or, worse still, the Tartaros, but on the way to the right to the Elysium, to the islands of the blessed, or to the gods on Mount Olympus. That is why they wanted to make a sacrifice or through relatives regularly leave a drink-offering or libation at the grave. It was also an attempt to achieve reconciliation, to reconcile the gods, or to achieve peace. But since no one of the gods died on behalf of the dead, not even one of the relatives, all that remained was a pious request and hope to achieve reconciliation with the gods. On the other hand, of course, Paul does not seek reconciliation in this way: For him, the cause of salvation is the grace of God in the death of Jesus. Jesus's sacrifice brings reconciliation, which opens the new eschatological dimension.

I would now like to clarify what has been said about Paul in the context of the Greek people and their eschatological orientation—that is, with regard to their hope for the afterlife.

THE HOPE OF GREEKS FOR A CHANCE OF POSITIVE AFTERLIFE

As you may know, there are many Greek texts that contain positive ideas about the afterlife. They show that in the contemporary Greek world, in which apostolic activity took place, there was a very strong longing for a positive after death fate.²² This longing was massive and very human-oriented: people wanted to have a good and enjoyable life in the afterlife. What were your chances of that? An example to this:

> This grave contains a beautiful figure who died—alas!—too soon. Because you, who were 16 years old or a little more, were led by Kure, the wife of Pluteus, to Hades. But the immortal gods had compassion and did not let your soul submerge into the house of Hades; she flies in the air; With the gods Stratonike has the same fate as the heroines. If anyone ever saw her alive who is now in this grave, he would not be able to pass this tomb without tears.²³ (translation my own)

Stratonike can experience this positive eschatological future simply because of her beautiful figure (καλὸν δέμας), her young death, and the "grace" of the immortal blessed gods (θεοὶ μάκαρες) who were compassionate (οἰκτείραντες: merciful, compassionate). The soul of Stratonike does not come down to dark Hades, but into the upper spheres, into the etheric heaven, where she can continue to live as a demigoddess in the circle of heroines. Hephaistion also expects similarly glorious life after death:

> The heaped-up earth embraces the famous son of Euboulus, who received from the goddesses of fate only a short existence under the sky; Hephaistion, good in his nature, excellent in his appearance; he was honoured by everyone—young and old alike—because even though he was still young, he had the wisdom of an old man and a pleasant manner of speaking. Klotho, who let forgetting (Lethe) approach, destroyed the child's Hyachintos age before the soft fluff sprang up on his cheek. So all the people shared the grief when the virtuous ephebe had died. But the children of pious men (Hermes) Kyllenios brings, leading them with his staff, not to the hated Acheron, but turn them towards the Elysian field, and there Pluteus has appointed (the deceased) as companion to the most just heroes.²⁴ (translation my own)

The epigram expresses the conviction that the young man Hephaistion, as the deceased of Pluteus, will get the place in the afterlife among the just heroes as the one equal to them. The prerequisites for this are his former good nature and character (φυὴ ἀγαθή), the beauty of his appearance (εἶδος ἄριστον), his honor (τείμα) and the recognition of young and old, his pleasant manner of speaking (μείλιχος ἐπὶ γλώσσῃ), and his mind (νοῦς) and relationship with the elderly. His very advantageous human skills secure him the way to the beautiful eschatological fate, the companion (ἐφέστιος) of the just heroes (ἡρώσσιν ἀκροδίκοισιν), which means that he is also considered highly just (ἀποκροδίκοιος) in the afterlife. It is the reward they have earned for their human virtue.

We could ceaselessly cite similar examples from the Greek epitaphs. A direct voice sounds from the tomb text of Demetrias (3rd year BCE), which—despite its sadness, fear, and distress—shows very nicely the arguments for valuable afterlife in front of the "judgment seat" of the underground goddess Persephone.

> Terrible Persephoneia, welcome a pious man, Agathocles, descending to you, a role model of all virtue and honesty. On the meadow of the pious let him take up residence; because truly, his soul was pure and just when he was on earth.[25] (translation my own)

Agathocles was a pious man who is presented as a role model (πρύτανις), who mastered all virtue and honesty. His soul (ψυχή) was pure (καθαρά), truthful, and sincere (ἀληθής) in earthly life, and he lived a righteous (δίκαιος) life. Someone from his relatives, who provided the inscription and his grave, pleads with the goddess Persephone with these arguments: May she let him dwell in the afterlife on the meadow of the pious (εὐσεβέων λειμῶνα κατοίκισον).

At the end another example: Diogenes from Eretria (3rd year BCE), on his tomb script is qualified as respectable (δίκαιος) and pious (εὐσεβής)—that is why he longs for a life of deity (κἀγὼ θεός εἰμι δικαίως).[26]

In summary, this section shows that the grave texts generally also contain wishes or prayers: May you (Hades, Persephone, Aiakos, Hermes, gods, etc.) lead the deceased to good places or give these to them (e.g., in the Elysium, on the Blessed Islands, in Heaven, or on Mount Olympus). It can be seen from the personal requirements that the Greeks expected a beautiful afterlife as a reward for their life, their good works, their faith, and their virtue (ἀρετή).

PERSONAL REQUIREMENTS FOR THE HOPEFUL AFTERLIFE: PAUL AND THE GREEKS

We assume that Paul was naturally interested in the Hellenistic world. It was the mission field for him. According to Hans-Heinrich Schade, "Paul takes statements from the primitive Christian mission and church sermons that express the salvation of believers through Christ from the judgment of annihilation."[27] However, he was attentive and thoughtful toward his coworkers. As we learn from his letters, he currently also reacts to the problems of eschatological hope (hopelessness), not only in terms of the time horizon but also in the theological meaning. In 1 Thess 4:13 he reacts to the concrete situation of the already deceased, those "asleep," which made it difficult for the Thessalonians to believe in the resurrection. In 1 Corinthians 15, Paul explains to the Corinthians the importance of the historical resurrection of Jesus and the eschatological resurrection in the case of all Christians—against the denial of the latter. Later, in his further letter, he writes just as up to date about the interim state of the naked soul in death and a new body, as well as about the judgment seat of Jesus (2 Cor 5:1–10) as an important borderline to eternal life. Earlier, in Athens, he responded in his Areopagic speech to the many divine statues (and gravestones?), which he saw while walking through the city. Here he led his speech to the eschatological exacerbation with reference to the eschatological judgment and the resurrection of Jesus (Acts 17:30–31). Even earlier in Lystra, he had to dissuade the crowd from sacrificing to them and deifying him and Barnabas (Acts 14:18). That, too, was a concrete reaction to a very difficult situation. Finally: Paul also writes to the Christians in Rome that the Gentiles nevertheless carry the law within them because it is written in their hearts, and that on an eschatological day God through Jesus Christ will judge everything that is hidden among men.[28] "The fact that the Gentiles are a law to themselves is not expressed by any philosophy, but only by the existence of the deed, which corresponds to the Jewish law."[29] Paul thus bound the Hellenistic world (with its nature law) and his apostolic eschatology together in the thought of the last judgment.[30]

All this shows that in his behavior and theological reasoning Paul answered the specific questions or problems of his listeners, members of the congregations, or opponents. We can imagine, as has already been shown, that Paul knew the world of thought of his Hellenistic environment well, including post-mortem folk beliefs and ideas about the afterlife. Yes, he also had to know the Hellenistic "cemetery poetry"[31] well. On his travels he often had to go to cities where there were many epitaph stones and gravestones with rich texts on the edges of streets. He knew how the Greeks wanted to secure a positive afterlife for themselves. All positive human qualities and abilities should serve them for this purpose. This was actually all that was available to the Greeks as an argument when they stood before the judgment seat of the gods.[32] Paul certainly knew these Greek popular religious opinions and the zeal to be saved for the afterlife. He could certainly understand it as a human, but he could not accept it theologically. This could give him an important signal or inspiration for the application; because he knew of another hope of eternal life for the Ἰουδαίον τε πρῶτον καὶ Ἕλληνα (Rom 14:10). The reason for this hope was not in man himself but in the reconciliation through Jesus.[33] For Paul, the personal requirements for the hope of the afterlife were not rooted in the best human qualities but in the personal faith in Jesus Christ and his reconciliation.[34]

We can ask: Why does Paul touch and use these images and theological thoughts from the Hellenistic world of belief and imagination? It is helpful to consider the statement of Jürgen Becker, who says: "In the concept of the final judgment as an end-of-time forensic court scene, there is continuity from Paul the Pharisee to the apostle to the Gentiles. It is based on a pictorial view that in the ancient world everyone could experience in the audience and court scenes of rulers, generals and provincial governors."[35] There are enough examples of this in Paul[36] but also in other New Testament writings.[37] In my opinion, Paul first thought and spoke as a Pharisee in the formulation of his theology of justice and reconciliation, but it is important to add that he also argues in the "Greek" way as a Hellenistic theologian through his knowledge of Greco-Roman cemetery hopes. The fact that this can be so is also shown by the corresponding word field, in which Paul uses many such words and terms[38] that have their firm place in the sphere of the Greek ideas about afterlife and epigraphs.

POSSIBLE CONSEQUENCE(S)

It can be seen from what has been said so far how it is possible to see the apostle Paul between Judaism and Hellenism and to define him as a "bridge theologian."

In my chapter, however, I did not define the entire scale of what it means: Judaism of Paul, and Hellenism of Paul, and where his exceeded limits are, where he thinks and acts in a kind of mixed manner. However, a basic question comes to mind here as to whether it is really and at all possible. Can that be clearly defined? I think a lot of effort is still needed.

I have a dream, namely: in my research I am trying to compile a list, or rather *a catalogue* of concrete Pauline words, deeds, arguments, and efforts where he expresses his Judaism and Hellenism. That—i.e., the concept of this observation—I would like to introduce *Deo volente* to you at the next potential conference(s) here in Bratislava, if time and my health allow me. But I wonder if it is at all possible. I hope it is. And therefore, I would like to cordially invite all of you to this work on Paul to "catalogue" his Jewish, Hellenistic, and/or mixed words, deeds, arguments, and efforts (simply said: *Logia Pauli*). This goal needs many good theologians—as you all are—from both sides: us, as the "Jews" and also as the "Hellenists." I know it is not that easy. But we need each other to compile this catalogue, then sort, check, and also correct the results. In this way we could see Paul more clearly and get to know him better. It is a challenge. It would be very nice to participate in this goal together in a warm and friendly way. We could really shed more light on the Pauline personality, but we could also probably set the Judaism of Paul's time in a new perspective.[39]

SUMMARY

It is not easy to orient oneself in the current discussion on Paul and his theological thinking. He is already a relatively complex person since he has a twofold background and also his field of work is divided into the Judaic and Hellenistic area, although his apostolic and missionary activities concerned mostly Hellenistic churches. The new research on Paul currently focuses on his roots in Judaism and sets him into a context of so-called "new perspectives on Paul." This chapter investigates the question whether we can see and at the same time ignore the Hellenistic background of Paul's work and his theology. In five chapters the author tries to define how to understand "Paul's Hellenism" and at the same time provides evidence for his Hellenism. As arguments he names Paul's quoting of Greek authors, the defense of the Hellenistic churches, the Hellenistic formulation of his letters (*The Hellenistic Letter-Formula and the Pauline Letter-Scheme*), his attitude towards pagan gods, his opinion about meat offered to idols, the question of his persecution of the Christians, etc. The analysis of his opinion on the reconciliation with God and the eschatological hope before God's judgment seat makes its own chapter, where he starts from the analysis of Paul's teaching on the law (evidence from Judaism) and provides also Hellenistic epitaphs and analyzes their hope for a good life after death based on personal human premises (good ethical behavior, physical ability, physical beauty, wisdom, godliness, etc.). These should weigh before the underworld gods so that they would give them a good place in Hades or let them to the gods on Olympus where they get immortality or a godly status (divinization). At the end the author provides two consequences: (1) He allows that in Paul traces of both Judaism and Hellenism appear. He can therefore be considered a "bridge-theologian" who in his person and teaching connects both: Judaism and Hellenism. To what extent, we do not know yet. This would still require a great deal of research. (2) Hence he suggests for the following conference to start research to precisely define Paul's teaching, words and speeches, and create from them a catalogue (*Logia Pauli*). This way we could not only more precisely shed light on Paul, but also set the Judaism of his time in a new perspective.

NOTES

1. This work was supported by the Scientific Grant Agency of the Ministry of Education, Science, Research and Sport of the Slovak Republic and the Slovak Academy of Sciences (VEGA), as part of the research project entitled "Paul within Judaism—New Perspectives" (VEGA 1/0103/18), with its home base at Comenius University in Bratislava, at the Evangelical Lutheran Theological Faculty.

2. See Albert Schweitzer, *Geschichte der paulinischen Forschung von der Reformation bis auf die Gegenwart* (Tübingen: Mohr Siebeck, 1911). Last print of the book: Hildesheim, Georg Olms Verlag, 2004.

3. Alexander J. M. Wedderburn, "Eine neuere Paulusperspektive?," in *Biographie und Persönlichkeitdes Paulus*, ed. Eve-Marie Becker and Peter Pilhofer, WUNT 187 (Tübingen: Mohr Siebeck, 2009 [2005]), 46–63.

4. See Troels Engberg-Pedersen (ed.), *Paul in His Hellenistic Context* (Minneapolis, MN: Fortress Press, 1995).

5. See Jörg Frey, "Paulus und die Apostel. Zur Entwicklung des paulinischen Apostel-begriffs und zum Verhältnis des Heidenapostels zu einen Kollegen," in *Biographie und Persönlichkeitdes Paulus*, ed. Eve-Marie Becker and Peter Pilhofer. WUNT 187 (Tübingen: Mohr Siebeck, 2009 [2005]), 192–226.

6. See Aratus (Acts 17:28), Euripides (Acts 26:14), Menander (1 Cor 15:33).

7. See, e.g., Gal 5:11; 1 Cor 4:12; and 2 Tim 3:11. See also Acts 14:19–20; 2 Cor 11:25 (23–27).

8. See Detlev Dormeyer, *The Hellenistic Letter-Formula and the Pauline Letter-Scheme*, in *The Pauline Canon*, ed. Stanley E. Porter, PAST 1 (Leiden: Brill, 2004), 59–93.

9. Dormeyer, *The Hellenistic Letter-Formula and the Pauline Letter-Scheme*, 81–82.

10. See Imre Peres, "A vallások konfrontációja a páli kereszténységben (Apostle Paul and gods)," in *Vallási pluralizmus, vallásközi párbeszéd és kortárs ideológiák*, ed. Ábrahám Kovács (Budapest: Kálvin Kiadó, 2013), 250–67.

11. See 1 Tim 1:13.

12. He talks about it more times in his letters.

13. Andreas Lindemann, "Sünde, Schuld, Vergebung? Paulus als Verfolger der Kirche und als Apostel Jesu Christi," in *Studia Theologica Debrecinensis—Sonderheft* (2012): 76 (53–80).

14. See to this, e.g., Heinrich Schmid, "Gesetz und Gnade im Alten Testament," in *Gesetz und Gnade im Alten Testament und im jüdischen Denken*, ed. Robert Brunner (Zürich: Zwingli Verlag, 1969), 3–29; Kurt Hruby, "Gesetz und Gnade in der rabbinischen Überlieferung," in *Gesetz und Gnade im Alten Testament und im jüdischen Denken*, ed. Robert Brunner (Zürich: Zwingli Verlag, 1969), 30–63.

15. Christian Wolff, *Der zweite Brief des Paulus an die Korinther*. THKNT 8 (Berlin: Evangelische Verlagsanstalt, 1989), 133–34.

16. Helmut Merkel, "καταλλαγή," *EWNT* 2 (1981): 646.

17. Otfried Hofius, "Erwägungen zur Gestalt und Herkunft des paulinischen Versöhnungsgedanken," *ZThK* 77 (1980): 186–99.

18. Peter Stuhlmacher speaks about a different and a general possibility: "Paul's ... used words 'to reconcile' and 'reconciliation' mean, in the outside Biblical Greek language, above all the peace between people who are hostile to each other; 'Reconciliation' is an end to enmity." (*Der Brief an die Römer.* NTD 6 [Göttingen: Vandenhoeck & Ruprecht, 1998], 76).

19. Joachim Gnilka, *Az Újszövetség teológiája (Die Theologie des Neuen Testaments)* (Budapest: Szent István Társulat, 2007), 81.

20. Wolfgang Speyer, "Religionen des griechisch-römischen Bereichs: Zorn der Gottheit, Vergeltung und Sühne," in Wolfgang Speyer, *Frühes Christentum im antiken Strahlungsfeld*, WUNT 50 (Tübingen: Mohr Siebeck, 1989), 145ff. (140–59).

21. See, e.g., Andrea Korečková, "Záhrobná láska ženy podľa gréckych náhrobných kameňov, [Jenseitsliebe der Frau in den griechischen Grabinschriften]," in *Tempus clausum: Festschrift für Pavel Procházka*, ed. Imre Peres (Banská Bystrica: Pedagogická fakulta Univerzity Mateja Bela, 2012), 97ff. (93–109).

22. See, e.g., Imre Peres, "Positive griechische Eschatologie," in *Apokalyptik als Herausforderung neutestamentlicher Theologie*, ed. Markus Öhler and Michael Becker, WUNT 2.214 (Tübingen: Mohr Siebeck, 2006), 267–82.

23. Reinhold Merkelbach and Josef Stauber, *Steinepigramme aus dem griechischen Osten* (Stuttgart/Leipzig: BG Teubner, 1998), n° 03/02/67 = J. J. E. Hondius (ed.), *Supplementum epigraphicum Graecum, Vol. 26* (Leiden/Amsterdam, 1934), n° 1280; Ernst Pfuhl and Hans Möbius, *Die ostgriechischen Grabreliefs* (Mainz am Rhein: Von Zabern, 1977), n° 808; Hermann Vetters (ed.), *Die Inschriften griechischer Städte aus Kleinasien, Band 16: Die Inschriften von Ephesos* (Bonn: Rudolf Habelt Verlag, 1980), n° 2104.

24. Merkelbach and Stauber, *Steinepigramme aus dem griechischen Osten*, n° 04/12/09.

25. Werner Peek, *Griechische Grabgedichte* (Berlin: Akademie Verlag, 1960), n° 208 = Werner Peek, *Griechische Vers-Inschriften* (Berlin: Akademie Verlag, 1955), n° 1572; Imre Peres, *Griechische Grabinschriften und neutestamentliche Eschatologie*, WUNT 157 (Tübingen: Mohr Siebeck, 2003), 62. Archeological finds in Demetrias.

26. Peres, *Griechische Grabinschriften und neutestamentliche Eschatologie*, 73 = Peek, *Griechische Grabgedichte*, n° 220; Peek, *Griechische Vers-Inschriften*, n° 1126; Johannes Kirchner (ed.), *Inscriptiones Graecae, Vol. XII* (Berlin: Reimer, 1915), n° 290.

27. Hans-Heinrich Schade, *Apokalyptische Christologie bei Paulus*. GTA 18 (Göttingen: Vandenhoeck & Ruprecht, 1984), 47. See 1 Thess 1:9–10; 5:9–10.

28. See Rom 2:14–16; 1 Cor 4:5.

29. Christian Maurer, *Die Gesetzeslehre des Paulus, nach ihrem Ursprung und in ihrer Entfaltung dargelegt* (Zürich: Evangelischer Verlag, 1941), 78.

30. Ulrich Luz, "Neutestamentliche Lichtblicke auf die dunklen Seiten Gottes. Überlegungen zu den Gerichtsaussagen der Paulustradition," in *Gott wahr nehmen: Festschrift für Christian Link*, ed. M. L. Frettlöch and H. P. Lichtengerger (Neukirchen-Vluyn: Neukirchener Verlag, 2003), 257–76.

31. See Georgius Kaibel, "Griechische Friedhofspoesie," *Deutsche Revue* 19 (1894): 367–80.

32. See Ulrich Luz, *Das Geschichtsverständnis des Paulus*. BEvTh 49 (München: Chr. Kaiser Verlag, 1968), 310–17.

33. See Daniel Patte, *Paul's Faith and the Power of the Gospel* (Philadelphia, PA: Fortress Press, 1983), 77ff.

34. Luz, *Das Geschichtsverständnis des Paulus*, 258.

35. Jürgen Becker, *Paulus. Der Apostel der Völker*. UTB (Tübingen: Mohr Siebeck, 2009), 97.

36. See, e.g., just the statements in the Romans: 2:6, 12, 16; 3:4, 6; 5:16, 18; 8:1, 3; 13:2; 14:10–12: Klaus-Michael Bull, "'Wir werden alle vor den Richterstuhl Gottes gestellt werden' (Röm 14,10). Zur Funktion des Motivs vom Endgericht in den Argumentationen des Römerbriefes," in *Apokalyptik als Herausforderung neutestamentlicher Theologie*, ed. Markus Öhler and Michael Becker, WUNT 2.214 (Tübingen: Mohr Siebeck, 2006), 125–43.

37. See, e.g., Matt 25:31ff.; Mark 15:1ff.; John 18:18ff.; Acts 18:12ff.; Rev 4; Barn. 21:1–6.

38. See, e.g., my "small catalogue" of all words in the Greek and apostolic eschatology: Imre Peres, *Griechische Grabinschriften und neutestamentliche Eschatologie*, 264–65.

39. See Willam David Davies, *Jewish and Pauline Studies* (Philadelphia, PA: Fortress Press, 1984), 259–60.

BIBLIOGRAPHY

Becker, Jürgen. *Paulus. Der Apostel der Völker*. UTB. Tübingen: Mohr Siebeck, 2009.

Bull, Klaus-Michael. "'Wir werden alle vor den Richterstuhl Gottes gestellt werden' (Röm 14,10). Zur Funktion des Motivs vom Endgericht in den Argumentationen des Römerbriefes." In *Apokalyptik als Herausforderung neutestamentlicher Theologie*, edited by Markus Öhler and Michael Becker, 125–43. WUNT 2.214, Tübingen: Mohr Siebeck, 2006.

Davies, William David. *Jewish and Pauline Studies*. Philadelphia, PA: Fortress Press, 1984.

Dormeyer, Detlev. *The Hellenistic Letter-Formula and the Pauline Letter-Scheme*. In *The Pauline Canon*, edited by Stanley E. Porter, 59–93. Pauline Studies 1. Leiden/Boston: Brill, 2004.

Engberg-Pedersen, Troels, ed. *Paul in His Hellenistic Context*. Minneapolis, MN: Fortress Press, 1995.

Frey, Jörg. "Paulus und die Apostel. Zur Entwicklung des paulinischen Apostelbegriffs und zum Verhältnis des Heidenapostels zu einen Kollegen." In *Biographie und Persönlichkeitdes Paulus*, edited by Eve-Marie Becker and Peter Pilhofer, 192–226. WUNT 187. Tübingen: Mohr Siebeck, 2009 [2005].

Gnilka, Joachim. *Az Újszövetség teológiája (Die Theologie des Neuen Testaments)*. Budapest: Szent István Társulat, 2007.

Hofius, Otfried. "Erwägungen zur Gestalt und Herkunft des paulinischen Versöhnungsgedanken." *ZThK* 77 (1980): 186–99.

Hondius, J. J. E., ed. *Supplementum epigraphicum Graecum, Vol. 26*. Leiden/Amsterdam: 1934.

Hruby, Kurt. "Gesetz und Gnade in der rabbinischen Überlieferung." In *Gesetz und Gnade im Alten Testament und im jüdischen Denken*, edited by Robert Brunner, 30–63. Zürich: Zwingli Verlag, 1969.
Kaibel, Georgius. "Griechische Friedhofspoesie." *Deutsche Revue* 19 (1894): 367–80.
Kirchner, Johannes, ed. *Inscriptiones Graecae, Vol. XII*. Berlin: Reimer, 1915.
Korečková, Andrea. "Záhrobná láska ženy podľa gréckych náhrobných kameňov [Jenseitsliebe der Frau in den griechischen Grabinschriften]." In *Tempus clausum: Festschrift für Pavel Procházka*, edited by Imre Peres, 93–109. Banská Bystrica: Pedagogická fakulta Univerzity Mateja Bela, 2012.
Lindemann, Andreas. "Sünde, Schuld, Vergebung? Paulus als Verfolger der Kirche und als apostel Jesu Christi" *Studia Theologica Debrecinensis—Sonderheft* (2012): 53–80.
Luz, Ulrich. *Das Geschichtsverständnis des Paulus*. BEvTh 49. München: Chr. Kaiser Verlag, 1968.
———. "Neutestamentliche Lichtblicke auf die dunklen Seiten Gottes. Überlegungen zu den Gerichtsaussagen der Paulustradition." In *Gott wahr nehmen: Festschrift für Christian Link*, edited by M. L. Frettlöch and H. P. Lichtengerger, 257–76. Neukirchen-Vluyn: Neukirchener Verlag, 2003.
Maurer, Christian. *Die Gesetzeslehre des Paulus, nach ihrem Ursprung und in ihrer Entfaltung dargelegt*. Zürich: Evangelischer Verlag, 1941.
Merkel, Helmut. "καταλλαγή." *EWNT* 2 (1981): 644–50.
Merkelbach, Reinhold and Josef Stauber, *Steinepigramme aus dem griechischen Osten*. Stuttgart/Leipzig: BG Teubner, 1998.
Patte, Daniel. *Paul's Faith and the Power of the Gospel*. Philadelphia, PA: Fortress Press, 1983.
Peek, Werner. *Griechische Grabgedichte*. Berlin: Akademie Verlag, 1960.
———. *Griechische Vers-Inschriften*. Berlin: Akademie Verlag, 1955.
Peres, Imre. *Griechische Grabinschriften und neutestamentliche Eschatologie*. WUNT 157. Tübingen: Mohr Siebeck, 2003.
———. "Positive griechische Eschatologie." In *Apokalyptik als Herausforderung neutestamentlicher Theologie*, edited by Markus Öhler and Michael Becker, 267–82. WUNT 2.214. Tübingen: Mohr Siebeck, 2006.
———. "A vallások konfrontációja a páli keresztyénségben (Apostle Paul and gods)." In *Vallási pluralizmus, vallásközi párbeszéd és kortárs ideológiák*, edited by Ábrahám Kovács, 250–67. Budapest: Kálvin Kiadó, 2013.
Pfuhl, Ernst and Möbius Hans. *Die ostgriechischen Grabreliefs*. Mainz am Rhein: Von Zabern, 1977.
Schade, Hans-Heinrich. *Apokalyptische Christologie bei Paulus*. GTA 18. Göttingen: Vandenhoeck & Ruprecht, 1984.
Schmid, Heinrich. "Gesetz und Gnade im Alten Testament." In *Gesetz und Gnade im Alten Testament und im jüdischen Denken*, edited by Robert Brunner, 3–29. Zürich: Zwingli Verlag, 1969.
Schweitzer, Albert. *Geschichte der paulinischen Forschung von der Reformation bis auf die Gegenwart*. Tübingen, Mohr Siebeck, 1911. Last print of the book: Hildesheim: Georg Olms Verlag, 2004.

Speyer, Wolfgang. "Religionen des griechisch-römischen Bereichs: Zorn der Gottheit, Vergeltung und Sühne." In Wolfgang Speyer, *Frühes Christentum im antiken Strahlungsfeld*, 140–59. WUNT 50. Tübingen: Mohr Siebeck, 1989.

Stuhlmacher, Peter. *Der Brief an die Römer*. NTD 6. Göttingen: Vandenhoeck & Ruprecht, 1998.

Vetters, Hermann, ed. *Die Inschriften griechischer Städte aus Kleinasien, Band 16: Die Inschriften von Ephesos*. Bonn: Rudolf Habelt Verlag, 1980.

Wedderburn, Alexander J. M. "Eine neuere Paulusperspektive?" In *Biographie und Persönlichkeitdes Paulus*, edited by Eve-Marie Becker and Peter Pilhofer, 46–63. WUNT 187. Tübingen: Mohr Siebeck, 2009 [2005].

Wolff, Christian. *Der zweite Brief des Paulus an die Korinther*. THKNT 8. Berlin: Evangelische Verlagsanstalt, 1989.

Part II

THE SPECIFICS OF PAUL'S MESSAGE CONCERNING END-TIME REDEMPTION OF ISRAEL AND ITS ROLE TOWARDS THE NATIONS (*ETHNĒ*)

Chapter Eight

Israēl (and Israēlitēs) in Paul, Particularly in Galatians

Michael Bachmann

INTRODUCTION

This topic may seem a bit strange to those familiar with Paul. After all, the word *Israēlitēs* is completely absent from the Letter to the Galatians—in the title above, too, it appears only in parentheses—and the indeclinable proper noun *Israēl* occurs only once in the letter—namely towards the end, in (Gal) 6:16. Do these findings really require an entire chapter to explain them? This question is especially relevant given that the situation is quite similar in the First Letter to the Corinthians and in Philippians (where we find only *Israēl*, namely in 1 Cor 10:18 and Phil 3:8); and in the field of the so-called proto-Paulines,[1] First Thessalonians and Philemon do not feature either of the terms of this word family.

Nonetheless, I believe it is useful, even essential, to investigate this topic. For *one thing*, we must ask ourselves whether—as Udo Schnelle, for instance, believes—the difference between Galatians and Romans, particularly in terms of this word family, could indicate that "in the wake of the Galatian crisis, [. . .] Paul distinguishes his Christology [. . .] as being *Israel-friendly*"[2]—*after* the Letter to the Galatians, and not in the letter itself.[3] *Secondly*, the interpretation of the phrase "the Israel of God" in 6:16 is open for debate. While Gottlob Schrenk argued in 1949/1950 that "the expression must refer to 'Judaism,'"[4] and although Peter Richardson made a similar assertion in 1969,[5] Hans-Dieter Betz stated in his 1979 commentary on the Letter to the Galatians that he continued to support "[t]he usual interpretation," namely "equating 'the Israel of God' with the Christian church."[6,7] Even now, this view is still promoted enthusiastically and often.[8] Of course, there is no lack of other positions. It is worth mentioning corresponding statements by Andreas Lindemann, Susan G. Eastman, Christiane Zimmermann, and John

121

M. G. Barclay,[9] as well as my own.[10] If one also considers the initial question above—namely, how Israel-friendly Paul's arguments are in the Letter to the Galatians—and whether they might in fact contain anti-Jewish leanings—then the title of this chapter, which at first seems somewhat strange, does in fact address a very important issue.

For this reason, we will (in the first section) first turn our attention to the proto-Pauline instances of the terms *Israēl* and *Israēlitēs*, and then (in the second subsection) specifically to those found in Rom 9:6, 1 Cor 10:18, and Gal 6:16, since the three passages are frequently linked.[11] After that (in the second section), attention will naturally need to be paid to Gal 6:16, beginning with synchronous observations (in the first subsection), followed by diachronous ones (in the second subsection).

One diachronous matter, by no means insignificant for the reception history of New Testament statements, should be mentioned here: At the latest by the second century CE, and certainly in Justin's *Dialogue with Trypho*, the noun *Israēl* already does not actually refer to the Jewish people—who are often meant by this in Old Testament texts (see, e.g., 2 Sam 8:15; 1 Kgs 4:1; Ez 37:16, 19–21)—but rather to the church. For instance, *Dial.* 11:5 (following 11:4, which associates "the new law and the new covenant" with "all people") states, "The true spiritual Israel, and descendants of Judah, Jacob, Isaac, and Abraham [. . .], are *we* who have been led to God through this crucified Christ."[12] This linguistic usage in particular plays a major role in shaping the expression over the following centuries.[13] This can be seen, for instance, in some (German) hymns. Two examples appear in the text of the well-known 1644 Protestant song "Nun preiset alle Gottes Barmherzigkeit" by Johannes Apelles von Löwenstern (1594–1648).[14] Echoing the first verse, the fifth verse reads:[15]

> Drum preis und ehre [*du*] seine Barmherzigkeit;
> Sein [nämlich: Gottes] Lob vermehre, *werteste Christenheit*!
> *Uns* soll hinfort kein Unfall schaden;
> freue *dich, Israel,* seiner Gnaden,
> freue *dich, Israel,* seiner Gnaden!

> Wherefore [*you*, sg.] now praise his mercifulness;
> Multiply His [God's] praise, *worthy Christianity*!
> Henceforth no misfortune shall harm *us*;
> *Israel,* enjoy his mercy!
> *Israel,* enjoy his mercy!

For this reason, too, it should come as no surprise that the "interpretation of the 'Israel of God' as a metaphor for Christianity [. . .] determined the understanding of the Letter to the Galatians in New Testament scholarship over the entire past century"[16]—and in fact, as just indicated, far longer than that. Thus it is even more important to ask whether the situation in the (proto-)Pauline letters might already be similar, at least to some extent.

ISRAĒL AND *ISRAĒLITĒS* IN THE PROTO-PAULINES— INCLUDING THE LETTER TO THE GALATIANS

The proto-Pauline evidence

Overview of Findings

The demonym *Israēl* occurs approximately 68 times in the New Testament, and the gentilic *Israēlitēs* appears 9 times.[17] The Corpus Paulinum fits in quite nicely here, with its 17 (or 18, if we follow the majority-text in Rom 10:1) plus 3 instances, in other words a total of 20.[18] However, the term *Israēlitēs* does not appear at all outside the letters, whose Pauline origin is fairly uncontroversial; and the term *Israēl* occurs there only once, namely in Eph 2:12. According to this verse, incidentally, the addressees (i.e., the "Gentiles by birth" [Eph 2:11]) would "at that time [have been] excluded from citizenship in Israel and foreigners to the covenants of the promise." In light of the proto-Paulines, if we exclude Eph 2:12, there are three passages that refer to *Israēlitēs*: Rom 9:4, 11:1, and 2 Cor 11:22, and 16 instances of the term *Israēl*. The latter occurs twice each in Rom 9:6 and 9:27, and once (each) in Rom 9:31, 10:19, 21, 11:2, 7, 5, 26, 1 Cor 10:18, 2 Cor 3:7, 13, Gal 6:16, and Phil 3:8. The distribution is also quite remarkable. Of these 19 instances in total, no fewer than 13 are found in the Rom 9–11 section, which can be considered a "self-contained line of thought" and which regards "the paradoxical reality of election" and thus also the "question of Israel's fate."[19]

Thematically, it is fairly clear that this is connected to at least Phil 3:5 and 2 Cor 11:22. In the former, Paul says he must—rhetorically—"boast" (see esp. Phil 3:3–4) of being and/or coming from "the people of Israel, [. . .] the tribe of Benjamin," among other things. The claim is similar in 2 Cor 11, where the apostle indulges in a "foolishness-speech" (see vv. 16–33), and there he refers to opponents—or "fools" (v. 19)—in verse 22 like this: "Are they Hebrews? So am I! Are they Israelites? So am I! Are they Abraham's descendants? So am I!" In a certain sense, in part based on the *en sarki* in Phil

3:3–4 and the *kata sarka* in 2 Cor 11:18, we could also include 1 Cor 10:18 in this series. Following references to the desert generation (see vv. 1–13), and particularly the negative events associated with them (see vv. 5–10/13), this example begins: "Consider the Israel *kata sarka*!" Also related are the examples in 2 Cor 3:7 and 13, which refer to the situation of Moses and the people after the creation of the new stone tablets—in other words, to the situation of Exod 34:29–35. The verses of 2 Cor 3 explain the significance that the "radiance of" Moses' "face" (v. 7) and the "veil over his face" (v. 13) had and/or still has for "the sons of Israel."

In Rom 9–11 itself, the *Israēlitai* (9:4), as well as Paul, the *Israēlitēs* (11:1), clearly have a positive connotation. The statement in 11:26, namely that "all Israel will be saved," must of course be seen similarly. As an "eschatological" "solution," it is in a sense opposed to several much more cautious formulations. The latter describe a partial "hardening" of "Israel" (11:25, also 11:7) and include a critical—though not overcritical—statement of Elijah (11:2 [–5]), and other equally critical and moreover biblically based opinions, 10:19, (20–)21 and 9:27(–28). Embedded here, in 9:31, is the following assessment: "the people of Israel, who pursued the law of righteousness, has not attained the law." Towards the beginning, in 9:6, the apostle—freely translated —states: "Not all who are descended from Israel are Israel."[20]

The genitive conjunction "the Israel of God," which is used in Gal 6:16, has not yet come up in our present overview. But it should probably also be considered, not least in light of the other 18 proto-Pauline instances. Reference here is frequently made to Rom 9:6 in particular, as well as to 1 Cor 10:18.[21]

Rom 9:6, 1 Cor 10:18, and Gal 6:16

The first of these three instances—Rom 9:6, 1 Cor 10:18, and Gal 6:16—as just mentioned, does not consider everyone "descended from Israel" to be part of "Israel." The second refers to "the Israel *kata sarka*," and the third offers the expression "the Israel of God." Michael Wolter, for instance, sees a fairly close connection between these formulations. Accordingly, in his 2011 book on Paul,[22] he states:

> Paul distinguishes [. . .] between an "empirical" or "external" Israel (1 Cor 10:18) and a "real" or "actual/true" [in German: eigentliches] Israel that is created solely by *God* and which can be perceived only through the Christian faith's understanding of reality (Gal 6:16). However, it must also be considered

that the "actual/true" Israel of Rom 9:6 and the "Israel of God" in Gal 6:16 have different denotations, namely because they describe different groups of people. In Rom 9:6, Paul is referring to the Christian Jews, and in Gal 6:16 to all Christians.

In my opinion, given the tenuous connection between these three passages, it is essential to build on the distinction made between the "Christian Jews" and the totality of "all Christians." In order to create a precise differentiation here, I will also draw on my "Proposal for a new 'set-theoretical' description of the relevant Pauline terminology," published 2002 under the keyword "Verus Israel."[23] In that paper I defined the following categories Canadians (citizens of Canada), true Canadians ("who particularly emphasize their Canadian-ness"), other (or nominal) Canadians, 'true Canadians' (who feel somehow Canadian despite not having this citizenship) and—now (beginning and ending) with *two* quotation marks!—"true Canadians" (namely people who belong to the group of true Canadians or 'true Canadians'), and I assigned them the letters A, B, C, D, and E as well as the following set-theoretical sketch (which also allows us, for instance, to clearly approach the complement of A [namely the non-Canadians]) (see Figure 8.1.).[24]

(a)

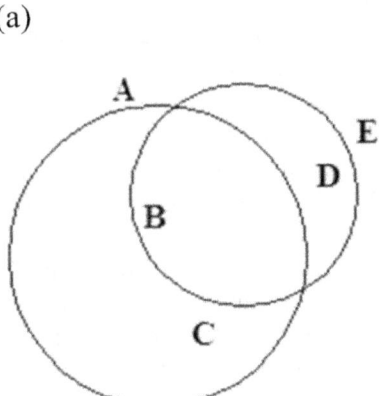

Figure 8.1.

These letters can also be applied analogously to Jews—and naturally also to Israelites (or Israel). The result can then be captured in a graph, i.e., in Figure 8.2.[25]:

(b)

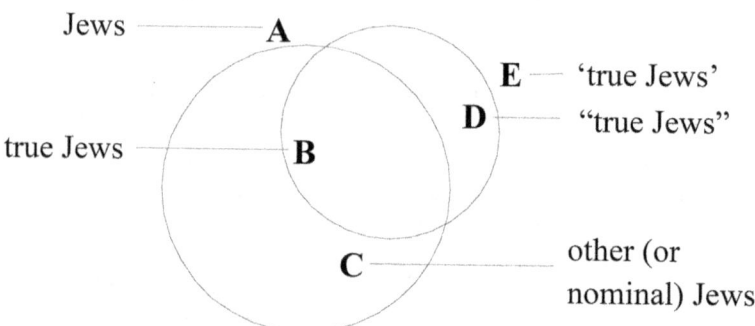

Figure 8.2.

The "set-theoretical" tools (a) and (b) should help us speak more precisely about the three passages under consideration.

Rom 9:6, then, particularly where it says, "not all who are descended from Israel are Israel," is describing a subset of Israel associated with Circle A, namely C; in this regard, we can also think about the complement of C within Circle A, namely B, the true Israelites (and thus of course also about A, the Israelites as a whole) without having to automatically associate them with "the Christian Jews." Thus a connection between C and E, the 'true Israelites,' is not immediately suggested. It follows that Rom 9:6 is not actually meant to evoke the idea of a totality of "all Christians," and so it is not in fact necessary to interpret "the Israel of God" in Gal 6:16 as referring to this particular community.

The expression "the Israel *kata sarka*" in *1 Cor 10:18*, if we consider the preceding context (see once again vv. 1–13, esp. vv. 5–10/13), initially also brings us to something like Circle-segment C, since Paul speaks here about "most of them"—in other words, of those who were all "under the cloud and [. . .] passed through the sea" (vv. 2–3) during the Mosaic era—with whom "God was *not* pleased" (v. 5). Here, too, then, there is no direct connection to E. Though verses 6–13 (see esp. v. 6 [*typoi*] and v. 11 [*typikōs*]) clearly accentuate the "typological" relevance of the occurrences during and after the exodus from Egypt, this does not simply mean a transfer to E. Rather, it has to do with the illustrative nature of C and B's interrelations and oppositions, as well as with the illustrative nature of the "subset" C.[26] For instance, verse 10 (see also v. 9) states, "do not grumble, as some of them did—and were killed by the destroying angel." Therefore it is also more logical to consider the Circle-segment B for the expression "Israel according to the spirit"—

suggested by the formulation "the Israel *kata sarka*"—;[27] this would then serve as a "typos," specifically for an "antitypos" within E.

So Rom 9:6 and 1 Cor 10:18 yield almost nothing in terms of "the Israel of God" in Gal 6:16. It is also far from obvious that the genitive "of God" here could simply be a clear reference to (even) a metaphorically understood usage of this syntagm. For, as Christiane Zimmermann puts it,[28] "the addition of the genitive attribute *tou theou* does not indicate a redefinition of Israel, since comparable attributes that express God's particular closeness with Israel—integrated into a blessing as in Gal 6:16—can be found in early Jewish documents," e.g., in Ps 125:2, 5 (LXX: Ps 124:2, 5), which states (in v. 5), "Peace be on Israel," immediately following a reference in verse 2 in which it says "his [the Lord's] people" (cf. Ps 127[128]:1, 5, 6).

In any case, our overview of the findings in the proto-Pauline texts has shown that in each case—three times—the gentilic *Israēlitēs* refers to persons who can be ethnically categorized as Jews (or to one such person, Paul). In addition, the word *Israēl*, at least outside Gal 6:16, also consistently applies to this ethnos—naturally also in Rom 10:1. Even Rom 9:6 and 1 Cor 10:18, as we just observed, are—technically speaking—discussing C, and in a certain sense perhaps also even B, but not D or E. Therefore we must ask whether Gal 6:16, and *only* Gal 6:16, is different—in other words, whether this passage could potentially be referring to non-Jews or *also* to non-Jews.

Synchronous and diachronous observations on Gal 6:16

Synchronous Observations

It seems appropriate here to briefly mention at least the most important pieces of relevant data—and, in light of earlier papers that touch on or address the topic,[29] this may even suffice. First we will make a few observations about Gal 6:15–16 before shifting our focus to earlier statements made in the Letter to the Galatians, so that by gradually expanding our perspective, we can ultimately also look at the letter as a whole.

In *6:15–16*, the wish for peace in verse 16—for "all who follow this 'rule'"—naturally stands out. The standard for this is set in the previous verse 15, as follows: "Neither circumcision nor uncircumcision means anything; what counts is the new creation." This is so striking (following the very similar statement in 5:6, which also refers to "Christ Jesus") that the wish for peace is an obvious successor. However, the proximity and succession of "peace" and "mercy"—i.e., the nouns connected (among other things) by *kai* and following *stoichēsousin*—is less obvious.[30] For another thing, the role of *kai* in the phrase "*and* over the Israel of God," placed behind *eleos*—the role of the third *kai*, in v. 16—is disputed. Should it be understood as epexegetic, explanatory, or is it attempting to add something new?[31] Now, while "the reading order of the verse [. . .] shows that the first *kai* is a simple copula between the clauses, [. . .] *eirēnē* and *eleos*, on the other hand, are linked as subjects by the second *kai*"; and "the third *kai* is overshooting," says Christiane Zimmermann.[32] We must make a similar judgment, in part because the combination of "peace" and "mercy" found in verse 16 "is not an exception insofar as in Paul with respect to the conclusions of the letters at least 'a quite large regularity' can be detected and insofar as in these conclusions often 'another benediction occurs before the concluding wish for grace,' which for the most part speaks of 'the God . . . of peace' (see Rom [15:33 and] 16:20; 2 Cor 13:11; Phil 4:7, 9 [and 4:19]; 1 Thess 5:23 [. . .])—so that in these cases *eirēnē* stands before *charis*."[33]

Since the term *Israēl*—and of course also the syntagm "the Israel of God"—does not occur in the Letter to the Galatians before 6:16, as mentioned earlier,[34] it has not been introduced. And, unlike the descendancy from Abraham and the characterization as being sons of God,[35] no groundwork is or has been laid to suggest that the (non-Jewish) addressees of the Letter to the Galatians (see 4:8–10) could somehow be part of Israel.[36] So there is no reason to interpret the third *kai* in the verse (6:16) as having an epexegetic role.[37] The term "the Israel of God" would thus indicate ethnic Jews, and the future *stoichēsousin* was probably chosen not least in order to express some kind of eschatological hopes for the Jewish people.[38] Thus Paul, in this fairly polemical letter (see, for instance, 1:6–9; 5:12), at least towards the end, is not found to be making an anti-Jewish argument. Quite the contrary!

Looking at the whole passage 6:11–18, written personally by Paul (see once again 6:11), two traits can easily be combined to underpin an ethnic understanding of the syntagm "the Israel of God" that is used in verse 16. This letter in 6:11–13 for the first time explicitly[39] accuses Paul's "opponents" of requiring the circumcision of Galatian (Gentile) Christians. Thus the idea of "oppositional" Judaizing Jewish Christians—of Jews!—is at least obvious.[40] It also, as indicated by the juxtaposition of 2:3 and 3:28, raises the issue of Jewish identity and being Jewish.[41] Secondly, it is noteworthy—especially *in contrast* to the other proto-Paulines[42]—that the final verse, 6:18, describes the (at least largely) Gentile Christian addressees specifically as *adelphoi*, as "brothers." *If* the previous term "the Israel of God" had referred to the Jewish people, this *adelphoi*-anomaly would naturally be quite understandable. After all, an eschatocol is generally expected, as a rule, to refer to the addressees.

Without a doubt, the corresponding wish that "the grace of our Lord Jesus Christ be with your spirit, brothers," and the explicit mention of these "brothers," would fit in here *if* this formulation had immediately been preceded by some kind of a hopeful word with regard to the Jewish people—i.e., with regard to another group.[43]

Now let us quickly turn our attention to *5:2–6:10*. In these verses, Paul treats the intended circumcisions (of [or among] Gentiles) in a remarkably coarse manner (see 5:2, 12).[44] However, this by no means signifies that he also had a negative opinion of Jewish ethics—namely, the ethics of the Torah. Rather, the section emphasizes the behavioral principles indicated by the *nomos*. In particular, this highlights its focus on the commandment to love, which is named in 5:13 according to Lev 19:18 (LXX), in the sense of a summary of the "law." This seems to be also the case in 6:2 (cf. 6:6, 10[45]); here the phrase "the law of Christ" should be understood in the light of the strongly emphasized connection between the faithful and Christ as well as *agapan* in 2:20. Accordingly, located in a sense between 5:13–15 and 6:2 (or 6:1–10), we find the ground rule, formulated in the indicative present[46] in 5:25: "If we live in the Spirit, let us also walk in the Spirit."

Often, *4:21–5:1*, the Hagar-Sara "allegory" (see 4:24) was and is still understood in an anti-Judaic sense, "equating Hagar with the Jewish people and obedience to the law, and Sara with 'Christianity' and freedom from the law."[47] However, the warning expressed in 5:1, using *palin* in a restitutive sense[48] and regarding a return to "bondage," also refers to Galatian *Gentile* Christians, as the context (see 4:8–10) makes clear. Therefore, "the birth of the 'free' has nothing to do with ethnicity."[49] And Paul, the Jew (2:15), includes himself by the first person plural, along with the Gentile Christian addressees of the letter, the "brothers," in the group of the free—the Sara group: "So, brothers, we are not children of the slave but of the free woman" (4:31).[50] In light of this pericope, it is thus difficult to claim anti-Judaism here.

Now let us attempt to survey the entire section of the letter which begins with the less-than-sedate salutation "Oh, you foolish Galatians!"—i.e. *3:1, 6:17–18*. Here—as well as for the observational steps that follow—it may be helpful to include a structural tableau (see Table 8.1) that I used in the 2016 *Festschrift* for Friedrich Wilhelm Horn:[51]

Table 8.1.

PRÄSKRIPT (1,1–5)		
Wende im Leben des Verfassers (1,6–2,14)		
PROOEMIUM (1,6–10)/NARRATIO (1,11–2,14) – endend mit PARTITIO (2,14b)		
Wende im Leben von Judenchristen (2,15–21)		
ARGUMENTATIO I		
2,15–17a: die durch Christus bedingte Wende (Stichwort: ouketi [2,20!])	2,17b–18: die Gefahr des Rückschritts dahinter (Stichwort: restitutives palin [V. 18])	2,19–21: das durch Christus bestimmte Leben (sprachl. Indiz: Präsens [V. 20])
Wende im Leben von Heidenchristen (3,1–6,17)		
ARGUMENTATIO II		
3,1–4,7: die durch Christus bedingte Wende	4,8–5,1: die Gefahr des Rückschritts dahinter	5,2–6,17: das durch Christus bestimmte Leben
(Stichwort: ouketi [3,18.25; 4,7])	(Stichwort: restitutives palin [4,9b; 5,1])	(sprachl. Indiz: Präsens [5,25])
3,1–14 (3,13: „Wir"; 3,14a: ethné) 3,15–29 (3,23–25: „Wir"; 3,26–29: „Ihr")	4,8–11: Freiheit/ Knechtschaft	5,2–12 (u.a.: Beschneidung?)
	4,12–20: (u.a.: Gefahr des Ausgeschlossenwerdens [V. 17])	5,13–6,10 (u.a.: Liebe/ Gesetz)
4,1–7 (4,3.5b: „Wir"; 4,6a: „Ihr")	4,21–5,1: Freiheit/Knechtschaft; Gefahr des douleuein (V. 25; [vgl. V. 8f.]; anders V. 3: Passiv von douloun)	6,11–17 (Beschneidungsfreiheit/Heilsgeschichte)
ESCHATOKOLL (6,18)		

The first thing that strikes us here is that the ethical passage 5:2–6:17—which, as mentioned above,[52] is characterized not least by the use of the present tense in 5:25—is preceded by several paragraphs that are somewhat different. There is one section addressing the risk of regression, recognizable—as also mentioned earlier[53]—by the restitutive *palin* in 5:1 as well as in 4:9b—namely, 4:8–5:1— and another section, 3:1–4:7, that discusses the previous—and now apparently threatened—"turning point caused by Christ" among the (Gentile Christian) addressees. In order to answer our question about whether the Letter to the Galatians supports an ethnic understanding of the syntagm "the Israel of God" as found in 6:16, it is now particularly important to note that the argumentative structure of 3:1–4:7 can already be determined by the *ouketi* in

3:18; 3:25, and 4:7, which the restitutive *palin* of 4:9b and 5:1 opposes in the sense of annulling what has been achieved (through the "turning point"). In my opinion—and not only mine[54]—what seems very important is what I describe, following an essay of Terrence L. Donaldson.[55] It hints at another triple transition, namely the transition from the Judeo-Christian "we" (3:13; 3:23–25; 4:25b) to the corporation of the *ethne* (3:14a), the non-Jews, or to the addressees indicated by "*you* (pl.)" (3:26–29; 4:6a).[56] The point here, as Donaldson in my opinion correctly states, is the "idea found, e.g. in Tob 14:5–7 and in the Book of Isaiah, regarding the 'inclusion of non-Jews'" in the salvific history that begins in the Jewish realm.[57] In other words, according to Gal 3:1–4:7, God's actions are clearly determined by a kind of preference for the Jewish people. An ethnic denotation of the expression "the Israel of God" in 6:16 and a corresponding understanding of the here formulated wish for such a community would fit in harmoniously here.

In *2:15–21*, a very densely formulated passage, we find the same sequence of a "turning point," "risk of regression thereafter," and "life determined by Christ," which also characterizes 3:1–6:17. In fact 2:15–17a precedes 2:17b–18 (see v. 18: restitutive *palin*) and 2:19–21 (see v. 20: present tense) in this sense—even if *ouketi* does not appear before verse 20.[58] Since here, according to 2:15, the discussion is of Jews by nature who, as it says in 2:16–17, "have found [themselves] among the sinners" due to an encounter with "Christ Jesus,"[59] this prioritizing of Jewish Christian experience over that of Gentile Christians—in other words of 2:15–21 over 3:1–6:17—significantly strengthens the emphasis on salvific history, that was already to observe in 3:1–4:7,[60] along with the ethnic interpretation of the phrase in 6:16 that concerns us.

Verses *1:6–2:14*, as we have seen, introduce the two "turning point" passages, 2:15–21 and 3:1–6:17, and this with a few autobiographical statements. Naturally, it is impossible to carry out a detailed exegesis of the section here. But this much is clear in any case: the subject also is a kind of "turning point," a "turning point in the life of the author," namely in connection with an appropriate understanding of the Gospel of Christ (see 1:7; cf. 1:6; 2:2, 5, 7, 14). Paul learned of this "through a revelation of Jesus Christ" (1:[11–]12), and it transformed the man who according to 1:13–14 had advanced very far within *Ioudaismos*[61]—and had "persecuted the church of God"—who had even been "extremely zealous for the traditions of my [i.e., his] fathers." The revelation from the God who in a sense had watched over him "in my [i.e., his] mother's womb" (1:15), particularly moved Paul to "preach him [i.e., God's son] among the Gentiles" (1:16). In this area, there is no shortage of confusion under "Jews" (see 2:13, 14; cf. 2:15), and we also find the problem of "Judaizing Gentiles/non-Jews" (see 2:14: *ioudaizein*, furthermore: *Ioudaikōs*). The Pauline "turning point," too—behind which, according to 1:1–5, we find "God the Father," who "raised him," Jesus Christ, "from the dead" (v. 1)—

speaks to an ethnic understanding of the expression "the Israel of God" that is used in 6:16. (S. G.) "Eastman pointed out the clear parallels that exist in a non-metaphorical reading [of this syntagm] between Paul's biography, i.e. his calling while still in his mother's womb, and the revelation of Christ through God, and his hope of a corresponding revelation for the Israel of God in the Letter to the Galatians."[62] This result of our synchronous observations, which will shortly also be considered from a diachronous perspective, particularly on the expression "the Israel of God" in 6:16, may be represented by another graphic (Figure 8.3.):[63]

(c)

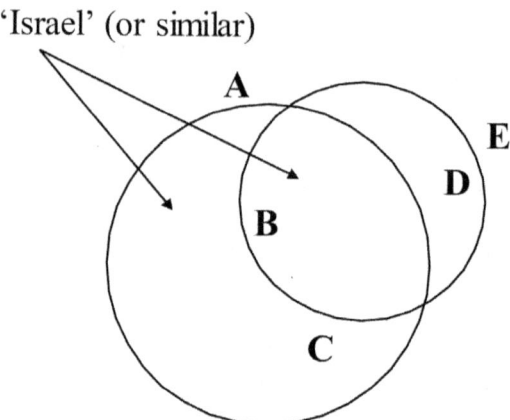

Figure 8.3.

This—at least preliminary—result is all the more noteworthy because it is *not* analogous to other conceptual contexts relating to Judaism, at least within the proto-Paulines. With regard to being sons of God (see [once again] 3:26) or descendants from Abraham (see [once again] 3:29), this may be observed in the Letter to the Galatians.[64] The circumstances may be illustrated more generally as follows (Figure 8.4.):[65]

(d)

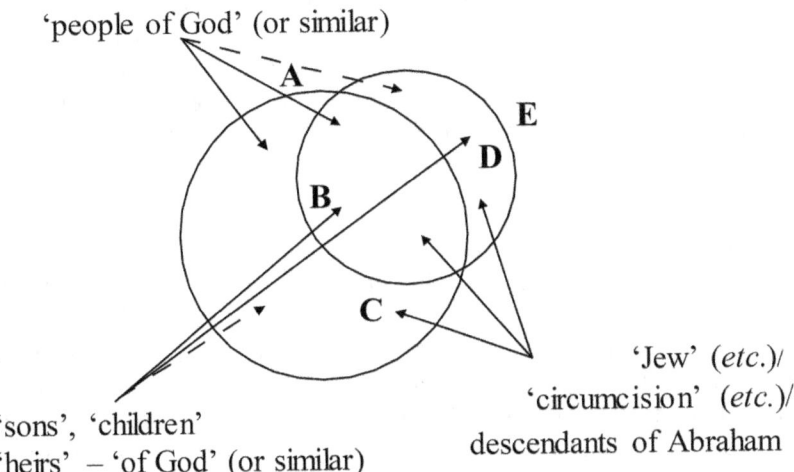

Figure 8.4.

For the most part, it will suffice if I cite a brief earlier explanation of this graphic:[66]

> It indicates that in his vocabulary concerning Judaism, Paul, at least to a large extent, knows in addition to a literal understanding also something like a transferred application (i.e., so to speak, particularly also for the subset D). This is unquestionably the case with the word *Ioudaios* (see Rom. 2.28–29), also with the circumcision terminology and the conceptualization of descent from Abraham (see Rom. 2.26, 29; 4.17–18). In a weakened manner it is in particular valid for the 'sons', 'children' and 'heirs' of God (see Rom. 8.14-21), though, however, even with Gal. 4.1–5 '[a] candid characterization of all Jews—. . . also the ones belonging to the subset C—as heirs of God (or also as his sons or children) is . . . not' simple to state. Things are somewhat different with the expression 'people of God', more exact: with 'my [i.e., God's] people' (Rom. 9.25,26), respectively with 'his [i.e., God's] people' (Rom. 11.1, 2; 15.10; 2 Cor. 6.16); because here, despite Rom. 9.25–26, a clear reference to non-Jews is not at all given, and so Paul says in Rom. 15.10 with regard to Deut. 32.42 that the nations should rejoice with his, that is, with God's people—with the Jews. When the apostle goes back to the Old Testament here and also in his five other 'people of God' instances, it fits in a certain sense with the fact that Paul does not, seen from a traditional-historical point of view, break ranks too with the other terms of this tableau.

We can round out this quotation and the graphic (d) with a few other comparable non-Pauline passages. For the concept outlined at bottom right, see Jer 4:4 (see also Deut 10:16; 30:6); for the concept at bottom left, let us mention only *Jos. Asen.* 19:8, and for the syntagm mentioned above, the "people of God," Zech 2:11. These brief notations[67] already involve diachronous aspects. Such observations will now a bit more thoroughly be pursued, as mentioned earlier, with regard to the words *Israēl* and *Israēlitēs*.

Diachronous Observations

Two things remain to be studied from a diachronous perspective. For one, the use of the term *Israēl* in particular, up to the time of the Apostle Paul, must be considered. The question is whether it makes sense, given the relevant findings, to relate the syntagm "the Israel of God" (found in Gal 6:16) to a Jewish community. For another, we will pursue the occasionally posited thesis that "the Israel of God" is a kind of "neologism," breaking open the linguistic customs of the time at least a little bit. It makes sense to begin with the latter problem.

The theory that this term "Israel" is a new coinage was already suggested above—i.e., in M. Wolter's statements on the "Israel of God" in Gal 6:16.[68] Gordon D. Fee is very explicit about this New Testament passage: "Those who follow him," Christ, "are now designated by Paul with this neologism: they are God's Israel, the real thing."[69] However, a closer look forces us to conclude that, while the term "the Israel of God" seems not to appear anywhere before Gal 6:16 (nor in any other places in the proto-Paulines), this phrase is clearly suggested by Jewish formulations. We have already mentioned Ps 125 (LXX: Ps 124) and Ps 128 (LXX: Ps 127).[70] Ps 124(125):5 and Ps 127(128):6 each include the phrase *eirēnē epi ton Israēl*, and in the first example the group has previously (in Ps 124[125]:2) been described as "his people," the people of the "Lord" (cf. Ps 127[128]:1, 4, 5). For this reason alone, we have to judge that the "expression *ho Israēl tou theou*" used in Gal 6:16 "cannot be considered unprepared."[71] Aside from the fact that both psalms—like Gal 6:(15–)16 (see once again *stoichēsousin* [future])—feature a moment of futurity (see Ps 124[125]:1–2; 127[128]:2), this is also significant for the comparison with the Letter to the Galatians in that the wish for peace *concludes* both Ps 124(125) and Ps 127(128).[72] The same is also true in two Hebrew documents, of which the second—and possibly also the earlier one—is a letter.[73] 4QMMT C30–31, in other words the last (two) lines of this much-discussed (reconstructed) Qumran text, which mentions "the end of the time" in C30 in a quite hopeful tone, includes a two-part statement: "[. . .] for your own welfare and for the welfare of Israel."[74] "Similarly, at the end of a far less religious letter composed during the Bar Kochba revolt [. . .] it says:

'Best wishes [. . .] to you and all Beth-Israel' (papMur 42:7)," where "you" means "the addressee, Yeshua son of Galgula (line 2)."[75] In short, the expression "the Israel of God" in Gal 6:16 is not really a neologism, and the syntagm fits very nicely—especially as the second element of a wish relating to the future—in the conclusion of a letter written by a Jew (see once again 2:15).[76]

Peter J. Tomson presented a thorough and thoughtful study in 1986 on the (early) Jewish use of the word "Israel" in particular (namely, "The Names Israel and Jew in Ancient Judaism and in the New Testament").[77] Discussing it here would exceed the limitations of the present chapter. However, it can and should be said that in this material, "confined to the Persian and Greco-Roman periods,"[78] "the Jewish speech duality" is noteworthy: with "'Israel' as the inner-Jewish name and 'Jew' as the outside self-designation." Thus it is permissible "to make a general division of the various categories of ancient Jewish texts into texts with an inner-Jewish framework and those written in a non-Jewish perspective." In this context, many of the New Testament writings can be understood such that "the Jewish speech duality, i.e. the socially distinct use of both names, operates in the New Testament as it does in the Jewish writings."[79] For the Corpus Paulinum, the negatively connoted use of *Ioudaios* or *Ioudaikos* in 1 Thess 2:14(–15) and in Tit 1:14 falls out of the frame.[80] However, this is not the case for the term *Israēl*, even in the Gal 6:16 example.[81] Where Paul is concerned, Tomson says: "It is his use of the name Israel which is most interesting. It designates the people of Israel, to which he himself belongs. He does use this inner-Jewish name, however, in communication with non-Jewish Christians. This transcends the limits of the Jewish speech duality [. . .]: In Paul's approach, the name Israel evokes a dynamic of identification which encompasses gentile Christians. In other words, gentiles are invited to call the Jews by the cherished inner-Jewish name of the Covenant People: Israel."[82] This, he says, does not correspond at all to the linguistic use within the church, since "the Church reserved for itself the 'inside' name of Israel, leaving the Jews their 'outside' name as a dishonour."[83] Of course, "Paul's approach has invited much misunderstanding, and this happened from an early stage on [. . .]. The most prominent misunderstanding is that for Paul the name Israel would represent a spiritual reality only."[84]

What Tomson expresses regarding the (early) Jewish use of the word "Israel" in particular is largely convincing,[85] and in my opinion,[86] one must also agree with what he says about the proto-Paulines beyond Gal 6:16. If only because Gal 6:16, as we stated earlier, fits in with some concluding remarks seen in the Psalter as well as with 4QMMT C30–31 and papMur 42:7, the expression "the Israel of God" as found in Gal 6:16 must also necessarily be interpreted as referring to ethnic Jews.

REVIEW AND OUTLOOK

A few short concluding observations will suffice. If the syntagm "the Israel of God" used in Gal 6:16 means (ethnic) Jews, and the verse wishes them "peace [. . .] and mercy" ([evidently:] from God) as was just granted to those Christians who "will walk" according to the "canon" of v. 15 ("neither circumcision nor uncircumcision means anything; what counts is the new creation"), then this doubtless corresponds to the constellation and the moment of hope in Rom 9–11, particularly Rom 11:25–32/36. Thus it would be difficult to argue that Paul's arguments become "Israel-friendly" only in the time after the Letter to the Galatians, but not yet in the letter to the Galatian communities. This text, which admittedly does not dispense with a polemical tone (see once again, for example, Gal 5:12), is unquestionably what G. Schrenk calls a "fighting epistle."[87] But its structure and its statements—and in my opinion, the passage Gal 3:19–20 (and/or 3:15/16–20/22) is no exception[88]—are nonetheless largely determined by the idea of a "salvific history" that particularly also applies to Jewish matters. In addition, a positive expectation for "Israel," for "the Israel of God," is definitively not abandoned in this letter. Thus the idea of "anti-Judaism" cannot be claimed here[89]—in part also because of the "blessing" in Gal 6:16.[90]

Of course, scholarship on the Letter to the Galatians in particular, as previously addressed, often sees things differently. Justin's *Dialogue with Trypho* (see once again *Dial.* 11:5) is informative here—namely, the "great hiatus between Gal. 6:16 and Justin's *Dialogue*."[91] P. Richardson thus begins his monograph "Israel in the Apostolic Church" with the following sentence: "The word 'Israel' is applied to the Christian Church for the first time by Justin Martyr *c.* A.D. 160."[92] Many centuries, as shown by hymns and exegetical scriptures/studies, provide analogous examples. (These in turn have shaped European as well as non-European history, often in a very detrimental way.) One important reason for this is clearly sociological. As P. J. Tomson says, "Christianity evolved from a Jewish messianic sect into a religion of non-Jews," and he concludes that this is associated with "a decisively ambivalent attitude to the Jews and their tradition."[93] This can also be graphically illustrated (and in a bit more detail), as I showed (first in 2002[94] and) most recently in 2017,[95] once again using "set theory" Circles in which the primarily white areas represent Jews and the gray areas—shaded only to make them more identifiable—represent Christians (not least: Gentile Christians).

"What can be understood in 'situation (i)' [Figure 8.5] as a friendly or lively exchange within a single societal entity that usually includes differing movements may be very different given the assumptions for 'situation (ii)' [Figure 8.6]: namely as a statement directed against the society—Judaism—with which the

(i) (ii)

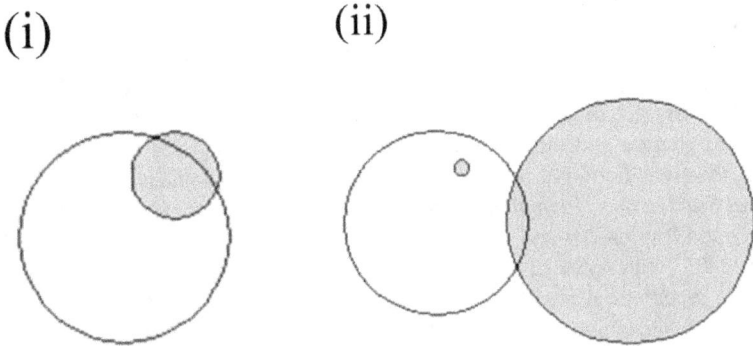

Figure 8.5.   **Figure 8.6.**

connection has almost vanished due to the significant increase in the number of Gentile Christians."[96] This supports the idea that we now—after the Holocaust, which *also* did entail a significant sociological shift—can come to a better understanding of many biblical texts. This is true at least for the Pauline word *Israēl*, and particularly for its use in Gal 6:16.

NOTES

1. See, for instance, Michael Bachmann, "Paulus," in *Der Neue Pauly. Supplemente 8. Historische Gestalten der Antike: Rezeption in Literatur, Kunst und Musik*, ed. Peter von Möllendorff, Annette Simonis, and Linda Simonis (Stuttgart/Weimar: J. B. Metzler, 2013), 735–750, 735: "Nicht weniger als 13nt. Briefe nennen P. als Absender; davon gelten heute zumeist 7 als authentisch: Röm; 1/2Kor; Gal; Phil; 1Thess; Phlm"—i.e., the proto-Paulines. Cf. Bachmann, "The Anti-Judaic Moment in the 'Pauline' Doctrine of Justification—A (Protestant) Misinterpretation of the Relevant Statements in Paul's Letters," in *The Message of Paul the Apostle within Second-Temple Judaism*, ed. František Ábel (Lanham, MD: Lexington Books/Fortress Academic, 2019), 21–59, 31–32.

2. Udo Schnelle, "Gibt es eine Entwicklung in der Rechtfertigungslehre vom Galater–zum Römerbrief?" in *Paulus—Werk und Wirkung. Festschrift für Andreas Lindemann zum 70. Geburtstag*, ed. Paul-Gerhard Klumbies and David S. du Toit (Tübingen: Mohr Siebeck, 2013), 303 (289–309). Cf. Michael Theobald, "'Geboren aus dem Samen Davids . . .' (Röm 1, 3). Wandlungen im paulinischen Christus-Bild?" *Zeitschrift für Neues Testament* 102 (2011): 235–60, especially 259–60.

3. See Schnelle, "Entwicklung in der Rechtfertigungslehre," especially 296–97, 303–4.

4. Hans Dieter Betz, *Der Galaterbrief. Ein Kommentar zum Brief des Apostels Paulus an die Gemeinden in Galatien*, trans. Sibylle Ann. Hermeneia (Munich: Chr. Kaiser, 1988), 546. It is stated a little bit differently in the English original: "Gottlob Schrenk

argues that the term must refer to 'Jewish Christianity'" (H. D. Betz, *Galatians. A Commentary on Paul's Letter to the Churches of Galatia*. Hermeneia [Philadelphia, PA: Fortress Press, 1979], 322). Cf. also Gottlob Schrenk, "Was bedeutet 'Israel Gottes'?" *Judaica* 5 (1949): 81–94, esp. 93; Schrenk, "Der Segenswunsch nach der Kampfepistel. Antwort," *Judaica* 6 (1950): 170–90, esp. 182, 185. See also Michael Bachmann, "The Church and the Israel of God: On the Meaning and Ecclesiastical Relevance of the Benediction at the End of Galatians," in *Anti-Judaism in Galatians? Exegetical Studies on a Polemical Letter and on Paul's Theology*, trans. Robert L. Brawley (Grand Rapids, MI and Cambridge, U.K.: Eerdmans, 2009 [1999]), 85–100, 176–95, 102–03 (with notes 13–17).

5. See Peter Richardson, *Israel in the Apostolic Church*. MSSNTS 10 (Cambridge: Cambridge University Press, 1964), 74–84, esp. 82 ("Israel is not yet the Christ-believing Jews, it is those who are still to believe") and 84 ("The 'Israel of God' is, when Galatians was written, a part of the Israelite nation").

6. Citations: H. D. Betz, *Galatians*, 322.

7. Betz, Galatians, (322–)323. For more on (older) advocates of such an opinion see Bachmann, "The Church and the Israel of God," 102 with note 12; and on interpretations differing from these positions see Bachmann, "The Church," 103 with note 17. Cf. Paula Fredriksen, "The Question of Worship: Gods, Pagans, and the Redemption of Israel," in *Paul within Judaism. Restoring the First-Century Context to the Apostle*, ed. Mark D. Nanos and Magnus Zetterholm (Minneapolis, MN: Fortress Press, 2015), 195 (175–201).

8. Cf, for instance: Frank J. Matera, *Galatians*. Sacra Pagina 9 (Collegeville, MN: The Liturgical Press, 1992), 226–27; Ferdinand Hahn, "Die Stellung des Paulus zum Judentum und zur Tora," in *Die Verwurzelung des Christentums im Judentum: Exegetische Beiträge zum christlich-jüdischen Gespräch. Ferdinand Hahn zum 70. Geburtstag*, ed. Cilliers Breytenbach (Neukirchen-Vluyn: Neukirchener Verlag, 1996), 95 (85–98); J. Louis Martyn, *Galatians*, Anchor Bible 33A (New York, NY: Doubleday, 1997), (574–)577; Atsuhiro Asano. *Community-Identity Construction in Galatians: Exegetical, Social-Anthropological and Socio-Historical Studies*. JSNT.S 285 (London/New York, NY: T&T Clark, 2005), 217 (with note 32); Gordon D. Fee, *Galatians*. Pentecostal Commentary (Dorset, U.K.: Deo Publishing, 2007), 253; Wilfried Eckey, *Der Galaterbrief* (Neukirchen-Vluyn: Neukirchener Verlagsanstalt, 2010), 334; Douglas J. Moo, *Galatians*. Baker Exegetical Commentary (Grand Rapids, MI: Baker Academic, 2013), 400–403; Mark A. Seifrid, "Answered Lament: Paul's Gospel, Israel, and the Scriptures in Romans," in *Paulinische Schriftrezeption. Grundlagen—Ausprägungen—Wirkungen—Wertungen*, ed. Florian Wilk and Markus Öhler. FRLANT 268 (Göttingen/Bristol, CT: Vandenhoeck & Ruprecht, 2017), 210 n. 105 (175–215).

9. See: Andreas Lindemann, "Israel und sein 'Land' im Neuen Testament," in *Glauben, Handeln, Verstehen. Studien zur Auslegung des Neuen Testaments II*. WUNT 282 (Tübingen: Mohr Siebeck, 2011), 149–89 (first [a little bit differently] 1999, 157–58), 172; Susan Grove Eastman, "Israel and the Mercy of God: A Re-reading of Galatians 6.16 and Romans 9–11," *NTS* 56 (2010): 367–95, esp. 385–89, 394; Christiane Zimmermann, "Kirche und Israel Gottes im Galaterbrief," in *Mazel Tov. Interdisziplinäre Beiträge zum Verhältnis von Christentum und Judentum. Festschrift*

anlässlich des 50. Geburtstages des Instituts Kirche und Judentum, ed. Markus Witte and Tanja Pilger (Leipzig: Evangelische Verlagsanstalt, 2012), 121–40, esp. 132–34 (see also Christiane Zimmerman, *Gott und seine Söhne. Das Gottesbild des Galaterbriefs*. WMANT 135 [Neukirchen-Vluyn: Evangelische Verlagsanstalt, 2013], 133–41); John M. G. Barclay, *Paul and the Gift* (Grand Rapids, MI/Cambridge, U.K.: Eerdmans, 2015), 420–21 with note 73. Cf. also Hermann L. Strack and Paul Billerbeck, *Kommentar zum Neuen Testament aus Talmud und Midrasch*, Volume 3: Die Briefe des Neuen Testaments und die Offenbarung des Johannis (Munich: C. H. Beck'sche Verlagsbuchhandlung, 1926), 578–79; Franz Mussner, *Der Galaterbrief*. HThK 9 (Freiburg/Basel/Vienna: Herder, 1974), 417; Frederick F. Bruce, *The Epistle of Paul to the Galatians. A Commentary on the Greek Text* (Exeter: Paternoster Press, 1982), 274–75; Peter J. Tomson, "The Names Israel and Jew in Ancient Judaism and in the New Testament," *Bijdragen* 47 (1986): 285 (266–289); James D. G. Dunn, *The Epistle to the Galatians*. Black's New Testament Commentaries (London: A&C Black, 1995), 343–46; Kjell Arne Morland, *The Rhetoric of Curse in Galatians. Paul Confronts Another Gospel*. Emory Studies in Early Christianity 5 (Atlanta, GA: Scholars Press, 1995), 232–33; Francesco Bianchini, *Lettera ai Galati. Nuovo Testamento—commento esegetico e spiritual* (Roma: Città Nuova Editrice, 2009), 162; Peter Oakes, *Galatians. Paideia Commentaries on the New Testament* (Grand Rapids, MI: Baker Academic, 2015), 192. Also the conference-paper of Paula Fredriksen, "'And Peace upon the Israel of God': A Non-Reformation Reading of Paul's Letter," supports the thesis (cf. already Fredriksen, *Paul, the Pagans' Apostle* [New Haven, CT, and London, U.K.: Yale University Press, 2017], 67–68 [with note 12] and 114 [with note 39]).

10. Bachmann, "The Church and the Israel of God" (first: 1999). Cf. also: Bachmann, "Bemerkungen zur Auslegung zweier Genitivverbindungen des Galaterbriefs: 'Werke des Gesetzes' (Gal 2,16 u.ö.) und 'Israel Gottes' (Gal 6,16)," in *Von Paulus zur Apokalypse—und weiter. Exegetische und rezeptionsgeschichtliche Studien zum Neuen Testament (including English summaries)*. NTOA/StUNT 91 (Göttingen and Oakville, CT: Vandenhoeck & Ruprecht, 2011), 277–95 (first: 2010), 287–95; Bachmann, "Paul, Israel and the Gentiles: Hermeneutical and Exegetical Notes," in *Paul and Judaism. Crosscurrents in Pauline Exegesis and the Study of Jewish-Christian Relations*, ed. Reimund Bieringer and Didier Pollefeyt, Library of New Testament Studies 463 (London: T&T Clark, 2012), 79–89, 103–04 (72–105); Bachmann, "Important and Delicate—Borders according to Paul," in *Borders. Terminologies, Ideologies, and Performances*, ed. Annette Weissenrieder, WUNT 366 (Tübingen: Mohr Siebeck, 2010), 363–68 (359–82); Bachmann, "The 'New Perspective on Paul' und 'The New View of Paul,'" in *Paulus Handbuch*, ed. Friedrich Wilhelm Horn (Tübingen: Mohr Siebeck, 2013), 36 (30–38); Bachmann, "Neues Testament und Antijudaismus—z.B. Bergpredigt und Galaterbrief," in *Update-Exegese 2.1. Ergebnisse gegenwärtiger Bibelwissenschaft*, ed. Wolfgang Kraus, Martin Rösel, mit einem Geleitwort von Heinrich Bedford-Strohm (Leipzig: Evangelische Verlagsanstalt, 2015), 236–48 (first [a little bit differently]: 2014), esp. 244–45; Bachmann, "Zu temporalen Momenten des Galaterbriefs. Beschneidungsfreiheit für Heidenchristen und Heilsgeschichte," in *Paulus und Petrus: Geschichte—Theologie—Rezeption*.

Festschrift für Friedrich Wilhelm Horn zu seinem 60. Geburtstag, ed. Heike Omerzu and Eckart David Schmidt (Leipzig: Evangelische Verlagsanstalt, 2016), 132–34 (101–36); Bachmann, *Das Freiburger Münster und seine Juden* (Regensberg: Schnell & Schneider, 2017), 186, 191–93.

11. Cf. below (at) notes 21–22.

12. Citation(s): Peter Häuser, *Des Heiligen Philosophen und Märtyrers Justins Dialog mit dem Juden Tryphon aus dem Griechischen übersetzt und mit einer Einleitung versehen*. BKV 33 (Kempten/Munich: Verlag der J. Kösel'schen Buchhandlung, 1917), 17–18 (italics: Michael Bachmann) (similarly stated in *Dial*. 123:7–9; 135:3; cf. also 116:3). Peter Richardson, *Israel in the Apostolic Church* (MSSNTS 10 [Cambridge: Cambridge University Press, 1964]) comments: "The transference from Israel to the Church is complete, but, and this point we wish to make, Justin's dialogue with Trypho is the first time in Christian literature that such an explicit claim has been made" (9) (cf. below [at] notes 91–92). Cf. for instance Bachmann, "The Church and the Israel of God," 103.

13. On this see Martin Meiser, *Galater*. Novum Testamentum Patristicum 9 (Göttingen: Vandenhoeck & Ruprecht, 2007), 319 (with notes 102–6) ("Die [. . .] Formel 'Israel Gottes' (Gal 6,16) wird von den Vätern außerhalb der Kommentarliteratur zum Galaterbrief selten rezipiert und m.W. durchgehend auf die Kirche der Glaubenden bezogen")—and also Christopher Levy, *The Letter to the Galatians*. The Bible in Medieval Literature (Grand Rapids, MI and Cambridge, U.K.: Eerdmans, 2011), esp. 130 (Haimo of Auxerre) and (183–)384 (Bruno the Carthusian). Cf. below (at) note 16.

14. The "Evangelische Gesangbuch" (EG), now in use, lists the hymn under no. 502. Probably two more examples can be found in Martin Luther's "Aus tiefer Not schrei ich zu dir" (EG no. 299; 1524), in the last stanzas, where one first reads the expression "Israel rechter Art," and at the end: "Er...[nämlich: Gott] ist allein der gute Hirt,/der Israel erlösen wird / aus seinen Sünden allen."

15. Italics: Michael Bachmann. Cf. for instance Bachmann, *Das Freiburger Münster und seine Juden*, 191–92.

16. Zimmermann, "Kirche und Israel Gottes im Galaterbrief," 131 (with note 32). Cf. Zimmerman, *Gott und seine Söhne*, 134 (with note 4)—also above (at) note 13.

17. Cf. Robert Morgenthaler, *Statistik des neutestamentlichen Wortschatzes* (Zürich and Stuttgart: Gotthelf-Verlag, 1958), 107.

18. On this see statistical data at Morgenthaler, ibid., 21. Cf. Zimmermann, *Gott und seine Söhne*, 134 (at) note 8.

19. Citations: Ulrich Wilckens, *Der Brief an die Römer 2: Röm 6–11*. EKK VI/2 (Zürich/Einsiedeln/Cologne/Neukirchen-Vluyn: Benziger/Neukirchener Verlag, 1980), 181.

20. Differently Klaus Wengst, *"Freut euch, ihr Völker, mit Gottes Volk!" Israel und die Völker als Thema des Paulus—ein Gang durch den Römerbrief* (Stuttgart: W. Kohlhammer, 2008), 293–98, who understands 9:6b "als rhetorische Frage" (297; cf. also: "Sind denn nicht alle aus Israel eben Israel?" [293])—and also William S. Campbell in his conference-paper (in this volume), "'But It Is not as though the Word of God Had Failed' (Romans 9:6a): Israel as the Sub-Text in Romans." But the *oude* of 9:7a, following the *ou* of 9.6b—i.e., the *oude* "with a neg. preceding"—normally should be translated by "nor" (Liddell/Scott, *A Greek-English Lexicon*, 1268 [*oude*];

cf. Bauer, *Griechisch-Deutsches Wörterbuch zu den Schriften des Neuen Testaments*, 1196–97 [*oude*], 1196 ["und nicht, noch," esp. following *ou*]).

21. Cf., for instance, Martinus C. de Boer, *Galatians: A Commentary*. NTL (Louisville, KY: Westminster John Knox Press, 2011), 405–6, and Moo, *Galatians*, 402–3. Cf. above (at) note 11.

22. Michael Wolter, *Paulus. Ein Grundriss seiner Theologie* (Neukirchen-Vluyn: Neukirchener Verlagsanstalt, 2011), 413–14. Cf. pp. 93–94, where Wolter (presumes "einen [. . .] metaphorischen Genitiv" [93] and) says: "Ein besonders schönes Beispiel ist der Ausdruck 'Israel Gottes', der es Paulus ermöglicht, die Christen in metaphorischer Weise als 'wirkliches', weil 'Gottes' Israel zu bezeichnen." The Bonn exegete adds: "Das Gegenüber ist das 'Israel nach dem Fleisch' (1Kor 10,18), d.h. das vorfindliche Israel" (94 note 77). Cf. below (at) note 68.

23. Michael Bachmann, "*Verus Israel*: Ein Vorschlag zu einer mengentheoretischen Neubeschreibung der betreffenden paulinischen Terminologie," *NTS* 48 (2002): 500–12 (now also in Bachmann *Von Paulus zur Apokalypse*, 79–91).

24. Ibid., 502.

25. Bachmann, "Paul, Israel and the Gentiles," 82 (and also Bachmann, "Borders According to Paul," 365).

26. See also Wolfgang Schrage, *Der erste Brief an die Korinther 2*: *1Kor 6,12–11,16*, EKK VII/2 (Solothurn/Düsseldorf/Neukirchen-Vluyn: Benziger/Neukirchener Verlag, 1995), (442–)443 (cf. Zimmermann, *Gott und seine Söhne*, 134–35 [with note 12]). Differently the conference-paper of Joshua Garroway—i.e., "Gentiles in the End: Remnant Theology."

27. Cf. Bachmann, "The Church and the Israel of God," 112, with notes 70–72, hinting at Wolfgang Schrage, "Israel nach dem Fleisch (1Kor 10,18)," in *"Wenn nicht jetzt, wann dann?" Aufsätze für Hans-Joachim Kraus zum 65. Geburtstag*, ed. Hans-Georg Geyer et al. (Neukirchen-Vluyn: Neukirchener Verlag, 1983), 143–51, esp. (144–)50: "W. Schrage thinks that it is quite probable that one should think of 'Israel, insofar as it does not offer sacrifice to God but to the idols.' If one boldly wished to bring in the counterpart term *ho Israēl kata pneuma* [. . .], particularly as the desert generation according to 1Cor 10:3–4 received 'spiritual food' and 'spiritual drink,' this expression could be understood 'as an *oppositum*' and it would not mean 'another Israel in the form of the new people of God, but those in whom God delighted because they did not belong to the people who pursued idolatry.'"

28. Zimmermann, "Kirche und Israel Gottes im Galaterbrief," 132–33, with note 39, hinting at "the 18th benediction of the Palestinian recension of the Shmone Esre ('Israel your people'), Ps 124,5.2; 127,6; 4QMMT C31–32; PapMur 42." Cf. Zimmerman, *Gott und seine Söhne*, 137 (with note 17)—and also below (at) note 70–76.

29. Cf. Bachmann, "The Church and the Israel of God," "Bemerkungen zur Auslegung zweier Genitivverbindungen des Galaterbriefs," esp. 287–95.

30. On this see, for instance, Bachmann, "The Church and the Israel of God," 108–10.

31. Ibid., 108–9.

32. Citations: Zimmermann, *Gott und seine Söhne*, 138–39 note 24 (cf. Zimmermann, "Kirche und Israel Gottes im Galaterbrief," 136, note 51). Cf. Theodor Zahn,

Der Brief des Paulus an die Galater. KNT 9 (2nd ed.; Leipzig: A. Deichert'sche Verlagsbuchhandlung, 1907), 283, and also Bachmann, "The Church and the Israel of God," 108(–9).

33. Citations: ibid., 115(–16) (with notes 93–94, hinting at and/or citing Nils A. Dahl, "Zur Auslegung von Gal. 6,16:" *Judaica* 6 [1950]: 164–65, esp. 164 [161–70]).

34. Cf. above at note 1.

35. See esp. 3:29 ("Abraham's seed you are" [cf. 3:7, 14, 16, 28]) and 3:26 ("for you are all sons of God through faith" [cf. 4:6, 7]). Cf. below at note 64.

36. On this see Zimmermann, "Kirche und Israel Gottes im Galaterbrief," 133–34 (cf. Zimmermann, *Gott und seine Söhne*, 135–37).

37. Cf., for instance, Bachmann, "The Church and the Israel of God," 108–10, and Zimmermann, "Kirche und Israel Gottes im Galaterbrief," 129–35.

38. Cf., for instance, Bachmann, "The Church and the Israel of God," 108, 110, 112, and Zimmermann, *Gott und seine Söhne*, 137–38, 140–41.

39. This may be pointed out indirectly earlier, especially in 2:3, 7–9 and in 5:2, 6, 11.

40. See my paper "Die 'Opponenten' des Paulus im (heilsgeschichtlich profilierten) Galaterbrief. Alte und neue Zugänge," which will be published in *Zeitschrift für Neues Testament*.

41. See Otto Betz, "*peritomē*," in *EWNT* 3 (1983): 186–89, esp. 187. Cf., for instance, Gen 14:4–14, esp. v. 14, and Rom 3:28–31.

42. Not even the "brother" instances before the final verse 1 Thess 5:28, i.e., 1 Thess 5:25, 26, 27—are true parallels to Gal 6:18. Cf.: Mussner, *Galaterbrief*, 421 (with note 86); H. D. Betz, *Galaterbrief*, 551; Oakes, *Galatians*, 194.

43. See Bachmann, "The Church and the Israel of God," 107–8 (with note[s] [44–]45).

44. Cf. Bachmann, "Die 'Opponenten' des Paulus im (heilsgeschichtlich profilierten) Galaterbrief. Alte und neue Zugänge," (see note 40), for instance at note 136.

45. See Zimmermann, *Gott und seine Söhne*, 139–40.

46. Cf. below at note 52.

47. Guido Baltes, "'Freiheit vom Gesetz'—eine paulinische Formel? Paulus zwischen jüdischem Gesetz und christlicher Freiheit," in *Der jüdische Messias Jesus und sein jüdischer Apostel Paulus*, ed. Armin D. Baum, Detlef Häußer, and Emmanuel L. Rehfeld, WUNT 2.425 (Tübingen: Mohr Siebeck, 2016), 295 (265–314). Baltes more precisely says: "dem Heidentum (oder Christentum) und der Gesetzesfreiheit."

48. See Bachmann, *Sünder oder Übertreter. Studien zur Argumentation in Gal 2,15ff*, WUNT 59 (Tübingen: Mohr Siebeck, 1992), 124–29. Cf. Bachmann, "Die 'Opponenten' des Paulus im (heilsgeschichtlich profilierten) Galaterbrief. Alte und neue Zugänge," (see note 40), (at) note 132 (where I refer to the linguist Roland Harweg, hinting moreover at Bauer, *Griechisch-Deutsches Wörterbuch zu den Schriften des Neuen Testaments*, 1227–28 [*palin*], 1227)—and below at note 53.

49. Barclay, *Paul and the Gift*, 412, note 64 (hinting at Bachmann, "The Other Woman. Synchronic and Diachronic Observations on Gal 4:21–5:1," in *Anti-Judaism in Galatians?*, 85–100, 176–95 [first: 1998], esp. 85–100; Robert L. Brawley, "Contextuality, Intertextuality, and the Hendiadic Relationship of Promise and Law in

Galatians," *Zeitschrift für das Neue Testament* 93 [2002]: 99–119). Cf. Zimmermann, *Gott und seine Söhne*, 105–8, and "Kirche und Israel Gottes im Galaterbrief," 133–34.

50. See Michael Bachmann, "The Other Woman," esp. 94–97. Cf. Baltes, "Freiheit vom Gesetz"—eine paulinische Formel?," esp. 295–96.

51. Bachmann, "Zu temporalen Momenten des Galaterbriefs," 130, here "Tableau (2).''

52. Cf. above at note 46.

53. Cf. above at note 48.

54. For instance: Matera, *Galatians*, 120; Jan Lambrecht, "The Universalistic Will of God. The True Gospel in Galatians," in *Pauline Studies. Collected Essays*. BEThL 115 (Leuven: University Press, 1994), 304–05 (299–306); Barclay, *Paul and the Gift*, 419 (with note 71).

55. Terence L. Donaldson, "The 'Curse of the Law' and the Inclusion of the Gentiles. Galatians 3.13–14," *NTS* 32 (1986): 94–112, esp. 99–102.

56. On this see: Bachmann, *Sünder oder Übertreter*, 136–39 (with note 196 [on Gal 4:5b, understood by me as referring only to Jewish Christians]); Bachmann, "The Other Woman," 95, with note 52.

57. This is the attempt of a summary at: Bachmann, "Die 'Opponenten' des Paulus im (heilsgeschichtlich profilierten) Galaterbrief" (see note 40), at note 138 (hinting at Karl O. Sandnes, *Paul Perceived. An Interactionist Perspective on Paul and the Law*, WUNT 412 [Tübingen: Mohr Siebeck, 2018], 88). Of course the Old Testament writings also present other views concerning the fate of the Gentiles. See also František Ábel, "The Role of Israel Towards the Gentiles in the Context of Romans 11:25–27," short paper, presented on August 1, 2019, in Marburg (SNTS congress), hinting, for instance, at Jer 30:11.

58. See Bachmann, *Sünder oder Übertreter*, 124, with note 129.

59. Cf. ibid., 82, 87–88.

60. Cf. Gottlob Schrenk, "Der Segenswunsch nach der Kampfepistel. Antwort." *Judaica* 6 (1950): 180–83 (170–90).

61. On this, also on *ioudaizein* and *Ioudaikōs*, see Bachmann, "Die 'Opponenten' des Paulus im (heilsgeschichtlich profilierten) Galaterbrief" (see note 40), at notes 97, 135. Cf., for instance, Martyn, *Galatians*, 154, and Oakes, *Galatians*, 52–54.

62. Zimmermann, *Gott und seine Söhne*, 139 with note 26, where she hints at Eastman, "Israel and the Mercy of God" 360–95, 390–94/95 (see esp. 391–92). Zimmermann agrees.

63. Bachmann, "Paul, Israel and the Gentiles," 84 (and "Borders according to Paul," 366).

64. See above (at) note 35.

65. Bachmann, "Paul, Israel and the Gentiles," 83 (and "Borders according to Paul," 365).

66. Bachmann, "Paul, Israel and the Gentiles," 83 (and "Borders according to Paul," 365–66)—citing Bachmann, "*Verus Israel*," 83.

67. Cf. Bachmann, "*Verus Israel*," (83–)90.

68. See above (at) note 22.

69. Fee, *Galatians*, 253. Cf., for instance, Longenecker, *Galatians*, (298–)299: "The phrase itself is not found in the extant writings of Second Temple Judaism or later rabbinic Judaism, and does not appear elsewhere in Paul's letters. So it may be postulated that it arose amongst the Judaizers and became part of their message to Paul's Galatian converts. If that be the case, then Paul here climaxes his whole response to the judaizing threat in something of an ad hominem manner."

70. Above (at) note 28.

71. Bachmann, "The Church and the Israel of God," 117.

72. Cf. ibid., 117.

73. Cf. ibid., 116–17.

74. Elisha Qimron and John Strugnell, eds. *Qumran Cave 4. Vol. V: Miqṣat Ma'aśe Ha-Torah*. DJD X (Oxford: Clarendon Press, 1994), (62–)63.

75. Bachmann, "The Church and the Israel of God," 116–17. Cf. Dennis Pardee, *Handbook of Ancient Hebrew Letters. A Study Edition*. SBL.SBibSt 15 (Chico, CA: Scholars Press, 1982), 122–28, esp. (123–)24 (cf. p. 127: "Signatures, lines 8–12")— and also Tomson, "The Names Israel and Jew," 130.

76. Cf.: Tomson, "The Names Israel and Jew," esp. (130 and) 285; Klaus Wengst, "'Universale Heilsbedeutung Jesu' und bleibende Besonderheit Israels nach dem Römerbrief," in *Christsein mit Tora und Evangelium. Beiträge zum Umbau christlicher Theologie im Angesicht Israels* (Stuttgart: W. Kohlhammer, 2014), 144–57, 209–10 (first: 2010), 149; Zimmermann, "Kirche und Israel Gottes im Galaterbrief," esp. 132–37 (and also: Zimmermann, *Gott und seine Söhne*, esp. 134–39); Barclay, *Paul and the Gift*, 420–21; Oakes, *Galatians*, 192.

77. Cf. above at note 9.

78. Tomson, "The Names Israel and Jew," 121.

79. Citations: ibid., 289.

80. See ibid, 284, 286–88.

81. See ibid., 284–88, esp. 285.

82. Ibid., 287–88. Though Jennifer Eyl ("'I Myself Am an Israelite': Paul, Authenticty and Authority," *JSNT* 40 [(2017)]: 148–68), regarding his use of the words *Israēl* and *Israēlitēs*, accentuates "Paul's need to be authorized by antiquity," she concedes: "My argument is not an outright rejection of insider/outsider claims" (164)— proposed not least by Peter J. Tomson (on this cf. pp. 159–63, with notes 34–44).

83. Tomson, "The Names Israel and Jew," 121.

84. Ibid., 288.

85. Cf., for instance, Bachmann, "Paul, Israel and the Gentiles," 84 (at note 56), and Zimmerman, *Gott und seine Söhne*, 134 (at note 10).

86. See above, esp. (at) notes 17–28.

87. See above, note 4 (i.e., Schrenk, "Segenswunsch nach der Kampfepistel," 170).

88. See Michael Bachmann, "Investigation on the Mediator: Gal 3:20 and the Character of the Mosaic Law," in *Anti-Judaism in Galatians?*, 60–84, 153–75 (first [a little bit differently]: 1997), esp. 77–83.

89. Cf. Bachmann, *Anti-Judaism in Galatians?* (see above, note 4). Cf. below at note 94.

90. See above, note(s) 4 (and 87).
91. Richardson, *Israel in the Apostolic Church*, 83, note 2.
92. Ibid., 1. Cf. above (at) note 12.
93. Tomson, "The Names Israel and Jew," 122.
94. Michael Bachmann, "Zur Entstehung (und zur Überwindung) des christlichen Antijudaismus," in *Von Paulus zur Apokalypse*, 439–92 (first: 2002), 484.
95. Bachmann, *Das Freiburger Münster und seine Juden*, 188(–189).
96. Ibid., 188.

BIBLIOGRAPHY

Asano, Atsuhiro. *Community-Identity Construction in Galatians: Exegetical, Social-Anthropological and Socio-Historical Studies*. JSNT.S 285. London, U.K. and New York, NY: T&T Clark, 2005.

Bachmann, Michael. *Anti-Judaism in Galatians? Exegetical Studies on a Polemical Letter and on Paul's Theology*. Translated by Robert L. Brawley). Grand Rapids, MI, and Cambridge, U.K.: Eerdmans, 2009 (original German: 1999).

———. *Das Freiburger Münster und seine Juden: Historische, ikonographische und hermeneutische Beobachtungen*. Regensburg: Schnell & Steiner, 2017.

———. "Important and Delicate—Borders according to Paul." In *Borders. Terminologies, Ideologies, and Performances*, edited by Annette Weissenrieder, 359–82. WUNT 366. Tübingen: Mohr Siebeck, 2010.

———. "Neues Testament und Antijudaismus—z.B. Bergpredigt und Galaterbrief." In *Update-Exegese 2.1. Ergebnisse gegenwärtiger Bibelwissenschaft*, edited by Wolfgang Kraus and Martin Rösel. Mit einem Geleitwort von Heinrich Bedford-Strohm, 236–48. Leipzig: Evangelische Verlagsanstalt, 2015.

———. "The 'New Perspective on Paul' und 'The New View of Paul.'" In *Paulus Handbuch*, edited by Friedrich Wilhelm Horn, 30–38. Tübingen: Mohr Siebeck, 2013.

———. "Paul, Israel and the Gentiles: Hermeneutical and Exegetical Notes." In *Paul and Judaism. Crosscurrents in Pauline Exegesis and the Study of Jewish-Christian Relations*, edited by Reimund Bieringer and Didier Pollefeyt, 72–105. Library of New Testament Studies 463. London: T&T Clark, 2012.

———. *Sünder oder Übertreter. Studien zur Argumentation in Gal 2,15ff*. WUNT 59. Tübingen: Mohr Siebeck, 1992.

———. "*Verus Israel*: Ein Vorschlag zu einer mengentheoretischen Neubeschreibung der betreffenden paulinischen Terminologie." *New Testament Studies* 48 (2002): 500–12.

———. *Von Paulus zur Apokalypse—und weiter. Exegetische und rezeptionsgeschichtliche Studien zum Neuen Testament (including English summaries)*. NTOA/StUNT 91. Göttingen and Oakville, CT: Vandenhoeck & Ruprecht, 2011.

———. "Zu temporalen Momenten des Galaterbriefs. Beschneidungsfreiheit für Heidenchristen und Heilsgeschichte." In *Paulus und Petrus: Geschichte—Theologie —Rezeption. Festschrift für Friedrich Wilhelm Horn zu seinem 60. Geburtstag*, edited by Heike Omerzu and Eckart David Schmidt, 101–36. Leipzig: Evangelische Verlagsanstalt, 2016.

Baltes, Guido. "'Freiheit vom Gesetz'—eine paulinische Formel? Paulus zwischen jüdischem Gesetz und christlicher Freiheit." In *Der jüdische Messias Jesus und sein jüdischer Apostel Paulus*, edited by Armin D. Baum, Detlef Häußer, and Emmanuel L. Rehfeld, 265–314. WUNT 2.425. Tübingen: Mohr Siebeck, 2016.

Barclay, John M. G. *Paul and the Gift*. Grand Rapids, MI, and Cambridge, U.K.: Eerdmans, 2015.

Bauer, Walter. *Griechisch-Deutsches Wörterbuch zu den Schriften des Neuen Testaments und der frühchristlichen Literatur*, edited by Kurt Aland and Barbara Aland. 6th, completely revised edition. Berlin and New York, NY: Walter de Gruyter, 1988.

Betz, Hans Dieter. *Der Galaterbrief. Ein Kommentar zum Brief des Apostels Paulus an die Gemeinden in Galatien*. Hermeneia. Munich: Chr. Kaiser, 1988 (translated by Sibylle Ann).

———. *Galatians. A Commentary on Paul's Letter to the Churches of Galatia*. Hermeneia. Philadelphia, PA: Fortress Press, 1979.

Bianchini, Francesco. *Lettera ai Galati*. Nuovo Testamento—commento esegetico e spiritual. Roma: Città Nuova Editrice, 2009.

Brawley, Robert L. "Contextuality, Intertextuality, and the Hendiadic Relationship of Promise and Law in Galatians." *Zeitschrift für das Neue Testament* 93 (2002): 99–119.

Bruce, Frederick Fyvie. *The Epistle of Paul to the Galatians. A Commentary on the Greek Text*. Exeter: Paternoster Press, 1982.

Dahl, Nils Aistrup. "Zur Auslegung von Gal. 6,16." *Judaica* 6 (1950): 161–70.

De Boer, Martinus C. *Galatians: A Commentary*. NTL. Louisville, KY: Westminster John Knox Press, 2011.

Donaldson, Terence L. "The 'Curse of the Law' and the Inclusion of the Gentiles. Galatians 3.13–14." *New Testament Studies* 32 (1986): 94–112.

Dunn, James D. G. *The Epistle to the Galatians*. Black's New Testament Commentaries. London: A&C Black, 1995.

Eastman, Susan Grove. "Israel and the Mercy of God: A Re-reading of Galatians 6.16 and Romans 9–11." *New Testament Studies* 56 (2010): 367–95.

Eckey, Wilfried. *Der Galaterbrief*. Neukirchen-Vluyn: Neukirchener Verlagsanstalt, 2010.

Eyl, Jennifer. "'I Myself Am an Israelite': Paul, Authenticty and Authority." *Journal for the Study of the New Testament* 40 (2017): 148–68.

Fee, Gordon D. *Galatians*. Pentecostal Commentary. Dorset, U.K.: Deo Publishing, 2007.

Fredriksen, Paula. *Paul, the Pagans' Apostle*. New Haven, CT, and London, U.K.: Yale University Press, 2017.

———. "The Question of Worship: Gods, Pagans, and the Redemption of Israel." In *Paul within Judaism: Restoring the First-Century Context to the Apostle*, edited by Mark D. Nanos and Magnus Zetterholm, 175–201. Minneapolis, MN: Fortress Press, 2015.

Hahn, Ferdinand. "Die Stellung des Paulus zum Judentum und zur Tora." In *Die Verwurzelung des Christentums im Judentum: Exegetische Beiträge zum christlich-jüdischen Gespräch. Zum 70. Geburtstag von Cilliers Breytenbach*, edited by Cilliers Breytenbach, 85–98. Neukirchen-Vluyn: Neukirchener Verlag, 1996.

Häuser, Peter. *Des Heiligen Philosophen und Märtyrers Justins Dialog mit dem Juden Tryphon aus dem Griechischen übersetzt und mit einer Einleitung versehen.* BKV 33. Kempten/Munich: Verlag der J. Kösel'schen Buchhandlung, 1917.

Lambrecht, Jan. "The Universalistic Will of God. The True Gospel in Galatians." In *Pauline Studies. Collected Essays*, 299–306. BEThL 115. Leuven: University Press, 1994.

Levy, Christopher. *The Letter to the Galatians.* The Bible in Medieval Literature. Grand Rapids, MI and Cambridge, U.K.: Eeerdmans, 2011.

Liddell, Henry George, and Robert Scott, eds. *A Greek-English Lexicon.* The Ninth Edition. Edited by Henry Stuart Jones. Oxford: Clarendon Press, 1940.

Lindemann, Andreas. "Israel und sein 'Land' im Neuen Testament." In *Glauben, Handeln, Verstehen. Studien zur Auslegung des Neuen Testaments II*, 149–89. WUNT 282. Tübingen: Mohr Siebeck, 2011.

Longenecker, Richard N. *Galatians.* Word Biblical Commentary 41. Dallas, TX: Word Books, 1990.

Martyn, J. Louis. *Galatians.* Anchor Bible 33A. New York, NY: Doubleday, 1997.

Matera, Frank J. *Galatians.* Sacra Pagina 9. Collegeville, MN: The Liturgical Press, 1992.

Meiser, Martin. *Galater.* Novum Testamentum Patristicum 9. Göttingen: Vandenhoeck & Ruprecht, 2007.

Moo, Douglas J. *Galatians.* Baker Exegetical Commentary. Grand Rapids, MI: Baker Academic, 2013.

Morgenthaler, Robert. *Statistik des neutestamentlichen Wortschatzes.* Zürich and Stuttgart: Gotthelf-Verlag, 1958.

Morland, Kjell Arne. *The Rhetoric of Curse in Galatians. Paul Confronts Another Gospel.* Emory Studies in Early Christianity 5. Atlanta, GA: Scholars Press, 1995.

Mussner, Franz. *Der Galaterbrief.* HThK 9. Freiburg/Basel/Vienna: Herder, 1974.

Oakes, Peter. *Galatians.* Paideia Commentaries on the New Testament. Grand Rapids, MI: Baker Academic, 2015.

Pardee, Dennis. *Handbook of Ancient Hebrew Letters. A Study Edition.* SBL.SBibSt 15. Chico, CA: Scholars Press, 1982.

Qimron, Elisha, and John Strugnell, eds. *Qumran Cave 4. Vol. V: Miqṣat Maʿaśe Ha-Torah.* DJD X. Oxford: Clarendon Press, 1994.

Richardson, Peter. *Israel in the Apostolic Church.* MSSNTS 10. Cambridge: Cambridge University Press, 1964.

Sandnes, Karl Olav. *Paul Perceived. An Interactionist Perspective on Paul and the Law.* WUNT 412. Tübingen: Mohr Siebeck, 2018.

Schnelle, Udo. "Gibt es eine Entwicklung in der Rechtfertigungslehre vom Galater– zum Römerbrief?" In *Paulus—Werk und Wirkung. Festschrift für Andreas Lindemann zum 70. Geburtstag*, edited by Paul-Gerhard Klumbies and David S. du Toit, 289–309. Tübingen: Mohr Siebeck, 2013.

Schrage, Wolfgang. *Der erste Brief an die Korinther 2: 1Kor 6,12–11,16*. EKK VII/2. Solothurn/Düsseldorf/Neukirchen-Vluyn: Benziger/Neukirchener Verlag, 1995.

———. "Israel nach dem Fleisch (1Kor 10,18)." In *"Wenn nicht jetzt, wann dann? Aufsätze für Hans-Joachim Kraus zum 65. Geburtstag*, edited by Hans-Georg Geyer et al., 143–51. Neukirchen-Vluyn: Neukirchener Verlag, 1983.

Schrenk, Gottlob. "Was bedeutet 'Israel Gottes'?" *Judaica* 5 (1949): 81–94.

———. "Der Segenswunsch nach der Kampfepistel. Antwort." *Judaica* 6 (1950): 170–90.

Seifrid, Mark A. "Answered Lament: Paul's Gospel, Israel, and the Scriptures in Romans." In *Paulinische Schriftrezeption. Grundlagen—Ausprägungen—Wirkungen —Wertungen*, edited by Florian Wilk and Markus Öhler, 175–215. FRLANT 268. Göttingen/Bristol, CT: Vandenhoeck & Ruprecht, 2017.

Strack, Hermann L., and Billerbeck, Paul. *Kommentar zum Neuen Testament aus Talmud und Midrasch*. 4 volumes. München: C. H. Beck'sche Buchhandlung, 1922–1928.

Theobald, Michael. "'Geboren aus dem Samen Davids . . .' (Röm 1, 3). Wandlungen im paulinischen Christus–Bild?" *Zeitschrift für Neues Testament* 102 (2011): 235–60.

Tomson, Peter J. "The Names Israel and Jew in Ancient Judaism and in the New Testament." *Bijdragen* 47 (1986): 266–289.

Wengst, Klaus. *Christsein mit Tora und Evangelium. Beiträge zum Umbau christlicher Theologie im Angesicht Israels*. Stuttgart: W. Kohlhammer, 2014.

———. *"Freut euch, ihr Völker, mit Gottes Volk!" Israel und die Völker als Thema des Paulus—ein Gang durch den Römerbrief.* Stuttgart: W. Kohlhammer, 2008.

Wilckens, Ulrich. *Der Brief an die Römer 2: Röm 6–11*. EKK VI/2. Zürich/Einsiedeln /Cologne/Neukirchen-Vluyn: Benziger/Neukirchener Verlag, 1980.

Wolter, Michael. *Paulus. Ein Grundriss seiner Theologie*. Neukirchen-Vluyn: Neukirchener Verlagsanstalt, 2011.

Zahn, Theodor. *Der Brief des Paulus an die Galater*. KNT 9. Second edition. Leipzig: A. Deichert'sche Verlagsbuchhandlung, 1907.

Zimmermann, Christiane. *Gott und seine Söhne. Das Gottesbild des Galaterbriefs*. WMANT 135. Neukirchen-Vluyn: Evangelische Verlagsanstalt, 2013.

———. "Kirche und Israel Gottes im Galaterbrief." In *Mazel Tov. Interdisziplinäre Beiträge zum Verhältnis von Christentum und Judentum. Festschrift anlässlich des 50. Geburtstages des Instituts Kirche und Judentum*, edited by Markus Witte and Tanja Pilger, 121–40. Leipzig: Evangelische Verlagsanstalt, 2012.

Chapter Nine

Bending Knees and Acknowledging Tongues (Phil 2:9–11)

The Nations' Loyalty to the God of Israel in the Shadow of the Empire

Kathy Ehrensperger

Philippians 2:6–11 has attracted more scholarly attention than any other Pauline text, not only in the present but parts of it are among the most cited passages in early Christian literature.[1] Contemporary secondary literature has accumulated to an almost unsurpassable mountain,[2] and I certainly do not intend to climb that mountain—or tunnel through it for that matter. I think the best way to understand this narrative poem or poetic narrative (I do not think it is a hymn) is via the last two verses—10–11. As my perception is based on the presupposition that Paul and his way of arguing are and remained part of Jewish tradition of the first century CE, I consider also this text as belonging to this tradition—resonating significantly with tunes of Roman imperial power.

The verses Phil 2:9–11 are providing assurance that this is what will be—in the future:[3]

διὸ καὶ ὁ θεὸς αὐτὸν ὑπερύψωσεν
καὶ ἐχαρίσατο αὐτῷ τὸ ὄνομα
  τὸ ὑπὲρ πᾶν ὄνομα,
ἵνα ἐν τῷ ὀνόματι Ἰησοῦ
πᾶν γόνυ κάμψῃ
ἐπουρανίων καὶ ἐπιγείων καὶ καταχθονίων
καὶ πᾶσα γλῶσσα ἐξομολογήσηται ὅτι
κύριος Ἰησοῦς Χριστὸς
εἰς δόξαν θεοῦ πατρός

The addressees in the present are confronted with serious problems due to their loyalty to this κύριος Ἰησοῦς Χριστὸς: they are involved in struggles with Roman authorities as is Paul himself (Phil 1:27–30). In my view, it is in relation to precisely this context, that they are given firm assurance that this is a temporarily limited issue when seen in light of the hope and trust in which they are now rooted. Despite the fact that their struggles might seem to be evidence to the contrary, they actually live already in anticipation of the alternative to the current all-dominating power of the Roman empire. Their lives and relationships are already, and should continue to be, firmly permeated by this trust. They live in anticipation of the cosmic rulership of the one and only God in the here and now, that is, in the firm trust that in and through the Christ-event God has already initiated the process towards the revelation and establishing of his cosmic rule. The current situation is not yet the time of fulfilment, hence the powers of this world are still having some impact on those who are awaiting God's rulership over the cosmos. But the time of the powers of this world is deemed to be limited.

THE CONTEXT

As mentioned, the Philippian Christ-followers had to face up to conflicts with Roman authorities—at least this is what Paul seems to imply when he mentions early on in the letter[4] that "you are having the same struggle that you saw in me and now hear that I still have" (1:30). Paul is concerned that they live their lives Μόνον ἀξίως τοῦ εὐαγγελίου τοῦ Χριστοῦ πολιτεύεσθε (1:27) under difficult circumstances. What follows in Philippians 2 is intrinsically linked to this concern. Immediately after the poetic passage of 2:6–11, in vv. 12–18 Paul takes up the issue of these struggles again, encouraging and strengthening the addressees to "hold fast to the word of life" (2:16) and to "be without blemish in the midst of a crooked and perverse generation" (2:15). This literary context directs the attention to the real-live context to which the letter related and into which the poetic text is actually formulated. Its purpose is thus intrinsically related to the flow of the argument intertwined with issues and topics which permeate the letter as a whole.

The context in which the addressees live is dominated by Rome. The fact that Philippi was a Roman colony, despite its population most likely being in the majority Greek and Thracian,[5] means that the public discourse and the visual display of power was thoroughly Roman in the first century CE and must have had significant impact on the population of the colony.[6]

There are a few aspects which seem specifically important when reading Phil 2:6–11. The authorities with whom Paul and the Philippians are in conflict had developed not only the military means to conquer and maintain power and domination over conquered areas and peoples through a sophisticated administrative system, they also had developed a broad ideological discourse to legitimize their rulership over the *oikoumene*—their imperium. It included not only claims to divinity via divine sonship on the part of the actual emperor, but more widely, the military success in violent conquests was interpreted as proof of favoritism by the gods—that is, Roman rulership was considered to be divinely instigated and sanctioned. The *populus Romanus* was considered as favored, even elect by the gods, destined to rule over the *oikoumene*, and thus legitimized to exploit subjugated peoples and provinces. The fact that these had been conquered and subjugated was inherent evidence that they were destined to be slaves[7]—whereas the Romans were destined to exploit the subjugated for their own advancement and benefit.[8] This rulership was regarded to be eternal, hence the attribute to Rome as *Roma eterna*. The issue here is not emperor cult in the narrow sense or as such, but the perception of the rulership of the *populus Romanus* which had developed over the course of centuries and was magisterially condensed, and consciously put into narrative form by Augustus in support of the permanent establishment of imperial rule and the role of the emperor as principal ruler.[9] It was not merely the divinity of the Caesars, as sons of their deified fathers which mattered, but the perception of the divinely ordained and approved rule of the people of Rome as such, represented by the emperor and his representatives in the provinces. The cult of the Capitoline Trias—Jupiter, Juno, and Minerva—was established in Roman colonies all over the empire and was an intrinsic part of Roman colonial administration.[10]

As a Roman colony Philippi was organized and administered according to Roman parameters, a kind of mini-Rome in that institutions of Rome were replicated as in any other colony. And of course there had to be cult places dedicated to the Capitoline Trias honoring the main deities of Rome in the most prominent place of the colony.[11] Moreover, the Roman dominance in the first century CE is evident through the preponderance of Latin inscriptions in Philippi.[12] The official life of the colony was imprinted by Roman organization, customs, the display of Roman power, the Roman calendar, and Latin as the official language when communicating with the "rulers" as represented by their magistrates.[13]

Christ-followers in Philippi, most likely recruited from god-fearing non-Jews who already had some interest in Jewish traditions and were familiar to some extent with these,[14] could not avoid being exposed to this dominant Roman presence and interact, with Roman representatives. Even if it was two generations after the confiscation and reallocation of land to army veterans, the memory of humiliation was most likely still vivid among people at the time of Paul. The building of the Roman Forum in the middle of the first century CE in a previously built-up area means that people must have been relocated some losing their most likely modest properties through confiscation. This was the immediately felt context of Paul's presence in, and letter to, Philippi. It is evident that the implications for the local population were unavoidable—they were not in charge of their own city, they were no longer owners of the land, now possibly working as day-laborers or slaves, they could not participate in the running of the affairs of the colony, and they could not be citizens of the colony.[15]

JEWISH WAYS OF NEGOTIATING IMPERIAL POWER

The Christ-followers from the (conquered) nations (ἔθνη) in the colony of Philippi most likely had already some familiarity with Jewish traditions before joining the Christ-movement. Jewish traditions had for centuries been exposed to foreign rule and had developed ways to relate to such whilst maintaining their own traditions, their identity, and their own perception of the "world" and events. Intrinsic to this was their refusal to consider their defeat or conquest as evidence of the defeat of their God. Irrespective of specific eschatological or messianic expectations, respective traditions maintained that he continued to be the supreme ruler of the cosmos, the creator of the universe to whom all and everything was subject. Hence any equivalent claim, whoever might have raised it, was inherently refuted.[16] Their narrative of belonging provided an alternative to dominating narratives from whichever angle these might have come. This did not necessarily lead to clashes and open conflicts, but to a relativization of any power claims made over the Jews in their own perspective, and thus to a certain critical distancing from such claims.

Even Philo, who to some extent accepted Roman rule, never affirms Roman claims that their rule was the result of divine providence. Divine providence (πρόνοια) rather sustains, and provides for the functioning of the universe, caring especially for the well-being of the Jews.[17] It is never mentioned in relation to any other people but the Jews, who are protected by God when they are put at risk by the Romans (*Legat.* 220). Thus, Katell Berthelot concludes that "Philo never writes that God helped the Romans conquer so vast an empire, that it was achieved by His will, that He stood by their side, or anything of the kind."[18] Whatever the Romans had achieved was granted to them by Fortuna (τύχη) in Philo's view, a view similar to that of some Greek authors implying that there is no intrinsic value to what has been granted by her. What has been granted by Fortuna has nothing to do with God's ultimate will. It could only be a temporary issue granted for a limited time.

Roman rule could not only cause problems for Jews at the socio-political level. The claim to be the people divinely ordained to rule the world eternally clashed diametrically with Jewish perceptions of the world as God's creation and their specific role within the purpose of their God. Their tradition was prone not to buy into Roman ideology and constituted by its mere existence an implicit counternarrative to these claims.[19] These Jewish narratives did not emerge in a vacuum but in concrete socio-political contexts. The narrative of Daniel is contextualized in the period of Seleucid rule.[20] And the fact that since the Babylonian exile there was an ongoing Jewish presence in the realm of subsequent rulerships rendered the awareness that Roman claims to eternal domination of the whole *oikoumene* relative to say the least. The ongoing contact between Jews east and west rendered any totalizing claims to power evidently wrong since the socio-political map and conditions revealed such claims as ideological postulations rather than facts.

But this distancing discourse did not imply open conflict for most of the periods under the domination of different imperial powers. For most of the time some accommodation could be found, both in practical as well as in ideological terms. The rulership could be considered as actually instigated for a limited period of time by God, the foreign domination thus getting integrated into the narrative of the Jewish people. Thus Josephus is convinced that God is on the side of the Romans since they could not rule such a vast empire without God's permission (*B.J.* 2.390; 5.367–68). Josephus thereby does not see a transfer of ultimate power to the Romans but rather asserts that in all of these events leading up to the Jewish War and the destruction of the Temple and Jerusalem, God was the agent. This implies that despite all of this God had not been defeated and "the relationship between God and Israel was not ruptured by the events of 70 CE."[21] Rather than being in contradiction to the differentiating traditions noted above, this is a variation to that theme in that whatever power was granted to, e.g., Roman authorities was granted to them by the God of Israel for a limited time. Thus, the sovereignty of their God and the agency to integrate events into their own narrative of belonging were maintained.

CHRIST-FOLLOWERS FROM THE NATIONS—STRUGGLING IN PHILIPPI

The god-fearing non-Jews who joined the Christ-movement thus associated with a tradition and a narrative of belonging which presented, if not actual opposition, a certain distancing from the dominating ideology.[22] Jews over the course of time had negotiated imperial claims and found ways to play and not to play the game of acculturation, including a way to express subordination to Roman rule through the daily offering in Jerusalem for the well-being of the imperial household. The question was how these non-Jewish Christ-followers could negotiate the claims of the dominating power.

To some extent they could certainly orient themselves on practices and ways and means Jews had developed. But they were not Jews. Up to a certain point this was not relevant from an outside perception—they could possibly pass as Jewish. After all they related to the Jewish God, they adhered to Jewish ethics, they learned from the Jewish scriptures and considered these as authoritative, they adhered to some Jewish practices; and they most likely had ceased to participate in the cultic practices at house and crossroad shrines so prevalent in the everyday life of non-elite people. So there were many good reasons why they could well have passed as Jews in the perception of outsiders. But they were not Jews and should not become Jews, as Paul is adamant to insist in other letters. Not because there was something wrong in being Jewish and living a Jewish way of life—this is precisely what Paul and the other earliest Jewish followers of Christ continued to do—but because of the time in which they lived, the dawning of the age to come inaugurated by the Christ-event. Now people from the non-Jewish nations gathered to glorify the God of Israel together with his people Israel, as representatives of the nations.[23] To them Paul writes and provides assurance:

διὸ καὶ ὁ θεὸς αὐτὸν ὑπερύψωσεν
καὶ ἐχαρίσατο αὐτῷ τὸ ὄνομα
τὸ ὑπὲρ πᾶν ὄνομα,
ἵνα ἐν τῷ ὀνόματι Ἰησοῦ
πᾶν γόνυ κάμψῃ
ἐπουρανίων καὶ ἐπιγείων καὶ καταχθονίων
καὶ πᾶσα γλῶσσα ἐξομολογήσηται ὅτι
κύριος Ἰησοῦς Χριστὸς
εἰς δόξαν θεοῦ πατρός.

Therefore God exalted him
And gave him the name
Above every name
So that in the name of Jesus
Every knee should bend/bow
In heaven and on earth and the underworld
And every tongue shall/should swear in loyalty that
Lord is Jesus Christ
To the glory of God Father.
(Phil 2:9–11)

Given the context in which they live—this is a strong message, a message which relativizes, even challenges the claim to eternal rulership by Rome or in the name of the *populus Romanus*.

Of course the entire narrative poem resonates with the specific context of the addressees in Philippi—that is, the wider political context of the addressees, as well as with Jewish traditions of negotiating life under foreign rule. More specifically, it resonates—as is obvious in the allusion to LXX Isa 45:23 in vv. 10–11—with scriptural passages. It is in light of this scriptural allusion that we need to consider the entire passage.

Exaltation and Naming (v.9)

διὸ καὶ ὁ θεὸς αὐτὸν ὑπερύψωσεν
καὶ ἐχαρίσατο αὐτῷ τὸ ὄνομα
τὸ ὑπὲρ πᾶν ὄνομα,

From verse 9 onward God is the agent of events. The humiliation of the Christ is juxtaposed with the exaltation and the bestowing of the name above every name on the executed one. The significance of this seems obvious after almost two millennia of Christianity. But we should try to listen to these verses in a context where there was only the tradition of a small people at the margins of the sphere of influence of this overwhelming imperial power. This people had learned to negotiate and maintain its way of life and identity under various foreign powers and developed a critical stance over against the self-glorification and absolute power claims of any rulers.

God's exaltation and thus vindication of the one who had been executed on a Roman cross, has already happened (whether this refers to the resurrection or ascension is not decisive here), the name has been attributed to him, he is Lord Jesus Christ. As has been noted, the claim of the title Lord is not directed specifically at the Emperor Cult. In Paul's world there were many lords and gods[24]—but for those in Christ there was only one Lord, Messiah Jesus, and one God, thus the affirmation.

Living in Anticipation (vv.10–11)

ἵνα ἐν τῷ ὀνόματι Ἰησοῦ
πᾶν γόνυ κάμψῃ
ἐπουρανίων καὶ ἐπιγείων καὶ καταχθονίων
καὶ πᾶσα γλῶσσα ἐξομολογήσηται ὅτι
κύριος Ἰησοῦς Χριστὸς
εἰς δόξαν θεοῦ πατρός.

The bowing of knees and the praising of every tongue (or in every language), however, is anticipated in the future. It clearly is not the reality of the here and now. The nomination of the Lord, the naming has happened, but this is not yet the time of consummation, the subordination of those dehumanizing powers has not happened as yet, as the aorist subjunctive clearly indicates (ἐξομολογήσηται). But this understanding of the fate of Christ provides already in the here and now affirmation for those who trust in him. What they see now will be transformed—they were convinced in the very near future—and the one who was already exalted would eventually be the one in whose name those powers that are now dominating and subjugating them would recognize him as Lord, to the glory of God.[25] The allusion to LXX Isa 45:23 is evident. This is a text which is explicitly also cited in Rom 14:11.[26] Here, as in Rom 14, the one who is in view is God himself. In all of these events it was not the powers of the *kosmos*—these many lords and gods above, on earth, and below—who were in charge as agents of the events, but it was God in Christ, so Paul affirms with this narrative poem.

The messianic expectation that with the dawning of the age to come the nations or representatives of the nations would join Israel in acknowledging and honoring God was of course a long-standing notion among possible end time scenarios. The fate of Israel and the nations is seen as intertwined, and although this is not spelled out explicitly here or anywhere else in Philippians, the citation and allusions in the narrative poem render aspects of this implicit notion in all likelihood present here. Thus, the entire poem resonates not only with specific Roman imperial topoi but at the same time with notions found in LXX Isaiah 45, and possibly other Isaiah texts. For understanding the assurance that "every knee will bow/bend" and "every tongue will confess/swear loyalty" (in the name of Jesus) to the glory of God, Isaiah 45 as a whole is decisively relevant.

LXX ISAIAH 45 AS AN ECHO CHAMBER OF PHILIPPIANS 2:9–11

Rather than merely taking account of Isa 45:23, the whole chapter 45 serves as an echo chamber of the notions presented here. Some key words which occur in Phil 2:6–11 are found in LXX Isaiah 45:

There is an anointed one (Christos 45:1) who is called by name (45:3–4); it is asserted in no uncertain terms in several verses that it is God, the one and only God of Israel who acts through this anointed one; he is the only God, all others are not gods, he is the Creator of all that is above and on earth (45:7, 12); there are the survivors of the nations (45:20)—if they turn, they shall come near (45:21), and all of this is for the sake of his people Israel.

Of course in Isaiah 45 this anointed one is Cyrus—who is attributed a saving role, assigned to him by God by giving him a name. This name-giving is associated with God who identifies himself in no uncertain terms—he is the One and only, and above all, the God of Israel! This anointed one is given a name so that he recognizes the uniqueness of the one God of Israel. It has a specific purpose: ἕνεκεν Ιακωβ τοῦ παιδός μου καὶ Ισραηλ τοῦ ἐκλεκτοῦ μου ἐγὼ καλέσω σε τῷ ὀνόματί σου καὶ προσδέξομαί σε, σὺ δὲ οὐκ ἔγνως με—*For the sake of my servant Jacob, and Israel my elect, I will call you by your name, and accept you.* (LXX Isa 45:4) The role of this anointed one is clearly for the sake of the people Israel.

A few verses later there is the call to the nations: "Assemble, come, all of you gather round, survivors from the nations.[27] They have no knowledge, who parade their wooden idols and pray to a god that cannot save" (συνάχθητε καὶ ἥκετε, βουλεύσασθε ἅμα, οἱ σῳζόμενοι ἀπὸ τῶν ἐθνῶν. οὐκ ἔγνωσαν οἱ αἴροντες τὸ ξύλον γλύμμα αὐτῶν καὶ προσευχόμενοι ὡς πρὸς θεούς, οἳ οὐ σῴζουσιν [Isa 45:20]). And further it says: "Turn to me, and you shall be saved, you that *come* from the end of the earth: I am God, and there is none other" (45:22) (ἐπιστράφητε πρός με καὶ σωθήσεσθε, οἱ ἀπ' ἐσχάτου τῆς γῆς· ἐγώ εἰμι ὁ θεός, καὶ οὐκ ἔστιν ἄλλος).

All of these allusions here refer to notions that the intervention of God, that is, the naming and role of the anointed one, the calling of people from the nations—and their recognition of the one God of Israel—is on behalf of his people Israel. The analogies of the topics in Phil 2:6–11 and LXX Isaiah 45 are striking—despite the differing literary and historical contexts.

The sole sovereignty of the one and only God of Israel is repeatedly emphasized in the Isaiah passage. Such aspects resonate also here in Phil 2:9–11 —and since more than vague allusion to LXX Isaiah 45 can be found here, it should not come as a surprise that other aspects of the passage resonate here as well. In the Christ-movement these hopes and convictions that God intervenes on behalf of his people—with implications for those of the nations who turn to him also—are seen as being actualized in this anointed one who was executed on a Roman cross, exalted, and given a name above every name.

That he was given a name above every name should be seen not only as resonating with the Isaiah text but contextually also in relation to the namelessness of slaves, and the intention on the part of the executioners to obliterate any trace of memory of such a nobody.[28] This intention is countered by the bestowing of the name above every name[29]—and enhanced by the conviction that in the future it will be precisely in the name of this one, Jesus, who was executed on a cross, that the powers on, below, and above the earth will recognize in him the Lord—and glorify the one and only God—of Israel. The assertion of a future loyalty of all powers to this one God presents a direct challenge to the power claims of Rome. Thus we have a telling example here of a double resonance—on the one side with Isaiah traditions, understood in messianic terms, and at the same time actualized in the concrete situation, by resonating also strongly with the context of the Roman imperial domination.

PHILO AND THE *THIRD SIBYLLINE ORACLE*

In addition to the echo chamber of LXX Isaiah 45, there are Second Temple traditions which consider the intertwined fate of Israel and the nations in various ways.[30] I will only refer to two examples here.

Philo can generally consider the role of Israel in relation to the nations as one of priesthood (*Abr.* 98; *Spec.* 2.162–67; *Mos.* 1.149); as examples for the rest of humankind they are sparks of wisdom wherever they are (*Prob.* 71). Philo also refers to the "conversion" of non-Jews to the one God of Israel and the true democratic constitution in *De Virtutibus* at length, demonstrating with rational arguments the benefit of such a turn or repentance as he calls it (*Virt.* 175–86). Of course Philo sees all of this not in light of messianic expectations but interestingly nevertheless, although not actively advocating proselytizing, notes that those who so turn to the one God should be welcomed and regarded as:

> "our friends and kinsmen since they display that greatest of all bonds with which to cement friendship and kindred, namely, a pious and God-loving disposition, and we ought to sympathise in joy with and to congratulate them, since even if they were blind previously they have now received their sight, beholding the most brilliant of all lights instead of the most profound darkness" (*Virt.* 179).

Although in Philo the specific phrasing of "bending/bowing one's knees" is not found, the turning of people from idolatry to the God of Israel implies of course that they worship him, that is bend their knees to him—if body language were used.

In the messianic-oriented *Third Sibylline Oracle* on the other hand, there is the expectation of a king who will come from the east and overturn the rule of Egypt whereupon there will be a "mass conversion" (lines 618–23) and "all the people will bend their knee to God and the handmade works of men will be cast into the fire" (616–18). Following the destruction of Egypt and the throwing away of idols, God will cause a peaceful period for all humanity giving them great joy (χάρμημεγάλη). It is evident that the abandonment of idolatry signifies entering into relations with the one and only God of Israel.

This turning of the nations to the one God is expected here after the decisive intervention of God, expressed in several parts of the *Sibyllines* (*Sib. Or.* 570; 601–23; 702–61; 767–808); the nations then will flock to the Temple in Jerusalem (715–23), looking to the people Israel for instruction in the worship of the true God. This also matches the role of the people of God laid out earlier on in lines 192–96 ("And then the nation of the Mighty God will be again powerful, that nation which will be to all mortals the guide of life.").

There are numerous allusions in the *Third Sibylline* to topics also found in Phil 2:11, and resonating with Isaiah 45. That in these visions of the *Sibylline* the bending of knees (and thus touching the ground) as expression of the turning of the nations to the one God occurs more than once is striking. It occurs again in lines 716–17: "δεῦτε, πεσόντες ἅπαντες ἐπὶ χθονὶ λισσώμεσθα ἀθάνατον βασιλῆα, θεὸν μέγαν ἀέναόν τε" ("Come on, let us all fall to the ground and pray to the Immortal king, the great and eternal God.")

CONCLUSIONS

The notion that in the context of eschatological events the non-Jewish nations and their idols will actually repent and turn exclusively to the one God is obviously part of the pool of Jewish traditions which circulated in the first century CE. It is noteworthy that in the *Third Sibylline Oracle* the role of Israel is that of a guide and prophet; Israel is not seen as triggering events or 'converting' the nations. The turning of the nations happens at, or after, a decisive intervention of God whereupon these realize his truth and faithfulness, and not least, his love for his people Israel.

By analogy, in the Christ poem of Philippians 2 (as of course elsewhere) the decisive agent in the Christ-event is God. In and through Christ it is God who is acting. This is the focus also in Phil 2:11: those who bend their knees and swear loyalty to him, the one God. They do this in the name of Christ Jesus. There is no Christ worship here, but in the name of this one who has been exalted and given a name above every name—a reference to his status as eschatological Lord Messiah—all powers will bend their knees and swear loyalty to the one and only God. The emphasis on the one and only God is found in Isaiah 45—this is the emphasis of the Philo texts, this is the emphasis of the *Third Sibylline Oracles*. Hence what emerges is evidence for a pool of traditions and notions of eschatological events. The Christ-followers perceived and interpreted their experiences of the Christ-event in light of, and resonating with, notions from this pool of traditions. There is nothing non-Jewish in this—the Christ-poem in Philippians 2 is a Jewish messianic poem—explicating to non-Jews Jewish notions of the nations turning to the one God, inaugurated through the Christ-event as they saw it.

Although Israel and the nations are not explicitly mentioned in Phil 2:9–11, nor in the narrative poem, nor is it an issue discussed explicitly in Philippians, it is a topic present as an echo chamber or intertext, which resonates certainly in this narrative poem. The entire Christ narrative is permeated with eschatological notions of Israel and the nations. However, what role Israel plays in Paul's view in relation to the turning of the nations is not spelled out here. One option would be the one found in the *Sibylline Oracles*. Could it be that Paul, in his role as apostle to the nations, remembered as a teacher of the nations, could have seen this as the role of Israel? He himself then would have taken on a role in relation to the nations, that he would have perceived in analogy to the *Sibylline Oracles*, as an aspect of Israel's role in the messianic age. This would imply that what he deplores in Romans 10 is specifically what his compatriots cannot see, that their role now is that of teachers and prophets to the nations. It cannot be ruled out.[31] Paul does present himself as a teacher (1 Cor 4:17) and is remembered as precisely that in 1 Timothy (2:7). Be this as it may, the theme of Israel and the nations is present in Phil 2:9–11 since there can be no perception of a turning of the nations, and eventually a bowing of every knee and swearing of loyalty of every tongue to the glory of the God of Israel apart from or at the exclusion of Israel.

NOTES

1. Clement of Alexandria, *Excerpts from Theodotus* (*Exc.* 19, 43); Tertullian, *Adversus Marcionem* (*Marc.* 5.20.3–4), *Adversus Praxean* (*Prax.* 10); Origen, *Commentarii in evangelium Joannis* (*Comm. Jo.* 10.23), *Homiliae in Genesim* (*Hom. Gen.* 1.13); Novatian, *De trinitate* (*Trin.* 13.1–2); Eusebius, *Historia ecclesiastica* (*Hist. Eccl.* 11.19.4). Cf. also Benjamin Edsall and Jennifer R. Strawbridge, "The Songs We Used to Sing? Hymn 'Traditions' and Reception in Pauline Letters," *JSNT* 37, no. 3 (2015): 290–311.
2. The literature on Phil 2:6–11 is virtually unmanageable.
3. Cf. Paul A. Holloway, *Philippians. A Commentary*. Hermeneia (Minneapolis, MN: Fortress Press, 2012), 128.
4. I do not discuss any partition theories here, but consider the letter in its canonically transmitted form as one letter. In this I follow Heiko Wojtkowiak, *Christologie und Ethik im Philipperbrief: Studien zur Handlungsorientierung einer frühchristlichen Gemeinde in paganer Umwelt*. FRLANT 243 (Göttingen: Vandenhoeck & Ruprecht, 2012), 73–79.
5. François Mottas, "La population de Philippes et ses origines a la lumière des inscriptions," *Études des Lettres* 239 (1994): 15–24.
6. Robert Brawley, "An Alternative Community and an Oral Encomium: Traces of the People in Philippi," in *The People beside Paul: The Philippian Assembly and History from Below*, ed. Joseph A. Marchal (Atlanta, GA: SBL Press, 2015), 223–46; Angela Standhartinger, "Letter from Prison as Hidden Transcript: What It Tells Us About the People in Philippi," in *The People beside Paul: The Philippian Assembly and History from Below*, ed. Joseph A. Marchal (Atlanta, GA: SBL Press, 2015), 107–40; Cédric Brélaz, "First Century Philippi: Contextualizing Paul's Visit," in *The First Urban Churches 4: Roman Philippi*, ed. James R. Harrison and Larry L.

Welborn (Atlanta, GA: SBL Press, 2018), 153–88; Peter Oakes, *Philippians: From People to Letter* (Cambridge: Cambridge University Press, 2001).

7. Cicero, *De provinciis consularibus* (*Prov. cons.* 5.10).

8. Cf. Cicero, *De republica* (*Resp.* 3.35–37), *Pro Flacco* (*Flac.* 1–16).

9. Although of course the fiction of the upholding of the *res publica* and the role of the senate were skillfully maintained for centuries.

10. See the requirements of the institutional setup in the Lex Ursoniensis for the colony of Urso in 44 BCE, discussed in Jörg Rüpke, *From Jupiter to Christ: On the History of Religion in the Roman Imperial Period* (Oxford: Oxford University Press, 2014), 113–34.

11. As noted by Mantha Zarmakoupi, "The forum zone was first established in the middle of the first century CE, in an area that was previously occupied by a residential district, and finalised in the second century CE. In its final phase it consisted of three terraces built up-slope the southwest face of the Acropolis hill. The highest terrace featured three central temples related to the worship of the Capitoline ("Urban Space and Housing in Roman Macedonia: Thessaloniki, Philippi, Amphipolis, and Dion," in *Les Communautiés du Nord Égéen au Temps de l'Hégémonie Romaine. Entre Ruptures and Continuités*, ed. Julien Fournier and Marie-Gabrielle G. Parissaki [Athènes: Fondation Nationale de la Recherche Scientifique/Institut de Recherches Historiques, 2018], 281 [263–97].

12. Peter Pilhofer, *Philippi. Band 2: Katalog der Inschriften von Philippi*, 2nd rev. ed., WUNT 119 (Tübingen: Mohr Siebeck, 2009); also James R. Harrison, "From Rome to the Colony of Philippi: Roman Boasting in Philippians 3:4-6 In its Latin West and Philippian Epigraphic Context," in *The First Urban Churches 4: Roman Philippi*, ed. James R. Harrison and Larry L. Welborn (Atlanta, GA: SBL 2018), 307–70.

13. On Philippi under Rome see James R. Harrison, "Excavating the Urban and Country Life of Roman Philippi and its Territory," in *The First Urban Churches 4: Roman Philippi*, ed. James R. Harrison, Larry L. Welborn (Atlanta, GA: SBL Press, 2018), 1–61; Peter Pilhofer, *Philippi. Band 1: Die erste christliche Gemeinde Europas*, WUNT 1.87 (Tübingen: Mohr Siebeck 1995).

14. Cf. my *Paul at the Crossroads of Cultures–Theologizing in the Space–Between* (London, U.K. and New York, NY: Bloomington T&T Clark, 2013), 126–31, also Paula Fredriksen, "If It Looks like a Duck, and It Quacks Like a Duck: On *Not* Giving Up the Godfearers," in *A Most Reliable Witness: Essays in Honor of Ross Shepard Kraemer*, ed. Susan Ashbrook Harvey et al. (Providence, RI: Brown Judaic Studies 2015), 25–33. This is also implied in the narrative of Acts 16:14, which may be legendary rather than precisely historical, but it nevertheless presents a narrative of events which are historically plausible for people towards the end of the first century CE.

15. Cf. my "The Politeuma in the Heavens and the Construction of Collective Identity in Philippians," in *Citizens of Heaven, Residents of Philippi: Studies in Philippians* (Lanham, MD: Lexington Books/Fortress Academic, forthcoming).

16. For example, in the narrative of 2 Maccabees in analogy and possibly application of Deut 32, the foreign rule can only be exercised due to God's power which is granted to Antiochos IV in this case for a limited time (cf. 2 Macc 7).

17. See, e.g., *De sobrietate* (*Sobr.* 63), *Quis rerum divinarum heres sit* (*Her.* 58), *De decalogo* (*Decal.* 58).

18. Katell Berthelot, "Philo's Perception of the Roman Empire," *JSJ* 42 (2011): 179 (166–87).

19. As noted above, of course there were others who distanced themselves from the Roman claim, but this was mainly so in terms of philosophical arguments or critical stances against particular rulers. Cf. James Harrison, *Paul and the Imperial Authorities at Thessalonica and Rome.* WUNT 273 (Tübingen: Mohr Siebeck, 2011), 177–85.

20. Anathea Portier-Young, *Apocalypse against Empire: Theologies of Resistance in Early Judaism* (Grand Rapids, MI: Eerdmans, 2011), 140–75.

21. Jonathan Klawans, *Josephus and the Theologies of Ancient Judaism* (Oxford: Oxford University Press, 2012), 190.

22. Cf. my *Paul at the Crossroads of Cultures*, 142–52, and also "Paul, Emasculated Apostle or Manly Man? Gendered Aspects of Cultural Translation" in *Searching Paul: Conversations with the Jewish Apostle to the Nations. Collected Essays.* WUNT 429 (Tübingen: Mohr Siebeck, 2019), 73–90. Samuel Vollenweider also maintains that Phil 2:6–11 "ist nicht einfach als eine Reaktionsbildung auf Alexander oder Caligula bzw. den Herrscherkult anzusprechen. Unser Christuslob kommt von biblischen und jüdischen Traditionen her, worin Gottes Königtum zu den Weltmächten einen scharfen Kontrast bildet". ("'Raub' der Göttlichkeit: Ein religionsgeschichtlicher Vorschlag zu Phil 2.6[(11)]," *NTS* 45 [1999]: 425 [(413–33)].

23. William S. Campbell, *The Nations in the Divine Economy: Paul's Covenantal Hermeneutics and Participation in Christ* (Lanham, MD: Lexington Books/Fortress Academic, 2018), 225–54.

24. Eric Heen, "Phil 2:6–11 and Resistance to Local Timocratic rule: Isa theō and the Cult of the Emperor in the East," in *Paul and the Roman Imperial Order*, ed. Richard A. Horsley (Harrisburg, PA: Trinity Press International, 2004), 125–53; also Albert Harrill who notes that references to Lord do not have the emperor cult in view but the lordship of all so acclaimed. However, the political dimension of this title cannot be denied in my view. See J. Albert Harrill, *Paul the Apostle: His Life and Legacy in Their Roman Context* (Cambridge: Cambridge University Press, 2012), 88.

25. Cf. also Rom 15:7, 1 Cor 10:31, etc.

26. Further similarities between formulations in Romans and Philippians would need to be explored as, e.g., the theme of welcoming.

27. This could refer to the dispersed among the non-Jewish nations as well as to the those from the nations who turn away from idols; thus it is open to interpretation.

28. Significantly with reference to the Lord's supper there is an emphasis on precisely the remembrance of the crucified: τοῦτο ποιεῖτε εἰς τὴν ἐμὴν ἀνάμνησιν (1 Cor 11:24b).

29. The discussion whether the name refers to the name of God—or as Holloway argues in his commentary rather to a name-bearing angel—meaning here then that the one crucified and exalted has been elevated to an angelic status cannot be discussed here, but either option is not excluded by the dimension of the name-

giving highlighted here; it is the one who had been executed and thereby sentenced to the *damnatio memoriae* who is given the name above every name (Holloway, *Philippians*, 125–27).

30. Cf., e.g., also my "The Pauline Ἐκκλησίαι and Images of Community in Enoch Traditions," in *Searching Paul: Conversations with the Jewish Apostle to the Nations. Collected Essays*, WUNT 429 (Tübingen: Mohr Siebeck, 2019), 111–36.

31. I cannot elaborate on this further in this contribution. This is a topic for another paper.

BIBLIOGRAPHY

Berthelot, Katell. "Philo's Perception of the Roman Empire." *JSJ* 42 (2011): 166–87.

Brawley, Robert. "An Alternative Community and an Oral Encomium: Traces of the People in Philippi." In *The People beside Paul: The Philippian Assembly and History from Below*, edited by Joseph A. Marchal, 223–46. Atlanta, GA: SBL Press, 2015.

Brélaz, Cédric. "First Century Philippi: Contextualizing Paul's Visit." In *The First Urban Churches 4: Roman Philippi*, edited by James R. Harrison and Larry L. Welborn, 153–88. Atlanta, GA: SBL Press, 2018.

Campbell, William S. *The Nations in the Divine Economy: Paul's Covenantal Hermeneutics and Participation in Christ.* Lanham, MD: Lexington Books/Fortress Academic, 2018.

Edsall, Benjamin, and Jennifer R. Strawbridge. "The Songs We Used to Sing? Hymn 'Traditions' and Reception in Pauline Letters." *JSNT* 37, no. 3 (2015): 290–311.

Ehrensperger, Kathy. *Paul at the Crossroads of Cultures–Theologizing in the Space-Between.* London, U.K. and New York, NY: Bloomington T&T Clark, 2013.

———. "Paul, Emasculated Apostle or Manly Man? Gendered Aspects of Cultural Translation." In *Searching Paul: Conversations with the Jewish Apostle to the Nations. Collected Essays*, 73–90. WUNT 429. Tübingen: Mohr Siebeck, 2019.

———. "The Politeuma in the Heavens and the Construction of Collective Identity in Philippians." In *Citizens of Heaven, Residents of Philippi: Studies in Philippians.* Lanham, MD: Lexington/Fortress Academic, forthcoming.

———. *Searching Paul: Conversations with the Jewish Apostle to the Nations. Collected Essays.* WUNT 429. Tübingen: Mohr Siebeck, 2019.

Fredriksen, Paula. "If It Looks like a Duck, and It Quacks like a Duck: On *Not* Giving Up the Godfearers." In *A Most Reliable Witness: Essays in Honor of Ross Shepard Kraemer*, edited by Susan Ashbrook Harvey et al., 25–33. Providence, RI: Brown Judaic Studies 2015.

Harrill, Albert. *Paul the Apostle: His Life and Legacy in Their Roman Context.* Cambridge: Cambridge University Press, 2012.

Harrison, James R. "Excavating the Urban and Country Life of Roman Philippi and Its Territory." In *The First Urban Churches 4: Roman Philippi*, edited by James R. Harrison and Larry L. Welborn, 1–61. Atlanta, GA: SBL Press, 2018.

———. "From Rome to the Colony of Philippi: Roman Boasting in Philippians 3:4-6 in Its Latin West and Philippian Epigraphic Context." In *The First Urban Churches 4: Roman Philippi*, edited by James R. Harrison and Larry L. Welborn, 307–70. Atlanta, GA: SBL Press, 2018.

———. *Paul and the Imperial Authorities at Thessalonica and Rome*. WUNT 273. Tübingen: Mohr Siebeck, 2011.

Heen, Eric. "Phil 2:6–11 and Resistance to Local Timocratic rule: Isa theō and the Cult of the Emperor in the East." In *Paul and the Roman Imperial Order*, edited by Richard A. Horsley, 125–53. Harrisburg, PA: Trinity Press International, 2004.

Holloway, Paul A. *Philippians. A Commentary*. Hermeneia. Minneapolis, MN: Fortress Press, 2012.

Klawans, Jonathan. *Josephus and the Theologies of Ancient Judaism*. Oxford: Oxford University Press, 2012.

Mottas, François. "La population de Philippes et ses origines a la lumière des inscriptions." *Études des Lettres* 239 (1994): 15–24.

Oakes, Peter. *Philippians: From People to Letter*. Cambridge: Cambridge University Press, 2001.

Pilhofer, Peter. *Philippi. Band 1: Die erste christliche Gemeinde Europas*. WUNT 1.87. Tübingen: Mohr Siebeck, 1995.

———. *Philippi. Band 2: Katalog der Inschriften von Philippi*. 2d rev. ed. WUNT 119. Tübingen: Mohr Siebeck, 2009.

Portier-Young, Anathea. *Apocalypse against Empire: Theologies of Resistance in Early Judaism*. Grand Rapids, MI: Eerdmans, 2011.

Rüpke, Jörg. *From Jupiter to Christ: On the History of Religion in the Roman Imperial Period*. Oxford: Oxford University Press, 2014.

Standhartinger, Angela. "Letter from Prison as Hidden Transcript: What It Tells Us about the People in Philippi." In *The People beside Paul: The Philippian Assembly and History from Below*, edited by Joseph A. Marchal, 107–40. Atlanta, GA: SBL Press, 2015.

Vollenweider, Samuel. "'Raub' der Göttlichkeit: Ein religionsgeschichtlicher Vorschlag zu Phil 2.6(–11)." *NTS* 45 (1999): 276 (413–33).

Wojtkowiak, Heiko. *Christologie und Ethik im Philipperbrief: Studien zur Handlungsorientierung einer frühchristlichen Gemeinde in paganer Umwelt*. FRLANT 243. Göttingen: Vandenhoeck & Ruprecht, 2012.

Zarmakoupi, Mantha. "Urban Space and Housing in Roman Macedonia: Thessaloniki, Philippi, Amphipolis, and Dion." In *Les Communautiés du Nord Égéen au Temps de l'Hégémonie Romaine. Entre Ruptures and Continuités*, edited by Julien Fournier and Marie-Gabrielle G. Parissaki, 263–97. Athènes: Fondation Nationale de la Recherche Scientifique/Institut de Recherches Historiques, 2018.

Chapter Ten

'But It Is Not As Though the Word of God Had Failed'

Israel as a Sub-Text in Romans?

William S. Campbell

INTRODUCTION

In any reading of Romans, it is clear that Paul's mission to the nations occupies a central place, discussed even within chapters 9–11. In this chapter I want also to study the presentation of Paul's mission to the nations in its relation to Jews and to the future of Israel. The issue is, how may these two themes, the one relating to Paul's mission to the nations and the other to his explicitly noted concern for his own people, be connected in any interpretation of Romans? We can relate these under the general theme of Jews, "gentiles," and the gospel, but I think we need to be more specific. If we keep in mind that Paul writes to the Romans not only because of their needs as reported to him, but also because of what it is that Paul wants or hopes for from them, a *link may be made between Paul's mission to the non-Jews in Rome and his strong emphasis in Romans on Israel in the divine purpose.*

My proposal is that reactions to Paul's reported teaching about God's dealings with Israel in the light of the coming of Christ had caused serious misrepresentations of his message such that Paul's future mission to Spain via Rome is being put in jeopardy. Likewise, biased reporting of Paul's attribution of insensibility by his own people to God's purpose in Christ[1] may prevent a peaceful receipt of the collection when he visits Jerusalem. So Paul finds it necessary to repudiate misconceptions and to establish himself as "apostle to the nations,"[2] including the gentile Christ-followers at Rome. Hence, he asserts that his primary work, his διακονία to the nations, has another anticipated outcome in view in making his fellow Jews jealous and so to win some of them (11:13–14). In Paul's perspective, the apostleship to the nations demonstrably excludes his portrayal as the enemy of Israel since the mission to the nations is inherently related also to the salvation of Israel. And yet it is only non-Jews who are addressed, the content of Romans is targeted for the ἔθνη—Jews are referred to in the third person. *We need to distinguish addressees from subject matter.*

Diversity among groups seems to have typified the Christ-movement in Rome following the similar fragmented character of Roman Judaism.[3]

REPORTS OF PAUL'S GOSPEL AS THE SOURCE OF THE QUESTIONS IN ROM 3:1–8

From the questions, objections, and inferences which Paul lists in 3:1–8 we can deduce that Paul's gospel for the nations contained not only teaching concerning the sinfulness of the world generally, but also some specific explanation about the failure of Israel as a whole to respond favorably to Jesus as the Christ. Paul, while addressing only non-Jews in Romans, somewhat surprisingly teaches about the Jewish people within God's purpose, particularly in chapters 2–4, 9–11, and 15. This is the peculiar problem that concerns Paul here—how his teaching to non-Jews about God's dealings with Israel has been misunderstood as indicating a displacement of Israel by ἔθνη in Christ, particularly as it raises doubts about God's impartial rule over all peoples, including Israel (and Rome) (Rom 2:5–11).

Paul's message to the nations is really an explanation of a divine purpose which tells both of God's opposition to human sin and failure, including Roman exploitation and injustice, and of how God through Christ is now dealing with this in relation to Jews and also the gentile world.[4] The people of Israel are central to this message as is the fact that opportunity for repentance has now been given to the *ἔθνη*.

This raises two main issues in 3:1–8—not all Jews have responded positively to the coming of Christ (3:3), and how can God still judge the world righteously (3:6), if he has tolerated human sin until now? Why does he still find fault? Paul's reply is to speak of a divine will to demonstrate God's power and wrath, involving patient forbearance "ἀνοχή" (3:26) and μακροθυμία (9:22).[5] The righteousness of God demands and ensures God's total opposition to unrighteousness, and the coming of Christ reveals this. *Paul views this revelation in terms of a divine purpose, which we might conceive as being delineated in the actual content of the (his) gospel.*

In Pauline perspective, God had a purpose which includes not only the Jews but also the ἔθνη which has only now been revealed through the revelation of righteousness in Christ.

It is striking that Paul gives such a strong condemnation of the gentile condition in 1:18–32. This may be accentuated because of the Roman context as suggested by a gentile misunderstanding of sin and grace as, e.g., 6:1; 6:15. But I think it is the gentile condition, qua gentiles,[6] of which Paul reminds the Romans both in 1:18–32 and in 11:13–24. This "condition" was critically perceived by Jews like Paul as life in an idolatrous world that merited the righteous opposition and judgment of the God of Israel. Paul not only informed those from the nations that now (e.g., 3:21; 5:9) a new era had dawned in which fresh options had been opened up to non-Jews, but included an explanation why, for various reasons, a majority of Israel had not responded favorably.

Also, the fact that Paul's mission work was deliberately confined to non-Jews, seemed to confirm that the divine purpose for Israel had been completed, and that God had turned instead to the nations, evidenced by their increasing numbers joining the Christ-movement, and the poor response from Jews (cf. 3:3).

God had temporarily rendered insensible to the gospel the hearts of a majority of his people so as to ensure the success of his purpose of gentile inclusion in Christ as representatives of the nations.[7] But this theological explanation that Paul offered was not well understood even by those ἔθνη who were willing to join the Christ-movement. Yet Paul will later in the letter, in chapters 9–11, maintain that the purpose of the God of Israel was not hindered by Israel's failure to recognize Jesus as the Christ, since this insensibility was itself part of the divine purpose that encompassed the incoming of the nations.

THE DIATRIBE STYLE AS KEY TO PAUL'S FORM OF ARGUMENTATION IN ROMANS

My view of Romans as a letter is that Paul chose a diatribe, i.e., an interactionary, question-response style—in order to present indirectly his own position in reaction to the content of negative responses to his mission that may have originated elsewhere but are now already present in Rome (3:8).[8] These, repeated in the voice of an imagined interlocutor, normally formed as a fictitious representative for the letter's audience, enable Paul to "respond in advance to potential objections to what is being uttered in the letter."[9] As noted above, following the dialogue introduced in 2.1 directly addressing someone in the second-person singular,[10] Paul in 3:1–8 lists a number of questions and his reactions to them. From the subject of the first question, the advantage of "the Jew," we get evidence that the interlocutor is gentile. The succeeding questions concerning the value of circumcision and the issue of some Jews being unfaithful are similar in perspective. Verse 3—"Does this nullify the faithfulness of God?"—is not so clear. But the first-person plural reference—"If our wickedness serves to show the righteousness of God, is God then unjust to punish us?"—is again clearly from a gentile perspective. The issues raised in these questions re-emerge throughout Romans 3–11: e.g., 4:1 (Abraham's paternity); 6:1, 15 (grace and continuing to sin); 7:7, 13 (the law as a source of sin); 11:1, 11 (has God rejected his people Israel?). When it is noted that it is a gentile audience that is addressed, and also that some of the vocabulary used in chapter 3 has connections with 1:18–32, then it emerges that in Romans Paul's focus is on the place of the nations alongside a related issue, the future of Israel. Paul's gospel does have a universal outreach, but not in the form espoused by historic Paulinism, forcing Paul to conform to an ideology of sameness.[11] Rather, the proselyte-related discussion of Romans 2 indicates that in Romans Paul affirms the distinctiveness of Jew and non-Jew (as Matthew Novenson's interpretation suggests to me[12]).

It seems that when Paul sought to explain the incoming of the nations, he found it necessary to do so via God's dealings with his people Israel. So, to situate his gentile mission in the divine purpose which differentiates Jew and non-Jew in accordance with the covenant, Paul had to give an explanation of Israel's status and identity in the divine plan. Moreover, this has to be explained so as to correlate with the new status and identity of those from the nations according to his gospel, and how his gentile mission relates to Israel. *In order to establish an identity for ἔθνη in Christ, Paul has to explain the place of Israel within God's purpose for the world now revealed in Christ.*[13]

In the immediate context of 3:4, Paul strongly repudiates with his first use of μὴ γένοιτο,[14] followed by a scriptural citation, any suggestion that human failure puts God's faithfulness in doubt. In v. 5 following, he moves away from the question concerning unfaithfulness to a discussion of divine justice, δικαιοσύνη—i.e., the character of a God who uses human sin to promote his own glory whilst still condemning the sinners. The use of ἀδικία and ἁμαρτολός here indicates that it is God's character particularly in relation to the idolatrous non-Jewish world so strongly condemned in 1:18–32 that is in view.[15] Since Romans is clearly designated as a letter to the ἔθνη, Paul's reference to 'our unrighteousness' in 3:5, in contrast to the third-person references to the Jews in 3:1–2, must be to gentile ἀδικία, wickedness, most often typified as idolatry;[16] thus these questions clearly represent gentile misunderstandings about the role of Israel in Paul's gospel.[17] Paul is aware of the misunderstandings possibly wrongly attributed to him and his mission. *In Romans he makes clear that God's dealings with Israel have not failed, and that Israel continues to occupy a central role in the divine purpose leading to both the "fullness of the nations" and the salvation of "all Israel"* (11:25–27).

Since he wishes to exercise leadership among the non-Jewish Christfollowers in Rome both now and on his way to Spain, though his entire letter addresses only the ἔθνη,[18] he deliberately argues his case indirectly so as to cause less offence, especially since he has not yet visited Rome.[19] Firstly, he sets up specific negative suggestions or responses and then immediately rejects these with a repeated μὴ γένοιτο. By this means he introduces the (mainly) negative questions he wishes to address, and immediately makes clear that he rejects these, thereby exposing stances he does not hold, and about the denial of which, particularly in relation to Israel, he wants to make sure there can now be no duplicity. His chosen manner of indirect address in the voice of a fictitious non-Jewish interlocutor, one of the ἔθνη, probably a proselyte, indicates Paul's carefully considered manner of address. He can indict the interlocutor sharply without offending his actual addressees.[20]

Secondly, in a more positive vein, rather than always giving a fierce response to an inference or objection as with the repeated use of μὴ γένοιτο, Paul can also refine or revise interpretations of his message, repeating the explicatory introductory formula τί οὖν [ἐροῦμεν], in order to prevent further misunderstanding. This pattern of address thus indicates Paul's own response to the perversions of the gospel message with which he has been charged. In these instances, where Paul does not wish to reject outright, but merely to refine stances or opinions, he can vary the introductory formula (τί οὖν ἐροῦμεν)—e.g., 3:1 begins only with τί οὖν, whereas 3:5 includes the ἐροῦμεν but omits the οὖν. The normal pattern occurs in 4:1; 6:1; 7:7; 8:31; 9:14 and 9:30. The links between the gospel and the Law (3:31) and between the Law and sin (7:7, 13) are thus indicated as significant, as derivatives of one of the two most important themes.[21] Who are Abraham's children i.e. of whom is Abraham father (4:1) is also likely to be one of the important questions Paul wishes to address (cf. 4:9) linking also to 9:14; 9:30; 11:1; and 11:11 where issues about Israel dominate. The diatribe style, though variable, permeates Rom 2–11, and to a lesser extent 12–15,[22] and must be viewed as a significant element in how Paul chose to present himself and his gospel in any attempt to give an overview of the argument.

One of the most significant critical objections Paul lists relates to the status of Israel. Already in chapter 2, he discusses who is a Jew, and this then continues into chapter 3 where he discusses the advantage of the Jew, the value of circumcision as the mark of a Jewish way of life. This is only a preliminary introduction to the issue which is explicitly raised again in 11:1 and 11:11, "Has God rejected his people?" and "Have they stumbled so as to be rejected?" These two negative questions are paralleled in relation also to the Law in 7:7 and 7:13, "Is the Law (the source of) sin?" and "Did that which was good bring death to me?" These two issues—i.e., the people of God and their Law—are the two most important issues from the gentile interlocutor which Paul wishes to introduce in this diatribe pattern,[23] and his reaction in good Jewish "question and response" style enables him to be explicit about how his mission to the nations fits into God's purpose for the mending of creation, including the redemption of Israel.[24] In the divine purpose, Paul's mission to the nations is bound up with the salvation of Israel, it is not an independent or oppositional activity. But we note that the texts in 3:2 and 9:4–5 both begin with references to the Jews in the third person, indicating that they are not the addressees.

Paul's assertion in 9:6a–b, though partly in the form of diatribal questioning, claims that God's word cannot possibly have failed. In this way he presents the basic issue concerning Israel by arguing that if there should be any doubt about Israel's future existence, if Israel as the people of grace-gifts and promises were to fail, this would mean that God's word, God's glorious revelation of righteousness has come to nought.[25] For Paul this is entirely inconceivable.

As noted, the common presupposition behind Paul's words of grief in Rom 9:1–3 is that a majority of Israelites have not responded positively to the message that he and others proclaimed—that is, that 'a new messianic time has been inaugurated in Christ'.[26] It is also probable, as mentioned above, that there were some Christ-followers in Rome who, based upon this presupposition and for other reasons, considered that Israel had put herself on the side of God's enemies, rather than of Christ, and therefore had been rejected as his people.[27] But Paul describes only his sorrow and *does not supply* its cause. We must not read in psychological perspectives on Paul's grieving such as Stendahl deplored in relation to the Western introspective conscience, nor use it as a reason for pessimism about Israel's future. In any case, it is not warranted to claim that it is Israel's failings alone that makes Paul grieve—Paul laments Israel in the context of Roman domination in a sinful world[28] where the weak and powerless are down-trodden. There are no strong grounds here for anticipating judgment rather than hope for Israel. Israel's future at this point in Rom 9 remains entirely open. So Paul commences the chapter by making his own stance towards Israel absolutely clear—God must be, and will be, faithful to Israel.

ROMANS 9:6b:
NEGATIVE STATEMENT OR RHETORICAL QUESTION?

Paul begins chapter 9 by a unique listing of the privileges of Israel, leaving little doubt as to his appreciation of that heritage from which stems the Messiah, through the lineage of promise. Paul protests that he speaks the truth in Christ about his concern for Israel, that he is not lying and his conscience bears witness to this through the Holy Spirit. Whilst it is likely that Paul means to put strong emphasis upon his appreciation of his Israelite heritage, the strength of his emphasis might suggest more than this—Paul is at pains to maintain that there is no duplicity in his attitude to his own people and their heritage. Paul's powerful denial here evidences the negative attitude to Israel of which he must have been suspected—i.e., of being less than fully committed to his ancestral faith.[29] So it is to be expected that in 9:6b, Paul in order to counteract the scepticism some attribute to him, would continue to affirm his confident hope for Israel despite her failure to recognize Christ. A closer look at the text confirms this expectation.

Paul commences the chapter by making his stance absolutely clear.[30] The depth of his concern for his brothers, his kin, is demonstrated by his willingness to be cut off from Christ if this would be advantageous to them. Then he rehearses the glorious blessings which Israel still enjoys: "They are Israelites, and to them belong (present tense) the sonship, the glory, the covenants, the giving of the law, the worship and the promises; to them belong the patriarchs, and from them by human descent is the Christ . . ." (9:4–5). Paul makes it plain that he identifies with the people of Israel and that he is confirming the abiding blessings God has given them. Paul's primary emphasis is not upon the failings of Israel despite her variegated history. If Israel is perceived as rejected by some, it is the word of God to Israel that is being despised, and Paul does not anticipate that the word that initially called Israel to blessing has failed or is likely to fail.

After such an exalted description of the heritage of Israel,[31] one would not anticipate that Paul would immediately dilute or diminish what he has now so fully elaborated and in which his own commitment to Israel is included. This factor is further emphasized by the very next verse, 9.6a, which the RSV translates as "But it is not as though the word of God had failed." Thus, first we have a full list of Israel's advantages, followed by a denial that God's promise to Israel has failed—i.e., the "word of God" refers back to the gifts of God's grace previously noted in 3:2 and elaborated in 9:4–5.[32] It would be most inconsistent immediately following on this introduction to the chapter for Paul then to begin apparently to retract on the claims he has just advanced.

But this is exactly what we are asked to believe if we read 9:6b with the RSV as a statement, "For not all who are descended from Israel belong to Israel." If this is what Paul knew he was going to write in this verse, it seems he chose a very poor preface as it does not in any way prepare for the partial denial of Israel's call by the sudden introduction of what would amount to a redefinition of Israel[33] that actually contradicts much of what he has just so strongly emphasized. Following on from 9:4–5, we would anticipate that Paul would be tending to argue in the opposite direction—i.e., that the non-acceptance by (part of) Israel of the message about Jesus as the Christ does not mean that God's grace-gifts to Israel have been nullified.

Thus, in terms of consistency, it would seem more likely that Paul would here be arguing for the ongoing validity of God's election of Israel rather than redefining Israel or denying her election. And, if the word of God has not failed (9:6a), then with Otto Michel we would expect v. 6b, if it is presumed to oppose the positive content of v. 6a, to start with an adversative ἀλλά ("but"), or even with a μὴ γένοιτο exclamation[34], rather than γάρ ("for")—which would suggest that the thought of the first part of the verse is being further elaborated rather than negated.[35] But if it is negated, even partially, what precedes it is almost completely devalued if Paul then juggles with the definition of "Israel,"[36] and possibly according to some readings, also includes those from the nations within the term "Israel," because if the content of the title "Israel" can be changed in one direction, it is thus open to change in others.

What then are we to make of the *apparent* contradiction, or at least hiatus in Paul's statements concerning Israel following the common translations of these verses? It would seem that what is claimed in vv. 4–5—that Israel according to the flesh was designated bearer of the promise and the recipient of sonship—is, in vv. 6b–7 partly and, following on from this in v. 8, fundamentally, disputed.[37] Those following closely Paul's train of thought would have anticipated that here in vv. 6b–7 Paul would have added to or developed his immediately preceding affirmation of Israel's election and blessing. But astonishingly, what we find is not affirmation but denial, or at least qualification of an extreme kind—the Israel first presented here is in fact not the real Israel; only a part is truly "Israel."

It seems as if Paul suddenly realized the problem of what he had just claimed, God's word to Israel has not failed, and yet Israel has not accepted his estimate of Christ. The solution since Justin in the second century[38] has been to solve the problem by a redefinition of the word "Israel," so it is now taken to mean that Judaism has no validity apart from Christ since it has been superseded. Only a part of Israel is actually Israel. But this solution gives a poor image of Pauline rhetoric if we remember that it is Paul himself who creates this dissonant discussion in the space of a few verses. Even if he is dealing with a topic that is incredibly difficult, Paul could have introduced it better.[39]

Struggling to find a coherent and consistent interpretation of Rom 9, I had, after many attempts, decided that part of the problem lies in the fact that Paul is really concentrating in the first half of the chapter on how Israel came into being, on the initial call that first constituted the people of Israel, so that 9:6b–13 is really a discussion that could precede 9:1–5 in that it defines who Israel is and how she was created. The explanations based upon the distinction between descendants as τέκνα or as σπέρμα now made sense of the limitation within Abraham's progeny that first constituted Israel. But it was only when I found Klaus Wengst's proposal that 9:6b–7 be read not as a redefining statement but as a rhetorical question[40] followed by an adversative in v. 7 that I was able to find a coherent reading such as I am following here.

In keeping with the dominant rhetorical patterns established in 3:1–8, and continuing in the succeeding chapters, such rhetorical patterns do not lead us to expect the statement in 9:6b, "For not all who are descended from Israel belong to Israel." A more fitting reading suggests instead a rhetorical question expecting an affirmative answer—"Is it not the case that all who are descended from Israel are Israel?"[41] The question points to an anticipated positive outcome, such as "Yes, it is true that all of Israel are Israel." This is similar to the question in 11:1 which we note Ross Wagner paraphrases as "God has not rejected his inheritance, has he?"[42] In the verse immediately following after 6b, a clarification helps to remove any negative inference behind the question in 6b.

In v. 7 Paul changes the subject somewhat in that he now speaks not of Israel's descendants but of Abraham's. Thus v. 7 is read adversatively, "But not all are σπέρμα because they are his τέκνα." Walter Bauer reads 9:6b as a negative sentence and then he prioritizes the reading οὐδέ in v. 7 as "and not", thus making v. 7 a continuation and equivalent of this supposedly negative sentence in 6b. But only v. 7 should be read adversatively, as a limitation among the wider family of Abraham. It appears that Paul now sets out to explain in detail how Israel both is and remains Israel. Paul clarifies that within Abraham's descendants there is a selection. "(But) not all of Abraham's children (τέκνα) are his seed (σπέρμα)."[43] Moreover, it is also stated that it is (only) through the line of Isaac that the promises continue, "in Isaac shall your σπέρμα be named," citing Gen 21:12 (LXX). Then this line of thought is consistently developed and explained in v. 8, "This means that it is not the children of the flesh (fleshly descent only) who are the children of God, but it is the children of promise (the line of descent thorough Isaac) who are reckoned as σπέρμα."[44] Reading 6b not as a negating statement but as a rhetorical question expecting an affirmative answer does, in fact, continue the positive presentation of Israel from vv. 4–5, and the qualification and limitation regarding Abraham's descendants introduced in v. 7, does not contradict the affirmation of Israel, since it does not apply to her. This alternative reading is thus not in tension with the rhetorical patterns that precede, and likewise resonates well with what succeeds. It is also more consistent with Paul's hope for Israel affirmed in 11:25–27.

Not only does this reading avoid the contradiction with the vivid, positive depiction of "Israelites" and their heritage in v. 4, and what immediately succeeds it, but it coheres well with the differentiation Paul goes on to stress in 9:8–13 that Abraham's descendants were not all included in Israel, the people of the covenant, but were according to Gen 18:10 limited to those within the line of Isaac. We note here that this reading is a differentiation *within* Abraham's descendants. So this differentiation, since it draws a distinction between τέκνα and σπέρμα within the descendants of Abraham, cannot be read as eliminating Israelites from the people of promise, nor is it a repudiation of normal human descent, but rather a limitation within this.[45] It refers to a limitation, or selection within the τέκνα of Abraham, not to a selection within Israel, nor does it suggest that there will be any selection *of this kind* in future among the people Israel whom God has chosen to be his own. This refers to a unique calling in which God *first* chooses Israel for his own purposes.

Thus, when Paul proceeds to develop his argument, he demonstrates through the example of Isaac, the promised son to aged parents, and Jacob (rather than Esau despite being twins) that Israel is constituted by people of descent *and promise*, rather than simply by those of fleshly descent from Abraham. Further, the items Paul sets in contrast are not works and faith, as might have been anticipated, but rather human works and God's call; it is these that constitute the foundation of the historic "faith versus works" dichotomy. Thus, Paul is stressing that those who are merely related to Abraham by physical descent are not his σπέρμα. What is more, no amount of human achievement can bring a people within the lineage of promise[46] since these are constituted, not by human worth, but by the call of God. *There is a real possibility that such an argument about Israel's identity has some relation to, and bearing upon, the status of proselytes and God-fearers in Rome.*

In Rom 9:1–13 Paul is setting out what makes Israel distinctive, how Israel was called. He goes back to Israel's beginnings to explain Israel's identity from her earliest origins. Israel is called from among the descendants of Abraham as the recipient of the promise, and thus is called to be the bearer of this promise in accordance with the divine "purpose of election" (9:11). It is the choice by God to make Israel the bearer of the promise that makes her distinctive.[47] Once Israel is identified, she is differentiated from other descendants of Abraham. Thus, there is only one Israel here, and not an Israel within Israel—Paul's reading precludes such a perception. Paul will go on to make a distinction in 11:7 between a holy remnant within Israel and the rest of Israel, but this is not the same distinction as in the traditional reading of Rom 9:6b–13, where a distinction is created among the descendants of Abraham generally, whereas this relates to a division within the line of promise itself.

CONCLUSION

What is noteworthy in chapter 9 in the narrative of Abraham's descendants is that where families are closely related, difference between them is introduced. To make the point, Paul first turns to the narrative of Isaac, the son of promise (9:7–9), and then to that of Jacob and Esau (9:10–12). Had it not been for the divine intervention, Sarah would never have had a son, so all the future progeny originates from the combination of this promise and of natural descent. The lineage of Jacob is by both promise and fleshly descent, no one outside this line of descendants of Abraham, Isaac, and Jacob is included. The statement in Rom 9:8 "it is not the children of the flesh who are the children of God, but the children of the promise are reckoned as σπέρμα" is not a general principle that applies outside of the Abraham, Isaac, and Jacob lineage of descent. Nor is it an ongoing principle continuing to operate. This is a specific commentary on this particular lineage, indicating only that though others, as descendants of Abraham, are related to Abraham and to one another, and thus count as his τέκνα—i.e., children—they are not because of this reckoned σπέρμα—i.e., heirs—to the promise.[48] Noteworthy here also is Paul's use of terminology—in 9:8 he uses the term λογίζεται, the same terminology that he used in relation to Abraham in chapter 4, e.g., v. 4, where the wages of the one working for a reward are not λογίζεται κατὰ χάραν.[49] By this Paul indicates, in both chapter 4 and chapter 9,[50] how those called by God live in a grace/faith relation rather than in a works/merit contract. Since the unborn twins Esau and Jacob were incapable of doing either good or bad deeds, the difference between them was because of the lineage of divine call and promise rather than by works that might earn them merit, "not because of works but because of His call" (9:11).

Paul's intention here might be summarized as being to demonstrate that Israel is chosen not because of any human qualities or achievements, that Israel's status rests on God's call alone. What the people of Israel have, they have only in relation to their God, and not in any sense from their own merit.[51] They did not achieve it, it is instead "reckoned to them" in a system of divine accounting radically different from any human systems of measuring worth.[52] In Rom 9:1–13 Paul has sought only to establish the origin of Israel as a distinct people by differentiating them from Abraham's other descendants—this is not the end of the story, though it is a crucial initial distinction. Once Israel has been constituted by divine choice, then she is called to live in covenant with her God, and the keeping of this covenant will determine Israel's future history in relation to the rest of the world. At this point, that history is still open in that Paul has now sought only to establish Israel's origins. Significantly, he has yet to consider within Romans 9–11 how Israel's existence and identity is affected by the coming of the Christ in the opening of the kingdom to those from the nations. This good news has not persuaded Israel that Jesus is the Messiah who is to enlighten the nations. She has heard but apparently not understood first (10:18–19) as had been anticipated.[53] Paul now hopes that after the nations, rather than preceding them, Israel and the nations will jointly worship the one God. This Paul will discuss in the remainder of chapters 9–11. But the affirmation that all Israel is Israel already points towards a positive conclusion.

NOTES

1. The problem for Paul is not that the reports are entirely inaccurate—they are not; but wrong inferences are drawn from these which Paul must disclaim.

2. Johannes Munck alerted us to the special task and status Paul believed himself to have been allocated in the purpose of God for the nations, noting Paul's daring in comparing himself with Moses, and his thinking in terms not of individuals but of peoples. For Munck, Paul's theology arises from his work as apostle and directly serves that work (*Paul and the Salvation of Mankind* [London: SCM Press, 1959], 66–68).

3. Cf. Daniel R. Schwartz, "Rome and Alexandria: Why Was There No Jewish Politeuma in Rome?" in *Jewish and Christian Communal Identities in the Roman World*, ed. Yair Fürstenberg (Leiden: Brill, 2016), 153–66.

4. Cf. Kathy Ehrensperger, "Bending Knees and Acknowledging Tongues (Phil 2:9–11): The Nations' Loyalty to the God of Israel in the Shadow of the Empire," in *Israel and the Nations: Paul's Gospel in the Context of Jewish Expectation*, ed. František Ábel (Lanham, MD: Lexington Books/Fortress Academic, 2021), 149–64.

5. The terms ἀνοχή and ἀνέχειν frequently mean not forbearance in a positive sense of forgiveness but God's delaying of punishment. As Stanley K. Stowers states, "God shows his goodness towards Israel by meting out punishment now so that his wrath does not accumulate. But for the gentile peoples, who have entirely rejected him, he patiently overlooks their sin in anticipation of a horrible day of reckoning" (*A Rereading of Romans: Justice, Jews and Gentiles* [New Haven, CT: Yale University Press, 1994], 105–8. Thus in Romans Stowers views Paul as making the same assumptions about God's judgment as 2 Maccabees and other Jewish writings, and reinterprets these in light of Paul's beliefs about Jesus Christ. Similarly, Runar M. Thorsteinsson notes the close parallel between Wisdom of Solomon 15:8 and Paul's indictment of non-Jews in Rom 1:18–32 in that both shared the convictions that sinful gentiles would not escape God's judgment. He notes also that Paul does not turn Jewish belief on its head since Paul's rhetorical questions imply that by his sinful behavior, the gentile interlocutor is manifesting his disrespect for the great kindness, forbearance, and patience which in strong Jewish traditions God has shown towards gentiles (*Paul's Interlocutor in Romans 2: Function and Identity in the Context of Ancient Epistolography* [Stockholm: Almqvist & Wiksell International, 2003], 167–72).

6. Thorsteinsson's terminology by which he stresses not just the former sinful life of those from the nations, but also their ongoing life in the gentile world permeated with idolatry: "Paul regards it as his duty to remind his gentile addressees of their actual position *qua* gentiles" (*Paul's Interlocutor in Romans 2*, 173–77). Thorsteinsson states in relation to Paul's hortatory request in 12:1–2, the occasion of which is the preceding discourse as a whole, "the antithesis of the existence delineated here to the one in 1:18–32 is striking and seems deliberate" (176).

7. In Romans Paul clearly speaks corporately of Jews and those from the nations rather than as individuals (cf. my paper, "Fulfilment Language in Paul?" SBL San Diego, November 2019).

8. Cf. Karl Olaf Sandnes, *Paul Perceived: An Interactionist Perspective on Paul and the Law*, WUNT 412 (Tübingen: Mohr Siebeck, 2018), 16–23.

9. Cf. Runar M. Thorsteinsson, Matthew Thiessen, and Rafael Rodriguez, "Paul's Interlocutor in Romans," in *The So-Called Jew in Paul's Letter to the Romans*, ed. Rafael Rodriguez and Matthew Thiessen (Minneapolis, MN: Fortress Press, 2016), 1–37 (19–20).

10. And continuing through chapters 3–11, cf. Thorsteinsson, *Paul's Interlocutor*, 137–43.

11. In contrast, in recent Pauline research, a covenantal perspective originates from a continuing differentiation between Jews and non-Jews in the divine purpose (cf. my *The Nations in the Divine Economy: Paul's Covenantal Hermeneutics and Participation in Christ* [Lanham, MD: Lexington Books/Fortress Academic, 2018], 79–82, 244–46).

12. Matthew Novenson "The Self-Styled Jew of Romans 2 and the Actual Jews of Romans 9–11," in *The So-Called Jew in St. Paul's Letter to the Romans*, ed. Rafael Rodriguez and Matthew Thiessen (Minneapolis, MN: Fortress Press, 2016), 133–62.

13. Gentile identity as the term "gentile" itself suggests, describes the non-Jewish world from a Jewish perspective, thus giving non-Jews a merely derivative identity status with an identity that is meaningful only in a context that includes Jews. These Christ-followers need to learn what it means to be a "gentile" (cf. Stephen Fowl, "Learning to Be a Gentile," in *Christology and Scripture: Interdisciplinary Perspectives*, ed. Andrew T. Lincoln and Angus Pattison [London: T&T Clark, 2007], 12–40).

14. Cf. Novenson, "The Self-Styled Jew," 138.

15. The idolatry referred to here may not arise from normal Jewish reaction to this aspect of pagan life, but may be more specific, indicating the idolizing of the Caesar and the divine destiny of the Roman people. Cf. Kathy Ehrensperger, "Bending Knees and Acknowledging Tongues: (Phil 2:9–11)," 149–64 in this volume. On the political aspect of Paul's thought, see especially Neil Elliott, "Paul's Political Christology: Samples from Romans," in *Reading Paul in Context: Explorations in Identity Formation: Essays in Honour of William S. Campbell*, ed. Kathy Ehrensperger and J. Brian Tucker (London: T&T Clark, 2010), 39–51. Edward Adams has noted in relation to Abraham in Romans 4, that underlying Paul's thought is a tradition depicting Abraham as a former idolater who reasoned from the creation to the creator, in contrast to the idolaters in 1:18–32 ("Abraham's Faith and Gentile Disobedience: Textual Links

between Romans 1 and 4," *Journal for the Study of the New Testament* 65 [1997]: 47–66).

16. This is a rhetorical diatribal pattern, and it needs to be considered whether the questions put in 3:1–8 are part of a continuous sequence with a common theme and group being always referenced, or rather a listing of items to be dealt with later as e.g., in 6:1–23 to which 3:8 is actually related by Paul. On 2:1–5 in this connection, see Thorsteinsson, *Paul's Interlocutor in Romans 2*, 188–94.

17. We might well ask why it is only against Paul's teaching that objections are raised, rather than other apostles or teachers. My view is that these concern the mission to the nations in which Paul is a recognized leader, and where reactions encountered differ from the experiences of those working among the circumcision. The additional factor must be that Paul's gospel is related closely to Israel, "to the Jew first and also to the Greek" (1:16) and "but they have not all responded positively to the gospel" (10:16). Paul wishes those from the nations to be informed about such things which he holds essential for ἔθνη in Christ to understand. These reactions then represent responses from the ἔθνη about Israel and constitute "the primary exigence of the letter" (cf. Neil Elliott, *The Arrogance of Nations: Reading Romans in the Shadow of Empire* [Minneapolis, MN: Fortress Press, 2008], 20).

18. Cf. my paper "The Implied Audience of Paul's Letter to Rome: Indications in Romans 4," given in the "Paul within Judaism" and "Pauline Epistles Groups," SBL Denver, November 2018.

19. Thus Paul addresses the Romans cautiously, noting it is not his normal policy to build on another man's foundation (15:20), that they who once were slaves of sin have become obedient to the *didache* to which they were committed (6:17), that their faith is widely applauded, and that he has long intended to visit them, not only for their benefit but for mutual upbuilding (Rom 1:8–13). He gives no indication that they worshipped together in one place, but chapter 16 suggests that there were different (house) groups, some being slaves in the homes of non-Christ-following masters. Cf. Peter Lampe, who considers that there were seven or possibly eight "christliche Inseln" in Rome at this time ("Urchristliche Missionswege nach Rom: Haushalte paganer Herrschaft als jüdische-christliche Keimzellen," *ZNW* 92 [2001]: 123–27 ([126]). Cf. also Philip F. Esler, *Conflict and Identity in Romans* [Minneapolis, MN: Fortress Press, 2003], 120–28. Aristobolus and Narcissus are not Christ-followers as they are not greeted, only those in their family who belong to the movement (cf. Peter Lampe, *From Paul to Valentinus: Christians at Rome in the First Two Centuries* (Minneapolis, MN: Fortress Press, 2003), 165–67). It seems there may be a parallel between the differing Christ-groups in Rome and the lack of a unified structure for the synagogues there (in contrast to the *politeuma* of the Jews in Egypt) (cf. Daniel R. Schwartz, "Rome and Alexandria: Why Was There No Jewish Politeuma in Rome?", 153–66).

20. Cf. Thorsteinsson, *Paul's Interlocutor in Romans 2*, 234. Thus Paul is most careful in Romans to speak not only about imparting some spiritual gift among them, as among other ethnē, but about mutual encouragement (1:11–12). He treads very carefully on the matter of his authority, even acknowledging that he is speaking boldly (15:15), whilst still stressing his apostleship to the nations. He also is careful to leave the explicit issue of Israel's future until later in the letter in a bid to reduce

misunderstanding by not dealing at first with what seriously disturbs him, but building rapport with his audience, (cf. Ben Witherington III, *Paul's Letter to the Romans: A Socio-Historical Commentary* [Grand Rapids, MI: Eerdmans, 2004], 17).

21. I view Israel and the Law as the two most important issues although altogether inferences or objections are rejected ten times, i.e., 3:3; 3:5; 3:31; 6:1; 6:15; 7:7; 7:13; 9:14; 11:1, 11.

22. Changwon Song, *Reading Romans as a Diatribe*. Studies in Biblical Literature 59 (New York: Peter Lang, 2004).

23. Cf. Stanley K. Stowers, *The Diatribe and Paul's Letter to the Romans*. SBLDS 57 (Chico: Scholars Press,1981). Cf. also Neil Elliott, *The Rhetoric of Romans: Argumentative Constraint and Strategy and Paul's Dialogue with Judaism* (Minneapolis, MN: Fortress Press, 2007), 120–26.

24. Cf. Krister Stendahl, *Final Account: Paul's Letter to the Romans (Sheffield: Sheffield Academic Press, 1990)*.

25. We take τὰ λόγια τοῦ θεοῦ here in its broadest sense, meaning the promises or revelation of God to Israel; cf. the same terminology in 3:2, where the question of Israel is first raised. Thus, if Israel fails, in Paul's view, God's word has failed, because it was to Israel that God revealed himself. Paul's terminology here resonates with texts concerning God's relation with Israel such as Deuteronomy 32 and Isaiah 65 which are echoed in Romans 9–11. Cf. J. Ross Wagner, *Heralds of God: Isaiah and Paul in Concert in the Letter to the Romans* (Leiden: Brill, 2003), 265–76. The failure of Israel would have severe repercussions for understanding God's power and faithfulness, basic themes in the interpretation of Romans. Thus in 3:26 the revelation of God's righteousness in Christ is not meant only to "justify the one who has faith in Jesus", but firstly "to prove that he himself is righteous."

26. But these words must not be used negatively in an argument against a positive outcome for Israel despite her present resistance. These represent primarily Paul's own repudiation of the charge that he is not really concerned about Israel in God's purpose.

27. If Paul had opposed or was reported to oppose non-Jews becoming proselytes, because a new era had dawned in which another form of access to the kingdom was now available to non-Jews, this may have caused some to infer from this that Israel had been bypassed, i.e., rejected (and therefore it would be pointless to become a proselyte). Indeed, if Paul seeks to convince non-Jews that there is no longer any need to become a Jew in order to have access to God's promised blessings, then this could be heard as a claim of Israel's redundancy.

28. As Ehrensperger notes, "The *populus Romanus* was considered as favoured, even elect by the gods, destined to rule over the *oikumene,* and thus legitimized to exploit subjugated peoples and provinces. The fact that these had been conquered and subjugated was inherent evidence that they were destined to be slaves-whereas the Romans were destined to exploit the subjugated for their own advancement and benefit" ("Bending Knees and Acknowledging Tongues [Phil 2:9–11]," 151 in this volume).

29. There was probably a suspicion that he enfranchised gentile believers at the expense of disinheriting the Jews (cf. Philip F. Esler, *Conflict and Identity in Romans,* 182).

30. As he does also in the exordium and conclusion of his letter to the Romans; the gospel is promised beforehand in the scriptures, and Jesus the "final messiah," "God's eschatological champion" is descended from David; as the "root of Jesse" he will rule the gentiles (cf. Rom 1:1–4, and 15:8–12; cf. Paula Fredriksen, *Paul, the Pagans' Apostle* [New Haven, CT, and London, U.K.: Yale University Press, 2017], 141–45.

31. Contra John M. G. Barclay, *Paul and the Gift* (Grand Rapids, MI: Eerdmans, 2015), 356–62. Barclay argues that conceptions of Judaism as Paul's former cultural capital no longer constitute his "salient currency of worth" (360). Cf. my comments on "Paul's Hierarchy of Values" in *The Nations in the Divine Economy*, 141–45).

32. So Klaus Wengst, "*Freut euch, ihr Völker, mit Gottes Volk: Israel und die Völker als Thema des Paulus-ein Gang durch den Römerbrief* (Stuttgart: Kohlhammer, 2008), 294–95.

33. As Udo Schnelle describes this, "Das Gottesvolk als Volk *neu definiert*," in *Paulus: Leben und Denken* (Berlin: de Gruyter, 2003), 380.

34. On the use of μὴ γένοιτο in Paul's discussion see also n. 21 above.

35. As Otto Michel states, "Schwierigkeiten macht die logische Verbindung zwischen v. 6a und 6b: statt des γάρ wäre eigentlich ein ἀλλά zu erwarten", in *Der Brief an Die Römer*, KEK 4 (Göttingen: Vandenhoeck & Ruprecht, 1957), 231. This is the outcome when 6b is read as a statement.

36. Cf. Hans Hübner, *Gottes Ich und Israel. Zum Schriftgebrauch des Paulus in Römer 9–11*, FRLANT 136 (Göttingen: Vandenhoeck & Ruprecht, 1984), 17.

37. See Ernst Käsemann, *Commentary on Romans*, trans. G. W. Bromiley (London: SCM Press, 1980), 251.

38. On Justin's life see Peter Lampe, *From Paul to Valentinus*, 272–84. On his views about Jews see Harold Remus, "Justin Martyr's Argument with Judaism," in *Anti-Judaism in Early Christianity, Vol. 2. Separation and Polemic*, ed. Stephen G. Wilson (Waterloo, ON: Canadian Corporation for Studies in Religion, 1986), 59–80.

39. Cf. Wengst, *Israel und die Völker*, 293–340.

40. Cf. Wengst, *Israel und die Volker*, 297–300.

41. Reading 9.6b as a rhetorical question does in fact cohere well with the diatribe style Paul uses frequently throughout Romans as noted above. J. Ross Wagner similarly paraphrases 11:11 (*Heralds of the Good News*, 40, 265–66). The rhetorical question, Rom 9:6b, serves as introduction of a possible suggestion envisaging a negative outcome for (part of Israel), but which is refined and thus refuted in v. 7 by distinguishing Abraham's σπέρμα from his τέκνα, and further explained in v. 8. The rhetorical questions, of which there are over twenty in Rom 9–11, typically occur at points where there is a break or transition in the thought of the letter, such as here, thus providing a structure to Paul's discussion, the conclusion of one section serving also as introduction to the next issue. Those issues seem to cohere as a *refutatio* of the misunderstanding by gentile Christ-followers of the heritage of Israel throughout the letter rather than only in 9–11 (contra Ben Witherington III, *Paul's Letter to the Romans*, 17).

42. Cf. *Heralds of the Good News*, n. 41 above.

43. Careful attention is required because Paul here uses τέκνα, children, to refer to Abraham's descendants generally but limits his use of σπέρμα, seed of promise, to

the descendants of Isaac and Jacob. Thus, v. 7 does not follow smoothly as an addition to the thought of v. 6b but is to be taken antithetically "but not all are σπέρμα of Abraham because they are his τέκνα"; only the children of the promise are reckoned as heirs, σπέρμα. Thus, there is a selection within the descendants of Abraham, but *not within the descendants of Isaac and Jacob*. See the careful exegesis of Rom 9:6–13 by Klaus Wengst (*Israel und die Völker*, 293–302). Wengst shows that his reading of 9:6b as a rhetorical question is supported by a similar construction using οὐδέ (v. 7) in Heb 9:25, contrary to Walter Bauer who prioritizes "and not" (*Wörterbuch*, 1196, cf. *BDR* §445, 2). Bauer in this reading of 9:6b thus connects this supposedly negative sentence with a negative equivalent in 9:7. However, when 9:6b is read as a rhetorical question, only 9:7 should be read adversatively, hence the translation of οὐδέ with "but not" is entirely feasible (cf. Liddell and Scott, *Lexicon* 11, 1268). Failure to note the change of subject from descendants of Israel in 9:6b to descendants of Abraham in 9:7 leads to confusion (cf. Wengst, 298–99).

44. We clarify the meaning of σάρξ here in order to prevent Paul's words being generalized in a dualistic critique of "flesh" inapplicable to Paul—cf. 4:1 where Abraham is specifically defined as "our forefather according to the flesh," not denigrating flesh, but referring to ethnic Israel to signal positive relation to Israelite corporate identity. See Philip F. Esler, *Conflict and Identity in Romans*, 185–94. Cf. also my "Abraham in the Divine Purpose according to Paul: The Reception of Abraham Tradition in Romans 4 and Romans 9," in *The Message of Paul the Apostle within Second Temple Judaism*, ed. František Ábel (Lanham, MD: Lexington Books/Fortress Academic, 2020), 145–65.

45. As with every other human attribute, there is nothing wrong with recognizing human descent, though it is not the basis of God's call. It is only when this attribute becomes a ground of boasting that human descent becomes a "fleshly" rather than a "spiritual" possession. Cf. the useful discussion by Thorsteinsson, Thiessen, and Rodriguez in "Paul's Interlocutor in Romans: The Problem of Identification," in *The So-Called Jew in Paul's Letter to the Romans*, 1–37.

46. Cf. Beverly Gaventa's claim that "Israel was never defined by birth but only by God's creation, it is not a biological but a theological category." I agree with the first part of her statement, but would add that it is not *only* a theological category but has also a social dimension. See "On the Calling into Being of Israel. Rom. 9.6–9," in *Gospel and Election: Explorations in the Interpretation of Romans 9–11*, ed. Florian Wilk and J. Ross Wagner, WUNT 257 (Tübingen: Mohr Siebeck, 2010), 255–69. Further, see Kathy Ehrensperger, "Narratives of Belonging: The Role of Paul's Genealogical Reasoning," in *Searching Paul: Conversations with the Jewish Apostle to the Nations. Collected Essays*. WUNT 429 (Tübingen: Mohr Siebeck, 2019), 229–47. On ethnic essentialist argument in Paul, cf. Paula Fredriksen, "God Is Jewish, but Gentiles Don't Have to Be: Ethnicity and Eschatology in Paul's Gospel," in *The Message of Paul the Apostle within Second Temple Judaism*, ed. František Ábel (Lanham, MD: Lexington Books/Fortress Academic, 2020), 3–19, see n. 44 above.

47. Cf. John Scheid's warning to be critical of the strand of British liberal thought that "tends to reduce all events to the free choice of individuals while denying any deterministic role to the social or institutional frameworks within which these choices

are made." Scheid is critical of the view that religion can exist without any need for social institutions (*The Gods, the State and the Individual: Reflections on Civic Religion in Rome,* trans. Clifford Ando [Philadelphia, PA: University of Pennsylvania Press, 2016], 1).

48. On this see Matthew Thiessen's argument that "non-eighth-day circumcision was not a sign of the covenant" and that "Paul like the author of *Jubilees* thought that gentiles gained no benefit from circumcision and law observance." (*Paul and the Gentile Problem* [Oxford and New York, NY: Oxford University Press, 2016], 95 and 100). The other possibility is that Paul shared Philo's view which accepts the possibility of converts but they can become members of the assembly only after the third generation (*Virt.* 108*)*. Cf. Kathy Ehrensperger, "Trouble in Galatia: What Should Be Cut? (On Gal 5:12)," in *The Message of Paul the Apostle within Second Temple Judaism,* ed. František Ábel (Lanham, MD: Lexington Books/Fortress Academic, 2020), 179–94.

49. The occurrence of ἐλογίσθη in Rom 4:3 indicates the close connection in Paul's thought between the language of election and that of justification, and supports our thesis that the primary contrast is between call and works rather than faith and works. As Wengst notes, "Aufgrund der Erwählung besteht daher ein kategorialer Unterschied zwischen Israel und den Völkern, der auch dadurch nicht aufgehoben wird, das Israel Jesus nicht als Messias akzeptiert"(*Israel und die Völker,* 300).

50. See my "Abraham in the Divine Purpose according to Paul" (n. 44 above).

51. Cf. Deut 7:7 in rabbinical reception; Rabbi Eliezer interpreted the verse: "Not because you are more in number than any people did the Lord desire you and choose you, for you were the fewest of all peoples" as follows: The Holy One, blessed be he, said to the Jewish people: I desire you, since even at a time that I bestow greatness upon you, you diminish i.e. humble yourselves", bChullin 89a:5.

52. Here I agree with aspects of Barclay's *Paul and the Gift.*

53. In terms of sequence Israel heard first, but this does not mean that Israel understood, hence Paul's second question. Cf. Theodor Zahn who proposed to connect πρῶτος with Israel rather than with Moses, cf. *Der Brief des Paulus an die Römer.* Kommentar zum Neuen Testament 6 (Leipzig: Deichert, 1910), 490–91.

BIBLIOGRAPHY

Adams, Edward. "Abraham's Faith and Gentile Disobedience: Textual Links between Romans 1 and 4." *Journal for the Study of the New Testament* 65 (1997): 47–66.

Barclay, John M. G. *Paul and the Gift.* Grand Rapids, MI: Eerdmans, 2015.

Barth, Markus. *Justification.* Grand Rapids, MI: Eerdmans, 1971.

Bauer, Walter. *Griechisch-deutsches Wörterbuch zu den Schriften des Neuen Testaments und der frühchristlichen Literatur,* 6. Aufl. bearb. v. Viktor Reichmann. Berlin and New York: de Gruyter, 1988.

Bormann, Lukas. "Abraham's Family in the New Testament." In *Abraham's Family: A Network of Meaning in Judaism, Christianity, and Islam,* edited by Lukas Bormann, 207–34. WUNT 415. Tübingen: Mohr Siebeck, 2018.

Bultmann, Rudolf. *Der Stil der paulinischen Predigt und die kynisch-stoische Diatribe*. Göttingen: E. A. Huth, 1910 (Repr. Vandenhoeck & Ruprecht, 1984).

Campbell, William S. "Abraham in the Divine Purpose according to Paul: The Reception of Abraham Tradition in Romans 4 and Romans 9." In *The Message of Paul the Apostle within Second Temple Judaism*, edited by František Ábel, 145–65. Lanham, MD: Lexington Books/Fortress Academic, 2020.

———. "Fulfilment Language in Paul." Paper read at the Society for Post-Supersessionist Theology, AAR/SBL annual meeting, San Diego, 2019.

———. "The Implied Audience of Romans: Indications in Romans 4." Paper read in the joint session of the "Paul within Judaism" and "The Pauline Epistles Groups." SBL Denver, 2018.

———. *The Nations in the Divine Economy: Paul's Covenantal Hermeneutics and Participation in Christ*. Lanham, MD: Lexington Books/Fortress Academic, 2018.

Dahl, Nils A. "Missionary Theology in the Epistle to the Romans." In *Studies in Paul*, 70–94. Minneapolis, MN: Augsburg Press, 1977.

———. *Studies in Paul*. Minneapolis, MN: Augsburg Press, 1977.

Ehrensperger, Kathy. "Bending Knees and Acknowledging Tongues (Phil 2:9–11): The Nations' Loyalty to the God of Israel in the Shadow of the Empire." In *Israel and the Nations: Paul's Gospel in the Context of Jewish Expectation*, edited by František Ábel, 149–64. Lanham, MD: Lexington Books/Fortress Academic, 2021.

———. "'Called to Be Saints': The Identity-Shaping Dimensions of Paul's Priestly Discourse in Romans." In *Reading Paul in Context: Explorations in Identity Formation: Essays in Honour of William S. Campbell*, edited by Kathy Ehrensperger and Brian Tucker, 90–109. London, U.K,. and New York, NY: Bloomsbury, 2010.

———. "Narratives of Belonging: The Role of Paul's Genealogical Reasoning." In *Searching Paul: Conversations with the Jewish Apostle to the Nations. Collected Essays*, 229–47. WUNT 429. Tübingen: Mohr Siebeck, 2019.

———. *Searching Paul: Conversations with the Jewish Apostle to the Nations. Collected Essays*. WUNT 429. Tübingen: Mohr Siebeck, 2019.

———. "Trouble in Galatia: What Should Be Cut? (On Gal 5:12)." In *The Message of Paul the Apostle within Second Temple Judaism*, edited by František Ábel, 179–94. Lanham, MD: Lexington Books/Fortress Academic, 2020.

Eisenbaum, Pamela. "A Remedy for Having Been Born of Woman: Jesus, Gentiles, and Genealogy in Romans." *JBL* 123, no. 1 (2004): 670–702.

Elliott, Neil. *The Arrogance of Nations: Reading Romans in the Shadow of Empire*. Minneapolis, MN: Fortress Press, 2008.

———. "Paul's Political Christology: Samples from Romans." In *Reading Paul in Context: Explorations in Identity Formation: Essays in Honour of William S. Campbell*, edited by Kathy Ehrensperger and J. Brian Tucker, 39–51. London: T&T Clark, 2010.

———. *The Rhetoric of Romans: Argumentative Constraint and Strategy and Paul's Dialogue with Judaism*. Sheffield: Sheffield Academic Press, 1990.

Esler, Philip F. *Conflict and Identity in Romans*. Minneapolis, MN: Fortress Press, 2003.

Fowl, Stephen. "Learning to Be a Gentile." In *Christology and Scripture: Interdisciplinary Perspectives*, edited by Andrew T. Lincoln and Angus Pattison, 12–40. London: T&T Clark, 2007.

Fredriksen, Paula. "God Is Jewish, but Gentiles Don't Have to Be: Ethnicity and Eschatology in Paul's Gospel." In *The Message of Paul the Apostle within Second Temple Judaism*, edited by František Ábel, 3–19. Lanham, MD: Lexington Books/ Fortress Academic, 2020.

———. *Paul: The Pagan's Apostle*. New Haven, CT, and London, U.K.: Yale University Press, 2017.

Gaventa, Beverly. "On the Calling into Being of Israel. Rom. 9.6–9." In *Gospel and Election: Explorations in the Interpretation of Romans 9–11*, edited by Florian Wilk and J. Ross Wagner, 255–69. WUNT 257. Tübingen: Mohr Siebeck, 2010.

Glombitza, Otto. "Welche Sorge treibt den Apostel Paulus zu den Sätzen Röm. xi 25ff?" *Novum Testamentum* 7 (1964–1965): 312–18.

Haas, Peter J. *Responsa: The Literary History of a Rabbinic Genre*. Atlanta, GA: Scholars Press, 1996.

Hays, Richard B. "Have We Found Abraham to Be Our Forefather according to the Flesh? A Reconsideration of Romans 4:1." *Novum Testamentum* 27, no. 1 (1985): 76–98.

Hübner, Hans. *Gottes Ich und Israel. Zum Schriftgebrauch des Paulus in Römer 9–11*, FRLANT 136. Göttingen: Vandenhoeck und Ruprecht, 1984.

Jewett, Robert. *Romans: A Commentary*. Edited by Eldon J. Epp. Hermeneia Series. Minneapolis, MN: Fortress Press, 2007.

Käsemann, Ernst. *Commentary on Romans*. Translated by G. W. Bromiley. London: SCM Press, 1980.

Lampe, Peter. *From Paul to Valentinus: Christians at Rome in the First Two Centuries*. Minneapolis, MN: Fortress Press, 2003.

———. "Urchristliche Missionswege nach Rom: Haushalte paganer Herrschaft als jüdisch-christliche Keimzellen." *ZNW* 92 (2001): 123–27.

Liddell, Henry George, Scott Robert. *A Greek-English Lexicon, Vols I & II*. New Edition by Henry Stuart Jones. Oxford: Oxford University Press, 1925.

Malherbe, Abraham J. "ME GENOITO in the Diatribe and Paul." *HTR* 73 (1980): 231–40.

Michel, Otto. *Der Brief an Die Römer*, 11th edition. KEK 4. Göttingen: Vandenhoeck & Ruprecht, 1957.

Munck, Johannes. *Paul and the Salvation of Mankind*. London: SCM Press, 1959.

Nanos, Mark D. *The Mystery of Romans: The Jewish Context of Paul's Letter*. Minneapolis, MN: Fortress Press, 1996.

———. *Reading Paul within Judaism. Collected Essays of Mark D. Nanos, Vol.1*. Eugene, OR: Cascade Books, 2017.

Novenson, Matthew. "The Self-Styled Jew of Romans 2 and the Actual Jews of Romans 9–11." In *The So-Called Jew in Paul's Letter to the Romans*, edited by Rafael Rodriguez and Matthew Thiessen, 133–62. Minneapolis, MN: Fortress Press, 2016.

Patte, Daniel. *Romans: Three Exegetical Interpretations and the History of Reception, Vol. 1. Romans 1:1–32*. London, U.K. and New York, NY: Bloomsbury Academic, 2018.

Remus, Harold. "Justin Martyr's Argument with Judaism." In *Anti-Judaism in Early Christianity, Vol.2. Separation and Polemic*, edited by Stephen G. Wilson, 59–80. Waterloo, ON: Canadian Corporation for Studies in Religion, 1986.

Rodriguez, Rafael. *If You Call Yourself a Jew: Reappraising Paul's Letter to the Romans*. Eugene, OR: Cascade Books, 2014.

———. "Romans 5–8 in Light of Paul's Dialogue with a Gentile Who 'Calls Himself a Jew.'" In *The So-Called Jew in Paul's Letter to the Romans*, edited by Rafael Rodriguez and Matthew Thiessen, 101–31. Minneapolis, MN: Fortress Press, 2016.

Rodriguez, Rafael and Matthew Thiessen, eds. *The So-Called Jew in Paul's Letter to the Romans*. Minneapolis, MN: Fortress Press, 2016.

Sandnes, Karl Olaf. *Paul Perceived: An Interactionist Perspective on Paul and the Law*. WUNT 412. Tübingen: Mohr Siebeck, 2018.

Scheid, John. *The Gods, the State, and the Individual: Reflections on Civic Religion in Rome*. Translated and with a foreword by Clifford Ando. Philadelphia, PA: University of Pennsylvania Press, 2016.

Schmeller, Thomas. *Paulus und die "Diatribe": Eine vergleichende Stilinterpretation*. NtAbh 19. Gütersloh: Aschendorf, 1987.

Schnelle, Udo. *Paulus: Leben und Denken*. Berlin: de Gruyter, 2003.

Schwartz, Daniel R. "Rome and Alexandria: Why Was There No Jewish Politeuma in Rome?" In *Jewish and Christian Communal Identities in the Roman World*, edited by Yair Fürstenberg, 153–66. Leiden: Brill, 2016.

Song, Changwon. *Reading Romans as a Diatribe*. Studies in Biblical Literature 59. New York, NY: Peter Lang, 2004.

Stendahl, Krister. "The Apostle Paul and the Introspective Conscience of the West." *HTR* 56 (1963): 190–215.

———. "Bragging Gentile Converts over against the Jewish People." In *In No Other Name: Christian Witness and the Jewish People*, edited by A. Sovik, 48–53. Geneva: Lutheran World Federation, 1976.

———. *Final Account: Paul's Letter to the Romans*. Minneapolis, MN: Fortress Press, 1995.

Stowers, Stanley. *The Diatribe and Paul's Letter to the Romans*. SBLDS 57. Chico, CA: Scholars Press, 1981.

———. *A Rereading of Romans: Justice, Jews and Gentiles*. New Haven, CT: Yale University Press, 1994.

Thiessen, Matthew. *Paul and the Gentile Problem*. Oxford and New York, NY: Oxford University Press, 2016.

———. "Paul's So-Called Jew and Lawless Law-Keeping." In *The So-Called Jew in Paul's Letter to the Romans*, edited by Rafael Rodriguez and Matthew Thiessen, 59–83. Minneapolis, MN: Fortress Press, 2016.

Thorsteinsson, Runar M. *Paul's Interlocutor in Romans 2: Function and Identity in the Context of Ancient Epistolography*. Stockholm: Almqvist & Wiksell International, 2003.

Tucker, J. Brian. *Reading Romans after Supersessionism: The Continuation of Jewish Covenantal Identity*. Eugene OR: Wipf & Stock Publishers, 2019.

———. *"Remain in Your Calling": Paul and the Continuation of Social Identities in 1 Corinthians*. Eugene, OR: Pickwick Publications, 2014.

Van der Lans, Birgit. "Belonging to Abraham's Kin: Genealogical Appeals to Abraham as a Possible Background for Paul's Abrahamic Argument." In *Abraham, the Nations, and the Hagarites: Jewish, Christian, and Islamic Perspectives on Kinship with Abraham*, edited by Goodman Martin, George H. van Kooten, and Jacques T. A. G. M. van Ruiten, 307–18. Leiden and Boston, MA: Brill, 2010.

Van Ruiten, Jacques T. A. G. M. "Abraham, and the Nations in the Book of Jubilees." In *Abraham, the Nations, and the Hagarites: Jewish, Christian, and Islamic Perspectives on Kinship with Abraham*, edited by Goodman Martin, George H. van Kooten, and Jacques T. A. G. M. van Ruiten, 105–16. Leiden and Boston, MA: Brill 2010.

Wagner, J. Ross. *Heralds of God: Isaiah and Paul in Concert in the Letter to the Romans*. Leiden: Brill, 2003.

Wengst, Klaus. *Christsein mit Tora und Evangelium: Beiträge zum Umbau christlicher Theologie im Angesicht Israels*. Stuttgart: Kohlhammer, 2014.

———. *„Freut Euch ihr Völker mit Gottes Volk!" Israel und die Völker als Thema des Paulus-ein Gang durch den Römerbrief. Israel und die Völker als Thema des Paulus-ein Gang durch den Römerbrief*. Stuttgart: Kohlhammer, 2008.

Wisdom, John R. *Blessing for the Nations and the Curse of the Law*. WUNT 2.133 Tübingen: Mohr Siebeck, 2001.

Witherington III, Ben. *Paul's Letter to the Romans: A Socio-Historical Commentary*. Grand Rapids, MI: Eerdmans, 2004.

Zahn, Theodor. *Der Brief des Paulus an die Römer*. Kommentar zum Neuen Testament 6. Leipzig: Deichert, 1910.

Chapter Eleven

The Ins and Outs of Paul's Israelite Remnant

Joshua Garroway

Shaye J. D. Cohen's 1999 exploration of Jewish identity, *The Beginnings of Jewishness*, opens with a joke: "There are two kinds of people in the world: those who divide the world into two kinds of people, and those who do not."[1] Jews, he says, are in the first group. Cohen goes on to note that "Jews see the world in bipolar terms: Jews versus gentiles, 'us' versus 'them,'" and this dualistic view of the world, he claims, "prevailed in Graeco-Roman antiquity no less than it does today."[2] I doubt anyone would dispute this contention. Jewish literature from the Second Temple and Rabbinic periods, whether from the land of Israel or the Diaspora, often exhibits the assumption that the world is divided between God's people, Israel, and the nations of the world.

The pervasive distinction between Israel and the nations is not the only important division displayed in this literature, however. Especially in sectarian literature, one sees further the isolation of a certain refined element within Israel opposed to Israel generally. Most notably, the Dead Sea Scrolls distinguish between God's elect, the righteous among God's people, over and against the evil ones among God's people, not to mention the Gentiles.[3] Still a third division arises within apocalyptic literature when the end of days is envisaged—namely, the soteriological distinction between the saved and the damned, those who will pass muster when God culminates history in cosmic judgment, and those will not. Where these three distinctions are found, they rarely coincide, which is why the authors of the Scrolls, like the authors of 4 Ezra, 2 Baruch, and 1 Enoch, are found negotiating simultaneously the historic distinction between Israel and the nations, the present distinction between the elect and the rest, and the future distinction between the saved and the damned. The result is a complicated literature that often confounds its interpreters.

My proposal in this chapter is that Paul, too, is an apocalyptic Jewish author, and Romans 9–11 is the *locus classicus* for his sectarian, apocalyptic negotiation of the literal ins and outs of God's people—past, present, and future. In Romans, Paul takes pains to demonstrate the intricate, even mysterious, relationship between the historic Israel, the present Israel, and the future Israel, the last of which, Paul proclaims in Rom 11:26a, will eventually be saved. For Paul, these three entities are not the same, varying both in constituency and in criteria for membership.

APOCALYPTIC CONTEMPORARIES

To distinguish between past, present, and future Israel, Paul draws upon three doctrines well attested in the sectarian and apocalyptic literature of his contemporaries: (1) the venerable prophetic concept of the remnant; (2) the deterministic foreknowledge of God; and (3) the expectation of an end-of-times introduction of Gentiles into the people of God.

A Predetermined Remnant

Any reader of the Hebrew prophets is familiar with the concept of the surviving remnant. Micah and Isaiah deployed it with reference to those who endured the annihilation of Israel, and much of Judah, by the Assyrians; Jeremiah, Ezekiel, Zephaniah, and Ezra did so generations later in response to the Babylonian conquest.[4]

It is no wonder, then, that the sectarian and apocalyptic Jews of the Second Temple period drew upon this refrain either to differentiate themselves from the unrighteous multitudes in their midst or to anticipate the selective salvation of the upright in the end. The preservation of the few features prominently in 1 Enoch, indebted as it is to the deliverance of Noah as the paradigmatic event in human history.[5] The theme of the remnant likewise peppers the Dead Sea Scrolls. The community that produced these writings understood itself to be the elect remnant within Israel, perhaps even the true Israel, that would be vindicated soon. No chapter of this length could possibly review the bevy of passages in 1 Enoch and the Dead Sea Scrolls that appeal to the concept of the remnant, nor for that matter those in Jubilees, 4 Ezra, and 2 Baruch.[6] Such an investigation would require something like the 760 pages Mark Elliott needed to treat the subject comprehensively in *The Survivors of Israel* (2000).[7] Following his exhaustive survey of texts, Elliott comes to the same conclusion reached by Joachim Jeremias more than half a century earlier, namely that the idea of the remnant was pervasive in Jewish thought of the first century BCE. As Jeremias put it,

> We therefore get an impression of just how extensively the religious thinking of Jesus' environment was influenced by the notion of the remnant, and how the entire *Religionsgeschichte des Spätjudentums* was shaped by the efforts to establish a voluntary holy remnant within the wider community.[8]

The tone here is admittedly hyperbolic, but one should also note that Jeremias was writing well before the contents of the Dead Sea Scrolls were known. Whether their inclusion would warrant the claim that Judaism was "entirely" consumed by the idea of the remnant remains debatable. Nonetheless, there can be no blinking at the currency of the remnant in apocalyptic Jewish thought of Paul's day.

The Foreknowledge of God

Among the many Second Temple texts that identify their communities as a remnant, or that anticipate a future judgment in which they become a remnant, one common feature is the foreknowledge of God. The notion of free will is not abandoned, but it is invariably intermingled with the conviction that the choices made by the righteous and the unrighteous were determined by God long ago. The *Rule of the Community* and the *Hodayot^a* from Qumran are the most obvious examples.[9] 1QS 3:15–16 baldly declares that "from the God of Knowledge stems all there is and all there shall be. Before they existed he established their entire design. And when they have come into being, at their appointed time, they will execute all their works according to his glorious design, without altering anything."[10] Likewise, 1 QH^a 9:19–24 says that "everything has been engraved before you with the stylus of remembrance," and tells God that "in the wisdom of your knowledge you have determined their course before they came to exist."[11] Similar citations from the Scrolls could be adduced at great length.

The embrace of determinism by 1 Enoch, 4 Ezra, and 2 Baruch is less enthusiastic, but each text features passages indicating an acknowledgment that God has long known the identity of the righteous or the manner in which the world will be consummated.[12] The Astronomical Book of 1 Enoch suggests that the heavenly tablets have prerecorded "all the actions of people and of all humans who will be on the earth for the generations of the world,"[13] while, in the Similitudes, one of the divine secrets is the name of every righteous person on earth.[14] According to 4 Ezra, God planned the end of the present age before anything occurred, including the evil designs of the wicked and the sealing of the righteous.[15] 2 Baruch speaks of the Most High marshaling nations "whom he had prepared before" for the final battle.[16] While these texts do not share the same thoroughgoing commitment to predestination exhibited in the scrolls, they indicate that apocalyptic authors often thought that remnant theology went hand in hand with a recognition of the foreknowledge of God or with a belief that the course of future (or present) events has been determined.

The Inclusion of Gentiles

Another concern often addressed in Second Temple texts featuring restorationist eschatology is the fate of the Gentiles. There is hardly unanimity on this score, no doubt owing to the variety of views expressed already by the Hebrew prophets.[17] A passage like Jub. 15:26, which decrees that anyone not included in the Abrahamic covenant is destined to be destroyed, resembles proclamations by Isaiah (34:2), Jeremiah (10:25), Zephaniah (2:8–9), and others.[18] Isaiah in particular, however, elsewhere foresaw not obliteration, but subservience on the part of future Gentiles (Isa 18:7; 49:23; 60:12–14), an expectation found also in 1 En. 48:4 and elsewhere.[19] In still other verses, the prophets anticipated the participation of Gentiles alongside Israel in redemption (Isa 2:2–4; Mic 4:1–2; Zech 8:23), and this view, too, held esteem among apocalyptic Jewish writers.[20] Indeed, sometimes all three expectations about Gentiles appear together in the same work, even the same chapter. Psalms of Solomon 17, for example, anticipates the day when God's anointed king will "destroy the unlawful nations with the word of his mouth" (17:24), but also the day when he will "have gentile nations serving him under his yoke" (17:30), and the day when "he shall be compassionate to all the nations (who) reverently (stand) before him" (17:34).[21] As Paula Fredriksen has observed, the juxtaposition of destruction and inclusion in such passages probably presumes a distinction within the nations—destruction awaiting the unrighteous, subordination and/or inclusion awaiting the righteous.[22]

Among the apocalyptic texts describing gentile inclusion, two seem especially pertinent to the scenario Paul envisages in Romans 9–11. Much like Paul, the authors of 2 Baruch and 1 Enoch envision a redeemed community comprised of a righteous Jewish remnant alongside a select group of righteous Gentiles brought on board in the final hour. In 2 Baruch 41–42, the issue is couched in terms of theodicy: How will the final triumph of Jews over Gentiles be fair, the seer asks God, if apostate Jews survive? By the same token, what will happen to those Gentiles that "have abandoned their emptiness and have fled under your wings"?[23] God's answer is clear: Jews who have chosen to live like Gentiles will be damned like Gentiles in the end, while Gentiles who have chosen to live like Jews will be saved like Jews in the end.

The animal apocalypse of 1 En. 90:30–33 suggests a similar scenario, though its rendering in ovine symbolism makes precise interpretation more difficult. It appears, at least, that the author foresees a remnant of obedient Israelites, represented by sheep, and the remnant of obedient Gentiles, represented by other animals, rejoicing together with the messiah in the new Jerusalem.

ROMANS 9–11

Paul, an apocalyptic Jew and rough contemporary of pseudo-Baruch, espoused a remnant theology featuring both divine foreknowledge and the redemption of righteous, "justified" Gentiles. In Romans 9–11, he says explicitly that the constituency of God's redeemed people, comprised of an Israelite remnant alongside Gentiles brought aboard in the final hour, had been determined and foreseen by God in ages past.

Paul may not invoke specific remnant terminology until his citation of Isa 10:22 in Rom 9:27, but the concept of the remnant informs his entire argument in chapter 9. He draws upon it to answer the question implied by his opening lament: if most Israelites have forsaken Christ, Paul wonders, does that mean that God has forsaken his promise to redeem Israel? It does not, Paul insists, because Israelites who forsake Christ are not Israel. They may descend from Israel, but membership in God's covenant people is determined by God's individual election rather than descent. Paul could not make this any clearer in his analysis of the patriarchs at the outset of his argument (Rom 9:6–8):

> [6] It is not as though the word of God has faltered, because not all those descended from Israel are Israel. [7] Nor is it that all the seed of Abraham are children, for "your seed will be called through Isaac"; [8] which is to say it is not the children according to the flesh who are children of God, but the children of the promise are reckoned to be the seed.

In but three verses Paul effects what I have elsewhere called the "unfleshing" of historic Israel.[24] The very first generation establishes the paradigm. Abraham had two sons, Ishmael and Isaac. Though he was a son, Ishmael was not *reckoned* a son because such status can only be conferred by God. The same principle held in the second generation, as Paul clarifies in the subsequent verses. Isaac also had two sons, Esau and Jacob. Though he was a son, Esau was not reckoned one because God decreed—prior to his birth, no less—that he would be rejected. Isaac and Jacob thus represent the prototype for God's separation of a chosen remnant from among the descendants of Israel. Nor is God's pruning limited to the patriarchal generations. In Rom

11:2–6, Paul reveals that the same paradigm was operative in the monarchic period. Although the men who killed Elijah's peers, demolished God's altars, and bowed to Baal were the sons of Israelites, they were not reckoned as such. Only Elijah and his 7,000 comrades received God's gracious appointment to the remnant of that time.

Paul thus broadens the role of the remnant concept by transforming it from a sectarian or eschatological indicator of exclusivity into an operative principle in all Israelite history. In every generation since Abraham, Paul suggests, or at least at important moments in time, God has pruned Israel by eliminating some constituents while preserving others. God's method of selection, unfair as it may seem, is nothing other than God's inscrutable, irresistible will, God's βούλημα (Rom 9:19). Poor Esau never had a chance. Before Esau was even born, God's πρόθεσις (Rom 9:11), or purpose, had been determined; God's ἐκλογή (Rom 9:11), or election, had been made; and God's call had been offered to someone other than Esau. Presumably the same was true for Esau's uncle, Ishmael, and Elijah's adversaries, and it would become true for the scores of Israelites down through the years who, in Paul's reckoning, were destined for God's wrath rather than his mercy. It does not seem fair, Paul concedes in Rom 9:20, but fairness from a human vantage point is irrelevant before the molder of humanity itself.

No less unfair might seem Paul's other innovation in remnant theology, the one he introduces in Rom 9:25—namely, the election of certain people who are not even descended from Israel to be included in the final manifestation of the remnant. As we saw especially in 2 Baruch 41–42, Paul was not the only apocalyptic Jew to envision an eschatological inclusion of Gentiles concomitant to the final paring down of Israelites. Paul did not merely envision it, however; he believed that he was seeing it unfold before his very eyes. Writing in what he figured were the final moments of history, Paul took the notion of Gentile inclusion a step further than his prophetic forebears and apocalyptic contemporaries by proposing that Gentiles, through Christ, are saved not as Gentile hangers-on but as constitutive members of the Israelite remnant itself. The final version of God's people Israel, Paul insists, comprises a remnant of graciously elected descendants of Israel alongside graciously elected descendants of the nations. The two groups combine to constitute the Israel that will be saved in the end.

Accordingly, the prophecy Paul adduces to introduce his innovation, Hos 2:23, is aptly chosen. The ancient prophet has God declaring that a group not previously known as "my people" (λαός μου) will be called "my people." If "my people" refers to God's covenant people Israel, as "his people" (λαός αὐτοῦ) certainly does in Rom 11:1–2, then Hosea can be said by Paul to have foreseen a group of Gentiles at the end of days that would be called Israel.

The word "call" is of utmost importance here, for in Paul's estimation the "call" of God goes hand in hand with the election of God. Paul just made this connection in Rom 9:11 when he noted that God's choice of Jacob was made *in utero* so that "God's purpose of election might continue, not by works but by his call." Election and call go together. Indeed, they go together for the Israelites who remain in the covenant no less than for the Gentiles who are brought in, which is why Paul's language about Israelites in Rom 9:7–13 and Rom 11:1–6 so closely resembles his description of Gentiles in Rom 8:28–33. Before coming to his treatise on Israel in Romans 9–11, Paul had described the Gentiles in Rome to whom he is writing, those who love God, as "called according to his purpose" (τοῖς κατὰ πρόθεσιν κλητοῖς οὖσιν). They are likewise "foreknown" (οὓς προέγνω), just like the remnant from among the Jews in Rom 11:2 (ὃν προέγνω), and because they are foreknown they are predestined to be conformed to the image of God's son; they are called, justified, and glorified; and they become identified as God's "elect."

Paul thus speaks with the same language about the descendants of Israel and the descendants of the nations that have been chosen to be part of the final remnant. The individuals in both groups are "called," "foreknown," and "elected" according to grace, and both groups together comprise the "us" to whom Paul refers in Rom 9:24, the "us whom he has called, not only from the Jews but also from the Gentiles." To support this twofold eschatological remnant scripturally, Paul juxtaposes two complementary prooftexts in Rom 9:25–29: first, the prophecy of Hosea describing the Gentiles predestined to be part of God's final people Israel; and second, the conflated prophecies from Hosea and Isaiah describing the Jews predestined to be part of God's final people Israel. They are two remnant components of a single Israel.

Were these prophecies not enough to clinch the point, Paul takes yet another tack when he returns to the idea in chapter 11. The image of the olive tree illustrates two remnants brought together as a single people.[25] The native branches not lopped off represent the remnant called from among the Jews who have exhibited faith, while the wild shoots detached from their wild plants and grafted into the cultivated tree represent the remnant called from among the Gentiles. God has ripped them from their native peoples and grafted them into the constituency of Israel. Now, it is true that Paul does not present these two constituencies as equal participants. The Jews are "natural" branches that belong there, while the Gentiles, the "unnatural" branches, are eschatological interlopers tenuously attached by faith. Moreover, Paul holds out hope that some Jews—not all Jews, but some Jews, as Paul says in Rom 11:14—might realize where they belong before it is too late and reattach themselves to Israel. In this way, Paul's remnant remains an open remnant for the few weeks, months, or perhaps years that might remain before Christ's return, an open remnant similar to the one described in the Dead Sea Scrolls according to a recent study by Joel Willitts. According to Willitts,

> Membership in the [Qumran] community—and, thus, membership in the remnant—remained a present possibility for all Israel at least for a short time while the Messiah(s) tarried. It was, in this way, an "open remnant": individual Jews could join the remnant by entering the "new covenant" through initiation rites. Therefore, in the understanding of the DSS community, the remnant did not replace Israel—it was not a new Israel—but was the elect from among Israel with whom and through whom God will ultimately fulfill his covenant promises.[26]

Paul would have put it a bit differently than the Qumranites: membership in the community of Israel—and, thus, membership in the remnant—remained a present possibility for all Israel—and Gentiles!—at least for a short time while the Messiah(s) tarried. For Paul, inclusion in the remnant remained a possibility for unbelieving Jews, and he zealously pursued his mission among the Gentiles in the hope that jealousy might spur his kinsmen to see the light before it was too late. This open remnant would be filled out in short order by the full number of predetermined Gentiles and, hopefully, by many Jews roused by jealousy to accept Jesus as Christ. When the time is up and the remnant is complete, then "all Israel," drawn from among Jews and Gentiles, "will be saved" (Rom 11:26).

To the objection that "all Israel" cannot refer to but a small remnant of Jews because Paul elsewhere uses "Israel" only to describe the full complement of the descendants of Israel, Paul's statement in Rom 9:6b poses an insurmountable challenge. Although it is just one verse, as opposed to the six from Romans in which Paul uses "Israel" clearly to mean the descendants of Israel, it is the operative verse in Paul's entire argument. It is Paul's thesis statement, his proposition: Not all those descended from Israel are Israel. Indeed, as Paul goes on to say in the next three chapters, most are not.

To the objection that Paul would never use the term "Israel" to describe the handful of Gentiles graciously predestined to become a part of God's people in the end, Gal 6:16 and 1 Cor 10:18 pose high hurdles. Whether or not the "Israel of God" in Gal 6:16 refers to believers in Christ is admittedly debatable, as studies by Susan Grove Eastman and others have demonstrated, but Paul's instruction to his Corinthian audience to consider the cultic practices of "Israel according to the flesh" (Ἰσραὴλ κατὰ σάρκα) implies unmistakably the conception of an Israel determined by some criterion other than the flesh.[27] Whether Paul means "according to the spirit" (κατὰ πνεῦμα), "according to grace" (κατὰ χάριν), "according to God" (κατὰ θεὸν), "according to election" (κατ' ἐκλογὴν), or "Israel of God" (Ἰσραὴλ τοῦ θεοῦ) is anyone's guess, but Paul would never have referred to Jews as "Israel according to the flesh" if the word "Israel" by itself necessarily meant Israel as determined by the flesh. For Paul, "Israel" as it is constituted in the final hour of history is not the same thing as "Israel according to the flesh." Israel is rather a dynamic entity that has changed from generation to generation as a result of God's ongoing (or periodic) pruning—and, in the end of days, God's miraculous grafting as well. Which is why Paul can tell the same Corinthian audience to recall their past, "when you were Gentiles" (1 Cor 12:2).[28] They *were* Gentiles, but now they are Israel—not Israel according to the flesh, of course, but Israel in its miraculous, eschatological phase as a remnant drawn from both Jews and Gentiles.

CONCLUSION

The theme of this volume, and of the conference upon which it is based, is Paul's thought vis-à-vis Jewish eschatological notions concerning Israel's role towards the nations. As such, the subject covered in this chapter might at first glance appear out of place. What has the idea of an Israelite remnant to do with ancient Jewish views about their role toward Gentiles? Prior to Paul, no Jewish writer envisioned Gentiles constituting that Israelite remnant in so thorough and explicit a way. Paul was an innovator.

I would note, however, that the very presence of remnant theology in Second Temple Judaism—indeed, possibly its ubiquity—sets the stage for Paul by destabilizing any hard and fast dichotomy between Israel and the nations, the us-and-them mentality described at the outset of this chapter. The doctrine of the remnant makes the boundary of Israel permeable. To say, as the Qumranites did, that a remnant of Israel obtains now, is to suggest that a portion of Israel has slipped through the boundary and ceased to be Israel in any meaningful way. To say, as other apocalyptic texts did, that a remnant of Israel will form in the future, is to suggest that a portion of Israel as it is presently constituted will one day cease to be Israel in any meaningful way. In other words, remnant theology moves the boundary between Israel and the Gentiles, either now or in the future. By narrowing the inner circle, it turns Israelites into non-Israelites, ins into outs.

Paul followed course. For him, the boundary between Israel and the nations was in constant flux. From Ishmael and Esau, to Elijah's adversaries, to the branches in Israel's family tree lopped off for lack of faith, innumerable Israelites had over time been dropped from the fold. In his customary fashion, however, Paul took the fluidity and dynamism afforded by a contemporary Jewish idea and ratcheted it up a notch. By incorporating Gentile inclusion into his remnant theology, Paul made movement across the final boundary of Israel bi-directional.

NOTES

1. Shaye J. D. Cohen, *The Beginnings of Jewishness: Boundaries, Varieties, Uncertainties* (Berkeley: University of California Press, 1999), 1.

2. Cohen, *Beginnings of Jewishness*, 1.

3. Among the many studies that explore this theme in the literature from Qumran, see Sigurd Grindheim, *The Crux of Election: Paul's Critique of the Jewish Confidence in the Election of Israel*, WUNT 2.202 (Tübingen: Mohr Siebeck, 2005), 55–69; Joel Willitts, "The Remnant of Israel in 4QpIsaiah[a] (4Q161) and the Dead Sea Scrolls," *JJS* 57, no.1 (2006): 11–25; Markus Bockmuehl, "1QS and Salvation at Qumran," in *Justification and Variegated Nomism*, ed. D. A. Carson, Peter T. O'Brien, and Mark A. Seifrid, WUNT 2.140 (Tübingen: Mohr Siebeck, 2001), 381–414.

4. for example, Isa 10:22; 37:4; Mic 2:12; 4:6–7; Jer 8:3; 23:3; 31:1–14; Ezek 9:8; 11:13; Zeph 2:3–9; Ezra 9:8. The passages from Micah may reflect post-exilic editing. Note that remnant terminology in the Hebrew Bible can be applied to both Israel and Judah, as well as to other nations—to any group that has survived the annihilation of the larger whole. According to Lester V. Meyer ("Remnant," in *The Anchor Bible Dictionary*, ed. David Noel Freedman [New York: Doubleday, 1992), 5:669–71), the term can have both a negative connotation (i.e., the survival of a remnant indicates just how catastrophic the destruction was) or a positive connotation (i.e., the remnant indicates the mercy of God, the worthiness of the survivors, or the possibility of renewal).

5. On the flood paradigm in 1 Enoch and Jubilees, see Mark Adam Elliott, *The Survivors of Israel: A Reconsideration of the Theology of Pre-Christian Judaism* (Grand Rapids, MI: Eerdmans, 2000), esp. 424–32, 577–90. See also James C. VanderKam, "Studies in the Apocalypse of Weeks (*1 Enoch* 93:1–10; 91:11–17)," *CBQ* 46, no. 3 (1984): 515.

6. According to Richard A. Taylor (*Interpreting Apocalyptic Literature: An Exegetical Handbook* [Grand Rapids, MI: Kregel, 2016], 81), Daniel also refers to a remnant, namely "the wise" in Dan 11:15 and 12:3 who endure the final tribulation.

7. Elliott, *Survivors of Israel*.

8. Joachim Jeremias, "Der Gedanke des 'Heiligen Restes' im Spätjudentum und in der Verkündung Jesu," *ZNW* 42 (1949): 184–94, cited here at 191.

9. On predestination in early Judaism, see Günter Röhser, *Prädestination und Verstockung: Untersuchungen zur frühjüdischen, paulinischen und johanneischen Theologie* (Tübingen: Franke, 1994), 63–90. On the *Hodayot*[a], see Eugene H. Merrill, *Qumran and Predestination: A Theological Study of the Thanksgiving Hymns* (Leiden: Brill, 1975).

10. Florentino García Martínez and Eibert J. C. Tigchelaar, eds., *The Dead Sea Scrolls Study Edition* (Leiden: Brill, 1997), 1:75.

11. García Martínez and Tigchelaar, *Dead Sea Scrolls*, 1:159–61.

12. For recent studies of 4 Ezra and 2 Baruch, see esp. Gabriele Boccaccini and Jason M. Zurawski, eds., *Interpreting 4 Ezra and 2 Baruch* (London: Bloomsbury, 2014).

13. 1 En. 81:2, translated in George W. E. Nickelsburg and James C. Vanderkam, eds., *1 Enoch: The Hermeneia Translation* (Minneapolis, MN: Fortress, 2012), 111.

14. 1 En. 43:4.
15. 4 Ezra 6:1–6.
16. 2 Bar. 70:7, translated in Michael E. Stone and Matthias Henze, eds., *4 Ezra and 2 Baruch: Translations, Introductions, and Notes* (Minneapolis, MN: Fortress, 2013), 130.
17. On Jewish expectations in the Second Temple period regarding the eschatological fate of Gentiles, see especially Paula Fredriksen, "Judaism, the Circumcision of the Gentiles, and Apocalyptic Hope: Another Look at Galatians 1 and 2," *JTS* 42, no. 2 (1991): 532–64; Terence L. Donaldson, *Judaism and the Gentiles: Jewish Patterns of Universalism (to 135 CE)* (Waco, TX: Baylor University Press, 2007), esp. 670–78.
18. Similar expectations of destruction appear in the Dead Sea Scrolls, especially the *War Scroll* (1QM), as well as in other texts from the Second Temple period (e.g., T. Mos. 10.7; Sir 36:8–9; Sib. Or. 3.517–19, 669–72). For further discussion, see Fredriksen, "Judaism, the Circumcision of the Gentiles, and Apocalyptic Hope," 544; E. P. Sanders, *Jesus and Judaism* (Philadelphia, PA: Fortress Press, 1985), 212–21.
19. E.g., Jub. 32:18–19; Tg. Isa. 16:1.
20. E.g., Tob 14:6; T. Levi 4.3–4; T. Benj. 9.2.
21. Translations of the Psalms of Solomon by R. B. Wright in James H. Charlesworth, ed., *The Old Testament Pseudepigrapha, Volume 2* (New York, NY: Doubleday, 1985), 667–68.
22. Fredriksen, "Judaism, the Circumcision of the Gentiles, and Apocalyptic Hope," 544.
23. 2 Bar. 41:3, translated in Stone and Henze, *4 Ezra and 2 Baruch*, 107.
24. Joshua Garroway, *Paul's Gentile-Jews: Neither Jew nor Gentile, but Both* (New York, NY: Palgrave, 2012), 150.
25. On Paul's metaphor as an ancient "family tree," see Caroline Johnson Hodge, *If Sons, Then Heirs: A Study of Kinship and Ethnicity in the Letters of Paul* (Oxford: Oxford University Press, 2007), 143.
26. Willitts, "The Remnant of Israel in 4QpIsaiah[a] (4Q161) and the Dead Sea Scrolls," 25.
27. Susan Grove Eastman, "Israel and the Mercy of God: A Re-reading of Galatians 6.16 and Romans 9-11," *NTS* 96 (2010): 367–95.
28. On Paul's construction of ambiguous identities in the Corinthian correspondence, see Cavan Concannon, *"When You Were Gentiles": Specters of Ethnicity in Roman Corinth and Paul's Corinthian Correspondence* (New Haven, CT: Yale University Press, 2014).

BIBLIOGRAPHY

Boccaccini, Gabriele, and Jason M. Zurawski, eds. *Interpreting 4 Ezra and 2 Baruch*. London: Bloomsbury, 2014.

Bockmuehl, Markus. "1QS and Salvation at Qumran." In *Justification and Variegated Nomism*, edited by D. A. Carson, Peter T. O'Brien, and Mark A. Seifrid, 381–414. WUNT 2.140. Tübingen: Mohr Siebeck, 2001.

Charlesworth, James H., ed. *The Old Testament Pseudepigrapha, Volume 2*. New York: Doubleday, 1985.

Cohen, Shaye J. D. *The Beginnings of Jewishness: Boundaries, Varieties, Uncertainties*. Berkeley: University of California Press, 1999.

Concannon, Cavan. *"When You Were Gentiles": Specters of Ethnicity in Roman Corinth and Paul's Corinthian Correspondence*. New Haven, CT: Yale University Press, 2014.

Donaldson, Terence L. *Judaism and the Gentiles: Jewish Patterns of Universalism (to 135 CE)*. Waco, TX: Baylor University Press, 2007.

Eastman, Susan Grove. "Israel and the Mercy of God: A Re-reading of Galatians 6.16 and Romans 9–11." *NTS* 96 (2010): 367–95.

Elliott, Mark Adam. *The Survivors of Israel: A Reconsideration of the Theology of Pre-Christian Judaism*. Grand Rapids, MI: Eerdmans, 2000.

Fredriksen, Paula. "Judaism, the Circumcision of the Gentiles, and Apocalyptic Hope: Another Look at Galatians 1 and 2." *JTS* 42, no. 2 (1991): 532–64.

Garroway, Joshua. *Paul's Gentile-Jews: Neither Jew nor Gentile, but Both*. New York, NY: Palgrave, 2012.

Grindheim, Sigurd. *The Crux of Election: Paul's Critique of the Jewish Confidence in the Election of Israel*. WUNT 2.202. Tübingen: Mohr Siebeck, 2005.

Hodge, Caroline Johnson. *If Sons, Then Heirs: A Study of Kinship and Ethnicity in the Letters of Paul*. Oxford: Oxford University Press, 2007.

Jeremias, Joachim. "Der Gedanke des 'Heiligen Restes' im Spätjudentum und in der Verkündung Jesu." *ZNW* 42 (1949): 184–94.

Martínez, Florentino García, and Eibert J. C. Tigchelaar, eds. *The Dead Sea Scrolls Study Edition*. Leiden: Brill, 1997.

Merrill, Eugene H. *Qumran and Predestination: A Theological Study of the Thanksgiving Hymns*. Leiden: Brill, 1975.

Meyer, Lester V. "Remnant." In *The Anchor Bible Dictionary*, edited by David Noel Freedman, 5:669–71. New York, NY: Doubleday, 1992.

Nickelsburg, George W. E., and James C. Vanderkam, eds. *1 Enoch: The Hermeneia Translation*. Minneapolis, MN: Fortress, 2012.

Röhser, Günter. *Prädestination und Verstockung: Untersuchungen zur frühjüdischen, paulinischen und johanneischen Theologie*. TANZ 14. Tübingen: Franke, 1994.

Sanders, E. P. *Jesus and Judaism*. Philadelphia, PA: Fortress Press, 1985.

Stone, Michael E., and Matthias Henze, eds. *4 Ezra and 2 Baruch: Translations, Introductions, and Notes*. Minneapolis, MN: Fortress, 2013.

Taylor, Richard A. *Interpreting Apocalyptic Literature: An Exegetical Handbook*. Grand Rapids, MI: Kregel, 2016.

VanderKam, James. C. "Studies in the Apocalypse of Weeks (*1 Enoch* 93:1–10; 91:11–17)." *CBQ* 46, no. 3 (1984): 511–23.

Willitts, Joel. "The Remnant of Israel in 4QpIsaiah[a] (4Q161) and the Dead Sea Scrolls." *JJS* 57, no.1 (2006): 11–25.

Chapter Twelve

The Gentile as Insider and Outsider in Paul's Letter to the Romans

Kenneth Atkinson

The letters of the Apostle Paul are insightful for the light they shed on the world of the first century C.E. Paul's personality is evident on every page of his writings. It is evident from reading them that he was a zealous missionary of the nascent Christian faith. Yet, Paul was unique among all the New Testament's authors because he believed his gentile mission was the culmination of Israel's divinely assured destiny. In other words, when Paul read Scripture, he believed he was in it. This explains his passion to bring the gentiles into the new faith in Jesus despite immense obstacles from pagans, Jews, and his fellow believers.

This chapter proposes that Paul did not write his Letter to the Romans as a systematic theology of his thought. Rather, he composed it to deal with specific and unique problems facing the community in Rome. A look at the early Jesus movement and some clues in this epistle helps us understand its theology. This historical background shows that Paul greatly complicated his mission by creating a unique understanding of the gentile as both insider and outsider that subsequently proved problematic for later generations of Christians.

THE INTEGRITY OF ROMANS

The first issue any scholar must face in dealing with Romans is its literary integrity. How we interpret it depends on the number of chapters we include. Ancient testimony suggests our present form of Romans is not identical with Paul's original letter. Origen claimed that Marcion deleted chapters 15 and 16 from it.[1] Some Latin manuscripts provide evidence to support Origen's claim. Papyrus[46] (mid-second century CE) from the Chester Beatty Papyrus collection is the most important surviving copy of the book. It places the doxology of 16:25–27 after 15:32, suggesting that Romans originally contained fifteen chapters. Phoebe's recommendation letter (16:1–27) was apparently later appended to Romans.[2] She likely carried this epistle of Paul and her reference letter to Rome. If so, this would explain why both were placed together to form a single book.

If we look at 16:1–16 from a literary perspective, it reads like a Greco-Roman letter of recommendation. This suggests it was not part of the original book. It introduces Phoebe, states her identity, and requests her favorable treatment by the recipients. However, Harry Gamble proposes that chapter sixteen was part of the original letter and that it is similar to the conclusions of Paul's other authentic writings.[3] If correct, then Phoebe played a major role in the dissemination of the Letter to the Romans to the community in Rome.

The majority of manuscripts include chapter sixteen, showing that it became part of Romans at an early date. The differences in our copies reveal that our present text of Romans has been altered to such an extent that it is impossible to reconstruct its original appearance with certainty. Nevertheless, there is general agreement among scholars that chapter sixteen is a genuine Pauline composition. Regardless of whether it was part of Romans, it contains some important information that greatly helps us understand the book's recipients. It also sheds some light on the historical reasons that led Paul to propagate his unique understanding of the gentile as insider and outsider.

THE CONTENT OF CHAPTER SIXTEEN

The names in chapter sixteen of Romans shed much light on Paul's relationship with the church in Rome. He knows many of the twenty-six persons in this list, plus the mother and sister of two of these individuals.[4] He also greets an unspecified number of brothers and sisters in the church there and in the households of several believers. This brings the number of individuals he knows in the city to over twenty-six. The names of the members he mentions are insightful. Twenty-one are Greek.[5] Ten are Latin.[6] A few appear to be Jewish; some may go back to a Hebrew name.[7] If we assume the language of these individuals represents the primary tongues they spoke, then Greek would have been the most common, Latin the second, and Aramaic or Hebrew the third. This suggests the recipients of Paul's letter in Rome were thoroughly Hellenized.

The names in chapter sixteen that appear outside the New Testament generally belong to freedmen, slaves, and artisans.[8] No one Paul mentions in chapter sixteen appears particularly prominent. This suggests that the congregation in Rome consisted of those from the lower classes: the same profile we find of believers mentioned in Paul's other letters and in early churches.[9] Although it is not surprising that the community in Rome appears similar to other gatherings of Jesus believers of the first century CE, there is something puzzling about it.

Paul expresses his desire to visit the congregation in Rome (15:24). Although it is theoretically possible that chapter sixteen postdates the Book of Romans, and that Paul had traveled to the city by the time he wrote Phoebe's recommendation letter, this is unlikely. Paul certainly would have mentioned his visit to Rome and thanked those who helped him there. How, then, did he know so many believers in Rome?

Paul likely met many of the individuals in chapter sixteen during his extensive travels, some of which the author of the Book of Acts recounts in a dramatic and novelistic fashion.[10] A specific historical event may explain why Paul met many of them outside Rome. This incident led him to develop his unique understanding of the gentile in Romans as insider and outsider.

THE EXPULSION OF THE JEWS

According to Acts 18:2, the emperor Claudius ordered all Jews to leave Rome. Because he ruled from 41–54 CE, this expulsion took place sometime before his reign ended in 54 CE. Some scholars believe that the dates provided by Orosius and the tenure of the Proconsul Gallio reveal that it occurred between 49 to 53 CE.[11] We likely have extra-biblical confirmation of this incident. Writing in approximately 120 CE, the Roman historian Suetonius states that the emperor Claudius "expelled from Rome Jews who were making constant disturbances at the instigation of Chrestus" (*Iudaeos impulsore Chresto assidue tumultuantis Roma expulit*).[12] Although several scholars argue this is not a reference to Jesus, it is difficult to imagine that Seutonius is referring to another Jew who caused trouble in Rome whose name was similar to Christ.[13]

Chrestos, meaning useful, good, and valuable, was a common Greek name for slaves and freedmen. Seutonius likely confused the name Christ with Chrestus since they must have sounded alike to someone unacquainted with the newly developing Christian faith. Greek and Latin historians, moreover, recorded names in different ways since there was no standard spelling in antiquity. Later Greek funerary inscriptions from Phrygia, for example, call followers of Jesus both Christians and Chrestians. One uses both terms together and reads "Christians for Chrestians." Based on this historical evidence, some scholars have proposed that pagans used both terms to refer to Christians.[14]

Early followers of Jesus by the second century CE appear to have used the designation Christians for their faith. Such lexical diversity is not surprising since Christianity was still a new religion in the second century CE. Its institutions and language were not fully developed. Paul was not merely writing to these early Christian communities, but he was helping to create the new faith.

Claudius issued his expulsion edict to end some dispute between Jews and Jewish believers in Jesus over Jesus's identity as the Messiah. Although the Romans' tolerance of Jews is well known, they did not permit social unrest among Jews or members of any faith.[15] We can understand why Claudius expelled the Jews from Rome if inner-Jewish disputes over Jesus had threatened the social order by dividing families and communities, and possibly threatening commerce. The extant evidence suggests that Roman authorities were increasingly troubled by Judaism.

Claudius was concerned with religious conflicts during his reign. His decrees attest to growing animosity between Jews and their pagan neighbors in the first century CE. This should not be surprising since Jews could never integrate into Roman society since their monotheism kept them apart from the pagan rituals and celebrations that bound citizens together. According to Josephus, Claudius dealt with Jewish disturbances in Rome and Egypt that erupted over the differing religious practices of the two faith communities. Claudius instructed Egyptian Jews not to "despise" the religious observances of the pagans and "not to show a contempt of the superstitious observances of other nations, but only to observe their laws."[16] Although we do not know the exact circumstance behind this warning, it shows that Jews, because of their unique faith, faced problems living among gentiles.

Because there is no evidence that Claudius's decree expelling the Jews from Rome was permanent, a substantial portion of the city's Jewish community likely returned by the time the seventeen-year-old emperor Nero succeeded Claudius. Prisca and Aquila, whom Paul, according to Acts 18:2, met in Corinth were among them. Both appear in Romans chapter sixteen, which, if this section of the letter dates late in Paul's life, shows they had resettled in the city. Paul probably urged them to go home to prepare for his arrival, and likely to help resolve problems that had arisen in the church in Rome during their absence. Many other Jews likely made it back to Rome by the time Paul wrote his letter to the community there. Paul hints that their arrival strained relations with the gentile followers of Jesus in the city. The two groups had grown apart and were fighting.[17] This had the potential to draw the attention of the Romans and lead to punishment. To appreciate this fear, we must look at where the Jews lived in the city to understand the historical background of Paul's letter.

THE JEWS IN ROME

It is uncertain when the first Jews arrived in Rome. Some likely moved there during the early Maccabean period when Judas sent envoys to the city around 160 BCE to establish an alliance with the Roman Republic.[18] By the first century BCE, Rome possessed a large Jewish community. The Roman general Pompey likely brought many Jews to Rome as slaves following his 63 BCE conquest of Jerusalem. By the first century BCE, there were likely 50,000 Jews in Rome.[19] They had become a recognized minority in Roman society. Josephus preserves a letter acknowledging their right to worship in Rome. Seutonius mentions that many Jews were prominent among the mourners at Julius Caesar's funeral.[20] Philo tells us that by Augustus's reign, most Jews had settled in a large section of Rome across the Tiber River; many were emancipated slaves.[21] This community somehow ran afoul of Roman authorities early during the reign of Tiberius and again when Claudius came to power. The emperor Claudius also expelled Jews from Rome and warned Egypt's Jewish community to cease its religious conflicts with gentiles. Much of Paul's theology in Romans is a reaction to the anti-Jewish measures of Tiberius and Claudius. It was Tiberius's eviction of the Jews that provides some valuable information for understanding why Paul wrote Romans.

Josephus, Tacitus, and Suetonius mention that in 19 CE, Tiberius suppressed the Isis-cult in Rome and expelled the city's entire Jewish community.[22] A fragment from the writings of Dio Cassius likely preserves a reference to this event. Philo mentions it twice in his books.[23] The exact reason for Tiberius's actions is unknown.

Josephus claims Tiberius expelled Rome's Jews because four Jewish scoundrels from Palestine had convinced a wealthy Roman woman proselyte named Fulvia to make a substantial donation of gold to the Jerusalem temple. They agreed to take her gift to Jerusalem but absconded with the money. This rather fantastic story fails to explain Tiberius's rage. Dio claims Tiberius expelled the Jews from Rome because they were converting many native Romans to Judaism. Seutonius and Tacitus support Dio's account.

Josephus's improbable explanation for Claudius's edict is important because it suggests that gentile conversions to Judaism had become a major issue in first-century-CE. Rome.[24] Seutonius states that Tiberius ordered proselytes to receive the same punishment as the Jews, which was expulsion from Rome and military conscription. Tacitus says that a *senatus consultum* authorized its implementation. This shows that Tiberius's eviction of Rome's Jews was not a rash act solely undertaken on his part. Rather, the city's politicians debated and authorized it. What happened that so worried the Senate and Tiberius? The philosopher Seneca may provide an answer.

In his letter to his friend Lucilius, Seneca "the Younger" (4 BCE–65 CE) describes his study of Pythagoras. Under the influence of this Greek sage, Seneca adopted vegetarianism. Then Tiberius issued his expulsion order of the Jews. Seneca mentions in his correspondence the problem this edict created for him:

> I was convinced by his [=Pythagoras] teaching and began to abstain from animal food at the end of a year. It was as pleasant as it was easy. I was beginning to feel that my mind was more active; though I could not positively state whether it was or not. Do you want to know how I came to abandon the practice? It happened this way. The days of my youth coincided with the early part of the reign of Tiberius Caesar. At that time, some foreign rites were being introduced, and abstinence from certain kinds of animal food was set down as a proof of interest in them. At the request of my father, who did not fear prosecution, but who detested philosophy, I returned to my previous habits. It was no very hard matter to induce me to dine more comfortably.[25]

In this letter, Seneca's father feared that his son's adoption of vegetarianism would cause the Roman authorities to identify him as a proselyte of a banned cult. This suggests that the Romans identified vegetarianism as a prominent feature of Judaism during Tiberius's reign.[26] His letter shows that the avoidance of meat by pagan converts to Judaism in Rome was upsetting the social order. Juvenal also mentions that the issue of conversions to Judaism was a growing problem in Roman society. He denounces Jews alone in his *Satires* for their proselytism and their exclusiveness.[27] Gentile converts were becoming outcasts in Roman society since they could no longer participate in the ordinary pagan activities of daily life. This issue provides an important backdrop to Paul's Letter to the Romans and shows that gentile converts to the Jesus movement threatened its very existence. However, the conflict was not only with Roman officials, but with fellow members of the Jesus movement.

Like Claudius's expulsion, Tiberius's eviction, was not permanent. Jews quickly returned to Rome. Their numbers so increased that Claudius cast them out again. Neither of these actions appears to have adversely affected Rome's Jewish community, which continued to prosper during the first century CE. Thousands of funerary inscriptions from Rome's catacombs reveal that its Jewish population was grouped into 13 synagogues. This should not be understood to refer to buildings constructed for worship. In contrast to the word *proseuchē*, which refers to the place where Jews gathered for prayer, *synagōgē* at this time appears to refer to gathering of Jews or a congregation.[28] This evidence shows that Rome's Jewish population was substantial in Paul's day and highly organized. Rome's Jews appear to have lived in close proximity to one another in the city, which complicated matters for gentile believers in Jesus.

Historical texts, inscriptions, and the writings of Philo indicate that most Jews in Rome resided on the right bank of the Tiber in the area known as Trastevere. Many were likely shopkeepers or perhaps worked in occupations connected with the adjacent harbor, its transportation system, and its vast trade network. They resided in small cramped apartments (*insulae*) resembling tenements along with their pagan neighbors.[29] If Romans sixteen accurately reflects the social status of Rome's Jesus movement, then the audience of Paul's letter met in the same small cramped quarters in which most of the city's lower class resided.

The Book of Acts (20:7–12) offers us the earliest glimpse of a gathering of believers in Jesus in its rather entertaining story of how Eutychus fell out of a third-story window while Paul was preaching. Although many today regard this as a comical tale and consider Eutychus the first, certainly not the last, person to fall asleep during a sermon, he was likely not responsible for his unfortunate accident. The author assumes that the reader knows the cultural context—namely, that Paul spoke to a late-night gathering of tired believers in a small and overcrowded apartment. The author states that this room was full of fumes from burning lamps. Roman literature is replete with descriptions of life in such dwellings. Writers frequently complained about their noxious odors due to the lack of toilets and plumbing.[30] We can assume Paul's Letter to the Romans was read aloud to the city's Jesus believing community in a similar room to tired and dirty members in a smelly apartment full of noxious vapors from the parishioners' oil lamps. Congregants had to bring these lights with them to walk down several flights of unlit stairs in cramped tenements to make it safely home.

Those who heard Paul's letter read aloud in Rome certainly met in small confined spaces in apartments. If we offer the estimate of forty meeting places in Rome, then there were likely fewer than 100 followers of Jesus when Paul wrote his letter to the community there.[31] This number would have dwindled when Claudius expelled Rome's Jewish population. What happened to the early Christian community when these Jews left? Paul likely wrote his letter to the Romans partly to address this issue.

It is unlikely that Tiberius and Claudius included gentile followers of Jesus in their expulsion orders. Christianity was not yet a recognized religion, but merely a deviant form of Judaism. Many ordinary Romans undoubtedly viewed gentile believers in Jesus who did eat meat as followers of some strange oriental mystery religion in which Jesus was the cult's patron deity. Rome's gentile believers in Jesus initially had a great advantage over their fellow Jewish members. As gentiles and former pagans, they were full participants in Roman society and not regarded as outsiders. Once the Jewish believers had left Rome, it is doubtful that the gentile members continued to worship in the Jewish sections of Trastevere. Rather, it is probable they gathered in their apartments in their pagan neighborhoods each Sunday where they would have attracted the attention of their neighbors. We can imagine when the Jewish believers returned to Rome, they found that the gentile congregants were assembling elsewhere. These former pagans had apparently taken over leadership of the community of Jesus followers in the city; some likely still embraced elements of their former faith to remain members of their pagan communities.[32] This seems to provide the background of Paul's Letter to the Romans. But he also addresses a greater concern in this composition.

It appears that some of Rome's Jewish believers in Jesus had convinced gentile members to follow Jewish law, including the avoidance of meat tainted by paganism. This led Rome's population to regard these gentiles as different. Many in the city undoubtedly viewed these followers of Jesus as antisocial like the Jews Tiberius and Claudius had banished from Rome. Paul had to somehow remedy this dangerous situation.

Paul wrote his Letter to the Romans for Jews and gentiles. Its context, particularly Romans 15:7–12, makes this clear. Here, he stresses the mutual acceptance of Jews and gentiles in the Christian community in Rome. Chapters 9–11 of the epistle deal with Jewish and gentile relations. Some passages presuppose halakhic issues. These include 14:14 where Paul states that "nothing is unclean in itself" (14:14). Here, Paul uses the Greek word *koinon*, meaning common, while six verses later he uses *katharos*, "clean." He chose these Jewish words to emphasize that all foods are kosher. Paul also highlights Torah observances such as sacred days (14:5–6) and circumcision (15:8). From the context of 14:2, it appears that some Jewish followers of Jesus in Rome had become vegetarians to avoid eating non-kosher, gentile, food. This caused trouble for Jewish and gentile believers in Jesus alike. Pagans would have viewed this as another example of Jews converting native Romans to Judaism, causing them to become anti-social and abandon their former way of life.

Paul's discussion of Jewish law suggests that Jewish believers in Jesus who still followed the Torah's precepts were arguing with their gentile members over the issue of kosher food. Because some former pagans still consumed meat, the Jewish members of Rome's community of Jesus followers were upset. It is doubtful that they were eating kosher food as meat was ordinarily consumed in pagan contexts as part of meals dedicated to the gods or blessed in a temple before sold or eaten.[33] Some Jews wanted gentiles to adopt Jewish law to avoid such practices. Paul's letter to Rome shows that the early community of Jesus followers, despite the testimony in Acts 15 about the verdict of the so-called Council of Jerusalem, had not settled the issue whether gentile believers had to follow Jewish law.

The problem Paul addresses in his Letter to the Romans is this growing schism between Jewish and gentile believers in Jesus. It appears that the Jewish members of the community who still followed the Torah's halakhic commands and likely attended synagogue sat in judgment over gentile believers. Gentiles who followed Jesus's teachings who did not observe the Torah appear to have had a condescending attitude toward Jewish believers who followed biblical halakah. Paul wanted to settle this debate. He realized that reaching a compromise was difficult since both groups claimed a privileged status for their respective positions. In Rom 15:1, the Jews assert their biblical heritage and the covenant, while the gentiles claimed they had a higher standing in the city of Rome. Here, Paul addresses this conflict directly when he states, "We who are strong ought to put up with the failings of the weak, and not to please ourselves."[34]

Resolving the debate over Jewish halakah was essential to preserving the Jesus community in Rome. The insistence that gentile believers had to follow Jewish law upset the religious and social fabric of Roman society. Gentiles who adopted Jewish law could not associate with their neighbors by eating food blessed in the name of pagan gods. They could no longer join associations and dine with members of their trades, participate in the guild's social activities, or bless their patron deities.[35] Such pagans could no longer celebrate the many holidays in the pagan calendar. This type of behavior had the potential to cause many pagans to fear that the Jews were out to destroy Roman society and religion. Such antisocial behavior could have led to another expulsion of Jews from Rome. This time, Paul certainly feared, gentile believers would be included.

Paul tried to heal the growing rift in Rome's congregation by commanding Jews and gentiles there not to pass judgment on members because of what they ate (14:3–4). Gentiles, according to Paul, could eat food offered to pagan gods and appear to be members of Roman society in good standing while recognizing Jesus as the messiah. Paul's insistence that Jews must respect their pagan members who adopt selected elements of pagan culture is reminiscent of Claudius's instructions to the Egyptian-Jewish community not to despise the religious practices of others or show contempt for their beliefs and observances.[36] Although Paul was not the first to preach to the gentile community and to have dealt with these issues, he is the only person who claims God chose him from the womb to do so (Gal 1:15). This, and his assertion that Jesus appeared to him after his crucifixion, Paul believes, gives him the right to dictate policy for all believers (Gal 1:11–12). His problem was that some Jews thought they had a claim of superiority on their side—namely, God's eternal covenant with the Jewish community preserved in the Torah. This, they believed, allowed them to determine the requirements for membership in Rome's Jesus community.

The nascent Christian faith, unlike Judaism, did not have a sacred Scripture. Consequently, Jewish believers in Rome felt they had the right to criticize their fellow gentile members because God had promised them a special relationship in their Scripture. According to their sacred text, God banned all elements of paganism and required His followers to observe special food laws. Eating pagan meat defied God's will. Paul tries to deal with this issue by pointing out that not all Jews followed every tenant of God's law.

In Rom 2:5–11, Paul calls into question the benefit of the covenant for Jews who failed to observe all its stipulations. He objects to the view that Jews by being Jews will be safe from God's wrath and awarded with eternal life. Rather, in 2:5–11, Paul states that God will repay each person according to their deeds. There will be anguish and distress for everyone who does evil, first for the Jews and then for the gentiles.[37] He insists the criterion of judgment is deeds. Undoubtedly, to the disgust of many of Rome's Jewish believers in Jesus, Paul says that certain gentiles will fare better than Jews on the Day of Judgment. But what is unique about Paul's theology of the gentiles is that he does not want them to become like their Jewish brethren.

Although Paul accepts gentiles in the believing community, he does not insist on their conversion. Rather, he makes it clear that gentiles are accepted as gentiles: these pagans join with Israel; they do not join Israel.[38] In chapter 15, Paul emphasizes this point by including a catena of scriptural citations regarding gentiles. Here, he selects biblical passages he believes demonstrate that gentiles are included in Israel's redemption, but only as gentiles.

Although Paul does not require the conversion of gentiles, he insists they show their belief in the one God by rejecting idolatry. His letters all integrate ethics and doctrine: Paul emphasizes that belief in the one God is connected with conduct.[39] Paul emphasizes that gentiles must live under God's will, mainly the Torah. Yet, they are not part of God's covenant community described in Scripture. Consequently, they do not have to observe Jewish law. Instead, Paul believes gentiles are reconciled with God through their abandonment of idolatry, which the Torah mandates for Jews and gentiles alike.[40]

Paul's understanding of gentile believers in Jesus creates some unique problems. He forbids them from becoming Jews but demands that they renounce what makes them gentiles, namely paganism. Yet, he complicates matters by insisting that gentiles become a third category that Jews and gentiles would not have recognized. They are gentiles who do not follow Jewish law but who reject the elements of paganism that bind Romans together. Yet, Rome's Jewish community is critical of some of these gentiles because they are still eating non-kosher meat, which would have been blessed in the name of pagan gods (14:1–4). Pagan members of the Jesus community would have been forced to become vegetarians unless they consumed kosher beef to avoid offending the Jewish members of their congregation. If they did, these gentiles, like Seneca, had to worry about possible Roman reprisals for their new lifestyle. Despite the problems their faith caused, Paul insists that gentile followers of Jesus are insiders. His injunction not to judge them for their dietary choices can be taken as giving them latitude to continue to eat pagan meat (14:1–4). Yet, as gentile followers of Jesus, Paul is demanding they become outsiders to their gentile world by renouncing paganism. His gentiles are, moreover, not Jews although they closely associate with Jewish believers in Jesus, some of whom still practice Jewish law. Paul is effectively requiring gentile believers to become a non-entity that neither Jew nor gentile would recognize.

Paul had a difficult time accounting for God's eternal covenant to the Jews described in Scripture while maintaining that God has granted gentiles the same salvation as the Jews. He presents several arguments to support this belief. In chapter 4, he addresses a question someone certainly posed to him—namely, why was Abraham circumcised if uncircumcised gentiles enjoy the same benefits of salvation as the Jews? He insists that because gentiles are not part of the covenant community, they are not under the Torah. Rather, they are children of Abraham since God promised the patriarch that through him the nations would be blessed (Gen 22:18). Gentiles, Paul insists, must follow Abraham's example before he was circumcised and accompany their faith with deeds. For Paul, God's promise to Abraham that all nations would be blessed has begun in the end-of-the-ages resurrection of Jesus.[41]

In 2:12–16, Paul states that although the Law distinguishes between Jews and gentiles, it is not the deciding factor at God's judgment. This was undoubtedly a rather hard argument for Paul's Jewish believers to understand. He takes another approach through an allegory to explain this difficult concept. In 11:16–17, he makes a rather unusual and problematic argument to illustrate that gentiles are saved without following Jewish law. Here, he alludes to the prophet Jeremiah's statement that God burns up the "evil branches" from the olive tree of Israel. God, Paul asserts, has not changed the rules. Rather, God is cutting off only those of Israel who have forfeited their standing through covenantal unfaithfulness.[42] This is not the first time the majority of Israel has rejected God, for Paul's allusion to Jeremiah (23:1–8; 33:14–16) refers to the idolatry of the ancient kingdoms of Israel and Judah.

Paul uses Jeremiah's metaphor of the branches to argue that God has grafted the gentiles onto the olive tree of Israel. Like the Jews of the past, they have failed to understand that election is no guarantee of salvation. Rather, all must remain faithful and dependent on God to be saved. God even cuts off the Jewish branch. However, Paul insists that Jews are still elect by their nature and can easily be reincorporated into Israel. He asserts that the Jewish branches are born into the tree by nature and can only be cut off for unfaithfulness. Gentiles must come into the tree by an unnatural process but, like the Jews, can be cut off for unfaithfulness. Deeds matter for both. But by being grafted into this tree, Paul's gentiles are neither Jew nor gentile.[43]

Paul appeals to the covenant to argue that God's promises to the Jews are eternal. In chapters 9–11, especially in 11:25–27, he claims that "all Israel" is a larger entity than just the Jews. Unfortunately, his metaphor of the olive tree to explain the relationship between Jew and gentiles is difficult to understand in light of these passages. It certainly perplexed many Jewish and gentile followers of Jesus in Rome. If any of his recipients in Rome had read his earlier Letter to the Galatians, they would have found his understanding of the Torah quite puzzling. In his famous and controversial passage in Galatians 3:19–22, Paul praises the Torah. Then, a few verses later, he writes, "There is no longer Jew or Greek, slave or free, male or female, but all are one in Christ Jesus" (Gal 3:28). This contradicts the tenor of Romans, where Paul erects a dividing wall between Jews and gentiles to show they are different and must remain so.[44]

In his Letter to the Romans, Paul wants to erect a dividing wall to prevent gentiles from being confused with Jews. In light of the earlier expulsions of the Jews from Rome, we can understand why he was so concerned with Roman perceptions of the Jesus community. Paul feared Jews would be charged with undermining the social order by converting native Romans to Judaism. Although Paul was concerned with Roman perceptions, another factor that greatly contributed to his understanding of the gentile in his Letter to the Romans complicated his mission.

Part of the messiness of Paul's theology in Romans is due to his apocalyptic mindset. The New Testament, unlike the Hebrew Bible, describes the world as dominated by demons. Paul, like the other writers of the New Testament, believed these powers seek to turn humans from God. These evil entities control the world. However, their domination will soon end, for in Romans 13:11 Paul assures his audience that "salvation is nearer to us now than when we became believers." Paul believes that the resurrected Jesus signifies the beginning of eschatological times.[45] This accounts for the difficulty in understanding Paul's theology in Romans and his other authentic letters: he wrote all of them in light of his growing expectation that the end is rapidly approaching.

In his Letter to the Romans, Paul distinguishes between the weak earthly and crucified Jesus and the all-powerful Messiah who, when he appears, will resurrect the dead, establish God's kingdom, and subdue the forces of darkness. This is especially clear in the book's opening (1:4) where Paul states that Christ was predestined not by his resurrection from the dead, but by the resurrection of the dead. Paul wanted to bring the gentiles into the fold so that they would join the imminent general resurrection of all the dead. We can sense some desperation in Paul's explanation of God's plan to incorporate the gentiles in Romans. The end has not come, and many are questioning whether Jesus will soon return. Paul's letters all reflect his growing unease with this delay. In his Letter to the Romans, one senses that he is still struggling to maintain his belief that Jesus is about to return with his growing fear that he is wrong and he and many in his congregations will die before judgment day.

The Deutero-Pauline letters can help us understand Paul's theology in Romans. These letters were written in Paul's name to resolve problems with his theology. Their authors also composed them to make the new faith in Jesus compatible with the Roman lifestyle. The writer of 2 Thessalonians gives a list of events that must first take place before the Kingdom's arrival to show that it will come in the distant future. In keeping with the New Testament's belief in cosmic powers, Colossians stresses that these forces have been disarmed and that we have been raised with Christ (Col 3:1). The Pastoral Epistles focus on church organization to bring order to the community and urge followers of Jesus to obey the authorities, namely the Roman governing officials. Slavery and the subjugation of women are acceptable.[46] In other words, the hope of unity in Christ and the breaking down of barriers is not something to be experienced in this life, but in the next. The message of the Pastorals is that women and slaves must remain in their traditional places of subjugation. This would have made the new religion based on Jesus less threatening to Romans.

Paul's understanding of God and the gentiles is firmly grounded in the ancient world. The God of Israel, like the pagan gods, is an ethnic deity who protects his group. As a Jew, Paul believed in Jewish ethnocentrism and therefore could not reject God's covenantal promises to Israel and God's history with the Jewish nation. In Romans 11, Paul stresses that election is God's form of intervention in the world and cannot be separated from God's past promises to the Jews.

Paul's theology is problematic because he is concerned with bringing unity to the small community of Jesus followers in Rome. He was convinced there was little time to do so since the end was near. The only thing that mattered was to gain gentile and Jewish followers in Jesus and keep them from fighting one another. This was vital to avoid creating problems with Roman authorities. Any theological inconsistencies in Paul's letters and preaching ultimately did not matter to him as long as he achieved these goals. He was convinced

God would soon sort out all theological difficulties in his theology: Paul expected Jesus to return shortly after he wrote Romans. The problem is that Paul is creating deviant gentiles whose unusual beliefs and renunciation of idolatry could arouse the wrath of the Roman officials should Jesus not return soon.[47]

The problem with Paul's theology is that he maintains a belief in an ethnic God who favors the Jewish people. Yet, he also claims gentile members of the believing community are saved although they do not share the ethnic features of the Jews. By giving up idolatry, the gentiles are no longer gentiles; however, they are not Jews. They remain both insider and outsider. The only ethnic identity of Paul's gentile believers is their non-Jewishness.[48]

For the gentile believers in Rome, the difficulty is that they no longer fit into their surrounding world. This has the potential to cause great difficulty for the nascent Christian community. It could lead to its expulsions or persecution. Paul's theology in Romans and his other epistles are often messy. Rather than try to make sense of Paul's conflicting doctrines in his writings and force them into a coherent systematic theology, we should recognize their problematic nature as the authors of the Pastoral Epistles did—namely, that the root of his theological inconsistencies in his letters is due to his conviction that Jesus' return was imminent.

NOTES

1. Origen, Commentaria in Epistolam B. Pauli ad Romanos, 10:43 in Patrologia Graeca, 14.1290.

2. Philip Wesley Comfort, *A Commentary on the Manuscripts and Text of the New Testament* (Grand Rapids, MI: Kregel, 2015), 312–16; Joseph A. Fitzmyer, *Romans: A New Translation with Introduction and Commentary*, AB 33 (New York, NY: Doubleday, 1993), 59.

3. Harry Gamble, *The Textual History of the Letter to the Romans: A Study in Textual and Literary Criticism* (Grand Rapids, MI: Eerdmans, 1977), esp. 35–47. The presence of the Greek particle *de* in 16:1 implies that something preceded the verse.

4. In addition to Phoebe, Paul appears to know a dozen of the persons in verses 14–15: Prisca, Aquila, Epaenetus, Andronicus, Junia, Ampliatus, Stachys, Apelles, Urbanus, Persis, and Rufus along with his mother. Seven of these are women (Prisca, Mary, Junia, Tryphaena, Typhosa, Persis, and Rufus's mother) and five are men (Aquila, Andronicus, Urbanus, Apelles, and Rufus). See further, Fitzmyer, *Romans*, 728.

5. Greek names: Andronicus, Apelles, Aristobulus, Asyncritus, Epaenetus, Erastus, Hermes, Jason, Narcissus, Nereus, Olympas, Patrobas, Persis, Philologus, Phlegon, Sosipater, Stachys, Timotheos, Tryphaena, and Tryphosa.

6. Ampliatus, Aquila, Caius, Julia, Junia, Lucius, Quartus, Rufus, Tertius, and Urbanus.

7. Mary, Rufus, Julia.

8. For further discussion and bibliography, see Fitzmyer, *Romans,* 733–44, 747–56.

9. See further, Wayne A. Meeks, *The First Urban Christians: The Social World of the Apostle Paul* (New Haven, CT: Yale University Press, 1983), 9–73.

10. Richard I. Pervo, *Profit with Delight: The Literary Genre of the Acts of the Apostles* (Philadelphia, PA: Fortress Press, 1987), 12–57.

11. Orosius (*Historia contra Paganos* 7.6.15) dates it to 49 CE Cassius Dio (*History* 6.6.6) claims there were so many Jews in Rome that Claudius could not evict them all from the city. Consequently, he allowed them to follow their traditional lifestyle but forbade gatherings. For a discussion of the extant sources that likely form the basis for the event mentioned in Acts 18:2, see further Richard I. Pervo, *Acts: A Commentary* (Minneapolis, MN: Fortress Press, 2009), 445–47.

12. *Life of Claudius* (*Claud.* 25.4).

13. Smallwood argues that the term "Chrestus" refers to Christ and that Seutonius describes Christian missionaries among Rome's Jewish community. They caused problems because Claudius, in 41 CE, had suspended the Jews' right of assembly (see E. Mary Smallwood, *The Jews under Roman Rule: From Pompey to Diocletian* [Leiden: Brill, 1976], 210–16). Slingerland has argued against the identification of "Chrestus" with "Christ." For his most recent presentation of this thesis, see Dixon Slingerland, *Claudian Policymaking and the Early Imperial Repression of Judaism at Rome* (Atlanta, GA: Scholars Press, 1997), 151–217. Nanos has adopted Slingerland's theory and uses it to argue against reading Romans in light of Claudius's edict (see Mark D. Nanos, *The Mystery of Romans: The Jewish Context of Paul's Letter* [Minneapolis, MN: Fortress, 1996], 372–87). Neither of these authors is aware of the Seneca correspondence examined in the present study that suggests otherwise. For evidence supporting the historicity of Suetonius's account of Jewish expulsion during Claudius's reign, see Robert Van Voorst, *Jesus outside the New Testament: An Introduction to the Ancient Evidence* (Grand Rapids, MI: Eerdmans, 2000), 29–39.

14. See further, F. Blass, "ΧΡΙΣΤΙΑΝΟΣ—ΧΡΗΣΤΙΑΝΟΣ," *Hermes* 30 (1895): 468–70; Elsa Gibson, *The "Christians for Christians" Inscriptions of Phrygia* (Missoula, MT: Scholars Press, 1978), esp. 15–17; Antonio Ferrua, "Una nuova iscrizione montanista," *Rivista di archeologia cristiana* 31 (1955): 97–100.

15. See further, Leonard Victor Rutgers, "Roman Policy towards the Jews: Expulsions from the City of Rome during the First Century C.E.," *Classical Antiquity* 13 (1994): 56–74.

16. *Antiquities* (*Ant.* 19.290).

17. For the conflict between Jewish and gentile Jesus followers in Rome as the backdrop of Paul's letter to the congregations there, see H.-W. Bartsch, "Die historische Situation des Römerbriefes," in *Studia Evangelica IV,* ed. F. L. Cross (Berlin: Akademie, 1968), 281–91.

18. For the early Hasmonean treaties with the Romans, see further Kenneth Atkinson, *The Hasmoneans and Their Neighbors: New Historical Reconstructions from the Dead Sea Scrolls and Classical Sources* (London: Bloomsbury T&T Clark, 2018), 3–8.

19. For estimates, see Eric S. Gruen, *Diaspora: Jews amidst Greeks and Romans* (Cambridge: Harvard University Press, 2002), 15.

20. *Life of Julius Caesar* (*Jul.* 85).

21. *Legatio ad Gaium* (*Legat.* 281–83).

22. Josephus, *Antiquities* (*Ant.* 18.81–84); Tacitus, *Annuals* (*Ann.* 2.85.5); Seutonius, *Life of Tiberius* (*Tib.* 36.1).

23. Cassius Dio, 57.18.5a; Philo, *In Flaccum* (*Flacc.* 1); *Legatio ad Gaium* (*Legat.* 159–61).

24. For additional evidence, see E. Mary Smallwood, "Some Notes on the Jews under Tiberius," *Latomus* 15 (1956): 314–29.

25. *Epistle* 103.22. For Tiberius's decree and Seneca's fear of being identified as a Jew, see further Margaret H. Williams, "The Expulsion of the Jews from Rome in A.D. 19," *Latomus* 4 (1989): 765–84.

26. Several philosophers discussed Pythagoras's prohibition against eating meat. See: Diogenes Laertius, *Lives of the Philosophers* (*Vitae Philosophorum* 8.3); Ovid, *Metamorphoses* (*Metam.* 15.75–142); Empedocles, fragments 11 and 124 in Brad Inwood, *The Poem of Empedocles*, rev. ed. (Toronto: University of Toronto Press, 2001), 115 and 139. Plato's earlier comments show that even followers of ascetic lifestyles questioned the practice of vegetarianism. (*Republic* [*Respublica* 372a–d]; *Laws* [*Leges* 781e–783b]). Defenders of vegetarianism were rare. For the most prominent, see Porphyry, *On Abstinence from Animal Flesh* (*De abstinentia* I.4; II.13); Plutarch, *On the Eating of Flesh* (*De esu carnium* 993c–994b, 995d–996a; 006E–997A); *Precepts for Preserving Health* (*Moralia* 131F–132A). For reasons discussed in the present study, Seneca clearly refers to vegetarianism that some pagans, and likely many Jews as well, had adopted under the influence of Judaism to avoid consuming meat tainted by paganism.

27. Juvenal (*Satirae* 6.542–47; 14.96–106) denounces Jews for their aversion to pork and for their begging in Rome.

28. On the literary evidence, see Anders Runesson, Donald D. Binder, and Birger Olsson, *The Ancient Synagogue from Its Origins to 200 C.E.: A Source Book* (Leiden: Brill, 2008), 230–37.

29. For the archaeological evidence, see Glenn R. Storey, "Regionaries-Type Insulae 2: Architectural/Residential Units at Rome," *American Journal of Archaeology* 106 (2002): 411–34.

30. See, Ann Olga Koloski-Ostrow, *The Archaeology of Sanitation in Roman Italy: Toilets, Sewers, and Water Systems* (Chapel Hill, NC: University of North Carolina Press, 2015), esp. 84–101.

31. For the small size of early gatherings of Jesus believers in homes, see Meeks, *First Urban,* 75–76.

32. For this thesis, see further Karl Paul Donfried, "A Short Note on Romans 16," *Journal of Biblical Literature* 89 (1970): 441–49. See also H.-W. Bartsch, "Die historische Situation," 281–91.

33. For the problem eating meat caused for gentile Christians, see further Ramsay MacMullen, *Paganism in the Roman Empire* (New Haven, CT: Yale University Press, 1981), 42–48. Because Romans rarely consumed beef, which was far too expensive

for them to purchase, any animal slaughtered by a Jewish purveyor of meat would have been out of the price range for most of Rome's citizens, whether gentile or Jewish. Meat, moreover, was rarely consumed in antiquity outside of a cultic context; fish provided the major source of protein. For examples, see further Margaret H. Williams, *Jews in a Graeco-Roman Environment*, WUNT 312 (Tübingen: Mohr Siebeck, 2013), 155–66.

34. Nanos, although adopting a slightly different interpretation of Paul's "weak" and "strong," comments that Paul wrestled with the tension of maintaining that the Law continued to be operative for Jews but that its observance was not necessary for gentiles to become coparticipants in Israel's blessings (*The Mystery of Romans*, 84–165).

35. See further, Stephen G. Wilson, "Voluntary Associations: An Overview," in *Voluntary Associations in the Graeco-Roman World*, ed. John S. Kloppenborg and Stephen G. Wilson (New York, NY: Routledge, 1996), 1–15.

36. Paul's earlier thoughts on eating meat in 1 Cor 8:1–9 is similar to Claudius's edict to the Egyptian Jews since he wants to avoid offending gentiles.

37. Chris VanLandingham, *Judgment & Justification in Early Judaism and the Apostle Paul* (Peabody, MA: Hendrickson, 2006), 222–23.

38. Paula Fredriksen, *Paul: The Pagans' Apostle* (New Haven, CT: Yale University Press, 2017), 74–75; Pamela Eisenbaum, *Paul Was Not a Christian* (New York, NY: HarperOne, 2009), 159–72. See also Daniel Boyarin, *A Radical Jew: Paul and the Politics of Identity* (Berkeley, CA: University of California Press, 1994), 50–53, 152–57.

39. František Ábel, *The Psalms of Solomon and the Messianic Ethics of Paul*. WUNT 2.416 (Tübingen: Mohr Siebeck, 2016), 82–83.

40. VanLandingham, *Judgment*, 18.

41. Mark Nanos, "Paul and Judaism," in *The Jewish Annotated New Testament*, ed. Amy-Jill Levine and Marc Zvi Brettler (Oxford: Oxford University Press, 2011), 551–54.

42. Jason A. Staples, "What Do the Gentiles Have to Do with '"All Israel'? A Fresh Look at Romans 11:25–27," *Journal of Biblical Literature* 130 (2011): 384.

43. Caroline Johnson Hodge comments on the identity of gentiles in Paul's writings: "They are not Jews and, in my view, they are not Christians; and they are not really gentiles any longer either.'", ("The Question of Identity: Gentiles as Gentiles—but also Not—in Pauline Communities," in *Paul within Judaism: Restoring the First-Century Context to the Apostle*, ed. Mark D. Nanos and Magnus Zetterholm [Minneapolis, MN: Fortress, 2015], 153–55).

44. Ishay Rosen-Zvi, "What If We Got Rid of the Goy?: Rereading Ancient Jewish Distinctions," *Journal for the Study of Judaism* 47 (2016): 21–22.

45. Ábel, *Psalms of Solomon*, 84.

46. 1 Cor 7:21; 1 Tim 6:1–2; 1 Peter 2:18; Eph 6:5–8; Col 3:22–24; Titus 2:9–10.

47. Kahl astutely comments that Paul's insistence that uncircumcised gentiles must cease practicing paganism would have appeared as disorderly, lawless, and un-Roman and a threat to the public order. It would have created problems for both Jews and Gentiles alike. See further, Brigitte Kahl, *Galatians Re-Imagined: Reading with the*

Eyes of the Vanquished (Minneapolis, MN: Fortress Press, 2010), 210–43. See also Josephus, *J.W.* 2.194; Tacitus, *Historiae* (*Hist.* 5.6).

48. Rosen-Zwi, "What If We Got Rid," 28.

BIBLIOGRAPHY

Ábel, František. *The Psalms of Solomon and the Messianic Ethics of Paul.* WUNT 2.416. Tübingen: Mohr Siebeck, 2016.

Atkinson, Kenneth. *The Hasmoneans and Their Neighbors: New Historical Reconstructions from the Dead Sea Scrolls and Classical Sources.* London: Bloomsbury T&T Clark, 2018.

Bartsch, H.-W. "Die historische Situation des Römerbriefes." In *Studia Evangelica IV*, edited by F. L. Cross, 281–91. Berlin: Akademie, 1968.

Blass, F. "ΧΡΙΣΤΙΑΝΟΣ—ΧΡΗΣΤΙΑΝΟΣ." *Hermes* 30 (1895): 468–70.

Boyarin, Daniel. *A Radical Jew: Paul and the Politics of Identity.* Berkeley, CA: University of California Press, 1994.

Comfort, Philip Wesley. *A Commentary on the Manuscripts and Text of the New Testament.* Grand Rapids, MI: Kregel, 2015.

Donfried, Karl Paul. "A Short Note on Romans 16." *Journal of Biblical Literature* 89 (1970): 441–49.

Eisenbaum, Pamela. *Paul Was Not a Christian.* New York, NY: HarperOne, 2009.

Ferrua, Antonio. "Una nuova iscrizione montanista." *Rivista di archeologia cristiana* 31 (1955): 97–100.

Fitzmyer, Joseph A. *Romans: A New Translation with Introduction and Commentary.* AB 33. New York, NY: Doubleday, 1993.

Fredriksen, Paula, *Paul: The Pagans' Apostle.* New Haven, CT: Yale University Press, 2017.

Gamble, Harry. *The Textual History of the Letter to the Romans: A Study in Textual and Literary Criticism.* Grand Rapids, MI: Eerdmans, 1977.

Gibson, Elsa. *The "Christians for Christians" Inscriptions of Phrygia.* Missoula, MT: Scholars Press, 1978.

Gruen, Eric S. *Diaspora: Jews amidst Greeks and Romans.* Cambridge: Harvard University Press, 2002.

Hodge, Caroline Johnson. "The Question of Identity: Gentiles as Gentiles—but also Not—in Pauline Communities." In *Paul within Judaism: Restoring the First-Century Context to the Apostle,* edited by Mark D. Nanos and Magnus Zetterholm, 153–73. Minneapolis, MN: Fortress, 2015.

Inwood, Brad. *The Poem of Empedocles,* rev. ed. Toronto: University of Toronto Press, 2001.

Kahl, Brigitte. *Galatians Re-Imagined: Reading with the Eyes of the Vanquished.* Minneapolis, MN: Fortress Press, 2010.

Koloski-Ostrow, Ann Olga. *The Archaeology of Sanitation in Roman Italy: Toilets, Sewers, and Water Systems.* Chapel Hill, NC: University of North Carolina Press, 2015.

MacMullen, Ramsay. *Paganism in the Roman Empire*. New Haven, CT: Yale University Press, 1981.
Meeks, Wayne A. *The First Urban Christians: The Social World of the Apostle Paul*. New Haven, CT: Yale University Press, 1983.
Nanos, Mark D. *The Mystery of Romans: The Jewish Context of Paul's Letter*. Minneapolis, MN: Fortress Press, 1996.
———. "Paul and Judaism." In *The Jewish Annotated New Testament*, edited by Amy-Jill Levine and Marc Zvi Brettler, 551–54. Oxford: Oxford University Press, 2011.
Pervo, Richard I. *Acts: A Commentary*. Minneapolis, MN: Fortress Press, 2009.
———. *Profit with Delight: The Literary Genre of the Acts of the Apostles*. Philadelphia, PA: Fortress Press, 1987.
Rosen-Zwi, Ishay. "What If We Got Rid of the Goy?: Rereading Ancient Jewish Distinctions." *Journal for the Study of Judaism* 47 (2016): 1–34.
Runesson, Anders, Donald D. Binder, and Birger Olsson. *The Ancient Synagogue from Its Origins to 200 C.E.: A Source Book*. Leiden: Brill, 2008.
Rutgers, Leonard Victor. "Roman Policy towards the Jews: Expulsions from the City of Rome during the First Century CE." *Classical Antiquity* 13 (1994): 56–74.
Slingerland, Dixon. *Claudian Policymaking and the Early Imperial Repression of Judaism at Rome*. Atlanta, GA: Scholars Press, 1997.
Smallwood, E. Mary. *The Jews under Roman Rule: From Pompey to Diocletian*. Leiden: Brill, 1976.
———. "Some Notes on the Jews under Tiberius." *Latomus* 15 (1956): 314–29.
Staples, Jason A. "What Do the Gentiles Have to Do with, 'All Israel'? A Fresh Look at Romans 11:25–27." *Journal of Biblical Literature* 130 (2011): 371–90.
Storey, Glenn R. "Regionaries-Type Insulae 2: Architectural/Residential Units at Rome." *American Journal of Archaeology* 106 (2002): 411–34.
VanLandingham, Chris. *Judgment & Justification in Early Judaism and the Apostle Paul*. Peabody, MA: Hendrickson, 2006.
Van Voorst, Robert. *Jesus outside the New Testament: An Introduction to the Ancient Evidence*. Grand Rapids, MI: Eerdmans, 2000.
Williams, Margaret H. "The Expulsion of the Jews from Rome in A.D. 19." *Latomus* 4 (1989): 765–84.
———. *Jews in a Graeco-Roman Environment*. WUNT 312. Tübingen: Mohr Siebeck, 2013.
Wilson, Stephen G. "Voluntary Associations: An Overview." In *Voluntary Associations in the Graeco-Roman World*, edited by John S. Kloppenborg and Stephen G. Wilson, 1–15. New York, NY: Routledge, 1996.

Chapter Thirteen

"If you are called a Judean..." (Rom 2:17)

Paul and His Interlocutor

Markus Öhler

The question of who is behind the Ἰουδαῖος that Paul addresses in Rom 2:17 has led to numerous publications in recent times. The following chapter aims to contribute to this discussion by contextualizing the formulation εἰ δὲ σὺ Ἰουδαῖος ἐπονομάζῃ within the ancient use of language and by examining the different interpretative approaches for their inner logic.

Before I deal with these specific questions, some basic statements about my understanding of the Epistle to the Romans are necessary: In my opinion Paul addresses this letter exclusively to Christ-believers from the nations, as he does by the way in all his letters. It is well known that this is already implied in Rom 1:5–6: When Paul describes the assignment of his apostleship "to bring about the obedience of faith among all the nations for the sake of his name, including yourselves who are called to belong to Jesus Christ," it is clear that Judeans are not among his intended readers. In my view this doesn't change throughout the entire letter. Neither the numerous references to the Septuagint nor the discussions on individual ethical questions such as food, etc., make it necessary to repeal the unambiguous salutations addressed exclusively to members of the nations (see also 11:13).[1] At the same time, of course, this does not mean that Paul wrote only about affairs of the nations. This is already evident in Rom 9–11 and is, of course, possible for the entire letter. So at no point is it ruled out that the apostle might express his views on Judeans and the Judean culture and religion.[2]

"IF YOU ARE CALLED A JUDEAN"

Origen on Rom 2:17

The question of who is actually meant by the Ἰουδαῖος in Rom 2:17 has always been a central subject for the exegesis of the Letter to the Romans.[3] Before we turn to more recent interpretations, I would like to quote Origen as part of the exegetical history. In his commentary on Romans (*Comm. Rom.*), a late work (243/244 CE) preserved only in the Latin translation of Rufinus, Origen said the following on 2:17 (book 2.11):

> The first thing to notice here, that he does not say about him: "You're a Jew, though.", but: "You are called a Jew" (*Iudaeus cognominaris*). It's not the same thing to be a Jew or to be called a Jew (*cognominari Iudaeum*).[4] For Paul himself teaches that the one who is truly a Jew is one who is it "in concealment" circumcised by the circumcision of the heart, who keeps the law "in spirit and not according to the letter", "whose glory comes not from men but from God". But the one who is "visibly circumcised in the flesh" and observes the law in order to be seen by men, is not in truth, but is only called a Jew (*cognominatur Iudaeus*). . . . So it has become clear that we are dealing with different people, and likewise who is truly a Jew and who, on the other hand, is just called that (*cognominetur*). . . . Even one who is called a Jew (*cognominatur*) and boasts that he has the Mosaic law by the letter is accused of breaking the law if he does not believe Christ. . . . So for the sake of those who are called Jews (*dicuntur Iudaei*) and are not, the name of God is blasphemed among the Gentiles. . . . It is true that the apostle says all this to the one who is a Jew by name, not by deed (*qui nomine, non opere Iudaeus est*). . . . These words can also be applied to heretics: They too are called Christians (*cognominatur Christiani*). . . . But one must know that the apostle speaks to the Jews here with irony.[5]

So for Origen it is clear: Paul writes about an actual "Jew," even if he doesn't use the word "is."[6] The Ἰουδαῖος is not a proselyte nor a Christian, even if an allegorical interpretation in the latter direction is also brought forward. Whether this Ἰουδαῖος calls himself so or is called that way, however, is not clear. Origen does not write about what is meant by the passive form ἐπονομάζῃ, although he is very much concerned with whether someone is actually a "Jew" or is merely referred to as such/presents himself as such. In the remark that the supposed Ἰουδαῖος keeps the law to be seen by others (*ut videatur ab hominis*), we can glimpse a hint of Origen's understanding of the expression: not as a reflexive but actually as a passive one. However, in the end this remains ambiguous, although I presume Origen would have elucidated it had it not been the usual passive understanding.[7]

ἐπονομάζῃ—Passive or Middle Voice?

Before we address the question of the interlocutor's identity, let us first examine the formulation εἰ δὲ σὺ Ἰουδαῖος ἐπονομάζῃ in more detail. From my point of view a closer look on it provides us with a first indication of what Paul's intention was and what background of interpretation he could draw on.

A Brief History of Interpretation

If we take a leap into the 16th century, it becomes clear that the rendering of this short sentence was already controversial by that time. While Luther had formulated in his translation from 1522, "Du heyssist eyn Jude," his opponent Hieronymus Emser critically examined Luther's translation of Rom 2:17 and referred to Origen. In Emser's view, it should be translated as passive: "So du aber ein Jud genennt wirst."[8]

A closer look into the exegetical literature of the 20th and 21st centuries shows the increasing popularity of the middle voice/reflexive understanding. The earliest commentator I've found who renders ἐπονομάζῃ as a medium/reflexive is Theodor Zahn in his commentary from 1910.[9] In an effort to prove his understanding, he points to the following clauses in Rom 2:17 and concludes that ἐπονομάζῃ must also describe the behavior of the interlocutor.[10] And indeed, the Ἰουδαῖος is surely the subject of ἐπαναπαύῃ νόμῳ καὶ καυχᾶσαι ἐν θεῷ and, according to Zahn, this must also be assumed for ἐπονομάζῃ. Also in 1910 the dictionary on New Testament Greek by Erwin Preuschen was published, who also translated the phrase as: "du nennst dich e. Juden."[11] The fact that this interpretation was not taken up at that time, however, is shown by Walter Bauer, who altered it in his edition of Preuschen's dictionary (1928): "du läßt dich e. Juden nennen" appears like a compromise between passive and medium.[12]

In further consequence it is interesting that especially exegetes who like Zahn refer to the pride of the Ἰουδαῖος assumed the medial/reflexive meaning.[13] E. Käsemann, for instance, translated the phrase without further discussion as: "Wenn du dich aber 'Jude' nennst"[14], and U. Wilckens almost identically: "Wenn aber du dich Jude nennst."[15] As Zahn's, Wilckens's interpretation is derived from the assumption that the religious self-claim of the Ἰουδαῖος is an expression of high self-esteem and boasting. Like the following statements about resting on the law and the pride of having a special relationship with God, being "Jewish" would accordingly be a statement that would constitute the boast of the fictitious opponent.[16] While C.E.B. Cranfield noticed a trace of irony in Paul's designation of the interlocutor as a "Jew" and preferred the rendition "be known to be, claim to be," A. Nygren explicitly rejected this notion,[17] whereas M.-J. Lagrange on the other hand favored the passive meaning.[18]

At present, the medial rendering of ἐπονομάζῃ has become dominant in most Bible translations, both in German and in English.[19] For the most part this line is continued in current commentaries. R. Jewett, e.g., points to the "emphatic pronoun 'you' and the dynamics of the diatribe" to sustain the interpretation of ἐπονομάζῃ as middle voice.[20] Only J. Dunn translates ἐπονομάζῃ as passive, but does not address the interpretive issues further.[21]

Passive or Medium—a Revaluation

In any case, regarding this question it might be helpful to take a closer look at the contemporary use of ἐπονομάζειν. The findings are clear: the reflexive interpretation has no linguistic background.[22] Multiple examples from Hellenistic literature demonstrate that it was always employed by others to name an object or place, a person or a group.[23] For the early imperial period I would like to provide the following examples.

Philo of Alexandria uses ἐπονομάζειν five times altogether (four of them in quotations from the LXX), and only once in the passive voice (in a quotation from Exod 15:23). The only original formulation with ἐπονομάζειν (*Praem.* 23) is in the active and denotes the naming of a person (τοῦτον Ἕλληνες μὲν Δευκαλίωνα, Χαλδαῖοι δὲ Νῶε ἐπονομάζουσιν). Josephus uses ἐπονομάζειν three times in the passive, each time referring to a place (*Ant.* 2.1; 4.207; *B.J.* 1.119). The evidence from LXX again is completely unambiguous: ἐπονομάζειν is employed to designate places (Gen 4:17; 21:31; etc.) or persons (Gen 4:25–26; 5:2–3; etc.). Four times the use of the name of God JHWH is thus expressed (Lev 24:11; Deut 12:5; 1 Chr 28:3; 2 Chr 12:13). The only indication of passive voice is found in the context of naming a place (Exod 15:23: διὰ τοῦτο ἐπωνομάσθη τὸ ὄνομα τοῦ τόπου ἐκείνου πικρία).

In Strabo we encounter ἐπονομάζειν time and again, so we can concentrate on the use in the passive voice. Twice the word is used to explain why a place is called by a special name (*Geogr.* 4.4.6; 11.7.1), twice in order to designate persons:. One time it is regarding a clarification of an epithet for Zeus: ἴσως δὲ καὶ ὁ Λαρίσιος ἐκεῖθεν ἐπωνόμασται (*Geogr.* 9.5.19). The other time it is applied to designate Egyptian migrants in the Kingdom of Saba: ἐπονομάζονται δὲ Σεμβρῖται, ὡς ἂν ἐπήλυδες (*Geogr.* 16.4.8).

In the Compendium of Greek theology by Cornutus the word is often employed in the passive voice, since the author explains the epithets of the gods (16.5, 21; 20.20; 34.1; 35.3). Nobody would ever assume that the gods called themselves that way in this context. In the anabasis of Arrian ἐπονομάζειν in the passive voice is used to introduce a surname of Alexander (*Anab.* 3.27.4), in a similar way Appian employs the word in his account of the civil war (1.11.97; 3.12.84). Also in Dio Chrysostom ἐπονομάζειν is found in passive voice, there to designate Zeus (*Or.* 1.39; 12.75).

Plutarch particularly often employs ἐπονομάζειν, so only a few examples shall be given here. Usually the author uses the verb to explain the surnames of gods or persons. Concerning our context, for example, it is interesting that the designation as "sow" is justified by ethos and bios (*Thes.* 9.2). As a rule, reasons are given for designations that refer to the person's activity (*Rom.* 16.6; 21.2; *Fab.* 1.3; *Flam.* 9.6; *Sert.* 18.3). It is always clear that others assigned these names and that the persons in question did not call themselves that. Also in the *Moralia* there is no other use of the terminology (e.g. in 426A; 675E; 676D; 869F; 1001B; 1112A). Especially interesting is Plutarch *Mor.* 472A–B, because at this point the evaluation of Stoics by others is equated with the naming of the gods:

> But some think that the Stoics are dancing when they hear that amongst them the wise man is termed (προσαγορευόμενον) not only prudent and just and brave, but also an orator, a poet, a general, a rich man, and a king; and then they count themselves worthy (ἀξιοῦσι) of all these titles, and if they don't get them (μὴ τυγχάνωσιν), are distressed. Yet even among the gods different gods hold different powers: one is called (ἐπονομάζεται) "war-like," another "oracular," another "gain-bringing."

In later Christian literature, ἐπονομάζειν is rarely found in the passive, apart from the evidence referring to Rom 2:17. From the 2nd century, Justin is to be mentioned, who in his apology points to the origin of the designation Χριστιανοί: Ἰησοῦς Χριστός, ἀφ' οὗ καὶ τὸ Χριστιανοὶ ἐπονομάζεσθαι (*1 Apol.* 12.9).[24] However, it is highly improbable that Justin actually assumed that Christians designated themselves in this manner, since in Acts 11:26 the origin of the title is explicitly attributed to outsiders (χρηματίσαι τε πρώτως ἐν Ἀντιοχείᾳ τοὺς μαθητὰς Χριστιανούς).[25]

If we take a closer look at the simplex ὀνομάζειν, the finding is also clear: in the LXX the passive form always stands for the naming or mentioning of names by others, never for self-designation (e.g., 1 Chr 12:32; *Sap.* 14:8; Jer 3:16; etc.). Paul himself uses the simplex twice: In Rom 15:20 it is undoubtedly a matter of the name of Christ being invoked (ὅπου ὠνομάσθη Χριστός), which is tantamount to proclaiming the gospel. At first glance, 1 Cor 5:11 is somewhat less clear: ἐάν τις ἀδελφὸς ὀνομαζόμενος can also be understood to mean that an evildoer, to whom some vices are subsequently attributed, calls himself a brother. But the participle passive ὀνομαζόμενος should rather be interpreted that way: Someone who is called "brother" by other church members, because he is part of the community, turns out to be unworthy of the ecclesia. A translation with "he calls himself brother" contradicts *de facto* that Paul here demands the exclusion of persons who had until then belonged to the community.[26] Other evidences for the use of ὀνομάζειν in the passive voice in the New Testament also are clearly non-reflexive (Eph 1:21; 3:15; 5:3).

A brief side glance on Epictetus: In his often cited references to philosophers[27] who call themselves Stoics while not keeping their teachings, the author applies reflexive constructions or other forms to make his case clear. He does not use ἐπονομάζειν, but other formulations: τί οὖν Στωικὸν λέγεις σεαυτόν (*Diatr.* 2.9.19), εἰ δὲ μή, οὐδὲν διοίσεις ἡμῶν τῶν λεγομένων Στωικῶν (3.7.17), and τί οὖν Στωικὸν σαυτὸν εἶναι λέγεις (3.24.41). Epictetus does not utilize medium/passive voices, but adds a reflexive σεαυτόν to mark that someone is calling himself something. A reflexive pronoun is obviously necessary to make clear that the identity of the Stoic is a self-predication.

In my opinion, all these examples make it very probable that the translation of ἐπονομάζῃ with "you call yourself"[28] runs contrary to the ordinary use of language in the 1st century CE. Neither in the LXX, which was certainly linguistically influential for Paul, nor in contemporary authors is the verb used this way. The phrase εἰ δὲ σὺ Ἰουδαῖος ἐπονομάζῃ should therefore be translated as "if you are called a Judean."[29]

The Context in Rom 2:17

But what about the argument put forward since T. Zahn that the following verbs would suggest a medial understanding of ἐπονομάζῃ? The full sentence, which is an anacoluthon, runs as follows (Rom 2:17–18):

    Εἰ δὲ σὺ Ἰουδαῖος   ἐπονομάζῃ
    καὶ   ἐπαναπαύῃ   νόμῳ
    καὶ   καυχᾶσαι   ἐν θεῷ
    καὶ   γινώσκεις   τὸ θέλημα
    καὶ   δοκιμάζεις   τὰ διαφέροντα
    κατηχούμενος ἐκ τοῦ νόμου.

Zahn's notion is that the following two forms (ἐπαναπαύῃ and καυχᾶσαι) are both obviously medium and thus determine the interpretation of ἐπονομάζῃ.[30] Indeed, there is a great deal of evidence for ἐπαναπαύεσθαι and καυχᾶσθαι in the LXX and in Paul himself, so there can be no doubt about it: the Ἰουδαῖος rests on the Torah and boasts of God. But does this really shift the obvious meaning of the first word into a completely diverging one? In addition, it should be considered that the last two verbs in this sentence are in active, so that a series of passive–medium–active voices is created, which ranges from the external perception to the self-understanding and then goes on to the actual action of the interlocutor.

And finally, we must bear in mind that in the following verses Paul is definitely referring to the fact that the fictitious Ἰουδαῖος is perceived by others—namely, by the nations (v. 24): "For the name of God is blasphemed because of you among the nations." In my opinion, it is therefore obvious that this first verb is not intended to refer to a self-understanding attributed to the opponent. Rather it is implied that his self-awareness, which Paul understands as resting on the Torah and boasting of the relationship with God, developed out of the perception by others and was triggered by this. If, then, we take the passive ἐπονομάζῃ seriously, we can see that right from the beginning Paul not only has in mind the self-conception of the opponent, but at this point already addresses the perspective of others—that is to say, of the nations, his addressees.[31]

ἸΟΥΔΑΙΟΣ AS A TITLE

The fact that the fictitious interlocutor of Paul is called Ἰουδαῖος raises the question what meaning this designation has here.[32]

Very probably it is not a name, because on the one hand this usage is hardly documented,[33] on the other hand it is not very likely in this context. It might be more probable that Paul refers to an origin from Judea. But although this meaning could be substantiated, it is not really plausible in Rom 2:17.[34] After all, the actions of the Ἰουδαῖος in Rom 2 that follow this designation have no connection whatsoever with the land of Judea.

So one must reckon with the fact that Ἰουδαῖος is used here titularly. The opponent is called or addressed as Ἰουδαῖος. A designation as Judean is quite common in literary contexts as well as in epigraphic and papyrological sources. Generally it means that someone is a member of the Judean people, whereby such identifications are usually found in the Diaspora. In some examples, however, the term is also used to refer to persons who do not belong to the Judean people as such, but who have either been forcibly integrated into them or have joined them voluntarily. Especially in the latter instance it was decisive that the joining of the Judean people was connected with a specific religious and cultural reorientation. As a rule, this led to the abandonment of traditional ties and a new affiliation.

In Josephus' depiction of the Idumean king Izates it becomes very clear that he became a Judean through circumcision (*Ant.* 20.38–47). Under the Hasmoneans, coercive measures were carried out several times in order to turn members of other peoples into Judeans.³⁵ In his book on Herod, the historian Ptolemais wrote that the Idumeans were forced to be circumcised, in order to belong to the people (ἔθνος) and to follow their customs. Therefore they were called Judeans (ἐκλήθεσαν Ἰουδαῖοι).³⁶ In Cassius Dio (*Roman History*) it is stated that not only the Judeans, who are named so after the landscape of Judea, are called that way, but also those who belong to a different tribe.³⁷ Also, in the philosophical tradition there are examples of a metaphorical use of the title Ἰουδαῖος. Usually, Epictetus is rightly referred to for this (*Diatr.* 2.9.19–21):

> Why, then, do you call yourself a Stoic? Why do you deceive the many? Why do you feign a Judean, while being a Greek? Do you not see in what sense men are severally called (λέγεται) a Judean, how a Syrian how an Egyptian? And when we see a man playing a double game, we are accustomed to say: He is not a Judean, but he is feigning it. But when he has assumed the attitude of mind, in which he immersed himself and took them over, then he is in fact one and is called (καλεῖται) a Judean. So are we false dyers, according to reason Judeans, but according to the work something else, unaffected by reason, far from holding those things which we say, but priding ourselves upon them as being men who know them.³⁸

Beyond all interpretive problems with which this paragraph, which plays on anti-Jewish resentment, is permeated, it is clear that Epictetus is alluding to the reality that individual persons conform to Judaism to such an extent that they are called Judeans. It remains open, however, whether they are so called by their pagan environment or by the Judeans themselves.

Epigraphic evidence also—albeit rarely—demonstrates the possibility to call proselytes Judeans. Williams names three relevant instances, all from Rome and dated to the 3rd or 4th century: One is a *Crescens Sinicerius Iudeus proselitus* (Noy II 491); the second is an Εἰρήνη προσήλυτος (Noy II 489); the third one is dubious.³⁹ However, the epigraphical evidence that Ἰουδαῖος simply refers to Judeans of course makes up for the vast majority.⁴⁰ None of these multiple instances bears any indication whatsoever that the person described as a Judean was a proselyte.

If we look at the literary tradition, the significance changes even more. In both the LXX and the New Testament, all occurrences of Ἰουδαῖος refer exclusively to Judeans, never to proselytes or sympathizers of Judaism. The evidence for this does not need to be listed here, only the references from the letters of Paul are really important. On the one hand those texts are to be mentioned in which Paul puts together Judeans and Greeks or Judeans and the nations, mostly with the intention to take the whole of humanity into consideration.⁴¹ Judeans without any naming of other nations are also mentioned very often.⁴² There is also no distinction between singular or plural. Paul is always speaking of real Judeans, who are either believers in Christ (Gal 2:13–14; 3:28) or unbelieving Judeans (e.g., 1 Thess 2:14).[43]

For Rom 2:17 this means that the probability that the addressed Ἰουδαῖος is actually a Judean is much higher than the likelihood that it is a man of the nations. However one cannot be sure if Rom 2:17 might not be the sole exception of the rule, although this seems to be rather unlikely.

THE IDENTITY OF THE INTERLOCUTOR

In recent literature on Paul a wide range of possibilities for an identification of the Ἰουδαῖος is considered. This overview may not be complete, but it should provide a review over the essential lines of interpretation.

The Ἰουδαῖος Is a Typical Ἰουδαῖος

This interpretation is undoubtedly the most widespread and is widely represented in commentary literature. Wolter takes the view that this Ἰουδαῖος is a fictitious Jewish interlocutor of Paul, who is drawn in an ideal-typical manner and therefore represents all Jews.[44] Likewise Jewett is of the opinion that the Ἰουδαῖος is a Jew, even if "far from his [Paul's] audience," but nevertheless endowed with all supposed advantages of Judaism.[45] According to D. Moo "'To be named a Jew,' refers to the religious status of anyone who belonged to the covenant people."[46]

What are the given reasons for this interpretation? First of all, it should be pointed out that the term Ἰουδαῖος is actually quite unambiguous in the Pauline letters, as we have seen. Subsequently, ἐπονομάζῃ is taken as an expression of pride in Judaic descent. Most exegetes representing this line of interpretation therefore understand the passive form ἐπονομάζῃ always reflexively (see above). The Ἰουδαῖος would thus express that he considers himself to be somewhat better than the rest of humanity, i.e., the nations. According to this view, Paul's further explanations refer to Israel's classical assets: the knowledge of God's will and the ability to discern between good and evil. Both are based on the familiarity with the law and are God's gifts to his chosen people.

My doubts about this very widespread interpretation are based on three points: First, one should not easily ignore the fact that Paul is not writing that the interlocutor is a Jew, but that he is called so. If the passive is taken seriously, then it cannot any longer be understood as a matter of self-exaltation, articulating pride in belonging to the Judean people. In my opinion Paul forms the bridge to verse 24 already in the beginning of this paragraph: "The name of God is blasphemed among the nations because of you." It is much more likely that people from the nations perceive him as a Ἰουδαῖος, who teaches Torah. However, because he himself does not keep the law, as Paul states in vv. 21–23, the name of God is also blasphemed by this: If people from a pagan background admire a Judean as a Judean *teacher* but have to realize that he does not do what he demands of others, this leads to a rejection of the worship of God.

Secondly, it must be noted that this hypothetical exemplary Judean is certain of two things: he rests on the law and boasts of his relationship with God. In addition, he sees himself as a teacher of the nations, a guide for the blind, a light in the darkness. At no point does Paul criticize this. What he doesn't approve of is when these teachings are not covered by one's own behavior.

Thirdly, teaching is not necessarily the ultimate characteristic of the Jewish people. Therefore, it cannot be assumed that the teacher is actually representative of the Jewish people as a whole. Rather, Paul describes the Interlocutor with such characteristics, which give him a special profile that also has its original historical roots (see below).

The Ἰουδαῖος is a Proselyte or a Sympathizer of Judaism

One major argument for this interpretation of Ἰουδαῖος ἐπονομάζῃ rests predominately on the rhetorical form of the first two chapters in Romans.[47] According to R. M. Thorsteinsson a change of the interlocutor within a letter should be indicated explicitly.[48] The Ἰουδαῖος is therefore the same person as in 2:1–5, a gentile, and accordingly a representative of the intended audience of the letter.[49] He calls himself a Jew (or as Thorsteinsson also puts it "wants to call himself a Jew"[50]), although he is no Jew.[51] R. Rodriguez offers a slightly different interpretation: In his view there is a difference between the gentile in 2:1–5 and the so-called Ἰουδαῖος in 2:17. Whereas the first is a "moralizing pagan gentile", the second is "a gentile proselyte to Judaism".[52] So while he plays down the rhetorical argument a little bit, he takes up the direction of Thorsteinsson and others: the Ἰουδαῖος is not an ethnic Jew, but a proselyte.

Proponents of this view also refer to a few instances which might indicate that Ἰουδαῖος was used to label proselytes. Two inscriptions could be interpreted as such, although in my opinion this is rather a long stretch.[53] In addition the earlier mentioned passages in Cassius Dio (*Hist.* 37.17) and Epictetus (*Diatr.* 2.9.19–21) play an important role for this understanding.[54]

However, I think that this line of interpretation has a number of arguments against it. On the one hand, Paul would have had several clearer possibilities to describe the supposed opponent as a proselyte. The word ἐπονομάζῃ does not do the job. Secondly, it is also striking that in the further course of the discussion the apostle doesn't make anything at all out of the (rather improbable) circumstance that the opponent should be a proselyte. His polemic is not about him being a proselyte, but about the fact that this hypocritical man sees himself as a teacher. Thirdly, this interpretation depends heavily on the reflexive interpretation of ἐπονομάζῃ, which is rather improbable, as we saw above. Fourthly, in the immediate context, namely in Rom 2:29 and 3:1, Ἰουδαῖος is again quite naturally used as a term for a member of the people of Israel. And finally: The change from one interlocutor to another is clearly marked by the use of σὺ Ἰουδαῖος in 2:17, which indicates that the opponent is a different person than before in 2:1 (ἄνθρωπος). Paul is sufficiently clear on that.

The Ἰουδαῖος Represents the Teachers of the Jewish Synagogues in Rome

One way to interpret the Ἰουδαῖος is to make out a historical point of reference among the addressees. Francis Watson did so by identifying the Ἰουδαῖος with the leaders of the Roman synagogues.[55] These are attacked by Paul because he held them responsible for resisting the proclamation of the Gospel. On the one hand their attempts to win over proselytes had led to anti-Jewish measures by the Roman magistrate (see below), on the other hand they had taken action against the Jewish believers in Christ. With his polemical portrayal Paul wanted to increase the distance of the faithful in Christ to the Jewish community in Rome.

The major problem with this explanation is certainly that it presupposes Jewish Christ-believers among the addressees of the letter, which I do not believe to be the case. In addition, one can also point out that the letter does not give the impression as if Paul has had available such concrete information about the present circumstances of the Christ-believers in Rome or their struggles with the Judean minority in the city. Moreover, a number of contents are assigned to the teaching Ἰουδαῖος, but not the requirement of circumcision. He refers to the commandments (which he himself does not keep), but he's not directly promoting becoming a Jew.

The Ἰουδαῖος Is a Judean, but Paul Denies His Judean Identity

In detail, this assumption, which in a way is already mentioned in Origen (*Comm. Rom.* 2.11), means: Paul would deny his fictitious interlocutor to be a real Judean, because he just does not abide by what he teaches others to do. Only a strictly Torah-observant Judean is a real Judean. One could understand this as a parallel to Rev 2:9; 3:9: the apocalypticist, looking at the members of the "Synagogue of Satan," states that they say they are Judeans, although according to him they are not. The verb to express this in Revelation is λέγω, and ἑαυτός is explicitly used. So the statement is much clearer than in Rom 2:17.

One argument against this assumption is that it is difficult to understand why Paul would emphasize the doctrinal activity of the Ἰουδαῖος when it is a question of a false attribution of identity. The Judean is not attacked as a Judean per se, but as an unauthentic teacher. An attack merely on the basis of a false identity would therefore have to take place in a tone similar to that in the book of Revelation in order to be unambiguous. For the self-contradiction of the Ἰουδαῖος does not consist in his alleged Judean existence, but in the teacher's lack of authenticity as a teacher.[56]

The Ἰουδαῖος is not a Representative for Judaism

Nowadays it has become a standard opinion that ancient Judaism was polymorphic, some even speak of Judaisms.[57] In my opinion, this has not been sufficiently taken into account for our discussion of Rom 2:17. When Paul was writing of someone who is called a Ἰουδαῖος we have to take a closer look on how he describes this Ἰουδαῖος, in the following clauses.

The Ἰουδαῖος rests firmly within the Law, he boasts about his relationship with God, he knows God's will, he can demonstrate what's good and what's bad in the eyes of the Law. The Ἰουδαῖος is described as a teacher: leader of the blind, light for those in darkness, educator of fools, instructor of minors, who has the embodiment of knowledge and truth in the Law. The juxtaposition of claim and reality in the actions of the Ἰουδαῖος is opened with the rhetorical question: "You, who teach someone else, do not teach yourself?"

Who are those people of antiquity for whom such a qualification is plausible at all? It is clear: Not every Judean in antiquity understood himself as a teacher. But who actually taught, explained, and commented on the law so that Paul could attribute precisely these peculiarities to the interlocutor?

For an answer, a glance at concrete events in Rome seems to be helpful, which Jan Dochhorn has recently reviewed again and with detailed arguments.[58] Dochhorn starts out with a problem that is also put forward by representatives of the "Paul within Judaism" perspective.[59] In Rom 2:22 Paul writes that the Ἰουδαῖος robs temples.[60] Now this does not really seem to suit a Judean, because robbing of temples is not explicitly included in the offenses that were reported of Judeans. Of all the explanations given so far for the use of ἱεροσυλεῖν,[61] the reference to an incident from the year 19 CE reported by Josephus best fits the setting of the letter as a writing to people actually living in Rome.[62]

The story Josephus tells in *Ant.* 18.81–84 is about a deceitful Judean (ἀνὴρ Ἰουδαῖος) who pretended to be a teacher of the Torah (ἐξηγεῖσθαι σοφίαν νόμων τῶν Μωυσέως). He had been accused of violating laws in Judea (παραβάσεων νόμων) and had therefore fled to Rome. However, as it turns out, this nameless Judean was in fact a teacher of the law who himself had not followed his teachings. Together with three henchmen, he convinced a Roman proselyte named Fulvia to donate purple and gold for the Jerusalem Temple. But the false teacher and his accomplices kept the riches for themselves. When Fulvia's husband Saturninus found out, he reported this to the emperor Tiberius, who banished the entire community of Judeans from Rome. Furthermore, 4,000 Judeans were conscripted as soldiers to Sardinia. "And so because of the wickedness of four men the Judeans were banished from the city."[63]

The story carries quite a bit of historical plausibility, although Josephus may have dramatized it a little.[64] Above all, it is significant that the accusation of temple robbery can be derived quite well from this story.[65] The withholding of the donated property is nothing other than such theft of the Jerusalem Temple. Also the accusation in Rom 2:24 according to which the teacher's actions led to the mockery of the nations can be deduced very well from the events that followed the deception. The reputation of the Judeans in Rome (and thus that of their God) was damaged for years.[66]

In my opinion, Paul can therefore safely assume that Roman readers of the letter recognized that the brief description in Rom 2:21–24 contains an allusion to a teacher who strove to teach non-Jews but was a deceiver. Against such a Ἰουδαῖος the polemic is directed.[67] It is not intended against Judaism or righteousness by works or against pride in the identity markers of the Judean people.[68] It is rather aimed at making clear that it is not the talking about the law but the actual observance of the law which is decisive.[69] This is illustrated with a historical example, which of course is kept so general that it can be understood without being aware of this particular background.

EPILOGUE

The interpretation of Ἰουδαῖος in Rom 2:17–24 is certainly not limited to the historical background which Paul brought to the point of presenting this fictitious and at the same time also somehow historical figure to the readers. For there is yet also a personal dimension to it: Paul saw himself as a teacher of the nations, and so he is the direct counterpart of this opponent whom he draws in such dark colors.[70] In my view, it could well be said that this figure also reflects some of the events that shaped Paul's past and present. However, for now we must close with only a hint to this line of interpretation, which cannot be pursued any further here.[71]

NOTES

1. The fact that Paul asks his addressees to send greetings to Judeans in chapter 16 (Prisca and Aquila, Andronicus and Junia, Herodion) is by no means to be interpreted in such a way that there are Judeans among the intended readers. On the contrary, they are through these greetings indirectly identified as being not part of the addressees. Passages like 1:16; 4:1; 7:1; 15:7 also do not correct the identification of Paul's intended addressees as Non-Jews.

2. Apart from that, I date Romans to the time around 56 CE and Corinth as the place of composition.

3. Rafael Rodriguez, *If You Call Yourself a Jew: Reappraising Paul's Letter to the Romans* (Eugene, OR: Cascade Books, 2015), 51, considers it as "the fork in the road for our reading of Romans as a whole."

4. In a summary of Thorsteinsson's study on Romans 2:17, M. Thiessen also quotes Origen, but only in an English translation that varies between a passive and a reflexive rendering. The wording of Rufin's translation, however, does not support this differentiation (Runar M. Thorsteinsson, Matthew Thiessen, and Rafael Rodriguez, "Paul's Interlocutor in Romans: The Problem of Identification," in *The So-Called Jew in Paul's Letter to the Romans*, ed. Rafael Rodriguez and Matthew Thiessen [Minneapolis, MN: Fortress, 2016], 25).

5. For the Latin text see Origen, *Commentarii in Epistulam ad Romanos*, ed. Theresia Heither, FC 2/1 (Freiburg a.o.: Herder, 1990), 238.

6. This is also acknowledged by Runar M. Thorsteinsson, *Paul's Interlocutor in Romans 2: Function and Identity in the Context of Ancient Epistolography*, CB.NT (Stockholm: Almqvist & Wiksell, 2003), 198–199; Thorsteinsson, Thiessen, and Rodriguez, "Interlocutor," 25; but see, e.g., William S. Campbell, *Paul and the Creation of Christian Identity* (London: T&T Clark, 2008), 108, n. 23; Jacob P. B. Mortensen, *Paul among the Gentiles: A 'Radical' Reading of Romans*, NET (Tübingen: Narr Francke Attempto, 2018), 125. A reconstruction of the text of Rom 2:17 according to Rufin's version runs *si autem tu iudaeus cognominaris*; see Caroline P. Hammond Bammel, *Der Römerbrieftext des Rufin und seine Origenes-Übersetzung*, AGLB (Freiburg: Herder, 1985), 509.

7. A short word about the Ambrosiaster: the source text reads as in the Vulgate "Si autem tu Judaeus cognominaris." The commentator understands Judaeus as a family name on the one hand. On the other hand, he sees it as expressing the Abrahamic lineage, the greatness which should be recognizable in the descendants. Finally, however, the name Judaeus would stand for Christ. "Jews who do not understand this defend the name of the fleshly Judah for themselves" (*Quod Judaei non intelligentes, nomen sibi carnalis Judae defendunt*); see Theodore S. de Bruyn, Stephen A. Cooper, and David G. Hunter, *Ambrosiaster's Commentary on the Pauline Epistles: Romans*. Writings from the Greco-Roman World (Atlanta, GA: SBL Press, 2017), 48.

8. Hieronymus Emser, *Auß was was grund vrsach Luthers dolmatschung vber das nawe testament dem gemeines man billich vorbotten sey* (Leipzig: Stöckel, 1523).

9. Exegetes from 19th century like A. Tholuck, H. A. W. Meyer, or B. Weiss naturally interpreted the expression as passive. See August Tholuck, *Commentar zum Brief an*

die Römer (5th ed.; Halle: Eduard Anton, 1856), 110; Heinrich August Wilhelm Meyer, *Kritisch-Exegetisches Handbuch über den Brief des Paulus an die Römer* (Göttingen: Vandenhoeck & Ruprecht, 1881), 95; Bernhard Weiss, *Der Brief an die Römer*. 8th ed. KEK; (Göttingen: Vandenhoeck & Ruprecht, 1891), 120.

10. Theodor Zahn, *Der Brief des Paulus an die Römer*. KNT (Leipzig: Deichert, 1910), 135–36: "Der Jude jener Zeit nannte sich noch mit Stolz einen Juden und liebte es, auch in der Öffentlichkeit seinem Eigennamen die Bezeichnung als Jude hinzuzufügen. Eben das ist mit Ἰουδαῖος ἐπονομάζῃ gesagt: denn erstens kann dies Verbum ebenso wie alle folgenden nur ein Verhalten des Angeredeten bezeichnen, ist also als Medium, nicht als Passivum zu fassen, und zweitens wird es zwar auch von der Verleihung eines Namens an etwas vorher namenloses gebraucht, hier aber nicht, da doch jeder Jude einen Eigennamen hat, zu welchem Ἰουδαῖος nur als Epitheton hinzutreten kann."

11. Erwin Preuschen, *Vollständiges griechisch-deutsches Handwörterbuch zu den Schriften des Neuen Testaments und der übrigen urchristlichen Literatur* (Gießen: Töpelmann, 1910), 443.

12. Walter Bauer, *Griechisch-Deutsches Wörterbuch zu den Schriften des Neuen Testaments und der übrigen urchristlichen Literatur* (Berlin: De Gruyter, 1928), 475. This was also taken up in the new edition of this lexicon by K. and B. Aland which is still used in German-speaking universities; see Walter Bauer, Kurt Aland, and Barbara Aland, *Griechisch-deutsches Wörterbuch zu den Schriften des Neuen Testaments und der frühchristlichen Literatur* (Berlin/New York: Walter de Gruyter, 1988), 618. F. W. Danker changed it in his English reedition to "you call yourself a Judean (Jew)" (*A Greek-English Lexicon of the New Testament and Other Early Christian Literature*, 3rd ed. [Chicago/London: University of Chicago Press, 2000], 387). In LSJ the reflexive use of ἐπονομάζειν is only mentioned once with a reference to Themistius, an author from the fourth century CE (*Or.* 31.354b). There is also no hint to a reflexive use in Franco Montanari, *The Brill Dictionary of Ancient Greek*, ed. Madeleine Goh et al. (Leiden/Boston: Brill, 2015), s.v.

13. See, e.g., Hans Lietzmann, *An die Römer*, 4th ed. HNT, (Tübingen: Mohr Siebeck, 1933), 42; Adolf Schlatter, *Gottes Gerechtigkeit: Ein Kommentar zum Römerbrief* (Stuttgart: Calwer Verlag, 1935), 101; Paul Althaus, *Der Brief an die Römer*. NTD (Göttingen: Vandenhoeck & Ruprecht, 1966), 26; Otto Michel, *Der Brief an die Römer*, 5th ed. KEK, (Göttingen: Vandenhoeck & Ruprecht, 1978), 126: "Wenn du dich aber stolz einen Juden nennst."

14. Ernst Käsemann, *An die Römer*, 3rd ed. HNT, (Tübingen: Mohr Siebeck, 1974), 63. See also Michel, *Röm*, 128. References to epigraphical testimonies on epitaphs, which are supposed to prove the special pride of the Judeans, overlook the fact that ethnic designations were used again and again by members of all peoples; see e.g. David Noy, *Foreigners at Rome: Citizens and Strangers*, 2nd ed. (London: Duckworth, 2002), 5–7; Laurens E. Tacoma, *Moving Romans: Migration to Rome in the Principate* (Oxford: Oxford University Press, 2016), 211–13. On Ἰουδαῖος in inscriptions see Ross S. Kraemer, "On the Meaning of the Term 'Jew' in Greco-Roman Inscriptions," *HThR* 82 (1989): 35–53, and the critique by Pieter W. van der Horst, *Ancient Jewish Epitaphs: An Introductory Survey of a Millenium of Jewish*

Funerary Epigraphy (300 BCE–700 CE). CBET (Kampen: Kok Pharos, 1991), 68–72, and Margaret H. Williams, "The Meaning and Function of *Ioudaios* in Graeco-Roman Inscriptions," *ZPE* 116 (1997): 249–62.

15. Ulrich Wilckens, *Der Brief an die Römer. Röm 1–5*, 2nd ed. EKK, (Zürich/Neukirchen-Vluyn: Benzinger/Neukirchener, 1978), 146.

16. Wilckens, *Röm I*, 147–48. Richard N. Longenecker, *The Epistle to the Romans: A Commentary on the Greek Text*. NIGTC (Grand Rapids, MI: Eerdmans, 2016), 299, also took the same line of argument; see also Nicholas T. Wright, "Romans 2:17–3:9: A Hidden Clue to the Meaning of Romans?" *JSPL* 2 (2012): 15 (1–25).

17. Charles E. B. Cranfield, *The Epistle to the Romans*. ICC (Edinburgh: T&T Clark, 1975), 164; Anders Nygren, *Der Römerbrief* (Göttingen: Vandenhoeck & Ruprecht, 1951), 99.

18. Marie-Joseph Lagrange, *Saint Paul Épitre aux Romains*, Etudes Bibliques (Paris: J. Gabalda, 1950), 51.

19. The only exception is the King James Version, which both originally and in its revision of 1769 translates as "Behold, thou art called a Jew." Active translations like "If you bear the name of a Jew" can be found in the English Revised Version (1885) or the New American Standard (1977). An exception in the German-speaking world is the "Bibel in gerechter Sprache" (2006): "Wenn du nun Jüdin oder Jude genannt wirst."

20. Robert Jewett, *Romans: A Commentary*, ed. Eldon J. Epp, Hermeneia Series (Minneapolis, MN: Fortress Press, 2006), 221. See also Douglas J. Moo, *The Epistle to the Romans*, NICNT (Grand Rapids, MI: Eerdmans, 1996), 159, n. 8, who is undecided between an intransitive sense ("bear the name") or a reflexive sense ("call yourself"). Stanley K. Stowers (*A Rereading of Romans: Justice, Jews, and Gentiles* [New Haven/London: Yale University Press, 1994], 148), does not discuss this question at all, while translating "This person 'merely calls (*onomazō*) [sic!] himself a Jew.'" See also Michael Wolter, *Der Brief an die Römer: Vol. I: Röm 1–8*. EKK (Neukirchen-Vluyn/Ostfildern: Neukirchener/Patmos, 2014), 190, and Gerd Theißen and Petra Von Gemünden, *Der Römerbrief. Rechenschaft eines Reformators* (Göttingen: Vandenhoeck & Ruprecht, 2016), 97.

21. James D. G. Dunn, *Romans 1–8*, WBC 38A (Dallas, TX: Word Books, 1988), 109: "But if you are called a Jew."

22. See generally J. H. Moulton, *Moulton's Grammar of New Testament Greek: Vol. I: The Prolegomena*, ed. Stanley E. Porter (London et al.: T&T Clark, 2019 [1906]), 155: "As a matter of fact, the proportion of strictly reflexive middles is exceedingly small"; similar Nigel Turner, *Moulton's Grammar of New Testament Greek: Vol. 3: Syntax* (London et al.: T&T Clark, 2019 [1906]), 54. Moulton, *Moulton's Grammar I*, 163, concludes his deliberations about the distinction between passive and middle with the succinct statement: "The context must decide the interpretation", but he never refers to Rom 2:17.

23. The use of ἐπονομάζειν in epigraphic and papyrological evidence is extremely sparse and not sufficient to further clarify the issue.

24. See also Origen, *Expositio in Proverbia* (MPG 17,245): ὁ δὲ Θεὸς καὶ Πατὴρ τοῦ Κυρίου ἡμῶν Ἰησοῦ Χριστοῦ, τοὺς κατὰ Χριστὸν ἐπονομαζομένους.

25. Thorsteinsson, *Interlocutor*, 197 n. 132, mentions this reference in Justin as "an interesting example," while not seeing that it contradicts his translation. Other earlier instances from Christian literature for the passive form are Justin, *Dial.* 75.2–3; 90.4; 131.4; 132.1; *1 Apol.* 9.3; 46.5; 61.10; Clement of Alexandria, *Paed.* 1.7.57.2; 2.8.71.5; *Strom.* 1.21.106.5; 1.27.174.1; 6.3.32.2. None of them suggests a reflexive understanding.

26. *Pace* Matthew Thiessen, "Paul's Argument against Gentile Circumcision in Romans 2:17–29," *NT* 56 (2014): 374–75 (373–91); Matthew V. Novenson, "The Self-Styled Jew of Romans 2 and the Actual Jew of Romans 9–11," in *The So-Called Jew in Paul's Letter to the Romans*, ed. Rafael Rodriguez and Matthew Thiessen (Minneapolis, MN: Fortress Press, 2016), 141.

27. See above all Stanley K. Stowers, *The Diatribe and Paul's Letter to the Romans*, SBL.DS (Chico, CA: Scholars Press, 1981), 96–97, and similar then among others Rodriguez, *If You Call . . .* , 52.

28. Incidentally, the reflexive translation is also represented by all researchers who see a proselyte in 2:17 in the background; see, e.g., Matthew Thiessen, "Paul's So-Called Jew and Lawless Lawkeeping," in *The So-Called Jew in Paul's Letter to the Romans*, ed. Rafael Rodriguez and Matthew Thiessen (Minneapolis, MN: Fortress, 2016), 81; Novenson, "Self-Styled Jew," 139; Michele Murray, "Romans 2 within the Broader Context of Gentile Judaizing in Early Christianity," in *The So-Called Jew in Paul's Letter to the Romans*, ed. Rafael Rodriguez and Matthew Thiessen (Minneapolis, MN: Fortress, 2016), 163; Thorsteinsson, Thiessen, and Rodriguez, "Interlocutor," 25; Mortensen, *Paul*, 124–26.

29. See also Lionel J. Windsor, *Paul and the Vocation of Israel: How Paul's Jewish Identity Informs His Apostolic Ministry, with Special Reference to Romans.* BZNW (Berlin/Boston: De Gruyter, 2014), 148: "This verb is frequently used in the LXX and Josephus to describe the act of giving a publicly available name to an individual or place. Neither the LXX nor Josephus ever use this verb in the middle voice, since such public names are conferred by others or come about through general consensus, never simply through the will of the named individual. The passive voice is, however, used in the LXX and Josephus to mean 'publicly known by the name . . .' This suggests that the verb in Rom 2:17 should also be understood in the passive voice. Hence we should paraphrase, 'you are publicly acknowledged as entitled to the name Jew.'"

30. Whereas καυχᾶσθαι is a deponent verb, (ἐπ-)αναπαύω is also used in active voice in Paul (1 Cor 16:18; Phlm 20).

31. Thorsteinsson, *Interlocutor*, 198, n. 136, plays down the relevance of the passive/medium-question. The significance for the question of the interlocutor's identity is made clear, for example, by R. Rodriguez's formulation: "This gentile has taken on the name [*eponomazē*] 'Jew' and gone on to assume the signs of the Mosaic covenant" (Rodriguez, *If You Call . . .* , 50). See also Campbell, *Paul*, 108: "Most noteworthy is the fact that Paul does not say that the person addressed in 2.17 is a Jew but only that he claims to be a Jew, wants to be called a Jew or simply calls himself a Jew." Mark D. Nanos, "Paul's Non-Jews Do Not Become 'Jews,' But Do They Become 'Jewish'?

Reading Romans 2:25–29 within Judaism, Alongside Josephus," *JJMJS* 1 (2014): 41 (26–53), leaves a precise determination open.

32. On the translation of Ἰουδαῖος see the overview on the debate in David M. Miller, "The Meaning of Ioudaios and Its Relationship to Other Group Labels in Ancient Judaism," *CBR* 9 (2010): 98–126; David M. Miller, "Ethnicity Comes of Age: An Overview of Twentieth-Century Terms for Ioudaios," *CBR* 10 (2012): 293–311; David M. Miller, "Ethnicity, Religion and the Meaning of Ioudaios in Ancient 'Judaism,'" *CBR* 12 (2014): 216–65; Markus Öhler, "Judäer oder Juden? Die Debatte 'Ethnos vs. Religion' im Blick auf das 2. Makkabäerbuch," in *Die Makkabäer*, ed. Friedrich Avemarie et al., WUNT 382 (Tübingen: Mohr Siebeck, 2017), 157–85.

33. Only in CIJ I 2710 and 7131: Both documents are from Delphi (162 resp. 119 BCE). This is a very special use, which is not representative; see also Williams, "Meaning," 258.

34. Williams, "Meaning," 251–52, is rather skeptical about this use, at least in inscriptions. A prominent instance might be IJO II 40 (=CIJ II 742), which mentions a group οἱ ποτὲ Ἰουδαῖοι. For a discussion of this puzzling inscription see Walter Ameling, ed., *Inscriptiones Judaicae Orientis. II: Kleinasien*, TSAJ (Tübingen: Mohr Siebeck, 2004), 177–79.

35. See on that Benedikt Eckhardt, *Ethnos und Herrschaft: Politische Figurationen judäischer Identität von Antiochos III. bis Herodes I.* SJ (Berlin/Boston: De Gruyter, 2013), 309–14.

36. Ptolemais in Ammonius, *De Adfinium Vocabulorum Differentia* 243, according to the Greek text in Menahem Stern, *Greek and Latin Authors on Jews and Judaism: Vol. I. From Herodotus to Plutarch*, 3rd ed. (Jerusalem: Israeli Academy of Sciences and Humanities, 1976), no.146, which reads Ἰουδαῖοι instead of Ἰδουμαῖοι.

37. Cassius Dio, *Hist.* 37.17: ἔχουσι δὲ καὶ ἕτερον ὄνομα ἐπίκτητον· ἥ τε γὰρ χώρα Ἰουδαία καὶ αὐτοὶ Ἰουδαῖοι ὠνομάδαται· ἡ δὲ ἐπίκλησις αὕτη ἐκείνοις μὲν οὐκ οἶδ' ὅθεν ἤρξατο γενέσθαι, φέρει δὲ καὶ ἐπὶ τοὺς ἄλλους ἀνθρώπους ὅσοι τὰ νόμιμα αὐτῶν, καίπερ ἀλλοεθνεῖς ὄντες, ζηλοῦσι. καὶ ἔστι καὶ παρὰ τοῖς Ῥωμαίοις τὸ γένος τοῦτο, κολουσθὲν μὲν πολλάκις, αὐξηθὲν δὲ ἐπὶ πλεῖστον, ὥστε καὶ ἐς παρρησίαν τῆς νομίσεως ἐκνικῆσαι ("They have also another name that they have acquired: the country has been named Judaea, and the people themselves Judeans. I do not know how this title came to be given them, but it applies also to all the rest of mankind, although of alien race, who affect their customs. This class exists even among the Romans, and though often repressed has increased to a very great extent and has won its way to the right of freedom in its observances" [ed./trans. E. Gary/H.B. Foster, LCL 53, 126–27). However, for this text it's doubtful that proselytes are meant. Dio might distinguish Judean inhabitants of Judea from Judeans in the Diaspora. The idea that they actually belong to a different tribe could be explained as a misunderstanding by Dio. Either he meant that Diaspora Judeans are basically a different people, or—which is more likely—he was thinking that they actually belong to the *ethnos* in which they were born—that is, Romans, Greeks, etc. and therefore ἀλλοεθνεῖ; *pace* Williams, "Meaning," 253. Steve N. Mason (*A History of the Jewish War: AD 66–74* [Cambridge: Cambridge University Press, 2016], 238), thinks that Dio refers to the Idumeans.

38. τί οὖν Στωικὸν λέγεις σεαυτόν, τί ἐξαπατᾷς τοὺς πολλούς, τί ὑποκρίνῃ Ἰουδαῖον ὢν Ἕλλην; οὐχ ὁρᾷς, πῶς ἕκαστος λέγεται Ἰουδαῖος, πῶς Σύρος, πῶς Αἰγύπτιος; καὶ ὅταν τινὰ ἐπαμφοτερίζοντα ἴδωμεν, εἰώθαμεν λέγειν 'οὐκ ἔστιν Ἰουδαῖος, ἀλλ' ὑποκρίνεται'. ὅταν δ' ἀναλάβῃ τὸ πάθος τὸ τοῦ βεβαμμένου καὶ ᾑρημένου, τότε καὶ ἔστι τῷ ὄντι καὶ καλεῖται Ἰουδαῖος. οὕτως καὶ ἡμεῖς παραβαπτισταί, λόγῳ μὲν Ἰουδαῖοι, ἔργῳ δ' ἄλλο τι, ἀσυμπαθεῖς πρὸς τὸν λόγον, μακρὰν ἀπὸ τοῦ χρῆσθαι τούτοις ἃ λέγομεν, ἐφ' οἷς ὡς εἰδότες αὐτὰ ἐπαιρόμεθα (ed. W. A. Oldfather. LCL 131, 266).

39. Williams, "Meaning," 258, reads [. . . Ἰο]υδέα προσή[λυτος . . .], but Noy, *Inscriptions II*, 392, does not complete it with [. . . Ἰο]υδέα.

40. Williams lists 35 clear instances, inscriptions of synagogues not included ("Meaning," 258–61).

41. Judeans and Greeks (Rom 1:16; 2:9–10; 3:9; 10:12; 1 Cor 1:22, 24; 10:32; 12:13; Gal 3:28), Judeans and the nations (Rom 3:29; 9:24; 1 Cor 1:23; Gal 2:14–15).

42. Rom 2:28–29; 3:1; 1 Cor 9:20; 2 Cor 11:24; Gal 2:13; 1 Thess 2:14.

43. And even to critics of this position it is obvious that "Paul always uses Ἰουδαῖος to refer to those who were ethnically Jewish" (see Thiessen, "Argument," 374).

44. Wolter, *Röm I*, 190; see also John M. G. Barclay, *Paul and the Gift* (Grand Rapids, MI: Eerdmans, 2015), 469.

45. Jewett, *Romans*, 221.

46. Moo, *Romans*, 159.

47. See, e.g., Thorsteinsson, *Interlocutor*, passim; Thiessen, "Argument," 379; Rodriguez, *If You Call* . . . , esp. 47–72; Thorsteinsson, Thiessen, and Rodriguez, "Interlocutor," 1–37; Mortensen, *Paul*, 123–31.

48. Thorsteinsson, *Interlocutor*, 144, 208–9.

49. Thorsteinsson, *Interlocutor*, 233: "The interlocutor, whose identity as a proselyte (i.e. a circumcised gentile) is sometimes blurred, is singled out as a potential, imaginary representative of the audience."

50. Thorsteinsson, *Interlocutor*, 198. See also the formulations in Campbell, *Paul*, 108: "He claims to be a Jew, wants to be called a Jew or simply calls himself a Jew."

51. See also Thiessen, "Argument," 384–90.

52. Rodriguez, *If You Call* . . . , 50.

53. Thus however Thorsteinsson, *Interlocutor*, 201–2; Campbell, *Paul*, 108. On the really scarce and late evidence for that see above.

54. See, e.g., Thorsteinsson, *Interlocutor*, 200–201; Mortensen, *Paul*, 126–27.

55. Francis Watson, *Paul, Judaism and the Gentiles*, SNTS.MS (Cambridge et al.: Cambridge University Press, 1986), 113–15. J. Brian Tucker (*Reading Romans after Supersessionism: The Continuation of Jewish Covenantal Identity* [Eugene, OR: Cascade Books, 2018], 47–48), opts for "an ideal in-Christ Jewish teacher of gentiles," which I think is rather implausible. The opponent does not have a single characteristic that would suggest a belief in Christ.

56. Nanos, "Paul's Non-Jews," 42: "The criticism is not of boasting, as so often stated, or of bigotry; what is circumscribed is hypocrisy." David Frankfurter ("Jews or Not? Reconstructing the 'Other' in Rev 2:9 and 3:9," *HThR* 94 [2001]: 419ff.), uses Rom 2:17 as a means to understand Rev 2:9; 3:9: In his view Paul was talking of a

Gentile considering himself an "inward" Jew, and consequently the author of Revelation did also mean gentile "Judaizers."

57. See, e.g., Jacob Neusner, *A Short History of Judaism: Three Meals, Three Epochs* (Minneapolis, MN: Augsburg Fortress, 1992), 3–5.

58. See Jan Dochhorn, "Der Vorwurf des Tempelraubs in Röm 2,22b und seine politischen Hintergründe," *ZNW* 109 (2018): 101–17; see also Windsor, *Paul*, 164–65.

59. See, e.g., Thorsteinsson, *Interlocutor*, 212–18; Rodriguez, *If You Call* . . . , 55; Mortensen, *Paul*, 129.

60. The plural "temples" is misleading, since the word ἱεροσυλεῖν does not necessarily presuppose that several sanctuaries are robbed or desecrated. The following interpretation is also valid if one understands ἱεροσυλεῖν as committing a sacrilege, which can also consist in taking possession of goods that are assigned to the temple; see on that, e.g., Novenson, "Self-Styled Jew," 146–47.

61. For an overview see Dochhorn, "Vorwurf," 106–8.

62. First mentioned in 1856 by Tholuck, *Römer*, 113. Barclay (*Paul*, 470, n. 53) considers this as possible, though not necessary for the argument. Novenson ("Self-Styled Jew," 146) regards a reference to Josephus's account to be too subtle a manoeuvre, although he admits that the interpretation of Ἰουδαῖος as an actual Judean could be verified with it. Instead, he considers the interpretation of Ἰουδαῖος as proselytes to be more economical—hardly! The advantage of a historical positioning of the charge against the nevertheless fictitious Judean is that it has an actual background within the addressees. So it is by no means necessary to point out that only people from the nations rob temples, as long as one does not become stiff on the fact that the word ἱεροσυλεῖν is not used in Josephus's story.

63. Καὶ οἱ μὲν δὴ διὰ κακίαν τεσσάρων ἀνδρῶν ἠλαύνοντο τῆς πόλεως (ed./transl. L. H. Feldman, LCL 433, 60–61).

64. For the historical details and the composition by Josephus see Dochhorn, "Vorwurf," 109–13.

65. The fact that this accusation can also be found in ancient lines of moral misconduct may have influenced the formulation; see Wolter, *Röm I*, 196. All the offenses mentioned in Rom 2:21–23 are of course also rejected by non-Jews.

66. A notice in Cassius Dio, *Hist.* 57.18.5 (preserved in Joh. Ant., fr.70 §4b), reports that Judeans in Rome converted natives to their customs and therefore the majority of the Judeans were banned by Tiberius.

67. Windsor (*Paul*, 162–68) generalizes this to a description of the mainstream synagogue, which I find not convincing.

68. For a different view see Simon J. Gathercole, *Where Is Boasting? Early Jewish Soteriology and Paul's Response in Romans 1–5* (Grand Rapids, MI: Eerdmans, 2002), 199: "This Jew is not merely an individual but a representative of the nation."

69. That is the main theme of the entire second chapter of Romans. See, e.g., Oda Wischmeyer, "Römer 2.1–24 als Teil der Gerichtsrede des Paulus gegen die Menschheit," *NTS* 52 (2006): 359: "Die beiden Redeabschnitte Röm 2.1–10 und 17–24 zielen zunächst auf eine ethische Grundwahrheit: Nur das gelebte Ethos zählt, nicht die ethische Überzeugung oder Lehre."

70. It is therefore indeed true that Paul does not condemn teaching the nations; see also Nanos, "Paul's Non-Jews," 42: "Moreover, the teaching of the nations as a spokesperson from Israel is precisely Paul's own purpose."

71. But see, e.g., Stowers, *Rereading*, 150–53; Wright, "Romans," 13; Nanos, "Paul's Non-Jews," 42; Theißen and Von Gemünden, *Römerbrief*, 388–90.

BIBLIOGRAPHY

Althaus, Paul. *Der Brief an die Römer.* NTD. Göttingen: Vandenhoeck & Ruprecht, 1966.

Ameling, Walter, ed. *Inscriptiones Judaicae Orientis. II: Kleinasien.* TSAJ. Tübingen: Mohr Siebeck, 2004.

Barclay, John M. G. *Paul and the Gift.* Grand Rapids, MI: Eerdmans, 2015.

Bauer, Walter. *Griechisch-Deutsches Wörterbuch zu den Schriften des Neuen Testaments und der übrigen urchristlichen Literatur.* Berlin: De Gruyter, 1928.

Bauer, Walter, Kurt Aland, and Barbara Aland. *Griechisch-Deutsches Wörterbuch zu den Schriften des Neuen Testaments und der frühchristlichen Literatur.* Berlin/New York: Walter de Gruyter, 1988.

Campbell, William S. *Paul and the Creation of Christian Identity.* London: T&T Clark, 2008.

Cranfield, Charles E. B. *The Epistle to the Romans.* ICC. Edinburgh: T&T Clark, 1975.

Danker, Frederick William. *A Greek-English Lexicon of the New Testament and Other Early Christian Literature,* 3rd ed. Chicago/London: University of Chicago Press, 2000.

de Bruyn, Theodore S., Stephen A. Cooper, and David G. Hunter. *Ambrosiaster's Commentary on the Pauline Epistles: Romans.* Writings from the Greco-Roman World. Atlanta, GA: SBL Press, 2017.

Dio Cassius. *Roman History,* Books 36–40. Edited and translated by Earnest Gary with Herbert B. Foster. LCL. Cambridge, MA: Harvard University Press, 1914.

Dochhorn, Jan. "Der Vorwurf des Tempelraubs in Röm 2,22b und seine politischen Hintergründe." *ZNW* 109 (2018): 101–17.

Dunn, James D. G. *Romans 1–8.* WBC 38A. Dallas, TX: Word Books, 1988.

Eckhardt, Benedikt. *Ethnos und Herrschaft: Politische Figurationen judäischer Identität von Antiochos III. bis Herodes I.* SJ. Berlin/Boston: De Gruyter, 2013.

Emser, Hieronymus. *Auß Was Was Grund Vrsach Luthers Dolmatschung Vber Das Nawe Testament Dem Gemeines Man Billich Vorbotten Sey.* Leipzig: Stöckel, 1523.

Epictetus. *Discourses 1–2.* Edited and translated by W. A. Oldfather. LCL. Cambridge, MA: Harvard University Press, 1925.

Frankfurter, David. "Jews or Not? Reconstructing the 'Other' in Rev 2:9 and 3:9." *HThR* 94 (2001): 403–25.

Gathercole, Simon J. *Where Is Boasting? Early Jewish Soteriology and Paul's Response in Romans 1–5.* Grand Rapids, MI: Eerdmans, 2002.

Hammond Bammel, Caroline P. *Der Römerbrieftext des Rufin und seine Origenes-Übersetzung.* AGLB. Freiburg: Herder, 1985.

Jewett, Robert. *Romans: A Commentary.* Edited by Eldon J. Epp. Hermeneia Series. Minneapolis, MN: Fortress Press, 2006.

Josephus, *Jewish Antiquities, Books 18–19.* Edited and translated by Louis H. Feldman. LCL. Cambridge, MA: Harvard University Press, 1965.

Käsemann, Ernst. *An die Römer,* 3rd ed. HNT. Tübingen: Mohr Siebeck, 1974.

Kraemer, Ross S. "On the Meaning of the Term 'Jew' in Greco-Roman Inscriptions." *HThR* 82 (1989): 35–53.

Lagrange, Marie-Joseph. *Saint Paul Épitre aux Romains.* Etudes Bibliques. Paris: J. Gabalda, 1950.

Lietzmann, Hans. *An die Römer,* 4th ed. HNT. Tübingen: Mohr Siebeck, 1933.

Longenecker, Richard N. *The Epistle to the Romans. A Commentary on the Greek Text.* NIGTC. Grand Rapids, MI: Eerdmans, 2016.

Mason, Steve N. *A History of the Jewish War: AD 66–74.* Cambridge: Cambridge University Press, 2016.

Meyer, Heinrich August Wilhelm. *Kritisch-Exegetisches Handbuch über den Brief des Paulus an die Römer.* Göttingen: Vandenhoeck & Ruprecht, 1881.

Michel, Otto. *Der Brief an die Römer,* 5th ed. KEK. Göttingen: Vandenhoeck & Ruprecht, 1978.

Miller, David M. "Ethnicity Comes of Age: An Overview of Twentieth-Century Terms for Ioudaios." *CBR* 10 (2012): 293–311.

———. "Ethnicity, Religion and the Meaning of Ioudaios in Ancient 'Judaism,'" *CBR* 12 (2014): 216–65.

———. "The Meaning of Ioudaios and Its Relationship to Other Group Labels in Ancient Judaism." *CBR* 9 (2010): 98–126.

Montanari, Franco. *The Brill Dictionary of Ancient Greek,* edited by Madeleine Goh, Chad Schroeder, Gregory Nagy, and Loenard Muellner. Leiden/Boston: Brill, 2015.

Moo, Douglas J. *The Epistle to the Romans.* NICNT. Grand Rapids, MI: Eerdmans, 1996.

Mortensen, Jacob P. B. *Paul among the Gentiles: A 'Radical' Reading of Romans.* NET. Tübingen: Narr Francke Attempto, 2018.

Moulton, James H. *Moulton's Grammar of New Testament Greek. Vol. I: The Prolegomena.* Edited by Stanley E. Porter. London et al.: T&T Clark, 2019 (1906).

Murray, Michele. "Romans 2 within the Broader Context of Gentile Judaizing in Early Christianity." In *The So-Called Jew in Paul's Letter to the Romans,* edited by Rafael Rodgriguez and Matthew Thiessen, 163–82. Minneapolis, MN: Fortress, 2016.

Nanos, Mark D. "Paul's Non-Jews Do Not Become 'Jews,' but Do They Become 'Jewish'? Reading Romans 2:25–29 within Judaism, alongside Josephus." *JJMJS* 1 (2014): 26–53.

Neusner, Jacob. *A Short History of Judaism: Three Meals, Three Epochs.* Minneapolis, MN: Augsburg Fortress, 1992.

Novenson, Matthew V. "The Self-Styled Jew of Romans 2 and the Actual Jew of Romans 9–11." In *The So-Called Jew in Paul's Letter to the Romans*, edited by Rafael Rodriguez and Matthew Thiessen, 133–62. Minneapolis, MN: Fortress Press, 2016.

Noy, David. *Foreigners at Rome: Citizens and Strangers*, 2nd ed. London: Duckworth, 2002.

———. *Jewish Inscriptions from Western Europe, Volume 2: The City of Rome.* Cambridge: Cambridge University Press, 1995.

Nygren, Anders. *Der Römerbrief.* Göttingen: Vandenhoeck & Ruprecht, 1951.

Öhler, Markus. "Judäer oder Juden? Die Debatte ‚Ethnos vs. Religion' im Blick auf das 2. Makkabäerbuch." In *Die Makkabäer*, edited by Friedrich Avemarie, Predrag Bukovec, Stefan Krauter, and Michael Tilly, 157–85. WUNT 382. Tübingen: Mohr Siebeck, 2017.

Origen. *Commentarii in Epistulam ad Romanos.* Edited by Theresia Heither. FC. Freiburg a.o.: Herder, 1990.

Origen. *Expositio in Proverbia.* MPG. Paris, 1857.

Preuschen, Erwin. *Vollständiges griechisch-deutsches Handwörterbuch zu den Schriften des Neuen Testaments und der übrigen urchristlichen Literatur.* Gießen: Töpelmann, 1910.

Rodriguez, Rafael. *If You Call Yourself a Jew: Reappraising Paul's Letter to the Romans.* Eugene, OR: Cascade Books, 2015.

Schlatter, Adolf. *Gottes Gerechtigkeit: Ein Kommentar zum Römerbrief.* Stuttgart: Calwer Verlag, 1935.

Stern, Menahem. *Greek and Latin Authors on Jews and Judaism. Vol. I: From Herodotus to Plutarch*, 3rd ed. Jerusalem: Israeli Academy of Sciences and Humanities, 1976.

Stowers, Stanley K. *The Diatribe and Paul's Letter to the Romans.* SBL.DS. Chico, CA: Scholars Press, 1981.

———. *A Rereading of Romans: Justice, Jews, and Gentiles.* New Haven/London: Yale University Press, 1994.

Tacoma, Laurens E. *Moving Romans: Migration to Rome in the Principate.* Oxford: Oxford University Press, 2016.

Theißen, Gerd, and Petra Von Gemünden. *Der Römerbrief: Rechenschaft eines Reformators.* Göttingen: Vandenhoeck & Ruprecht, 2016.

Thiessen, Matthew. "Paul's Argument against Gentile Circumcision in Romans 2:17–29." *NT* 56 (2014): 373–91.

———. "Paul's So-Called Jew and Lawless Lawkeeping." In *The So-Called Jew in Paul's Letter to the Romans*, edited by Rafael Rodgriguez and Matthew Thiessen, 59–83. Minneapolis, MN: Fortress, 2016.

Tholuck, August. *Commentar zum Brief an die Römer,* 5th ed. Halle: Eduard Anton, 1856.

Thorsteinsson, Runar M. *Paul's Interlocutor in Romans 2: Function and Identity in the Context of Ancient Epistolography.* CB.NT. Stockholm: Almqvist & Wiksell, 2003.

Thorsteinsson, Runar M., Matthew Thiessen, and Rafael Rodriguez. "Paul's Interlocutor in Romans: The Problem of Identification." In *The So-Called Jew in Paul's*

Letter to the Romans, edited by Rafael Rodgriguez and Matthew Thiessen, 1–37. Minneapolis, MN: Fortress, 2016.

Tucker, J. Brian. *Reading Romans after Supersessionsim: The Continuation of Jewish Covenantal Identity.* Eugene, OR: Cascade Books, 2018.

Turner, Nigel. *Moulton's Grammar of New Testament Greek: Vol. 3: Syntax.* London et al.: T&T Clark, 2019 (1906).

van der Horst, Pieter W. *Ancient Jewish Epitaphs. An Introductory Survey of a Millenium of Jewish Funerary Epigraphy (300 BCE–700 CE).* CBET. Kampen: Kok Pharos, 1991.

Watson, Francis. *Paul, Judaism and the Gentiles.* SNTS.MS. Cambridge et al.: Cambridge University Press, 1986.

Weiss, Bernhard. *Der Brief an die Römer,* 8th ed. KEK. Göttingen: Vandenhoeck & Ruprecht, 1891.

Wilckens, Ulrich, *Der Brief an die Römer. Röm 1–5.,* 2nd ed. EKK. Zürich/ Neukirchen-Vluyn: Benzinger/Neukirchener, 1987.

Williams, Margaret H. "The Meaning and Function of *Ioudaios* in Graeco-Roman Inscriptions." *ZPE* 116 (1997): 249–62.

Windsor, Lionel J. *Paul and the Vocation of Israel. How Paul's Jewish Identity Informs His Apostolic Ministry, with Special Reference to Romans.* BZNW. Berlin/ Boston: De Gruyter, 2014.

Wischmeyer, Oda. "Römer 2.1–24 als Teil der Gerichtsrede des Paulus gegen die Menschheit." *NTS* 52 (2006): 356–76.

Wolter, Michael. *Der Brief an die Römer: Vol. I: Röm 1–8.* EKK. Neukirchen-Vluyn/ Ostfildern: Neukirchener/Patmos, 2014.

Wright, Nicholas T. "Romans 2:17–3:9: A Hidden Clue to the Meaning of Romans?" *JSPL* 2 (2012): 1–25.

Zahn, Theodor. *Der Brief des Paulus an die Römer.* KNT. Leipzig: Deichert, 1910.

Chapter Fourteen

"All Israel Will Be *Saved*" or "*Kept Safe*"? (Rom 11:26)

Israel's *Conversion* or *Irrevocable Calling to Gospel the Nations*?

Mark D. Nanos

In Romans 11:26 Paul declares that "all Israel σωθήσεται"—universally translated "*will be saved.*"[1] Commentators generally discuss *when* this event will occur,[2] what mechanism will trigger it,[3] and whether "all Israel" here refers to all or most Jews, to only Jews who believe in Jesus, or includes as well those who believe in Jesus from the nations ("Gentiles"), the option usually referred to in replacement (and anachronistic) theological terms as "the Church."[4] However, what "saved" means is considered self-evident. For example, in the field's most academically detailed commentary on Romans, Robert Jewett summarily notes that there is "little doubt that the verb σωθήσεται ('they shall be saved') refers to evangelical conversion. . . ."[5] Exegetical discussion is thereby foreclosed.

I suspect Jewett and other commentators correctly assume that most of their readers can follow their arguments without explaining what they mean by "saved."[6] I have not only been able to do so, but my earliest published work on this passage, which preceded Jewett's commentary, assumed the same, even if I read the mechanism and timing differently, and did not come to the same conclusions overall.[7] But for me, in 2015, that changed. I realized that everything else in the chapter and letter did not point in the direction of that assumed definition of salvation in evangelical terms or the premises upon which it depended, which provoked me to consult the lexicons rather than assume the gloss "saved" was self-evident, as well as what that signified.[8] What I discovered therefore challenged not only the received views, it challenged my own.

This conference provides a good venue for presenting more details of this new reading because what I propose—in concert with other indicators in 9–11 and throughout the letter—offers a new "Paul within Judaism" based perspective that significantly alters the questions to be asked and the possible answers in investigating the theme, "Israel and Nations: Paul's Gospel in the Context of Jewish Expectation."

In short, what the lexicons reveal, to which we will return below in more detail, is that the Greek word σῴζω and cognates were normally used to refer to *protecting* and *keeping safe*—before and besides Paul's supposed use, that is. This word group was not used to discuss someone or thing that had been *lost* being *returned* in the evangelical salvation sense that it has come to denote—*converted* in common parlance—but to *prevent* someone or something from becoming lost, or from the threat thereof; in this case, to preserve these Israelites in their covenant standing as Israel during this anomalous period so that all Israel could complete the *calling* to bring the "news of good" to the nations:[9] the *gift* of the *entrustment with God's oracles* was *irrevocable* (cf. 11:28–29 with 3:1–2).

QUESTIONING THE PREMISES OF THE EVANGELICAL SALVATION PARADIGM

The premise that Paul believed Jews needed to share his convictions about Jesus to be *saved* in the evangelical construal logically requires the accompanying premise that Paul considered those Jews already to have become somehow, at sometime, *lost*. Just what lost means or how and when or why they became lost so as to now be in need of salvation are not considered in any depth, beyond the supposition that they rejected the gospel claims for Jesus. Perhaps most importantly, interpreters do not explain what *all Israel*[10] required salvation *from* or *to* in terms that would make sense to a Jew of the time who did not share their (later) Christian evangelical soteriological premises, or, if I may say so, to Jews since then.[11]

The common refrain, that "Jews are in need of salvation, being sinners just like Gentiles," ignores the historical reality that when Paul wrote, the Temple was still operating, and thus there was a sacrificial system in place for any sins committed. Paul could thus proclaim, "according to righteousness that is in the Torah, being blameless" (Phil 3:6).[12] Paul still assessed himself and Peter to be different from non-Jews because they were "Jews from birth/nature [φύσει]" and thereby distinguished from "sinners from the nations," even if now equals in standing among the righteous ones in Christ within these Jewish subgroups (Gal 2:15–17).[13]

Whether or not commentators use the term *lost*, their reader is expected to understand that the Jews Paul was referring to were no longer counted among the *saved* who "believe the gospel," as if *saved* and *lost* represented states of being.[14] As commentators move through Romans before reaching 11:26, and following this verse, *lostness* is communicated implicitly when not explicitly named in the following ways: they are also no longer among those who have "faith" or among "the righteous" (1:16–17; 9:30–33; 11:20, 23), or "the justified" and "the forgiven" (3:21–26), or "the children of God" (8:19–21), since those are identifications only gained by believing the gospel; they are no longer to be properly understood as "the Jew" or "the circumcision" (2:25–29) or within the Abrahamic (4:1–25; 9:7) or even the Mosaic covenant (9:4–6).[15] They are instead, e.g., "under judgment" (2:1–16), "under sin" (3:9–20), "disobedient" (10:21; 11:30–32), and, of particular relevance within Rom 9–11, they are no longer even "Israel" per the received view of 9:6.[16] For replacement theological readings ("Israel" = "Church") that is the case in 11:26 as well;[17] like a vessel made for wrath, Israel has been "destroyed" (9:22).[18] Not only are these Jews often classified as "*unbelieving*," they are even judged to be "enemies *of God*" (11:28, per NRSV, although tellingly, "of God" does not appear in any Greek manuscripts). Many other negative descriptions follow from the binary contrasts developed to identify what those who shared Paul's faith in Christ had been like, such as "of the flesh," "slaves of sin," "condemned," and so on. Contextually relevant for discussing chapter 11, in metaphorical terms these Jews are described as *branches broken off* of the olive tree and *hardened*, which is often described as stubborn refusal to believe the truth and analogized with Pharaoh's hardness of heart. The ostensibly generous idea that these Jews can *be grafted back in* is a good metaphorical example of how *are lost* but *will be saved* is generally understood to function in this soteriological paradigm.[19]

I have challenged the elements in this list of supposed support for the lost/saved paradigm, and the results are naturally relevant to any challenge to the reading of 11:26 at the heart of that paradigm. Here I can only briefly offer a few details focused on elements in chapter 11, and direct the reader to the research that warrants building upon them herein.[20]

As already noted, I did not begin the specific research leading to this chapter because I initially questioned the received translation and interpretation of σωθήσεται per se; quite the contrary, I accepted it, for example in my 1996 monograph, *The Mystery of Romans*, disputing merely matters such as the mechanism and timing. My basic acceptance continued in several subsequent essays in spite of discovering that many of the elements just listed to which the evangelical salvation premises appealed were far from self-evident, especially related to the language in chapter 11 regarding the olive tree, and immediately before and after that allegory. I continually found that many of the details in the received views represented the less likely lexical option and were inconsistent with the arguments Paul was otherwise widely recognized to be making, not least for expressing his metaphorical imagery. Upon reflecting later on the fact that these textual details did not support the evangelically construed lost/saved paradigm for the 2015 paper on Paul's view of his fellow Jews, I began to question whether Paul's culminating argument was that all Israel needed to be saved in such terms (as if having lost covenantal standing for not already believing in Jesus as Messiah) rather than protected in covenantal status until this temporary—mysterious—period of suffering estrangement by "some" Israelites (which connoted "most" other than the "some" within Paul's subgroup) had completed its course.[21]

After all, Paul argued throughout the chapter that the anomalous "mystery" of the divided response of Israelites was but a temporary development, that the purpose of his message was not to pass judgment on Israel or the Israelites not (yet) joining him in his convictions about Jesus and thus in announcing this news to the nations, but to challenge any nascent resentment among the Christ-following non-Jews addressed toward those Israelites, or indifference or smugness toward their plight in comparison with their own newly enjoyed receipt of God's mercy. He made the case in several direct statements, and by way of several metaphors. The translator and interpreter should be expected to explore which alternatives for each word and phrase best communicates Paul's stated rhetorical goals, at least question any choices that subvert or reverse them. Many current translations fail to do so, and one may wonder whether that remains the case even in historical-critical commentaries because of the underexamined influence of the evangelical salvation paradigm. Consider this brief survey of some elements in the argument of Romans 11, both before and after the statement in v. 26a.

In the metaphor in vv. 11–15, the prevailing readings make it clear that Paul insisted that although some Israelites were "stumbling" over the gospel claims and thus "falling behind" over taking up the task of bringing this news to the nations alongside of Paul, they nevertheless were absolutely not in any way to be understood to have "fallen (down)." He follows that with a more developed metaphor (hence, an allegory) about an olive tree in vv. 17–24, which involves some branches suffering ἐξεκλάσθησαν, which is usually translated "were broken off" (v. 17). Yet it makes little sense for Paul to follow his vehement denial of falling down in the previous metaphor with an allegory based upon those same Israelites portrayed as "branches broken *off*," and all the less that the one wild shoot grafted in "among them [ἐν αὐτοῖς]" had been instead put "in their place," per the NRSV. I found many reasons to question those translations.[22] The Greek nouns, which should agree in gender, indicate that the wild branch is grafted "among" the "broken" branches, which makes no sense if those branches have been removed from the tree. Paul does not identify the tree as Israel, or state that non-Jews were "grafted into Israel," although that is a common refrain (and although people are not grafted into people much less trees); instead, he portrays the natural branches as Israelites and the wild branch stands for the non-Jews in Christ now brought in alongside them in the tree, thereafter drawing from the same root. Paul appears to use the tree's branches to represent those rooted in the Abrahamic family of promise, whether natural to the tree as are the genealogical descendants (Israel), or of foreign origin (from the other nations) but grafted in (adopted), together representing the prophetic hope of shalom in the age to come, when all of the nations are promised to be blessed (i.e., rooted) in Abraham's seed.[23]

In this image, Paul's argument makes better sense if the experience of ἐξεκλάσθησαν suffered by the natural branches is translated not as "were broken *off*" but as "were *bent* (aside)" in v. 17.[24] That is a temporary state and corresponds to the previous assertion that they were stumbling but had not fallen. The singular "wild shoot" was grafted in among these bent branches, who represent that part of Israel suffering to make space for the newly introduced (and singular) wild shoot, not as "enemies" but as temporarily "*estranged* for your sake" (v. 28). Although Paul's explanation is constrained by zero sum logic, his goal was to express concern that all Israel—that is, even the distressed branches (the "some" Israelites)—will be protected/kept safe in the meantime, metaphorically, by way of a temporary "callus [πώρωσις]" so that the safety of the entire tree as well as of the impaired branches is not compromised (v. 25).[25] Thus the tree can bear the fruit for which it was designed—if not from every branch just yet, then in God's due time.

But what about vv. 23–24 within the olive tree allegory, where translations today read "*to graft* them in again" for πάλιν ἐγκεντρίσαι αὐτούς, which logically suggests that they had been detached? The translation reflects the prior decision that the natural branches have been broken (or cut) *off* (NRSV/NABRE/DRB/NJB), and vice versa. But if the natural branches were understood to remain on the tree, albeit broken as in bent or cracked, then this phrase would warrant the translation, "again *to invigorate* them," which reflects the normal thrust of the verb ἐγκεντρίζω, "to goad" or "to spur on."[26] This reading would logically suggest that the branches remained on the tree in a distressed state. Note that Paul changes from cognates of ἐκκλάω, which he used initially to describe the broken natural branches in vv. 17–20, to cognates of ἐκκόπτω in vv. 22–24 in the diatribe with the wild shoot—which has actually experienced being "cut off" of its natural tree—regarding its own fate should it become unfaithful to its role by becoming arrogant toward the bent aside natural branches.[27] In other words, the wild shoot is being told that if it can be grafted in among the natural branches, how much more natural would it be for those natural branches that have been damaged to be spurred on to bearing fruit "for their own olive tree." That message reflects precisely what Paul argued prior to the olive tree allegory, that the catching up of those which have fallen behind is in the best interests of those who have joined in during the meantime (vv. 11–15), and what he will argue after the allegory, to which we now turn.

As Paul moves toward wrapping up his case in vv. 30–32, the judgment of his fellow Jews is represented in translations today to be because of their "disobedience." That decision expresses the evangelical soteriological paradigm's premise that these Jews have refused to believe or act according to what they are presumed to have been already convinced. Leaving aside for a moment the problematic nature of that logical premise, translating the cognates of ἀπειθέω in Paul's argument here in terms of disobedience rather than *persuasion* should also be questioned. Paul is explaining why some of his fellow Jews are presently "unpersuaded" or "doubtful,"[28] just as the non-Jews he is addressing had been previously. Doubtful of what? In the case of those Jews, doubtful of the gospel claim that God's mercy was now being shown to those from the nations, which might reasonably be expected when the age to come begins *if* an Israelite is persuaded that is the case and thus "justified." This reading also makes more sense of Paul's appeal to a parallel development for the Christ-following non-Jews, who were not previously *disobedient to* so much as *unpersuaded about* (if not also, for most of them, like the Jews Paul is discussing, mutatis mutandis, *unaware of*) the One God Israel proclaimed. Thus Paul concludes that all were joined together in need of God's kindness so that all could escape their respective *doubts* about the mystery Paul herein seeks to reveal. Rather than undermine Paul's emphatic claim that these Israelites remain "beloved for the sake of the fathers" and that "the gifts and calling of God are irrevocable" in vv. 28–29, this translation affirms these assertions; hence, while this anomalous scenario unfolds, "all Israel will be kept safe."

In addition to these kinds of exegetical warrants for reconsidering what Paul most likely meant by "all Israel σωθήσεται," there are a number of logical problems with the consensus soteriological arguments that remain unexamined. To begin with, there is the often repeated reasoning that these Jews need to be saved because they have *refused* to believe, they have *rejected* Jesus or the gospel or God's grace, and so on. But consider: How many Jews in Paul's time (or since) were *rejecting* what they were *convinced* was *true*, or that not being persuaded by a particular Jewish subgroups' claims for a Judean martyr constituted *refusal* to accept fulfillment of *God's* promises?[29] And at what moment did all these Jews become lost? And why? For example, was it when Jesus died, or when he rose from the dead? Yet these events were witnessed by only a few of the millions of Jews at the time. Does it make sense to apply to all Jews culpable knowledge of claims first heard only by a few of the Jews alive in Paul's time? Did even those few experience a personal revelation, such as Paul appeals to for himself—who, unlike most Jews, was neither unaware of nor indifferent to these claims before that revelation—to be persuaded? Also unexplained is where it would have been clear from Scripture or Jewish traditions or even from Paul's arguments that Jews must have *faith* in *any,* much less *the Messiah* to be *saved*? And, as already noted, saved by a Messiah from what to what? And even if convinced about the need for *a* Messiah, however understood, were any Jews really rejecting Jesus as a figure they actually believed *to be* the Messiah? Or were most Jews if even aware of the claims on Paul's terms—which is assuming a lot—more than likely (from their perspective anyway, and if the translation proposed above is granted, then also from Paul's) simply *unpersuaded*? Were they rejecting Jesus, or that which Paul otherwise assesses negatively in Gal 1:1–12: merely claims made by humans (or even angels) for Jesus? And after the founding of Christianity and its creeds and way of life that were not only no longer Jewish but in many ways anti-Jewish (e.g., post-Theodosian codes and Crusades and Inquisition and Pogroms and the Shoah), how can lack of *persuasion* be presented in the case of contemporary Jews as *rejecting* what was or is believed to be true and compelling for themselves *on Jewish terms,* all the more as *rejecting* what Paul was wrestling with in his pre-Christianity context (who was still making his case within Judaism) while writing Romans?[30]

What was (or is) the compelling empirical proof that accounts for assessing such a high level of culpability from the reading of Romans? Should no place be given for covenantal faithfulness in the face of what was, for most Jews anyway, understood to represent a threat to that which God had commanded them to uphold in the face of competing claims, and easily interpreted to represent claims to incorporate into Judaism the worship of additional gods?

These kinds of logical problems in the premises for these judgments of the other as "lost," combined with the lexical and contextual reasons to question the evangelical salvation tropes briefly sketched above, provide substantial reasons to question whether 11:26 refers to salvation in the usual evangelical terms.

THE LEXICAL CASE FOR "ALL ISRAEL WILL BE *KEPT SAFE*"?

In addition to the exegetical and logical reasons to question whether Paul was making a case for the evangelical salvation of all Israel in chapter 11, there are good philological reasons to reconsider how to best translate and interpret σῴζω in v. 26a.

The Greek word σῴζω was usually used to indicate being "saved" in the sense of "protected" or "kept safe," more so than in the sense of "returned" as in "found" after being "lost," or "revived" after being "dead," from which the received interpretations proceed. A few glosses from *LSJ* make the point: the verb σῴζω was used, in terms of persons, to "save [from death/destruction]" (meaning, that one did not die or experience complete destruction), to "keep alive," "protect," "escape," "rescue" from danger/threat; in the passive: to "be delivered," "kept alive," "preserved."[31] In medical terms, σῴζω was commonly used to refer to being "healed," to "recover from sickness." Likewise, σωτηρία was used for "deliverance," "preservation," "keeping safe," "bodily health," and "well-being."[32] To refer to the work of a doctor, σῴζω was not used to describe bringing the patient back to life but for keeping someone healthy and bringing someone back to health when sick or dying. Note that the Gospels do not use σῴζω to describe Jesus bringing anyone back to life who has died in the sense of resuscitated or raised up.[33] The Septuagint (and the Hebrew equivalents) used σῴζω and cognates similarly.[34] Not without significance for our passage, which trades in plant metaphors, the agricultural specialist Theophrastus regularly used σῴζω and cognates to refer to the safekeeping and preservation of plants and their various parts.[35]

We use "saved" in English to signify protected and kept safe as well, but as Jewett's appeal to the self-evident meaning demonstrates, the use of *saved* for reading Paul has become so synonymous with the Christian evangelical salvation paradigm that it inhibits further examination of what Paul meant in this context. To avoid that commonplace, I suggest that we translate Paul's phrase "all Israel will be *kept safe*" or "*protected*." Doing so allows us to explore whether Paul meant that Israel had *lost* its active relationship with God (been *destroyed, cut off, hardened*, become *enemies of God* or *of the saved*) and needed to be returned by being *saved* (*grafted back in again*) as usually conceptualized, or whether the relationship was still intact but those within it faced some kind of threat from which they needed to be *protected* or *rescued*, which aligns with translation alternatives such as *bent, callused, estranged*, and *reinvigorated*, for which I have argued already. One might even contend that "*safed*" has defamiliarizing usefulness in the way that it plays off of "saved," and thus translate the phrase, "will be *safed*." The reader would encounter the unfamiliar, but at the same time recognize that this new translation derived meaning in part from the tension it creates with that which was familiar, which would be arguably useful for encouraging deep engagement with the text.

Although I am unaware of anyone since Paul developing the implications in the direction I propose, I am not the first to notice that this is the natural meaning of the Greek: Jerome translated this phrase with "salvus fieret" ("will be kept safe/protected") for the Vulgate.³⁶ In his effort to capture the literal sense of the Latin, Wycliffe then translated this phrase from the Vulgate into English as, "schulde be maad saaf" (1385); in modern English this reads: "shall be made safe" (WYC, on the web).³⁷ Such translations allow for the inference that the limbs remain on the tree, even if, as far as I am aware, their own interpretations and the Pauline tradition did not explore this alternative.

The lexemes σῴζω and *salvus* as well as "broken" can all be used to indicate injury short of removal of a limb or limbs, and thus to question the underexamined evangelical salvation paradigm in more detail. In short, there are both sound exegetical and promising ideological grounds for reading σωθήσεται as *"will be kept safe"* or *"protected," "safe-d,"* if you will, rather than *"saved."* Like "will be saved," the basically interchangeable translations "will be safed," "kept safe," and "protected" raise a number of questions, not least, protected from what, and to what purpose or end.

"JUST AS HAS BEEN WRITTEN": THE WARRANT FOR PAUL'S CLAIM THAT "ALL ISRAEL *WILL BE KEPT SAFE*"

Paul's declaration of the safety of all Israel until those who have not taken up yet the entrusted task of declaring the good news to the nations is followed by an appeal to Scriptural warrant ("just as has been written"). In his citation, Paul conflated two texts from Isaiah, whom he drew from throughout the letter.

In the balance of what has come to be designated v. 26,³⁸ the sentence continues with a citation from LXX Isa 59:20: "The Deliverer will come out of/from [ἥξει ἐκ] Zion; he will turn away [or: aside; or: bend back]³⁹ ungodliness [or: impiety/disloyalty (ἀσεβείας)]⁴⁰ from Jacob" (cf. Isa 40:6–11). Paul continued in v. 27 by citing from Isa 59:21a: "And this is my covenant with them . . . ." But rather than complete the sentence by continuing to cite from Isa 59:21, Paul wrote: ". . . when[ever] [ὅταν] I [would (subj.)] take away [ἀφέλωμαι]⁴¹ their sins [or: "failings/faults/shortcomings" (ἁμαρτίας)]," which introduces a clause from LXX Isa 27:9b.

Paul chose these passages to warrant his claim for all Israel's protection in spite of present circumstances, although why he mixed them together, all the more why he omitted elements in those texts to create the proof-text that results, are difficult to ascertain. It was common to conflate two or more texts,⁴² yet this case is curious for several reasons. Paul seemingly could have made his case by citing from statements in the extant Masoretic or Septuagint versions (assuming he had what we have) that are not included, either from chapter 59, including the rest of v. 21,[43] or following closely after that in chapter 60,[44] or from more of the text in chapter 27.[45]

As Christopher Stanley helpfully explores, the language in his citations could represent traditions that had already developed in various Jewish groups of which he was aware, been invented or construed by Christ-following Jews before he joined them, or been altered by Paul. Moreover, the variations from the wording in the extant manuscripts could also be for any number of reasons, from manuscripts he had that we do not have, traditional substitutions already made before him, or from substitutions made by his choice, perhaps due to lapses of memory and lack of concern with literalism in order to make the points he wanted to highlight.[46]

I wonder if perhaps Paul did not cite elements from those texts because the case he sought to explain had not yet reached the point of fulfillment that they declared: the entrusted task of heralding the good news to the nations had not been taken up yet by all Israel. Instead, from his viewpoint, some Israelites still needed to be rescued from their failure to receive and thus announce these words. Therefore, the time addressed was closer to the concern raised in these parts of the texts from Isa 59:21 and 27:9, but not the other parts, even though he drew from the contextual concerns for Israel's eventual rescue and role as messenger expressed throughout those chapters.

Isaiah 59 and 27 declare that God will come to rescue Israel when all others fail to do so. Although the details are hardly set out in an orderly fashion, the overall message, both on their own or as Paul combined them, is detectable: Israel will eventually repent (59:12–15) and experience forgiveness and return from captivity to enjoy the presence of the Lord and provide light to the nations (59:15–16:22); those responsible for her current distress will be judged and subdued (60:11–14); and this will transpire in spite of Israel's sins and the present appearance of abandonment.[47] The optimistic catalog of the reversal of fortunes as a result of God's mercy toward Israel continues to 63:7 (from which Paul arguably drew in Rom 11:30–36).[48] Many other Second Temple texts expressed relatively similar hopes for the future, albeit with many variations on these themes (e.g., *Pss. Sol.* 17:21–32).[49] We must leave aside further discussion of supporting texts, or consideration of what Paul did not cite.

Returning to the text of Rom 11:26, the citation appeals to the activity of "the *Deliverer*," "*Redeemer*," or "*Protector*" (ὁ ῥυόμενος), from Isa 59:20. Paul could have used this to refer to Jesus as a or the messianic figure. Paul did not change this to ὁ σωτήρ, but followed the LXX translator's choice, ὁ ῥυόμενος, "the one who delivers/rescues/protects."[50] This supports the translation "kept safe/protected" for Paul's use of σώζω in v. 26a, since, as just argued, this primarily communicates saving in the sense of *keeping safe*. The point of the passage cited is that God will act on behalf of those with whom God already has a covenant relationship, and that action will be to deliver/protect them when in harm's way but no one else has come to their aid.

Often noted, the manuscripts that have survived do not refer to the Protector coming *out of* or *from* [ἐκ] Zion, but *for the sake of* [ἕνεκεν] Zion (Heb.: *come to/enter* [בְּ אָ]). If Paul altered the preposition intentionally,[51] the change away from the extant LXX use of ἕνεκεν is remarkable, because ἕνεκεν would have expressed better what he has asserted if what he was seeking to describe was, as traditionally proposed, a future time when the Messiah will return to evangelically "save" those Jews who have not believed the gospel during Paul's time, or since.[52] That the action anticipated will be from Zion rather than to Zion does not support the idea that Paul was referring to a time when the nations will go to Jerusalem; rather, it indicates a time when God or God's servant(s) will go out in the service of those descended from Jacob who are not in Jerusalem but in the rest of Judea, or who are scattered throughout the nations, that is, the diaspora. And yet Isa 59 does not seem to envisage Israel in exile, but in need of rescue within the land itself. Whatever else this reference to *"from* Zion" meant to Paul (or Isaiah and earlier readers, if original but unattested in the extant manuscripts),[53] the ones the deliverer/protector will come to deliver or protect are already in the covenant made with Jacob/Israel; they are not being saved in the sense of being introduced into that relationship.

What Paul did cite favors translating σωθήσεται in the direction of saved as in *rescued*, which thus supports the translation, "will be kept safe/protected"—"safed," if you will. That is the case in spite of the present ostensibly contrary indicator: many are suffering estrangement for not having faithfully carried out the entrusted task. This sense of "preserved" and "kept safe" is also the most likely inference earlier, when Paul appealed to the example of the remnant seven thousand God had "left behind for himself [κατέλιπον ἐμαυτῷ]" in the story of Elijah's misreading of his situation, just as the situation of Paul could be misread with respect to the question whether God had "pushed back [ἀπώσατο]" Israel. Paul used this example to substantiate his judgment that this was most certainly *not* the case (11:1–6; 1 Kings 19:10, 18).[54]

The texts that Paul cites do not signal that Israel *will be saved* in the way usually imagined, as if some Israelites have *rejected* the gospel, been *cut out* of Israel or the covenants made with Abraham and Israel and Moses but are *to be saved back into* covenant standing. No mention is made of either *faith* or of *belief* in *the Messiah*, or of the need for these Jews to realize that they are *sinners* in need of being *saved just like gentiles*. In neither Paul's argument nor the texts he cites is the Deliverer or Protector coming to remove sinners, but rather sins.[55] Thus Israelites have not been and are not being excluded from their standing as members of all Israel.[56] The citations also do not support the idea that "all Israel" signifies the inclusion of non-Jews who become followers of Jesus. The protector comes to rescue from the present suffering those who are *in* the covenant made with *Jacob*; that is, genealogical descendants of Israel.

CONCLUDING REFLECTIONS

I am concerned about the risk involved in challenging the widely held, good-willed conclusion that Paul was affirming "all Israel *will be saved*." For all of its logical problems and negative judgments about non-Christian Jews, the promise of eventual salvation has also served to check the Christian theological legacy of understanding such Jews not only to be superseded and replaced by Christians, but no longer to retain their covenantal relationship with God as Israel, logically reversing Paul's assertion a few verses later, that "the gifts and calling of God are irrevocable" (v. 29).[57]

The Catholic Church, among others, in recent years (against their own interpretive traditions) has appealed to the affirmation of all Israel's salvation to conclude that these Jews remain in their covenant relationship with God as Israel, and that *God* will act on their behalf, thus God will do what is necessary to save them. This has led to calls for a new level of mutual respect for Jews "in our times" and to taking a stand against continued *Church* efforts to evangelize Jews.[58]

Although my reading challenges the premise of the need for salvation that remains central to this reconsideration of the mechanism, I am convinced that what I have discovered offers a more promising way forward in Christian-Jewish relations *from* rather than *in spite of* Paul's voice. My proposal not only changes the focus to Paul's view of his fellow Jews in terms of a temporary development with respect to their role as heralds to the nations, but it offers an explanation that does not perpetuate the premise that, for Paul, Jews who did not share his convictions about Jesus had lost their covenantal status and were thus in need of being saved as usually understood.

Some readers may be tempted to classify my argument as another expression of the various *Sonderweg* and Two Covenant alternatives. It should not be. Although I appreciate the sensibilities they express, my proposal does not reason from the (perhaps unrecognized) soteriological premises that they share with the traditional alternatives; that is, that Paul's language about Israel here signifies evangelical salvation, since the Jews discussed would require to be saved on such terms, even if by way of different means, such as by observing Torah rather than believing in Jesus.[59] As noted earlier, their focus on subverting the mechanism for accomplishing that salvation leaves unasked and unanswered why Jews would need to be saved at all in those paradigmatic terms. In my view, that does not seem warranted by Paul's arguments here, or elsewhere. My reading thus offers a new approach to the topic and should be engaged on its own terms.

As I understand Paul, he confessed Jesus as Messiah and upheld that his fellow Jews should do the same, but not in order to be saved in evangelical salvation-based terms by any mechanism, period. For Paul, that was a truth claim made within Judaism; it did not involve Jews being saved in evangelical soteriological terms because they were never lost in the logical way that paradigm requires. What he promoted was a chronometrically based propositional claim that an awaited event, when the reign of God would arrive to rescue those who were already in a living covenant relationship from sinfulness, from sinners, from enemies, and so on—so that they could complete their calling to bring the gospel announcement to the nations—had begun. That premise, central to the gospel, should shape the thoughts and lives of the non-Israelites he addressed toward humble concern for the well-being of those Israelites who were not persuaded that was the case yet: they remained the "beloved" because of the promises made to their fathers, not least to "Jacob/Israel." To argue that Israelites were being *protected* during this anomalous period of alienation while retaining continued covenant standing is not the same as the later evangelical concept that Jews need to believe in Jesus Christ to become saved, which empties their historical covenantal standing as "irrevocable" of the substance that Paul labors to explain.

Paul's conviction that Jews should profess a Jewish Messiah was conceptualized within Jewish communal life; the calling of Israel was to announce this news to the nations. Israelites who were doubtful of the claims made by the gospel and thus that it was the appropriate time to herald this news to the nations needed "to be kept safe" until they were persuaded.

Much has changed since Paul's time; the gospel is not part of Judaism. Paul's concern was thus very different than, even the opposite of, later Christian calls to profess Jesus Christ that required Jews to become Christians and leave Judaism and Jewish communal life, and just as commonly, to spurn continued valuation of the genealogical identity marker, Jew.[60]

The quest to understand Paul's aims in his context remains relevant, even if that context is different than our own, even if events did not develop in the direction he imagined and sought to describe. Besides engaging in the challenge to interpret Paul's texts with historical rigor so that we might understand him and the origins of a movement that shaped our world with the highest degree of probability, it is my hope that this project demonstrates how a critical, within-Judaism reading might also contribute to a more mutually respectful, fruitful future for Christian-Jewish relations.

NOTES

1. Although this chapter focuses on English language translations and interpretive discussions, this habit is reflected in other modern language translations; see, e.g., Edition de Genèva (1979): "sera sauvé"; Nuova Riveduta (1994): "sarà salvato"; Reina–Valera Revisión 1909: "será salvo"; Die Bibel, Luther (1973): "wird . . . gerettet...werden"; (1912): "selig werde."

2. With good cause; this clause in v. 26a is part of a sentence that begins in v. 25, and the sentence includes several references to time elements and arguably to a sequence of events (the citation that follows in vv. 26b–27 also includes temporal and arguably sequential elements; discussion below). In v. 25, Paul proceeds to explain how a mystery is or will unfold, which includes the statement, "until the fullness of the nations begins [ἄχρι οὗ τὸ πλήρωμα τῶν ἐθνῶν εἰσέλθῃ]," and the full clause in v. 26a that follows that clause is, "and thus [or: in this way/then (οὕτως)] all Israel σωθήσεται." Also ἀπὸ μέρους in v. 25 arguably adds another temporal element to Paul's language.

3. For example, following "the fullness of the nations begins" as a sign, the common view is that these Jews will believe Jesus is Messiah at the *parousia*, or at the final judgment, or as a result of the completion of the apostolic mission to the nations.

4. Most conclude that "all Israel" refers either to the genealogical descendants of Israel ("according to the flesh") who become Christ-followers (for some that is the whole of or many Israelites; for others it is simply the remnant, even if only a few), or that here this refers to all Christ-followers (usually "Christians") inclusive of Jews and non-Jews—i.e., "the Church" = "Israel." For a useful survey of the prevailing contemporary readings of this passage, although to different conclusions than mine, and preceding several new elements I have brought to the discussion, see Christopher Zoccali, *Whom God Has Called: The Relationship of Church and Israel in Pauline Interpretation, 1920 to the Present* (Eugene, OR: Pickwick Publications, 2010), 91–117; Zoccali, "'And So All Israel Will Be Saved': Competing Interpretations of Romans 11.26 in Pauline Scholarship," *JSNT* 30, no. 3 (2008): 289–318; earlier, James M. Scott, "'And Then All Israel Will Be Saved' (Rom 11:26)," in *Restoration: Old Testament, Jewish, and Christian Perspectives*, ed. James M. Scott (Leiden, Boston, MA, and Köln: Brill, 2001), 489–527. Also of interest is the tradition that Elijah was implicitly the one who would convince these Jews about Jesus, although this tradition fell out of discussion after the Reformation, which remains the case; see Joel A. Weaver, *Theodoret of Cyrus on Romans 11:26: Recovering an Early Christian Elijah Redivivus Tradition*, Series VII: Theology and Religion, 249 (New York, NY: Peter Lang, 2007). The "special way"/*Sonderweg* alternative is discussed below.

5. Robert Jewett, *Romans: A Commentary*, ed. Eldon J. Epp. Hermeneia Series (Minneapolis, MN: Fortress Press, 2006), 702.

6. A survey of the current commentaries supports Jewett's claim. Michael G. Vanlaningham (*Christ, the Savior of Israel: An Evaluation of the Dual Covenant and* Sonderweg *Interpretations of Paul's Letters*, EDIS 5 [Frankfurt am Main: Peter Lang, 2012] undertakes an entire monograph to challenge recent alternatives to the traditional understanding of the mechanism for the salvation of the Jews, such as

the Two Covenant and *Sonderweg* approaches, with many detailed descriptions and arguments that, in my view, successfully challenge major tenets of those approaches. Yet Vanlaningham does not labor over the evangelical construal itself, likely because those alternatives accepted the basic paradigm of salvation, although they challenged certain aspects, especially the mechanism (Torah or *parousia*) for triggering that salvation for Jews versus the mechanism (of Christ) for non-Jews. Although I deeply appreciate the respectful sensibilities they express, the acceptance of the paradigmatic concept of the need for salvation for Jews in traditionally construed evangelical terms undermines their usefulness. I want to be clear that I do not subscribe to the Two Covenant and *Sonderweg* alternatives; rather, I am offering a different paradigm that questions the very premise that Paul was arguing that these Jews needed to be saved in the Christian evangelically constructed terms that those alternatives share with the traditional approaches. Terrance L. Donaldson's useful, earlier critique in "Jewish Christianity, Israel's Stumbling and the Sonderweg Reading of Paul" (*Journal for the Study of the New Testament* 29.1 [2006]: 27–54), is problematic for the same reasons as Vanlaningham's.

7. In my *The Mystery of Romans: The Jewish Context of Paul's Letter* (Minneapolis, MN: Fortress Press, 1996), 239–88.

8. This realization followed a return to study Romans 9–11 that began with research for a conference paper in 2008, available in my "'Broken Branches': A Pauline Metaphor Gone Awry? (Romans 11:11–36)," in *Between Gospel and Election: Explorations in the Interpretation of Romans 9–11*, ed. Florian Wilk and J. Ross Wagner (Tübingen: Mohr Siebeck, 2010), 339–76. This led to several other investigations in papers and essays, which are now collected, along with "Broken Branches," including revisions to reflect what I had continued to discover up until the completion of my *Reading Romans within Judaism: The Collected Essays of Mark D. Nanos, Vol. 2* (Eugene, OR: Cascade, 2018), a process discussed in the preface (xxi–xxix) and demonstrated in the "Appendix: Translating Romans 11:11—12:1a within Judaism: Literal-Oriented and Expanded Versions," 285–92. I began to explore the alternative translation and interpretation of σῴζω for "Are Jews outside of the Covenants If Not Confessing Jesus as Messiah?: Questioning the Questions, the Options for the Answers Too," a paper presented at the Society of Biblical Literature Annual Meeting, November 23, 2015, in Atlanta, in the "Paul within Judaism" session entitled, "For Paul, Do Jews Have to Become Christians to Be Saved?" I have presented facets of this new research in my annotations for "Romans," in *The Jewish Annotated New Testament, Revised Edition*, ed. Amy-Jill Levine and Marc Zvi Brettler (New York, NY, et al: Oxford University Press, 2017), 285–320. More details about my process of discovery are discussed in "Paul: Why Bother? A Jewish Perspective," *Swedish Theological Quarterly (STK)* 95, no. 4 (2019): 271–87.

9. I am indebted to Lloyd Gaston *Paul and the Torah* [Vancouver: University of British Columbia Press, 1987], 116–34, 135–50), for recognizing that what Paul found fault with among his fellow Jews was failure to join him in fulfilling Israel's role to enlighten the nations with the gospel, which Gaston contrasted with the idea of them needing to join him in believing that Jesus was Messiah, although I disagree that Paul did not also believe his fellow Jews should believe in Jesus as Messiah, and

I do not accept the premise that at issue was evangelically construed salvation by way of observing Torah anymore than by way of believing in Jesus as Messiah. Cf. John G. Gager, *The Origins of Anti-Semitism: Attitudes toward Judaism in Pagan and Christian Antiquity* (New York, NY: Oxford University Press, 1985), 250; Stanley Kent Stowers, *A Rereading of Romans: Justice, Jews, and Gentiles* (New Haven, CT: Yale University Press, 1994), 286, 296.

10. *Israel* and *Jew* here and throughout this chapter, unless otherwise stated, are used to denote genealogical descendants of Israel, both *Jews* who were not declaring Jesus the Christ and those who were, which was how Paul identified himself as well as the other Jews he was discussing in Romans 9–11. There is not space to discuss this matter in any detail here, but it makes no sense to suppose that Paul switched to using Israel to signify Christ-following Jews only here, all the less that Israel for Paul included Christ-following non-Jews, since he continued to identify the non-Jews in Christ explicitly as *ethnē* whom he was informing about "them"—i.e., about the Jews/Israelites to whom promises were made and gifts given even though they were not presently persuaded about the gospel. Neither of those common options would have been useful to challenge the concern with arrogance toward Jews/Israelites who did not already subscribe to the gospel. See my "Paul's Non-Jews Do Not Become 'Jews,' but Do They Become 'Jewish'?: Reading Romans 2:25–29 within Judaism, alongside Josephus," *Journal of the Jesus Movement in Its Jewish Setting (JJMJS)* 1, no. 1 (2014): 26–53, available in my *Reading Paul within Judaism: The Collected Essays of Mark D. Nanos, Vol. 1* (Eugene, OR: Cascade, 2017), 127–54; and *Mystery of Romans*, chapter 5.

11. Cf. Jeremy Cohen, "The Mystery of Israel's Salvation: Romans 11:25–26 in Patristic and Medieval Exegesis," *Harvard Theological Review* 98, no. 3 (2005): 247–81.

12. A point Krister Stendahl made central for his challenge to the traditional views, in *Paul among Jews and Gentiles, and Other Essays* (Philadelphia, PA: Fortress Press, 1976).

13. I have explored this dynamic in several essays, most recently in "How Could Paul Accuse Peter of 'Living *Ethné*-ishly' in Antioch (Gal 2:11–21) If Peter Was Eating according to Jewish Dietary Norms?" (*Journal for the Study of Paul and His Letters* 6, no. 2 [2016]: 199–223) and "Reading the Antioch Incident (Gal 2:11–21) as a Subversive Banquet Narrative" (*Journal for the Study of Paul and His Letters* 7, no. 1–2 [2017]: 26–52). These and related essays will be included in my *Reading Galatians within Judaism: The Collected Essays of Mark D. Nanos, Vol. 3* (Eugene, OR: Cascade, forthcoming).

14. Matthew Novenson, in the discussion of my study, affirmatively noted that "saved" was not a state of being.

15. If no longer "Israel," logically they were no longer the recipients of the promises in 9:4–5, including the covenants and cult of the Mosaic covenant. From Galatians, we could add that the received interpretations of the allegory in Gal 4:21–30 also propose that these Jews were not sons of Sarah but of Hagar, not of promise but of flesh, not of freedom but of slavery. Some interpreters approach these Jews as if under the Mosaic covenant but separated from the Abrahamic except through

Hagar and thus as slaves. Logically, however, if still under the Mosaic covenant, that requires them to be still in a covenant relationship with the God of Abraham through Isaac/Jacob-Israel, etc., which undermines their interpretive paradigm's relegation of their genealogy to the line of Hagar. In my view, Paul's allegory does not describe Jews as genealogical descendants of Hagar; he was not discussing genealogical Jews/Israelites. He was arguing that there were *two models for the incorporation of non-Jews* into the Abrahamic family: one, via the model of Hagar/Ishmael for slaves, to which Paul analogizes the model on offer of completing the rites of proselyte religio-ethnic transformation; or two, via the model he asserts that his non-Jew Christ-following addressees have already experienced, miraculous birth by God's spirit, just *like* Isaac, even though not descended from Isaac, as Jews are. Thus they are those who have joined the family line through adoption rather than natural genealogical descent, by which they already have become co-participants in the family with Jews, including non-Christ-following Jews. I presented these views in my "Reading Paul's Allegory (Gal 4:21–5:1) as Haftarah: A Jewish Liturgical Explanation for Paul's Characterization of 'Jerusalem Presently in Slavery with Her Children,'" a paper presented in the Jewish-Christian Dialogue and Sacred Texts section, Society of Biblical Literature Annual Meeting, San Antonio, Texas, November 19-22, 2016; a revised version for publication is in development for *Reading Galatians within Judaism*.

16. I have challenged the received view in "'The Gifts and the Calling of God Are Irrevocable' (Romans 11:29): If So, How Can Paul Declare That 'Not All Israelites Truly Belong to Israel' (9:6)?" *Studies in Christian-Jewish Relations [SCJR]* 11, no. 1 (2016): 1–17; available in *Reading Romans within Judaism*, vol. 1, 214–34.

17. See the critiques of replacement theology options by Zoccali, *Whom God Has Called*.

18. Note that those Christians who read "all Israel" in 11:26 to signify "all Christians" (however labeled) do not apply the judgment in 9:6 to themselves as Christian readers: they do not read Israel in the replacement terms that they advocate, which logically would become "not all Christians are Christians." But that substitution of terms is logically required if this applied to themselves on the same terms that they read it to apply to the genealogical descendants, understanding that not all Jews are Israel, but all Christians are, except perhaps those whom they do not regard as proper Christians either. And if Paul now considered those Christ-followers to be the Israel he is describing in 11:26a, then they must be the "enemies" (better: "the ones alienated") "for your sake" in v. 28, that is, the Christ-followers whom Paul is addressing, which just does not make any sense. Likewise, vv. 30–32 continue the argument by referring to "they/them" without explicit mention of Israel or Israelites or Jews, and, again, this is not understood to refer to Christ-following non-Jews because that would not make any sense (nor would filling in Christ-following Israelites like Paul as the "them/they"); instead the Christ-following non-Jews remain the "you" addressed about the "them" non-Christ-following Jews/Israelites throughout this argument too.

The same inconsistency is evident in 2:25–29: although interpreting Paul to be calling "Christians" the "true Jews" or "circumcised" and dismissing this identification as any longer properly applicable for Jews who do not become Christians, the same interpreters nevertheless read the rest of the comments about Jews to apply only to Jews from genealogical descent, especially if understood to be critical. If Paul was claiming the titles Jew, Israel, and circumcised (cf. Phil 3:3 also) for Christians (to name a few common elements in replacement theology), and all the more if doing so involved Paul denying these to be rightful ("true/real/spiritual") descriptive titles now for those Jews who were not Christians, would not one expect this to show up in how Paul (or Acts) addressed and identified his audiences in the rhetorical world he was creating for them? See my "Paul's Non-Jews Do Not Become 'Jews,' But Do They Become 'Jewish'?" (included in *Reading Paul within Judaism*, 127–54). For just this kind of move later by Justin Martyr and the Patristic authors, see Peter Richardson, *Israel in the Apostolic Church*, SNTSM 10 (London: Cambridge University Press, 1969). The regular appeals to Gal 6:6, "the Israel of God," for example, to argue that Paul calls the "Church" Israel involve the same kind of interpretive reasoning that is under dispute, because this text can be read to include a wish for peace and mercy "even" for the genealogical descendants who are not Christ-followers. Paul perhaps added that point because he realized his respect for their continued covenantal identity might be questioned following the polemicizing he undertook in the letter to dissuade them from undertaking proselyte conversion to gain identity as members of Israel.

19. This point was not lost on Chrysostom, although he turned it to an even more disparaging accusation against the Jews; see Vasile Mihoc, "Paul and the Jews according to St. John Chrysostom's Commentary on Romans 9–11," in *Greek Patristic and Eastern Orthodox Interpretations of Romans*, ed. Daniel Patte and Vasile Mihoc, RHCS, 9 (London et al.: Bloomsbury T&T Clark, 2013), 74 (63–82).

20. In addition to the notes provided to my arguments as I listed off the received views above, the various challenges are demonstrated in the annotations and glosses for "Romans" in *JANT*; and in the papers and essays collected in *Reading Romans within Judaism*, supplemented by arguments made in the other collected volumes in that series; some elements were already argued in *The Mystery of Romans*.

21. Introduced in my paper, "Are Jews Outside of the Covenants If Not Confessing Jesus as Messiah?: Questioning the Questions, the Options for the Answers Too" (unpublished).

22. See esp. my "'Broken Branches.'"

23. See my *Mystery of Romans*, chapter 4; and "Paul and the Jewish Tradition: The Ideology of the *Shema*," in *Celebrating Paul. Festschrift in Honor of Jerome Murphy-O'Connor, O.P., and Joseph A. Fitzmyer, S. J.*, ed. Peter Spitaler, CBQMS 48 (Washington, DC: Catholic Biblical Association of America, 2012), 62–80; available in *Reading Paul within Judaism*, 108–26.

24. Cf. Lev 1:17; Pausanias, *Graeciae descriptio* 8.40.2 (Loeb; transl. W. H. S. Jones).

25. See my "'Callused,' Not 'Hardened': Paul's Revelation of Temporary Protection until All Israel Can Be Healed," in *Reading Paul in Context: Explorations in Identity Formation: Essays in Honour of William S. Campbell*, ed. Kathy Ehrensperger and J. Brian Tucker (London, U.K., and New York, NY: T&T Clark, 2010), 52–73.

26. *LSJ*, 471, references LXX Wisdom of Solomon 16:11, which refers to the motiving "bite" of a serpent. The example from Theophrastus, *Hist. Plant.* 2.2.5, does seem to indicate grafting onto an almond tree rather than planting seed, but normally Theophrastus uses ἐμφυτεύω and ἐμφύτεία for grafting (*Caus. Plant.* 1.6.1–10, where he explains the process of grafting, and the olive bud specifically). In *Hist. Plant.* 2.1.4, just prior to the example given, Theophrastus notes that he will take up the topic of grafting later, so it is not so clear that what he is referring to for almond trees in 2.2.5 is grafting rather than some other form of goading growth when possible versus planting a new tree. Note also κεντέω, *LSJ*, 939: "generally, *prick, stab.*" The addition of ῥίζω to κεντέω may suggest the idea of stimulating the root (ῥιζόω), drawing from the point made in 11:17 (ῥίζα) that the newly added wild shoot is now drawing its life from the same root as the branches, including those suffering a break/bend.

27. Notice the turn from describing "them" to admonishing (even threatening) "you" in v. 21.

28. In addition to my own arguments for this in several essays in *Reading Romans within Judaism*, and in the notes for "Romans" in *JANT*, see now the case made that the meaning revolves around not being persuaded throughout the NT (Matthew D. Jensen, "Some Unpersuasive Glosses: The Meaning of ἀπείθεια, ἀπειθέω, and ἀπειθής in the New Testament," *JBL* 128, no. 2 [2019]: 391–412).

29. Notably representative, Nicholas T. Wright (*Paul and the Faithfulness of God*, COQG 4 [Minneapolis, MN: Fortress Press, 2013], 1264), sees Paul's problem with Judaism in just such culpability-oriented judgmental terms: "Israel's God had kept his promises, but Israel had refused to believe it."

30. Should not exegetes at least alert their readers to differentiate the judgments they attribute to Paul about Jews of his time from those that they make about Jews thereafter, and especially in their own time?

31. *LSJ*, 1748, and cognates on 1751; so too *L&N*, 241; W. Foerster, *TDNT* 7:965–1024, allowing for the theologizing toward the evangelical salvation paradigm assumed in the NT and some later Christian (including Gnostic) usages versus the cases in LXX and other Jewish and Greek literature; *Sqicq TLNT* 3:344–57, and *BDAG*, 982–86, both with caveat similar to *TDNT*. See also Johan C. Thom, "God the Savior in Greco-Roman Popular Philosophy," in *Sōtēria: Salvation in Early Christianity and Antiquity: Festschrift in Honour of Cilliers Breytenbach on the Occasion of His 65th Birthday*, ed. David S. du Toit (Leiden and Boston, MA: Brill, 2019), 86–100.

32. *LSJ*, 1751.

33. Note that when NT texts refer to issues around coming back from the dead, the language of raised or resurrected rather than saved is employed. For example, in John 11:12 the disciples talk about Lazarus being saved as in protected [σωθήσεται] because they suppose that he has fallen asleep; Jesus then explains in v. 24 that he is not asleep but dead and refers to raising [ἀναστήσεται] him, not to saving him. In Lk 23:35 Jesus is mocked when on the cross because "he saved [ἔσωσεν] others but cannot save [σωσάτω] himself." Jesus was not dead, so the point was not readmission to life, but rather whether he could *protect* himself from dying in his present crucified condition.

34. The Hebrew equivalent יָשַׁע and cognates refer to saved in the sense of rescued, kept safe, liberated, and victorious (cf. Deut 33:29 NRSV: "Happy are you, O Israel!

Who is like you, a people saved [LXX: σῳζόμενος; MT: נוֹשַׁע] by the LORD, the shield of your help, and the sword of your triumph! Your enemies shall come fawning to you, and you shall tread on their backs.") There are places where σῴζω is used for the return of exiles from Babylon or the deported northern tribes coming back to the land, and all that is related to that hope. That does have a sense of readmitted but not into covenantal identity; rather, they remain Israel/Judah being rescued from the state of discipline and punishment of a specific nature for a specific period of time, during which these Israelites remain members of Israel, even if suffering exile. Likewise, the idea of eschatological salvation concerns deliverance and rescue, heralding a time when instead of enduring defeat Israel will enjoy victory.

35. *Caus. Plant.* 1.7.2; 19.5; 21.5; 22.2; 2.16.5; 17.5; 5.16.2; 18.4.

36. I am grateful to Paula Fredriksen for confirming this observation and translation from Latin into English after the conference, who noted, "this might sound odd to our RSV-habituated ears," and, moreover: "how I'd translate it if I didn't know that the phrase occurred in 11:26." Paula also brought to my attention that this was already the translation used before Jerome, in Rufinus of Aquileia's Latin translation of Origen's Greek Commentary on Romans (ca. 406), which uses "saluus fieret" (Origen, *Commentaire sur l'Épître aux Romains*, ed. Caroline P. Hammond Bammel, Luc Brésard, and Michel Fédou, Sources Chrétiennes 3 [Paris: Éditions du Cerf, 2009], 362). This Latin translation with some spelling variations is attested in many other early examples, (see H. A. G. Houghton et al., eds., *The Principal Pauline Epistles: A Collation of Old Latin Witnesses* [Leiden and Boston, MA: Brill, 2019], 128).

37. Douay–Rheims (1582), however, translates: "should be saved."

38. I cannot herein discuss v. 25 in the detail warranted, or how it supports the reading of v. 26a that I now advocate. The "mystery" Paul articulated involved disclosing the way that he was currently conducting his ministry in order to provoke his fellow Jews to reconsider the claims he was making for these non-Jews as evidence of the awaited arrival of the age to come, rather than toward a future *parousia-based* event as usually conceptualized. For details, see *Mystery of Romans*, chapter 5, and my essays "'Broken Branches'" and "'Callused,'" as well as the translations offered in the "Appendix," in *Reading Romans within Judaism*.

39. To the degree that Paul's language is judged to be still drawing metaphorically on the olive tree allegory, we might choose the alternative "bend back/aside" [ἀποστρέψει] to indicate the state of some of the branches; see *LSJ*, 220; so too שָׁבַע indicates "to turn back/away" (*BDB*). This could reflect the reasoning in the chapter's metaphors in the sense that they are bent back or aside for "lack of loyalty" yet to herald the gospel.

40. *LSJ*, p. 255; פֶּשַׁע "transgression/rebellion" (*BDB*).

41. The verb ἀφαιρέω was used to refer to atonement (Num 14:18; Lev 10:17).

42. See Christopher D. Stanley, *Paul and the Language of Scripture: Citation Technique in the Pauline Epistles and Contemporary Literature*, SNTSMS, 69 (Cambridge, U.K., and New York, NY: Cambridge University Press, 1992), 289–91, 304–6, 321–23, 333–37, 341–42.

43. Although Paul did not cite the rest of 59:21, the message therein supports the thesis that the issue was protection for Israel until ready to complete the task of her-

alding the good news to the nations: "my spirit that is upon you, and my words that I have put in your mouth, shall not depart out of your mouth, or out of the mouths of your children, or out of the mouths of your children's children, says the LORD, from now on and forever" (NRSV).

44. 60:1–3: $_1$Arise, shine; for your light has come, and the glory of the LORD has risen upon you. $_2$For darkness shall cover the earth, and thick darkness the peoples; but the LORD will arise upon you, and his glory will appear over you. $_3$Nations shall come to your light, and kings to the brightness of your dawn' (NRSV). Note also v. 21.

45. Isa 27 is a song of God's care for the vineyard, which might account for Paul's choice, and v. 6 is especially of interest because Jacob/Israel will blossom and the world will be covered with fruit: "[In days] to come Jacob shall strike root, Israel shall sprout and blossom, [a]nd the face of the world [s]hall be covered with fruit" (JPS). There are other interesting elements here too, which could be read to indicate the relative harm or blessing that results from how the nations treat God's vineyard, Israel, during God's temporary period of disciplining Israel for idolatry (v. 9) prior to restoration, followed by those lost from Assyria and Egypt coming to Jerusalem to worship (cf. Isa 5:1–7, whose judgment this text reverses). LXX Isa 27:9a: "Because of this the lawlessness of Jacob will be taken away/removed, and this is his blessing." NRSV from Hebrew: $_{9a}$"Assuredly, by this alone [s]hall Jacob's sin be purged away; $_{9b}$[t]his is the only price [f]or removing his guilt." In the Masoretic text, the rest of the verse and vv. 10–11 involve jumbled descriptions of judgment that include broken and dried up branches, but that may indicate the judgment on the nations when Jacob is restored; the LXX does not mention branches but rather the drying up of green grass upon which cattle graze. Paul could use this to warn the non-Jews, also to describe judgment on Jews who do not get on board, but he seems to use it to indicate that all Israelites are being protected rather than that some will fail. The text in Isaiah is hardly clear. Isaiah may draw here on LXX Jer 38:33a, 34d (MT 31:33a, d).

46. Christopher D. Stanley, "'The Redeemer with Come ἐκ Σιὼν': Romans 11:26–27 Revisited," in *Paul and the Scriptures of Israel*, ed. Craig A. Evans and James A. Sanders (Sheffield: JSOT Press, 1993), 118–42.

47. The citation from Isa 59:20 in Rom 11:26–27 refers to God coming to deliver/protect Jacob, not to observing Torah to be saved, contra some Two Covenant arguments. In Isaiah (and elsewhere in Tanakh) those in covenant relationship should observe the Torah; nevertheless, even those who have done so are suffering presently, and Isaiah expresses the view that their success requires God's action to rescue them.

48. Cf. Stanley, "'The Redeemer,'" 128–29.

49. Note also b. *Menachot* 53b, which argues that Israel is like an olive tree because just as the leaves remain in summer and winter, Israel will never be undone, and that "just as the olive produces its oil only after pounding, so Israel mends her ways only after suffering."

50. Kasch, "ῥύομαι," *TDNT* 6:998–1003, albeit laced with theological twists, notes that the basic sense is to guard or protect or deliver, often in the sense of to keep intact when threatened, accomplished variously by humans and things as well as divine figures. He observes, in keeping with what I am arguing for Paul's use of the citation to confirm his claim that "all Israel will be kept safe" in their covenant

standing rather than returned to it after supposedly having become lost "just like Gentiles," that "[s]alvation in the OT is preservation from being snatched out of the sphere of salvation established by Yahweh" (1001).

Kasch makes several interesting observations that led me to wonder if Paul did not use cognates of ῥύομαι to refer to all Israel as "will be delivered/protected" because, although the choice in LXX Isaiah, it was a less rarely used word group, whereas σῴζω was common. Yet Paul did use cognates of ῥύομαι in Rom 7:24; 15:31; also 2 Cor 1:10; 1 Thess 1:10—so that may not explain the choice of the synonym σῴζω here. But since Kasch notes that the verb is less common and has a narrower range of meaning than σῴζω, "which results in the fact that σῴζω can always be used for it whereas ῥύομαι is a synon. of σῴζω only where the latter has the special sense 'to deliver,' 'to protect'" (999), this supports the possibility that Paul was highlighting the sense of "kept safe" in this particular use of σῴζω followed by the citation with ῥύομαι. In the case of Paul's citation of Isa 59:20, Kasch argues that the "Savior does not actually bring in the time of salvation but does the preliminary work which is its presupposition, namely, that of abolishing ungodliness" (1003). Greeks used σωτηρες to refer to "saviors" who protect humans and rescue them from circumstances beyond their control. Throughout Second and Third Isaiah cognates of σῴζω are used to describe the expectation that God will rescue Israel when no one else will, including from the various negative circumstances, and several of these passages may shape Paul's thinking in the direction for which I am arguing (e.g., 49:24–25 [where σῴζω and ῥύομαι are used as synonymous couplets]; 59:1; 60:16; 61:10 [σωτηρίου]; 63:9; 66:19 ["and I will set a sign among them. From them I will send *survivors* (σεσῳσμένους) to the nations, to Tarshish, Put, and Lud—which draw the bow—to Tubal and Javan, to the coastlands far away that have not heard of my fame or seen my glory; and they shall declare my glory among the nations"; NRSV]). Note that the Heb ישׁע is translated in the LXX by both σῴζω and ῥύομαι, and גאל by ῥύομαι (i.e., to deliver in the sense of redeem; see e.g., Isa 48:17, 20; 49:7, 25–26; 51:10; 52:9; 54:5, 8; 59:20; 63:16) and by λυτρόω (e.g., Isa 59:3; 62:12; 63:9 with σῴζω for ישׁע).

51. Stanley ("'The Redeemer,'" 134–36), notes that ἕνεκεν Σιων only appears in the LXX in 59:20; in the other cases the normal phrase is ἐκ Σιων (Ps 13:7; 109:2; Joel 4:16; Amos 1:2; Obad 1:21; Mic 4:2), thus making the basis for the substitution quite easy to understand among Diaspora Jews (and 138).

52. We cannot know if Paul was aware of an alternative tradition using ἐκ, or, if working from memory, did not remember accurately, or altered the text, raising the question "Why?" Cf. LXX Ps. 13:7 for ἐκ Σιων, where not only a similar sentiment is expressed, but arguably a better proof text is offered for Paul's point (so too 14:7 MS); for restoration of Israel and the nations, e.g., Isa 2:2–3; *Pss. Sol.* 17:30–31. Stanley ("'The Redeemer,'" 133–36), offers an excellent discussion of the explanations that have been offered. Cf. J. R. Daniel Kirk, "Why Does the Deliverer Come ἐκ Σιὼν (Romans 11:26)?," *JSNT* 33.1 (2010): 81–99, where the difference from my reading emerges from his view (which is the prevailing view) that Israel said "No" (88: "Israel's rejection of the gospel" rather than "some Israelites . . . ."). I argue instead that Paul is a representative of Israel's "Yes," even if only by the other "some" of Israel,

until the rest come around to "Yes" also; that is why the "Yes" of the nations is so critical, and what Paul is trying to communicate about a suffering, divided Israel.

53. For example, whether this refers to God, to Jesus, or even to Paul or the apostles responsible for taking this message from Jerusalem to Judea and the nations. In *Mystery of Romans*, 280–84, I argued that Paul could be referring to himself and those others whose feet were declaring the good news to the nations (Rom 10, citing from Isa 52), and also that Paul may not be describing so much an eschatological *parousia* as the recognition by the other Israelites that that which he and the apostles were doing was the undertaking of the task of heralding that the other Jews also awaited when the hoped for age began. He hoped they thus would be convinced of the gospel and join the Christ-followers, being protected until such time arrived, which God designed and knew. Although Paul sought to explain this mysterious development here in order to influence the situation in Rome, at the end of the chapter he more or less throws up his hands in admission that God's ways are beyond comprehension or counsel by humans, including his own (11:33–36).

54. Cf. 1 Kings 20:15, where "all the Israelites—7000 strong," intriguingly ties together the number who are unrecognized but faithful in 19:18 to the number that can later be mustered to take up the task at hand.

55. Note also that Paul, whether he invented this version or cited an existing one, does not use "the sin of him" (αὐτοῦ τὴν ἁμαρτίαν; Isa 27:9) but "the sins of them" (τὰς ἁμαρτίας αὐτῶν), which arguably supports the point that Paul has in mind the some Israelites who are not performing rather than Israel per se not performing (after all, he and some others are), or an overall judgment of sin. Stanley ("'The Redeemer,'" 122–23) observes the choice, but argues quite differently that this does not reflect Paul's point of view, and thus was already a tradition with which he felt for some reason compelled to work.

56. I have explained how Rom 9:6 in context also confirms this interpretation of Paul's view, against the received readings, in "'The Gifts and the Calling of God Are Irrevocable' (Romans 11:29)."

57. For the history of ignoring when not reversing this affirmation in just such ways, see Joseph Sievers, "'God's Gifts and Call Are Irrevocable': The Reception of Romans 11:29 through the Centuries and Christian-Jewish Relations," in *Reading Israel in Romans: Legitimacy and Plausibility of Divergent Interpretations*, ed. Cristina Grenholm and Daniel Patte (Harrisburg, PA: Trinity Press International, 2000), 127–73.

58. Vatican II, *Nostra Aetate* 4—although there remains some room for various interpretations of both of these conclusions, and there are many who argue otherwise. Some argue that the decision not to evangelize Jews is to deny them the opportunity to experience salvation. Such reasoning is predicated upon the premise of need for evangelical salvation I seek to challenge. Such statements also fail to appreciate that what Paul advocated, even if understood in evangelistic salvation terms, was for Jews to be loyal to a Messiah interpreted in first-century Jewish terms, not those of later Christian concepts of Christ, which involve converting Jews out of Judaism into Christianity, and all that has come to represent. See the many essays on this topic by Philip A. Cunningham, and a joint essay we authored, "Implications of Paul's

Hopes for the End of Days for Jews and Christians Today: A Critical Re-evaluation of the Evidence," *Studies in Christian-Jewish Relations (SCJR)* 9.1 (2014): 1–45 (included in *Reading Romans within Judaism*, 249–84); also see my "The Translation of Romans 11 since the Shoah: What's Different? What's Not? What Could Be?" in *Exploring Bible, Church and Life. Essays in Celebration of the 100th Anniversary of Lutheran Theological Seminary, Hong Kong, China (Theology and Life Annual Theological Journal No. 36)*, ed. Dieter Mitternacht and Nicholas Thai (Hong Kong, China: Lutheran Theological Seminary, 2013), 167–77; included in *Reading Romans within Judaism*, 200–13.

59. In addition to accepting the Christian evangelical paradigm's requirement to offer an alternative mechanism for gaining salvation, appeal to obeying Torah runs the risk of playing to the long-standing Christian binary way of characterizing Judaism as works-righteousness based versus Christianity as grace and faith based.

60. Note that Paul is not interpreted to have opposed the parallel group-boundary-marking identifiers Christian, or Christ-followers, or in-Christ, and so on, which betrays the problematic logic at work in the New Perspective on Paul (and in traditional Pauline discourse) reasoning that Paul supposedly objected to the identifier Jew on those grounds. I discuss examples of important NPP interpreters like Dunn and Wright denying the continued value of even the identification Jew, as well as that of the practice of Judaism, in my "Paul and Judaism: Why Not Paul's Judaism?" in *Paul Unbound: Other Perspectives on the Apostle*, ed. Mark Douglas Given (Peabody, MA: Hendrickson, 2010), 117–31 (117–60); updated in *Reading Paul within Judaism*, 3–17 (3–59).

BIBLIOGRAPHY

Cohen, Jeremy. "The Mystery of Israel's Salvation: Romans 11:25–26 in Patristic and Medieval Exegesis." *Harvard Theological Review* 98, no. 3 (2005): 247–81.

Donaldson, Terence L. "Jewish Christianity, Israel's Stumbling and the Sonderweg Reading of Paul." *Journal for the Study of the New Testament* 29, no. 1 (2006): 27–54.

Gager, John G. *The Origins of Anti-Semitism: Attitudes toward Judaism in Pagan and Christian Antiquity.* New York, NY: Oxford University Press, 1985.

Gaston, Lloyd. *Paul and the Torah.* Vancouver: University of British Columbia Press, 1987.

Houghton, H. A. G., C. M. Kreinecker, R. F. Maclachlan, and C. J. Smith, eds. *The Principal Pauline Epistles: A Collation of Old Latin Witnesses.* NTTSD, 59. Leiden and Boston, MA: Brill, 2019.

Jensen, Matthew D. "Some Unpersuasive Glosses: The Meaning of ἀπειθεία, ἀπειθέω, and ἀπειθής in the New Testament." *JBL* 128, no. 2 (2019): 391–412.

Jewett, Robert. *Romans: A Commentary.* Edited by Eldon J. Epp. Hermeneia Series. Minneapolis, MN: Fortress Press, 2006.

Kirk, J. R. Daniel. "Why Does the Deliverer Come ἐκ Σιών (Romans 11:26)?" *JSNT* 33, no. 1 (2010): 81–99.

Mihoc, Vasile. "Paul and the Jews according to St. John Chrysostom's Commentary on Romans 9–11." In *Greek Patristic and Eastern Orthodox Interpretations of Romans*, edited by Daniel Patte and Vasile Mihoc, 63–82. Romans through History and Culture Series, 9. London et al.: Bloomsbury T&T Clark, 2013.

Nanos, Mark D. "Appendix: Translating Romans 11:11–12:1a within Judaism: Literal-Oriented and Expanded Versions." In *Reading Romans within Judaism: The Collected Essays of Mark D. Nanos, Vol. 2*, 285–92. Eugene, OR: Cascade, 2018.

———. "Are Jews Outside of the Covenants If Not Confessing Jesus as Messiah?: Questioning the Questions, the Options for the Answers too." Paper presented at the Society of Biblical Literature Annual Meeting, Atlanta, November 23, 2015.

———. "'Broken Branches': A Pauline Metaphor Gone Awry? (Romans 11:11–36)." In *Between Gospel and Election: Explorations in the Interpretation of Romans 9–11*, edited by Florian Wilk and J. Ross Wagner, 339–76. Tübingen: Mohr Siebeck, 2010.

———. "'Callused,' Not 'Hardened': Paul's Revelation of Temporary Protection until All Israel Can Be Healed." In *Reading Paul in Context: Explorations in Identity Formation: Essays in Honour of William S. Campbell*, edited by Kathy Ehrensperger and J. Brian Tucker, 52–73. London, U.K, and New York, NY: T&T Clark, 2010.

———. "'The Gifts and the Calling of God Are Irrevocable' (Romans 11:29): If So, How Can Paul Declare That 'Not All Israelites Truly Belong to Israel' (9:6)?" *Studies in Christian-Jewish Relations* 11, no. 1 (2016): 1–17.

———. "How Could Paul Accuse Peter of 'Living *Ethné*-ishly' in Antioch (Gal 2:11–21) If Peter Was Eating according to Jewish Dietary Norms?" *Journal for the Study of Paul and His Letters* 6, no. 2 (2016): 199–223.

———. *The Mystery of Romans: The Jewish Context of Paul's Letter.* Minneapolis, MN: Fortress Press, 1996.

———. "Paul and Judaism: Why Not Paul's Judaism?" In *Paul Unbound: Other Perspectives on the Apostle*, edited by Mark Douglas Given, 117–60. Peabody, MA: Hendrickson, 2010.

———. "Paul and the Jewish Tradition: The Ideology of the Shema." In *Celebrating Paul. Festschrift in Honor of Jerome Murphy-O'Connor, O.P., and Joseph A. Fitzmyer, S.J.*, edited by Peter Spitaler, 62–80. CBQMS, 48. Washington, DC: Catholic Biblical Association of America, 2012.

———. "Paul: Why Bother? A Jewish Perspective." *Swedish Theological Quarterly (STK)* 95, no. 4 (2019): 271–87.

———. "Paul's Non-Jews Do Not Become 'Jews,' But Do They Become 'Jewish'?: Reading Romans 2:25–29 within Judaism, alongside Josephus." *Journal of the Jesus Movement in Its Jewish Setting (JJMJS)* 1, no. 1 (2014): 26–53.

———. *Reading Galatians within Judaism: The Collected Essays of Mark D. Nanos, Vol. 3.* Eugene, OR: Cascade, forthcoming.

———. "Reading Paul's Allegory (Gal 4:21–5:1) as Haftarah: A Jewish Liturgical Explanation for Paul's Characterization of 'Jerusalem Presently in Slavery with Her Children.'" Paper presented in the Jewish-Christian Dialogue and Sacred

Texts section, Society of Biblical Literature Annual Meeting, San Antonio, Texas, November 19–22, 2016.

———. *Reading Paul within Judaism: The Collected Essays of Mark D. Nanos, Vol. 1.* Eugene, OR: Cascade, 2017.

———. *Reading Romans within Judaism: The Collected Essays of Mark D. Nanos, Vol. 2.* Eugene, OR: Cascade, 2018.

———. "Reading the Antioch Incident (Gal 2:11–21) as a Subversive Banquet Narrative." *Journal for the Study of Paul and His Letters* 7, no. 1–2 (2017): 26–52.

———. "Romans." In *The Jewish Annotated New Testament*, edited by Amy-Jill Levine and Marc Zvi Brettler, 253–86. New York, NY, et al.: Oxford University Press, 2011. Revised Edition, 2017, 285–320.

———. "The Translation of Romans 11 since the Shoah: What's Different? What's Not? What Could Be?" In *Exploring Bible, Church and Life. Essays in Celebration of the 100th Anniversary of Lutheran Theological Seminary, Hong Kong, China (Theology and Life Annual Theological Journal No. 36)*, edited by Dieter Mitternacht and Nicholas Thai, 167–77. Hong Kong, China: Lutheran Theological Seminary, 2013.

Nanos, Mark D., and Philip A. Cunningham. "Implications of Paul's Hopes for the End of Days for Jews and Christians Today: A Critical Re-Evaluation of the Evidence." *Studies in Christian-Jewish Relations (SCJR)* 9, no. 1 (2014): 1–45.

Origen. *Commentaire sur l'épître aux Romains.* Edited by Caroline P. Hammond Bammel, Luc Brésard, and Michel Fédou. Sources Chrétiennes. Paris: Éditions du Cerf, 2009.

Richardson, Peter. *Israel in the Apostolic Church.* SNTSM 10. London: Cambridge University Press, 1969.

Scott, James M. "'And Then All Israel Will Be Saved' (Rom 11:26)." In *Restoration: Old Testament, Jewish, and Christian Perspectives*, edited by James M. Scott, 489–527. Leiden; Boston, MA; and Köln: Brill, 2001.

Sievers, Joseph. "'God's Gifts and Call Are Irrevocable': The Reception of Romans 11:29 through the Centuries and Christian-Jewish Relations." In *Reading Israel in Romans: Legitimacy and Plausibility of Divergent Interpretations*, edited by Cristina Grenholm and Daniel Patte, 127–73. Romans through History and Culture Series. Harrisburg, PA: Trinity Press International, 2000.

Stanley, Christopher D. *Paul and the Language of Scripture: Citation Technique in the Pauline Epistles and Contemporary Literature.* SNTSMS, 69. Cambridge, U.K., and New York, NY: Cambridge University Press, 1992.

———. "'The Redeemer with Come ἐκ Σιὼν': Romans 11:26–27 Revisited." In *Paul and the Scriptures of Israel*, edited by Craig A. Evans and James A. Sanders, 118–42. Sheffield: JSOT Press, 1993.

Stendahl, Krister. *Paul among Jews and Gentiles, and Other Essays.* Philadelphia, PA: Fortress Press, 1976.

Stowers, Stanley Kent. *A Rereading of Romans: Justice, Jews, and Gentiles.* New Haven, CT: Yale University Press, 1994.

Thom, Johan C. "God the Savior in Greco-Roman Popular Philosophy." In *Sōtēria: Salvation in Early Christianity and Antiquity: Festschrift in Honour of Cilliers*

Breytenbach on the Occasion of His 65th Birthday, edited by David S. du Toit, 86–100. Leiden and Boston, MA: Brill, 2019.

Vanlaningham, Michael G. *Christ, the Savior of Israel: An Evaluation of the Dual Covenant and* Sonderweg *Interpretations of Paul's Letters.* EDIS, 5. Frankfurt am Main: Peter Lang, 2012.

Weaver, Joel A. *Theodoret of Cyrus on Romans 11:26: Recovering an Early Christian Elijah Redivivus Tradition.* Series VII: Theology and Religion, 249. New York, NY: Peter Lang, 2007.

Wright, Nicholas Thomas. *Paul and the Faithfulness of God.* COQG 4. Minneapolis, MN: Fortress Press, 2013.

Zoccali, Christopher. "'And So All Israel Will Be Saved': Competing Interpretations of Romans 11.26 in Pauline Scholarship." *JSNT* 30, no. 3 (2008): 289–318.

———. *Whom God Has Called: The Relationship of Church and Israel in Pauline Interpretation, 1920 to the Present.* Eugene, OR: Pickwick Publications, 2010.

Chapter Fifteen

Paul, the Israelite, on Israel and the Gentiles at the End of Time

Reflections on Rom 9–11

Karl-Wilhelm Niebuhr

In his argument in Romans 9–11 Paul combines three different levels of reasoning. First, a personal or biographical level: Paul, the Israelite and apostle to the Gentiles. Second, a tradition historical level: quotations from Scripture and expectations in ancient Jewish traditions on Israel and the Gentiles. Third, a level of theology or salvation history: Paul's own proclamation of the gospel as part of the eschatological events and its credibility.[1] The correlation between Paul's understanding of his gospel and his statements about the fate of Israel and the Gentiles at the eschatological time of revelation of Jesus Christ is a determining parameter for the exegetical interpretation of this section of Paul's letter to the Romans. The three levels of interpretation stand out from each other methodologically, but the meaning of the text as a whole is accessible only by observing their diffusion or permeation. The text-pragmatical peculiarity of the passage results from the combination of biographical arguments, references to Scripture, and statements about Israel's standing vis-à-vis God. Paul acts as agent in the events of God's salutary agency over against Israel and the nations. As apostle called to proclaim the gospel to the Gentiles, he at the same time represents Israel at the end of time. Paul understands himself as an eschatological messenger according to the model of the biblical prophets.[2]

THE BIOGRAPHICAL LEVEL—PAUL, APOSTLE TO THE GENTILES AND ISRAELITE

Four times in his argument in Romans 9–11 Paul refers to himself, his person, his task, and his aims, even his emotions.[3] Each time, he is concerned with his personal relationship to Israel, the people of God, to whom he counts himself. By pointing to his identity as Israelite (11:1)[4] Paul assures his existential bond to Israel, even to those from his people who actually are remote from Jesus Christ (9:1–5).[5] He substantiates this bond by continuous intercession in favor of their salvation (10:1),[6] and he proves it by tying his own lifework as apostle to the Gentiles to the goal to lead his own people to eschatological salvation (11:13).[7]

In view of such a subjective coloring of his argument,[8] we may ask how Paul exactly relates his identity as Israelite to his task as apostle to the nations. What, according to the contents of Paul's proclamation of Christ to the Gentiles, is the result of the history of God's people and its present situation in view of the Christ revelation? In which way does his expectation of the eschatological salvation of all Israel (11:26) affect his actual proclamation and his mission to the Gentiles? Is there any link between his propositions about the present status of Israel and the situation in the communities of Christ believers in Rome or the state of his missionary project as a whole?[9] By asking such questions, we notice that Paul's basic theological convictions closely relate to his individual experience as a missionary and to biblical and Jewish religious traditions as well.

Chapters 9–11 are part of the argumentative explication of the theme of the letter indicated in 1:16–17. God has revealed his righteousness in Jesus Christ to every believer, Jew or Gentile. In Romans 1–8 Paul explains how God has enforced his intention to save all human beings, Jews and Gentiles alike— that is, by faith in Jesus Christ.[10] In Romans 9–11, he ingrains the Christ event in the saving agency of God over against Israel by defining God as the one who calls Jews and Gentiles to his people and has mercy upon them.[11] The credibility of Paul's gospel to the Gentiles, therefore, stands and falls with the trustworthiness of God over against his people. That trustworthiness, however, seems to be in question, given the refusal of Christ in Israel, because Paul can interpret this refusal merely as an expression of Israel's turning away from God.[12] For Israel, if turning away from God, ends up under God's wrath. In Romans 9–11, therefore, the trustworthiness of God as the theological basis for Paul's credibility as apostle of Christ is in question due to the disbelief in Israel that brings Israel under conviction by God.

By manifesting his permanent solidarity to Israel even as apostle to the Gentiles and even in view of disbelief in Israel, Paul in his letter to the Romans intervenes in debates that arose in his churches due to his ministry.[13] When Paul asserts the faithfulness of God to Israel, even against appearance, he points his Roman audience to his ministry as apostle to the nations as performed by order of the God of Israel.[14] Likewise, he points them to his faith in Jesus Christ. His faith in Jesus Christ, in his view, is the same as his faith in the God of Israel. The addressees in Rome, as believers in Christ from the Gentiles, are called to believe in the God of Israel. On this ground, the apostle exhorts them not to react to the unbelief in Israel with self-praise and arrogance but with hope and expectation that God will save all Israel at the end of time.[15]

Romans 9:1–5

Paul's personal affirmation of his steadfast solidarity to Israel (9:1–5) follows a hymnal confession of communion to God in Jesus Christ (8:31–39).[16] His deep sorrow and unremitting grief in view of the present state of Israel is in stark contrast to his joy about the inseparable communion between the Christ believers and God as just expressed when Paul had claimed that nothing will be able to separate from the love of God those who are in Christ (8:39). However, by cursing himself, Paul expresses with highest emotions that he wished to be apart from Christ if this would help his fellow Israelites to be saved (9:3).[17] The relationship between Paul and Israel obviously is not only a biographical or personal link of parentage, but it belongs to his identity as apostle of Jesus Christ. Paul's immeasurable grief results from questioning his relation to Christ by the present unbelief in Israel.

The theological poignancy of the situation as initially expressed emotionally by Paul becomes a subject of his argument explicitly from 9:6ff,[18] but is already there implicitly in the exposition in 9:1–5. If Israel's refusal of Christ results in God's abandoning his promises to Israel, then indeed God would have rejected his people. Precisely this is the consequence explicitly pronounced four times by Paul in his argument, yet, only to deny it emphatically each time: "It is not the case that God's word has lapsed!" (9:6a); "Has God rejected his people? By no means!" (11:1); "So I ask, have they stumbled so as to fall? By no means!" (11:11); "For the gifts and the calling of God are irrevocable" (11:29). Therefore, from the beginning to the end of his argumentation, Paul never raises any doubts that God would be faithful to his promises to Israel. However, this does not suffice as a theologically satisfying solution for Paul's problem that at present part of Israel locks out themselves from God's saving agency in Christ. Here Paul's immeasurable sorrow has its roots.

However, this apparently desperate state of affairs at the beginning of Paul's argument has still another reason. For Paul, the faithfulness of God to Israel is at the same time the guarantee for his own proclamation to the Gentiles to be saved in Christ. If God would not be faithful even to his own people, how will they, as Gentiles who believe in Christ, trust him to fulfill his promise to all who turn to God by faith in Christ? Therefore, Paul's faithfulness as well as his self-understanding as apostle to the nations, founded by his call, is in question. The Pauline gospel proclaimed to the Gentiles and theologically justified by his letters depends on his belief in the God of Israel who puts into effect his promises unrestrictedly.[19]

Romans 10:1

In the light of the present state when Gentiles have come to righteousness in Christ already, but Israel on her way lead by the Torah has not yet arrived at the promised end of the Torah (9:30f),[20] Paul turns to God in prayer (10:1). His urgent request to God aims to Israel's salvation in the eschatological judgment. Thereby, Paul expresses to his audience his conviction that the present state of part of Israel far from salvation does not entail as its result Israel's ultimate rejection by God. Instead, Paul perceives from this situation a mandate from God to advocate energetically in favor of Israel's salvation.[21] Two convictions about Israel crucial for Paul's understanding of the gospel are plain: Salvation from God's judgment *is needed* for Israel as well as for the Gentiles as long as they lean on their own will and turn themselves against God.[22] Yet, salvation from judgment *is possible* for everyone (that is, also for every Israelite who does not believe in Christ) who submits him - or herself to the righteousness of God revealed in Jesus Christ.[23]

When Paul addresses his predominantly non-Jewish audience in Rome by pointing them to his prayer in favor of Israel, he testifies his enduring solidarity with his people, including its presently non-believing members. At the same time, he substantiates his judgment that those who do not believe in Christ are disobedient to God and therefore submitted to his wrath.[24] Thus, his testimony in favor of Israel implies a convicting judgment on Israel. All Israelites have the chance to be saved by faith in Christ now and then. Yet, those of Israel who refuse this possibility now, according to Paul, stand on par with the Gentiles before they turned themselves to God by faith in Christ.[25]

Romans 11:1

Paul, the Israelite, represents those from Israel who already have grasped this possibility.[26] Therefore, he can point to himself to exclude the assumption that God has abandoned his people altogether (11:1). Moreover, by hinting to himself, Paul not only manifests his belonging to the "remnant from Israel" (11:5).[27] By his self-designation as Israelite from the offspring of Abraham, from the tribe of Benjamin, he also refers to the numeration of the privileges of Israel at the beginning of his argument in 9:1–3. As an Israelite, he has a part in these privileges permanently, even now when he is proclaiming as God's agent the gospel to the nations. His particular task as apostle to the

Gentiles called by God is just to warrant that God did not abandon his own people. Thus, in a way, God had made Paul a sign for all Israel and for those in Israel in particular who at present do not believe in Christ. For, they all together own the promises of God that are fulfilled already in Paul as well as in the believers from Israel and from the Gentiles. Paul as Israelite and as apostle to the nations, therefore, is an apparent proof for the faithfulness of God over against his people.

Romans 11:13

In Rom 11:7–15, Paul deploys a thought that is crucial for his argumentation. God will bring all Israel to eschatological salvation on a way that leads just across the field where the gospel of Christ is proclaimed.[28] In the middle of the paragraph, Paul again points to himself. When he turns explicitly to his Gentile audience to highlight his mandate as apostle to the nations, he aims to bring close to them the salvific future of all Israel (11:13f).[29] If the invitation of the nations to have a part in eschatological salvation by faith in Christ indicates God's graceful richness already, it will be proved largely by his acceptance of all Israel in the future (11:15). Thus, if believers from the nations will come to salvation, this will result in a salutary future for all Israel (11:25–32).[30]

Paul's proclamation of the gospel to the Gentiles, therefore, cannot be separated from the salvific fate of all Israel. Israel for Paul is not just a means to save the nations, but Israel and the nations altogether are the addressees of the salvific message that Paul has to proclaim.[31] Salvation only for the nations that does not include Israel's participation would be thinkable for Paul only by abandoning the faithfulness of God to his promises—and that is an unthinkable possibility, for it destroys the theological basis for Paul's gospel.

Paul submits his ministry as apostle to the nations to the God of Israel who intends to grant his people eschatological salvation. Thereby, he attributes to his apostolic ministry a salvation historical function, even though he carefully marks the boundary between God's agency and his own work. Only God can take care of all Israel's salvation, yet Paul can contribute to this at least somewhat by proclaiming the gospel to the nations. If Israel, excited by believing Gentiles, will seek to participate in that eschatological salvation, then all Israel also will be saved—this is Paul's hope, at least. It seems, therefore, that Paul's biography—that is, his personal view on his ministry as apostle—relates inseparably to his understanding of God's agency over against Israel. In his proclamation of the gospel to the nations, Paul discovers an indispensable contribution to the enforcement of eschatological salvation for all Israel that God is going to realize. To avoid any accusation of hubris or even blasphemy,

Paul at the end of his argumentation points to the unsearchable ways of God (11:32–36). However, it is his deep conviction that the ways to salvation for Israel and for the Gentiles belong together and that these ways do not pass off Christ, a conviction that has always determined his ministry as Christ's apostle and has guided his theological reflection in Romans 9–11 as well.

THE TRADITION HISTORICAL LEVEL—ISRAEL AND THE NATIONS AT THE END OF TIME

A large number of quotations, allusions, or links to Scripture obviously draw through Paul's argument in Romans 9–11.[32] By this means, Paul at the same time takes up more or less explicitly a number of basic features of biblical and ancient Jewish expectations regarding the eschatological time. The relationship between Israel and the Gentiles at the end of time is one of such conceptions that is a given feature for Paul's argument.[33] Following a model of biblical and Jewish thinking on the human being(s), Paul understands what we today would call "humankind" according to the bipolar distinction between Israel and the Gentiles, and, at the same time, according to the bipolar distinction between faith and faithlessness in view of God's agency.[34] Three areas of biblical traditions are particularly crucial for Paul's argument: the prophetic tradition on Israel and the nations at the end of time, the sapiential tradition on the creation and the creatures in front of their creator, and the so-called 'Deuteronomistic model of history' about Israel and her members at the judgment of God. I can only go into the first mentioned item here a little bit more in detail.[35]

The picture of the nations as drawn by prophetic literature in Scripture in particular is ambivalent. On the one hand, Gentiles are the classic representatives of wrong religion submitted under God's judgment.[36] As such, they function as deterrent examples for Israel regarding wrong religion as well as liability to God's judgment.[37] On the other hand, aside this there is a considerable branch of tradition according to which the nations expect a positive fate in the eschatological events. Either they belong to those who draw near to Zion in a pilgrimage of peoples together with the Israelites scattered among the nations,[38] or they are part of all creation that will partake in the eschatological veneration of the God of Israel.[39] Nevertheless, according to the biblical writings God without question will act beneficially in the end to his own people. This basic idea appears in the book of Isaiah in its final shape (notwithstanding its earlier layers) and is apparent in the Dodekapropheton as well as in the canonical collection of prophetic writings as a whole. Apparently, this eschatological focusing of prophetic traditions on the salvation of

Israel was the result of a purposeful redaction of the biblical writings guided by conscious literary and theological reflection.

A brief look at selected Jewish writings may show how Paul's propositions about the fate of Israel and the Gentiles at the end of time appear as part of a spectrum of possibilities in early Judaism influenced by the biblical traditions just mentioned. For this purpose, I select only two examples from very different fields of the early Jewish literature. I thereby do not want to deviate Paul's propositions from such statements, neither by assumption of a literary nor a tradition historical dependency. I simply attempt to describe a conceivable spectrum of possibilities testified by contemporary Jewish writings available to determine the relationship between Israel and the nations at the end of time.

Book 3 of the Sibylline Oracles

Book 3 of the *Sibylline Oracles* provides an impressive insight into the reception of prophetic traditions in Hellenistic Judaism.[40] Extremely brutal descriptions of the fate of the nations inimical to God alternate to paradise-like depictions of the future life of the "righteous men" who easily can be identified as members of the people of Israel. Several times promises of eschatological salvation for Israel conclude predictions of judgment against the Gentiles. Thus, at the end of an apocalyptical periodization of history[41] the Sibyl says:

> And then the people of the great God will again be strong
> who will be guides in life for all mortals. (*Sib. Or.* 3.194–195)

As part of a reminiscence to the deportation of Israel to the Babylonian exile and to the existence in the diaspora[42] the people of God receive the annunciation:

> But a good end and a very great glory await you
> as immortal God decreed for you . . .
> And then the heavenly God will send a king
> and will judge each men in blood and the gleam of fire.
> There is a certain royal tribe whose race will never stumble.
> This too, as time pursues its cyclic course,
> will reign, and it will begin to raise up a new temple of God.
> All the kings of the Persians will bring to their aid
> gold and bronze and much-wrought iron. (*Sib. Or.* 3.282–292)

To characterize the "sacred race of pious men" in the future,[43] the Sibyl announces:

> Sharing in the righteousness of the law of the Most High,
> they will inhabit cities and rich fields in prosperity,
> themselves exalted as prophets by the Immortal
> and bringing great joy to all mortals. (*Sib. Or.* 3.580–583)

Finally, the "sons of the great God" will experience a salvific life around the temple protected by God[44] that leads the nations to wonder and to confess:

> How much the Immortal loves those men!
> For everything fights on their side and helps them,
> heaven, divinely driven sun and moon. (*Sib. Or.* 3.711–713)

It follows a description of adoration to the "great eternal God" of Israel by the nations. They will send gifts to the temple and "ponder the Law of the Most High God" so that they will repent their aberration from the Immortal by revering things made by hands.[45] Israel, according to such expectations, will not be alone at the end of time. It will be in contact and communication with the nations. The nations, however, clearly are subordinate to the people of God. They will be spectators at best, forced to accept the glorious fortune of Israel, to marvel about their fate and to praise the god of Israel for that.

Flavius Josephus, Bellum Judaicum

Flavius Josephus, a historian with theological ambitions, shows a completely different view on Israel and the Gentiles in early Judaism. In his particular historical situation, he contests any promise of salvation for Israel among the nations, as still was the hope for the *Sibylline Oracles* when they adopted respective aspects from the prophetic tradition. For Josephus, in contrast, there is no space any longer for a salvific future of Israel among or over against the nations. In his theological interpretation of the events of the *Jewish War* against Rome, probably caused by his personal and political motives, Josephus takes a position alongside the Romans. Nevertheless, Josephus too arranges his position in relation to the traditions of the biblical prophets, yet he now takes the role of a prophet of doom over Israel.

Thus, in *Bellum Judaicum*[46] he announces the judgment of God *against* Israel, whereas he promises salvation to Rome. According to the prophetic proclamation of Josephus, God himself had delivered Israel under the power of the Romans. Therefore, by regarding himself as God's servant, Josephus prays to God before surrendering to the Roman tribune Nikanor:

> Since it pleases thee, [...] who didst create the Jewish nation, to break thy work, since fortune has wholly passed to the Romans, [...] I willingly surrender to the Romans and consent to live. (*B.J.* 3.354)

Before the Romans conquer Jerusalem, Josephus once more wants to persuade those who try to defend the city to lay down their arms. Now, already alongside the Roman troops, Josephus tries to convince his fellow Jews by the argument:

> Fortune, indeed, had from all quarters passed over to them, and God who went the round of the nations, bringing to each in turn the rod of empire, now rested over Italy. (*B.J.* 5.367)

Finally, after an excursus about Israel's history, Josephus concludes:

> My belief, therefore, is that the Deity has fled from the holy places and taken His stand on the side of those with whom you are now at war. (*B.J.* 5.412)[47]

The Romans in the present time, according to Josephus, have occupied the position of the Babylonians in Israel's history, as is depicted in Ezek 10–11: In view of the siege and the conquest of Jerusalem, the prophet there observes how the glory of God leaves the temple. However, whereas the Book of Ezekiel ends in a glorious depiction of the restored eschatological temple,[48] such a salvific perspective is completely missing in Josephus.

Paul

The eschatological expectations in the third book of the *Sibylline Oracles* on the one hand and Josephus's interpretation of Israel's history on the other exhibit two poles of possible concepts in Hellenistic Judaism on the fate of Israel and the nations at the end of time. How do Paul's propositions range in relation to them? Probably, Paul comes closer to the Sibyl than to Josephus with regard to the future of Israel, although his own accents are obvious. This refers in particular to the inclusion of non-Jews into eschatological salvation, provided they turn to the God of Israel by faith in Jesus Christ. This certainly is more than what the *Sibylline Oracles* admitted them, for there, the nations are no more but spectators wondering and applauding the saving events in favor of Israel, if not being destroyed before. It is, however, much less than what Josephus offers them, who deems the Romans the heirs of God's promises to Israel. This sort of substitution theory, strangely enough, does not occur with Paul, the apostle of the Gentiles, or with any other Christian sources from the 1st century AD, but with the Jewish author Josephus who counts himself a pious member of Israel![49]

All three—Paul, the *Sibyllines,* and Josephus—perceive every Israelite as a member of the people of God. By parenetical exhortation, they attempt to prompt every single Israelite to follow the will of God in their individual everyday life, in their religious, ethical, or political decisions.[50] However, the individual situation of all Israelites relates inseparably to the fate of the people of God under eschatological perspective. Yet, the outcome of the eschatological events with regard to Israel, either salutary or catastrophic, does not lie in the hands of Israel or any of her members, but in God's hands alone.

THE THEOLOGICAL LEVEL— GOD'S AGENCY OVER AGAINST ISRAEL

Paul highlights the privileges of Israel and God's promises to his people (9:4–5) even before he articulates the problem with regard to Israel that brings him to utter his deeply felt sorrow and grief about them (9:6–29). The tension that results from this situation forces Paul to argue theologically, based on Scripture. At the end of his argument that leads him to the result that all Israel will be saved, Paul again emphasizes the graceful agency of God that is founded theologically in his mercy upon "all"—that is, upon Israel and the nations (11:30–36). Between these brackets, the principle of God's trustworthiness to his promises to Israel forms the theological basis for the construction of Paul's argument.[51]

Romans 9:6–29

The first deployment of the argument replies to the impossible assumption that God's word has lapsed (9:6a).[52] In this step of the argument, the leading idea refers to God who has always enforced his intent to save his people by calling them. This was true for Abraham and his offspring (9:7–10) as well as for Rebecca's sons (9:11–14). It can be shown for Moses likewise as for Pharaoh (9:14–18), and it follows the insight of the biblical wisdom and the prophets (9:19–21). When Paul in his argument turns from biblical times to the present time, his leading idea remains the same (9:22–29). God's calling is the only reason for salvation. Therefore, even now, even for "us"—that is, for Jews and Gentiles—God's promises to Israel have been fulfilled only because he has called us (9:24).

Israel, therefore, is the people to which God acts by enforcing his will when he calls them to salvation. Paul comes to a solution for the hard-pressing problem of disbelief in Israel only by arguing from the point of view of God's agency, not from the point of view of Israel's virtues or deeds. This arises clearly from Paul's argument in 9:22–29.[53] Given that currently not all "from Israel" are "Israel" (9:6b), Paul has to explain if and how God will stick to his promises to Israel in future. He does this by interpreting the present situation because of God's calling. This suits his former arguments with regard to the biblical examples mentioned in 9:9–18. God enforces his salutary promise to *all of* Israel by calling sovereignly *out of* Israel and the Gentiles those who believe in Christ (9:24). Certainly, this still leaves open the question of how God will comply his promises toward all of Israel, although there is no indication at all in this passage that God would have withdrawn or only restricted his promises or even have transferred them upon the nations in view of Israel's disbelief.

Romans 11:2–10

The next step of Paul's argument adopts the biblical idea of a remnant from Israel (11:2–10).[54] In the present time, the existence of such a remnant belonging to the saved already would indicate at least that God has not disowned his people completely, but has lead Israel to salvation at least partly by his calling. This means that presently all of Israel already faces God's intention to save them, but only part of them have accomplished God's will entirely. The rest are "hardened," as Paul calls it (11:7). To understand Paul's thoughts correctly, it is decisive that this "hardening" of part of Israel results from God's agency as well. Paul attributes a positive function to the rejection of Christ in Israel! This act of part of Israel is the precondition for believers from the nations who are called to salvation to enter the eschatological people of God. Thereby, the "hardened" part of Israel takes on a positive role when God enforces his salutary will over against Israel and the nations. In fact, all Israel has not yet come to salvation, but the part of Israel that has not yet arrived there, nevertheless, is exposed to the salvific agency of God that succeeded already by calling Jews and Gentiles alike to salvation through faith in Christ in the present time.

Romans 11:11–32

This opens a new perspective to the salvation of all Israel (11:12, 15). Turning to his predominantly non-Jewish audience in Rome, Paul in a parenetical argument first deploys this possibility by using the metaphor of the olive tree (11:16–24).[55] However, his point here is not the quality of the tree or its roots. Again, the decisive activity in the events of salvation is with God, not with Israel. The olive tree and its roots, therefore, do not represent Israel or the patriarchs, but refer to God in his salvific agency towards Israel and the nations. The olive tree embodies the space and the events where and when God enacts his salutary will. Israel's participation in the eschatological salvation as well as the participation of the Gentiles in it is due to God's will alone. It is the result of God's sovereign intention to put into effect his promises to his people.

What is expressed as a possibility in the parable of the olive tree is deployed as eschatological reality at the end of Paul's argumentation (11:25–27).[56] He calls it a "mystery" that all Israel will be saved when the hardening over Israel will have succeeded by opening the way to salvation for believing Gentiles. Then, the savior will come from Zion to take off all ungodliness from Jacob. Again, the theological basis for this idea is the conviction that God alone is acting in this event, by hardening as well as by saving his people.

This is the theological reason why Paul does not need to claim that all Israel in the end will *believe* in the savior Jesus Christ.[57] The nations, if at all, will be saved by faith in Christ alone. All Israel, however, at the end of time will be saved by the salvific eschatological act of the merciful God who will enforce his promises to his people out of his own will. This remains as a difference between Israel and the Gentiles, even at the time of the eschatological completion. This does not mean, however, that all Israel, according to Paul, will be saved by passing off Christ, and it also does not mean that Israel can be saved by passing off those from the nations who are saved by faith in Christ alone. When God will accomplish his promises to Israel, he acts as the one and only God of Israel who has revealed his salvific will toward all humankind—Jews and Gentiles—in Jesus Christ. That is how Paul sees it, the apostle to the Gentiles from Israel.

CONCLUSION

For Paul, the Israelite and the apostle to the Gentiles, every hope for eschatological salvation is rooted in the biblical promises. In Rom 9–11, Paul employs the fundamental consequences of his proclamation of the gospel in view of challenges resulting from his mission to the Gentiles. To his primarily Gentile audience in Rome, he declares the trustworthiness of God towards his promises in favor of Israel the fundamental basis for any belief in God. Therefore, Paul points even Gentiles, who have come to faith in Jesus Christ, to the promises to Israel as fundamental for their own "Christian" faith.

In his argument in Rom 9–11, Paul repeatedly refers to himself as Israelite and apostle to the Gentiles. This biographical fact has theological importance, for Paul sees himself as eschatological agent in the events when God is enforcing his salutary will over against Israel and the Gentiles. Paul finds a solution for the urgent problem of Israelites who refuse to believe in Jesus Christ by developing a scenario of how God is pursuing his aim to save all human beings, Jews and Gentiles. In his mandate to proclaim the gospel to the Gentiles, Paul identifies a means by which God is going to entice his own people. Thus, Paul's Gentile mission and his hope for Israel's salvation become parts of the same course of events.

The basic elements of Paul's hope for Israel and the Gentiles are rooted in biblical and early Jewish traditions about Israel and the nations at the end of time. Put in that context, Paul's particular ideas about the eschatological future prove to be shaped by such biblical traditions on the one hand, but on the other hand are fundamentally based on the faith that God has revealed his eschatological intent to save every human being—Jew and Gentile—in Jesus Christ.

NOTES

1. I have provided a thorough interpretation of Rom 9–11 in my habilitation thesis. See my *Heidenapostel aus Israel. Die jüdische Identität des Paulus nach ihrer Darstellung in seinen Briefen*, WUNT 62 (Tübingen: Mohr Siebeck, 1992), 136–78. A more recent collection of essays on these three chapters of Romans is *Between Gospel and Election. Explorations in the Interpretation of Romans 9–11*, ed. F. Wilk and J. R. Wagner. WUNT 257 (Tübingen: Mohr Siebeck, 2010), including my own "'Nicht alle aus Israel sind Israel' (Röm 9,6b). Röm 9–11 als Zeugnis paulinischer Anthropologie," 433–62. My argument in this chapter is based on the exegesis presented there in more detail.

2. Karl Olav Sandnes, *Paul—one of the prophets? A contribution to the apostle's self-understanding*. WUNT 2.43 (Tübingen: Mohr Siebeck, 1991).

3. Eve-Marie Becker ("Autobiographisches bei Paulus. Aspekte und Anliegen," in *Biographie und Persönlichkeit des Paulus*, ed. Eve-Marie Baker and P. Pilhofer, WUNT 187 [Tübingen: Mohr Siebeck, 2005], 67–87), completely ignores all references to Paul's identity as an Israelite in his letters, but his self-designation as "apostle to the Gentiles" in Rom 11:13 (introduced by εἰμι ἐγώ!) as well.

4. See my Niebuhr, *Heidenapostel aus Israel*, 167–71.

5. See my Niebuhr, *Heidenapostel aus Israel*, 163–65.

6. See my Niebuhr, *Heidenapostel aus Israel*, 163–67.

7. See my Niebuhr, *Heidenapostel aus Israel*, 171–75.

8. Cf. the highly emotional diction in 9:1–5.

9. A positive answer to this question has been the assumption of Francis Watson, *Paul, Judaism and the Gentiles: A Sociological Approach*, SNTS.MS 56 (Cambridge: Cambridge University Press, 1986), 88–105 (revised and expanded edition: *Paul, Judaism, and the Gentiles: Beyond the New Perspective* [Grand Rapids, MI: Eerdmans, 2007], 163–91); cf. also William S. Campbell, "The Addressees of Paul's Letter to the Romans: Assemblies of God in House Churches and Synagogues?," in *Between Gospel and Election*, 171–95.

10. For my own interpretation of Rom 1–8, see my "Menschenbild, Gottesverständnis und Ethik. Zwei paulinische Argumentationen (Röm 1,18–2,29; 8,1–30)," in *Anthropologie und Ethik im Frühjudentum und im Neuen*

Testament. Wechselseitige Wahrnehmungen, Internationales Symposium in Verbindung mit dem Projekt Corpus Judaeo-Hellenisticum Novi Testamenti (CJHNT) 17–20, Mai 2012, Heidelberg, ed. M. Konradt and E. Schläpfer, WUNT 322 (Tübingen: Mohr Siebeck, 2014), 147–58 (139–61).

11. Rom 9:22–24; see my *Heidenapostel aus Israel*, 150–51. See also Beverly Roberts Gaventa, "On the Calling-into-Being of Israel: Romans 9:6–29," in *Between Gospel and Election*, 255–69.

12. See my *Heidenapostel aus Israel*, 154–58; "'Nicht alle aus Israel sind Israel,'" 437–38.

13. Rom 11:13–31. Cf. William S. Campbell, *Paul and the Creation of Christian Identity* (London, U.K., and New York, NY: T&T Clark, 2008), 121–39; Mark D. Nanos, "'Broken Branches': A Pauline Metaphor Gone Awry? (Romans 11:11–24)," in *Between Gospel and Election*, 339–76 (also in, *Reading Romans within Judaism: Collected Essays* [Eugene, OR: Cascade, 2018], 112–52); Nanos, *The Mystery of Romans: The Jewish Context of Paul's Letter* (Minneapolis, MN: Fortress Press, 1996), 75–84.

14. For the whole argument, see Watson, *Paul, Judaism, and the Gentiles*, 301–43 (the whole section on Rom 9–11 is thoroughly reworked in the revised and expanded edition of 2007).

15. Cf. Campbell, "The Addressees of Paul's Letter to the Romans," 183–85.

16. Cf. Michael Wolter, *Der Brief an die Römer. Teilband 2: Röm 9–16*. EKK VI/2 (Ostfildern: Patmos Verlag, Göttingen: Vandenhoeck & Ruprecht, 2019), 25–43; Arland J. Hultgren, *Paul's Letter to the Romans: A Commentary* (Grand Rapids: Eerdmans, 2011), 353–60.

17. See my *Heidenapostel aus Israel*, 160–61; cf. Hans Dieter Betz, "Geschichte und Selbstopfer. Zur Interpretation von Römer 9,1–5," *Paulinische Theologie und Religionsgeschichte. Gesammelte Aufsätze V* (Tübingen: Mohr Siebeck, 2009), 71–86.

18. See my "'Nicht alle aus Israel sind Israel'", 433–38.

19. See my *Heidenapostel aus Israel*, 142–48.

20. Cf. Stephen Westerholm, "Paul and the Law in Romans 9–11," *Law and Ethics in Early Judaism and the New Testament*, WUNT 383 (Tübingen: Mohr Siebeck, 2017), 265–88. For recent debates on the phrase τέλος νόμου see the excursus in Wolter, *Romans*, 107–12.

21. See my *Heidenapostel aus Israel*, 154–56.

22. 10:2f, cf. 1:18–2:29!

23. Cf. 10:4–13.

24. Cf. Friedrich Avemarie, "Israels rätselhafter Ungehorsam. Römer 10 als Anomalie eines von Gott provozierten Unglaubens," in *Between Gospel and Election*, 299–320.

25. See my "'Nicht alle aus Israel sind Israel,'" 437–38.

26. See my *Heidenapostel aus Israel*, 167–71.

27. Cf. Andreas Lindemann, "Paulus und Elia. Zur Argumentation in Röm 11,1–12," in *Logos—Logik—Lyrik* (FS Klaus Haacker), ed. V. A. Lehnert and U. Rüsen-Weinhold (Leipzig: Evangelische Verlagsanstalt, 2007), 201–18.

28. Cf. Niebuhr, *Heidenapostel aus Israel*, 171–75.
29. Cf. Michael F. Bird, *An Anomalous Jew: Paul among Jews, Greeks, and Romans* (Grand Rapids, MI: Eerdmans, 2016), 69–107 ("Paul, Apostle to the Gentiles and Jews?").
30. Cf. Dieter Sänger, "'Er wird die Gottlosigkeit von Israel entfernen' (Röm 11,26). Kontinuität und Wandel in den Israelaussagen des Apostels Paulus," in *Between Gospel and Election*, 121–46.
31. Cf. Campbell, "The Addressees of Paul's Letter to the Romans," 192–95.
32. Cf. Richard Hays, *Echoes of Scripture in the Letters of Paul* (New Haven, CT, and London, U.K.: Yale University Press, 1989), 34–83; Florian Wilk, *Die Bedeutung des Jesajabuches für Paulus*, FRLANT 179 (Göttingen: Vandenhoeck & Ruprecht, 1998), passim; Robert B. Foster, *Renaming Abraham's Children: Election, Ethnicity, and the Interpretation of Scripture in Romans 9*, WUNT 2.421 (Tübingen: Mohr Siebeck, 2016), 151–238.
33. Cf. Wolfgang Kraus, *Das Volk Gottes. Zur Grundlegung der Ekklesiologie bei Paulus*, WUNT 85 (Tübingen: Mohr Siebeck, 1996), 16–110; Terence T. Donaldson, *Paul and the Gentiles: Remapping the Apostle's Convictional World* (Minneapolis, MN: Fortress Press, 1997), 51–78.
34. For an anthropological interpretation of Rom 9–11 see my "'Nicht alle aus Israel sind Israel,'" 433–44.
35. Cf. for the other two traditions, see my "'Nicht alle aus Israel sind Israel,'" 450–61.
36. Cf., e.g., Isa 14:26; 40:15–17; Jer 10:25; 30:11; 46:28; Ps 9:6–9, 16–21; for a more detailed interpretation see my "'Nicht alle aus Israel sind Israel,'" 445–46.
37. Cf. Deut 7:1–6; Exod 34:10–16.
38. Cf. Isa 2:2–5; Mic 4:1–5; Jer 16:19–21; Zech 8:20–23; 14:16; Isa 56:3–7.
39. Cf. Isa 66:23; Ps 22:28–32; 47:10; 86:9–10.
40. Critical Greek edition: Johannes Geffcken, *Die Oracula Sibyllina*, GCS 8 (Leipzig: J. C. Hinrichs'sche Buchhandlung, 1902); translations according to John J. Collins, "Sibylline Oracles (Second Century B.C.–Seventh Century A.D.)," in *The Old Testament Pseudepigrapha, Vol. 1*, ed. James H. Charlesworth (London: Darton Longman & Todd Ltd., 1983), 317–472. For critical discussion on introductory questions, see Rieuwerd Buitenwerf, *Book III of the Sibylline Oracles and Its Social Setting. With an Introduction, Translation, and Commentary*, SVTP 17 (Leiden, Boston: Brill, 2003); John J. Collins, "The Third Sibyl Revisited," *Jewish Cult and Hellenistic Culture. Essays on the Jewish Encounter with Hellenism and Roman Rule.* JSJ.S 100 (Leiden, Boston: Brill, 2005), 82–98; Albert-Marie Denis, *Introduction à la littérature religieuse Judéo-Hellénistique, Tome II (Pseudépigraphes de l'Ancien Testament)* (Turnhout: Brepols, 2000), 947–92.
41. *Sib. Or.* 3.167–195.
42. *Sib. Or.* 3.266–294.
43. Cf. *Sib. Or.* 3.573–600.
44. Cf. *Sib. Or.* 3.702–703.
45. *Sib. Or.* 3.715–726, cf. *Sib. Or.* 3.767–780. For the view on the temple in *Sib. Or.* 3 cf. Andrew Chester, "The Sibyl and the Temple," in *Templum Amicitiae.*

Essays on the Second Temple (FS E. Bammel), ed. W. Horbury, JSNT.S 48 (Sheffield: JSOT Press, 1991), 37–69.

46. Critical edition of the Greek text in *Flavius Josephus, De Bello Judaico/Der Jüdische Krieg. Griechisch und Deutsch*, ed. O. Michel and O. Bauernfeind. 3 vols. (München: Kösel, 1959–1969); translations according to H. St. J. Thackeray, *Josephus in Nine Volumes, II: The Jewish War, Books I-III, III: The Jewish War, Books IV–VII. With an English Translation* (London: William Heinemann Ltd., Cambridge, MA: Harvard University Press, 1927/1928).

47. Cf. also *B.J.* 7.359.

48. Cf. Ezek 40–48.

49. For an interpretation of Josephus's overall view on theologically interpreted history and its text-pragmatic intentions cf. John M. G. Barclay, *Jews in the Mediterranean Diaspora. From Alexander to Trajan (323 BCE–117 CE)* (Edinburgh: T&T Clark, 1996), 351–56.

50. For a primarily parenetical intention of *Sib. Or.* 3 cf., see my *Gesetz und Paränese. Katechismusartige Weisungsreihen in der frühjüdischen Literatur*, WUNT 2.28 (Tübingen: Mohr Siebeck, 1987), 169–85. For Josephus with regard to *Contra Apionem* 2.190–219 see op. cit., 31–72.

51. Cf. the interpretation of Rom 9–11 in John M. G. Barclay, *Paul and the Gift* (Grand Rapids, MI: Eerdmans, 2015), 520–61, who identifies the theological coherence in these chapters in "the fact that God's mercy (or grace) is given without regard to worth, and thus forms the creative root of God's purposes for the world" (521).

52. See my *Heidenapostel aus Israel*, 143–44.

53. See my *Heidenapostel aus Israel*, 150–51.

54. See my *Heidenapostel aus Israel*, 145–46, 151–54.

55. See my *Heidenapostel aus Israel*, 152–53.

56. See my *Heidenapostel aus Israel*, 146–47.

57. The verb πιστεύειν is missing here.

BIBLIOGRAPHY

Avemarie, Friedrich. "Israels rätselhafter Ungehorsam. Römer 10 als Anomalie eines von Gott provozierten Unglaubens." In *Between Gospel and Election. Explorations in the Interpretation of Romans 9–11*, edited by F. Wilk and J. R. Wagner, 299–320. WUNT 257. Tübingen: Mohr Siebeck, 2010.

Barclay, John M. G. *Jews in the Mediterranean Diaspora. From Alexander to Trajan (323 BCE–117 CE)*. Edinburgh: T&T Clark, 1996.

———. *Paul and the Gift*. Grand Rapids, MI: Eerdmans, 2015.

Becker, Eve-Marie. "Autobiographisches bei Paulus. Aspekte und Anliegen." In *Biographie und Persönlichkeit des Paulus*, edited by Eve-Marie Becker and Peter Pilhofer, 67–87. WUNT 187. Tübingen: Mohr Siebeck, 2005.

Betz, Hans Dieter. "Geschichte und Selbstopfer. Zur Interpretation von Römer 9,1–5. *Paulinische Theologie und Religionsgeschichte. Gesammelte Aufsätze V*, 71–86. Tübingen: Mohr Siebeck, 2009.
Bird, Michael F. *An Anomalous Jew: Paul among Jews, Greeks, and Romans*. Grand Rapids, MI: Eerdmans, 2016.
Buitenwerf, Rieuwerd. *Book III of the Sibylline Oracles and Its Social Setting. With an Introduction, Translation, and Commentary*. SVTP 17. Leiden, Boston: Brill, 2003.
Campbell, William S. "The Addressees of Paul's Letter to the Romans: Assemblies of God in House Churches and Synagogues?" In *Between Gospel and Election. Explorations in the Interpretation of Romans 9–11*, edited by Florian Wilk and J. Ross Wagner, 171–95. WUNT 257. Tübingen: Mohr Siebeck, 2010.
———. *Paul and the Creation of Christian Identity*. London, U.K., and New York, NY: T&T Clark, 2008.
Chester, Andrew. "The Sibyl and the Temple." In *Templum Amicitiae. Essays on the Second Temple* (FS E. Bammel), edited by William Horbury, 37–69. JSNT.S 48. Sheffield: JSOT Press, 1991.
Collins, John J. "Sibylline Oracles (Second Century BC.–Seventh Century A.D.)." In *The Old Testament Pseudepigrapha, Vol. 1*, edited by James H. Charlesworth, 317–472. London: Darton Longman & Todd Ltd., 1983.
———. "The Third Sibyl Revisited." *Jewish Cult and Hellenistic Culture. Essays on the Jewish Encounter with Hellenism and Roman Rule*, 82–98. JSJ.S 100. Leiden, Boston: Brill, 2005.
Denis, Albert-Marie. *Introduction à la littérature religieuse Judéo-Hellénistique, Tome II (Pseudépigraphes de l'Ancien Testament)*. Turnhout: Brepols, 2000.
Donaldson, Terence T. *Paul and the Gentiles: Remapping the Apostle's Convictional World*. Minneapolis, MN: Fortress Press, 1997.
Foster, Robert B. *Renaming Abraham's Children: Election, Ethnicity, and the Interpretation of Scripture in Romans 9*. WUNT 2.421. Tübingen: Mohr Siebeck, 2016.
Gaventa, Beverly Roberts. "On the Calling-into-Being of Israel: Romans 9:6–29." In *Between Gospel and Election. Explorations in the Interpretation of Romans 9–11*, edited by Florian Wilk and J. Ross Wagner, 255–69. WUNT 257. Tübingen: Mohr Siebeck, 2010.
Geffcken, Johannes. *Die Oracula Sibyllina*. GCS 8. Leipzig: J. C. Hinrichs'sche Buchhandlung, 1902.
Hays, Richard. *Echoes of Scripture in the Letters of Paul*. New Haven, CT, and London, U.K.: Yale University Press, 1989.
Hultgren, Arland J. *Paul's Letter to the Romans: A Commentary*. Grand Rapids, MI: Eerdmans, 2011.
Kraus, Wolfgang. *Das Volk Gottes. Zur Grundlegung der Ekklesiologie bei Paulus*. WUNT 85. Tübingen: Mohr Siebeck, 1996.
Lindemann, Andreas. "Paulus und Elia. Zur Argumentation in Röm 11,1–12." In *Logos–Logik–Lyrik* (FS Klaus Haacker), edited by Volker A. Lehnert and Ulrich Rüsen-Weinhold, 201–18. Leipzig: Evangelische Verlagsanstalt, 2007.

Michel, Otto, and Otto Bauernfeind, eds. *Flavius Josephus, De Bello Judaico/Der Jüdische Krieg. Griechisch und Deutsch*. 3 vols. München: Kösel, 1959–1969.

Nanos, Mark D. "'Broken Branches': A Pauline Metaphor Gone Awry? (Romans 11:11–24)." In *Between Gospel and Election. Explorations in the Interpretation of Romans 9–11*, edited by Florian Wilk and J. Ross Wagner, 339–76. WUNT 257. Tübingen: Mohr Siebeck, 2010 (also in *Reading Romans within Judaism: Collected Essays*, 112–52 [Eugene, OR: Cascade, 2018]).

———. *The Mystery of Romans: The Jewish Context of Paul's Letter*. Minneapolis, MN: Fortress Press, 1996.

Niebuhr, Karl-Wilhelm. *Gesetz und Paränese. Katechismusartige Weisungsreihen in der frühjüdischen Literatur*. WUNT 2.28. Tübingen: Mohr Siebeck, 1987.

———. *Heidenapostel aus Israel. Die jüdische Identität des Paulus nach ihrer Darstellung in seinen Briefen*. WUNT 62. Tübingen: Mohr Siebeck, 1992.

———. "Menschenbild, Gottesverständnis und Ethik. Zwei paulinische Argumentationen (Röm 1,18–2,29; 8,1–30)." In *Anthropologie und Ethik im Frühjudentum und im Neuen Testament. Wechselseitige Wahrnehmungen*. Internationales Symposium in Verbindung mit dem Projekt Corpus Judaeo-Hellenisticum Novi Testamenti (CJHNT) 17.–20. Mai 2012, Heidelberg. Edited by Matthias Konradt and Esther Schläpfer, 139–61. WUNT 322. Tübingen: Mohr Siebeck, 2014.

———. "'Nicht alle aus Israel sind Israel' (Röm 9,6b). Röm 9–11 als Zeugnis paulinischer Anthropologie." In *Between Gospel and Election. Explorations in the Interpretation of Romans 9–11*, edited by Florian Wilk and J. Ross Wagner, 433–62. WUNT 257. Tübingen: Mohr Siebeck, 2010.

Sänger, Dieter. "'Er wird die Gottlosigkeit von Israel entfernen' (Röm 11,26). Kontinuität und Wandel in den Israelaussagen des Apostels Paulus." In *Between Gospel and Election. Explorations in the Interpretation of Romans 9–11*, edited by Florian Wilk and J. Ross Wagner, 121–46. WUNT 257. Tübingen: Mohr Siebeck, 2010.

Sandnes, Karl Olav. *Paul—One of the Prophets? A Contribution to the Apostle's Self-understanding*. WUNT 2.43. Tübingen: Mohr Siebeck, 1991.

Thackeray, H. St. J. *Josephus in Nine Volumes, II: The Jewish War, Books I–III. With an English Translation*. London: William Heinemann Ltd., Cambridge, MA: Harvard University Press, 1927.

———. *Josephus in Nine Volumes, III: The Jewish War, Books IV–VII. With an English Translation*. London: William Heinemann Ltd., Cambridge, MA: Harvard University Press, 1927.

Watson, Francis. *Paul, Judaism and the Gentiles: A Sociological Approach*. SNTS. MS 56. Cambridge: Cambridge University Press, 1986; revised and expanded edition: *Paul, Judaism, and the Gentiles: Beyond the New Perspective*. Grand Rapids, MI: Eerdmans, 2007.

Westerholm, Stephen. "Paul and the Law in Romans 9–11." *Law and Ethics in Early Judaism and the New Testament*, 265–88. WUNT 383. Tübingen: Mohr Siebeck, 2017.

Wilk, Florian. *Die Bedeutung des Jesajabuches für Paulus*. FRLANT 179. Göttingen: Vandenhoeck & Ruprecht, 1998.

Wolter, Michael. *Der Brief an die Römer. Teilband 2: Röm 9–16*. EKK VI/2. Ostfildern: Patmos Verlag, Göttingen: Vandenhoeck & Ruprecht, 2019.

Chapter Sixteen

Pesher Concerning Righteousness (Romans 10:5–13) in Relation to the Response of Jews and Gentiles to the Gospel

František Ábel

INTRODUCTION

Among the later Second Temple Jewish eschatological conceptions, there come to the fore the notions of the end-time redemption of Israel related to messianic ideas.[1] This matter largely concerns the religious status and identity of the *ethnē* (ἔθνη), the non-Jewish nations (gentiles). Given the ambiguity of these notions, an important question arises about the precise status of the non-Jewish participants in Jewish restoration theology: Will they be fully incorporated into Israel as end-time proselytes, or do they continue to exist as non-Jews alongside Israel, or does some other version apply? Paul's message in Romans, chapters 9–11, makes an instructive and at the same time unique example of these eschatological concepts. The goal of this chapter is an examination of the *pesher* concerning divine righteousness in Romans 10:5–13, in the context of Paul's own notion of global salvation, which he describes as a "mystery."[2]

When discussing Second Temple Jewish eschatological notions of the end-time redemption of Israel, it is observable that all these concepts reflect the experiences of the Jewish population with non-Jewish populations. Jews[3] living within the first-century Greco-Roman world interacted daily with non-Jewish people, while the *modus vivendi* varied depending on the local geopolitical situation bearing upon the relationships between Jewish and non-Jewish people—"those of the nations."[4] As is well-known, the Jewish communities in the Diaspora had in many cases achieved a comfortable coexistence with the local non-Jewish majority urban population.[5] However, the situation in the territories with a majority Jewish population, primarily in Judea, especially at the turn of the era but also during the first century CE, was more complicated, often resulting in tensions and conflicts, and finally also in the first open revolt. The worsening situation in Galilee and Judea was increasingly reflected in the Diaspora, which resulted in the violent hostility of local populations toward Jews. Concerning these tensions, Josephus and Philo mention several instances of anti-Jewish riots and violence perpetrated on Jewish urban populations at the outbreak of the first revolt: in Alexandria (Philo, *In Flaccum* and *Legatio ad Gaium*, Josephus, *Ant.* 18.8.1), Caesarea (*J.W.* 2.18.1; 7.8.7), in Ptolemais (*J.W.* 2.18.5), in Damascus, (*J.W.* 2.20.2; cf. 7.8.7), in Gaza and Anthedon (*J.W.* 2.18.1), in Ascalon (*J.W.* 2.18.5), Hippus and Gadara (*J.W.* 2.18.1, 5), and in Scythopolis (*J.W.* 2.18.3–4; 7.8.7; *Life* 6).[6]

Importantly, all these reflections also had to be related to the long-anticipated fulfillment of God's promises of final redemption and salvation of Israel. In places where Jews lived in proximity to non-Jewish nations (gentiles), they had to consider, among other issues, the status of these nations before the God of Israel—the one, universal deity, the only God.[7] This reflection drives us to the specific theological concept of the eschatological redemption of Israel, with participation by the non-Jewish nations.[8] This matter largely concerns the religious status and identity[9] of the non-Jews in Jewish restoration theology. Notions of the eschatological redemption of Israel are related, especially among Pharisaic groups, to the concept of coming of the Messiah, including the last judgment. Since the messianic idea is a key element of Paul's message, it is possible to work on the assumption that eschatological notions concentrating on messianism were well-known to most of, if not to all, Jewish groups or schools of that time, especially those in Judea and Galilee.[10]

Moreover, these important questions are at work in Paul's message as a whole, primarily in Romans, especially in chapters 9–11, which make a specific example of this eschatological concept in the later Second Temple period. The goal of this chapter is to examine one of the important pericopes within that section, particularly the text of 10:5–13 with its *pesher* concerning divine righteousness, a strong support of Paul's argumentation in the epistle serving the purpose of convincingly and understandably describing "the triumph of divine righteousness in the gospel's mission to Israel and the Gentiles."[11]

BRIEF OUTLINE OF THE PERICOPE 9:1–11:36

First, we have to remind ourselves that the text I am focusing on in this study (Rom 10:5–13) is a part of the more broadly outlined section of the epistle, namely, Rom 9:1–11:36; this is not an appendix to the key theological exposition of Romans in Chapters 1–8, the subject of which is the doctrine of justification by faith, but rather is a key section of the epistle as a whole, or, as James Dunn aptly remarks, "the real climax of Paul's attempt to understand the place of Jew and Gentile within the purpose of God."[12] In other words, in this substantial section Paul maintains God's faithfulness and the irrevocability of the divine gifts and calling of Israel, and tries to understand, to the best of human abilities, God's purposes within the history of Israel and non-Jewish nations.

Robert Jewett calls this section "the triumph of divine righteousness in the gospel's mission to Israel and the Gentiles," and counts it as the third of four proofs of the thesis about the Gospel—as the powerful embodiment of the righteousness of God—and about its implications for the Roman congregations, with the central issue being "the faithfulness and reliability of God."[13] In my opinion, it is one of the most important features of Paul's message, stemming from his continual abiding the principles of Second Temple Jewish monotheism. The God of Israel, the only God, is and always remains faithful and reliable in relation to Israel. God's gifts of grace and the vocation of Israel are irrevocable (ἀμεταμέλητα γὰρ τὰ χαρίσματα καὶ ἡ κλῆσις τοῦ θεοῦ. [11:29]). Thus, Paul seeks out the true meaning and significance of God's vocation of Israel concerning the non-Jewish nations (*ethnē*).[14] After all, he was convinced that it is found in God's paradoxical acting in the Messiah Jesus, the outcome and implications of which Paul calls the "mystery" (Οὐ γὰρ θέλω ὑμᾶς ἀγνοεῖν, ἀδελφοί, τὸ μυστήριον τοῦτο, ἵνα μὴ ἦτε [παρ'] ἑαυτοῖς φρόνιμοι, ὅτι πώρωσις ἀπὸ μέρους τῷ Ἰσραὴλ γέγονεν ἄχρι οὗ τὸ πλήρωμα τῶν ἐθνῶν εἰσέλθῃ [11:25]). For Paul, this means that the gospel is about the salvation of Israel as well as gentiles. However, the salvation of the gentiles is not a side effect or consequence of Israel's redemption, which was to happen first (in its totality), but quite the opposite. First, the full number of the gentiles will come in, and only then, and in such a manner, will all Israel be saved.[15]

The structure of this part of the epistle (9:1–11:36) is well-worked out and elaborated.[16] First, Paul pays attention to the conundrum of the unbelief of most of Israel in the gospel and expresses his sorrow at it (9:1–5). Then, he presents an argument for Israel and the righteousness of divine election, followed by a diatribe refuting objections (9:6–29). In 9:30–10:4, Paul makes another diatribe on the failure to obey God's righteousness due to falsely directed zeal. Next is the *pesher* concerning righteousness, the goal of which is to confirm God's righteousness by faith (10:5–13), the focus of this chapter. In the next passage (10:14–21), Paul introduces a citation-chain concerning the gospel he is announcing among the gentiles, which is still being rejected by most of Israel. The content of the first ten verses of the eleventh chapter (11:1–10) represents another diatribe with the midrash concerning the status of Israel, which is followed by another diatribe with an allegory about the purpose of Israel's error concerning the gospel (11:11–24). The final part of the chapter (11:25–36) is dedicated to disclosure and interpretation of the mystery of universal salvation (vv. 25–32), which is followed by a hymn on God's majesty (vv. 33–36).[17]

In the following section, I concern myself only with the pericope 10:5–13, focusing primarily on the *pesher* concerning God's righteousness, in order to examine Paul's intent and goal by using it in terms of his own notion of universal salvation, Jews as well as the *ethnē*.

10:5–13: *PESHER* CONCERNING RIGHTEOUSNESS

Regardless of the answer to the question of whether a new pericope begins at v. 5 or at v. 14, I agree with the suggestion that vv. 5–13 make up a single pericope, since they provide a scriptural continuation of the theme of righteousness, about which Paul also wrote in 9:30–31 and 10:3–4.[18] Paul continually works on the assumption that all his arguments, in this place as well as elsewhere, have to be proven and attested by the Scriptures. Here, Paul uses in combination a classical Hellenistic rhetorical tool, the *prosopopeia*,[19] and a Hebrew *pesher*,[20] setting Lev 18:5 in contrast with compound citations from five biblical texts: Deut 8:14 (and 9:4); 30:11–14; Ps 106:26 (107:26 [BH]); Isa 28:16; and Joel 3:5.[21]

Traditionally—mainly within Protestant circles, based on the Reformers' uniformly insisted teaching that human depravity made it impossible for people to be saved by keeping the precepts of God's law—i.e., by doing what God commands; but solely by accepting in humility before God, in faith, what God works on our behalf in Jesus Christ, which is the "good news"—this section (10:5–13) is considered to be a theological "law"/"gospel" antithesis, as, for example Douglas Moo states, "as Paul contrasts the righteousness that is based on 'doing' the law (v. 5) with the righteousness that is based on faith (vv. 6–13)."[22] This approach to Paul's argumentation is still maintained by the majority of scholars.[23]

However, I am convinced that this interpretation is false, one still under the strong influence of a traditional interpretation of Paul's message as a "law"/"gospel" antithetical incongruity. Of course, we would agree with the antithetical character of these words of Paul's as such; however, the core of the antithesis lays elsewhere. It is Paul's focus on the addressees and their status and identity within God's universal salvific purposes that plays a key role and thus must be the basis of a proper interpretation of this antithesis. In other words, we should ask: Why is Paul using this antithesis, in what context and goal? And why does he use the *pesher* in this regard? He is primarily and still concerned about the divine vocation of Israel and her role toward the gentiles, the *ethnē*, and thereby also about Paul's Jewish divine vocation. Paul constantly works with Jewish restoration theology, which also includes the other (non-Jewish) nations (*ethnē*), and is convinced that his mission among the gentiles constitutes a fulfilling of Israel's divine vocation.[24] As Mark Nanos rightly remarks concerning the theme of the "broken branches" in 11:11–24, the problem is that "some Israelites are, according to Paul, more concerned with demonstrating the righteousness of Israel to the nations than they are with God using righteous Israel to gather in the nations as co-participants in the people of God, apart from becoming members of Israel (cf. chs. 9–10)."[25]

Now, let us proceed to the particular *pesher*, focusing on two quotations, or speeches, interacting in its content.[26] The introduction is formed by Moses's words from Lev 18:5, which are followed by the speech of a personified "righteousness by faith" speaking in the next five biblical quotations. As a whole, it is a well-worked out part of the epistle that serves as the basis for Paul's argumentation about the nature and goal of God's righteousness in universal perspective. Owing to space limitations, I shall only focus more closely on two, in my opinion, key quotations in this *pesher*, namely Lev 18:5 and Deut 30:11–14.

Lev 18:5 — First speech (v. 5)

At the beginning of the pericope, Paul cites the lawgiver Moses (Lev 18:5), with the crucial text for the self-understanding of Jewish identity, and then he goes on to interpret five subsequent texts, as Jewett aptly notes, "in a typical rabbinic fashion."[27]

> [5] Μωϋσῆς γὰρ γράφει τὴν δικαιοσύνην τὴν ἐκ [τοῦ] νόμου ὅτι *ὁ ποιήσας αὐτὰ ἄνθρωπος ζήσεται ἐν αὐτοῖς.*
>
> καὶ φυλάξεσθε πάντα τὰ προστάγματά μου καὶ πάντα τὰ κρίματά μου καὶ ποιήσετε αὐτά ἃ ποιήσας ἄνθρωπος ζήσεται ἐν αὐτοῖς ἐγὼ κύριος ὁ θεὸς ὑμῶν (Lev 18:5 [LXX])

First, we have to deal with the question of how this text was understood and practiced in Second Temple Jewishness: whether as an individual or as community, and what Paul's intent is in using it here. Despite the variedness of Second Temple Judaism, the relationship of Israel to the Mosaic law (the Torah) can be characterized properly and at the same time aptly by this very text: καὶ φυλάξεσθε πάντα τὰ προστάγματά μου καὶ πάντα τὰ κρίματά μου καὶ ποιήσετε αὐτά ἃ ποιήσας ἄνθρωπος ζήσεται ἐν αὐτοῖς ἐγὼ κύριος ὁ θεὸς ὑμῶν.[28]

These words indicate God's mercy as well as the obligation laid upon Israel, and set forth the most essential ideas for the life of God's people. Thus, this text and its historical interpretation leads us to an important insight about the Jewish way of life: to an understanding that the text stands in direct relationship with the daily life of the community of believers. It is not about a matter of mindlessly obeying God's commandments in order to achieve salvation by doing what is written in the law. The primary understanding of these words is, rather, to be mindful of the responsibility and consequences stemming from God's commandments toward Israel, God's chosen people. Since God's choice of Israel to become his people ("*a priestly kingdom and holy nation*"; Exod 19:6), is considered to be a manifestation of God's love and mercy, the status and privilege of Israel imply the obligation to be a "light to the nations" (Isa 42:6–7; 49:6); since the God of Israel is the one and only God, all people belong to him. In the end, it is about Israel's divine vocation and its fulfillment in worldwide perspective.

Most of Paul's Jewish contemporaries understood this vocation and role of Israel toward the gentiles primarily as being a charge to keep and teach the precepts of the law of Moses—the "light" given to Israel—and thus to serve as an exemplary witness to God's power and wisdom revealed to the whole world (Ps 119:105; Isa 2:2–5; 51:4–5; cf. Sir 24:23–24; Wis 18:4; see also Philo, *Somn.* 1.175–178; *Spec.* 1.320–323).[29] Paul does not deny that the Torah is a "light" for the other (non-Jewish) nations; however, he understands it differently. Paul is aware of the universal human subjection to sin, and thus of the universal human inability to keep all the precepts of the Torah.[30] Even Israel, which has the Torah and thus enjoys substantial epistemological privilege, does not always and everywhere respond rightly to the Torah's requirements (cf. Rom 2:9–13, 17–24; 3:3–8, 9–20; 9:4–5, 11:11–31).[31] Therefore, Paul is convinced that the Mosaic law serves to testify to the gospel of Christ, since Christ's crucifixion and resurrection is considered to be the goal, and thus also the fulfillment, of the law (Rom 10:4). Paul identifies himself as the "servant of the Lord" (Isa 40–55; especially 49:1–7), and the "light to the nations" (Isa 42:6–7; 49:6). He has a "zeal" for God's gospel, preaching and calling the addressees of his message to do likewise, to emulate his "good zeal." For Paul, then, "Jewish identity and vocation were expressed primarily in preaching the gospel of Christ to the Gentiles".[32]

However, at this place (v. 5), Paul uses this quotation as characteristic of Jewish identity (cf. 9:31–32; 10:3), a typical expression of Israel's awareness of her obligation and promise under the covenant (Deut 4:1; 5:32–33; 8:1; 16:20; 22:7; 30:15–20; Neh 9:29; Ezek 18:9, 17, 19, 21; 20:11, 13, 21; 33:15–16; *Pss. Sol.* 14:2–3; 4 Ezra 14:30; cf. Luke 10:28).[33] Paul is doing so intentionally, setting the identity in contrast to the different status and identity of the non-Jewish Christ believers in Rome. Paul does not intend to characterize Moses' law as that of the old epoch, now superseded by Christ.[34] Rather, Paul is merely explaining what God's acting in Jesus means for Jews as well as gentile nations. In this regard, I hold the view that "the righteousness which is from the law," which "Moses writes about," is the same as the righteousness which is available in Christ through faith (v. 6a), since Christ is the goal and fulfillment of the law (v. 4).[35] There is nothing to indicate that Paul wishes to challenge the validity of his fellow Jews' ability to live by the law, nor to disparage the Mosaic law as such. Paul is simply restating the traditional Jewish proposition of Israel's obligation to live by the law. In this way, he prepares the stage for the *pesher*, proving that the law itself points to faith in Christ, who is its goal and fulfillment.[36] As Mark Nanos remarks in this connection: "Paul himself wishes to do the Law, agrees with it in his inner self, and finds in Christ the victory enabling him to fulfill Torah; he expects the same of those whom he addresses (7:7–8:4; 10:4; 13:8–10)."[37] Thus, according to Paul, the problem lies not in any incompatibility of the law and the gospel, nor it is that Christ has superseded the Mosaic law.[38] The problem is elsewhere, located with some Israelites who failed to understand properly the purpose of God's righteousness and who are "zealous" for God, but in a wrong way (10:2), as Nanos aptly claims:

> Thus, according to Paul, some Israelites are being jealous for God in the wrong way (10:2), in ignorance that the righteousness/justice of God is pointing to the inclusion in Christ of members from the other nations alongside Israelites without discrimination of status according to whether one is Israelite or non-Israelite. This equal access to the blessing of being declared among the righteous ones must now be recognized to be a present reality (10:8–12). It must not be overlooked that Paul's stated goal is to provoke such fellow Israelites to get back on track, that is, to be restored (10:1) to their rightful role as heralds to the nations (10:14–11:15).[39]

All of this is crucial for a proper understanding of the whole pericope, including the next words, a so-called second speech, a personified "righteousness by faith," "'speaking' the next five citations"[40] among which the quotation from Deut 30:11–14 comes to the fore.

Righteousness by Faith — Second Speech (vv. 6–13)

Now, Paul changes speaker from Moses to the personified "righteousness by faith" (vv. 6–13). Concerning to ancient rhetorical skills, scholars highlight that there are several other biblical (Prov 8:21ff.; Isa 45:8; 55:10–11; Ps 85:10–13) as well as popular-philosophical parallels for such personification

(Theon *Prog.* 2.114.10–11; Hermogenes *Prof.* 9.4–6; *Rhet. Her.* 4.66; Cicero *Inv.* 99–100; Quintilian *Inst.* 9.2.31).[41] This form of "speech-in-character" is typical of ancient rhetoric, and is simply understood by the audience.[42]

Paul begins with an exhortation to gratitude and humility before God, taken from Deut 8:17 and 9:4, followed by a quotation from Deut 30:11–14, the core of his *pesher* on divine righteousness.

[6a] ἡ δὲ ἐκ πίστεως δικαιοσύνη οὕτως λέγει· *μὴ εἴπῃς ἐν τῇ καρδίᾳ σου·*
μὴ εἴπῃς ἐν τῇ καρδίᾳ σου. . . (Deut 8:17; 9:4 [LXX])

[6b] τίς ἀναβήσεται εἰς τὸν οὐρανόν; τοῦτ' ἔστιν Χριστὸν καταγαγεῖν·
οὐκ ἐν τῷ οὐρανῷ ἄνω ἐστὶν λέγων *τίς ἀναβήσεται ἡμῖν εἰς τὸν οὐρανὸν*
καὶ λήμψεται αὐτὴν ἡμῖν καὶ ἀκούσαντες αὐτὴν ποιήσομε (Deut 30:12
[LXX])[43]

[7] ἤ· τίς καταβήσεται εἰς τὴν ἄβυσσον; τοῦτ' ἔστιν Χριστὸν ἐκ νεκρῶν ἀναγαγεῖν.
οὐδὲ πέραν τῆς θαλάσσης ἐστὶν λέγων *τίς διαπεράσει ἡμῖν εἰς τὸ πέραν τῆς*
θαλάσσης καὶ λήμψεται ἡμῖν αὐτήν καὶ ἀκουστὴν ἡμῖν ποιήσει αὐτήν καὶ
ποιήσομεν (Deut 30:13 [LXX])
ἀναβαίνουσιν ἕως τῶν οὐρανῶν καὶ καταβαίνουσιν ἕως τῶν ἀβύσσων. . .
(Ps 106:26 [LXX]; 107:26 [BH])

First, the change of speakers, or speeches, from Moses to the personified "righteousness by faith" in v. 6, made by the opening conjunction δέ, does not have an adversative meaning—faith contrasting with Moses—as traditional scholars and interpreters have taken it to mean.[44] In that event, it would contradict Paul's thesis at 9:6 that God's word has not failed, and would undermine the proposition that the law must be performed.[45] Rather, as Jewett notes, "the change of voice substantiates the antithesis between the misguided zeal of 10:2 and the intent of the Mosaic revelation."[46]

We ought continually to recall that for Paul, the most important thing is to prove the faithfulness and reliability of God's word in the Scriptures. This is why Paul confirms the axiom that the righteousness by (or through) faith (faithfulness) is consistent with Scripture. He does so by quoting and reinterpreting these very passages from Deuteronomy, not in his own voice, but in the voice of a personified "righteousness by faith."[47] The core of Paul's reinterpretation is his explanatory statement that the object of this ascent into heaven is "to bring Christ down" (v. 6), and that of the descent into the abyss is "to bring Christ up from the real of the dead" (v. 7).[48] Contextually, Deut 30:11–14 is a passage about God's law as a whole (see Deut 11:22; 19:9, etc.),[49] and had importance in contemporary Judaism (it is cited in Bar 3:29–30; Philo *Post.* 84–85; *Tg. Neof.* on Deut 30:11–14).[50]

Concerning the historical context of Deut 30:11–14, it is generally accepted that chapters 29–30 consist of a distinct unit of thought within the book, and that—as a whole and along with Deut 4, with which the passage is associated in topic and language—these chapters "form a frame around the parenetic and legal core of Deuteronomy."[51] Verses 1–10 follow the context of destruction and exile in Deut 29 that challenges Israel to repent and reform. As such, this section looks into the future, beyond the frustration and failure of 29:21–27. Disobedience and its result, the curses, are no longer the subjects of the admonition but are replaced by the promise of restoration based on repentance and that assures prosperity contingent on obedience.[52] Verses 11–14 make a shift in portraying the future, turning back to the present situation, when Moses "takes up once again the decisive challenge for obedience set forth in 29:1–20 [ET 2–21]."[53] However, at this place, Moses is not warning or threatening, but rather persuading and encouraging, Israel, since the law and its understanding are not beyond human capacity, are not undisclosed, and are not remote. On the contrary, as Richard Nelson remarks: "This is a user-friendly law, easy to grasp and freely available. The essential point is simply to 'do it' (the last words of vv. 12, 13, and 14)."[54]

This historical context would resonate in Paul's purpose to use it in the form of this *pesher*. For Paul, there are two decisive aspects: the eschatological view of the end-time redemption of Israel, and, at the same time, the way for the non-Jewish nations to be co-participants in this process. Thus, it is clear that both of these quotations, or speeches, in this *pesher*, Lev 18:5 and Deut 30:12–14, are interrelated and serve Paul's purpose of explaining what is, in actual fact, the aim of the Mosaic law. Thus, it is not about the cessation or termination of the Mosaic law,[55] nor the ending of the law understood in terms of works,[56] nor about its superseding by Christ on the basis of that other righteousness now found only in Christ and only through faith in Christ due to his being the one who has brought the law to its climax and thus has ended its reign.[57] On the contrary, it is about the goal and fulfilling of the Torah,[58] or in other words, it is the goal of divine vocation of Israel in God's worldwide purposes by the reconciliation of Jews and gentiles to bring salvation to all.

Within the recontextualization of this passage, Paul intentionally omits the opening verse 11 about the commandment that is close and at hand, as well as the word "for us" (ἡμῖν) in verses 12–13, as he is able instead to emphasize the personified character of the "righteousness by faith." While recent scholarship points to the significance of the warning in Deut 9:4–5[59] against an assumption by Israel that the conquest of the promised land would be the result of her own righteousness and the holiness of her heart, I agree with Jewett who, taking into consideration the content of 10:3, remarks that Paul is focusing on those zealous Jewish parties who were seeking to validate their own righteousness based on their religious programs associated with the law, in order to hasten the coming of the divinely appointed Messiah (Χριστός) and usher in the messianic age (see, for example, Midrash *Exod. Rab.* 25.12).[60] Paul's strategy is based on his own experiences from the time when, as a zealous Pharisee, he was leading the rejection of Jesus as Messiah (Gal 1:13–14; Phil 3:4–6). Although Paul cannot be sure what particularly his addressees would hear and know about him, since most of them had never met him, he could, however, assume—at the least and with a high degree of probability—that they heard about his previous life when he persecuted the Christ-followers.[61] Now, he implicitly criticizes this kind of zeal on the part of some Jewish factions; thus, this way of interpretation of Paul's purpose in using the *pesher* corresponds best to the historical context and situation of his addressees. As Jewett aptly comments in this connection: "By the skillful combination of Lev 18:5; Deut 8:17; 9:4; and 30:12, the character called Righteousness by Faith shows that these zealous programs to usher in the messianic age through obedience to this or that law were repudiated by Scripture itself."[62]

Paul continues in his rhetorical purpose in verse 7 also, with its quotation of Deut 30:13. I agree with Jewett[63] that we should not follow those scholars who see here an exposition of the doctrine of Christ's resurrection from the dead[64] or the doctrine of Christ's descent into hell.[65] Equally, there is no reason to interpret that reaching heaven or the abyss merely as a metaphor for what is impossible for people in their present life.[66] Rather, Paul is following here the track of his argument in chapters 7, 9, and 10 about the problem of zealotry among some Jewish parties and factions. To bring the Messiah up from the abyss should be understood in the context of messianic expectations held by some Jewish factions that had not accepted "the righteousness by faith" in Christ Jesus as the inauguration of the messianic age heralded by major figures in Israel's history, such as Elijah and Enoch, who it was held would return from the dead at that decisive time.[67]

For Paul, the right answer of believers in Jesus as the Christ to the questions of Deut 30:12–13 is found in 30:14, the quotation of which he introduces by the formula, "But what does it say?" in v. 8:[68]

⁸ ἀλλὰ τί λέγει; *ἐγγύς σου τὸ ῥῆμά ἐστιν ἐν τῷ στόματί σου καὶ ἐν τῇ καρδίᾳ σου,* τοῦτ' ἔστιν τὸ ῥῆμα τῆς πίστεως ὃ κηρύσσομεν.
  ἔστιν σου ἐγγὺς τὸ ῥῆμα σφόδρα ἐν τῷ στόματί σου καὶ ἐν τῇ καρδίᾳ σου καὶ ἐν ταῖς χερσίν σου αὐτὸ ποιεῖν. (Deut 30:14 [LXX])

In this verse, Paul closes the *pesher* with the final explanatory formula "that is" (τοῦτ' ἔστιν). For Paul, this answer—derived from Deuteronomy—means the assurance that "the righteousness by faith" explains the consistency between the gospel proclamation (τὸ ῥῆμα τῆς πίστεως ὃ κηρύσσομεν) and the original intent of the Mosaic law.[69]

However, as was emphasized above, this is not to say that the gospel proclamation, or "the righteousness by faith" itself, replaces the Mosaic law as such. It concerns the end-time redemption of Israel with the participation of gentiles (*ethnē*), who in Christ have attained the new status of those drawn from the nations (*ethnē*), not as sympathizers with Jewishness (Godfearers) who could continue with their participation in gentile cults, nor by ethnic transformation like the proselytes, but rather through an entirely new way of life by adopting Jewish attributes and at the same time a strict rejection of idolatry.[70] Hence, they remained gentiles, albeit of a special sort.[71] Their faithfulness and trust (πίστις) in the gospel has become a foundation for their new righteous conduct (δικαιοσύνη) (Rom 12:1–2, 9–21; 13:8–14; cf. Gal 5:13–14, 22–25; 6:1–10).[72] Now, the gentiles (*ethnē*) in Christ have the freedom to disregard the previous criteria of distinction and competition for honor established under the constraints of the dominant cultural systems, which were visible in every city of the Roman Empire, where public life was centered around the quest for honor.[73] Now, the non-Jewish nations in Christ have a share in God's blessing imparted to Abraham and his descendants (Gen 22:16–18) and can expect the ultimate restoration and redemption of Israel. The abiding separateness of the gentiles in Christ from Israel is part of God's eschatological plan for the redemption of Israel, and, through Israel, also the redemption of other nations, so that the propositional claim can be confirmed that God is the one and only God: not God only to the Jews, but to the other nations also (3:29).[74] Paul is aware of the sincere "zeal" of those Jewish parties who do not accept Jesus as the Messiah and who seek to validate their own righteousness based on their religious programs associated with the law, in order to hasten the coming of the (in their opinion) true Messiah; nevertheless, he is convinced that this is not based on knowledge (ζῆλον θεοῦ ἔχουσιν ἀλλ' οὐ κατ' ἐπίγνωσιν; Rom 10:2). He thus expresses his eagerness and desire that even their "zeal" be value-redirected, like his own, since now, Paul as the apostle of the gentiles, "saw himself as assisting in the removal of hostility through the reconciliation of Jews and those from the nations, *as Jews and as non-Jews*, in the divine purpose."[75]

Finally, in verses 9–13, Paul explains how the "word" is near to believers, and what this means for God's eschatological purpose with Israel as well as the other nations. Paul bases his argumentation here on two further quotations: from Isa 28:16 (v. 11), concerning faith that is sustained, and from Joel 3:5 (v. 13), concerning salvation to everyone who calls upon the Lord:[76]

⁹ ὅτι ἐὰν ὁμολογήσῃς ἐν τῷ στόματί σου κύριον Ἰησοῦν καὶ πιστεύσῃς ἐν τῇ καρδίᾳ σου ὅτι ὁ θεὸς αὐτὸν ἤγειρεν ἐκ νεκρῶν, σωθήσῃ· ¹⁰ καρδίᾳ γὰρ

πιστεύεται εἰς δικαιοσύνην, στόματι δὲ ὁμολογεῖται εἰς σωτηρίαν. ¹¹ λέγει γὰρ ἡ γραφή· πᾶς ὁ πιστεύων ἐπ' αὐτῷ οὐ καταισχυνθήσεται.

διὰ τοῦτο οὕτως λέγει κύριος ἰδοὺ ἐγὼ ἐμβαλῶ εἰς τὰ θεμέλια Σιων λίθον πολυτελῆ ἐκλεκτὸν ἀκρογωνιαῖον ἔντιμον εἰς τὰ θεμέλια αὐτῆς καὶ ὁ πιστεύων ἐπ' αὐτῷ οὐ μὴ καταισχυνθῇ. (Isa 28:16 [LXX])

¹² οὐ γάρ ἐστιν διαστολὴ Ἰουδαίου τε καὶ Ἕλληνος, ὁ γὰρ αὐτὸς κύριος πάντων, πλουτῶν εἰς πάντας τοὺς ἐπικαλουμένους αὐτόν· ¹³ πᾶς γὰρ ὃς ἂν ἐπικαλέσηται τὸ ὄνομα κυρίου σωθήσεται.

καὶ ἔσται πᾶς ὃς ἂν ἐπικαλέσηται τὸ ὄνομα κυρίου σωθήσεται ὅτι ἐν τῷ ὄρει Σιων καὶ ἐν Ιερουσαλημ ἔσται ἀνασῳζόμενος καθότι εἶπεν κύριος καὶ εὐαγγελιζόμενοι οὓς κύριος προσκέκληται. (Joel 3:5 [LXX])

Paul is convinced that even though the difference between Israel and the gentiles continues and remains—Israel is and remains God's chosen people (*"treasured possession out of all the peoples . . . a priestly kingdom and holy nation"* [Exod 19:5–6])—nevertheless, in regard to God's universal salvific purpose, there is no difference. Although Paul stresses his divine vocation to be *"the apostle to the nations,"* this does not mean that his calling serves only in relation to gentile nations. As Campbell aptly notes: "Rather, he believed and hoped that a successful mission to non-Jews would have a salvific influence on Jews, so that together they would then achieve the goal of the divine purpose to join in harmonious worship of the God of Israel (Rom. 15.7–13)."[77] Also, Paul's frequent stress upon "all" (πᾶς, πάντες) is necessary to understand and interpret Paul's argument as including and categorizing together both Jews and non-Jews, always within the framework of what is his "Jewish understanding of creation that is inclusive of all humanity whether Jewish or non-Jewish. It is inclusive in terms of diversity, not via an imposed sameness that denies or seeks to overcome the diversity of creation."[78] This is proven very clearly by Paul's typical form of expression, "not to the Jew only, but also to the gentile" (Rom 3:29–30; 4:9) that, although inclusive, aptly depicts the abiding difference, while still resisting polarity.[79]

In this historical context, we should take into account and understand also the acclamation "Lord Jesus" in v. 9, that very early expression of allegiance to Christ, revealing one's own identity and commitment (cf. Phil 2:11; 1 Cor 1:2; 12:3).[80] In this way, Paul reminds and at the same time convinces his addressees in Rome that now, in their deeply emotional faith and trust in all that God has done in Jesus Christ, they belong to Christ (God's "anointed one"), and thus are under the dominion of the only true God. This means that they are no more under the dominion of other "powers," such as δαιμόνια, στοιχεῖα, ἄρχοντες, ἐξουσίαι, θεοί, κύριοι (cf. Gal 2:15; 5:19–21). The new identity they have gained in Christ is "evidence of having abandoned the traditional systems of earning honor and avoiding shame, because this Lord has the marks of the shameful cross on his resurrected body."[81] Now, through love, they are free to be slaves to one another (see Gal 5:1, 13).[82] At the same time, they should be aware that this does not mean that they have to become end-time proselytes. Their relation to Israel is other than that. They are, and remain, those from the other (non-Jewish) nations (*ethnē*), but in Christ have become "holy," a part of God's people—an eschatological community of Israel and the gentile (non-Jewish) nations.

In the next verse (v. 10), Paul clarifies the sequence of faith and confession (v. 9) by an explanatory comment, and in this way he closes the chiastic explanation in verses 9–10 of how the "word" is near to believers.[83] Unlike v. 9, where Paul—by using active verbs (ὁμολογήσῃς . . . πιστεύσῃς) in reverse order from the standpoint of missionizing—places the emphasis on the side of the believers, here he uses passive verbs (πιστεύεται . . . ὁμολογεῖται), making a succinct formulation joining the language of 1:16–17 with the details of the Deuteronomy quotation and "creating a fully plausible statement of the viewpoint of the character called Righteousness by Faith."[84] As it is in the whole epistle, so here, "Paul's purpose is missional rather than dogmatic."[85] Paul's purpose is to win the groups of non-Jewish Christ-believers in Rome for the gospel that he proclaims, as well as to explain what is their status and identity within God's universal salvific purpose, including their association with Israel. By quoting Isa 28:16 in v. 11—slightly adapted by adding the word πᾶς ("all")—Paul proves that there is no separate path to salvation through the law for Jewish believers. Jews and *ethnē* alike, everyone who believes and is trusting in God's universal salvific purpose, is included in the end-time redemption of Israel and the *ethnē*. They all will not be put to shame, but will become part and parcel of the universal reconciliation of God's creation. Paul emphasizes that this kind of faith and confession is not self-honorific. On the contrary, as Jewett asserts in this connection, "[t]o 'call on the name' of this Lord (Rom 10:13) is to abandon any prior claim of honor and to take one's place alongside the dishonored savior and his disheveled flock."[86]

Verses 12 and 13 sustain Paul's claim to be the apostle to the gentile nations. By using the expression Ἰουδαίου τε καὶ Ἕλληνος for the fifth and last time in this epistle (1:16; 2:9, 10; 3:9; 10:12), Paul repeatedly reflects his conviction that the God of Israel has, in the Messiah Jesus, erased the boundaries of honor and shame. This means that the prejudicial boundaries between social groups are being eliminated. The crucial fact that this is how all inequalities are overcome comes here, in v. 12, to its climactic assertion: οὐ γάρ ἐστιν διαστολή ("for there is no distinction").[87] As to distinctions, there are and remain differences—particularities like ethnicity, race, or culture. Jews are and still remain Jews—that is, Israelites, and the members of the other nations will not become Israelites,[88] but despite this, in Christ, they are equal to Israel. God in Jesus Christ is reconciling Jew and a non-Jew alike, a truth exemplified by living together without social discriminations based on the prevailing conventions that divided the Graeco-Roman world.

Finally, by using the fifth quotation of Joel 3:5 in this *pesher*, Paul confirms that God's love and mercy manifested in the event of Jesus Christ comes to all who call upon him—that is, God or Christ;[89] to all who, by faith and trust in God's doings in the event of Jesus Christ, confirmed by the quality of life which corresponds to God's reconciliation in Jesus Christ, are expressing their allegiance to God or Christ. That "all" includes Jew as well as gentile—those from the *ethnē*—and thus this proves the proposition that God is the one and only God, God of both Israel and the other nations. Thus Paul brings this important *pesher* concerning God's universal righteousness to its conclusion.[90]

CONCLUSION

The above analysis of the *pesher* concerning God's righteousness in Romans 10:5–13 substantiates that for Paul, the event of Jesus as Christ signifies not an annulment of God's covenant with Israel, nor a substitution of faith in Jesus Christ for the Mosaic law, and in no way the sublimation of Judaism to essential Christianity with the character of universal religion.[91] On the contrary, it signifies the eschatological fulfillment of the Mosaic law: the arrival of the end-time redemption of Israel as well as of the *ethnē* in Christ who are participants in this process. The end of the ages has dawned. To use Isaiah's phrasing, this is the beginning of the promised time when those from the non-Jewish nations join alongside Israel in the worship of the One and only God, and all the nations will recognize the God of Israel as the one and only God (Isa 2:2–4; 19:18–25; 25:6–8; 45:18–25; 56:7; 65–66).[92] For Paul, a first-century Jewish Christ-follower, it truly is a mystery, since this eschatological scenario, when compared to conventional Jewish eschatological notions of the end-time redemption of Israel,[93] occurs in reverse order: first, the full number of the non-Jewish nations will come in, and only then, and in such a manner, will all Israel be saved (11:25–27). Nevertheless, Paul is aware that this process began with Israel, in particular with a group of Jewish believers in Christ constituting "the present-time remnant of Israel" (11:5). At the same time, this means the differences between Israel and other, non-Jewish, nations, are to be maintained; but in full equality in the sight of the only God. On both sides, Israelites and the other nations, this social status has to be manifested and demonstrated by a life without discrimination or hostility. In other words, the *pesher* on God's righteousness expresses the very "truth of the gospel" that is God's universal salvific purpose for Jews as well as gentiles.

NOTES

1. Matthew V. Novenson has argued for a significant role of Jewish messianism for understanding the mission of Jewish Christ-followers among the non-Jews, especially Paul's mission. ("Jewish Messiahs, the Pauline Christ, and the Gentile Question," *JBL* 128.2 [2009]: 373 [357–73]). The significance of Jewish messianism in its relation to Gentile nations is attested also to Hasmonean state expansion during the rule of Hyrcanus. See in more detail Kenneth Atkinson, *The Hasmoneans and Their Neighbors: New Historical Reconstructions from the Dead Sea Scrolls and Classical Sources*, Jewish and Christian Texts 27 (London, U.K. and New York, NY: T&T Clark, 2018), 32–64.

2. This work was supported by the Scientific Grant Agency of the Ministry of Education, Science, Research and Sport of the Slovak Republic and the Slovak Academy of Sciences (VEGA), as part of the research project entitled "Paul within Judaism—New Perspectives" (VEGA 1/0103/18), with its home base at Comenius University in Bratislava, at the Evangelical Lutheran Theological Faculty. Some parts of the content are based upon previous studies and were partially included into my study titled "The Role of Israel towards the Gentiles in the Context of Romans 11:25–27" that was presented during the SNTS general meeting in Marburg 2019, in the Short Papers section. However, these chapters have been rewritten, supplemented, and updated on the basis of more recent literature.

3. The use of the terms "Jew/Jewish/Jewishness/Judean/Judaism/Israel/Israelites" and their cognates depends on the frame of reference from which we approach the issue. I use these terms in the meaning of the ancient members of God's people of Israel who maintain belief in Yahweh in its various forms, traditions, notions, and schools, and who consider themselves to be heirs of his promises; in other words, the ethnic (religio-ethnic) groups claiming descent from Abraham and Isaac (especially from Isaac's son Jacob); the nation which God selected to receive his revelation and with whom God chose to make a covenant (Exodus 19). From a chronological point of view, I mean the Second Temple era, the period between the construction of the second Jewish temple in Jerusalem in 515 BCE and its destruction by the Romans in 70 CE. For the various views and stances on this problematic, see in more detail William S. Campbell, *The Nations in the Divine Economy: Paul's Covenantal Hermeneutics and Participation in Christ* (Lanham/Boulder/New York/London: Lexington Books/Fortress Academic, 2018), 4–6; Stephen Mason, "Jews, Judeans, Judaizing, Judaism: Problems of Categorization in Ancient History," *Journal for the Study of Judaism* 38 (2007): 482–88; Philip F. Esler, *Conflict and Identity in Romans: The Social Setting of Paul's Letter* (Minneapolis, MN: Fortress Press, 2003), 19–76. See also other volumes mentioned by Campbell, *The Nations in the Divine Economy*, 4–6, including the notes (16–17).

4. As William S. Campbell rightly notes (*The Nations in the Divine Economy*, 3), this designation "is the typical Jewish way of corporately indicating non-Jews, the other nations among whom they lived." In this chapter, when using the term "gentiles/ gentile", I mean a social construct for the description of non-Jewish people or nations (*ethnē*), regardless of their national, cultural, or religious identity. In this regard, apart from the quotations, I am not using this term or cognate words with a capital, in order not to give the impression that it represents an actual group of people. I found inspiration for this usage in Campbell's aforementioned monograph (*The Nations in the Divine Economy*, 3).

5. On the interaction between Jews and non-Jews in the Hellenistic world, see: Erich S. Gruen, *Heritage and Hellenism: The Reinvention of Jewish Tradition* (Berkeley/Los Angeles/London: University of California Press, 1998); John J. Collins, *Between Athens and Jerusalem: Jewish Identity in the Hellenistic Diaspora*, 2nd ed. BRS (Grand Rapids, MI/Cambridge, U.K.: Eerdmans, 2000); Paula Fredriksen, "The Question of Worship: Gods, Pagans, and the Redemption of Israel," in *Paul within Judaism: Restoring the First-Century Context to the Apostle*, ed. Mark D. Nanos and Magnus Zetterholm (Minneapolis, MN: Fortress Press, 2015), 175–201; Neil Elliott, "The Question of Politics: Paul as a Diaspora Jew under Roman Rule", in *Paul within Judaism: Restoring the First-Century Context to the Apostle*, ed. Mark D. Nanos and Magnus Zetterholm (Minneapolis, MN: Fortress Press, 2015), 203–43.

6. For more detail, see Paula Fredriksen, "Judaism, the Circumcision of Gentiles and Apocalyptic Hope: Another Look at Galatians 1 and 2," in *The Galatians Debate: Contemporary Issues in Rhetorical and Historical Interpretation*, ed. Mark D. Nanos (Peabody, MA: Hendrickson, 2002), 254, including notes.

7. In this regard, Terence Donaldson remarks: "Jews believed that this God had chosen them out of all the nations of the world to be a special people, that the will and the ways of this God had been revealed uniquely in Israel's scripture, that the God who had created the cosmos was nevertheless uniquely present in the Jerusalem temple, and that despite the Jews' temporal misfortunes, eventually Israel would be vindicated and exalted to a position of preeminence over all other nations." See in more detail Terence Donaldson, *Judaism and the Gentiles: Jewish Patterns of Universalism (To 135 CE)* (Waco, TX: Baylor University Press, 2007), 1–2 (quotation from 2). In his book *Judaism and the Gentiles*, Terence Donaldson focuses on Jewish writings from the Second Temple period and synthesizes them by identifying four distinct patterns of universalism that arose out of the four broad textual categories of sympathizing, conversion, ethical monotheism, and eschatological participation. For further explanation of the term "universalism" as used by the author in regard to the world of late antiquity, especially in connection to Jewish "universalism," see Donaldson, in the introduction to *Judaism and the Gentiles*, 1–13.

8. However, in this context it must be emphasized that the non-Jewish nations are not always treated positively in Jewish eschatological traditions and notions. In Jewish scriptures, there are texts describing the fate of gentiles negatively and depicting them as Israel's enemies or idolaters that must be punished and defeated together with idolatry itself (for example, Isa 29:8; 49:22–23; 54:3; Jer 30:11, 16; Ezek 17:11–21; Mic 5:6–14; 7:16–17; Joel 4:9–21; Zeph 2:1–3, 9–15; 1 En. 91.9; Sir 36:1–10; Bar

4:25, 31–35; *Sib. Or.* 3.415–440, 669, 761; *Pss. Sol.* 17:24.30; 1QM 12.10–13). Gentiles are sometimes described as those who will be subservient to Israel or as submissive witnesses to Israel's vindication (Isa 18:7; 60:1–22; 66:18–21; Hag 2:21–22). Other notions present the eschatological inclusion of gentiles in Israel as a consequence of the restoration and redemption of Israel (for example, Isa 2:2–4/Mic 4:1–3; Isa 19:18–25; 25:6–8; 45:18–25; 56:7; 60:5–6; 66:19; Zech 8:21–23; Tob 13:11; 14:5–7; *Pss. Sol.* 17:31–41; Sir 36:11–17; 1 En. 90.30–38; 91.14; *Sib. Or.* 3.616, 702–723), resulting in the observance of the Torah by gentiles as well (Isa 2:2–4; Philo, *Mos.* 2.43–44; *T. Levi* 18.9; *T. Naph.* 3.2; *Sib. Or.* 3.791, 757–758; 5.264), yet there also are occurrences where the inclusion of gentiles with Israel does not assume the observance of the Torah (Isa 25:6–10; Zech 8:20–23; *Pss. Sol.* 17:28, 34; *Sib. Or.* 5.493; Tob 14:5–7; 1 En. 90.30–38; 2 Bar. 72). Instead, gentiles will renounce their idols and sinful ways, turn to the God of Israel, and worship God as those sharing in the blessing of the coming age (Isa 2:20–21; Jer 16:19–20).

9. In regard to the question of identity, Campbell (*The Nations in the Divine Economy*, 1–2), aptly remarks that "the meaning of the term *identity* is often not clear to those who wish a more precise or exact terminology." In seeking to clarify this potential difficulty, we can accept and use the definition of identity which Richard Jenkins comes up with in his *Social Identity* (London: Routledge, 1996) defining identity as follows: "Identity refers to the ways in which individuals and groups define themselves, and are defined by others on the basis of race, ethnicity, religion, language and culture" (4). Regarding this definition, Campbell points out further: "If identity is used to describe how an individual or a group describes themselves and are recognized by others, this seems straightforward and unproblematic. But if we say that identities can be trans-ethnic or overarching, we are using the same term for something that is particular to a specific location and also for another term that overarches or possibly modifies the term as originally used." (*The Nations in Divine Economy*, 2; on this issue, see further 129–52, 255–97).

10. On Jewish messianic ideas and notions, see: Marion Wyse, *Variations on the Messianic Theme: A Case Study of Interfaith Dialogue (Judaism and Jewish Life)* (Brighton, MA: Academic Studies Press, 2009), 185–95; William Horbury, *Jewish Messianism and the Cult of Christ* (London: SCM, 1998); Horbury, "Messianism in the Old Testament Apocrypha and Pseudepigrapha," *Messianism among Jews and Christians. Twelve Biblical and Historical Studies* (London/New York, NY: T&T Clark—Continuum, 2003), 35–64; John J. Collins, *The Scepter and the Star: The Messiahs of the Dead Sea Scrolls and Other Ancient Literature*, ABRL (New York, NY: Doubleday, 1995), 11–12; Collins, "Messianism and Exegetical Tradition: The Evidence of the LXX Pentateuch," in *Jewish Cult and Hellenistic Culture: Essays on the Jewish Encounter with Hellenism and Roman Culture*, ed. J. J. Collins. JSJSup 100 (Leiden: Brill, 2005), 58–81; James H. Charlesworth, ed., *The Messiah: Developments in Earliest Judaism and Christianity* (Minneapolis, MN: Fortress Press, 1992); Jacob Neusner, William S. Green and Ernest S. Frerichs, eds., *Judaisms and Their Messiahs* (Cambridge, U.K.: Cambridge University Press, 1987).

11. This is what Robert Jewett calls this section, and he regards it as the third of four proofs of the thesis about the Gospel—as the powerful embodiment of the

righteousness of God—and its implications for the Roman congregations. See Robert Jewett, *Romans: A Commentary*, ed. Eldon J. Epp. Hermeneia Series (Minneapolis, MN: Fortress Press, 2006), 148, 555–723.

12. James D. G. Dunn, *Theology of Paul the Apostle* (Grand Rapids, MI/ Cambridge, U.K.: Eerdmans, 2006 [1998]), 501. As James Dunn remarks in this regard: "In part this view stems from F. C. Baur, in his recognition that Paul's concern was not with individuals but with nations." See the quotations in Richard H. Bell, *Provoked to Jealousy: The Origin and Purpose of the Jealousy Motif in Romans 9–11*, WUNT 2.63 (Tübingen: Mohr Siebeck, 1994), 46–47; see also William S. Campbell, "The Freedom and Faithfulness of God in Relation to Israel," *Paul's Gospel in an Intercultural Context: Jew and Gentile in the Letter to the Romans*. Studies in the Intercultural History of Christianity 69 (Frankfurt: Peter Lang, 1991), 43–59. Stated by Dunn, *Theology*, 499–501, including n. 7.

13. Jewett, *Romans*, 555–56. For a thorough exegetical analysis of this passage of Romans (9:1–11:36), including a review of other relevant literature, see: Jewett, *Romans* 555–723; James D. G. Dunn, *Romans 9–16*, WBC 38B (Dallas, TX: Word, 1991 [1988]), 517–704; Douglas J. Moo, *The Epistle to the Romans*, NICNT (Grand Rapids, MI/ Cambridge, U.K.: Eerdmans, 1996), 547–744; Joseph A. Fitzmyer, *Romans: A New Translation with Introduction and Commentary*, AB 33 (New York, NY: Doubleday, 1993), 539–636. On the exegetical analysis of Rom 11:25–29, see also Mark D. Nanos, *The Mystery of Romans: The Jewish Context of Paul's Letter* (Minneapolis, MN: Fortress Press, 1996), 239–88.

14. As William S. Campbell notes in regard to Paul's mission among the gentiles, "Paul's concern for the gentile mission should not be viewed as antipathy toward Israel, but rather as evidence of his parallel concern for the ultimate restoration of Israel. Both of these perspectives emerge out of his zeal for the glory of God. What is seldom noted is that Paul's self-designation as apostle to the non-Jews inherently demonstrates Paul's continuing to operate within the ancient Israel-nations binary pattern, rather than his attempt to overcome this" (*The Nations in the Divine Economy*, 59–60).

15. As Campbell notes in this regard, "[w]hat had to be changed was not the certainty of eschatological blessing, but only the sequence of events. It was this perception, however it came to Paul—as a mystery revealed or otherwise—that affirmed his mission to the nations, giving it a specific function in relation to the salvation of Israel." (*The Nations in the Divine Economy*, 231–33; quotation from 232).

16. In this part, I follow the structural analysis made by Robert Jewett. See in more detail Jewett, *Romans*, 556–57, 570–73, 588–90, 607–8, 622–24, 635–37, 651–52, 668–72, 695–96, 713–15. For comparison see also Dunn, *Romans 9–16*, 518–21; Moo, *The Epistle to the Romans*, 553–54.

17. In regard to this part of Romans (Rom 11:25–32), especially to disclosure and interpretation of the "mystery" of universal salvation, see also Michael Wolter, "Ein exegetischer und theologischer Blick auf Röm 11.25–32," *NTS* 64 (2018): 123–42; Christopher Zoccali, "'And so all Israel will be saved': Competing Interpretations of Romans 11.26 in Pauline Scholarship," *JSNT* 30.3 (2008): 289–318.

18. The opinion held by, for example, Jewett, or Louw, 2:104–6. See in more detail Jewett, *Romans*, 622, including n. 1 and 2.

19. "Speech-in-character" (προςωποπεία). See Jewett, *Romans*, 27–28; see also Rudolf Bultmann, *Der Stil der paulinischen Predigt und die kynisch-stoische Diatribe* (Göttingen: Vandenhoeck & Ruprecht, 1984 [1910]), 87–88; Johann D. Kim, *God, Israel, and the Gentiles: Rhetoric and Situation in Romans 9–11*, SBLDS 176 (Missoula, MT: Scholars Press, 2000), 132; and Stanley K. Stowers, *A Rereading of Romans: Justice, Jews and Gentiles* (New Haven, CT: Yale University Press, 1994), 309, who, as Jewett remarks in this regard, "refers to this as an example of 'speech-in-character,' defined by Theon *Prog.* 2.114.10–11 as 'introducing into the discourse' a personified character who speaks 'words appropriate both to the character and the subject matter.'" (*Romans*, 622, n. 3).

20. As Jewett (*Romans*, 622, n. 6) explains in this regard: "A *pesher* cites a short section of a biblical text and then intersperses explanatory comments, often with 'that is . . .' or 'its interpretation is'" Fitzmyer (*Romans*, 588, speaks of the "midrashic fashion" in which Paul comments on Deut 30:11–14. Dunn, *Romans 9–16*, 602–3), remarks that "[t]here is some dispute as to whether Paul intended to quote Deut 30:12–14 or was simply using some of its language and imagery to make his own point without dependence on Deut 30:12–14 as such. . . . But Paul almost certainly does intend to cite Deut 30:12–14, or more precisely, to explain and expound it."

21. In this regard, Jewett notes: "Two voices interact in this *pesher*, with Moses 'writing' in the initial text from Leviticus, and a personified 'righteousness by faith' 'speaking' the next five citations. Each citation is interpreted in the light of the 'by faith' formula derived from Paul's earlier citation from Hab 2:4 in the thesis statement of Rom 1:16–17." (*Romans*, 622, emphasis original).

22. Moo, *The Epistle to the Romans*, 644.

23. Aptly attested by Moo's words: "For it is particularly the Jews who need to understand that the righteousness of the law that they are seeking is a righteousness based on 'doing' (v. 5, quoting Lev. 18:5). Such a righteousness, as Paul has already shown (9:31–32a; 10:3), is a phantom righteousness, for it cannot bring a person into relationship with a holy God (*The Epistle to the Romans*, 645, 647–50).

24. Then the *ethnē* would also share in the promised blessings of the age to come (Isa 2:2–4 [Mic 4:1–3]; 56:7; see also 18:7; 25:6; 60:5–6; 66:19; Hag 2:21–22; Zech 8:22). For the issue of Israel's divine vocation, in connection with Rom 9–11, see especially Lionel J. Windsor, *Paul and the Vocation of Israel: How Paul's Jewish Identity Informs His Apostolic Ministry, With Special Reference to Romans*, BZNW 205 (Berlin: de Gruyter, 2014), 195–254.

25. Mark D. Nanos, *Reading Romans within Judaism. Collected Essays of Mark D. Nanos, Vol. 2* (Eugene, OR: Cascade Books, 2018), 123.

26. Jewett calls it "voices." Here, I follow Jewett's analysis of this pericope (see Jewett, *Romans*, 622–23).

27. Jewett, *Romans*, 624. See also Dunn, *Romans 9–16*, 603.

28. I engage with this particular text, in connection with the comprehension of the Torah in the context of other Jewish Second Temple literature, in my monograph, *The Psalms of Solomon and the Messianic Ethics of Paul* WUNT 2.416 (Tübingen:

Mohr Siebeck, 2016), 15–27. In the following part of this chapter, I proceed from that source.

29. Windsor, *Paul and the Vocation of Israel*, 158–59.

30. As Campbell aptly notes in this regard: "Having acknowledged the sinfulness of all of humanity, he then introduces the possibility that Israel has been rejected and may even be no different from the nations, but then goes on to claim that though, at the present, there is only a remnant that responds positively to the message of the Christ movement, eventually 'all Israel will be saved.'" (The Nations in the Divine Economy, 64).

31. For more detail, see Windsor, *Paul and the Vocation of Israel*, 140–94.

32. Windsor, *Paul and the Vocation of Israel*, 248.

33. Dunn, *Romans 9–16*, 600–601. In regard to this quotation, Jewett (*Romans*, 624, including n. 17), notes that the rhetorical force of this *pesher* seems to be far removed from the possibility that Paul intended this citation to be understood in the light of Gal 3:10 and Rom 3:23 as a condemnation of Jewish noncompliance with the law, as some scholars suppose: Theodor Zahn, *Der Brief des Paulus an die Römer*. Kommentar zum Neuen Testament 6 (Leipzig: Deichert, 1910), 477; Ulrich Wilckens, *Der Brief and die Römer*, 3 vols., EKKNT 6 (Zürich: Benziger, 1978–82), 2:224; Johan Sijko Vos, "Die hermeneutische Antinomie bei Paulus (Galater 3.11–12; Römer 10.5–10)," *NTS* 38 (1992): 257–60 (254–70); Johan S. Vos, *Die Kunst der Argumentation bei Paulus. Studien zur antiken Rhetorik*, WUNT 149 (Tübingen: Mohr Siebeck, 2002), 120–34. This line of argument is criticized by Dietrich-Alex Koch, *Die Schrift als Zeuge des Evangeliums. Untersuchungen zur Verwendung und zum Verständnis der Schrift bei Paulus* (Tübingen: Mohr Siebeck, 1986), 291–92, as well as Dunn, *Romans 9–16*, 601.

34. So, for example, Dunn, *Romans 9–16*, 600.

35. For example, George E. Howard, "Christ the End of the Law: The Meaning of Romans 10:4ff.," *JBL* 88 (1969): 333–36 (331–37); Ragnar Bring, *Christus und das Gesetz* (Leiden: Brill, 1969), 54; Robert Badenas, *Christ the End of the Law: Romans 10:4 in Pauline Perspective*, JSNTSup 10 (Sheffield: JSOT Press, 1985), 120–25; Nicholas T. Wright, *Climax of the Covenant: Christ and the Law in Pauline Theology* (Minneapolis, MN: Fortress Press, 1991), 245. See also Moo, *The Epistle to the Romans*, 646, who, however, rejects this view.

36. See, Jewett, *Romans*, 624–25.

37. Nanos, *Reading Romans within Judaism*, 56.

38. In this regard, Jewett (*Romans*, 625, n. 20), refers to Andreas Lindemann ("Die Gerechtigkeit aus dem Gesetz: Erwägungen zur Auslegung und zur Textgeschichte von Römer 10,5," *ZNW* 73 [1982]: 240–45 [231–50], who argues "that the citations from Moses shows that both justification by works and justification by faith are included in Israel's law." In regard to Paul's using this quotation from Lev 18:5, Jewett comments that "[t]his is one more instance of Paul's skill in becoming 'one under the law' in order to win over 'those under the law' (1 Cor 9:20)." (625).

39. Nanos, *Reading Romans within Judaism*, 123, n. 25.

40. Jewett, *Romans*, 622.

41. See, in more detail, Jewett, *Romans*, 625, including the notes; Moo, *The Epistle to the Romans*, 590; Kim, *God, Israel, and the Gentiles*, 132; Thomas H. Tobin, *Paul's Rhetoric in Its Context: The Argument of Romans* (Peabody, MA: Hendrickson, 2004), 343–45.
42. Jewett, *Romans*, 625.
43. As Moo remarks in this connection, the LXX, which Paul follows closely, accurately translates the MT, "only omitting the first person plural dative (of advantage) pronoun, ἡμῖν, which comes between ἀναβήσεται and εἰς" (The Epistle to the Romans, 651, n. 27).
44. See Moo, *The Epistle to the Romans*, 650 (650–55); Dunn, *Romans 9–16*, 602; Wilckens, *Der Brief and die Römer*, 2:224; Charles E. B. Cranfield, *A Critical and Exegetical Commentary on the Epistle to the Romans*, 2 vols. ICC (Edinburgh: T&T Clark, 1975–79), 2:522.
45. So also Jewett, *Romans*, 625. See too, Badenas, *Christ the End of the Law*, 123.
46. Jewett, *Romans*, 625.
47. Jewett remarks that "the voice of Righteousness by Faith cites passages from Deuteronomy that repudiate efforts to usher in the messiah through zealous campaigns" (Romans, 625).
48. The significant difference in v. 7 from the Deuteronomy quotation, where Moses speaks about crossing the sea, will have been caused by the familiar wording of LXX Ps 106:26 that is echoed in the artful parallelism of this quotation. See in more detail, Jewett, *Romans*, 627–28.
49. See Moo, *The Epistle to the Romans*, 651.
50. Jewett, *Romans*, 626; Dunn, *Romans 9–16*, 603–05.
51. See in more detail Richard D. Nelson, *Deuteronomy: A Commentary*, OTL (Louisville, KY/London: Westminster John Knox Press, 2002), 346–47; quotation from 346.
52. See in more detail Nelson, *Deuteronomy*, 347–49.
53. Nelson, *Deuteronomy*, 349.
54. See in more detail Nelson, *Deuteronomy*, 349–50; quotation from 349.
55. For example, Rudolf Bultmann, "Christ the End of the Law," *Essays Philosophical and Theological,* trans. James G. G. Greig (London: SCM, 1955), 36–66; Peter Stuhlmacher, "Das Ende des Gesetzes: Über Ursprung und Ansatz der paulinischen Theologie," *ZThK* 67 (1970): 14–30; repr. in P. Stuhlmacher, *Versöhnung, Gesetz und Gerechtigkeit* (Göttingen: Vandenhoeck & Ruprecht, 1981), 166–91; Ernst Käsemann, *Commentary on Romans*, trans. G. W. Bromiley (Grand Rapids, MI: Eerdmans, 1980), 282–83; Wilckens, *Der Brief and die Römer*, 2:221–24; Franz Mussner, "Christus, des Gesetzes Ende zur Gerechtigkeit für jeden der glaubt (Röm 10,4)," in M. Barth et al., eds., *Paulus—Apostat oder Apostel? Jüdische und christliche Antworten* (Regensburg: Pustet, 1977), 31–44; Hans Hübner, "τέλος," *EDNT* 3 (1993): 347–48. Stated by Jewett, *Romans*, 619, n. 125.
56. Dunn, *Romans 9–16*, 589–91, 598.
57. Moo, *The Epistle to the Romans*, 636–42.
58. See Jewett, *Romans*, 619–20.
59. For example, Moo, *The Epistle to the Romans*, 651.

60. See in more detail Jewett, *Romans*, 626–27. At the same time, Jewett points out that "[t]his interpretation is sustained by the use of 'Christ' rather than 'Jesus Christ' in vv. 6 and 7" (627). In this connection, Jewett refers to Charles Kingsley Barrett, *A Commentary on the Epistle to the Romans*, 2d ed. BNTC/HNTC (London: Black; New York, NY: Harper, 1991), 199, who, among modern commentators, "has the clearest grasp of this background: 'the Messiah has appeared, and it is therefore impossible to hasten his coming (as some devout Jews thought to do) by perfect obedience to the law and penitence for its transgressions. (627).

61. See also, Jewett, *Romans*, 445.

62. Jewett, *Romans*, 627.

63. Jewett, *Romans*, 628.

64. For example, Cranfield, *Romans*, 2:525; Fitzmyer, *Romans*, 591; Moo, *The Epistle to the Romans*, 656.

65. See Otto Michel, *Der Brief an die Römer*, 14th ed. MeyerK 4 (Göttingen: Vandenhoeck & Ruprecht, 1978), 328; Käsemann, *Commentary on Romans*, 288; Dunn, *Romans 9–16*, 606; Moo, *The Epistle to the Romans*, 656.

66. Str-B 3:281; Dieter Zeller, *Der Brief an die Römer. Übersetzt und erklärt.* RNT (Regensburg: Pustet, 1985), 186; M. Jack Suggs, "The Word Is Near You: Rom 10:6–10 within the Purpose of the Letter," in *Christian History and Interpretation: Studies Presented to John Knox*, eds. W. R. Farmer, C. F. D. Moule, and R. R. Niebuhr (Cambridge, U.K.: University Press, 1967), 310–11 (289–312), referring to the "inaccessibility of Wisdom." Stated by Jewett, *Romans*, 628, n. 56.

67. See in this context Jewett, *Romans*, 628.

68. See in more detail Jewett, *Romans*, 628–29, including notes.

69. Jewett, *Romans*, 628.

70. Josephus describes it as a voluntary affiliation with Jewish way of life, the *politeia*: ὅσοι μὲν γὰρ θέλουσιν ὑπὸ τοὺς αὐτοὺς ἡμῖν νόμους ζῆν ὑπελθόντες δέχεται φιλοφρόνως οὐ τῷ γένει μόνον ἀλλὰ καὶ τῇ προαιρέσει τοῦ βίου νομίζων εἶναι τὴν οἰκειότητα τοὺς δ' ἐκ παρέργου προσιόντας ἀναμίγνυσθαι τῇ συνηθείᾳ οὐκ ἠθέλησεν (*Ag. Ap.* 2.210). See also Campbell, *The Nations in the Divine Economy*, 114–20.

71. See Caroline J. Hodge, "The Question of Identity: Gentiles as Gentiles—but Also Not—in Pauline Communities," in *Paul within Judaism: Restoring the First-Century Context to the Apostle*, eds. Mark D. Nanos and Magnus Zetterholm (Minneapolis, MN: Fortress Press, 2015), 172 (153–73).

72. As Paula Fredriksen interprets it: "Their *pistis* in Christ (steadfast confidence that he had died, been raised, and was about to return) righteoused them (through the conferring of *pneuma*, 'spirit') so that they could 'fulfil the Law,' meaning, quite specifically, the Law's Second Table, *dikaiosynē*." (The Question of Worship, 190–94 (175–201, quotation from 194). It would be characterized as the objective reality of qualitative righteousness. Chris VanLandingham argues for this interpretation in *Judgment and Justification in Early Judaism and the Apostle Paul* (Peabody, MA: Hendrickson, 2006), 272–332. See also Ábel, *The Psalms of Solomon and the Messianic Ethics of Paul*, 199–210, 265–84.

73. See in more detail Jewett, *Romans*, 46–91, including all referenced literature.

74. Hodge, "The Question of Identity," 172–73. However, at the same time it must be emphasized that this new identity of Paul's non-Jewish converts as proclaimed by Paul was, from the perspective of indigenous cultures, and most probably also from that of Jewish communities, generally unknown, and therefore it remained very suspicious, especially because—in contrast to God-fearers (*sebomenoi* or *phoboūmenoi*), who were attached to synagogues and permitted to continue their cultic practices—Paul's non-Jewish communities of Christ-followers were prohibited from such idolatry. By contrast, proselytism was a known, legal, and generally an accepted form of changing one's identity. In this regard, William Campbell remarks very aptly that the prohibition of idolatry results in them "experiencing an identity deficiency." (*The Nations in the Divine Economy*, 8).

75. Campbell, *The Nations in the Divine Economy*, 66 (emphasis original).

76. See in more detail Jewett, *Romans*, 629–33, including notes.

77. Campbell, *The Nations in the Divine Economy*, 65–66.

78. Campbell, *The Nations in the Divine Economy*, 61. Campbell stresses that "[b]ehind the problems in interpreting the universal aspects of Paul's gospel lies an assumed philosophical contrast between the universal and the particular. This is a modern assumption that owes much to the tendency toward binary thinking and shows the influence of Hegel's form of philosophy as exemplified in the thought of F. C. Baur" (62). In this regard, Campbell refers to Johannes Munck, who has asserted that "[t]he opposition between universalism and particularism is the product of a modern cosmopolitan outlook and has nothing to do with the biblical concept of the mission." *Paul and the Salvation of Mankind* (London: SCM Press, 1959), 71).

79. Campbell, *The Nations in the Divine Economy*, 61. See also Nanos, "Romans 9–11 from a Jewish Perspective on Christian-Jewish relations," in *Reading Romans within Judaism*, 103–11.

80. Jewett, *Romans*, 629–30; Dunn, *Romans 9–16*, 607.

81. Jewett, *Romans*, 630.

82. In regard to Galatians, Nils Dahl notes: "But they should serve one another in love and thus keep the commandment in which the whole law is fulfilled (5:13–14)"in ("Paul's Letter to the Galatians: Epistolary Genre, Content, and Structure,") in *The Galatians Debate: Contemporary Issues in Rhetorical and Historical Interpretation*, ed. Mark D. Nanos (Peabody, MA: Hendrickson, 2002), 137 (117–42). The new identity reveals the true nature of Paul's own vision of communal life in the Galatian churches (Gal 5:13–6:10) and explains what Paul really means by his paradoxical interpretation of freedom as slavery (5:13). See John M. G. Barclay, *Paul and the Gift* (Grand Rapids, MI: Eerdmans, 2015), 423–46. See also Barclay, *Obeying the Truth: A Study of Paul's Ethics in Galatians* (Edinburgh: T&T Clark, 1988), 152–54, 156, 166–69.

83. See in more detail Jewett, *Romans*, 629–30.

84. Jewett, *Romans*, 631. See also Dunn, *Romans 9–16*, 609.

85. Jewett, *Romans*, 631.

86. Jewett, *Romans*, 632.

87. In this connection, Jewett remarks that "[a]lthough scholars are agreed in translating διαστολή as 'distinction' or 'difference,' the search for parallels in papyri and classical sources has hitherto produced no exact parallel to Paul's usage ... Overlooked thus far is the parallel in Philo *Mos.* 2.158.4, 'of the distinction (διαστολήν) between things sacred and profane, things human and divine'" (*Romans*, 632, n. 106). See also Fitzmyer, *Romans*, 593; Moo, *The Epistle to the Romans*, 650.

88. Nanos notes: "Paul maintains the proposition that those from the nations who respond to this message of good news in Christ remain members of the other nations thereafter, joining alongside of Israelites in the worship of the One God of *all* the nations" (*Reading Romans within Judaism*, 106; emphasis original).

89. For the question of whom the word κύριος refers to in this verse, see in more detail Jewett, *Romans*, 633, including notes.

90. As Jewett aptly concludes on this passage of the epistle: "With this brilliant rhetorical device the *pesher* comes to a conclusion that is fully supportive of the missionary project that Paul wishes to promote: to preach the gospel of Christ crucified to the end of the known world and thus to overcome the destructive distinctions and imperial exploitations that had ruined the world" (*Romans*, 633).

91. Campbell, *The Nations in the Divine Economy*, 82. For the issue of reception and interpretation of Paul in contrast to Judaism, see in more detail, Campbell, 51–103.

92. Nanos remarks in this connection: "The non-Israelites thus cannot become Israelites, because then the proposition that the end of the ages has dawned, when all of the nations will recognize Israel's God as the one and only God, a propositional claim based in the confession of the *Shema' Israel*, will instead be undermined" (*Reading Romans within Judaism*, 106; emphasis original).

93. Philo, *Mos.* 2.43–44; *Sib. Or.* 3.702–723. See Donaldson, *Paul and the Gentiles: Remapping the Apostle's Convictional World* (Minneapolis, MN: Fortress Press, 1997), 219; Donaldson, "Jewish Christianity, Israel's Stumbling and the *Sonderweg* Reading of Paul," in *Journal for the Study of the New Testament* 29 (2006): 27–54.

BIBLIOGRAPHY

Ábel, František. *The Psalms of Solomon and the Messianic Ethics of Paul*. WUNT 2.416. Tübingen: Mohr Siebeck, 2016.

Atkinson, Kenneth. *The Hasmoneans and Their Neighbors: New Historical Reconstructions from the Dead Sea Scrolls and Classical Sources*. Jewish and Christian Texts 27. London, U.K., and New York, NY: T&T Clark, 2018.

Badenas, Robert. *Christ the End of the Law: Romans 10:4 in Pauline Perspective*. JSNTSup 10. Sheffield: JSOT Press, 1985.

Barclay, John M. G. *Obeying the Truth: A Study of Paul's Ethics in Galatians*. Edinburgh: T&T Clark, 1988.

———. *Paul and the Gift*. Grand Rapids, MI: Eerdmans, 2015.

Barrett, Charles Kingsley. *A Commentary on the Epistle to the Romans*, 2nd ed. BNTC/HNTC. London, U.K.: Black; New York, NY: Harper, 1991.

Bell, Richard H. *Provoked to Jealousy: The Origin and Purpose of the Jealousy Motif in Romans 9–11.* WUNT 2.63. Tübingen: Mohr Siebeck, 1994.

Betz, Hans-Dieter. *Galatians: A Commentary on Paul's Letter to the Churches in Galatia.* Hermeneia. Philadelphia, PA: Fortress Press, 1979.

Bring, Ragnar. *Christus und das Gesetz.* Leiden: Brill, 1969.

Bultmann, Rudolf. "Christ the End of the Law." In *Essays Philosophical and Theological*, 36–66. Translated by James G. G. Greig. London: SCM, 1955.

———. *Der Stil der paulinischen Predigt und die kynisch-stoische Diatribe.* Göttingen: Vandenhoeck & Ruprecht, 1984 [1910].

Campbell, William S. "The Freedom and Faithfulness of God in Relation to Israel." *Paul's Gospel in an Intercultural Context: Jew and Gentile in the Letter to the Romans*, 43–59. Studies in the Intercultural History of Christianity 69; Frankfurt: Peter Lang, 1991.

———. *The Nations in the Divine Economy: Paul's Covenantal Hermeneutics and Participation in Christ.* Lanham, MD: Lexington Books/Fortress Academic, 2018.

———. *Paul's Gospel in an Intercultural Context: Jew and Gentile in the Letter to the Romans.* Studies in the Intercultural History of Christianity 69. Frankfurt: Peter Lang, 1991.

Charlesworth, James H., ed. *The Messiah: Developments in Earliest Judaism and Christianity.* Minneapolis, MN: Fortress Press, 1992.

Collins, John J. *Between Athens and Jerusalem: Jewish Identity in the Hellenistic Diaspora.* 2nd ed. BRS. Grand Rapids, MI, and Cambridge, U.K.: Eerdmans, 2000.

———. "Messianism and Exegetical Tradition: The Evidence of the LXX Pentateuch." In *Jewish Cult and Hellenistic Culture: Essays on the Jewish Encounter with Hellenism and Roman Culture*, edited by John J. Collins, 58–81. JSJSup 100. Leiden: Brill, 2005.

———. *The Scepter and the Star: The Messiahs of the Dead Sea Scrolls and Other Ancient Literature.* ABRL. New York, NY: Doubleday, 1995.

Cranfield, Charles E. B. *A Critical and Exegetical Commentary on the Epistle to the Romans.* 2 vols. ICC. Edinburgh: T&T Clark, 1975–79.

Dahl, Nils A. "Paul's Letter to the Galatians: Epistolary Genre, Content, and Structure." In *The Galatians Debate: Contemporary Issues in Rhetorical and Historical Interpretation*, edited by Mark D. Nanos, 117–42. Peabody, MA: Hendrickson, 2002.

Donaldson, Terence. *Judaism and the Gentiles: Jewish Patterns of Universalism (To 135 CE).* Waco, TX: Baylor University Press, 2007.

———. *Paul and the Gentiles: Remapping the Apostle's Convictional World.* Minneapolis, MN: Fortress Press, 1997.

Dunn, James D. G. *Romans 9–16.* Word Bible Commentary 38B. Dallas, TX: Word Books, 1991 [1988].

———. *The Theology of Paul the Apostle.* Grand Rapids, MI, and Cambridge, U.K.: Eerdmans, 2006 [1998].

Elliott, Neil. "The Question of Politics: Paul as a Diaspora Jew under Roman Rule." In *Paul within Judaism: Restoring the First-Century Context to the Apostle*, edited by Mark D. Nanos and Magnus Zetterholm, 203–43. Minneapolis, MN: Fortress Press, 2015.

Esler, Philip F. *Conflict and Identity in Romans: The Social Setting of Paul's Letter*. Minneapolis, MN: Fortress Press, 2003.

Fitzmyer, Joseph A. *Romans: A New Translation with Introduction and Commentary*. AB 33. New York, NY: Doubleday, 1993.

Fredriksen, Paula. "Judaism, the Circumcision of Gentiles and Apocalyptic Hope: Another Look at Galatians 1 and 2." In *The Galatians Debate: Contemporary Issues in Rhetorical and Historical Interpretation*, edited by Mark D. Nanos, 235–60. Peabody, MA: Hendrickson, 2002.

———. "The Question of Worship: Gods, Pagans, and the Redemption of Israel." In *Paul within Judaism: Restoring the First-Century Context to the Apostle*, edited by Mark D. Nanos and Magnus Zetterholm, 175–201. Minneapolis, MN: Fortress Press, 2015.

Gruen, Erich S. *Heritage and Hellenism: The Reinvention of Jewish Tradition*. Berkeley/Los Angeles/London: University of California Press, 1998.

Hodge, Caroline J. "The Question of Identity: Gentiles as Gentiles—but Also Not—in Pauline Communities." In *Paul within Judaism: Restoring the First-Century Context to the Apostle*, edited by Mark D. Nanos and Magnus Zetterholm, 153–73. Minneapolis, MN: Fortress Press, 2015.

Horbury, William. *Jewish Messianism and the Cult of Christ*. London: SCM, 1998.

———. "Messianism in the Old Testament Apocrypha and Pseudepigrapha." *Messianism among Jews and Christians. Twelve Biblical and Historical Studies*, 35–64. London, U.K., and New York, NY: T&T Clark—Continuum, 2003.

Howard, George E. "Christ the End of the Law: The Meaning of Romans 10:4ff." *JBL* 88 (1969): 331–37.

Hübner, Hans. "τέλος." *EDNT* 3 (1993): 347–48.

Jenkins, Richard. *Social Identity*. London: Routledge, 1996.

Jewett, Robert. *Romans: A Commentary*. Edited by Eldon J. Epp. Hermeneia Series. Minneapolis, MN: Fortress Press, 2006.

Käsemann, Ernst. *Commentary on Romans*. Translated by G. W. Bromiley. Grand Rapids, MI: Eerdmans, 1980.

Kim, Johann D. *God, Israel, and the Gentiles: Rhetoric and Situation in Romans 9–11*. SBLDS 176. Missoula, MT: Scholars Press, 2000.

Koch, Dietrich-Alex. *Die Schrift als Zeuge des Evangeliums. Untersuchungen zur Verwendung und zum Verständnis der Schrift bei Paulus*. Tübingen: Mohr Siebeck, 1986.

Lindemann, Andreas. "Die Gerechtigkeit aus dem Gesetz: Erwägungen zur Auslegung und zur Textgeschichte von Römer 10,5." *ZNW* 73 (1982): 231–50.

Mason, Stephen. "Jews, Judeans, Judaizing, Judaism: Problems of Categorization in Ancient History." *Journal for the Study of Judaism* 38 (2007): 475–512.

Michel, Otto. *Der Brief an die Römer*, 14th ed. MeyerK 4. Göttingen: Vandenhoeck & Ruprecht, 1978.

Moo, Douglas J. *The Epistle to the Romans*. NICNT. Grand Rapids, MI, and Cambridge, U.K.: Eerdmans, 1996.

Munck, Johannes. *Paul and the Salvation of Mankind*. London: SCM Press, 1959.
Mussner, Franz. "Christus, des Gesetzes Ende zur Gerechtigkeit für jeden der glaubt (Röm 10,4)." In *Paulus—Apostat oder Apostel? Jüdische und christliche Antworten*, edited by Markus Barth et al., 31–44. Regensburg: Pustet, 1977.
Nanos, Mark D. *The Mystery of Romans: The Jewish Context of Paul's Letter*. Minneapolis, MN: Fortress Press, 1996.
———. *Reading Romans within Judaism. Collected Essays of Mark D. Nanos, Vol. 2*. Eugene, OR: Cascade Books, 2018.
Nanos, Mark D., and Zetterholm, Magnus, eds. *Paul within Judaism: Restoring the First-Century Context to the Apostle*. Minneapolis, MN: Fortress Press, 2015.
Nelson, Richard D. *Deuteronomy: A Commentary*. OTL. Louisville, KY, and London, U.K.: Westminster John Knox Press, 2002.
Neusner, Jacob, William S. Green, and Ernest S. Frerichs, eds. *Judaisms and Their Messiahs*. Cambridge, U.K.: Cambridge University Press, 1987.
Novenson, Matthew V. "Jewish Messiahs, the Pauline Christ, and the Gentile Question." *JBL* 128.2 (2009): 357–73.
Stowers, Stanley K. *A Rereading of Romans: Justice, Jews and Gentiles*. New Haven, CT: Yale University Press, 1994.
Stuhlmacher, Peter. "Das Ende des Gesetzes: Über Ursprung und Ansatz der paulinischen Theologie." *ZThK* 67 (1970): 14–30. Reprinted in Peter Stuhlmacher, *Versöhnung, Gesetz und Gerechtigkeit*, 166–91. Göttingen: Vandenhoeck & Ruprecht, 1981.
Suggs, M. Jack. "The Word Is Near You: Rom 10:6–10 within the Purpose of the Letter." In *Christian History and Interpretation: Studies Presented to John Knox*, edited by W. R. Farmer, C. F. D. Moule, and R. R. Niebuhr, 289–312. Cambridge, U.K.: University Press, 1967.
Tobin, Thomas H. *Paul's Rhetoric in Its Context: The Argument of Romans*. Peabody, MA: Hendrickson, 2004.
VanLandingham, Chris. *Judgment and Justification in Early Judaism and the Apostle Paul*. Peabody, MA: Hendrickson, 2006.
Vos, Johan S. "Die hermeneutische Antinomie bei Paulus (Galater 3.11–12; Römer 10.5–10)." *NTS* 38 (1992): 254–70.
———. *Die Kunst der Argumentation bei Paulus. Studien zur antiken Rhetorik*. WUNT 149. Tübingen: Mohr Siebeck, 2002.
Wilckens, Ulrich. *Der Brief and die Römer*. 3 vols. EKKNT 6. Zurich: Benziger, 1978–82.
Windsor, Lionel J. *Paul and the Vocation of Israel: How Paul's Jewish Identity Informs His Apostolic Ministry, With Special Reference to Romans*. BZNW 205. Berlin: de Gruyter, 2014.
Wolter, Michael. "Ein exegetischer und theologischer Blick auf Röm 11.25–32." *NTS* 64 (2018): 123–42.
Wright, Nicholas Thomas. *Climax of the Covenant: Christ and the Law in Pauline Theology*. Minneapolis, MN: Fortress Press, 1991.
Wyse, Marion. *Variations on the Messianic Theme: A Case Study of Interfaith Dialogue (Judaism and Jewish Life)*. Brighton, MA: Academic Studies Press, 2009.

Zahn, Theodor. *Der Brief des Paulus an die Römer*. Kommentar zum Neuen Testament 6. Leipzig: Deichert, 1910.

Zeller, Dieter. *Der Brief an die Römer. Übersetzt und erklärt*. RNT. Regensburg: Pustet, 1985.

Zoccali, Christopher. "'And so all Israel will be saved': Competing Interpretations of Romans 11.26 in Pauline Scholarship." *JSNT* 30.3 (2008): 289–318.

Index of Authors

Ábel, František, 215n39, 215n45, 289–316
Abelard, Peter, 37, 45, 45n61
Adamo, David Tuesday, 18n22
Adams, Edward, 177n15
Aland, Barbara, 233n12
Aland, Kurt, 233n12
Althaus, Paul, 233n13
Aratus, 104–5, 114n6
Arrian, 222–23
Asano, Atsuhiro, 138n8
Ascough, Richard S., 39n7
Atkinson, Kenneth, xi, xii, 199–217, 213n18, 303n1
Avemarie, Friedrich, 284n24

Bachmann, Michael, xi, xii, 121–48
Badenas, Robert, 308n35, 309n45
Bailey, Robert C., 19n30
Baltes, Guido, 142n47
Barclay, John M. G., 59n12, 69n3, 71, 121–22, 138n9, 142n49, 144n76, 180n31, 182n52, 237n44, 238n62, 286n49, 286n51, 311n82
Barth, Markus, 69n4, 70
Barthélemy, Dominique, 93–94, 101n15
Bartsch, H.-W., 213n17, 214n32
Bauer, Walter, 140n20, 142n48, 180n43, 221, 233n12

Bauernfeind, Otto, 288
Baur, Ferdinand Christian, 84n2, 311n78
Bayat, Ardeshir, 19n31
Becker, Adam H., 47
Becker, Eve-Marie, 283n3
Becker, Jürgen, 111–12, 116n35
Bell, Richard H., 306n12
Berger, Peter L., 39n10
Berlin, Adele, 19n26, 20
Berthelot, Katell, 152, 162
Bertram, Georg, 88, 100n7
Betz, Hans-Dieter, 121, 137n4, 138n7, 284n17
Betz, Otto, 142nn41–42
Bianchini, Francesco, 138n9
Billerbeck, Paul, 138n9
Binder, Donald D., 214n28
Bird, Michael F., 285n29
Blass, F., 213n14
Boccaccini, Gabriele, 196n12
Bockmuehl, Markus, 196n3
Boer, Martinus C. de, 141n21
Borgen, Peder, 40n15
Boyarin, Daniel, xi, xii, 17n1, 21, 83n1, 215n38
Brawley, Robert L., 142n49, 160n6
Brélaz, Cédric, 160n6
Brenner, Athalya, 18n22
Breytenbach, Cilliers, 107

Bring, Ragnar, 308n35
Bruce, Frederick F., 138n9
Bruyn, Theodore S. de, 232n7
Buitenwerf, Rieuwerd, 285n40
Bull, Klaus-Michael, 116n36
Bultmann, Rudolf, 307n19, 309n55
Byrskog, Samuel, 41n23, 47

Campbell, Douglas A., 42n31
Campbell, William S., xi, xii, 38n2, 43n36, 140n20, 162, 165–86, 232n6, 237n53, 283n9, 284n13, 284n15, 285n31, 300, 303n3, 304n4, 305n9, 306n12, 306nn14–15, 308n30, 310n70, 311nn74–75, 311nn77–79, 312n91
Cassius Dio, 203, 214n23, 226, 228, 236n37, 238n66
Celsus, Aulus, 6, 21
Charles, Ronald, 39n12, 47
Charlesworth, James H., 58n3, 59nn7–9, 305n10
Chester, Andrew, 69n8, 285n45
Cicero, 161nn7–8
Clarke, Frank, 69n10
Clement of Alexandria, 160n1, 235n25
Cohen, Jeremy, 258n11
Cohen, Shaye J. D., 17n1, 18n18, 18n22, 187, 196nn1–2
Collar, Anna, 41n20
Collins, John J., 59n8, 63, 285n40, 304n5, 305n10
Colson, F. H., 58n4
Comfort, Philip Wesley, 212n2
Concannon, Cavan, 197n28
Cooper, Stephen A., 232n7
Cover, Michael B., 71n28
Cranfield, Charles E. B., 221, 234n17, 309n44, 310n64
Cunningham, Philip A., 265n58, 268
Cyprian, 28, 45n58

Dahl, Nils A., 142n33, 311n82
Danker, F. W., 233n12
Davies, Willam David, 116n39

Denis, Albert-Marie, 285n40
Dibley, Genevive, xi, xii, 3–23, 20n42, 21, 71n31, 84n5
Dimant, Devorah, 69n8
Dio Cassius. *See* Cassius Dio
Dio Chrysostom, 223
Diogenes Laertius, 214n26
Dochhorn, Jan, 230, 238n58, 238n61, 238n64
Dodd, Charles H., 43n42
Donaldson, Terence L., 39n12, 40n14, 42n31, 43n37, 47, 62, 69nn5–7, 71n24, 83n1, 84nn5–6, 88, 100n2, 131, 143n55, 197n17, 256n6, 285n33, 304n7, 312n93
Donfried, Karl Paul, 214n32
Dormeyer, Detlev, 105, 114nn8–9, 116
Douay–Rheims, 262n37
Downs, David J., 64, 70n11
Dunn, James D. G., 100n1, 138n9, 222, 234n21, 290–91, 306n16, 306nn12–13, 307n20, 308nn33–34, 309n44, 309n56, 310n65, 311n84
Dunne, John, 18n22

Eastman, Susan Grove, 121–22, 138n9, 143n62, 194, 197n27
Eckhardt, Benedikt, 18n19, 236n35
Edsall, Benjamin, 160n1
Ehrensperger, Kathy, xi, xii, 38n2, 68n1, 149–64, 176n4, 177n15, 179n28, 181n46, 182n48
Eisenbaum, Paula, 20n40, 38n2, 46, 215n38
Elliott, Mark Adam, 188–89, 196n5, 196n7
Elliott, Neil, 177n15, 178n17, 179n23, 304n5
Empedocles, 214n26
Emser, Hieronymus, 221, 232n7
Engberg-Pedersen, Troels, 114n4
Enrietti, Mario, 55, 59n6
Epictetus, 224, 226, 228
Esler, Philip F., 179n29, 181n44, 303n3
Euripides, 104–5, 114n6

Eusebius, 160n1
Eyl, Jennifer, 144n82

Fee, Gordon D., 134, 138n8, 144n69
Feldman, Louis H., 17n13, 20n33, 59nn11–12
Ferguson, Mark, 19n31
Ferrua, Antonio, 213n14
Fitzmyer, Joseph A., 212n2, 213n8, 306n13, 307n20, 310n64, 311n87, 311n93, 312n87
Foerster, W., 261n31
Foster, Robert B., 285n32
Fowl, Stephen, 77n13
Fox, Michael V., 19n27, 21
Frankfurter, David, 237n56
Fredriksen, Paula, xi, xiii, 20n40, 30, 38n3, 43n35, 68n1, 71n28, 71n32, 138n7, 138n9, 146, 161n14, 180n30, 181n46, 190, 197n17, 197n18, 197n22, 215n38, 262n36, 304nn5–6, 310n72
Frey, Jörg, 114n5

Gager, John G., 257n9
Gamble, Harry, 200, 212n3
García Martínez, Florentino, 196nn10–11
Garroway, Joshua D., xi, xiii, 68n1, 187–98, 197n24
Gaston, Lloyd, 33, 44n45, 257n9
Gathercole, Simon J., 238n68
Gaventa, Beverly Roberts, 181n46, 284n11
Geffcken, Johannes, 285n40
Gemünden, Petra Von, 234n20
Georgi, Dieter, 64, 69n10
Gibson, Elsa, 213n14
Gilbert, Gary, 20n33
Gnilka, Joachim, 107, 114n19
Gollaher, David L., 17n10
Goodman, Martin, 41n23
Gowler, David B., 40n15
Grabbe, Lester L., 18n16, 21, 59n12, 100n5

Green, Peter, 21
Grindheim, Sigurd, 196n3
Gruen, Erich S., 18n16, 18n20, 214n19, 304n5
Gurtner, Daniel M., 85

Hahn, Ferdinand, 69n4, 107, 138n8
Hall, Robert, 6, 17n10, 21
Hammond Bammel, Caroline P., 232n6
Hanneken, Todd R., 20n37, 20n39
Harl, Marguerite, 100nn16–18, 101n13, 101nn16–18, 101n20
Harland, Philip, 39nn5–7
Harrill, Albert J., 70n15, 162
Harrison, James R., 161nn12–13, 162
Hata, Gohei, 20n33
Häuser, Peter, 140n12
Hays, Richard B., 69n9, 285n32
Heen, Eric, 162, 164
Hengel, Martin, 107
Henze, Matthias, 197n16
Herms, Ronald, 83n1
Hicks-Keeton, Jill, 69n8
Hodge, Caroline Johnson, 197n25, 215n43, 310n71, 311n74
Hofius, Otfried, 107, 114n17
Holloway, Paul A., 160n3, 162
Holofernes character, 11–12
Holtz, Gudrun, 83n1
Horbury, William, 69n8, 305n10
Horn, Friedrich Wilhelm, 129–30
Howard, George E., 308n35
Hruby, Kurt, 114n14
Hübner, Hans, 180n36, 309n55
Hultgren, Arland J., 284n16
Hunter, David G., 232n7

Inwood, Brad, 214n26
Iyaduria, Joshua, 19n29

Jaoko, Walter, 19n30
Jenkins, Richard, 305n9
Jensen, Matthew D., 261n28
Jeremias, Joachim, 188–89, 196n8, 308n40

Jewett, Robert, 222, 227, 234n20, 237n45, 243, 250, 256n5, 291, 298, 305n11, 306n13, 306n16, 307nn18–21, 307nn26–27, 308n36, 309nn41–42, 309nn45–48, 310nn60–63, 310nn66–69, 309n50, 309n55, 309n58, 311n73, 311n76, 311nn80–81, 311nn83–85, 312nn86–87, 312nn89–90, 314
Jipp, Joshua W., 71n32
Jobes, Karen H., 100n8, 101n25
Joosten, Jan, 100n10
Josephus, Flavius, 18n19, 153, 203, 214n22, 215n47, 222, 230–31, 235n29, 278–79, 286n49, 290, 310n70
Justin Martyr, 122, 136, 223, 235n25
Juvenal, 204, 214n27

Kahl, Brigitte, 215n47
Kaibel, Georgius, 115n31
Karlenzig, Bruce, 39n10
Kasch, 263n50
Käsemann, Ernst, 180n37, 221, 233n14, 309n55, 310n65
Keck, Leander, 70n11
Kim, Johann D., 307n19, 309n41
Kimber Buell, Denise, 45n57
Kirk, J. R. Daniel, 264n52
Klawans, Jonathan, 162, 164
Kloppenborg, John S., 39n5, 39n7
Koch, Dietrich-Alex, 69n9, 308n33
Koloski-Ostrow, Ann Olga, 214n30
Korečková, Andrea, 115n21
Kraemer, Ross S., 233n14
Kraus, Wolfgang, 285n33
Krey, Philip D. W., 45n61, 47

Lagrange, Marie-Joseph, 221–22, 234n18
Lambrecht, Jan, 143n54
Lampe, Peter, 178n19, 180n38
Last, Richard, 35–36, 39n5, 43n34, 47
Leeming, David A., 19n29

Levenson, Jon D., 19n26, 22
Levy, Ian Christopher, 45n61, 47, 140n13
Liddell, Henry George, 180n43
Lietzmann, Hans, 233n13
Lim, Timothy H., 69n9
Lindemann, Andreas, 106, 114n13, 121–22, 138n9, 284n27
Longenecker, Richard N., 144n69, 234n16
Louw, 307n18
Löwenstern, Johannes Apelles von, 122
Lucien, 42n28
Luther, Martin, 140n14, 221
Luz, Ulrich, 115n30, 115n32, 115n34

MacMullen, Ramsay, 214n33
Magid, Shaul, 18n22
Martial, 17n11
Martyn, J. Louis, 138n8, 143n61
Mason, Steve N., 236n37, 303n3
Matera, Frank J., 138n8, 143n54
Maurer, Christian, 115n29
McGrouther, Duncan, 19n31
McKnight, Scot, 100n8, 101n26
McLaren, James S., 40n14
Meeks, Wayne A., 213n9, 214n31
Meiser, Martin, 140n13
Menander, 104–5, 114n6
Merkel, Helmut, 107, 114n16
Merkelbach, Reinhold, 115nn23–24
Merrill, Eugene H., 196n9
Meyer, Heinrich August Wilhelm, 232n9
Meyer, Lester V., 196n4
Michel, Otto, 172, 180n35, 233n13, 233n14, 288, 310n65
Mihoc, Vasile, 260n19, 267
Miller, David M., 236n32
Minear, Paul S., 71n25
Minnis, A. J., 45, 45n61
Möbius, Hans, 115n23
Montanari, Franco, 233n12
Moo, Douglas J., 138n8, 227, 234n20, 237n46, 292, 306n13, 307nn22–23,

308n35, 309n41, 309n49, 309n56, 309n59, 309nn43–44, 310nn64–65, 312n87
Mordecai, 11, 19n25
Morgenthaler, Robert, 140nn17–18
Morland, Kjell Arne, 138n9
Mortensen, Jacob P. B., 38n2, 47, 232n6, 237n47, 237n54, 238n59
Mottas, François, 160n5, 164
Moulton, J. H., 234n22
Moxnes, Halvor, 69n4
Munck, Johannes, 64, 69n10, 176n2, 311n78
Murray, Michele, 235n28
Mussner, Franz, 138n9, 142n42, 309n55

Nanos, Mark D., xi, xiii, 17n3, 17n9, 20n33, 38n2, 41n25, 42n31, 43n37, 47, 213n13, 215n34, 215n41, 235n31, 237n56, 239nn70–71, 243–69, 284n13, 288, 293, 295, 306n13, 307n25, 308n39, 311n79, 312n88, 312n92
Nasrallah, Laura Salah, 38n2, 47
Nelson, Richard D., 297, 309nn51–54
Neusner, Jacob, 238n57, 305n10
Nickelsburg, George W. E., 59n8, 84n5, 196n13
Nickle, Keith F., 69n10
Niebuhr, Karl-Wilhelm, xi, xiii, 69n4, 271–88
Noffke, Eric, xi, xiii, 49–60, 101n24
Novatian, 160n1
Novenson, Matthew V., xi, xiii, 61–73, 70n21, 71n23, 100n4, 101n27, 168, 177n12, 177n14, 235n26, 238n60, 238n62, 258n14, 303n1
Noy, David, 237n39
Nygren, Anders, 221–22, 234n17

Oakes, Peter, 138n9, 143n61, 144n76, 164
Odoyo-June, Elijah, 19n30
Öhler, Markus, xi, xiii, 219–42, 236n32
Olsson, Birger, 214n28

Origen, 160n1, 212n1, 220, 229, 232n5, 234n24, 262n36, 268
Orosius, 201, 213n11
Orton, David E., 68n1
Ovid, 214n26

Pardee, Dennis, 144n75
Patte, Daniel, 115n33
Peek, Werner, 115nn25–26
Peres, Imre, xiii, 103–18
Pervo, Richard I., 213nn10–11
Pfuhl, Ernst, 115n23
Philo of Alexandria, 16, 52, 158–59, 203, 214n23, 222, 294, 312n87, 312n93
Pilhofer, Peter, 161nn12–13, 164
Plato, 214n26
Pliny the Sabinianus, 105
Plutarch, 223
Pope, Alexander, 45n60
Porphyry, 214n26
Porter, Stanley E., 17n2, 22
Portier-Young, Anathea, 162, 164
Pouchelle, Patrick, xi, xiii, 71n31, 87–102
Preuschen, Erwin, 221, 233n11
Ptolemais, 226, 236n36, 290

Qimron, Elisha, 144n74

Räisänen, Heikki, 68n1
Reed, Annette Yoshiko, 44n46, 47
Remus, Harold, 180n38
Richardson, Peter, 121, 136, 138n5, 140n12, 145nn91–92, 268
Robbins, Vernon K., 40n15
Roberts, J. J. M., 65, 70n20, 70nn17–18
Rodriguez, Rafael, 177n9, 181n45, 228, 232n6, 232nn3–4, 235n27, 235n28, 235n31, 237n47, 237n52, 238n59
Rogers, John H., 19n30
Röhser, Günter, 196n9
Rosen-Zwi, Ishay, 215n44
Rubinkiewicz, 55, 59nn7–8
Rudolph, David, 43n34, 47

Rufinus, 220, 262n36
Ruiz-Ortiz, Francisco-Javier, 19n27
Runesson, Anders, xi, xiii, 25–48, 42n28, 68n1, 214n28
Rüpke, Jörg, 161n10, 164
Rushdie, Salman, 9, 18n21, 23
Rutgers, Leonard V., 29, 42n29, 47, 213n15
Ryan, Thomas, 45n61, 47

Sacchi, Paolo, 59n6, 59n8
Sanders, E. P., 38n2, 62, 69n4, 197n18
Sandnes, Karl-Olav, 42n31, 47, 143n57, 177n8, 283n2, 288
Sänger, Dieter, 285n30, 288
Schade, Hans-Heinrich, 110, 115n27
Scheid, John, 181n47
Schiffman, Lawrence H., 20n33
Schlatter, Adolf, 233n13
Schmid, Heinrich, 114n14
Schnelle, Udo, 137nn2–3, 180n33
Schoeps, Hans-Joachim, 69n4
Schrage, Wolfgang, 141nn26–27
Schrenk, Gottlob, 121, 136, 137n4, 143n60, 144n87
Schwartz, Daniel R., 176n3, 178n19
Schweitzer, Albert, 103, 114n2
Scott, A. B., 45, 45n61
Scott, James M., 256n4, 268
Segal, Alan F., 38n4
Segal, Michael, 20n38
Seifrid, Mark A., 138n8
Seneca, 214n26
Seneca "the Younger," 204
Setzer, Claudia, 38n4
Sherwood, Aaron, 83n1, 84n6
Shutt, 58n2
Sievers, Joseph, 265n57, 268
Silva, Moisés, 100n8, 101n25
Sim, David C., 40n14
Simkovich, Malka Z., 88, 95, 100n3, 100n5, 100n11, 101n23
Slingerland, Dixon, 213n13
Smallwood, E. Mary, 213n13, 214n24
Smith, Eric C., 42n29

Smith, Ralph L., 101n14
Sonderweg, 32, 256n6
Song, Changwon, 179n22
Spencer, W. G., 6
Standhartinger, Angela, 160n6, 164
Stanley, Christopher D., 17n2, 69n9, 252, 262n42, 263n46, 263n48, 264n51, 268
Staples, Jason A., 215n42
Starling, David I., 84n4
Stauber, Josef, 115nn23–24
Stendahl, Krister, 33, 38n2, 179n24, 258n12, 268
Stern, Menahem, 236n36
Stone, Michael E., 197n16
Storey, Glenn R., 214n29
Stowers, Stanley Kent, 71n32, 176n5, 179n23, 234n20, 235n27, 239n71, 257n9, 268, 307n19
Strabo, 222
Strack, Hermann L., 138n9
Strawbridge, Jennifer R., 160n1
Strugnell, John, 144n74
Stuckenbruck, Loren T., xi, xiii, 75–86
Stuhlmacher, Peter, 69n4, 114n18, 309n55
Suetonius, 201, 203
Suggs, M. Jack, 310n66
Swatos, William H., Jr., 39n10

Tacitus, 203, 214n22, 215n47
Tacoma, Laurens E., 233n14
Tassin, Claude, 100n9
Taylor, Richard A., 196n6
Tcherikover, Victor, 59n12
Thackeray, H., 288
Theißen, Gerd, 234n20
Theobald, Michael, 137n2
Theophrastus, 261n26
Thiessen, Matthew, 4, 5, 15, 17nn4–8, 38n2, 42n31, 42n33, 71n28, 177n9, 181n45, 182n48, 232n4, 232n6, 235n26, 235n28, 237n43, 237n47, 237n51
Tholuck, A., 232n9, 238n62, 241

Thom, Johan C., 261n31, 268
Thorsteinsson, Runar M., 176n5, 177n6, 177nn9–10, 178n16, 178n20, 181n45, 228, 232n4, 232n6, 235n25, 235n28, 235n31, 237nn47–50, 237nn53–54, 238n59
Tigchelaar, Eibert J. C., 196nn10–11
Tiller, Patrick A., 84n5
Tobin, Thomas H., 309n41
Tomson, Peter J., 135, 136, 138n9, 144nn75–76, 144nn78–84, 145n93
Trophimus the Ephesian, 70n14
Tucker, J. Brian, 237n55
Turner, Nigel, 234n22

van der Horst, Pieter W., 233n14
VanderKam, James C., 5, 13, 20n35, 23, 196n5, 196n13
VanLandingham, Chris, 215n37, 215n40, 310n72
Vanlaningham, Michael G., 256n6, 269
Van Voorst, Robert, 213n13
Vital, Hayyim, 18n22
Vollenweider, Samuel, 162, 164
Vos, Johan S., 308n33

Wagner, J. Ross, 69n3, 70n21, 71n22, 71n27, 179n25, 180nn41–42
Watson, Francis, 229, 237n55, 283n9, 284n14, 288
Weaver, Joel A., 256n4, 269
Wedderburn, Alexander J. M., 114n3
Weiss, Bernhard, 232n9
Wengst, Klaus, 140n20, 144n76, 173, 180n32, 180n43, 180nn39–40, 182n49
Westerholm, Stephen, 284n20, 288
Whiston, William, 18n15, 18n17
Wilckens, Ulrich, 221, 234n15, 234nn15–16, 309n44, 309n55
Wilk, Florian, 69n9, 285n32, 288

Williams, Margaret H., 214n25, 214n33, 226, 233n14, 236n34, 236n37, 237nn39–40
Willitts, Joel, 43n34, 47, 193–94, 196n3, 197n26
Wilson, Stephen G., 215n35
Windsor, Lionel J., 235n29, 238n67, 307n24, 308n29, 308nn31–32
Winninge, Mikael, xi, xiii
Wischmeyer, Oda, 238n69
Witherington, Ben, III, 178n20, 180n41
Witt, R. E., 42n28
Wojtkowiak, Heiko, 160n4, 164
Wolff, Christian, 114n15
Wolff, H. W., 70n19
Wolter, Michael, 124–25, 134, 141n22, 227, 234n20, 237n44, 238n65, 284n16, 288, 306n17
Wright, Nicholas T., 234n16, 239n71, 261n29, 269, 308n35
Wycliffe, 251
Wyse, Marion, 305n10

Yee, Gale A., 18n22, 20

Zahn, Theodor, 141n32, 182n53, 221, 224, 233n10, 308n33
Zarmakoupi, Mantha, 161n11, 164
Zeller, Dieter, 310n66
Zetterholm, Karin Hedner, 44n46
Zetterholm, Magnus, 17n3, 38n2, 41n23, 42n31
Zimmermann, Christiane, 121–22, 127, 128, 138n9, 140n16, 140n18, 141n26, 141n28, 141n32, 142n45, 142nn36–38, 143n62, 144n76, 144n85
Zoccali, Christopher, 70n16, 256n4, 259n17, 269, 306n17
Zurawski, Jason M., 196n12

Index of Subjects

Abraham: Azazel and, 54–55, 59n6, 59n8; circumcision and, 3, 14; idolatry of, 177n15; *Israēl* (and *Israēlites*) and, 128, 132–33, *133,* 142n35; Israel related to, 172–73; in particularism and universalism, Gentile salvation, 31–32, 35, 43n41; text related to, 54–55, 58n5, 58n9; Torah and, 82; translation related to, 55, 59n10

Abrahamic covenant: of circumcision, 4–5; destruction of, 190; Greek standards and, 6, 17n10; Jews related to, 244–45, 258n15

Abrahamic faith, 82

Abraham's descendants, 181n44; calling of, 280; through Isaac, 173–74; through Isaac and Jacob, 180n43, 191, 192, 303n3

Achior, 11–12, 13

Adiabene, 43n37

admonishing, 247, 261n27

afterlife: Jewish Hellenism related to, 108–12, 113; Pharisees on, 26, 38n4

Agathocles, 110

Ahasuerus (king), 11, 19n23

Alexander the Great, 8

Alexandria anti-Jewish riots, 290

"all Israel saved," 249, 281–82; English on, 250, 251, 262n37; Greek language on, 250, 261n31, 261nn33, 262nn36–37; Hebrew on, 250, 261n34; Latin on, 250–51, 262n36

Ambrosiaster, 232n7

Ammonites, 11–12, 20n34

anacoluthon, 224

Ananias, 43n37, 56

angels, 53, 54, 82, 98; giants and, 79–81; Michael, 79–80; name and, 162n29

Animal Apocalypse, 63, 191

Animal Vision, 78, 84n5

annunciation, 277

anointed one, 156–57

Anthedon anti-Jewish riots, 290

anti-Jewish riots, 290

Antiochos (Antiochus) IV (king), 7–8, 9, 161n16

apocalyptic contemporaries, 188–91, 196n4, 196n6

apostle to the Gentiles, 272, 282, 283n3; all Israel related to, 275; end of times and, 111–12, 273–74

Aquila, 202

argumentative explication, 272

Aristeas, 50–53

325

Ascalon anti-Jewish riots, 290
ascent and descent, 296, 309n48
Aseneth, 53–54, 98
assimilation model, 94
Assyrian Empire, 11–12
Azazel, 54–55, 59n6, 59n8

Babylonia, 49
beauty, 109
bending knees and acknowledging tongues, 149; anointed one in, 156–57; Antiochos IV related to, 161n16; call to nations in, 157; challenges in, 154–55; Christ poem and, 159; contemporary secondary literature on, 149, 160n2; context of, 150–52; divine providence for, 152–53, 162n19; echo chamber in, 156–58; expectation of, 155–56, 158; historicity of, 151, 161n14; imperial power negotiation and, 152–53, 161n16, 162n19; Jews related to, 154; letter on, 150, 160n4; lordship in, 154–56, 162n24; memory of, 157, 162n28; naming in, 154, 156–58, 162n29; narrative poem related to, 155–56, 159–60; nations' Christ-followers and, 153–56; nations in, 157, 162n27; non-Jewish Christ-followers and, 153–56, 162n24, 162n26; Philo and, 152, 158–59; roles in, 160, 163n31; Roman culture and, 151; Roman dominance related to, 150–52, 161n14; Roman temples and, 151, 161n11; rulership in, 151, 161n9; temporariness of, 149–50; *Third Sibylline Oracle* and, 158–60; trust in, 150; verses in, 149; welcoming in, 156, 158, 162n26
biographical level, 271–76, 283n3
Bratislava conference, ix–xi, 112; participants at, xii–xiii
brothers, 223–24; in *Israēl* (and *Israēlites*), 128–29, 142n42

Caesar, Julius (emperor), 203
Caesarea, anti-Jewish riots in, 290
call: for Gentiles, 193; of God, 192–93
"called a Jew," 220
calling: of Abraham's descendants, 280; from God, 280–81
call to nations, 157
Catholic Church, 254, 265n58
"cemetery poetry," 111
Cephas, 44n49
chapter sixteen names, 200–201, 212nn4–6, 213n7
Chester Beatty Papyrus, 199–200
children, of God, 132–33, *133*
Chrestus, 201, 213n13
Christ: name of, 223; Torah related to, 295, 297. *See also specific topics*
Christ-followers, 150, 152, 153–56, 259n18
Christ-groups, 178n19
Christian identity, xii, 36
Christianity, 25; as Judaism, 205
Christians, term use, 201–2
Christians' persecution, 105–6, 131
Christology, 121–22
Christ poem, 159
church organization, 211
circumcision: Abraham and, 3, 14; Abrahamic covenant of, 4–5; attitude against, 15–16; compulsion of, 8–9, 226; eighth-day, 13–15; *first-order threat* of, 15; Galatians related to, 15–16, 20n41; in Gentiles' eschatological pilgrimage, 66, 71n22; God-fearer without, 14; inspection of, 11; *Israēl* (and *Israēlites*) and, 128, 129, 130, *130, 133*; of Izates, 56; Jesus related to, 57–58; as Jewish identity, 9, 18nn17–18; Jews in Rome and, 206, 209, 215n47; Jubilees on, 13–15, 20n36; line of inquiry on, 5–6; metonymic capacity of, 9; missionaries for, 58; in particularism and universalism,

Index of Subjects

mission, 34, 44n51; Philo on, 16, 182n48; Second Temple witnesses of, 16; of teachers, 229; timing of, 5, 13–15; Torah related to, 42n32. *See also* conversions; convert circumcision

circumcision surgical disguise *(epispasm)*, 6–7, 18n15

Claudius (emperor), 201–3, 204, 207, 213n11, 213n13

Closed-Ethnic religion, 28, 41n18

collection of money, 64, 70nn12–13

Comenius University (Bratislava), 303n2

commandments, 294

communities: of proselyte, 10–11

compassion, 109

compulsive conversion, 6–9, 18nn17–20

"congregations": joining of, 27; theology of, 26–27, 39n11; "why" of, 27, 39n12

contemporary secondary literature, 149, 160n2

content structure, text, xii

"conversion embodied," 98

conversion model, 87

conversions: of adults, 5; of Aseneth, 98; compulsive, 6–9, 18nn17–20; Hellenistic Jews and other nations and, 56–57, 59n12; of Jews in Rome, 203, 208; to Judaism, 204; meaning of, 12–13; mysticism related to, 54; of Paul, 69n6; self-preservation, 9–11, 18n22, 19n23, 19n25, 19n28, 29n32; of women, 20n41, 98. *See also* Israel's conversion

convert circumcision: desire for, 3; Paul against, 3–4, 17n2, 57–58

convert definition, 18n15

Corpus Paulinum, 123

Council of Jerusalem, 90–91

credibility, 272–73

cult of Isis, 29, 39n9, 41n20, 42n28, 203

curse, 96–97

Cyprian, 28, 41n22, 45n58

Cyrus, 156–57

Damascus anti-Jewish riots, 290

David (king) ("root of Jesse"), 64–65, 66–67, 89, 180n30

Delphic *gnōthi seauton,* 37, 45n60

Demetrias, 110

demigoddess, 109

Deo volente, 112

determinism, 189–90

Deutero-Isaiah's theological statements, 107

diachronous observations, 122, 134–35

Diaspora, 58, 83n1, 225, 236n37; annunciation related to, 277; in Babylonia, 49; messianic movement in, 27, 29

difference: in righteousness *pesher,* second speech, 301, 312n87

Diogenes from Eretria, 110

divine providence, 152–53, 162n19

divine righteousness, 296, 309n43. *See also* righteousness *pesher*

Dodekapropheton, 276

dual covenants, 32–33, 44n46

dualism, 187

echo chamber, 156–58

Egypt, 263n45; conquest of, 53; cult of Isis in, 29; exodus from, 18n22, 126; Jewish disturbances in, 202; rule of, 158; slavery in, 7

Egyptian-Jewish community, 178n19; warning to, 203, 207, 215n36

eighth-day circumcision, 13–15

ekklēsia, 57; division within, 30–31, 36, 44n47

Eleazarus (high priest), 50; Paul compared to, 57

Eleazer (Eleazar) the Galilean: Adiabene and, 41n24; Ananias compared to, 43n37; Izates and, 56; Paul and, 57; region of, 58

election, 209–10
Eliezer, Rabbi, 182n51
Elijah (prophet), 192, 256n4
emotions, 300; end of times related to, 273; of Paul, 271–72
end of times, 55; apostle to the nations and, 273–74; argumentative explication and, 272; biographical level, 271–76, 283n3; credibility in, 272–73; emotions related to, 273; eschatological salvation in, 275, 283; expectations of, 272–73; identity as Israelite in, 271–72, 274–75; Josephus and, 278–79; judgment and, 274, 276, 277; Paul in, 279–80; privileges related to, 274–75; prophetic traditions and, 276–78; Romans 9:1-5, 273–74; Romans 10:1, 274; Romans 11:1, 274–75; Romans 11:2-10, 281; Romans 11:6-29, 280–81; Romans 11:11-32, 281–82; Romans 11:13, 275–76; substitution theory and, 279; theological level, 280–82, 286n51; Torah and, 274; tradition historical level, 276–80
end-time redemption, xi, 289
English, on "all Israel saved," 250, 251, 262n37
Enoch tradition, 78, 80–83, 83n1
environment, 81
epispasm (circumcision surgical disguise), 6, 18n15
Esau, 175, 191, 192
eschatological expectation, 87
eschatological salvation, 275, 283
eschatological universalism: angels in, 79–80, 81–82; Animal Vision in, 78, 79, 84n5; Enoch tradition in, 78, 80–83, 83n1; faith in, 82; hope in, 77–78; Jerusalem in, 75, 76, 78, 83; Messiah in, 76–78, 84n4; nations in, 76–78, 84nn5–6; Noah related to, 80–82; promises related to, 76; righteous ones in, 80; Song of Moses in, 77; sources in, 75, 83n1; universal in, 75–76, 84nn2–3; worship in, 77–79, 80, 82, 85nn7–8
Esther, 9–11, 19n23, 19n25
ethical monotheism model, 87
ethnē (Gentile nations), ix–x, 258n10, 289
ethnic identity, 34–35, 44n50
ethnicities: of proselyte, 42n33
Ethnic Status, 28, 36, 45n57. *See also* particularism and universalism, ethnicity
Ethno-Ethic Mission, 28, 41n25
ethno-religious matters, 37
Eutychus, 205
Evangelical Lutheran Theological Faculty, 303n2
evangelical salvation paradigm: admonishing in, 247, 261n27; Israel in, 244–45, 258n10, 258n15, 259n18; persuasion related to, 248, 249, 261n28; rejection of, 248–49, 261n29; research on, 245–46; righteousness in, 244–45, 258n12; "saved" in, 244, 245, 258n14, 269nn18–19; timing of, 249, 261n30; translations and, 246–47
expectations, 87; of bending knees and acknowledging tongues, 155–56, 158; of end of times, 272–73; of Jews in Rome, 211–12
explicatory introductory formula, 169
expulsion of Jews, 201–2, 213n11, 213n13, 213n17
Ezra, 49, 188

faith, 175; Abrahamic, 82; Moses compared to, 296; in righteousness *pesher*, second speech, 296, 299–300, 301, 309n47. *See also* righteousness *pesher*, second speech
fear: for proselytes, 204
Fortuna, 152
freedom as slavery, 301, 311n82
Fulvia, 203, 231

Index of Subjects

Galilee anti-Jewish riots, 290
Gaza anti-Jewish riots, 290
Gentile as insider and outsider: chapter sixteen names and, 200–201, 212nn4–6, 213n7; expulsion of Jews in, 201–2, 213n11, 213n13, 213n17; integrity of Romans epistle in, 199–200; Orosius on, 201, 213n11. *See also* Jews in Rome
Gentile condition, 167, 177n6
Gentile inclusion. *See* particularism and universalism, ethnicity
Gentile nations *(ethnē)*, ix–x, 258n10, 289
Gentiles: call for, 193; identity of, 305n9; idolatry related to, 304n8; in Israel as sub-text, 166–67, 177n6; in Israel as sub-text, diatribe style, 168, 177n13; Israel compared to, 282; Jesus and, 27, 40n13; negative description of, 304n8; salvation and, 27, 39n14; term use of, 304n4; Torah for, 304n8. *See also* apostle to the Gentiles
Gentiles' eschatological pilgrimage: Animal Apocalypse in, 63; circumcision in, 66, 71n22; collection of money in, 64, 70nn12–13; divine governance in, 65; Isaiah on, 61, 63, 64–65, 68nn1–2, 70n16; Jerusalem in, 67, 71n28; Micah on, 61, 63, 68nn1–2; omissions related to, 62–63, 64–65, 68nn1–2, 70n16; options in, 67–68; Paul on, 62–63, 64, 69nn5–6, 70n16; "root of Jesse" in, 64–65, 66–67; *Sibylline Oracles* 3 on, 62; Zechariah on, 62, 63, 68nn1–2; Zion in, 66–67, 71n26. *See also* particularism and universalism, Gentile salvation
Gentiles' inclusion, 190–92, 304n8
Gershom, 14–15
giants, 79–81
globalized Christ, 30, 43n36

God: adoration to, 278; calling from, 280–81; call of, 192–93; children of, 132–33, *133*; faithfulness of, 291; of Hellenistic Jews and other nations, 50–51; in Israel as sub-text, negative statement or rhetorical question, 174, 175, 181nn46–47, 182n51; *Israēl* (and *Israēlites*) of, 14n39, 123, 124–25, 127–29, 131–32, *132,* 134, 136, 141n28, 142n39; mercy of, 286n51; mountain of, 61; names of, 50–51, 222, 225, 228; nations and, 61–62; rejection by, 273; trustworthiness of, 272, 273, 275, 282; Yahweh as, 303n3
God-fearers, 14, 87, 311n74
God of Israel: as God of nations, 30, 43n34; in Israel as sub-text, diatribe style, 170, 179nn25–27; in righteousness *pesher,* 290, 304n7
gods, names of, 222–23
God's chosen people, 300
God's delaying of punishment, 166, 176n5
God's plan, 35
God's promises, 31, 43n39
Gospels, 229, 250, 291; Torah compared to, 46n47
grace/faith relation, 175
grave texts, 110
Greco-Roman letter of recommendation., 200
Greek culture, 104
Greek epitaphs, 110
Greek language, 99; on "all Israel saved," 250, 261n31, 261nn33, 262nn36–37; Old Greek, 65–66, 71n22
Greek Magical Papyri, 29
Greek names, 200, 212n5
Greek positive afterlife, 108–10
Greek standards, 6, 17n10
"Greek-style" reconciliation, 107–8
Grk. Codes Panopolitanus, 79, 85n8

Hadassah. *See* Esther
Hagar/Ishmael, 258n15
Hagar/Sara, 129, 258n15
Hasmoneans, 225–26
Hasmonean state expansion, 303n1
Hebrew, 250, 261n34. *See also specific topics*
Helena (queen), 55–56
Hellenistic Jews and other nations, 49, 103; Abraham in, 54–55, 58n5, 59n6, 59n8; Aristeas and, 50–53; conversion and, 56–57, 59n12; Egypt in, 53–54; Eleazarus and, 50; God of, 50–51; idolatry related to, 51–52, 53; Izates in, 55–57, 59n12; Mosaic law and, 51; pagans and, 51, 52; seventy-two translators and, 50, 51; yearly celebrations for, 52–53
Hephaistion, 109
Herod (king), 226
historicity, 151, 161n14
Holofernes, 11–12
hopes, 108–11; in eschatological universalism, 77–78; for "just as has been written," 252, 263n49
human virtues, 109–10, 111
Hyrcanus (king), 303n1

identity, xii, 34–35, 36, 44n50, 174, 181n46; of Jesus, 202; Jews in Rome and, 12, 208–10, 215n43; meaning of, 305n9; in righteousness *pesher,* 290, 294–95, 305n9, 308n33. *See also* Jewish identity; Paul's interlocutor identity
identity as Israelite, 271–72, 274–75
idolatry, 54–55, 141n27, 263n45; Gentiles related to, 304n8; Hellenistic Jews and other nations related to, 51–52, 53; in Israel as sub-text, diatribe style, 168, 177n15, 178n16
Idumeans, 18n19
imperial power negotiation, 152–53, 161n16, 162n19

insulae (small apartments), 205
integrity of Romans epistle, 199–200
Inward Mission, 28, 41n26
Ioudaios: negative connotation of, 135; transferred application of term, 133
Isaac, 175, 191, 303n3; Abraham's descendants through, 173–74
Isaac and Jacob, 180n43, 191, 192, 303n3
Isaiah, 61, 68nn1–2
Ishmael, 191, 192
Isis cult, 29, 39n9, 41n20, 42n28, 203
Israel: Abraham related to, 172–73; boundaries of, 195; definitions of, 172, 194; in evangelical salvation paradigm, 244–45, 258n10, 258n15, 259n18; Gentiles compared to, 282; redemption of, 291; remnant from, 281; term use of, 303n3; twelve prophets and, 95–96
Israēl (and *Israēlites*), 258n10, 303n3; Abraham and, 128, 132–33, *133,* 142n35; boasting and, 123; brothers in, 128–29, 142n42; "Christian Jews" compared to "all Christians" and, 125; Christology and, 121–22; circumcision and, 128, 129, 130, *130,* 133; Corpus Paulinum and, 123, 135; diachronous observations on, 122, 134–35; of God, 14n39, 123, 124–25, 127–29, 131–32, *132,* 134, 136, 141n28, 142n39; Hagar-Sara and, 129; *Israēl* in, 134–35, 144n69, 144n82; *Israēlites* in, 124, 126, 127; Judaism related to, 121, 138nn4–5; *kata sarka* and, 122–23, 124, 126–27, 141n27; non-Jews' inclusion in, 131, 143n57; Protestant song and, 122, 140n14; proto-Pauline evidence and, 121, 123–27, *125, 126*; "salvific history" of, 136; set-theory tools and, *125,* 125–26, 136–37, *137*; synchronous observations on, 127–34, *130, 132, 133*; translations related to, 124, 126–27, 140n20,

141n27; turning point passages on, *130*, 130–32; wish for peace and, 127–28, 134–35

"Israel according to the flesh," 194–95

Israel as sub-text: "apostle to the nations" in, 165–67, 176n2, 177n7; Gentile condition in, 167, 177n6; God's delaying of punishment in, 166, 176n5; misconceptions in, 165, 166–67, 176n1, 177n6; Moses related to, 176n2; non-Jews in, 166–67, 177n6; reports in, 165, 176n1; revelations in, 166

Israel as sub-text, diatribe style, 167; Gentile in, 168, 177n13; God of Israel in, 170, 179nn25–27; ideology of sameness in, 168, 177n11; idolatry in, 168, 177n15, 178n16; Israel's status in, 169–70; leadership in, 168–69, 178nn19–20; major issues in, 169, 179n21; objections in, 168, 178n17, 179n21; *populus Romanus* in, 170, 179n28

Israel as sub-text, negative statement or rhetorical question: Abraham in, 173–75, 180n43, 181n44–45; *apparent* contradiction in, 172; circumcision in, 182n48; God in, 174, 175, 181nn46–47, 182n51; hearing and understanding in, 176, 182n53; Israelite heritage in, 170–71, 179n29; Israel's identity in, 174, 181n46; Israel's social dimension, 174, 181nn46–47; Justin on, 172; 9:6a-b in, 172, 180n35; 9:b in, 173, 180n41, 180n43; promises in, 171, 180n30; "word of God" in, 171; works/merit contract in, 175, 182n49

Israelite, 303n3; meaning of, 25, 37n1

Israelite heritage, 170–71, 179n29

Israelite remnant: apocalyptic contemporaries of, 188–91, 196n4, 196n6; within apocalyptic literature, 187; connotation of, 196n4; Daniel on, 196n6; Dead Sea Scrolls on, 188–89; division within, 187; dualism related to, 187; Elliott on, 188–89; foreknowledge of God and of, 189–90; Gentiles' inclusion and, 190–91; Jeremias on, 189; membership of, 187–88; predetermination of, 188–89, 196n4, 196n6; Romans 9–11 in, 191–95

Israel's conversion: "all Israel" in, 243, 256n4, 259n18; correction related to, 244, 257n9; mechanism of, 243, 256n3, 256n6; "saved" in, 243, 256n6, 257n8; timing of, 243, 256n2. *See also* "all Israel saved"; evangelical salvation paradigm; "just as has been written"

Izates (king), 20n33, 55–57, 59n12, 225

Jacob, 175, 180n43, 191, 192, 193, 303n3

Jacob/Israel, 255, 263n45

James (apostle), 44n49, 58n2

Jeremiah (prophet), 209

Jeremias, 189

Jerusalem: conquest of, 279; in eschatological universalism, 75, 76, 78, 83; in Gentiles' eschatological pilgrimage, 67, 71n28

Jerusalem Temple, 231

Jesus: Azazel and, 54–55; circumcision related to, 57–58; directive of, 75; identity of, 202; non-Jews and, 27, 40n13

Jesus compared to Messiah, 210–11

Jewish eschatological apocalyptical notions, xii

Jewish Hellenism: afterlife related to, 108–12, 113; afterlife requirements and, 110–12, 113; "bridge-theologian" in, 112, 113; catalogue on, 112, 113; Christians' persecution in, 105–6; fear related to, 108; Greek authors in, 104–5; Greek culture in, 104; Greek positive afterlife and, 108–10; "Greek-style" reconciliation

and, 107–8; "Hellenistic side" of, 104; Jesus and, 108; Jewish theologian in, 103; last judgment and, 111–12; letters related to, 104–5, 113; mission as, 105; new perspectives on, 103, 113; Pauline Hellenism as, 104, 114n12; Pauline Hellenism references and, 104–6; Pauline reconciliation and, 107–8, 114n18; Pharisee Paul and, 106; possible consequences and, 112; research on, 103; roots of, 106–7; self-righteousness and, 108; tolerance in, 105. *See also* Hellenistic Jews and other nations
Jewish identity, 128; circumcision as, 9, 18nn17–18; Moses on, 293; Paul's interlocutor and, 220, 232nn3–4
Jewish messianic movement, x
Jewish messianism, 289, 303n1
Jewish monotheism, x
Jewish-Pagan interaction, 49
Jewish speech duality, 135
Jewish way of life, 299, 310n70
Jews, 135, 258n10; Abrahamic covenant related to, 244–45, 258n15; fear of, 9–10; solidarity with, 274; term use of, 303n3; Ἰουδαῖος as, 227
Jews in Rome: circumcision and, 206, 209, 215n47; conversions of, 203, 208; denouncing of, 204, 214n27; diet of, 204, 206, 207, 208, 214n26, 214n33, 215n36; eschatological times and, 210–11; expectations of, 211–12; expulsion of, 203; gatherings of, 205, 214n31; identity and, 12, 208–10, 215n43; Jesus compared to Messiah and, 210–11; paganism and, 208–9, 212; residence of, 204–5; Torah of, 206–8, 209, 215n34
John, 75
joining to parting: Ethnic Status in, 36, 45n57; resurrection in, 35, 45n53; theology and institution in, 36, 45n56

Joseph, 53–54, 98
Josephus, 278–79
Judaism and the Gentiles (Donaldson), 304n7
Judaisms, 230; Christianity as, 205; conversions to, 204; diversity within, 57, 59n12; practice of, 25; term use of, 303n3
Judea, 289–90
Judeans: Paul's interlocutor, Ἰουδαῖος as title to, 226–27, 237n43; Paul's interlocutor identity and, 219; proselytes as, 204; Torah related to, 229
judgment, 111–12; end of times and, 274, 276, 277
Judith, 11–13, 20nn33–34
"just as has been written": v. 26 on, 251, 262nn38–40; v. 27 on, 251, 262n41; Catholic Church and, 254, 265n58; chapter 27 on, 251–52, 263n45; chapter 59 on, 251–52, 262n43; chapter 60 on, 251–52, 263n44; delivered/protected for, 252–53, 255, 263n50, 265nn53–54; disbelief in, 253, 264n52; hopes for, 252, 263n49; Isaiah on, 252, 263n47; Jacob/Israel and, 255, 263n45; NPP and, 266n60; substitution on, 253, 264nn51–52; Torah related to, 254–55, 266n59; traditions on, 252
Justin Martyr, 136, 140n12, 172

kata sarka, 122–24, 126–27, 141n27

Lamech, 80–81
languages, 200
last judgment, 111–12
Latin, 250–51, 262n36; names, 200, 212n6
letters: on bending knees and acknowledging tongues, 150, 160n4; Jewish Hellenism related to, 104–5, 113; Phoebe's recommendation, 200, 201

Letter to the Galatians, 15–16, 20n41
life after death. *See* afterlife
lordship, 154–56, 162n24
love, 53
Löwenstern, Johannes Apelles von, 122, 140n14
Lucianic recension, 89–90

Masoretic Text (MT), 65, 88–89, 90, 91, 92, 93, 94, 95, 96, 97, 99, 262, 263, 309n43
Mattathias, 8–9
Matthew: James compared to, 58n2; Paul compared to, 39n12
membership profiles, 29
memory, 157, 162n28
Menelaus (high priest), 7
The Message of Paul the Apostle within Second Temple Judaism, ix
Messiah: in eschatological universalism, 76–78, 84n4; Jesus compared to, 210–11; righteousness and, 297–98, 310n60
messianic ideas, ix–x
messianic movement, 27, 29
Micah, 61, 63, 68nn1–2, 92–93
Michael (angel), 79–80
middle voice. *See* passive or middle voice
Midnight's Children (Rushdie), 9
missionaries: for circumcision, 58
Moabites, 20n34
Mosaic covenant, 244–45, 258n15
Mosaic law, 51; aim of, 297; righteousness *pesher*, second speech and, 298–99, 302; in righteousness *pesher*, 294–95, 309n38
Moses: calling for, 280; faith compared to, 296; Israel as sub-text related to, 176n2; on Jewish identity, 293; persuasion of, 297; son of, 14–15
mountain, of God, 61
mysticism, 54

names, 201, 212n4, 213n7; angels and, 162n29; of Christ, 223; epigraphical evidence of, 226–27, 237n40, 237n43; feigning related to, 226, 236n37; of God, 50–51, 222, 225, 228; of gods, 222–23; Greek, 200, 212n5; Latin, 200, 212n6
naming, 154, 156–58, 162n29; in passive or middle voice, 235n29
narrative poem, 155–56, 159–60
nations, 30, 43n34; in bending knees and acknowledging tongues, 157, 162n27; in eschatological universalism, 76–78, 84nn5–6; *ethnē* as, ix–x, 258n10, 289; God and, 61–62; Paul's interlocutor identity and, 219, 232n1; in righteousness *pesher*, 289, 292–93, 302–3, 304n4, 307n24; in righteousness *pesher*, second speech, 301–2, 312n88; Ἰουδαῖος as, 227–28. *See also* Hellenistic Jews and other nations
nations' Christ-followers, 153–56
Nebuchadnezzar, 49
negative questions, 169
Nehemiah, 49
Nero (emperor), 55, 202
New Perspective on Paul (NPP), 266n60
Nikanor (Roman tribune), 278
Noah, 80–82
Non-Ethnic religion, 28, 41n20
non-Jewish Christ-followers, 153–56, 162n24, 162n26. *See also* Gentiles
NPP. *See* New Perspective on Paul
"Nun preiset alle Gottes Barmherzigkeit" (Löwenstern), 122, 140n14

observance of law, 231
Old Greek, 65–66, 71n22
Old Slavonic, 54–55, 58n5
olive tree grafting analogy, 261n27; allegory of, 246; "all Israel" related

to, 247, 282; catching up in, 247–48; election related to, 209–10; eschatological reality of, 281–82; remnants in, 193; temporariness in, 247; Theophrastus on, 261n26; wild shoot in, 247, 261n26
open-ethnic perspective, 29–30, 42n31
Open-Ethnic religion, 28, 41n19
"other," 28, 40n17. *See also* Hellenistic Jews and other nations

paganism, 208–9, 212. *See also* idolatry
papyrus, 199–200
paradigm shift, x–xi
particularism and universalism, 40n17, 87, 100n1; open-ethnic perspective in, 29–30, 42n31; recruitment in, 27–28; righteousness *pesher,* second speech related to, 300, 311n78
particularism and universalism, ethnicity, 28, 41nn18–20, 42n28, 43n44; Paul's original position on, 29–30, 42nn31–33; "unity in diversity" in, 30–31, 35, 36–37, 43n37, 44n51, 45n57
particularism and universalism, Gentile salvation, 36–37, 41n22, 43n42, 45nn58–59; Abraham in, 31–32, 35, 43n41; association in, 32, 43n43; dual covenants in, 32–33, 44n46; God's promises in, 31, 43n39; reconciliation in, 31, 43n40; salvation-inclusive religion in, 28, 31, 41n21
particularism and universalism, mission, 45n52; ethnic identity in, 34–35, 44n50; practices in, 33–35, 41nn23–26, 44n50; strategies of, 28–29, 44nn47–49, 44n51
parting to joining, 25–27
passive or middle voice, 235n28; brother and, 223–24; Cranfield on, 221–22; differentiation of, 232n4, 234nn22–23; "interesting example" in, 235n25; naming in, 235n29; of

Paul's interlocutor identity, 220–24, 232n4
Paul. *See specific topics*
Paul and the Gentile Problem (Theissen), 5–6
Paul and the Gentiles (Donaldson), 62, 69nn5–6
Pauline Hellenism, 104, 114n12
Pauline Hellenism references, 104–6
Pauline reconciliation, 107–8, 114n18
Paul's interlocutor, interpretation history, 232n9, 233n10, 234n19; medial/reflexive in, 221, 233n14; Nygren on, 221–22; reflexive use in, 233n12, 234n20
Paul's interlocutor, Ἰουδαῖος as title, 236n33, 237nn38–40; Cassius Dio and, 226, 236n37; Hasmoneans and, 225–26; to Judeans, 226–27, 237n43; origin in, 225, 236n34
Paul's interlocutor identity, 238n70; apostleship and, 219; audience of, 219, 220, 232n1, 232n3; Jewish identity and, 220, 232nn3–4; Judeans and, 219; nations and, 219, 232n1; Origen on Rom 2:17, 220–21, 232nn3–4; passive or middle voice of, 220–24, 232n4; Rom 2:17 context and, 224–25, 235nn30–31; translation about, 220, 232n4; Ἰουδαῖος as "called a Jew" and, 220; Ἰουδαῖος as Jewish teachers in, 229, 237n55; Ἰουδαῖος as proselyte or sympathizer of Judaism, 228–29, 237nn49–50; Ἰουδαῖος as typical Ἰουδαῖος in, 227–28
Paul's interlocutor identity, Ἰουδαῖος unrepresentative, 238n68; robbery of, 229–31, 237n56, 238n60, 238n62, 238nn65–67
Paul's Message and Jewish Eschatological Notions Concerning Israel's Role Towards the Nations, ix, xi–xii
Paul's primordialism, 4–5

Paul within Judaism Perspective, 4, 17n3
pericope 9:1–11:36 brief outline, 290–92, 306nn14–15
Persephone, 110
Persia, 18n22, 19n23, 19n25. *See also* self-preservation conversion
persuasion, evangelical salvation paradigm related to, 248, 249, 261n28
pesher 10:5-13, 292–93, 307n19, 307n21, 307nn23–24, 307n26; *pesher* definition in, 307n20. *See also* righteousness *pesher*
Pharisee Paul, 106
Pharisees: on afterlife, 26, 38n4; Josephus on, 38n4; Paul as, 44n48
philosophical parallels, 295–96
Phoebe's recommendation letter, 200, 201
piety, 109
plausibility structure, 26–27, 39n10
poetry, 111, 155–56, 159–60
Pompey (general), 203
primordial constructivist ethnicity construction., 4
Prisca, 202
promises, 76
pronoun, 222
prophetic traditions, 276–78
prophets, 12; Elijah, 192, 256n4; Jeremiah, 209
proselytes, 237n49; community of, 10–11; distinction of, 168; ethnicities of, 42n33; fear for, 204; issue of, 203; as Judeans, 204; sympathizers as, 228–29; welcoming of, 52, 56–57
proselytism, 311n74
Proselytizing Mission, 28, 41n24
prosopopeia (speech-in-character), 292, 307n19
Protestant song, 122, 140n14
proto-Pauline evidence, 121, 123–27, *125, 126*

Ptolemais anti-Jewish riots, 290
Ptolemy (king), 88

Qumran community membership, 194, 195
Qumranic sources, 83n1

reconciliation, 31, 43n40, 107–8, 114n18
recruitment, 27–28
redemption, of Israel, 291
rejection, of evangelical salvation paradigm, 248–49, 261n29
religious conversion, x
remnants, 281; in olive tree grafting analogy, 193; in righteousness *pesher,* 294, 308n30. *See also* Israelite remnant
remnant theology, 188–89, 191–95
repentance, 297
research, 245–46
resurrection, 15, 26, 35, 38n4, 45n53, 71n28, 211
revelations, 166
righteousness, 244–45, 258n12; Messiah and, 297–98, 310n60; self-, 108
righteousness *pesher,* 303n2, 305n11; 'by faith' formula in, 292, 307n21; commandments in, 294; end of time and, 289, 303n1; event sequence in, 291, 306n15; God of Israel in, 290, 304n7; identity in, 290, 294–95, 305n9, 308n33; Jewish messianism, 289, 290, 303n1; Jews in, 289, 303n3; Lev 18:5, first speech, 293–95, 308n30, 308n33, 308n38; Mosaic law in, 294–95, 309n38; nations in, 289, 292–93, 302–3, 304n4, 307n24; pericope 9:1–11:36 brief outline in, 290–92, 306nn14–15; *pesher* 10:5-13, 292–93, 307nn19–21, 307nn23–24, 307n26; *prosopopeia* in, 292, 307n19; remnant in, 294, 308n30;

speeches in, 293, 307n26; Torah in, 293, 308n28
righteousness *pesher*, second speech: "all" in, 302, 312n90, 312n92; ascent and descent in, 296, 309n48; difference in, 301, 312n87; divine righteousness in, 296, 309n43; faith in, 296, 299–300, 301, 309n47; freedom as slavery in, 301, 311n82; historical context in, 297; idolatry prohibition and, 299, 311n74; Jewish way of life in, 299, 310n70; Mosaic law and, 298–99, 302; nations in, 301–2, 312n88; new righteous conduct in, 299, 310n72; particularism and universalism related to, 300, 311n78; philosophical parallels in, 295–96; recontextualization in, 297–98, 310n60; salvific purpose in, 301
righteous ones, 80
robbery, 237n56, 238nn65–67; proselytes in, 238n62; sacrilege as, 238n60; teacher related to, 229–31
Roman culture, 151
Roman dominance, 150–52, 161n14
Romans, xi
Roman synagogues leaders, 229, 237n55
Roman temples, 151, 161n11
"root of Jesse" (David), 64–65, 66–67, 89, 180n30
Rule of the Community, 189
rulership, 151, 161n9
Ruth, 20n34

sacrilege, 64, 238n60
salvation, 28, 41nn21–22; non-Jews and, 27, 39n14. See also specific topics
salvation-exclusive religion, 28, 41n22
salvation-inclusive religion, 28, 31, 41n21

"salvific history," 136
Sarah, 175
Sarah/Hagar, 129, 258n15
"saved": in evangelical salvation paradigm, 244, 245, 258n14, 269nn18–19
scholars, xi
Scientific Grant Agency of the Ministry of Education, Science, Research and Sport of the Slovak Republic, ix, 303n2
Scythopolis anti-Jewish riots, 290
Second Temple era, 303n3
Second Temple Jewish monotheism, 291
self-preservation conversion, 9, 18n22, 19n23, 19n25; Septuagint on, 10, 19n28; timing of, 11, 29n32
self-reflection, 37, 45n60
self-righteousness, 108
senatus consultum, 203
set-theory tools, *125*, 126, 136–37, *137*
seventy-two translators, 50
Shema' Israel, 312n92
Sibyl, 277–78, 279
slavery, 7, 258n15; freedom as, 301, 311n82
Slovak Academy of Sciences (VEGA), ix, 303n2
small apartments *(insulae)*, 205
social dimension, of Israel, 174, 181nn46–47
socioreligious themes, 29–30
Sonderweg, 32, 254, 256nn4–6
Song of Moses, 77
speech, 93–94. See also righteousness *pesher*, second speech
speech-in-character *(prosopopeia)*, 292, 307n19
spells, 29
Stoics, 223, 224
Stratonike, 109
substitution theory, 279
supersessionist ideology, 84n2

Index of Subjects

The Survivors of Israel (Elliott), 188–89
"Synagogue of Satan," 229–30
synagogues. *See* "congregations"
synchronous observations, 127–34, *130, 132, 133*

TDNT. *See* Theological Dictionary of the New Testament
teachers, 230–31, 239n70; circumcision of, 229
text content structure, xii
theodicy, 190
Theological Dictionary of the New Testament (TDNT), 263n50
theological level, 280–82, 286n51
theology, definition of, 26–27, 39n11
theology and institution, 36, 45n56
theology of religions, 40n17
Thessalonians, 110–11
"those who are called Jews" *(dicuntur Iudaei)*, 220
Tiberius (emperor), 203–4, 231
timing: of circumcision, 5, 13–15; of evangelical salvation paradigm, 249, 261n30; of Israel's conversion, 243, 256n2; of self-preservation conversion, 11, 29n32
Titus, 64
Tolomaeus (king), 50
Torah, 80; Abraham and, 82; Christ related to, 295, 297; circumcision related to, 42n32; Donaldson on, 62, 69n6; end of times and, 274; for Gentiles, 304n8; Gospels compared to, 46n47; Greek translation of, 52; Izates and, 56; of Jews in Rome, 206–8, 209, 215n34; Judeans related to, 229; "just as has been written" related to, 254–55, 266n59; outlawing of, 8–9; Paul and, 4, 82, 83, 105, 107, 129, 206–7
tradition historical level, 276–80

translations, 50, 51, 243, 256n1; Abraham related to, 55, 59n10; evangelical salvation paradigm and, 246–47; *Israēl* (and *Israēlites*) related to, 124, 126–27, 140n20, 141n27; about Paul's interlocutor, 220, 232n4; twelve prophets and, 88, 90, 91–100
Trophimus, 64, 70n14
trust, 150, 299
trustworthiness, of God, 272, 273, 275, 282
twelve prophets: Aseneth and, 98; assimilation model and, 94, 101n29; Bertram and, 88; "conversion embodied" and, 98; Council of Jerusalem and, 90–91; curse and, 96–97; diaspora and, 95; Donaldson and, 87–88; history of transmission and, 90; Israel and, 95–96; less than open stance related to, 92–93; Lucianic recension and, 89–90; Micah in, 92–93; models related to, 87–88, 93–95; non-universalism related to, 91–92; patterns and, 88; Ptolemy related to, 88; refugees in, 96, 97, 98, 99–100; revenge and, 91–92; Simkovich and, 87–88, 91, 95, 98, 99; speech and, 93–94; strangers and, 96; systematic trend related to, 95–98; "to seek" related to, 90; translation and, 88, 90, 91–100; universalism and, 87–88, 89–95, 99; vocalization and, 93; "you" and, 97

"unity in diversity," 30–31, 36–37, 43n37, 44n51, 45n57
universal, 75–76, 84nn2–3
universalism, 27–28, 304n7. *See also* particularism and universalism

VEGA. *See* Slovak Academy of
    Sciences
vegetarianism, 204, 206, 209, 214n26,
    215n36
virgin, 53

welcoming, 156, 158, 162n26; of
    proselytes, 52, 56–57
women, 15, 39n9, 53, 129, 175, 258n15;
    conversions of, 20n41, 98; Esther,
    9–11, 19n23, 19n25; Fulvia, 203,
    231; Helena, 55–56; Ruth, 20n34

"word of God," 171
works/merit contract, 175
worship, 77–79, 80, 82,
    85nn7–8

Yahweh, 303n3

Zechariah, 62, 63, 68nn1–2
Zeus, 222
Zeus Hypsistos, 39n9
Zion, 66–67, 71n26
Zipporah, 15

Index of Scripture References and Ancient Sources

OLD TESTAMENT

Genesis (Gen)
  4:17, 222
  4:25–26, 222
  5:2–3, 222
  14:4–14, 142n41
  17:23–27, 14
  17:12, 4
  17:12–14, 13
  17:12a,14, 13
  17:14, 3, 4–5
  18:10, 173–174
  21:4, 4
  21:12, 173
  21:31; etc., 222
  22:16–18, 299
  22:18, 209
Exodus (Exod)
  4:24–26, 15
  15:23, 222
  19, 303n3
  19:5–6, 300
  19:6, 294
  34:10–16, 285n37
  34:29–35, 124
Leviticus (Lev)
  1:17, 260n24
  10:17, 262n41
  18:5, 292, 293–295, 297, 298, 307n23, 308n38
  19:18, 129
  24:11, 222
  26:13, 7
  26:25, 96
Numbers (Num)
  7:9, 94
  14:18, 262n41
  23:19, 45n52
Deuteronomy (Deut)
  4:1, 294
  5:32–33, 294
  7:1–6, 285n37
  7:7, 182n51
  8:1, 294
  8:14, 292
  8:17, 296, 298
  9:4, 292, 296, 298
  9:4–5, 297
  10:3, 297–298
  10:16; 30:6, *133*, 134
  11:22, 296
  12:5, 222
  16:20, 294
  19:9, 296
  22:7, 294
  29:1–20, 297
  29:11–14, 297
  29:12, 297
  29:13, 297
  29:14, 297
  29:21–27, 297
  30:1–10, 297
  30:11, 297
  30:11–14, 292, 293, 295, 296–297, 307n20
  30:12, 296, 298
  30:12–13, 297–298
  30:12–14, 297, 307n20
  30:13, 296, 298
  30:14, 298
  30:15–20, 294
  32, 161n16, 179n25
  32:43, 66
Judges (Judg)
  6:29, 90
  18:30, 15

1 Samuel (1 Sam)
  3:13, 91
2 Kingdoms (2 Kgdms)
  22:50, 66
2 Samuel (2 Sam)
  8:15, 122
  12:28, 89
1 Kings (1 Kgs)
  4:1, 122
  19:10, 18, 253
  19:18, 265n54
  20:15, 265n54
1 Chronicles (1 Chr)
  12:32, 223
  28:3, 222
2 Chronicles (2 Chr)
  12:13, 222
  22:8, 91
Ezra
  9:8, 196n4
Nehemiah (Neh)
  9:29, 294
Esther (Esth)
  8:10–12, 9–10
  8:17b, 9–10
  8:17, 19
  8:10–12, 9–10
  8:17, 19
  8:17b, 9–10 9:5–16, 11
Psalms (Ps)
  9:6–9, 285n36
  9:16–21, 285n36
  11:28–29, 296
  13:7, 264n51
  13:7 (LXX), 264n52
  22:28–32, 285n39
  47:10, 285n39
  85:10–13, 295–296
  86:9–10, 285n39
  93[94]:17, 97
  106:26, 292
  106:26 [LXX], 296, 309n48

  109:2, 264n51
  119:105, 294
  119[120]:6, 97
  124, 134
  124,5.2; 127,6, 141n28
  124:2, 5, 127
  124(125), 134
  124(125):5, 134
  124[125]:1–2;
  127[128]:2, 134
  124[125]:2, 134
  125, 134
  125:2, 5, 127
  127(128), 134
  127(128):6, 134
  127[128]:1, 4, 5, 134
  127[128]:1, 5, 6, 127
  128, 134
Old Greek Psalms
  17:50, 66
  17:50–51, 66
  116:1, 66
Proverbs (Prov)
  8:21ff., 295–296
Isaiah (Isa)
  2, 65, 67
  2:2–3, 264n52
  2:2–4, 61, 190, 302, 304n8, 307n24
  2:2–5, 285n38, 294
  2:3, 12, 92
  2:3–4, 65
  2:20–21, 304n8
  5:1–7, 263n45
  5:10–11, 263n45
  10:22, 191, 196n4
  11, 65, 68
  11:10, 64–65, 66, 70n16
  14:26, 285n36
  18:7, 190, 304n8
  19:18–25, 302, 304n8
  25, 65

  25:6–7, 68n2
  25:6–8, 302, 304n8
  25:6–10, 304n8
  27, 263n45
  27:9, 252, 265n55
  27:9a, 264n45
  27:9b, 251
  28:16, 67, 71n26, 292, 299–300, 301
  28:16 [LXX], 299–300
  29:8, 304n8
  31:33a, d, 263n45
  34:2, 190
  37:4, 196n4
  40–55, 294
  40:6–11, 251
  40:15–17, 285n36
  42:6–7, 294
  45, 156–158
  45:1, 156
  45:3–4, 156
  45:4, 157
  45:7, 12, 156
  45:8, 295–296
  45:18–25, 302, 304n8
  45:20, 156
  45:21, 156
  45:23, 156
  45:22, 157
  45:23, 155, 156
  59:20, 251
  48:17, 263n50
  48:20, 263n50
  49:1–7, 294
  49:6, 294
  49:7, 263n50
  49:22–23, 304n8
  49:23, 190
  51:4–5, 294
  51:10, 264n50
  52, 265n53
  52:9, 264n50
  54, 98

54:3, 304n8
54:5, 264n50
54:15, 96, 97
55, 98
55:5, 97
55:10–11, 295–296
56, 65
56:3, 96, 98
56:3–7, 285n38
56:6–7, 61
56:7, 68n2, 302, 304n8
56:65–66, 302
59:3, 264n50
59:12–15, 252
59:20, 67, 71n26, 252, 263n47, 264n50
59:21, 251, 252
59:21a, 251
60:1–22, 304n8
60:5–6, 304n8
60:11–14, 252
60:12–14, 190
61:9, 41n27
62:12, 264n50
63:7, 252
63:9, 264n50
63:16, 264n50
65, 179n25
65:1, 90
66, 65
66:14–21, 12
66:18–20, 61
66:18–21, 304n8
66:19, 304n8
66:20, 68n2
66:23, 285n39
Old Greek Isaiah, 70n21
11:10, 66
Jeremiah (Jer)
3:16, 223

4:4, *133,* 134
8:3; 23:3; 31:1–14, 196n4
10:25, 190, 285n36
16:19–20, 304n8
16:19–21, 285n38
23:1–8; 33:14–16, 209
27[50]:4–5, 96
27[50]:5, 98
30:11, 143n57, 285n36, 304n8
30:16, 304n8
38:33a (LXX), 263n45
46:28, 285n36
Ezekiel (Ez)
9:8; 11:13, 196n4
10–11, 279
17:11–21, 304n8
18:9, 294
18:17, 294
18:19, 294
18:21, 294
20:11, 294
20:13, 294
20:21, 294
33:15–16, 294
34:27, 7
37:16, 122
37:19–21, 122
40–48, 286n48
Daniel (Dan)
11:15, 196n6
12:3, 196n6
Hosea (Hos)
2:23, 192
Joel (Joel)
3:5, 292, 299–300, 302
4:9–21, 304n8
4:16, 264n51

Amos (Amos)
1:2, 264n51
9:11–12, 89–91
9:12, 88, 93, 99
Obadiah (Obad)
1:21, 264n51
21, 88, 91–92, 99
Micah (Mic)
2:12; 4:6–7, 196n4
4, 65
4:1–2, 61, 190
4:1–3, 304n8, 307n24
4:1–5, 285n38
4:2, 88, 92–93, 99, 264n51
4:2c, 12
5:6–14, 304n8
7:16–17, 304n8
Zephaniah (Zeph)
2:1–3, 304n8
2:3–9, 196n4
2:8–9, 190
2:9–15, 304n8
3:9–10, 88, 93–95
Haggai (Hag)
2:21–22, 304n8, 307n24
Zechariah (Zech)
2:11, *133,* 134
2:15, 88, 95–98, 99, 100
8, 65, 67
8:20–23, 285n38, 304n8
8:21–23, 304n8
8:22, 307n24
8:22–23, 62
8:23, 68n2, 190
14, 65
14:16, 62, 285n38

APOCRYPHA AND SEPTUAGINT

Additions to Esther
(Add Esth, Grk Esth),
6
8:17b, 10
Baruch (Bar)
4:25, 304n8
4:31–35, 304n8
Judith (Jdt), 6
5:16–21, 11
6:1–13, 12
14:10, 12
1 Maccabees (1 Macc), 6
1:14, 6
1:15a, 6

1:15b, 7
1:41, 7–8
1:42, 50, 7
1:43, 8
2:27, 8–9
2:44–46, 8
Septuagint (LXX),
87–102, 100n6,
299–300
Sirach (Sir)
24:23–24, 294
36:1–10, 304n8
36:8–9, 197n18
36:11–17, 304n8

Tobit (Tob)
13, 63
13:9–11, 63
13:11, 304n8
14:5–7, 131, 304n8
14:6, 197n20
Wisdom of Solomon
(Wis, Sap.)
14:8, 223
15:8, 176n5
16:11, 261n26
18:4, 294

OLD TESTAMENT PSEUDEPIGRAPHA

Apocalypse of Abraham
(Apoc. Ab.), 54
29.4–14, 55
29.19–20, 55
2 Baruch (2 Bar.), 54,
187, 188, 189–190,
196n12
41–42, 190, 192
41:3, 197n23
70:7, 197n16
72, 304n8
1 Enoch (1 En.), 187,
188, 189, 196n5
43:4, 197n14
48:4, 190
81:2, 196n13
90:29–31, 63
90:30–33, 191
90.30–38, 304n8
91.9, 304n8
91.14, 304n8
4 Ezra, 54, 67, 187,
188, 189, 196n12
6:1–6, 197n15

14:30, 294
Joseph and Aseneth
(Jos. Asen.), 15,
53–54, 98, 99
19:8, *133*, 134
Jubilees (Jub.), 6, 67
15:23–24, 14
15:25–26, 13
15:26, 190
15:26a, 5
32:18–19, 197n19
Letter of Aristeas (Let.
Aris.), 50, 52–53
139–140, 51
142–143, 51
295–297, 51
Psalms of Solomon
(Pss. Sol.)
14:2–3, 294
17, 190
17:21–32, 252
17:24.30, 304n8
17:28, 304n8
17:30–31, 264n52

17:31–41, 304n8
17:34, 304n8
Sibylline Oracles (Sib
Or.)
3.5.264, 304n8
3.167–195, 285n41
3.194–195, 277
3.266–294, 285n42
3.282–292, 277
3.415–440, 304n8
3.517–19, 197n18
3.517–19, 669–72,
197n18
3.573–600, 285n43
3.580–583, 277–278
3.616, 304n8
3.669, 304n8
3.702–703, 285n44
3.702–723, 304n8,
312n93
3.711–713, 278
3.715–719, 63
3.715–726, 285n45
3.757–758, 304n8

3.761, 304n8
3.767–780, 285n45
3.791, 304n8
5.493, 304n8
192–96, 158–159
570, 158
601–23, 158
702–61, 158
715–23, 158
767–808, 158

772–775, 63
Testament of Benjamin
 (T. Benj.) 9.2, 197n20
Testament of Levi
 (T. Levi)
 4.3–4, 197n20
 18.9, 304n8
Testament of Moses
 (T. Mos.) 10.7, 197n18

Testament of Naphtali
 (T. Naph.) 3.2, 304n8
Third Sibylline Oracle,
 63, 277–278, 286n50
 616–18, 158
 618–23, 158
 716–17, 159

NEW TESTAMENT

Matthew (Mt)
 2:1–2, 41n27
 7:21–23, 43n37
 8:5–13, 41n27
 10:5–6, 40n13, 41n27, 58n2
 15:21–28, 41n27
 15:24, 58n2
 23:15, 59n12
 25:31, 116n37
 25:31–46, 41n24, 44n44
 28:18–20, 41n24, 41n27
Mark 15:1, 116n37
Luke (Lk)
 10:28, 294
 23:35, 261n33
John
 11:12, 261n33
 13:35, 41n27
 18:18, 116n37
Acts
 11:26, 223
 13:47, 105
 14:6, 100
 14:18, 111
 14:19–20, 114n7
 15, 57, 58n2, 105, 206–207

15:5, 39n12, 44n48, 44n51
15:17, 89, 90
15:33, 105
16:14, 161n14
17:28, 105, 114n6
17:30–31, 111
18:2, 201, 202
18:12, 116n37
20:7–12, 205
21:20–22, 44n51
21:28–29, 64, 70n14
23:6–9, 38n4
26:14, 105, 114n6
Romans
 1–8, 272, 283n10, 290–291
 1:1–4, 180n30
 1:4, 210–211
 1:5, 58n1
 1:5–6, 219
 1:8–13, 178n19
 1:11–12, 178n20
 1:16, 178n17, 237n41, 301
 1:16–17, 245, 272, 301, 307n21
 1:16–2:13, 26
 1:18–32, 166–167,

 168, 176n5, 177n15
 1:23–24, 33
 1:28–32, 33
 2–11, 169
 2:1, 229
 2:1–5, 228
 2:1–16, 245
 2:4–11, 36
 2:5–11, 166, 208
 2:6, 116n36
 2:9, 301
 2:9–10, 237n41
 2:9–13, 294
 2:10, 301
 2:11, 36
 2:12, 116n36
 2:12–16, 209
 2:14–16, 115n28
 2:16, 116n36
 2:17, 219, 220, 221, 223, 224–225, 227, 229, 230, 232n4, 235n29, 237n56
 2:17–3:9, 234n16
 2:17–18, 224
 2:17–24, 294
 2:21–24, 231
 2:22, 230
 2:24, 231

2:25–29, 47, 235n31, 245, 259n18
2:26, 133, *133*
2:28–29, 133, *133*, 237n42
2:29, 133, 229
2 :28–29, 133, *133*
3–11, 168
3:1, 169, 229, 237n42
3:1–2, 244
3:1–4, 44n47
3:1–8, 166–168, 173
3:2, 170
3:3, 166, 167
3:3–8, 294
3:4, 116n36
3:4–5, 168
3:5, 169
3:6, 116n36
3:8, 167
3:9, 237n41, 301
3:9–20, 245
3:21–26, 245
3:23, 308n33
3:25–26, 35
3:25–31, 26
3:26, 166
3:28–31, 142n41
3:29, 30, 237n41
3:29–30, 300
3:29–31, 36, 44n47
4:1, 168, 169
4:1–25, 245
4:3, 182n49
4:9, 300, 301
4:10, 301
4:11, 16, 32
4:11–12, 31
4:16–17, 31
4:17–18, 133, *133*
5:10–11, 107
5:11, 43n40
5:16, 116n36
5:18, 116n36
6:1, 168, 169

6:17, 178n19
7:7, 168, 169
7:7–8:4, 295
7:13, 169
7:24, 264n50
8:1, 116n36
8:3, 116n36
8:14, 31, 32
8:14–21, 133, *133*
8:17, 32
8:19–21, 245
8:19–22, 40n14
8:28–33, 193
8:31, 169
8:31–39, 273
9–11, 71n27,123, 124, 136, 138n9, 165, 175–176, 179n25, 188, 190, 191–195, 197n27, 206, 210, 219, 235n26, 245, 258n10, 260n19, 271–286, 283n1, 284n14, 284n20, 285n34, 286n51
9–16, 208n33, 284n16, 306n13, 307n27, 309n50, 310n65, 311n80
9–20, 294
9:1–3, 170
9:1–5, 172, 272, 273–274, 283n8, 291
9:1–11:36, 290–291
9:1–13, 174
9:3, 37n1, 273
9:4, 123, 124
9:4–5, 37n1, 170, 171, 294
9:4–6, 245
9:6, 31, 122, 123, 124–127, 245, 259n16, 259n18, 265n56

9:6b, 170–174
9:6–8, 191
9:6–13, 180n43
9:6–29, 280–281, 284n11, 291
9:6a, 140n20, 171, 172, 273, 280
9:6b, 140n20, 180n41, 194, 280
9:6b–7, 172, 173
9:6b–13, 172
9:6b–13, 174
9:7, 180n43, 245
9:7–9, 175
9:7–13, 193
9:8, 175
9:8–13, 173–174
9:9–18, 281
9:10–12, 175
9:11, 175, 192, 193
9:11–14, 280
9:14, 169
9:14–18, 280
9:19, 192
9:19–21, 280
9:20, 192
9:22, 166, 245
9:22–24, 284n11
9:22–29, 280
9:24, 193, 237n41, 280, 281
9:25, 192
9:25–26, 133, *133*
9:25–29, 193
9:27, 123, 191
9:27(–28), 124
9:30, 169
9:30–10:4, 291
9:30–33, 245
9:31, 123
9:33, 67, 71n26
10, 160, 264n53
10:1, 123, 127, 272, 274, 295
10:2, 295, 299

Index of Scripture References and Ancient Sources   345

10:4, 294, 295
10:4ff, 308n35
10:5, 294–295
10:5–13, 289–312
10:6–13, 295–302
10:6a, 295
10:8–12, 295
10:9–13, 299
10:12, 237n41, 301
10:12–13, 36
10:13, 301
10:14–11:15, 295
10:14–21, 291
10:16, 178n17
10:18–19, 176
10:19, 123, 124
10:(20–)21, 124
10:21, 123, 245
11, 211
11:1, 25, 123, 169, 173, 272
11:1–2, 133, *133*, 192
11:1–3, 274
11:1–6, 193, 253
11:1–10, 291–292
11:2, 123, 124, 193
11:2–6, 191–192
11:2–10, 281
11:5, 123, 274, 302
11:7, 123, 124, 281
11:7–15, 275
11:11, 169, 180n41, 273, 274–275
11:11–12, 257n8
11:11–15, 246, 247–248
11:11–32, 281–282
11:11–24, 291–292
11:11–31, 294
11:11–36, 257n8
11:13, 272, 275–276, 283n3
11:13–14, 58n1, 165
11:13–24, 167
11:13–31, 284n13

11:13f, 275
11:14, 193
11:15, 31, 107, 275
11:16–17, 209
11:16–24, 281–282
11:17, 246, 247, 261n26
11:17–18, 27
11:17–20, 247
11:17–24, 246
11:20, 245
11:21, 251–252
11:22–24, 247
11:23, 245
11:23–24, 247
11:25, 35, 124, 247, 256n2, 291
11:25, 33–36, 33
11:25–26, 258n11
11:25–27, 143n57, 168, 173, 210, 215n42, 282, 302, 303n2
11:25–29, 306n13
11:25–32, 275, 292, 306n17
11:25–32/36, 136
11:25–36, 292
11:26, 31, 67, 71n26, 123, 124, 194, 243, 244–245, 249, 251, 252, 256n4, 264n52, 272
11:26–27, 263n46, 263n47
11:26–29, 33
11:26a, 188, 246, 249–251, 256n2, 259n18, 262n38
11:26b–27, 256n2
11:28, 245, 247
11:28–29, 31, 35, 244, 248
11:29, 254, 259n16, 265n57, 273, 291

11:30–32, 245, 248, 259n18
11:30–36, 252
11:32–36, 276
11:33–36, 33, 264n53, 292
11:1, 133
12:1, 35
12:1–2, 299
12:9–21, 299
13, 168
13:2, 116n36
13:8–10, 295
13:8–14, 299
13:11, 210
14, 31
14:1–4, 208–209
14:2, 206
14:3–4, 207
14:5–6, 206
14:10, 111
14:10–12, 116n36
14:11.26, 156
14:14, 206
15, 64, 70n12, 168, 208
15–16, 199
15:1, 207
15:7, 162n25
15:7–12, 206
15:7–13, 71n22
15:8, 206
15:8–9, 71n22
15:8–12, 66, 180n30
15:10, 133, *133*
15:12, 64–65, 66, 70n16
15:15, 178n20
15:16, 35, 68n2
15:18, 66–67
15:20, 178n19, 223
15:24, 201
15:25–28, 70n13
15:25–31, 64
15:31, 264n50

15:32, 200
15:33, 128
15:7–13, 300
15:10, 133, *133*
16:1–16, 200
16:1–27, 200
16:20, 128
16:25–27, 200
1 Corinthians (1 Cor)
1–13, 124
1:2, 300
1:22, 237n41
1:23, 237n41
1:24, 237n41
3:13–17, 26
4:5, 26, 115n28
4:12, 114n7
4:17, 160
5–10/13, 124
5:11, 223
7:14, 32
7:17–18, 30
7:17–24, 43n34, 44n47, 47
7:21, 215n46
8:1–9, 215n36
8:5–6, 105
9:20, 237n42, 308n38
10:1–13, 126
10:3–4, 141n27
10:18, 121, 122, 123–124, *126*, 126–127, 194
10:18.21, 124
10:31, 162n25
10:32, 237n41
11:24b, 162n28
11:29–32, 26
12:2, 195
12:3, 300
12:13, 36, 237n41
14:25, 68n2
15, 38n4, 111
15:33, 114n6
15:49–56, 26

15:54, 68n2
16:1–4, 64
16:18, 235n30
2 Corinthians (2 Cor)
1:10, 264n50
3, 124
3:7, 123, 124
3:13, 124
3.7, 124
3.13, 124
5:1–10, 111
5:10, 26
5:18–20, 107
6.16, 133, *133*
8:1–9:15, 64
11, 123
11:16–33, 123
11:18, 123–124
11:22, 25, 123
11:24, 237n42
11:25, 114n7
13, 123
13:11, 128
Galatians (Gal)
1, 57
1–2, 58n2, 64
1:1–5, 131
1:1–12, 249
1:4, 15
1:6, 15
1:6–2:14, 131
1:6–9, 5:12, 128
1:8–9, 15
1:10–12, 15
1:11–12, 207
1:13–14, 298
1:15, 131, 207
1:16, 58n1, 131
2, 57
2:1–3, 64
2:3, 128
2:9, 34
2:11–14, 44n49
2:11–21, 258n13
2:13, 131, 237n42

2:13–14, 226–227
2:14–15, 237n41
2:15, 25, 33, 135, 300
2:15–21, *130*, 131
2:15–17, 244
2:15–21, *130*, 131
2:18–21, 15
2:19–21, *130*, 131
3:1, 129
3:1–3, 15
3:1–4:7, 130, *130*, 131
3:1–6:17, *130*, 131
3:6–9, 31
3:10, 308n33
3:13, *130*, 131
3:15/16–20/22, 136
3:17, 43n39
3:18, *130*, 130–131
3:19–20, 136
3:19–22, 210
3:23–25, *130*, 131
3:25, *130*, 130–131
3:26, 132
3:26–29, *130*, 131
3:28, 36, 45n55, 128, 210, 226–227, 237n41
3:29, 132, *133*
3.11–12, 308n33
4:6a, *130*, 131
4:7, *130*, 130–131
4:8–10, 33
4:8–10, 128, 129
4:9b, *130*, 130–131
4:11, 15
4:20, 15
4:21–5:1, 129, 142n49, 258n15
4:21–30, 258n15
4:21–31, 71n28
4:25, 67
4:25b, *130*, 131
4:26, 67
4.1–5, 133, *133*

5:1, *130,* 130–131, 301
5:1–10, 15
5:2–6, 32
5:2–6:10, 129
5:2–6:17, 130
5:3, 42n32
5:3–4, 44n47
5:4, 30
5:11, 29–30, 34, 42n31, 46, 114n7
5:12, 15, 30, 39n12, 182n48
5:13, 301
5:13–6:10, 311n82
5:13–14, 299, 311n82
5:13–15, 129
5:16–21, 33
5:19–21, 300
5:22–25, 299
5:24, 33
5:25, 130, *130*
6:1–10, 299
6:11–18, 128
6:15–16, 127–128
6:16, 121, 122, 123, 124–127, 128, 130, *130,* 131–132, *132,* 134, 135, 137, 194
6:17, 15
6:17–18, 129
6:18, 128–129
6.16, 138n9, 140n13, 142n33, 197n27

6:(15–)16, 134
Ephesians (Eph)
1:21, 224
2:11, 123
2:12, 123
3:15, 224
5:3, 224
6:5–8, 215n46
Philippians (Phil)
1:27–30, 149–150
1:30, 150
2, 159
2:6–11, 149–164, 160n2, 162n24
2:9–11, 149, 154, 159, 160, 177n15, 179n28
2:11, 159, 300
2:12–18, 150
2:15, 150
2:16, 150
3:3, 259n18
3:3–4, 123–124
3:4–5, 25
3:4–6, 161n12, 298
3:5, 123
3:6, 244
3:8, 121, 123
4:7, 9, 128
4:18, 68n2
4:19, 128
Colossians (Col)
3:1, 211
3:22–24, 215n46

1 Thessalonians (1 Thess)
1:9–10, 115n27
1:10, 264n50
2:14, 226–227, 237n42
2:14(–15), 135
4:13–5:11, 26
5:9–10, 115n27
5:23, 128
5:25, 26, 27, 142n42
5:28, 142n42
1 Timothy
1:13, 114n11
2:7, 160
6:1–2, 215n46
2 Timothy
3:11, 114n7
Titus (Tit)
1:14, 135
2:9–10, 215n46
Philemon
20, 235n30
Hebrews (Heb)
9:25, 180n43
1 Peter
2:18, 215n46
2 Peter
3:15–16, 44n51
Revelations (Rev)
2:9, 229–230, 237n56
3:9, 229–230
4, 116n37

OTHER ANCIENT SOURCES

Dead Sea Scrolls (DSS), 188, 193–194, 197n18
1QH^a (Hodayot)
9:19–24, 189

1QM (War Scroll)
12.10–13, 304n8
1QS (Serek Hayaḥad)
3:15–16, 189

4Q161 (4QpIsa^a), 196n3, 197n26
4QMMT (Miqṣat Ma'aśê ha-Torah),

134, 135,
141n28
C30–31, 134, 135
C31–32, 141n28
Josephus
   Against Apion (*Ag.*
     Ap.) 2.210, 310n70
   Jewish Antiquities
     (*Ant.*, *A.J.*), 55–57
   2.1, 222
   4.207, 222
   12.5.1, 18n15
   12.241, 18n16
   13.9.1, 18n15,
     18n19
   13.395, 18n17
   18.8.1, 290
   18.81–84, 214n22,
     231
   19.290, 213n16
   20.34–48, 56
   20.38–47, 225
   20.38–48, 43n37
   Jewish War (*J.W.*,
     B.J.)
   1.119, 222

2.18.1, 290
2.18.3–4, 290
2.18.5, 290
2.20.2, 290
2.390, 153
3.354, 278
5.367, 279
5.367–68, 153
5.412, 279
7.8.7, 290
7.359, 286n47
Philo of Alexandria
   De Abrahamo (*Abr.*)
     98, 158
   De decalogo (*Decal.*)
     58, 162n17
   De migratione
     Abrahami (*Migr.*)
     89–93, 16
   De sobrietate (*Sobr.*)
     63, 162n17
   De somniis (*Somn.*)
     1.175–178, 294
   De specialibus legibus
     (*Spec.*)
     1.320–323, 294

2.162–67, 158
De virtutibus (*Virt.*)
   108, 182n48
   175–86, 158
De vita Mosis (*Mos.*)
   1.149, 158
   2.43–44, 52,
     304n8, 312n93
   2.158.4, 312n87
De posteritate Caini
   (*Post.*) 84–85, 296
Legatio ad Gaium
   (*Legat.*)
   159–161, 214n23
   220, 152
   281–83, 214n21
Quod omnis probus
   liber sit (*Prob.*) 71,
   158
Quis rerum divinarum
   heres sit (*Her.*) 58,
   162n17

RABBINIC LITERATURE

Avodah Zarah 24a, 94
Exodus Rabba (*Exod.*
   Rab.)
   25.12, 298
Letter from Beit-Mashiko
   to Yeshua b. Galgula
   (PapMur)

42, 141n28
42:7, 135
Mishnah *Menahot* (*m.*
   Menaḥ) 53b, 263n49
Mishnah *Shabbat* (*m.*
   Šabb.) 19:5, 20n36

Targum Isaiah (Tg. Isa.)
   16:1, 197n19

OTHER GRECO-ROMAN SOURCES

Arrian of Nicomedia
   Anabasis of Alexander
   (*Anab.*)

1.11.97, 222–223
3.12.84, 222–223
3.27.4, 222–223

Cassius Dio
   Roman History (*Hist.*),
   226

Index of Scripture References and Ancient Sources

6.6.6, 213n11
37.17, 228, 236n37
57.18.5, 238n66
Celsus
   De Medicina (Med.).
      7.25.1, 6
Cicero
   De inventione
   rhetorica (Inv.)
      99–100, 295–296
   De provinciis
   consularibus (Prov.
   cons.) 5.10, 161n7
   De republica (Resp.)
      3.35–37, 161n8
   In Flaccum (Flacc. 1),
      214n23
   Pro Flacco (Flac.)
      1–16, 161n8
Cornutus
   Compendium of Greek
   theology
      16.5, 222
      16.21, 222
      20.20, 222
      34.1, 222
      35.3, 222
Crescens Sinicerius
   Iudeus proselitus (Noy
      II 491), 226
Dio Chrysostom
   Discourses (Or.)
      1.39; 12.75, 223
      31.354b, 233n12
Diogenes Laertius
   Lives of the
   Philosophers (Vitae
   Philosophorum 8.3),
      214n26
   Vitae Philosophorum
      8.3, 214n26
Εἰρήνη προσήλυτος (Noy
   II 489), 226
Empedocles

fragments 11 and 124,
   214n26
Epictetus
   Diatribai (Diatr.)
      2.9.19, 224
      2.9.19–21, 226,
         228
      3.7.17, 224
      3.24.41, 224
Hermogenes
   Prof. 9.4–6, 295–296
   Rhet. Her. 4.66, 295–
      296
Juvenal
   Satirae 6.542–47;
      14.96–106, 214n27
Novatian
   De trinitate (Trin)
      13.1–2, 160n1
Ovid
   Metamorphoses
   (Metam.) 15.75–142,
      214n26
Pausanias
   Graeciae descriptio
      8.40.2, 260n24
Plato
   Leges 781e–783b,
      214n26
   Republic (Respublica
      372a–d), 214n26
Plutarch
   On the Eating of Flesh
   (De esu carnium
      993c–994b,
      995d–996a;
      006E–997A),
      214n26, 223
   Fabius Maximus
   (Fab.) 1.3, 223
   Precepts for
   Preserving Health
   (Moralia, Mor.)
      131F–132A,
      214n26

426A, 223
472A–B, 223
675E, 223
676D, 223
869F, 223
1001B, 223
1112A, 223
Romulus (Rom.)
   16.6, 223
   21.2, 223
Sertorius (Sert.) 18.3,
   223
Theseus (Thes.) 9.2,
   223
Titus Flamininus
   (Flam.) 9.6, 223
Porphyry
   De abstinentia I.4;
      II.13, 214n26
Quintilian
   Institutio oratoria
   (Inst.) 9.2.31, 295–296
Seneca
   Epistle 103.22,
      214n25
   Life of Julius Caesar
      (Jul.), 85, 214n20
Seutonius
   Life of Tiberius (Tib.
      36.1) 36.1, 214n22
Strabo
   Geographica (Geogr.)
      4.4.6, 222
      9.5.19, 222
      11.7.1, 222
      16.4.8, 222
Tacitus
   Annales (Ann.) 2.85.5,
      214n22
   Historiae (Hist.) 5.6,
      215n47
Theon
   Progymnasmata
      (Prog.) 2.114.10–11,
      295–296, 307n19

Theophrastus
De causis plantarum
(*Caus. Plant.*)
  1.6.1–10, 261n26
  1.7.2, 262n35
  2.16.5, 262n35
  5.16.2, 262n35
  17.5, 262n35
  18.4, 262n35
  19.5, 262n35
  21.5, 262n35
  22.2, 262n35
Historia plantarum
(*Hist. Plant.*)
  2.1.4, 261n26
  2.2.5, 261n26

EARLY CHRISTIAN SOURCES

Barnabas (Barn.)
  21:1–6, 116n37
Clement of Alexandria
  Adversus Praxean
  (*Prax.* 10), 160n1
  Excerpts from Theodotus (*Exc.*)
  19, 43, 160n1
  Homiliae in Genesim
  (*Hom. Gen.*) 1.13,
  160n1
  Paedagogus (*Paed.*)
  1.7.57.2; 2.8.71.5,
  235n25
  Stromata (*Strom.*)
  1.21.106.5;
  1.27.174.1;
  6.3.32.2., 235n25
Eusebius
  Historia ecclesiastica
  (*Hist. Eccl.*)
  11.19.4, 160n1
  Historia ecclesiastica
  (*Hist. Eccl.*) 11.19.4,
  160n1

Justin Martyr
  Dialogue with Trypho
  (*Dial*)
  11:4–5, 122
  75.2–3, 235n25
  90.4, 235n25
  116:3, 140n12
  123:7–9; 135:3,
  140n12
  131.4, 235n25
  132.1, 235n25
  First Apologia (*1 Apol.*)
  9.3, 235n25
  12.9, 223
  46.5, 235n25
  61.10, 235n25
Origen
  Commentarii in evangelium Joannis
  (*Comm. Jo.*),
  10.23, 160n1
  Commentarii in Romanos (Comm. Rom.)
  2.11, 220, 229
  Expositio in Proverbia
  (*Exp. Prov.*), MPG
  17,245, 234n24
  Homiliae in Genesim
  (*Hom. Gen.*),
  1.13, 160n1
Orosius
  Historia contra Paganos 7.6.15,
  213n11
Pseudo-Clementines
  (Homilies) 8.5–7,
  44n46
Tertullian
  Adversus Marcionem
  (*Marc*). 5.20.3–4,
  160n1
  Adversus Praxean
  (*Prax.* 10), 160n1

About the Contributors

František Ábel (Ph.D., Comenius University in Bratislava, Slovakia) is professor of New Testament at the Evangelical Lutheran Theological Faculty of Comenius University in Bratislava, Slovakia. His research focuses primarily on Second Temple Judaism and Paul's message. He is the author of *Z Galiley do Galiley: univerzalizmus spásy v kontexte Jn 1–4* [From Galilee to Galilee: The Universalism of Salvation in the context of John 1–4] (Comenius University Press, 2011) and *The Psalms of Solomon and the Messianic Ethics of Paul* (Mohr Siebeck, 2016), and the coauthor and editor of *The Message of Paul the Apostle within Second Temple Judaism* (Lexington Books/Fortress Academic, 2020).

Kenneth Atkinson (Ph.D., Temple University) is professor of history at the University of Northern Iowa in Cedar Falls (US). He specializes in biblical studies, Second Temple Judaism, the Dead Sea Scrolls, and ancient history and archaeology. His recent books include *The Hasmoneans and Their Neighbors: New Historical Reconstructions from the Dead Sea Scrolls and Classical Sources* (Bloomsbury T&T Clark, 2018) and *A History of the Hasmonean State: Josephus and Beyond* (Bloomsbury T&T Clark, 2016).

Michael Bachmann is professor (emeritus) at the University of Siegen (Evangelische Theologie, esp. New Testament). His study degrees are mathematics and Protestant theology. He wrote his dissertation and habilitation on New Testament topics. His books include *Anti-Judaism in Galatians?* (Eerdmans, 2009), *Das Freiburger Münster und seine Juden* (Schnell & Steiner, 2017), and *Gott, der 'Allmächtige'* (Herder, 2019), and the scholar is editor of *Lutherische und Neue Paulusperspektive* (Mohr Siebeck, 2005).

About the Contributors

William S. Campbell is senior research fellow at the Abraham Geiger Kolleg, University of Potsdam. His research focuses on the interpretation of Paul in his historical context, opposing anti-Jewish and ethnically invective readings, and the relevance of this for emerging Christian identity. He has published widely, including *Paul's Gospel in an Intercultural Context: Jew and Gentile in the Letter to the Romans* (Peter Lang, 1992), *Paul and the Creation of Christian Identity* (T&T Clark, 2008), *Unity and Diversity in Christ: Interpreting Paul in Context* (Cascade, 2013), and *The Nations in the Divine Economy: Paul's Covenantal Hermeneutics and Participation in Christ* (Lexington Books/Fortress Academic, 2018).

Genevive Dibley (Ph.D., University of California at Berkeley and the Graduate Theological Union) is Director of Religious Studies at Rockford University and chair of the Society of the Abolition of Modern-day Slavery. She is the author of *Abraham's Uncircumcised Children: The Enochic Precedent for Paul's Paradoxical Claim in Galatians 3:29* (UC Berkeley ETD, 2013) and *Uncovering Theologies in Genesis* (GlossaHouse, 2019).

Kathy Ehrensperger is research professor, New Testament in Jewish Context at the Abraham Geiger Kolleg, University of Potsdam, Germany. Her research focuses on the interplay between cultural translation, power dynamics, and identity formation, and questions of gender in first-century intercultural interaction. She has published widely, including, *That We May Be Mutually Encouraged: Feminism and the New Perspective on Paul* (T&T Clark, 2004), *Paul and the Dynamics of Power: Communication and Interaction in the Early Christ Movement* (T&T Clark, 2009), *Paul at the Crossroads of Cultures—Theologizing in the Space-Between* (T&T Clark, 2015), and *Searching Paul: Conversations with the Jewish Apostle to the Nations. Collected Essays* (Mohr Siebeck, 2019).

Joshua D. Garroway is Sol and Arlene Bronstein professor of Judaeo-Christian Studies at Hebrew Union College—Jewish Institute of Religion in Los Angeles, California. He has written *Paul's Gentile-Jews: Neither Jew nor Gentile, but Both* (Palgrave Macmillan, 2012) and *The Beginning of the Gospel: Paul, Philippi, and the Origins of Christianity* (Palgrave Macmillan, 2018).

Mark D. Nanos (Ph.D., University of St. Andrews, Scotland), is a lecturer at the University of Kansas. His books include *The Mystery of Romans: The Jewish Context of Paul's Letter* (Fortress, 1996); *The Irony of Galatians: Paul's Letter in First Century Context* (Fortress, 2002); edited volumes include *The Galatians Debate* (Baker Academic, 2002); *Paul within Judaism:*

Restoring the First-Century Context to the Apostle (coedited with Magnus Zetterholm; Fortress, 2015); and a four-volume series of his collected essays with Cascade: *Reading Paul within Judaism* (2017); *Reading Romans within Judaism* (2018); *Reading Galatians within Judaism* (forthcoming); *Reading Corinthians and Philippians within Judaism* (2017).

Karl-Wilhelm Niebuhr is professor for New Testament at the Theological Faculty of the University of Jena, Germany. His research includes Hellenistic-Jewish literature in relation to New Testament writings, in particular to the letters of Paul and the Epistle of James. He has edited and published several books—on early Jewish literature, *Gesetz und Paränese: Katechismusartige Weisungsreihen in der frühjüdischen Literatur* (Mohr Siebeck, 1987); on Paul, *Heidenapostel aus Israel: Die jüdische Identität des Paulus nach der Darstellung in seinen Briefen* (Mohr Siebeck, 1992); and on the Wisdom of Solomon, *Sapientia Salomonis (Weisheit Salomos)*, SAPERE 27 (Mohr Siebeck, 2015).

Eric Noffke is professor for New Testament at the Waldensian Theological Faculty in Rome. He studied theology at Rome, Heidelberg, and Princeton, and took his Ph.D. at the Faculty of Theology in Basel. His specialization fields are Middle Judaism, political readings of the New Testament, and Paul's letters and theology. His latest publications are *Giovanni battista: un profeta esseno?* (Claudiana, Torino 2008), *Ester* (San Paolo, Roma 2018), and *Beati i poveri: dalla legislazione mosaica alla predicazione di Gesù nel vangelo secondo Luca* (San Paolo, Cinisello Balsamo 2019).

Matthew V. Novenson is senior lecturer in New Testament and Director of the Centre for the Study of Christian Origins at the University of Edinburgh. He is the author of *Christ among the Messiahs* (OUP, 2012) and *The Grammar of Messianism* (OUP, 2017) and editor of the *Oxford Handbook of Pauline Studies* (OUP, forthcoming). His current project is a critical commentary on the Letter of Paul to the Philippians.

Markus Öhler (born 1967) is professor of New Testament Studies at the Protestant Theological Faculty of the University of Vienna. His main areas of research are the history of early Christianity and the Letter to the Romans. His latest publications are *Barnabas. Die historische Person und ihre Rezeption in der Apostelgeschichte* (Mohr Siebeck, 2003) and *Geschichte des frühen Christentums* (Göttingen: Vandenhoeck & Ruprecht, 2018).

Imre Peres is professor of New Testament at the Evangelical Lutheran Theological Faculty of Comenius University in Bratislava, Slovakia, and at the Reformed Theological University of Debrecen, Hungary. His main areas of interest are the theology of the New Testament, Hellenistic religion, and Ancient Greek epitaph texts. Presently, he is working on a volume of essays and studies entitled *Similarities and Interrelationships in Eschatology* and chiefly on the project *Life and Death in the Ancient Greek Epitaphs* at the Theological Faculty of the University of Zürich, with Prof. Dr. Jörg Frey. His work comprises a large number of editorial and publishing activities. Of particular importance are his book *Griechische Grabinschriften und neutestamentliche Eschatologie* (Mohr Siebeck, 2003) and his articles "Positive griechische Eschatologie" (Mohr Siebeck, 2007), "Sepulkralische Anthropologie" (Leuven, 2010), "Die eschatologischen Aussage kaiserzeitlicher Grabinschriften" (Mohr Siebeck, 2016), and "Sünde und Versöhnung aus eschatologischer Sicht bei Paulus" (Studia, Debrecen 2012).

Patrick Pouchelle (Ph.D., University of Strasbourg) is associate professor of Old Testament at Centre Sèvres (Paris, France). He is the author of *Dieu éducateur: Une nouvelle approche d'un concept de la théologie biblique entre Bible Hébraïque, Septante et littérature grecque classique* (Mohr Siebeck, 2015) and the coeditor with Eberhard Bons of *The Psalms of Solomon: Language, History, Theology* (SBL Press, 2018). His research focuses on the Septuagint, especially lexicography, and the Pseudepigrapha of the Old Testament, especially the Psalms of Solomon.

Anders Runesson (Ph.D., Lund University, Sweden) is professor of New Testament at the University of Oslo, Norway. He has published widely on issues relating to ancient Jewish and Christian interaction, as well as on the ancient institutions in which such interaction took place, including *Divine Wrath and Salvation in Matthew: The Narrative World of the First Gospel* (Fortress), *The Origins of the Synagogue: A Socio-Historical Study* (CBNTS 37; Almvist & Wiksell International), and *Judaism for Gentiles: Reading Paul beyond the Parting of the Ways Paradigm* (WUNT; Mohr Siebeck, forthcoming). He is the co-editor, with Dieter Mitternacht, of *Jesus, the New Testament, and Christian Origins: Perspectives, Methods, Meanings* (Eerdmans, 2021).

Loren T. Stuckenbruck is professor of New Testament Studies (with an emphasis on Ancient Judaism) at the Protestant Faculty of Theology in Ludwig Maximilian University of Munich. A specialist in Dead Sea Scrolls and early Jewish apocalyptic literature, he is the author of four monographs and over 150 articles, and has edited a number of volumes, most recently, with Daniel M. Gurtner, the *Encyclopedia of Second Temple Judaism* (London: T&T Clark, 2019).

www.ingramcontent.com/pod-product-compliance
Lightning Source LLC
Chambersburg PA
CBHW052141300426
44115CB00011B/1465